Hands-On Microsoft® Windows® Server 2016

Michael Palmer

CENGAGE Learning®

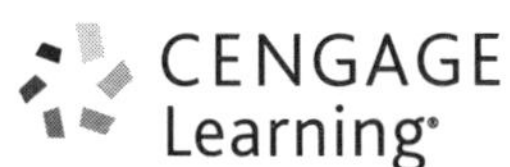

Australia • Brazil • Mexico • Singapore • United Kingdom • United States

Hands-On Microsoft® Windows® Server 2016
Michael Palmer

GM, Science, Technology, & Math: Balraj Kalsi

Sr. Product Director, Computing: Kathleen McMahon

Product Team Manager: Kristin McNary

Associate Product Manager: Amy Savino

Director, Development: Julia Caballero

Content Development Manager: Leigh Hefferon

Managing Content Developer: Alyssa Pratt

Senior Content Developer: Natalie Pashoukos

Product Assistant: Jake Toth

Marketing Director: Michele McTighe

Marketing Managers: Stephanie Albracht and Jeff Tousignant

Marketing Coordinator: Cassie Cloutier

Executive Director, Production: Martin Rabinowitz

Production Director: Patty Stephan

Senior Content Project Manager: Jim Zayicek

Art Director: Heather Marshall

Development Editor: Deb Kaufmann

Cover image(s): iStockphoto.com/blackdovfx

Library of Congress Control Number: 2016963026

ISBN: 978-1-305-07862-8

Cengage Learning
20 Channel Center Street
Boston, MA 02210
USA

Printed in the United States of America
Print Number: 02 Print Year: 2017

Dedication

I dedicate this book to Maria.

Brief Contents

Contents

CHAPTER 8
Managing Windows Server 2016 Network Services 327

CHAPTER 9
Configuring Remote Access Services 377

Introduction

Hands-On Microsoft® Windows® Server 2016 is the perfect resource for learning Windows Server 2016 from the ground up. Designed to build a foundation in basic server administration, this book requires no previous server experience. It covers all of the critical Windows Server 2016 features, including the features unique to this new server operating system. You learn how to choose the right server edition for your needs, and you learn to install, configure, customize, manage, and troubleshoot your server. If you are new to server administration, this book gives you the knowledge you need to manage servers on small to large networks. If you are an experienced server administrator, the book provides a fast way to get up to speed on Windows Server 2016 administration.

The book offers you administrator skills to install and configure Windows Server 2016, use Active Directory, set up server resources for clients, configure and manage printing services, manage data storage, manage network services, configure remote access for clients, create a virtual server, establish strong security, monitor a server, and create a reliable server environment.

Each chapter is written for easy understanding and the book contains over 135 hands-on activities to make what you learn come alive. These activities give you the experience you need to truly learn Windows Server 2016 and retain what you have learned.

In addition to the hands-on activities, the book is filled with many learning aids to help you maximize what you learn. The objectives at the start of each chapter give you an overview of what you will be able to accomplish and can be used for a fast review of the chapter contents. At the end of each chapter, there are chapter summaries for more in-depth point-by-point review. There also are review questions and realistic case studies to enable you to stretch your learning. The case studies put you in the shoes of a Windows Server 2016 consultant who works in all kinds of situations fulfilling the needs of clients. Other learning tools include a list of key terms that you have encountered in the chapter and application examples provided throughout to help you understand different ways to use Windows Server 2016.

The goal when you complete this book is to give you the knowledge and confidence to be a capable server administrator. The book also provides a foundation for pursuing a Microsoft certification in Windows Server 2016 server administration.

Intended Audience

Hands-On Microsoft Windows Server 2016 is intended for anyone who wants to learn and practice using Windows Server 2016. It also can be used as a starting block in preparing for the Microsoft Server administrator certification exam track. No prior server operating system experience is required, but some basic experience with client systems, such as Windows 7, 8/8.1, or 10, is helpful.

New to this Edition

- Step-by-step hands-on activities for learning nearly every phase of Windows Server 2016, with all activities tested by a technical editor, reviewers, and validation experts
- Broad training in planning, installation, configuration, security, networking, monitoring, and troubleshooting of Windows Server 2016
- Coverage of features critical or new to Windows Server 2016, including using the graphical user interface, Windows Server Core, Nano Server, Windows PowerShell, Hyper-V, Server Manager, security features, network services, role services, monitoring tools, and much more
- An appendix to cover using Windows Server 2016 with Hyper-V virtualization
- An appendix showing Windows PowerShell command examples for managing and troubleshooting a server

Chapter Descriptions

The chapters are balanced to provide a similar amount of coverage. There are twelve chapters and two appendices. The beginning chapters introduce the Windows Server 2016 operating system, and show how to plan for, install, and configure Windows Server 2016. Because it can be vital to a server installation, you also learn about Active Directory in the early portion of the book. The middle chapters address how to configure key services, such as file and folder services, printing, data storage, network services, and remote access. The chapters at the end of the book focus on configuring security, server and network monitoring, and ensuring server reliability. The appendices provide supplementary information about using virtualization through Hyper-V and a full range of Windows PowerShell command examples you can use in your work.

- **Chapter 1, Introduction to Windows Server 2016,** explains and compares each of the Windows Server 2016 editions. The chapter discusses client systems that can be used with Windows Server 2016, identifies important features, reviews introductory networking concepts, and shows how to plan a network model to use.
- **Chapter 2, Installing Windows Server 2016,** discusses how to prepare for an installation, describes different installation methods (including using virtualization), and steps through an actual installation. The chapter additionally discusses how to implement Windows Server Core, how to implement Windows Deployment Services, how to install service packs, how to troubleshoot installation problems, and how to uninstall the operating system.
- **Chapter 3, Configuring the Windows Server 2016 Environment,** starts by familiarizing you with the Server Manager management tool. You also learn how to install and uninstall server roles, how to use the Best Practices Analyzer, configure hardware, and configure and tune the operating system. Other topics include using the System File Checker, understanding the Registry, and using Windows PowerShell.
- **Chapter 4, Introduction to Active Directory and Account Management,** presents an extensive introduction to Active Directory, including how to install and configure it. You additionally learn how to create Active Directory containers, and how to create and manage user accounts and security groups. The chapter additionally provides an introduction to Azure Active Directory for cloud services.
- **Chapter 5, Configuring, Managing, and Troubleshooting Resource Access,** teaches you how to manage folders and files, particularly in relation to setting up security. You learn how to create shared objects, such as folders, and how to publish them in Active Directory.

You additionally learn how to troubleshoot security issues, how to use work folders, how to implement the Distributed File System, and how to establish disk quotas.

- **Chapter 6, Configuring Windows Server 2016 Printing,** provides information about the inner workings of Windows Server 2016 printing, including how to install local, network, and Internet printers. You implement the Print and Document Services role and learn about the XPS Print Path. You discover how to manage print jobs and how to troubleshoot printing problems. You also learn to use the Print Management tool.
- **Chapter 7, Configuring and Managing Data Storage,** shows you how to use the Disk Management tool to configure basic and dynamic disks. You learn about RAID, Storage Spaces, and other disk storage and fault tolerance options. You also learn to perform backups and restores and how to troubleshoot storage problems.
- **Chapter 8, Managing Windows Server 2016 Network Services,** focuses on how to configure the essential services needed for a smooth functioning Windows Server 2016 network, including DNS, DHCP, and Internet Information Services (Web Server). You also learn about network interface card teaming and about the IP Address Management tool.
- **Chapter 9, Configuring Remote Access Services,** enables you to learn how to set up and troubleshoot Windows Server 2016 as a virtual private network (VPN) for remote access, such as from the Internet. You additionally learn how to set up and use a DirectAccess server and how to configure and manage Remote Desktop Services for running applications directly on the server.
- **Chapter 10, Securing Windows Server 2016,** shows you a wealth of new and time-tested security features. You learn how to configure security policies, set up Active Directory rights, manage security on clients, create security templates, encrypt files and folders, use the powerful BitLocker Drive Encryption, implement Network Address Translation, configure Windows Firewall, and implement the Windows Defender virus checking software.
- **Chapter 11, Server and Network Monitoring,** teaches you how to monitor a server and a network for troubleshooting and to prevent problems. You learn how to use monitoring tools such as Resource Monitor, the Services tool, Task Manager, Performance Monitor, Data Collector Sets, and the SNMP service. Many of these tools have been enhanced in Windows Server 2016 to offer more functionality.
- **Chapter 12, Managing System Reliability and Availability,** enables you to develop problem-solving strategies for handling server difficulties. You learn how to resolve boot problems, use the Advanced Boot Options, use repair tools on the installation DVD, protect critical systems, use and configure Event Viewer, troubleshoot network problems, and how to remotely administer one or more servers.
- **Appendix A, Windows Server 2016 Virtualization and Hyper-V,** provides a foundation for understanding virtualization and virtual machines. After you learn about virtualization, you learn the ins and outs of Hyper-V, which is virtualization software included with Windows Server 2016. You also learn about using Hyper-V with Windows 8.1 Professional and above and Windows 10 and above.
- **Appendix B, Sample Windows PowerShell Cmdlets,** gives you 60 sample Windows PowerShell cmdlet examples to help you learn how to use this powerful tool. The cmdlets are presented by topical areas: file processing, system-related, network, and security.

Features

To help you better understand how Microsoft Windows Server 2016 and network management concepts and techniques are applied in real-world organizations, this book includes the following learning features:

- Chapter Objectives—Each chapter begins with a detailed list of the concepts to be mastered. This list provides you with a quick reference to the chapter's contents and is a useful study aid.

- Hands-On Activities—Over 135 hands-on activities are incorporated throughout the text, giving you practice in setting up, managing, and troubleshooting a server. The activities give you a strong foundation for carrying out server administration tasks in the real world. Many of the activities present questions for you to investigate and answer, such as by recording your answers in a Microsoft Word file. This is intended to help retention and to provide a study aid that you can go back to.

  For the activities in this book, you can obtain the free Windows Server 2016 evaluation installation DVD from Microsoft or make an installation DVD (or thumb drive) from an .iso file downloaded from Microsoft's download center website. Go to *www.microsoft.com* and search for downloads or click a link for downloads. Also, on a home or lab computer running Windows 8.1 Professional or above or Windows 10 Professional or above, you can use Hyper-V to create a Windows Server 2016 virtual machine running Windows Server 2016. You learn how to do this in Chapter 2, Installing Windows Server 2016, and in Appendix A, Windows Server 2016 Virtualization and Hyper-V.

- Screen Captures, Illustrations, and Tables—Numerous reproductions of screens and illustrations of concepts aid you in the visualization of theories, concepts, and how to use tools and desktop features. In addition, many tables provide details and comparisons of both practical and theoretical information and can be used for a quick review of topics. Some screen captures are cropped to emphasize the concept you are learning.
- Chapter Summary—Each chapter's text is followed by a summary of the concepts introduced in the chapter. These summaries provide a helpful way to recap and revisit the ideas covered in each chapter.
- Key Terms—All of the terms within the chapter that were introduced with boldfaced text are gathered together in the Key Terms list at the end of the chapter. This provides you with a method of checking your understanding of the terms introduced.
- Review Questions—The end-of-chapter assessment begins with a set of review questions that reinforce the ideas introduced in each chapter. Answering these questions will ensure that you have mastered the important concepts.
- Case Projects—Each chapter closes with a multipart case project. In this realistic case example, as a consultant at Aspen Consulting, you implement the skills and knowledge gained in the chapter through real-world setup and administration scenarios.

Text and Graphic Conventions

Additional information and exercises have been added to this book to help you better understand what's being discussed in the chapter. Icons throughout the text alert you to these additional materials. The icons used in this book are described below:

Tips offer extra information on resources, how to attack problems, and time-saving shortcuts.

Notes present additional helpful material related to the subject being discussed.

The Caution icon identifies important information about potential mistakes or hazards.

Each Hands-On Activity in this book is preceded by the Activity icon.

Case project icons mark the end-of-chapter case projects, which are scenario-based assignments that ask you to independently apply what you have learned in the chapter.

Instructor Resources

Everything you need for your course in one place! This collection of book-specific lecture and class tools is available online via *www.cengage.com/login*. Access and download PowerPoint presentations, the Instructor's Manual, and more.

- *Electronic Instructor's Manual*—The Instructor's Manual that accompanies this book includes additional instructional material to assist in class preparation, including suggestions for classroom activities, discussion topics, and additional quiz questions.
- *Solutions*—The instructor's resources include solutions to all end-of-chapter material, including review questions and case projects.
- *Cengage Testing Powered by Cognero*—This flexible, online system allows you to do the following:
  - o Author, edit, and manage test bank content from multiple Cengage solutions.
  - o Create multiple test versions in an instant.
  - o Deliver tests from your LMS, your classroom, or wherever you want.
- *PowerPoint presentations*—This book comes with Microsoft PowerPoint slides for each chapter. They're included as a teaching aid for classroom presentation, to make available to students on the network for chapter review, or to be printed for classroom distribution. Instructors, please feel free to add your own slides for additional topics you introduce to the class.

System Requirements

Hardware Listed in the Windows Server Catalog or has the Windows Server 2016 Certified sticker on the hardware, including:

- 1.4 GHz CPU or faster 64-bit processor
- 512 MB RAM or more (more is better)
- 36 GB or more disk space (more is better)
- Optical drive or USB drive or both
- Super VGA or higher resolution monitor
- Mouse or pointing device
- Keyboard
- Network interface card connected to the classroom, lab, or school network for on-ground students—or Internet access (plus a network interface card installed) for online students
- Printer (optional, but helps to practice setting up a network printer)

Software Windows Server 2016 Standard or Datacenter Edition

Virtualization Windows Server 2016 can be loaded into a virtual server environment, such as Microsoft Hyper-V orVMware. You can download from Microsoft's download center a free copy of Hyper-V for your Windows 8.1 Professional or above personal computer. Hyper-V is included with Windows 10 Professional or above. Using Hyper-V, you can create a virtual machine in which to run Windows Server 2016. See Chapter 2 and Appendix B for details.

About the Author

Michael Palmer is an industry consultant and teacher who has written numerous networking and operating systems books, including best-selling books about Windows Server systems and UNIX/Linux. He holds a Ph.D. degree from the University of Colorado at Boulder and has worked over 30 years in higher education and in the industry as a teacher/professor, systems and networking specialist, technical manager, and consultant. He is president of CertQuick, which provides computer and network consulting services, technical authoring services, and computer science curriculum development for schools. Dr. Palmer is the author of many other books in the industry.

Acknowledgments

Cengage always puts together an outstanding team of people for its publications and I've been fortunate to work with this kind of team. I am especially indebted to Deb Kaufmann, the Development Editor for this book, who is always there to provide guidance, ideas, encouragement, and sound advice. An author couldn't ask for a better Development Editor and true friend on the journey. Natalie Pashoukos has also been vital to this book as the Senior Content Developer, who puts together all the pieces to move it to completion. I also want to thank Kristin McNary, Product Team Manager, for her support from the beginning to make this book happen.

Serge Palladino and Danielle Shaw, the Technical Editors for this book, have also played a key role in reviewing every chapter and appendix for technical and conceptual content. Several Associate Program Managers for Lumina Datamatics Ltd. have also worked diligently on the production aspects of this book. I am also grateful to the peer reviewers who have throughout provided all kinds of essential advice, ideas, insights, and help. They have been important to helping ensure that the book is technically accurate and that it is tailored to the needs of students and teachers as well as general readers. Reviewers include:

Dave Braunschweig, MIS/M
Professor
Harper College
Palatine, IL

Todd Koonts, MSIT, CCE
Program Chair
CTI/Information Assurance and Digital Forensics
Central Piedmont Community College
Charlotte, NC

Dr. Zarreen Farooqi, Ph.D.
Professor, Computer Information Systems
University of Akron
Akron, OH

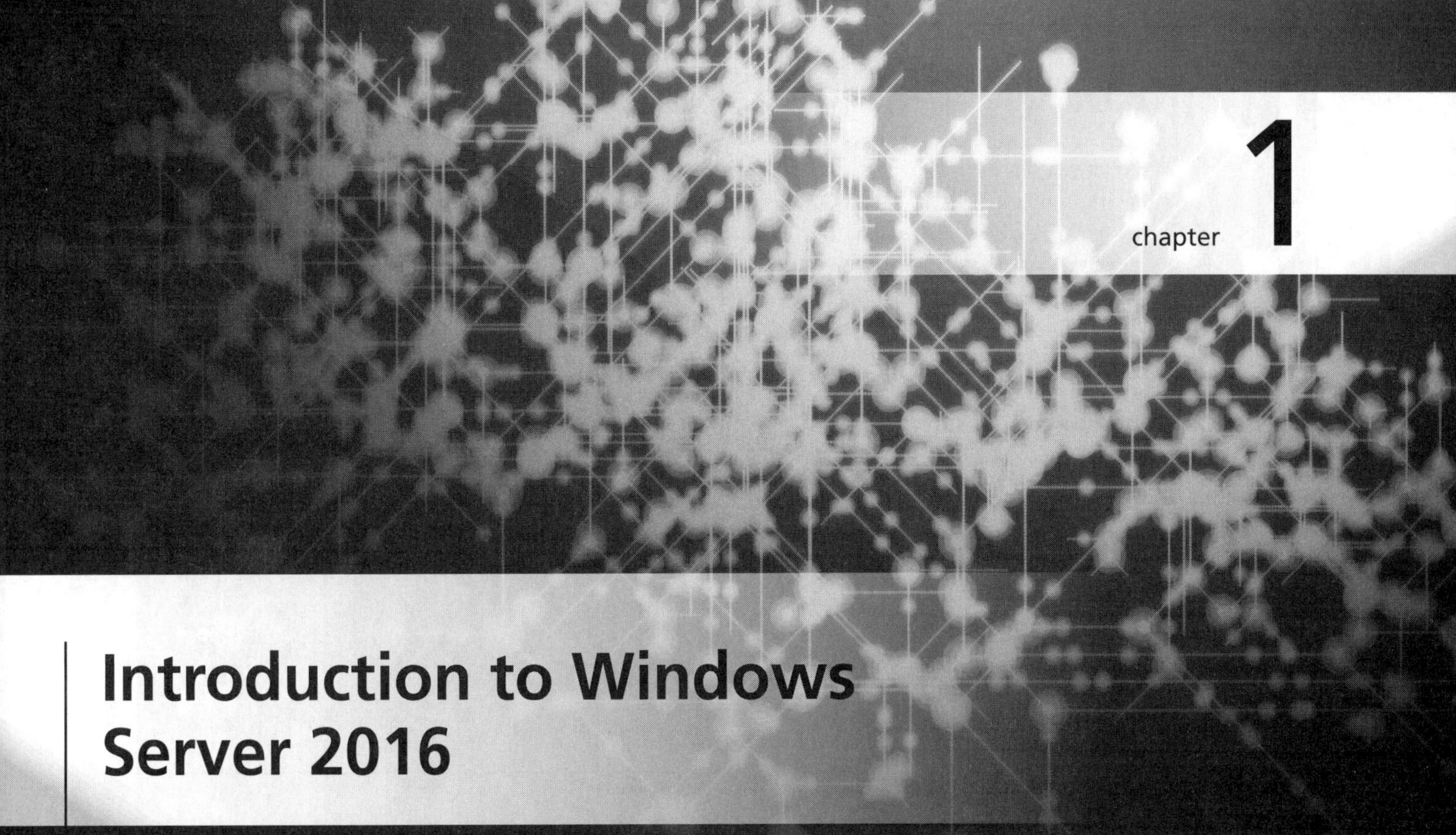

Introduction to Windows Server 2016

After reading this chapter and completing the exercises, you will be able to:

- Identify the key features of each Windows Server 2016 edition
- Understand the hardware requirements for Windows Server 2016
- Identify client systems that can be used with Windows Server 2016
- Understand important general features of Windows Server 2016
- Plan a Windows Server 2016 networking model
- Explore introductory concepts for the networking protocols, IPv4 and IPv6, used by Windows Server 2016
- Configure and enable TCP/IP in Windows Server 2016

Microsoft Windows Server systems are at the core of information access, productivity, and entertainment all over the world. Chances are that you access a Windows server when you store and access data in the cloud, purchase music on the Internet, stream a movie, open a spreadsheet at work, watch a movie on a plane, or send an email. Windows Server 2016 is Microsoft's newest server platform that offers even more roles for servers, better security, easier server management, new desktop features, and more reliable computing than its predecessors.

This book is intended to give you a solid grounding in how to install, administer, and use Windows Server 2016 for all types of computing situations. In this chapter, you begin your journey by learning about the different Windows Server 2016 editions, from the industrial-strength Datacenter Edition to the more basic Essentials Edition. You also learn how Windows Server 2016 works in tandem with client desktop systems such as Windows 7, Windows 8, Windows 8.1, and Windows 10.

Windows Server 2016 incorporates many new features, which you learn about in this chapter and go on to master in later chapters. After exploring the features, you review the networking models used by Windows Server 2016, from peer-to-peer to server-based networking. Finally, you learn basic networking protocol concepts and configuration techniques for effective Windows Server 2016 networking.

Windows Server 2016 Editions

Servers have a wide variety of uses designed to match the needs of users from small businesses to international corporations. They are also finding their way into homes and home offices. Because one size does not fit all needs, it is important to offer different types of server operating systems. Windows Server 2016 comes in several versions. All versions are built on the same foundation but offer unique capabilities to suit a home office or a business with branches all over the world.

The main Windows Server 2016 platforms are as follows:

- Windows Server 2016 Essentials Edition
- Windows Server 2016 Standard Edition
- Windows Server 2016 Datacenter Edition

Additional Windows Server 2016 platforms that are targeted for specific-purpose niches at this writing include:

- Windows Server 2016 Multipoint Premium Server
- Windows Storage Server 2016
- Windows Hyper-V Server 2016

These platforms are discussed in the next sections.

Windows Server 2016 Essentials Edition

For a business or organization with up to 25 users, Windows Server 2016 Essentials Edition is a good option. Another reason to consider Essentials Edition is when your business is relatively small now, but you expect it to grow up to 25 users and you want a system that can grow in the future.

At this writing, Windows Server 2016 Essentials Edition supports a maximum of:

- 25 users
- 16.8 million connections for file sharing through Server Message Block (SMB) services
- 2 central processor sockets
- 50 Remote Desktop connections
- 50 Routing and Remote Access connections

Maximum capabilities are provided at this point to help you understand the differences between editions and how to select the right edition for a specific use.

Besides the limitations of 25 users and 50 devices, Windows Server 2016 Essentials Edition cannot join a domain, other than to migrate files and data from one server to another. A domain is used to centrally manage a large number of users, server applications, and multiple servers (you learn more about domains later in this chapter as well as in Chapter 4, Introduction to Active Directory and Account Management).

Further, Windows Server 2016 Essentials Edition provides most but not all server roles. For example, it does not provide a role for hosting virtual machines, which is the Hyper-V role (you learn about virtual machines in the Windows Server 2016 Standard Edition section of this chapter). This also means that the Essentials Edition cannot provide cloud services to an organization. Even though Windows Server 2016 Essentials Edition cannot host virtual machines, it can be installed in Hyper-V as one of many virtual machines.

Microsoft has implemented features to Server 2016 Essentials Edition (also available on higher editions) to make it particularly attractive to small businesses and organizations. These features include:

- User groups can be created to manage clients and client access to Microsoft Office 365.
- Backups and restores can use file history information for each user instead of only for each device.
- Size and growth of a server folder can be managed through a space quota.
- Installation can be on a standalone physical server or as a virtual machine (guest server) on a virtual server, which means it can be a guest operating system on another server that houses multiple guest operating systems.
- Server Health Reports are automatically installed to be available at the time Essentials Edition is installed.
- Mobile devices can be managed using Dashboard, which is a tool within Server Manager for simplified management of the server.
- BranchCache is available so that data can be accessed quickly on a server running Essentials Edition at an offsite location.

See Table 1-1 to compare Essentials Edition to the other main Windows Server 2016 editions.

Table 1-1 Maximums for the main Windows Server 2016 editions

Limitations	Essentials Edition	Standard Edition	Datacenter Edition
Maximum users	25	Limited only by the number of user licenses and processor cores	Limited only by the number of user licenses and processor cores
Maximum server RAM	64 GB	4 TB	4 TB
Maximum CPU sockets	2	64	64
Can join a domain	Only to enable migration	Yes	Yes
Maximum SMB connections	16.8 million	16.8 million	16.8 million
Maximum Routing and Remote Access connections	50	No limit	No limit
Support for Hyper-V	No support	Yes	Yes
Windows Server containers	No support	No limit	No limit
Hyper-V containers	No support	Up to 2	No limit

Windows Server 2016 Standard Edition

Windows Server 2016 Standard Edition is designed to meet the everyday needs of small to large businesses and organizations. Standard Edition provides file and print services, secure Internet connectivity, centralized management of users, and centralized management of applications and network resources. This platform is built on technology from previous Windows Server systems, such as Windows Server 2003 through Windows Server 2012 R2—but includes many new features. Also, the program coding of old features is constantly enhanced for security and efficiency.

A small company or a department in a larger company might use Windows Server 2016 Standard Edition to manage its accounting and payroll software, for example. A medium-sized or large company might use it to manage email or network resources. Small to large companies might use Standard Edition to manage users' access to application software, such as Office 365.

New features in Windows Server 2016 Standard Edition include:

These new features also apply to the Essentials Edition that is derived from the Standard Edition. Some of these features were introduced with Windows Server 2012 R2 but merit listing here as well.

- The Start button and Start menu are back in the desktop interface after being removed in Windows Server 2012 (the Start button returned in Windows Server 2012 R2 and the Start menu in Server 2016).
- Active Directory, which is the cornerstone database for managing users, applications, and networking, is easier to set up and has improved file security.
- A domain controller, which houses Active Directory, can be cloned to quickly create additional domain controllers.
- **Generic Routing Encapsulation (GRE) tunneling** to enable virtual private networks to go over external networks, including wide area networks (a private communications tunnel over a cable- or public telephone-based network, for example)
- **Desired State Configuration** is used to monitor specific server states and roles so that desired states don't change as other elements are changed on one or many servers in the same server pool.
- **Windows Defender** is automatically included as an antivirus and antimalware program.
- **Storage tiering** allows selected blocks of data to be moved to different storage locations, such as moving data from hard drive storage to solid state storage.
- **Storage pinning** works with storage tiering to enable you to move (and ensure they stay) specific files to a desired type of storage, such as ensuring that customer service files that require fast access are always kept in solid state storage.
- A new network controller role that provides information about the network structure, such as about protocol services, virtual private networks, and the physical structure of a network.
- **Parallel rebuild** that enables a failed disk in RAID (a set of disks for redundant storage) to be rebuilt significantly faster.
- **Virtual desktops**—which is a capability that is also a part of Windows 10—enables you to run different desktops side-by-side, such as having one desktop working with programming tools and another desktop using server administration tools.

Included with Standard Edition is **Hyper-V**. Hyper-V enables Windows Server 2016 to offer a **virtualization** environment, which is a way to run more than one operating system on a single computer at the same time. Historically, organizations have used multiple servers for different operating systems, such as one server for Windows Server 2016 and one for Linux. The disadvantage of this approach is the cost of multiple computers. In organizations that require tens or hundreds of servers, the hardware costs rise fast. Also, additional costs are associated with housing the computers in temperature-controlled computer rooms, including the cost of security and cooling the machines. Virtualization offers a way to cut costs by using fewer computers.

As you learn about virtualization, it is useful to make a distinction between virtual server and virtual machine. A computer running virtual server software, such as Hyper-V, is typically referred to as a **virtual server**, while each instance of an operating system running within the software is a **virtual machine**. A virtual server is considered the host and each virtual machine is a guest. For example, a host computer running Hyper-V might be home to two operating systems, Windows Server 2016 Standard Edition and Linux, both running as guests in a virtual server host. Each operating system is running in its own virtual machine, for a total of two virtual machines.

In Windows Server 2016, Hyper-V is improved on many fronts including faster cloning and migration of individual virtual machines. Also, Hyper-V virtual machine information is stored in a new file format that protects virtual machine information from being directly edited (such as by an attacker or inexperienced administrator).

New to Windows Server 2016 is the option to use containers. Containers enable applications to run in an isolated fashion with the ability to execute multiple applications on one computer system. There are two types of containers: Windows Server containers and Hyper-V containers. Windows Server containers use isolation through domain namespace capabilities and by isolating running processes. In Hyper-V, isolation is achieved because each container runs within a "lightweight" virtual machine. Standard Edition supports unlimited Windows Server containers and up to two Hyper-V containers. You learn more about containers later in the chapter.

In addition to containers, Standard Edition provides basic server elements that enable file and printer sharing, essential network services, application sharing, user authentication, and many other server services. Historically, Standard Edition has paved the way for Windows Server operating systems to use **symmetric multiprocessor (SMP) computers**, which are computers that use more than one processor.

For companies that develop their own software, all editions of Windows Server 2016 are compatible with the common language runtime used in Microsoft .NET Framework and Microsoft Visual Studio .NET, and Windows Server 2016 enables computer programmers to develop and use program code in several programming languages.

Another feature of Windows Server 2016 Standard Edition is clustering. **Clustering** is the ability to increase the access to server resources and provide fail-safe services by linking two or more discrete computer systems so they appear to function as one (see Figure 1-1). An immediate advantage of server clustering is the increase in computer speed or capacity to complete server tasks faster. Also, server clustering provides more computing power for handling resource-hungry applications. With clustering, as an organization adds more users and requires more demanding applications, one or more computers can be added to the cluster to handle the growth. This is a faster, less-expensive approach than having to purchase a larger computer and transfer users and applications to a new system because the old one is overwhelmed. Standard Edition supports clusters of up to 16 computers.

Windows Server 2016 clustering enhancements include Cloud Witness, which enables more integration with Microsoft Azure for cloud computing and the ability to migrate Windows Server 2012 R2 to Windows Server 2016 without having to take servers offline. There is also the ability to create workgroup clusters, clusters all in the same domain, or clusters in different domains. You learn about workgroups and domains later in this chapter.

Windows Server 2016 Standard Edition maximums include (see Table 1-1):

- Number of users limited only by the number of user licenses purchased and number of server cores
- Up to 16.8 million connections for file sharing through SMB services
- Up to 64 central processor sockets
- Number of Remote Desktop connections limited only by the number of user licenses purchased

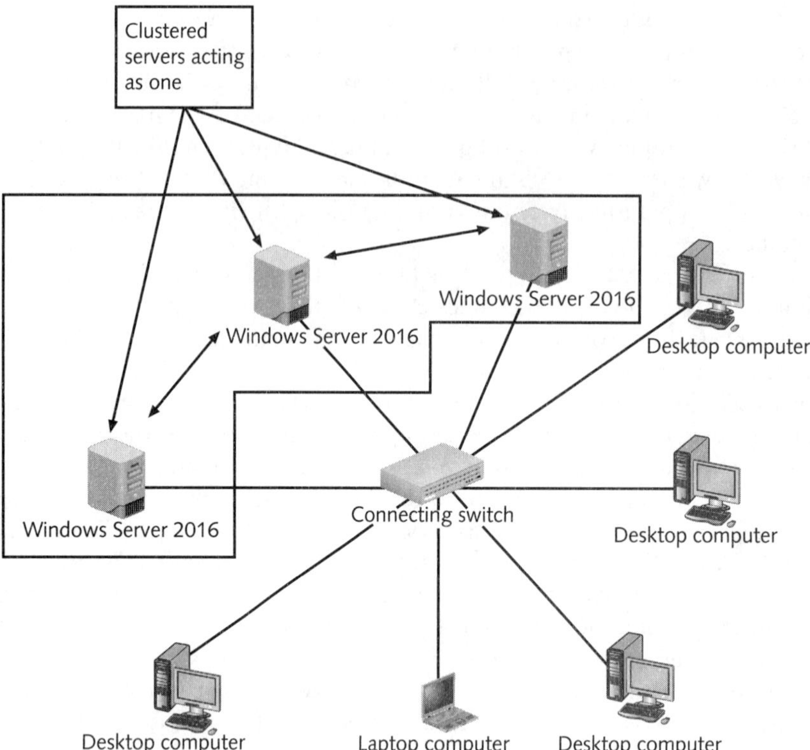

Figure 1-1 Three servers acting as one in a cluster

- Number of Routing and Remote Access connections limited only by the number of user licenses purchased
- No limit to the number of Windows Server containers and up to two Hyper-V containers

Windows Server 2016 Datacenter Edition

Windows Server 2016 Datacenter Edition is designed for environments with mission-critical applications, very large databases, very large virtualization requirements, cloud computing needs, and information access requiring high availability. This platform offers support for clustering with up to 64 computers. As with Standard Edition, Datacenter Edition uses SMP computers supporting up to 64 processor sockets.

The RAM capabilities for the Datacenter Edition are identical to Standard Edition, supporting up to 4 TB. The maximums for Datacenter Edition are (see Table 1-1):

- Number of users limited only by the number of user licenses purchased and number of server cores
- Up to 16.8 million connections for file sharing through SMB services
- Up to 64 central processor sockets
- Number of Remote Desktop connections limited only by the number of user licenses purchased
- Number of Routing and Remote Access connections limited only by the number of user licenses purchased
- No limit to the number of Windows Server containers and Hyper-V containers

The new features in Windows Server 2016 Standard Edition also apply to Datacenter Edition. The differences between the two editions focus on Datacenter Edition's industrial strength capabilities in the areas of virtualization, cloud computing, and database handling—which can all be interlinked on a massive scale. For example, Standard Edition supports only two virtual machines, whereas Datacenter Edition's support for virtual machines is limited only by the hardware resources and operating system licenses that you own—thus it is practically unlimited.

Windows Server 2016 Datacenter Edition does not come with database software, such as Microsoft **SQL Server**, but it is designed to provide the operating system resources to accommodate large database applications in any organization. A university alumni association might use it to house a database that tracks information on thousands of alumni all over the world. A large company, such as an automobile manufacturer, might use it for an integrated accounting system that stores information in a complex database. A national investment firm might use it to track and manage the investment holdings of its customers. Furthermore, with Datacenter Edition, such large databases can be tied into massive virtualization and cloud environments.

Windows Server 2016 Multipoint Premium Server

Multipoint services enable many users to share the same physical computer through each person connecting a keyboard, monitor, and mouse to a USB hub that is connected to a server. This approach, for example, might be used to connect users in a computer lab at a school.

Windows Server 2016 Multipoint Premium Server is offered to educational customers as a way to provide volume licensing for multipoint services. The Multipoint Services role is included as a regular server role in Windows Server 2016 Standard and Datacenter Editions. However, some educational institutions require volume licensing to run multiple computer labs, for example, and Windows Server 2016 Multipoint Premium Server fulfills this need.

Windows Storage Server 2016

Original equipment manufacturers (OEMs) that focus on storage solutions for organizations can offer Windows Storage Server 2016 on the server-based products they sell. Windows Storage Server 2016 turns a server into a central storage center for data in an organization and takes advantage of the storage utilities offered in Windows Server 2016. To learn more about the storage services, see Chapter 7, Configuring and Managing Data Storage.

Microsoft Hyper-V Server 2016

At this writing, Microsoft Hyper-V Server 2016 is a free download of a basic server system that enables you to use Hyper-V. You might use this if you want to learn more about how Hyper-V works or to set up a basic Hyper-V system, such as to load Windows Server Standard Edition into a virtual machine that is dedicated as a simple file and print server or as a DNS server.

Hardware Requirements for Windows Server 2016

Before you install any Windows Server 2016 edition, carefully consider the hardware needs for your installation. Table 1-2 lists the minimum hardware requirements, which is only a starting place. Your server installation should be planned on the basis of what you need to do with the server. Here are some general questions to consider:

- What role or roles will the server have in your organization? For example, is this a small business limited to file and printer sharing? Are you implementing a web server or an email server? Will your server offer remote access or will it be a source of applications for users?
- Do you need to deploy virtual machines, and if so how many? (Hyper-V will need a CPU that supports hardware virtualization, see Appendix A, Windows Server 2016 Virtualization and Hyper-V.)
- What databases will be used and how large are they?
- Will the server offer image libraries or multimedia to users?
- How many local and remote users are to be supported?
- What kind of support is needed from the hardware vendor?
- What redundancy features are needed to ensure the server continues running in the event of a hardware failure, such as a failed disk drive, power supply, or network interface card?
- What growth in server use and resources is expected in the next 3 to 5 years?

Table 1-2 Minimum hardware requirements for Windows Server 2016

Hardware	Minimums	Additional considerations
CPU	1.4 GHz 64-bit processor (includes support for NX, DEP, CMPXCHG16b, LAHF/SAHF, EPT, or NPT)	Processor clock speed, amount of processor cache, number of processor cores (more than one is needed for virtualization), and a processor that supports hardware virtualization for Hyper-V implementations
RAM	512 MB (2 GB for a server with the GUI desktop)	Each virtual machine requires 800 MB for setup (although this can be scaled back after setup is complete)
Hard disk	32 GB	32 GB is enough for using Server Core (command line installation) with web services, 36 GB is the minimum for installing the GUI mode
Network interface card	1 gigabit Ethernet adapter (such as 10/100/1000baseT) that is compatible with PCI Express architecture and Pre-boot Execution Environment (PXE)	Additional adapters are recommended for multiple virtual machines
Optical drive	DVD drive	DVD drive is needed (for installations from DVD media) or a USB drive can be used for installation from a thumb drive
Display	Super VGA at 1024 × 768 or higher resolution	Multiple servers can share one display via the use of a switch box
Interactive devices	Keyboard and pointing device	Multiple servers can share a keyboard and pointing device via the use of a switch box

These questions only provide a starting point for your planning. In a small business, much of the planning can be done with the help of the business owner. In medium and large businesses, the planning will likely require input from management, user departments, technical people, software providers, and hardware vendors.

You can do the hands-on activities in this book from a Windows Server 2016 server with or without virtualization. If you are not working from a virtual machine, just follow the steps as written. If you are using a virtual machine, such as in Hyper-V, you first need to access the server from within the virtual environment or over a network. The following steps show how to start and access a Hyper-V virtual server that is already installed on the local server and how to sign in to a virtual machine within the virtual server. You learn how to install a virtual server in Microsoft Hyper-V in Chapter 2, Installing Windows Server 2016.

Virtual Activity

To access a virtual server in Microsoft Hyper-V, follow these general steps:

1. Click Start, click Windows Administrative Tools, and click Hyper-V Manager.
2. In the Hyper-V Manager window under Virtual Machines, click the virtual machine (server), such as Windows Server 2016.
3. If the server is not already started (State is Off), click the Action menu and click Start as shown in Figure 1-2 (otherwise skip to Step 5). Note that some figures, such as this one, are cropped at the bottom or top for emphasis.
4. Wait for the server to start up.

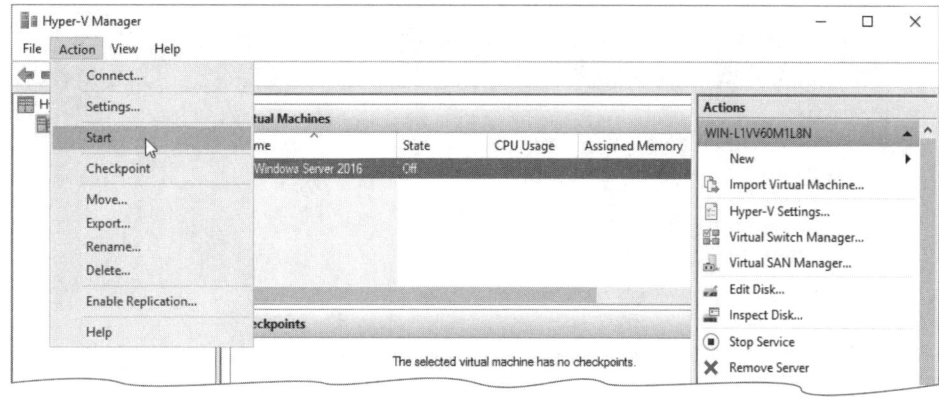

Figure 1-2 Starting a virtual machine in Hyper-V Manager

5. Right-click the name of the server and click **Connect** to open its working window, which is the Virtual Machine Connection window.
6. If you see the screen that says Press CTRL+ALT+DELETE to sign in (don't press CTRL+ALT+DELETE yet), click the Action menu under the title bar and click CTRL+ALT+DELETE.
7. Sign in using your account and password.
8. Click the Maximize square in the upper-right corner of the window to go into the full screen mode or use the View menu and select Full Screen Mode.
9. Whenever you are finished (and signed out of your account) and want to leave the full screen mode, click the Restore Down icon (two tiled squares) in the title bar at the top of the screen (as you would to go back to windowed mode in any application).
10. Close the Virtual Machine Connection window.
11. In the Hyper-V Manager window, if you want to shut down the server, select the server, click the Action menu, and click Shut Down to properly shut down the server. If you see the Shut Down Machine box asking if you are sure you want to shut down, click Shut Down.
12. Close Hyper-V Manager.

Some steps in the activities in this book include bulleted questions for you to answer. Plan to record your answers in a Microsoft Word document, in a course journal, in your class notes, or in the book margins for later personal reference or for your instructor to see. Additionally, for all of the activities in this chapter, you'll need an account with Administrator privileges. These activities can be completed on a virtual machine or computer, such as in Hyper-V.

Activity 1-1: Determining the Windows Server 2016 Edition

Time Required: Approximately 5 minutes
Objective: Determine the Windows Server 2016 edition installed on a computer.

Description: A computer room might have only a few or hundreds of servers. Sometimes it is important for a server administrator to verify which edition of Windows Server 2016 is running on a particular server. In this activity, you learn how to make a quick determination. You will need a server account provided by your instructor or server administrator.

1. Sign in to Windows Server 2016 using your account.
2. If Server Manager is not already open, click **Start** and click the **Server Manager** tile (or click **Start** and click **Server Manager** under S in the listing of selections).
3. Click **Local Server** in the left pane of Server Manager (see Figure 1-3).

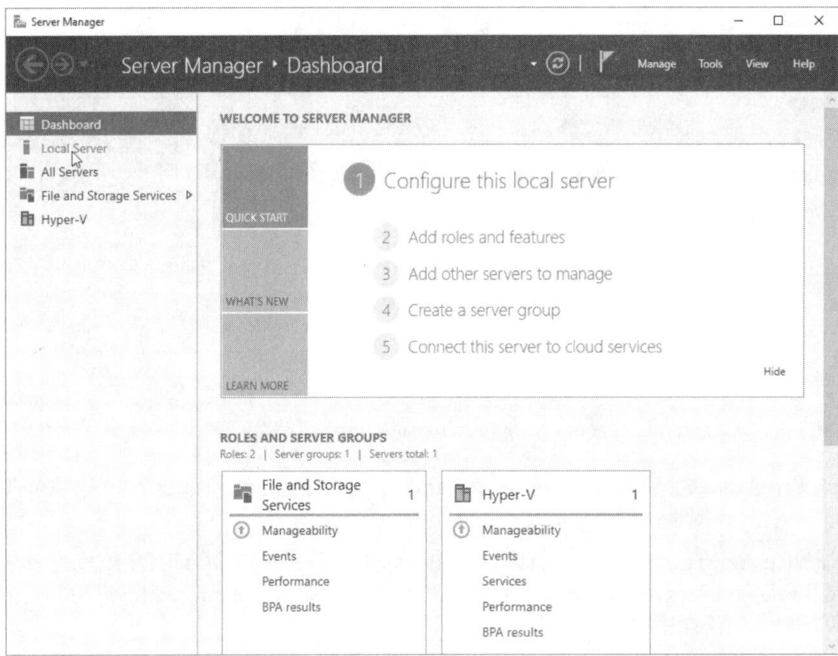

Figure 1-3 Selecting Local Server in Server Manager

4. Locate Operating system version under Properties in the right pane. Here you'll see the edition of Windows Server 2016, such as Microsoft Windows Server 2016 Datacenter or Microsoft Windows Server 2016 Datacenter Evaluation (if you are using an evaluation version).
   - Which version of Windows Server 2016 is installed on your computer?
5. Notice the other information available in this window.
   - Is the Windows Firewall turned on?
6. Leave Server Manager open for Activity 1-2.

Using Windows Server 2016 with Client Systems

The client workstation operating systems most compatible with Windows Server 2016 are Windows versions 7, 8, 8.1, and 10, with Windows 10 the most compatible in terms of client management. A **client** is a computer that accesses resources on another computer via a network or direct cable connection; a **workstation** is a computer that has its own central processing unit (CPU) and can be used as a stand-alone or network computer (often used for a combination of word-processing, spreadsheet, scientific, and other individual applications).

The overall goal of Microsoft is to use the Windows Server 2016 platforms and Windows versions 7 through 10 on the same network to achieve a lower TCO. The **total cost of ownership (TCO)** is the full cost of owning a network, including hardware, software, training, maintenance, and user support costs. Windows versions 7 through 10 are designed as reliable and secure workstation operating systems to be used in a business environment in a peer-to-peer network or as a member of a domain. A **domain** is a grouping of network objects, such as computers, servers, and user accounts, that provides for centralized management. Computers and users in a domain can be managed to determine what resources they can access, such as printers and shared folders. A domain is given a name, such as Microsoft.com for Microsoft. In addition, computers within a domain are given a unique name, which often parallels the name of a user, such as Brown, or is a favorite name or word, such as *antelope* or *popcorn*. You learn more about domains in Chapter 4, Introduction to Active Directory and Account Management.

Recognizing that professionals are highly mobile, Windows versions 7 through 10 are designed to work equally well on a desktop computer or on a laptop computer.

Windows 8 introduced touch screen computing to Windows desktop and laptop computers.

In terms of networking advancements, some of the advantages of using Windows Server 2016 and Windows versions 7 through 10 include the following:

- Enhanced capabilities to recover from many types of network communications problems
- Computer code for more efficient network communications
- More network diagnostic capabilities
- Computer code for better use of the network communications protocols, IPv4 and IPv6, with special emphasis on IPv6
- Continuing upgrades for Windows PowerShell commands and scripts in Windows Server 2016 as well as in Windows 7 through 10 (you learn more about Windows PowerShell later in this chapter)

Windows Server 2016 is intended to play a key management role on a network by hosting **Active Directory**—a database of computers, users, groups of users, shared printers, shared folders, and other domain resources—and by offering a multitude of network services. Windows versions 7 through 10 offer the best compatibility with the newest version of Active Directory in Windows Server 2016. By combining Windows versions 7 through 10, client workstations and Windows Server 2016 under the management of Active Directory, it is possible to centralize security, applications, application updates, desktop customizations, and automated client configuration via a server, thus reducing the TCO.

Another Microsoft long-term objective is to encourage users to convert all workstation operating systems on a network to the latest Windows client operating system, because the TCO for using the latest client operating system is less than for older workstation operating systems, such as Windows XP or Vista. The TCO is less because the latest Windows client operating system is able to use automated installation, configuration, desktop, and management policy features controlled through Windows Server 2016. Also, although older Windows client operating systems support Active Directory, they don't support some newer elements. Many desktop configuration settings (including software deployment) can be automated from Windows Server 2016 to Windows clients, so that the user can set up a client workstation with less technical knowledge or assistance.

In addition to Windows clients, Windows Server 2016 supports Linux computing options, through **Linux Integration Services (LIS)**, which enable Linux clients to access a Linux virtual machine in Hyper-V. These servers also provide greater functionality for Linux virtual machines. Some Linux distributions, such as Red Hat Enterprise Linux, already have certified drivers for Hyper-V.

The new capabilities in LIS that are included with Windows Server 2016 are:

- New software for enhanced desktop graphics performance on Linux clients
- Improved backup support functions
- Creation of kernel dumps for Linux virtual machines
- Better control of available RAM in Linux virtual machines

Most Linux distributions (distros) can run software called Samba, which enables a Linux computer to connect to a Windows Server system to access files and resources.

Windows Server 2016 Features

Windows Server 2016 offers many features that make it a solid server and network operating system. The following list is a sampling of features in Windows Server 2016 that deserve special focus:

- Server Manager
- Security
- Clustering
- Enhanced web services
- Windows Server Core and Nano Server
- Windows PowerShell
- Virtualization
- Reliability
- Multitasking and multithreading
- Physical and logical processors
- Containers

Each of these features is introduced in the sections that follow. You will learn more about these features as you continue through this book.

Server Manager

Windows Server 2008 introduced the Server Manager tool, and Windows Server 2016 adds even more enhancements to the tool. **Server Manager** enables the server administrator to manage critical configuration and management features with one tool. In earlier versions of Windows Server, you might have to look in several places to do different tasks. Server Manager puts the management tasks together in one place. When you first sign in with administrator privileges, Server Manager automatically starts. You can use this tool to do the initial setup of your server, as you learn in Chapter 2. After your server is configured, you use this tool to modify settings and manage one or more servers. Server Manager is used to:

- Configure a server from the beginning.
- View computer configuration information.
- Change server roles and system properties.
- Configure networking.
- Configure Remote Desktop.
- Configure security, including the firewall.
- Configure a multitude of server roles, from a basic file server to advanced network services.
- Add and remove features.
- Run diagnostics.
- Manage storage and backups.
- Manage multiple servers from one place.

In many cases, when the administrator selects a management function, Server Manager starts an automated process or wizard for step-by-step guidance through the task. Wizards are helpful for learning tasks and for reducing configuration errors. Server Manager is particularly useful for beginning and intermediate administrators but also centralizes common tasks for advanced administrators.

In Windows Server 2016, the new features of Server Manager include the following advantages:

- The Local Server option makes all of the local server properties available to manage.
- Multiple servers are easier to manage from one place.

- Servers can be grouped so that all the servers in a specific group receive one or more commands simultaneously.
- The Dashboard offers even more quick-start guidance for setting up one or more servers and establishing groupings used to manage specific kinds of servers.
- The Server Manager GUI has a new look different from Windows Server 2012 with added features, such as greater ability to add and manage remote servers.

Security

Windows Server 2016 is built to be even more secure than previous Windows Server systems. One important approach built in to Windows Server 2016 is implementing security by default. When you install Windows Server 2016, add a feature, or install a Windows component, an essential level of security is automatically implemented. This helps to ensure that no backdoors are left open for an attacker.

Windows Server 2016 additionally includes many basic security features, such as:

- File and folder permissions
- Security policies
- Encryption of data
- Event auditing
- Various authentication methods
- Server management and monitoring tools

Clustering and Clustering Tools

Clustering is an important feature of Windows Server 2016 because it not only makes a server system more powerful, but it also provides failover capabilities, so that if one server in a cluster fails, its work is automatically taken over by other servers in the cluster. Clustering also enables a large amount of disk storage to be made available to users, with failover for disk storage as well.

The power of clustering is only as good as the tools used to configure it. Windows Server 2016 offers tools to:

- Test a cluster to ensure it is set up to accomplish the tasks for which it is intended.
- Migrate configuration settings from one cluster to another.
- Quickly configure a cluster and troubleshoot problems.
- Set up storage used in a cluster.
- Create better cluster storage performance and reliability.
- Secure a cluster and enable it to use new network capabilities.

Enhanced Web Services

Windows Server 2016 comes with Microsoft **Internet Information Services (IIS)** to transform the server into a versatile web server. Consistent with Microsoft's emphasis on security, IIS is implemented in multiple modules. This design is intended to enable IIS to have a lower attack surface (vulnerable openings exposed to network attackers and malicious software). In addition to reducing the attack surface, individual modules handle specific security issues.

Another security feature is easy application of IIS patches. Microsoft often issues patches for its software as new attack techniques against its operating systems and applications are discovered. Easy patching means that system administrators are more likely to apply security patches in a timely way.

IIS is also redesigned to make it easy for network programmers to write network applications and configure applications for the web. Also, complementing the applications development enhancements, IIS has better management tools that are incorporated into the IIS Manager. Administrators also can manage IIS remotely for greater convenience and access.

Windows Server Core and Nano Server

Windows Server 2016 gives you the option to install a minimal server environment using Server Core or Nano Server. These two options are explained in the following sections.

Windows Server Core Windows Server Core is best understood not by what it has, but by what it does not have. **Windows Server Core** is a minimum server configuration, designed to function in a fashion similar to traditional UNIX and Linux servers. One of the advantages of UNIX and Linux systems is that they can be installed with a simple command-line interface and only the minimum services needed to get the job done. This offers three distinct advantages. First, there is reduced overhead by omitting the graphical interface, which means the CPU can be devoted to accomplishing the essential work of the computer. A second advantage is that less disk space and memory are needed for everyday tasks. The third advantage is that the computer has a much smaller attack surface. Some UNIX and Linux server administrators appreciate the flexibility, simplicity, and power of working at a command line. With Server Core, Windows server administrators can install the same type of system.

When you install Windows Server Core, you don't have the following:

- A graphical interface, just a command line
- Graphical tools to configure the server, such as Server Manager
- Extra services that you do not need
- A mouse pointer on the screen
- Windows Mail, Microsoft Word, search windows (in fact no windows), and other software

There are exceptions because there is some window and mouse functionality for certain applications, such as window-based Control Panel applets, the Registry editor, and Notepad for editing text files.

What you do have are the essential or core services needed to run a server. You can still create server accounts through commands at a command line. You can configure security measures and get operating system and software updates. You can install and configure hardware. You can configure a combination of roles for the server, such as file serving, print serving, or handling distributed shared files across multiple computers. You can open the Notepad screen editor to create and edit files. Windows Server Core is an installation mode available at the time you install your Windows Server 2016 edition.

You can remotely manage a server installed with Server Core using GUI tools.

Windows Nano Server **Windows Nano Server** is introduced as a new installation option in Windows Server 2016. Windows Nano Server is based on the same small footprint idea as Windows Server Core, but it is smaller still. Having a base image of only 400 MB, Nano Server is many times smaller than even Server Core. However, Nano Server still has fundamental elements, such as the **.Net Framework**, used to develop and execute applications. It can also host server roles as explained in Chapter 2. Windows Server 2016 developers at Microsoft describe Nano Server as a "remotely administered server operating system optimized for cloud and datacenters."

The idea behind Nano Server is to provide a basic foundation for server computing, particularly in the cloud, that can be used for the next 20 years. Nano Server is designed to run only 64-bit applications. It is intended to be faster and to need less maintenance than graphical Windows Server or Server Core, such as updates, because it is such a bare-bones operating system. Because you cannot sign in to Nano Server locally, it is not suitable to be housed in a single standalone computer box. Rather, it is designed to be installed on a modular server card (called a blade server) in an enclosed cabinet (called a blade enclosure) containing many such cards.

Microsoft views Nano Server as a platform on which to run a (an):

- DNS or DHCP server
- Applications server, such as from the cloud
- Web server
- Database or file server

Windows PowerShell

Server administrators who want command-line capability, but also want to install the full-fledged Windows Server 2016 operating system with the graphical user interface (GUI), can use **Windows PowerShell**. Windows PowerShell is a command-line interface that offers a **shell**, a customized environment for executing commands and scripts. **Scripts** are files that contain commands to be run by a computer operating system. Scripts save time because commands don't have to be typed individually by the user each time a particular set of activities needs to be accomplished, such as adding new data to a file.

Using scripts can save a computer user or administrator a lot of time because an involved sequence of commands is stored in a file to use time and time again—so you don't have to memorize the sequence. It's not unusual to hear a computer user (including this author) comment that he spent considerable time trying to figure out how to accomplish a task and a month later does not remember what the specific steps were. Recording the commands in a script solves this problem.

By using the commands available in Windows PowerShell, you can do the following types of tasks:

- Work with files and folders
- Manage disk storage
- Manage network tasks
- Set up local and network printing options
- Install, list, and remove software applications
- View information about the local computer, including user accounts
- Manage services and processes
- Lock a computer or sign out
- Manage IIS web services

Windows PowerShell is automatically integrated with Windows Server 2016 and offers several hundred command-line tools, also called **cmdlets**. A scripting language is also implemented in Windows PowerShell. Windows PowerShell is additionally integrated with Windows 8.1 and Windows 10—and is available for earlier Windows server and desktop versions through Windows Server 2003 and Windows XP with Service Pack 2. For people who manage an enterprise of different Windows computers, Windows PowerShell can be important for automating all kinds of tasks. For example, scripting is often used to create and set up user accounts or to import hundreds of users from an older server. Figure 1-4 shows Windows PowerShell using the Get-Childitem cmdlet to list the files in the current directory, which is the directory of the Administrator account.

PowerShell is also used in Server Core. Nano Server uses a smaller set of commands and cmdlets through PowerShell Core. The time you take to learn PowerShell commands and cmdlets can be very productive, because it applies to both the GUI and Server Core environments, and to Nano Server on a more limited basis.

Virtualization

The Hyper-V in Windows Server 2016 provides the ability to run two or more operating systems on a single computer. Virtualization has become important to organizations because it offers a way to save expenses and to provide more uptime for computing. Consider a scenario in which an organization has 30 servers and they want to reduce this number to 5 so they can put the servers in a smaller central computer room and use the space of the old room for other purposes. They can do this by using Hyper-V to install six operating systems on each server (using Datacenter Edition). Besides gaining space, virtualization simplifies server management by reducing the number of computers to manage. This offers cost savings because five computers use less energy than 30.

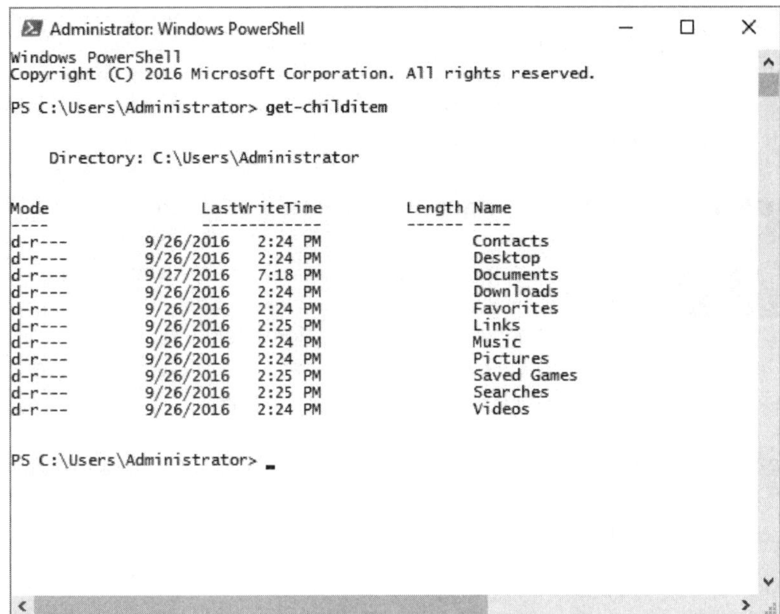

Figure 1-4 Using Windows PowerShell for a directory listing

Another situation that is common to organizations is the need to have a test platform for the development of new applications. Consider a small company that provides a nationwide database service to agricultural colleges. This company has four servers, one for applications and three containing databases. Two programmers develop specialized software for the database service. This type of software development must be done in a test environment before it is brought live for production. The company can use Hyper-V on the single applications server to create one system for production and one for testing.

Or, consider a retail business that takes product orders through web services, over the telephone, and through surface mail. The company is concerned about redundancy in case of fire or another disaster scenario. One way to have redundancy is to use Hyper-V on one or two servers that are in a different location and to perform regular backups to that location. This provides disaster recovery, so that operations could be continued from the remote location.

Hyper-V capabilities include the following:

- Compatible with clustering
- Can be used with Windows and Linux operating systems, which are commonly implemented for servers
- Compatible with different types of disk storage methods
- Enables fast migration from one computer to another
- Can host 64-bit and 32-bit operating systems

Reliability

Several features make Windows Server 2016 reliable and powerful. The operating system kernel runs in **privileged mode**, which protects it from problems created by a malfunctioning program or process. The **kernel** consists of the core programs and the computer code of the operating system. Privileged mode gives the operating system kernel an extra level of security from intruders and prevents system crashes due to poorly written applications.

In addition to privileged mode, Microsoft has implemented typical and protected processes in both Windows Server 2016 and Windows 7 through 10. A **process** is a computer program or portion of a program that is currently running. One large program might start several smaller programs or processes. A *typical process* is like one on previous Windows systems in which the process can be influenced by a user or other processes. A *protected process* is one for which outside influences are restricted. The concept of a protected process is important because some activities shouldn't be interrupted prematurely, such as updating a database.

Another feature that contributes to reliability is the implementation of powerful management tools, including Server Manager and a host of wizards that provide step-by-step guidance. These tools help ensure that the server administrator does not introduce errors or problems when configuring and managing a server. Server administrators can also use the Performance Monitor to identify trouble spots so they can be addressed.

Activity 1-2: Viewing Running Processes

Time Required: Approximately 5 minutes
Objective: View the processes running in Windows Server 2016 using Resource Monitor.

Description: Windows Server 2016 runs many processes at any one time. Some of the processes are used by a program you are using, such as Windows Explorer. Other processes are running in the background, such as a process for your desktop background. In this activity, you view the running processes using a tool in Windows Server 2016 called Resource Monitor.

1. Ensure your computer is signed in and make certain that Server Manager is already running. If Server Manager is not open, click **Start** and click the **Server Manager** tile; or click **Start** and click **Server Manager** under the S in the listing.
2. Click **Local Server** in the left pane of Server Manager.
3. In the menu bar at the top of the Server Manager window, click **Tools** to see a drop-down menu of administrative tools.
4. Click **Resource Monitor** (see Figure 1-5).
5. Ensure that the **Overview** tab is selected.
6. Move the cursor so that it is on top of the line just above the Disk section in Resource Monitor and you see an up and down arrow. With the up and down arrow displayed, drag the Disk section down to view more of the processes shown in the CPU section (see Figure 1-6).
7. Scroll through the CPU section and notice that ServerManager.exe is one of the running processes.
8. Using the scroll bar, examine all of the processes that are running.
   - Record the names of two processes other than ServerManager.exe.
9. Close Resource Monitor, but leave Server Manager open.

Multitasking and Multithreading

Windows Server 2016 and other recent Windows systems take full advantage of the multitasking and multithreading capabilities of modern computers. **Multitasking** is the ability to run two or more programs at the same time. For example, Microsoft Word can print a document at the same time that a Microsoft Excel spreadsheet can calculate the sum of a column of numbers. **Multithreading** is the capability of programs written to run several program code blocks, or

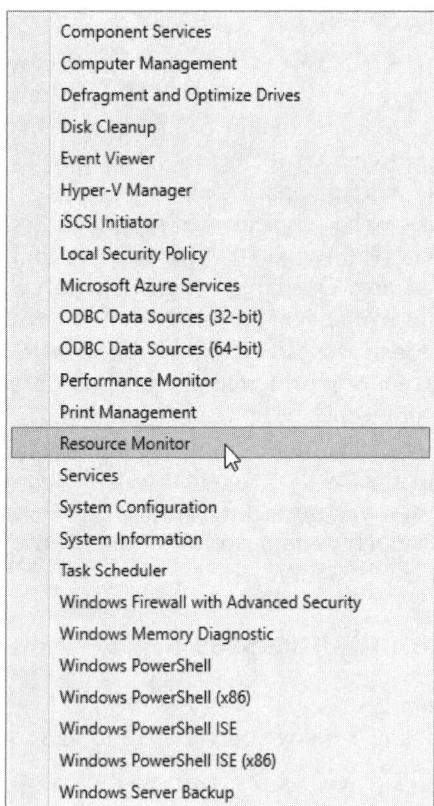

Figure 1-5 Selecting Resource Monitor on the Tools menu

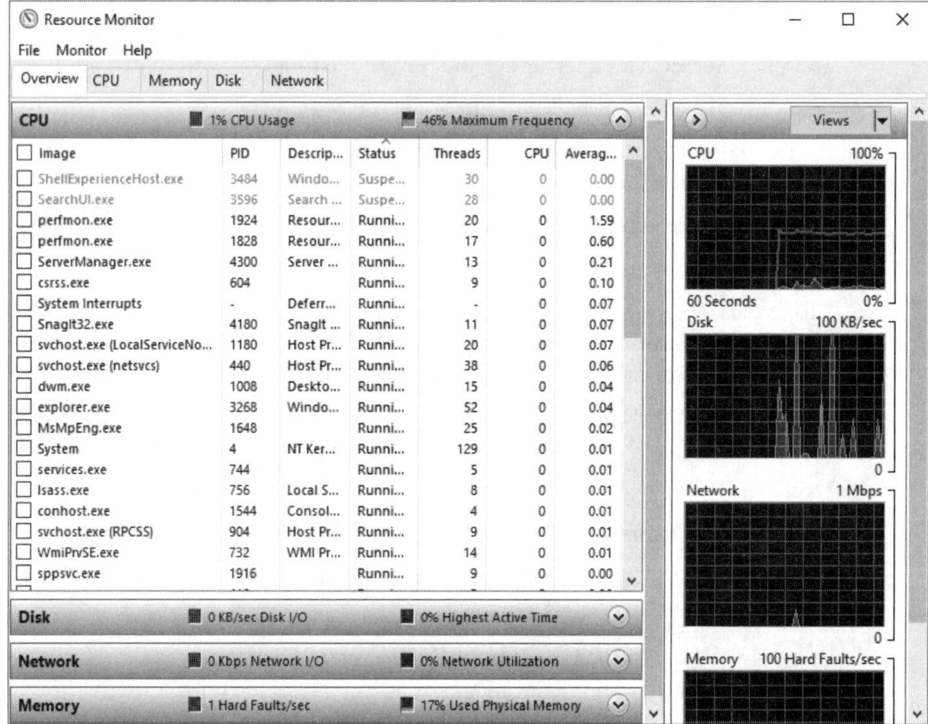

Figure 1-6 Viewing processes in Resource Monitor

"threads," at the same time. For instance, a Microsoft Access database query runs a thread to pull data out of the database, while another thread generates a subtotal of data already obtained.

The multitasking in Windows Server 2016 is called **preemptive multitasking**. This means each program runs in an area of memory separate from areas used by other programs. Early versions of Windows used cooperative multitasking, in which programs shared the same memory area. The advantage of preemptive multitasking is that it reduces the risk of one program interfering with the smooth running of another program, which increases reliability.

Physical and Logical Processors

One of the reasons why Windows Server has become such a versatile and powerful operating system is that it can be scaled upward in processor capacity. As more capacity is needed, more processors can be added.

A **physical processor** is plugged into a processor socket on the motherboard of the computer. As shown previously in Table 1-1, Windows Server 2016 can support up to 64 sockets for individual physical processors (SMP computers). Further, one physical processor can actually house several **logical processors**. Each logical processor is a core that can run its own executable threads. A physical processor might consist of four cores, for example, that enable it to function as four processors in one.

When a computer is functioning as a virtual server, each virtual machine can be set up to use logical processors and their cores as virtual processors. In this case, a **virtual processor** is a logical processor or one or more of its cores that function for the use of a specific virtual machine.

Without Hyper-V in use (no virtual processors), Windows Server 2016 can have up to 640 logical processors—using up to 64 sockets—which is a lot of processing capacity. With Hyper-V in use, Windows Server 2016 supports up to 320 logical processors—again with up to 64 sockets.

Containers

New to Windows Server 2016, **containers** enable you to isolate a specific application to run in its own environment. While running inside a container, it is as if that application has its own unique access to Windows Server 2016 operating system files— including running processes, using the file system, using the registry, and even a unique access to network communication addresses. The Windows Server 2016 implementation of containers is modeled after the same concept that is already successfully used in Linux distributions. Container technology is considered the next significant step in virtualization.

Using a container establishes a separate layer or engine for each application. You might think of it as having a special engine (the container) that runs within a main engine (the operating system). The idea is to increase the efficiency of the application operating environment, while keeping the total system footprint to a minimum. Using container technology enables an application to run more securely and with less contention from other applications than in operating systems without container technology. Reducing the overall footprint of a server system not only uses system resources more efficiently, it also makes operations less visible to attackers.

Windows Server 2016 offers two types of containers:

- *Windows server containers*, which run through process and user-mode isolation. This form of isolation still involves a base-level sharing of the operating system kernel. A drawback is that an application in one container that has become rogue due to malware might still attack other containers. Another drawback is that if there is an operating system patch installed that causes problems with applications, it can affect the applications running in multiple containers.
- *Hyper-V containers*, which involve a separate container for each virtual machine running in Hyper-V. There is only one container per virtual machine, which means there is a one-to-one relationship between the operating system kernel and virtual machine. This approach eliminates the chance that a rogue application in one container might attack other containers. Also, if an operating system patch adversely affects applications, only one application is affected, because the virtual machine has only one container.

- Figure 1-7 illustrates the architecture of Windows server containers versus Hyper-V containers.

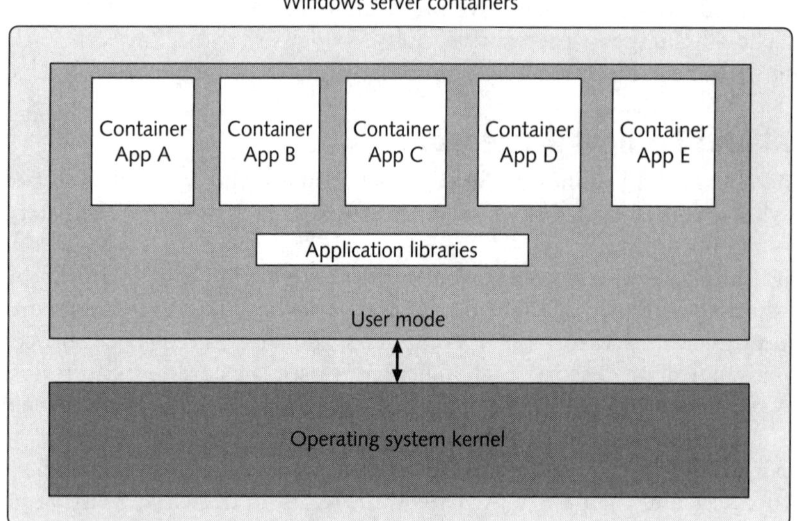

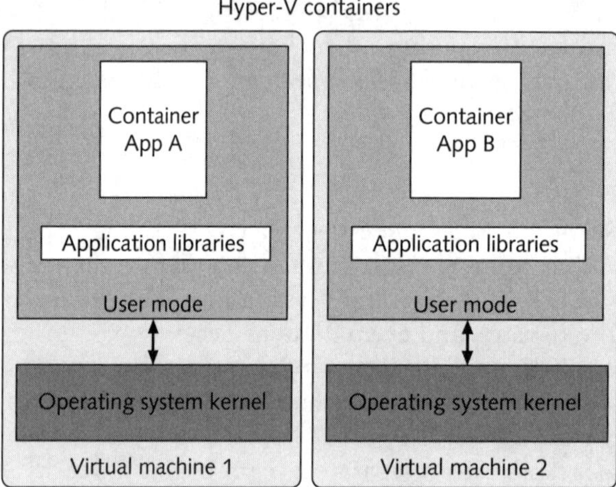

Figure 1-7 Windows Server versus Hyper-V containers

Planning a Windows Server 2016 Networking Model

In its simplest form, a network is two or more computers linked together. This provides users with the ability to share devices and applications, exchange files, and communicate via email or videoconferencing. The following sections introduce you to the two basic networking models used with Windows Server 2016 and its workstation clients (such as Windows 10): the peer-to-peer model and the server-based model.

As a network operating system, Windows Server 2016 is used to coordinate the ways computers access resources available to them on the network. A **network** is a communications system enabling computer users to share computer equipment, application software, data, voice, and video transmissions. Physically, a network contains computers joined by communications cabling or wireless communications. Networks can link users who are in the same office or building, in a different state, or anywhere in the world (see Figure 1-8).

A workstation or client network operating system is one that enables individual computers to access a network, and in some cases to share resources on a limited basis. As you learned earlier, a workstation is a computer that has its own central processing unit (CPU) and can

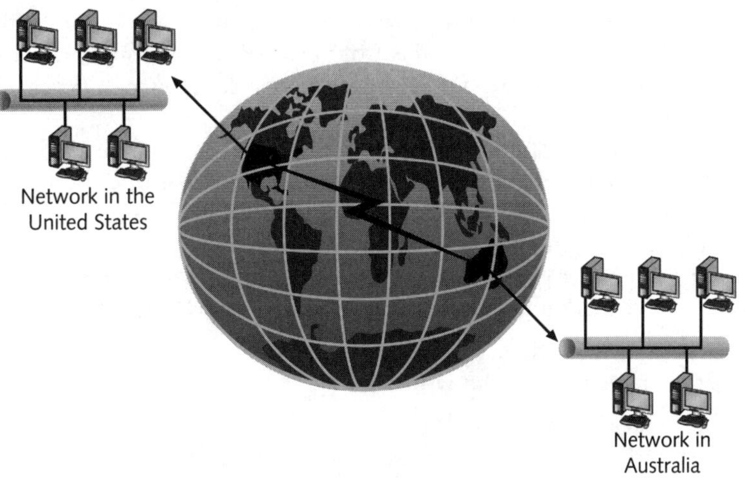

Figure 1-8 Networking across continents

be used as a stand-alone or network computer for word processing, spreadsheet creation, or other software applications. A client is a computer that accesses resources on another computer through a network or by a direct connection.

Windows Server 2016 can be implemented using either peer-to-peer networking, server-based networking, or a combination of both. **Peer-to-peer networking** focuses on spreading network resource administration among server and non-server members of a network, whereas **server-based networking** centralizes the network administration on one or more servers. Often small organizations use the peer-to-peer networking model, whereas medium-sized and large networks use the server-based model.

Peer-to-Peer Networking

A peer-to-peer network is one of the simplest ways to configure a network and is often used for home offices and small businesses. On a peer-to-peer network, workstations are used to share resources such as files and printers and to connect to resources on other computers. Windows Server 2016 and Windows 10 are examples of operating systems that can be used for peer-to-peer network communication. Files, folders, printers, applications, and devices on one computer can be shared and made available for others to access. No special computer is needed to enable workstations to communicate and share resources, although in some cases a computer with a server operating system (but no installed domain services) can be used as a powerful workstation (see Figure 1-9).

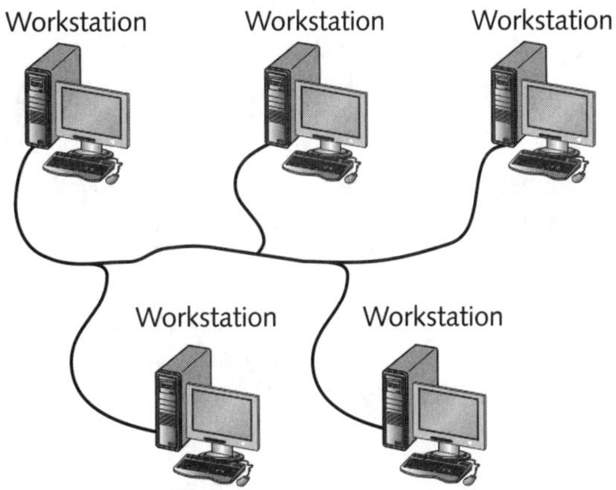

Figure 1-9 A simple peer-to-peer network without a server

Peer-to-peer networking can be effective for very small networks, but it does present some disadvantages. With this model, management of network resources is decentralized. As the network increases in size and the number of shared network resources increases, administration becomes more difficult.

Security of the resources is another important issue. Each of the users is responsible for the security of their own resources and must know how to set the proper permissions and security. Also, a client operating system is not designed to handle a growing load of clients in the same way as a server operating system.

Peer-to-peer networks are generally designed for about 10 workstations or less. As the number of workstations surpass this number, this model becomes less effective for the following reasons:

- Peer-to-peer networking offers only moderate network security because user account information must be managed on each workstation.
- This model provides no centralized storage of information for account management. As the number of network users grows, so does the need to have a central place to store and manage user account information and account security.
- Network management becomes more difficult because there is no point of centralized administrative control from which to manage users and critical files, including backing up important files.
- Workstation-based peer-to-peer networks can often experience slow response times because this model is not optimized for larger numbers of multiple users accessing one computer. If many workgroup members decide to access one shared drive on a non-server system or some other shared resource at the same time, all members are likely to experience slow response.
- On Microsoft networks, a **workgroup** is a number of users who share drive and printer resources, and it represents an alternative (generally for small networks) to organizing resources in a domain.

Activity 1-3: Determining if a Computer Is in a Domain or a Workgroup

Time Required: Approximately 5 minutes
Objective: Discover if a particular computer is in a domain or a workgroup.

Description: Some networks combine the use of domains and workgroups. Often workgroups are less secure and less tightly managed than a domain, leaving workgroup resources more susceptible to intruders and more likely to have problems with reliable access to shared resources, such as files. In this activity, you learn how to determine if a Windows Server 2016 computer is a member of a domain or workgroup.

1. Ensure Server Manager is started and that its window is open.
2. If necessary, click **Local Server** in the left pane of Server Manager.
3. Under Properties in the right pane, look to see if your computer is designated as in a domain or workgroup.
    - Is your computer identified as being in a workgroup or a domain? What name is used? Also, what is the computer name?
4. Leave Server Manager open.
5. Alternatively, you can determine if your computer is in a domain or workgroup from the System window. Right-click **Start** and click **System**. Look under the heading *Computer name, domain, and workgroup settings* (see Figure 1-10).
6. Close the System window.

Figure 1-10 System window showing the Workgroup or Domain membership and computer name

You can use the System window in Windows 7 through 10 to determine if a computer is in a workgroup or a domain. For example, in Windows 7, click Start, right-click Computer, and click Properties. In Windows 8 and 8.1, click Start, right-click This PC, and click Properties. In Windows 10, right-click Start and click System.

Server-Based Networking

Windows Server 2016 is a more scalable network operating system than a workstation operating system, such as Windows 10, and unlike Windows 10, Windows Server 2016 has features that make it a true server operating system. A **server** is a single computer that provides extensive multiuser access to network resources. For example, a single server can act as a file and print server, a web server, a network administration server, a database server, an email server, a streaming media server, or a combination of any of these. Depending on the hardware capabilities, the server can handle hundreds of users at once, providing fast response when delivering the shared resource, and less network congestion when multiple workstations access that resource. Figure 1-11 illustrates a Windows Server 2016 server-based network.

The server-based model offers a wide array of options for networking. For instance, implementing this model can provide the following advantages:

- Users only need to sign in once to gain access to network resources.
- Security is stronger because access to shared resources and to the network itself can be intentionally managed from one place—the server—rather than randomly managed on many independent peer-to-peer computers.
- All members can share computer files.
- Printers and other resources can be shared; they can also be located in a central place for convenience.
- All members can have email and send messages to other office members through an email server such as Microsoft Exchange Server.

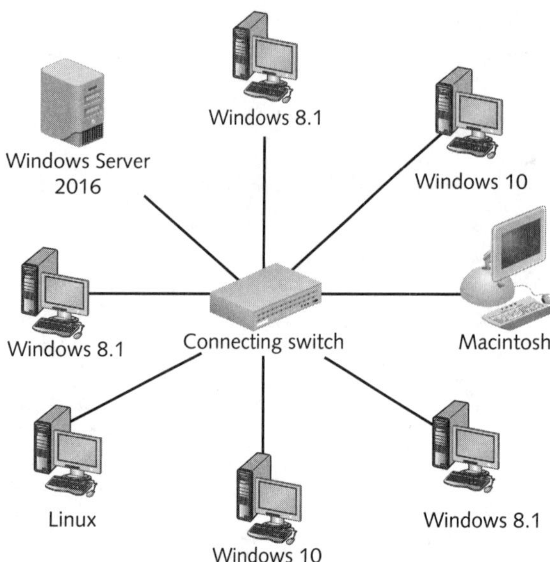

Figure 1-11 A server-based network

- Software applications, such as an accounting or a statistics package, can be stored and shared in a central location.
- Important databases can be managed and secured from one computer.
- All computers can be backed up more easily. With a network and server, the backups can be performed from one location and regularly scheduled to run from the server.
- Computer resource sharing can be arranged to reflect the work patterns of groups within an organization. For example, managing partners in a legal firm can be one group for the purpose of sharing management and financial information on the server.
- The server administrator can save time when installing software upgrades. For example, to implement the latest version of a statistics package, the administrator upgrades the software installation files on the server. Then statistics users on the network can upgrade their versions from the server.

The following information about network protocols and configuration in Windows Server 2016 is included so that you know how to get the latest operating system updates and to use network communications right away. If you have already learned these networking concepts and configuration information, you can move on to the Chapter Summary.

Protocols for the Windows Server 2016 Networking Model

Servers and clients on a Windows Server 2016 network communicate through a set of guidelines or rules called protocols. A **protocol** consists of guidelines for the following:

- How data is formatted into discrete units called packets and frames
- How packets and frames are transmitted across one or more networks
- How packets and frames are interpreted at the receiving end

Packets and **frames** are units of data transmitted from a sending computer to a receiving computer. These units might be compared with words in a language. In a language, people communicate by using words to compose sentences and paragraphs to convey a thought. The words

by themselves do not convey the full thought until they are placed in the context of a sentence or paragraph. Like words, packets and frames usually do not convey full meaning until the complete stream of information is received; and just as words must be properly placed in sentences and paragraphs, packets and frames must be received in the proper order to be understood.

Sometimes the terms *packet* and *frame* are used as if they have the same meaning. However, a packet operates at a higher level of communication than a frame. A packet's higher level of communication enables it to contain routing information so that it can be forwarded from one network to another.

Windows Server 2016 and its clients primarily use the **Transmission Control Protocol/ Internet Protocol (TCP/IP)**, which is actually a suite of protocols and utilities that support communication across LANs and the Internet. A **local area network (LAN)** is a network of computers in relatively close proximity, such as on the same floor or in the same building. TCP/IP has become the worldwide protocol of choice. One reason for this is that TCP/IP is the protocol used for Internet communication. As companies continue to utilize the Internet as an essential component of their businesses, it makes sense to use TCP/IP as the internal protocol, rather than dedicating additional network resources to use another one. TCP/IP is also popular because it is designed as an open standard, that is, no one owns TCP/IP. It can also be used to connect computers running almost any operating system. In addition, many people around the world are working on improving the standards on which TCP/IP is based.

Transmission Control Protocol

The **Transmission Control Protocol (TCP)** portion of TCP/IP provides for reliable end-to-end delivery of data by controlling data flow. Computers or network stations agree upon a "window" for data transmission that includes the number of bytes to be sent. The transmission window is constantly adjusted to account for existing network traffic. TCP/IP monitors for requests to start a communications session, establishes sessions with other TCP stations, handles transmitting and receiving data, and closes transmission sessions when they are finished. TCP is also considered a **connection-oriented communication** because it ensures that packets are delivered, that they are delivered in the right sequence, and that their contents are accurate.

Some applications use the **User Datagram Protocol (UDP)** with IP instead of using TCP. These are typically applications in which the reliability of the communication is not a major concern, such as for information used to boot diskless workstations over a network. UDP is a **connectionless communication** because it does not provide checking to make sure that a connection is reliable and that data is sent accurately. The advantage of UDP is that it is formatted as a smaller frame with less header information than TCP and so can be processed faster through network communications.

Internet Protocol

The **Internet Protocol (IP)** portion of the TCP/IP protocol provides network addressing to ensure data packets quickly reach the correct destination. **Internet Protocol Version 4 (IPv4)** and **Internet Protocol Version 6 (IPv6)** are the two versions of IP in use. In this section, you learn about IPv4; IPv6 is described in the section Internet Protocol Version 6.

IPv4 is used by default on most networks because it has been in existence for years and is well understood. It uses a system of addressing that consists of four numbers separated by a period, such as 129.77.15.182. IP also provides for routing data over different networks, so that data sent from one network only goes to the appropriate destination network instead of to all networks that are linked together. Routing is accomplished through a device called a **router** (or a network device with router capabilities), which connects networks, is able to read IP addresses (see the next section), and can route or forward packets of data to designated networks, as shown in Figure 1-12. IP also handles fragmenting packets because the packet sizes might vary from one network to another. IP is a connectionless communication because it relies on TCP to provide connection-oriented communications.

The combined TCP/IP protocol is particularly well suited for medium-sized and large networks, but it becomes important on any enterprise network or on a local area network that connects to a wide area network.

IP Addressing The **IP address** format is called the **dotted decimal notation.** It is 32 bits long and contains four fields of decimal values representing eight-bit binary octets. An IP address in binary octet format looks like this: 11000110.00110011.01100100.00000000, which converts to 198.51.100.0 in decimal format. Part of the address is the network identifier (NET_ID), and another part is the host identifier (HOST_ID), depending on the size of the LAN, how the LAN is divided into smaller networks, and if the packet is unicast or multicast. A **unicast** is a transmission in which one packet is sent from a server to each client that requests a file or application, such as a video presentation. Thus, if five clients request the video presentation, the server sends five packets per each transmission to the five clients. In the same example, a **multicast** means that the server is able to treat all five clients as a group and send one packet per transmission that reaches all five clients (see Figure 1-13). Multicasts can be used to significantly reduce network traffic when transmitting multimedia applications. A third type of communication is called a **broadcast**, which sends a communication to all points on a specific network (routers are often configured so that they do not forward broadcasts to other networks).

In a unicast on a typical medium-sized LAN, the first two octets are normally the network ID and the last two are the host ID. In a multicast transmission on the same network, the four

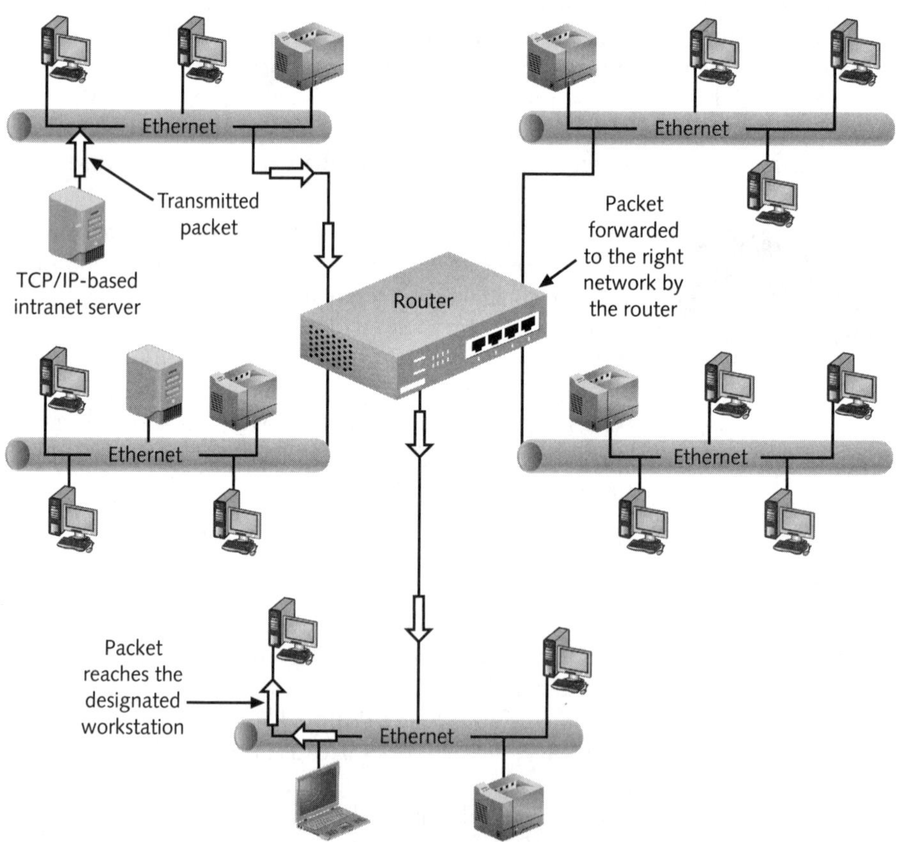

Figure 1-12 A router forwarding packets to a designated network

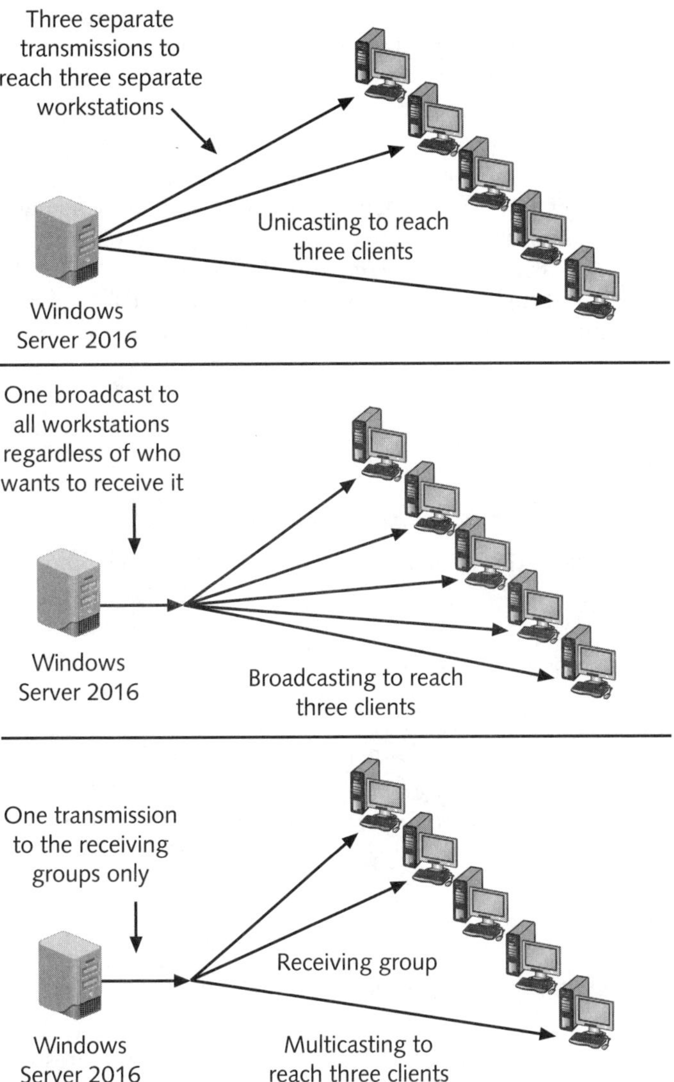

Figure 1-13 Unicasting, broadcasting, and multicasting

octets are used to specify a group of nodes to receive the multicast. Such a group usually consists of nodes that are multicast subscription members.

Another special-purpose form of addressing is the subnet mask. A **subnet mask** is used for two purposes: to show the class of addressing used and to divide a network into subnetworks or subnets to control network traffic. In the first instance, the subnet mask enables an application to determine which part of the address is for the network ID and which is for the host ID. For example, a subnet mask for a Class A network is all binary 1s in the first octet and all binary 0s in remaining octets: 11111111.00000000.00000000.00000000 (255.0.0.0 in decimal).

To divide the network into subnetworks, the subnet mask consists of a subnet ID within the network and a host ID, which is determined by the network administrator. For example, the entire third octet in a Class B address could be designated to indicate the subnet ID, which would be an octet of 11111111.11111111.11111111.00000000 (255.255.255.0). Another option would be to designate only the first five bits in the third octet as the subnet ID and the last three bits (and last octet as well) for the host ID, which would be 11111111.11111111.11111000.00000000 (255.255.248.0). This approach might be used to reduce the number of unused IP addresses, so that they are not wasted.

Many server administrators like TCP/IP because the ability to create subnets provides important versatility in controlling network congestion and in setting up security so that only authorized users can reach specific parts of a network or specific intranets.

IP Address Considerations When planning your TCP/IP implementation, you will need to consider a few specific rules. First, the network number 127.0.0.0 cannot be assigned to any network. It is used for diagnostic purposes. For example, the address 127.0.0.1 is known as the loopback address, and is used for diagnostic testing of the local TCP/IP installation. You might use the TCP/IP-based utility, *pathping*, as shown in Figure 1-14, to test connectivity using the loopback address.

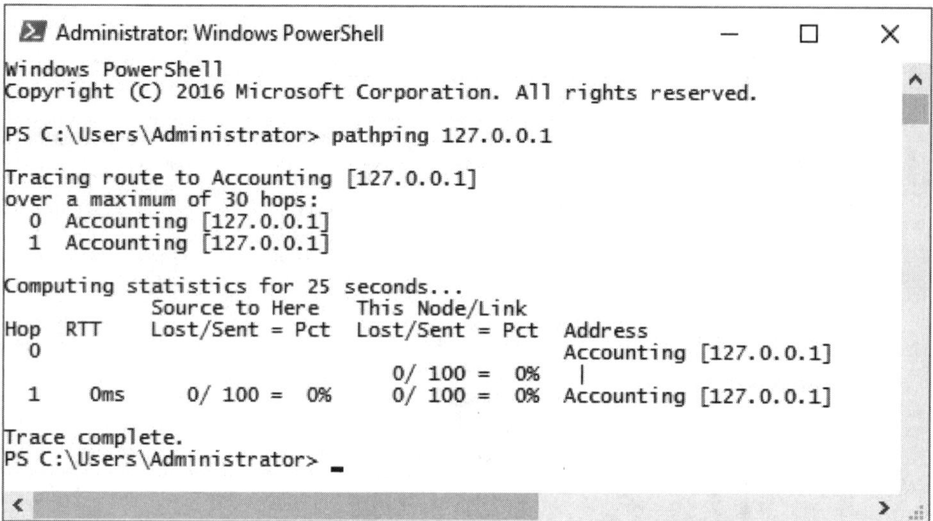

Figure 1-14 Testing a local TCP/IP installation using the loopback address

The standard implementation of TCP/IP also reserves a series of addresses known as private addresses. Table 1-3 shows the IP network numbers that have been reserved for such purposes.

Table 1-3 Reserved IP network numbers for private addresses

Network number	Subnet mask	IP address range
10.0.0.0	255.0.0.0	10.0.0.1 – 10.255.255.255
172.16.0.0 – 172.31.0.0	255.255.0.0	172.16.0.1 – 172.31.255.255
192.168.0.0	255.255.255.0	192.168.0.1 – 192.168.255.255

No one can use these IP addresses on the Internet. They are designed for use on a private network behind a **Network Address Translation (NAT)** device, such as a firewall or proxy server, or some routers. If you do have a NAT device, you can use any of these addresses on your own private network. A NAT device is used to disguise local or internal IP addresses from outside networks, such as the Internet. You learn more about NAT in Chapter 10, Securing Windows Server 2016.

You cannot assign a network number to a computer or any other host on the network. For example, your network number might be 198.51.100.0 (subnet mask 255.255.255.0). You cannot assign this number to a computer on the network.

You also cannot assign the highest number on a network to a host. In the preceding example, you cannot assign 198.92.4.255 to a host on the network. This address is interpreted as

a broadcast message for the subnet, and all of the computers on the subnet would receive the packet. On the network referred to here, any numbers from 198.92.4.1 to 198.92.4.254 are valid numbers for hosts.

Activity 1-4: Testing for IP Address and Connectivity

Time Required: Approximately 10 minutes
Objective: Practice using the Windows Server 2016 Windows PowerShell window with the *pathping* and *tracert* commands.

Description: Two tools that enable you to test IP-addressing issues and connectivity on a network are *pathping* and *tracert*. *pathping* is used to test connectivity to another network by using IP address information. *pathping* can also calculate the number of IP packets returned from each router through which *pathping* passes. *tracert* simply determines the number of routers, called hops, through which it passes. Because both utilities report IP addressing for the hops, you can use them not only to determine connectivity but also to identify malfunctioning routers by IP address. This activity enables you to practice both commands from the Windows Server 2016 PowerShell window (or you can use Windows 7 through 10). Before you start, obtain from your instructor an off-site network address or name that you can use, or use a name from a favorite website in the form of *myfavoritesitename.com*.

1. In Windows Server 2016, click **Start** and click the **Windows PowerShell** tile; or click **Start**, click the **Windows PowerShell** folder, and click **Windows PowerShell**. In Windows 10, click **Start**, click the **Windows PowerShell** folder, and click **Windows PowerShell**. For Windows 8 and 8.1, open the **Apps** screen and select **Windows PowerShell** under Windows System. In Windows 7 click **Start**, enter **PowerShell** in the Search programs and files box, and select **Windows PowerShell**.
2. At the prompt, type **pathping** plus the name or address of the computer you are contacting, such as *pathping myfavoritesitename.com*.
   - What results do you see?
3. Next, type **tracert** plus the name or address of the computer you are contacting, such as *tracert myfavoritesitename.com*.
   - What are the results?
4. Close the Windows PowerShell window.

Internet Protocol Version 6 IPv4 is a product of the early 1980s. By the mid-1990s, network professionals recognized that IPv4 had some limitations. Chief among the limitations was the 32-bit address, particularly when there were thousands of networks and millions of network users. IPv4 was literally running out of addresses. It was also limited because it had no provision for network security or for implementing sophisticated routing options, such as creating subnets based on specific levels of network service and performance. Also, IPv4 did not have many options, other than broadcast and multicast addressing, for handling different kinds of multimedia applications, such as streaming video or videoconferencing.

In response to the exploding use of networks and IP, the IP Next Generation (IPng) initiative was started by the Internet Engineering Task Force (IETF). By 1996, IPng resulted in a newly defined standard called IP Version 6 (IPv6). The purpose of IPv6 is to provide a logical growth path from IPv4 so that applications and network devices can handle new demands as they arise. Currently, IPv4 is used on most networks throughout the world, and the transition to IPv6 has moved rapidly since 2008. By early 2014, over 90 percent of the world's top-level domains supported IPv6 access simultaneously with IPv4 access. All major operating systems support IPv6 and cellular telephone companies have mandates for IPv6, particularly for 4G networks.

This section provides an introduction to IPv6 so you are aware of its existence, but the emphasis in this chapter is on IPv4 because it is so firmly entrenched in current network use.

Among the new features of IPv6 are:

- A 128-bit address capability
- A single address associated with multiple network interfaces
- Address autoconfiguration
- A 40-byte header instead of IPv4's 20-byte header (which means there is more information at the beginning of the packet)
- New IP extension headers that can be implemented for special needs, including more routing and security options
- Use of IP security (IPsec) to enhance network security
- More compact and efficient routing capabilities compared to IPv4

IPv6 is designed so that addresses can be configured using a wide range of options. This enables better communications for routing and subnetting. Plus, it offers options to create distinctions within a single address for network size, network location, organization, organization type, workgroups within an organization, and so on. IPv6 addressing is autoconfiguring, which reduces the workload of the network administrator in managing and configuring addresses.

In the addressing format, IPv6 uses eight 16-bit fields, each of which can be expressed as a hexadecimal number followed by a colon. The following is an IPv6 address example:

```
1042:0071:0000:0000:07ac:0522:210c:425b
```

One advantage of the IPv6 format is that leading zeros can be removed and contiguous fields containing only zeros can be represented as ::. The example given here can be rewritten as follows:

```
1042:71::7ac:522:210c:425b
```

In another example, the following address:

```
0082:05ad:41f8:0000:0000:0000:0000:36bd
```

can also be represented as:

```
82:5ad:41f8:0:0:0:0:36bd
```

or

```
82:5ad:41f8::36bd
```

The IPv6 addressing rules enable the use of address prefixes. The prefix without a slash shows fixed values in the addressing format, such as fixed values in a range of addresses, and the prefix with a slash shows the network portion of the address or network ID.

The network ID prefix is expressed as the actual prefix numbers followed by a slash and the prefix length. For example, 1042:71::/64 could be the network prefix for the IPv6 address 1042:71::7ac:522:210c:425b. Further, the 1042:71::/64 prefix can represent a subnet on a larger network. An IPv6 packet is one of three types: unicast, anycast, or multicast. A unicast packet is identified by its single address for a single interface (NIC) and is transmitted point-to-point. An **anycast** packet contains a destination address that is associated with multiple interfaces, usually on different nodes. The anycast packet goes only to the closest interface and does not attempt to reach the other interfaces with the same address. A multicast packet, like an anycast packet, has a destination address that is associated with multiple interfaces, but unlike the anycast packet, it is directed to each of the interfaces with that address. The end result is that IPv6 can handle multimedia traffic better than IPv4.

Considering today's concern about network attackers, the IP packet payload, or the TCP/UDP header and payload, can be encrypted for security. An encrypted packet makes snooping on networks more difficult, which can help to thwart attackers. IPv6 supports encryption techniques that are compatible with **Data Encryption Standard (DES)** security. DES is a network symmetric-key encryption standard developed by the **National Institute of Standards and Technology (NIST)** and the **American National Standards Institute (ANSI)**, which are both prominent standards organizations. The IPv6 encryption capability enables security over the Internet as well as over other types of LANs and WANs.

The downside to using IPv6 encryption is that it can increase the latency of network communications. **Latency** is the time it takes for networked information to travel from the transmitting device to the receiving device.

Static and Dynamic Addressing Each server and workstation needs a unique IP address, either specified at the computer or obtained from a server that assigns temporary IP addresses. Before setting up TCP/IP, you need to make some decisions about how to set up IP addressing on the network. The options are to use what Microsoft calls static addressing or dynamic addressing. **Static addressing** involves assigning a dotted decimal address that becomes each workstation's permanent, unique IP address. This method is used on networks, large and small, where the network administrator wants direct control over the assigned addresses. Direct control might be necessary where network management software is used to track all network nodes and the software depends on each node having a permanent, known IP address. Permanent addresses give consistency to monitoring network statistics and to keeping historical network performance information. The disadvantage is that IP address administration can be a laborious task on a large network. Most network administrators have an IP database to keep track of currently assigned addresses and unused addresses to assign as new people are connected to the network.

Dynamic addressing automatically assigns an IP address to a computer each time it is signed in. An IP address is leased to a particular computer for a defined period of time. This addressing method uses the **Dynamic Host Configuration Protocol** (DHCP), which is supported by Windows Server 2016 for dynamic addressing. The protocol is used to enable a Windows Server 2016 server with DHCP services to detect the presence of a new workstation and assign an IP address to that workstation. On your network, this would require you to load DHCP services onto a Windows Server 2016 server and configure it to be a DHCP server. It would still act as a regular server for other activities, but with the added ability to automatically assign IP addresses to workstations. A Windows Server 2016 DHCP server leases IP addresses for a specified period of time, which might be 1 week, 1 month, 1 year, or a permanent lease. When the lease is up, the IP address is returned to a pool of available IP addresses maintained by the server.

When you use DHCP, plan to apply it to client workstations and not to servers, so that servers have static addresses. Or, if you apply DHCP to servers, use the option to assign an individual non-changing address to each server.

Default Gateway In Windows Server 2016, if you statically configure the IP address, plan to supply the subnet mask information as well as the default gateway. The **default gateway** is the IP address of the router that has a connection to other networks. The default gateway address is used when the host computer you are trying to contact exists on another network. This could be compared with a room that has only one door. If you are in the room, you can talk to anyone else who is also in the room, but if you ever want to go to another room, you must use the door. The default gateway is like the door. If a computer is connecting only to local computers, it will never need the default gateway; but as soon as it needs to go outside the network, it needs to know the exit point.

For example, Table 1-4 shows the TCP/IP (using IPv4) configuration for ComputerA and ComputerC and their default gateways.

Table 1-4 Sample TCP/IP configurations

Computer	IP address	Subnet mask	Default gateway
ComputerA	133.229.143.72	255.255.0.0	133.229.1.1
ComputerC	133.225.143.92	255.255.0.0	133.225.1.1

When ComputerA tries to communicate with ComputerC, it determines that ComputerC is on a different network. ComputerA has to send the packet to a remote network, so it uses its default gateway as the exit to that network. Because the default gateway is set as the router (133.229.1.1), ComputerA sends the packet to the router, and the router forwards the packet to

ComputerC. When ComputerC replies to the message, it sends the packet to its side of the router (133.225.1.1), and the router forwards the packet to ComputerA.

Most of the time the default gateway (and the router IP address) are set as the first valid host number on a subnet, such as 133.229.1.1. There is no technical reason to do this; it simply makes it easier to remember the configuration.

Name Resolution Even when using the decimal notation for the IP address instead of the 32-bit number, most users still have difficulty remembering the IP addresses for their computers. Generally, computers are referred to by their names, which are **NetBIOS names** for older Windows-based systems and/or host names for computers on networks that use DNS servers. **Domain Name System (DNS)** is a TCP/IP application protocol that enables a DNS server to resolve (translate) domain and computer names to IP addresses or IP addresses to domain and computer names, in a process called **name resolution.**

Examples of names include CORPDC1, RAMRZ, ACCOUNTANT, or any name that an organization or user chooses to uniquely identify a computer on the network. The problem with using names is that they cannot be used by TCP/IP, which can only use the IP address when contacting another computer. Therefore, if computer names are going to be used to connect to other computers, there must be some method of determining the IP address that matches a computer name. Windows Server 2016 enables use of both NetBIOS and host names to resolve IP addresses to computer names.

NetBIOS Names Prior to Windows 2000 Server, the primary means of locating computers on a Windows-based network was by the computer's NetBIOS name. The Browse list and mapped drives were also based on NetBIOS names.

Windows Server 2016 still supports NetBIOS names for backward compatibility with previous versions of Windows. Every Windows Server 2016 computer can still be accessed using the NetBIOS name.

A number of methods are available to resolve NetBIOS names to IP addresses, but the preferred method is using a **Windows Internet Name Service (WINS)** server. WINS is a Windows Server (all versions) service that enables the server to convert NetBIOS workstation names to IP addresses. A WINS server stores a database of computer names and their corresponding IP addresses. The biggest advantage of WINS is its dynamic nature. When a WINS client computer is connected to the network and turned on, it automatically registers its name and IP address with the WINS server. Then, any other WINS client can query the WINS server for the IP address using the computer name.

NetBIOS names can also be resolved through the use of broadcasts and files called LmHosts files (Lm stands for LAN Manager, which was an early server operating system offered through Microsoft and IBM). However, these methods present two main problems. First, broadcasts can create a significant amount of network traffic, as all computers on a network have to look at the broadcast packets. Second, in most cases, broadcast messages do not cross routers. LmHosts are text files stored on each computer that list computer names and IP addresses. One problem with LmHosts files is that they are located on all computers and must be manually updated whenever computer names or IP addresses change (although it is also possible to centralize LmHosts to one file that all other LmHosts files use as a reference). In most cases, WINS is the best solution only if NetBIOS names are used.

WINS and NetBIOS are legacy network services that have been kept in recent server operating systems mostly for compatibility with older client systems, such as Windows NT, Windows 95, and Windows 98. Organizations are retiring the use of WINS and NetBIOS. Also, WINS and NetBIOS are not compatible with IPv6.

Host Names Using host names is the preferred method of resolving computer names to IP addresses in Windows Server 2016. In fact, you can turn off NetBIOS on a Windows Server 2016 computer so that host name resolution is the only method of name resolution that is available.

The best method in Windows Server 2016 for resolving host names to IP addresses is to use **Dynamic Domain Name System (DDNS)**. DDNS is a modern DNS application that enables client computers to automatically register their IP addresses in DNS without intervention by a user or network administrator.

If a DNS server is not available, HOSTS files and broadcasts can also be used to resolve IP addresses to host names. These methods, however, require far more effort to administer.

You learn much more about using DHCP, DNS, WINS, and DDNS in Chapter 8, Managing Windows Server 2016 Network Services.

Physical Addresses and the Address Resolution Protocol

In addition to the IP address, each network station also has a unique physical or device address. The **Address Resolution Protocol (ARP)** is used to acquire the physical address associated with a computer's **network interface card (NIC)**. Every NIC has a physical address, or **media access control (MAC) address.** A NIC is a card in a networked device that attaches that device to the network, through a wired or wireless connection. The MAC address is programmed on the NIC when it is manufactured, and no two NICs have the same MAC address. For computers to communicate with each other, they must know the MAC addresses of each other's network interface cards. Proper communications using TCP/IP rely on both IP addresses and MAC addresses.

For example, suppose that ComputerA is trying to connect with another computer on the same network (ComputerB) with an IP address of 192.168.1.200. In making the connection, the following occurs:

1. By examining the IP address and subnet mask, ComputerA determines that the two computers are on the same network. ComputerA then checks its ARP cache (storage area) to see if it already has the MAC address for the IP address of ComputerB.
2. If ComputerA does not have the address, then ARP sends out a packet to look for the address. The packet is a request for the MAC address for host 192.168.1.200 (see Figure 1-15).
3. All of the computers on the network examine the packet, but only the computer with the right IP address (ComputerB) responds. When ComputerB sees this request, it puts the MAC address for ComputerA into its own ARP cache and then sends back its MAC address to ComputerA.
4. ComputerA puts the MAC address into its ARP cache, and communication continues. The MAC address remains in the cache for 2 to 10 minutes, depending on how often the address is used. If the two computers are not on the same network and the information needs to cross a router, a similar process occurs, except that the ARP request asks for the MAC address of the router.

Every computer running Windows Server 2016 has an ARP cache that can include the recently resolved MAC addresses as well as statically assigned values in the ARP cache. To view the information in the ARP cache, open a Windows PowerShell window (in Windows Server 2008 through 2016 or Windows 7 through 10) and then type *arp -a*.

The *arp -a* command shows you the MAC addresses along with the corresponding IP addresses that the local computer currently has in its ARP cache. The dynamic entries are stored in the ARP cache for 2 minutes, unless the entry is used during those 2 minutes. If the entry is used within 2 minutes, then the entry will be stored for 10 minutes. The static entries stay in the ARP cache until the computer is rebooted or until the entry is removed using the *arp -d* command.

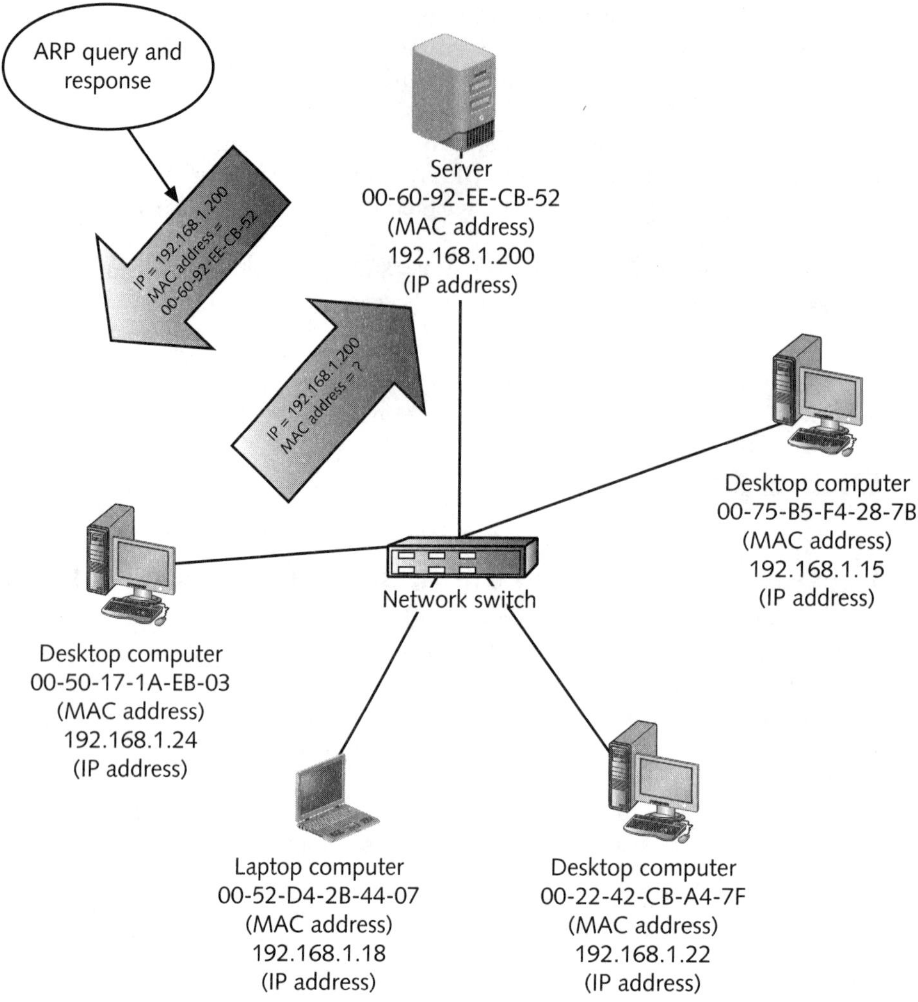

Figure 1-15 Using ARP to query the MAC address

The ***arp*** command, like many other network commands, such as ***tracert*** and ***pathping,*** can also be run from the Command Prompt window in most Windows operating systems. In Windows Server 2008 and Windows 7, click Start, type command prompt in the Search programs and files box, and select Command Prompt. In Windows Server 2012/2012 R2, Windows 8/8.1, and Windows 10, right-click Start and click Command Prompt or Command Prompt (Admin). In Windows Server 2016, click Start, click the Windows System folder, and click Command Prompt.

Activity 1-5: Using Sample Utilities for IP Address and Connectivity Testing

Time Required: Approximately 10 minutes

Objective: Practice using the Windows Server 2016 Windows PowerShell window and ARP command.

Description: The ARP command is a great addition to your toolkit of utilities for diagnosing a network problem. In this activity, you practice using the ARP tool with the *-a* option to view the contents of the ARP cache and the */?* option to view a listing of all ARP options. You need to be signed in to a computer running Windows Server 2016 (or Windows 7 through10) using an account provided by your instructor or an account with administrator privileges.

1. In Windows Server 2016, click **Start** and click the **Windows PowerShell** tile; or click **Start**, click the **Windows PowerShell** folder, and click **Windows PowerShell**. In Windows 10, click **Start**, click the **Windows PowerShell** folder, and click **Windows PowerShell**. In Windows 8/8.1, open the **Apps** screen and select **Windows PowerShell** under Windows System. In Windows 7 click **Start**, enter **PowerShell** in the Search programs and files box, and select **Windows PowerShell**.
2. At the prompt, type **arp -a** and press **Enter**. Your screen should look similar to the one in Figure 1-16.

```
Administrator: Windows PowerShell
Windows PowerShell
Copyright (C) 2016 Microsoft Corporation. All rights reserved.

PS C:\Users\Administrator> arp -a

Interface: 192.168.0.21 --- 0x2
  Internet Address      Physical Address      Type
  192.168.0.1           00-24-7b-b0-f1-a6     dynamic
  192.168.0.19          28-b2-bd-a6-6a-49     dynamic
  192.168.0.255         ff-ff-ff-ff-ff-ff     static
  224.0.0.22            01-00-5e-00-00-16     static
  224.0.0.252           01-00-5e-00-00-fc     static
  255.255.255.255       ff-ff-ff-ff-ff-ff     static
PS C:\Users\Administrator>
```

Figure 1-16 Using the ARP command in Windows Server 2016

3. Type **arp /?** and press **Enter** at the prompt.
   - What switches are displayed other than -a?
4. Close the Windows PowerShell window.

Implementing TCP/IP in Windows Server 2016

Implementing TCP/IP in Windows Server 2016 involves two tasks: verifying it is enabled and configuring it. Verifying that TCP/IP is enabled is the easiest part of the implementation. Configuring TCP/IP can be more complex, depending on whether your network uses static or dynamic addressing. You learn about enabling and configuring in the next sections.

Enabling TCP/IP

One of the most essential elements in network setup is understanding how to enable TCP/IP. TCP/IP is the only protocol that is installed by default when you install Windows Server 2016 (and, in fact, the option to remove it is disabled). However, TCP/IP itself can be disabled, which blocks network communication with Windows Server 2016.

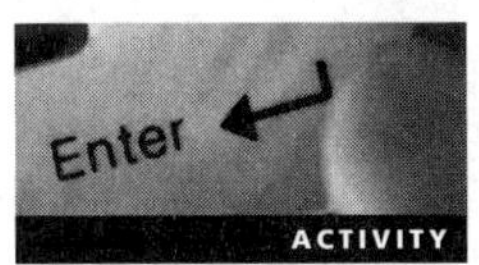

Activity 1-6: Verifying TCP/IP and the NIC Are Enabled

Time Required: Approximately 10 minutes

Objective: Ensure that TCP/IP and the computer's NIC are enabled in Windows Server 2016.

Description: If your network connection is not working, you can check to ensure that TCP/IP is enabled. It is important to know where to enable or disable TCP/IP to help troubleshoot network problems. Also, there might be times when you want to disable TCP/IP so users do not access a server while you are working on it. In addition, it is possible to disable a computer's NIC, which additionally prevents network communications to that computer. The following steps show you where to enable or disable TCP/IP and the NIC. You will need to sign in using an account that has Administrator privileges.

1. Ensure that your computer is physically connected to a network, such as through an Ethernet cable.
2. Open **Server Manager**, if it is not already open.
3. If necessary, click **Local Server** in the left pane of Server Manager.
4. In the right pane under Properties, find the network connection listing, such as Ethernet. Click the link to the right, such as the IPv4 address that is listed when a static address has been assigned or DHCP when it is used (you may also see that IPv6 is enabled; see Figure 1-17).

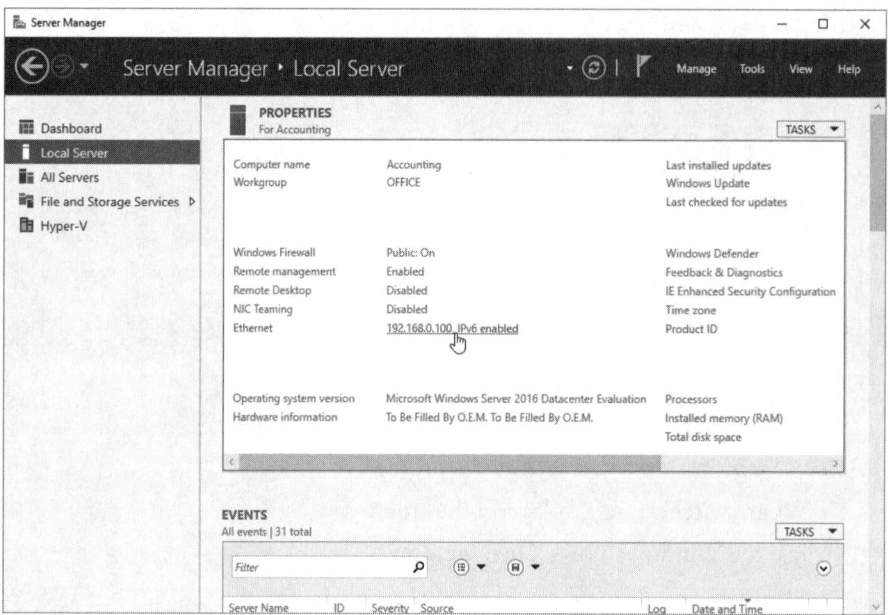

Figure 1-17 Selecting the Ethernet connection for the server

5. If necessary, click (one click only) the server's connection, such as **Ethernet**, to highlight and select the connection. Near the top of the Network Connections window, if the NIC is currently enabled, you will see an option to Disable this network device. If the NIC is disabled, you'll see an option to Enable this network device. Make sure you see the option to Disable this network device (which means it is enabled). Double-click the server's connection, such as **Ethernet**.
6. In the Ethernet Status window, ensure that the Media State shows Enabled. Click the **Properties** button.
7. In the Ethernet Properties window, scroll through the section entitled *This connection uses the following items:*. Check to see if TCP/IP is enabled. If it is currently enabled, you'll see one or both of Internet Protocol Version 6 (TCP/IPv6) and Internet Protocol Version 4 (TCP/IPv4) with checkmarks in their boxes, as shown in Figure 1-18.
   - What can you do to initiate configuring your NIC from the currently open window?
8. Leave the Ethernet Properties dialog box open for the next activity (unless you can't complete the next activity at this time).

If a server is running but not available on a network, checking to ensure that the NIC and TCP/IP are enabled can be important first steps in troubleshooting the problem. Also, if you want to prevent users from accessing the server, such as for maintenance, you can disable the NIC or TCP/IP (disabling the NIC is likely to be easier). Note that when you disable both TCP/IPv4 and TCP/IPv6, Windows Server 2016 also disables Client for

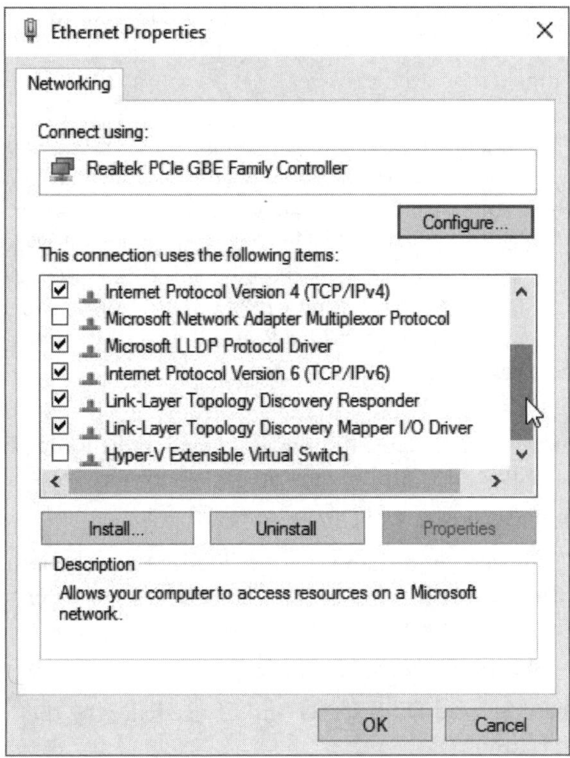

Figure 1-18 Viewing the network connection properties

Microsoft Networks and File and Printer Sharing for Microsoft Networks. When you're ready to enable networking, you'll need to enable these services as well as TCP/IPv4 and TCP/IPv6.

Configuring TCP/IP

As you learned earlier in this chapter, two basic approaches can be used to configure the TCP/IP settings, in Windows Server 2016: static addressing and dynamic addressing. In the following sections, you learn how to use each approach.

Using static addressing for all computers on a network can be time consuming. However, some organizations prefer this approach to maintain the ability to track network problems by IP address. Other organizations use static addressing for servers and certain other network devices, such as routers, but use dynamic addressing for their users' computers. When you use static addressing, ensure that all of the parameters are correctly entered to avoid duplicate or conflicting entries that might result in one or more computers that cannot access the network. This is particularly true when configuring a server that must be reliably available to a large number of users.

Activity 1-7: Configuring TCP/IP for Static Addressing

Time Required: Approximately 10 minutes

Objective: Learn how to manually configure TCP/IP for situations in which static addressing is used.

Description: Some organizations prefer to use a static IP address for some or all of the computers on the network. For example, servers are often given a static IP address that does not change, because if it did, there might be confusion about how to reliably access a particular server. In this activity, you learn how to configure the TCP/IP address information manually. Before you start, obtain an IP address, subnet mask, and default gateway from your instructor. Furthermore, obtain an IP address for the preferred DNS server, and if needed, an address for the alternate DNS server. For this activity, assume you are configuring IPv4. Also, you will need to sign in using an account that has Administrator privileges.

In Step 3, you'll need an IP address, subnet mask, and gateway to use in configuring IP addressing. Contact your instructor in advance for this information. Alternatively, if you are working from home, for example, you can use Windows PowerShell to obtain the configuration parameters that are currently in use and enter them in Step 3. Open Windows PowerShell (click Start and click the Windows PowerShell tile), type ***ipconfig /all*** at the prompt, and record the IP address, subnet mask, default gateway, and DNS server addressing information.

1. Make sure that the connection Properties dialog box, such as **Ethernet Properties**, is still open from the previous activity. If it is not, review Steps 1–7 in Activity 1-6.
2. Double-click **Internet Protocol Version 4 (TCP/IPv4)**.
3. Click **Use the following IP address**, and then type the IP address, Subnet mask, and Default gateway provided by your instructor for this computer. (If necessary, enter periods after each number set in the IP address to advance from box to box.)
4. If necessary, click **Use the following DNS server addresses**.
5. Type the IP address for the **Preferred DNS server** and, if needed, type the IP address for the **Alternate DNS server** (see Figure 1-19).
6. Click the **Advanced** button.
   - What tabs are available for advanced information?

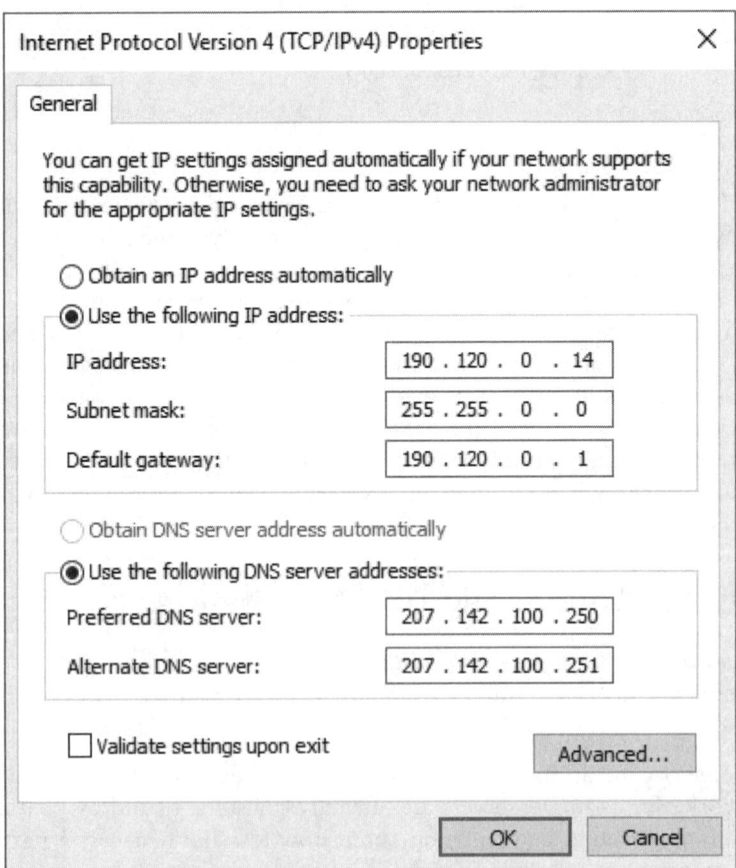

Figure 1-19 Using the Internet Protocol Version 4 (TCP/IPv4) Properties dialog box

7. Click each tab to see the specific information that you can enter. Click **Cancel**.
8. Click **OK**.
   - What would you click to start configuring IPv6?
9. Click **OK** in the Ethernet Properties dialog box. Close the Ethernet Status dialog box and the Network Connections window.
10. Close Server Manager.

Automated Address Configuration

Windows Server 2016 supports two automated addressing approaches. One is **Automatic Private IP Addressing (APIPA)**, which is used to automatically configure the TCP/IP settings for a computer without using a Dynamic Host Configuration Protocol (DHCP) server. The other approach is to use dynamic addressing through the use of a DHCP server.

Automated Addressing Through Automatic Private IP Addressing Notice in Figure 1-19 that you have the option to obtain an IP address automatically. When a computer that is configured to automatically obtain an IP address is switched on, it tries to find a DHCP server to obtain an IP address. As you learned earlier in this chapter, a DHCP server is a server that uses software and DHCP to automatically assign or lease an IP address from a pool of possible addresses. If there is no DHCP server available, the computer automatically assigns itself an IP address from the reserved range of 169.254.0.1 to 169.254.255.254 and a subnet mask of 255.255.0.0. The computer is not able to assign itself a default gateway or the IP address for a Windows Internet Name Service (WINS) or Domain Name System (DNS) server. As you learned earlier, WINS is a Windows Server 2016 service that enables the server to convert NetBIOS workstation names to IP addresses for Internet communication. DNS is a TCP/IP application protocol that enables a DNS server to resolve domain and computer names to IP addresses or IP addresses to domain and computer names. The main problem with automatic configuration is that the computer can only communicate with other computers on the same network that are also automatically configured.

Automatic configuration is appropriate for small organizations that have only one network segment and where the computers do not need to use DNS or access another network or the Internet. In an environment where a DHCP server is set up, but might be temporarily unavailable, automatic configuration can result in some computers having different IP addresses than the others on the network, which results in the computers not being able to communicate. In a situation like this, automatic configuration should be disabled.

Automatic configuration can be disabled through the Windows Server 2016 Registry. The **Registry** is a database used to store information about the configuration, program setup, devices, drivers, and other data important to the setup of Windows operating systems, such as Windows Server 2016. To disable automatic configuration, you use a Registry editor, such as regedit. The following are general steps you can follow to disable automatic configuration, but note that these are presented for your information and not as a hands-on activity. You will need access to the system using an account with administrator privileges to modify the Registry.

Always use great caution in the Registry editor to avoid inadvertently changing a value that might corrupt the operating system.

1. Open Windows PowerShell, such as by clicking Start and clicking the Windows PowerShell tile.
2. Create a restore point for the Registry as a precaution, so it is possible to restore back to this point in case you make an error. At the prompt, type checkpoint-computer and press Enter. At the Description prompt, type a name for the restore point, such as Before Registry Edit date (where date is today's date). Press Enter.

3. Type regedit at the prompt and press Enter. Click Yes if you see the User Account Control box.
4. In the Registry Editor window, browse to the key HKEY_LOCAL_MACHINE\SYSTEM\CurrentControlSet\Services\Tcpip\Parameters\Interfaces\adaptername (the adaptername is the reference to the network interface card in your computer).
5. Click Edit, point to New, and click QWORD (64-bit) Value.
6. Create the value IPAutoconfigurationEnabled as a REG_QWORD value. Assign the Value data as 0.
7. Close regedit.
8. Close the Windows PowerShell window.

Dynamic Addressing Through a DHCP Server Dynamic addressing through a DHCP server is a very common way to configure TCP/IP on many networks, particularly medium-sized and large networks. To enable this type of configuration, you must first install and configure a DHCP server on the network. This server can be configured to dynamically assign an IP address to all the client computers that are set up to automatically obtain an IP address. In addition to assigning the IP address, the DHCP server can also assign the subnet mask, default gateway, DNS server, and other IP settings.

Using a DHCP server can save you a great deal of administrative effort. You only need to configure one server and most of your TCP/IP management tasks are done. You learn how to configure a DHCP server in Chapter 8, Managing Windows Server 2016 Network Services.

To configure a Windows-based computer for dynamic configuration, you select Obtain an IP address automatically in the Internet Protocol Version 4 (TCP/IPv4) Properties dialog box shown in Figure 1-19. (The same capability applies if you are configuring IPv6 by selecting *Obtain an IPv6 address automatically* in the Internet Protocol Version 6 (TCP/IPv6) Properties dialog box.) After this option is configured, the computer contacts a DHCP server on its network to obtain an IP address.

Chapter Summary

- The Windows Server 2016 main platforms include Essentials Edition, Standard Edition, and Datacenter Edition. Standard and Datacenter Editions include Hyper-V for creating a virtual server, but if you need to use more than two virtual machines plan to obtain Datacenter Edition.
- Windows Server 2016 also offers specific-purpose platforms that include Windows Server 2016 Multipoint Premium Server, Windows Storage Server 2016, and Windows Hyper-V Server 2016.
- Windows Server 2016 includes many vital features for security, networking, clustering, virtualization, cloud computing, reliability, database handling, and multitasking and multithreading. Other important features include the enhanced Server Manager tool, Windows Server Core, Nano Server, Windows PowerShell, containers, and improved web services.
- The two types of networking models used by Windows Server 2016 are peer-to-peer networks and server-based networks.
- Peer-to-peer networking is intended for small networks. For most networks, a server-based networking model offers increased performance, scalability, security, and centralized management.
- TCP/IP is the default protocol installed with Windows Server 2016. TCP/IP is an industry-standard suite of protocols and application utilities that enable communication across local and wide area networks.

- The two versions of IP are IPv4 and IPv6. IPv4 is used in many places, while implementation of IPv6 is rapidly growing. Some networks implement both IP versions, which is a capability in Windows Server 2016. IPv6 offers the ability to have more network addresses, better security, and generally better communications capabilities compared to IPv4.
- Every network device, such as a computer or router, must have a unique IP address to ensure network connectivity and the delivery of data. An IPv4 address consists of four decimal numbers separated by a period and has two parts: the network identifier and the host identifier. Each IPv4 address also has an associated subnet mask to distinguish between the network part and the host part and to enable creating subnets for traffic management.
- An IPv6 address uses eight 16-bit fields in hexadecimal format separated by colons and includes addressing rules to enable address prefixes. A prefix with a slash shows the network portion of the address or network ID.
- IP addresses can be manually configured using static addressing or automatically configured, using APIPA or dynamic addressing through a DHCP server.

Key Terms

.NET Framework An environment that is built into Windows Server 2016 that is used to develop and execute applications.

Active Directory A central database of computers, users, shared printers, shared folders, other network resources, and resource groupings that is used to manage a network and enable users to quickly find a particular resource.

Address Resolution Protocol (ARP) A protocol in the TCP/IP suite that enables a sending station to determine the MAC or physical address of another station on a network.

American National Standards Institute (ANSI) An organization that works to set standards for all types of products, including network equipment.

anycast A packet that goes only to the closest interface and does not attempt to reach other interfaces with the same address.

Automatic Private IP Addressing (APIPA) Windows Server 2016 supports Automatic Private IP Addressing (APIPA) to automatically configure the TCP/IP settings for a computer. The computer assigns itself an IP address in the range of 169.254.0.1–169.254.255.254, if a DHCP server is not available.

broadcast A message sent to all computers on a network (but usually blocked to other networks by a router).

client A computer that accesses resources on another computer via a network or direct cable connection.

clustering Linking two or more discrete computer systems so they appear to function as though they are one, thus increasing the ability to access server resources and provide fail-safe services.

cmdlet A command-line tool available in Windows PowerShell. *See* Windows PowerShell.

connectionless communication Also called a connectionless service, a communication service that provides no checks (or minimal checks) to make sure that data accurately reaches the destination node.

connection-oriented communication Also called a connection-oriented service, this service provides several ways to ensure that data is successfully received at the destination, such as requiring an acknowledgement of receipt and using a checksum to make sure the packet or frame contents are accurate.

container An operating environment that enables applications to run in an isolated fashion and provides the ability to execute multiple applications on one computer system.

Data Encryption Standard (DES) A network symmetric-key encryption standard developed by the National Institute of Standards and Technology (NIST) and the American National Standards Institute (ANSI).

default gateway The IP address of the router that has a connection to other networks. The default gateway address is used when the host computer you are trying to contact exists on another network.

Desired State Configuration A feature of Windows Server 2016 that enables monitoring of specific server states and roles to ensure that desired server states are not inadvertently altered.

domain A grouping of resource objects—for example, servers, computers, and user accounts—to enable easier centralized management of these objects. On Windows Server 2016 networks, a domain is contained within Active Directory as a higher-level representation of how a business, school, or government agency is organized.

Domain Name System (DNS) Also called Domain Name Service, a TCP/IP application protocol that enables a DNS server to resolve (translate) domain and computer names to IP addresses or IP addresses to domain and computer names.

dotted decimal notation An addressing technique that uses four octets, such as 10000110.11011110.01100101.00000101, converted to decimal (e.g., 134.222.101.5) to differentiate individual servers, workstations, and other network devices.

dynamic addressing An IP address that is automatically assigned to a client from a general pool of available addresses and that might be assigned each time the client is started, or it might be assigned for a period of days, weeks, months, or longer.

Dynamic Domain Name System (DDNS) A form of DNS that enables client computers to update DNS registration information so that this does not have to be done manually. DDNS is often used with DHCP servers to automatically register IP addresses on a DNS server.

Dynamic Host Configuration Protocol (DHCP) A network protocol that provides a way for a server to automatically assign an IP address to a workstation on its network.

frame A unit of data that is transmitted on a network that contains control and address information, but not routing information.

Generic Routing Encapsulation (GRE) tunneling A protocol that encapsulates a packet payload for transport through a private tunnel over a network that goes from one point to another. One advantage of GRE tunneling is the ability to enable virtual private networks to use a private tunnel over an external network, such as through a wide area network.

Hyper-V Virtualization software developed by Microsoft that is included with Windows Server 2016 Standard and Datacenter Editions. *See* virtualization.

Internet Information Services (IIS) A Microsoft Windows Server component that provides Internet, web, FTP, mail, and other services to make the server into a full-featured web server.

Internet Protocol (IP) The Internet layer protocol responsible for addressing packets so that they are delivered on the local network or across routers to other networks or subnets.

Internet Protocol Version 4 (IPv4) The most commonly used version of IP, which has been in use for many years. IPv4 has a limitation in that it was not designed to anticipate the vast numbers of networks and network users currently in existence.

Internet Protocol Version 6 (IPv6) The newest version of IP that is designed for enhanced security and that can handle the addressing needs of growing networks.

IP address A logical address assigned to each host on an IP network. It is used to identify a specific host on a specific network.

kernel An essential set of programs and computer code that allows a computer operating system to control processor, disk, memory, and other functions central to its basic operation.

latency The time it takes for information to travel from the transmitting device to the receiving device.

Linux Integration Services (LIS) Services for Hyper-V that support Linux virtual machines and Linux clients.

local area network (LAN) A network of computers in relatively close proximity, such as on the same floor or in the same building.

logical processor A core within a multi-core processor that can run its own executable threads.

media access control (MAC) address Also called a physical or device address, the hexadecimal number permanently assigned to a network interface and used by the MAC sublayer (a communications sublayer for controlling how computers share communications on the same network).

multicast A single message is sent from one location and received at several different locations that are subscribed to receive that message.

multitasking The capability of a computer to run two or more programs at the same time.

multithreading Running several program processes or parts (threads) at the same time.

name resolution A process used to translate a computer's logical or host name into a network address, such as to a dotted decimal address associated with a computer—and vice versa.

National Institute of Standards and Technology (NIST) Established by the United States Congress, this agency is a physical science laboratory that works to research and standardize measurements and applied technologies. NIST is part of the U.S. Department of Commerce and was first created to help make U.S. businesses more competitive.

NetBIOS name A name or identifier used in older Windows systems to uniquely identify a computer.

network A communications system that enables computer users to share computer equipment, software, data, voice, and video transmissions.

Network Address Translation (NAT) Sometimes used by firewalls, proxy servers, and routers, NAT translates IP addresses on an internal or local network so that the actual IP addresses cannot be determined on the Internet, because the address seen on the Internet is a decoy address used from a pool of decoy addresses.

network interface card (NIC) An adaptor board or device to connect a workstation, server, or other network device to a network medium. The connection can be wired or wireless.

packet A unit of data transmitted on a network that contains control and address information as well as routing information.

parallel rebuild A Windows Server 2016 feature that enables a failed disk in RAID (a set of disks for redundant storage) to be rebuilt significantly faster.

peer-to-peer networking A network on which any computer can communicate with other networked computers on an equal or peer basis without going through an intermediary, such as a server or host.

physical processor A processor chip plugged into a processor socket on a motherboard in a computer.

preemptive multitasking Running two or more programs simultaneously so that each program runs in an area of memory separate from areas used by other programs.

privileged mode A protected memory space allocated for the Windows Server 2016 kernel that cannot be directly accessed by software applications.

process A computer program or portion of a program that is currently running. One large program might start several smaller programs or processes.

processor socket A receptacle on a computer motherboard into which a processor chip is plugged.

protocol A strictly defined set of rules for communication across a network that specifies how networked data is formatted for transmission, how it is transmitted, and how it is interpreted at the receiving end.

Registry A database used to store information about the configuration, program setup, devices, drivers, and other data important to the setup of Windows operating systems, such as Windows Server 2016.

router A device that connects networks, is able to read IP addresses, and can route or forward packets of data to designated networks.

script A file of shell commands that are run as a unit within the shell. The shell interprets the commands to the operating system one line at a time. To run the contents of a script, the name of that script usually must be entered at the command line. Scripts save time because commands don't have to be typed individually by the user. Another advantage is that the users do not have to memorize the exact sequence of a set of commands each time they want to accomplish a certain task.

server A single computer that provides extensive multiuser access to network resources.

server-based networking A model in which access to the network and resources, and the management of resources, is accomplished through one or more servers.

Server Manager A comprehensive server management tool offered through Windows Server 2016.

shell A command-line environment, also called a command interpreter, that enables communication with an operating system. Commands that are run within a shell are typically specific to that shell (although different shells sometimes use the same or similar commands, particularly in UNIX and Linux).

SQL Server A relational database system from Microsoft that is used to build enterprise databases.

static addressing An IP address that is assigned to a client and remains in use until it is manually changed.

storage pinning Used with storage tiering to enable you to move specific files to a given storage location and ensure that those files are always kept in that location.

storage tiering A Windows Server 2016 feature that allows selected blocks of data to be moved to specific locations, such as to solid state storage instead of disk storage.

subnet mask Used to distinguish between the network part and the host part of the IP address and to enable networks to be divided into subnets.

symmetric multiprocessor (SMP) computer A computer that uses more than one processor.

total cost of ownership (TCO) The cost of installing and maintaining computers and equipment on a network, which includes hardware, software, maintenance, and support costs.

Transmission Control Protocol (TCP) This transport protocol, which is part of the TCP/IP suite, establishes communication sessions between networked software application processes and provides for reliable end-to-end delivery of data by controlling data flow.

Transmission Control Protocol/Internet Protocol (TCP/IP) The default protocol suite installed with Windows Server 2016 that enables network communication.

unicast A message that goes from one single computer to another single computer.

User Datagram Protocol (UDP) A connectionless protocol that can be used with IP, instead of TCP.

virtual desktop Enables you to run different desktops side-by-side, such as having one desktop working with programming tools and another desktop using server administration tools.

virtual machine An instance of a discrete operating system running within virtual server software on one computer. Multiple virtual machines can run within the virtual server software on one computer.

virtual processor A logical processor in a computer that is used by a virtual machine.

virtual server A computer running virtual server software that enables configuring multiple virtual machines. *See* virtual machine.

virtualization Software that enables one computer to run two or more operating systems that are live at the same time and in which one application running in one operating system does not interfere with an application running in a different operating system.

Windows Defender Software available from Microsoft to protect against spyware, adware, viruses, and other malware.

Windows Internet Name Service (WINS) A Windows Server service that enables the server to convert NetBIOS computer names to IP addresses for network and Internet communications. (NetBIOS is an applications programming interface to provide programs with a consistent command set for using network services.)

Windows Nano Server An installation option in Windows Server 2016 that provides an even smaller footprint than Windows Server Core and is intended for a remotely administered server in a cloud or datacenter.

Windows PowerShell A Windows command-line interface that offers scripting capabilities as well.

Windows Server Core A minimum Windows Server 2016 configuration, designed to function in a fashion similar to traditional UNIX and Linux servers by offering a command-line interface and only the minimum services needed to get the job done.

workgroup As used in Microsoft networks, a number of users who share drive and printer resources in an independent peer-to-peer relationship.

workstation A computer that has its own central processing unit (CPU) and can be used as a stand-alone or network computer for word processing, spreadsheet creation, or other software applications.

Review Questions

1. The small company where you work needs to implement a second server for its accounting system but does not have the funds to purchase another computer until next year. Which of the following is a solution?
   a. Implement Active Directory.
   b. Use virtualization.
   c. Change to IPv6 with NAT.
   d. Replace the x86 processor in the computer with an x64 processor.
2. Which of the following are types of containers that can be used in Windows Server 2016?
   a. Windows Server containers
   b. Teaming containers
   c. preemptive containers
   d. Hyper-V containers
3. You are the administrative assistant for the Psychology Department in your college, and they have assigned you to set up a small server to provide basic file services to faculty, staff, and students in that department, which currently has 122 users. For example, faculty will use the server to post and receive class assignments. Which edition of Windows Server 2016 is most appropriate for this situation?
   a. Multipoint Premium Server Edition
   b. Essentials Edition
   c. Standard Edition
   d. Datacenter Edition
4. You work as the network administrator for an advertising company. While you are visiting on the top floor of the company's building, a server user sends you a text message that she cannot access the company's server. Since you are several floors away from the computer room, which of the following commands can you quickly use from a top-floor user's Windows 10 computer to test connectivity to the server?
   a. garp -a
   b. nettest
   c. fastping
   d. pathping

5. __________ enables a Windows Server 2016 system to run more than one program at the same time.
   a. Task managing
   b. Powershelling
   c. Micromanaging
   d. Multitasking
6. Which of the following can you accomplish with Windows PowerShell? (Choose all that apply.)
   a. Run a script.
   b. Install software.
   c. View information about local user accounts.
   d. View a listing of files in a folder.
7. Your company has many telecommuters who work at home three or more days a week. What new virtual private network feature in Windows Sever 2016 enables you to provide secure access to the company's network for these telecommuters?
   a. Secure Domain Name System (SDNS)
   b. Generic Routing Encapsulation tunneling
   c. IPvng2
   d. Windows client for networks
8. Command-line tools in Windows PowerShell are called __________.
9. __________ can be used to automatically assign IP addressing when a DHCP server is not available on a small network.
10. Your company needs to set up a new server that acts as a general file and print server and that has the smallest attack surface possible to reduce the risk of attackers obtaining company secrets. Which of the following installation options offers a reduced attack surface?
    a. Nano Server
    b. Network Access Authorization in Windowless Mode
    c. Windows Server Core
    d. GUI Mode
11. The work day has just started and you receive reports that the inventory management server is not accessible on your company's network. You recall that the new network administration assistant was working on that server last night. Which tool can you use to determine if the network administration assistant left that server's NIC disabled?
    a. netenable
    b. MAC Configuration Tool
    c. Server Manager
    d. System Window
12. Hyper-V enables Windows Server 2016 to operate as a __________ server.
13. One of the managers in your organization has seen older servers crash because of one malfunctioning program. What feature in Windows Server 2016 can help prevent this from happening?
    a. privileged mode for the kernel
    b. tunneling
    c. protected shell
    d. permissions for the shell

14. The three elements you can configure when you manually set up a static IPv4 address are ________, ________, and ________.
15. Which of the following are supported by Windows Server 2016 Essentials Edition? (Choose all that apply.)
    a. a 1.4 GHz 32-bit processor
    b. up to 25 users
    c. up to 50 Remote Desktop connections
    d. Hyper-V
16. The physical address of a NIC is its ________ address.
17. A Fedora Enterprise Linux workstation can access and use a Linux virtual machine in Hyper-V through which of the following?
    a. Microsoft Linux Address Protocol (LAP)
    b. a Red Hat Router
    c. Somba
    d. Linux Integration Services
18. ________ is the ability to translate a computer's logical or host name into a network address.
19. Your IT manager wants you to set up three computers to appear to users as one powerful Windows Server 2016 server. What capability in Windows Server 2016 accomplishes this?
    a. merging
    b. NAPing
    c. gateway converging
    d. clustering
20. An IPv6 address consists of which of the following? (Choose all that apply.)
    a. Four 8-bit fields
    b. Eight 16-bit fields
    c. Hexadecimal numbers separated by colons
    d. Octal numbers separated by dashes

Case Projects

One of the best ways to make the most of what you have learned is to apply that knowledge in practical experience. The case projects at the end of each chapter are designed to reinforce your learning by working through realistic situations that involve using Windows Server 2016. In the case projects, you are asked to step into the shoes of a consultant in a consulting firm. In this role, you work with Windows Server 2016 in many different kinds of organizations from small to large. Your cases and tasks are varied, just as they would be for any versatile consultant.

Your role involves working for Aspen Consulting, which has clients throughout the U.S. and Canada. Their staff specializes in server and network implementation, application development, and providing on-site and remote support. Aspen Consulting works with small businesses, departments in organizations, corporations, schools, universities, and government agencies.

Case Project 1-1: Choosing a New Operating System

Cutting Edge is a company with 122 employees who make cutting boards and a full line of knives and knife sets for home and commercial kitchens. The company is divided into several departments, including Development, Marketing, Business, Manufacturing, Information Systems (IS), and Inventory and Shipping. There is also a management team consisting of the company president, vice president, chief financial officer, and the managers of each department. The company is housed in one building that is fully networked. All employees have access to a desktop or laptop computer. These computers are a mixture of Windows 10, Windows 8.1, and Windows 7 machines. At this point, there is a Windows Server 2012 (without Release 2) server in each department, and the company is planning to gradually upgrade each server to Windows Server 2016. The IS Department is the smallest department, consisting of four very overworked employees. Considering the IS workload, the IS manager hires you to help assess the server needs of the company and make recommendations for the future.

1. The Marketing Department uses large name and address databases for catalog and other promotions. Some of the databases are ones they own and others are purchased from other catalog sales companies and from Internet companies. The databases are currently on a Windows Server 2012 (without Release 2), Standard Edition server, which is overloaded. When they perform sorts and queries of addresses, the computer operates extremely slowly. Which Windows Server 2016 edition do you recommend for them? Provide a justification for your recommendation.
2. The Marketing Department wants to establish an Internet business to supplement Cutting Edge's catalog and outlet businesses. Which Windows Server 2016 system would work for the Internet portion of the business? Be sure to justify your recommendation.
3. Because they like stability without dramatic change, the Business Department has an old Windows 2003 Server system and is concerned about security and reliability. To which Windows Server 2016 edition do you recommend they upgrade? Note some features that would be important for the Business Department.

Case Project 1-2: Management Tools

The IS staff wants to know about important management tools built into Windows Server 2016. Prepare a summary of two management tools that will be of use to them.

Case Project 1-3: Windows Server 2016 Features

The Cutting Edge management team wants to know more about Windows Server 2016 before proceeding with upgrades. In response to their questions, the IS manager asks you to deliver a presentation of Windows Server 2016 features. In your presentation, you should cover elements such as:

- Security
- Reliability
- Expansion options
- Other features valuable to Cutting Edge

If you have the access to Microsoft Office PowerPoint, consider putting your presentation in a slide show for the managers.

Case Project 1-4: IP Addressing Issues

Cutting Edge has been using static IP addressing for all computer systems on their network. One of the difficulties is that because the IS Department is understaffed, they give written NIC configuration instructions to employees, so that employees do their own network configurations. Often employees make mistakes that cause conflicts on the network, and the IS staff has to check out many connections anyway. Further, if the company decides on a wholesale upgrade to the latest Windows desktop operating system, this means all employees will be reconfiguring their computers at the same time. In this context, do you recommend staying with the practice of static addressing? How might an alternative method save time for the IS staff? Create a short report of your recommendations for the IS manager.

chapter 2

Installing Windows Server 2016

After reading this chapter and completing the exercises, you will be able to:

- Plan and make the appropriate preparations for installing Windows Server 2016
- Understand the different installation methods used and install Windows Server 2016
- Set up Windows Server 2016 using Server Manager
- Activate Windows Server 2016
- Install and configure Windows Deployment Services
- Install Windows Server Core
- Install service packs
- Troubleshoot installation problems
- Uninstall Windows Server 2016

Installing a server operating system might sound daunting because servers now offer so many options and features. At one time it was true that installing a server could be like going through a labyrinth with complex steps and confusing paths. Fortunately, the installation of Windows Server 2016 is highly automated to help avoid pitfalls. The Windows Server 2016 installation program takes much of the guesswork out of an installation by detecting hardware and simplifying how to respond by providing windows that step you through the process. Still, installation problems can occur. With advanced preparations as described in this chapter, you can side-step most installation problems.

In this chapter, you begin with the planning steps needed to help ensure a successful Windows Server 2016 installation. Next, you learn the installation methods that can be used and then install Windows Server 2016. Following the installation, you use Server Manager to complete essential configuration tasks, such as naming the server. You also activate the server with Microsoft. You learn how to use Windows Deployment Services to install multiple servers and to install servers in unattended mode. You also learn to implement service packs to update the operating system. In case there are any problems with the installation, you learn troubleshooting tips to solve them. Finally, you learn how to uninstall Windows Server 2016 so that a computer can be used with a different operating system in the future.

Preparing for Installation

Just as a trip goes better with advanced planning, so does an operating system installation. You are likely to work with the operating system for some time, so it makes sense to get off on a solid footing. When you follow the preinstallation tasks outlined in this section, you can ensure a more successful result and avoid problems later.

The following preinstallation tasks should be completed before installing any edition of Windows Server 2016:

- Identify the hardware requirements and check hardware compatibility.
- Determine disk partitioning options.
- Understand the file system.
- Determine upgrade options.
- Plan user licensing.
- Determine domain or workgroup membership.
- Choose a computer name.
- Determine whether to install Nano Server, Server Core, or the full GUI version.
- Identify the server roles to implement.
- Determine the immediate preparations.

Identifying Hardware Requirements and Determining Compatibility

The first step in planning the installation of any operating system is to determine the hardware requirements. Most operating systems come with a list of minimum hardware requirements, which must be met for the operating system to run, and often a list of recommended requirements. It is always better to exceed the minimum recommendations; by how much will be determined by what role the Windows Server 2016 will play on the network. For example, if your server will play the role of a file server, hosting things such as home folders and company-shared files and printers, additional hard drive space is needed beyond what is required to simply run the operating system. Exceeding the minimum requirements also makes your server more scalable and able to meet increased requirements as the organization grows.

With this in mind, you need to plan hardware based on the server role and projected growth, so as to exceed what is needed to:

- Accommodate the clients that will access the server
- Provide for extra software and services
- Match data storage needs

In Table 1-2 in Chapter 1, Introduction to Windows Server 2016, you reviewed the minimum requirements for a computer to run an edition of Windows Server 2016. When you develop the specifications for the server hardware you are planning to use, it is better to overestimate than to underestimate. In nearly all cases, this means purchasing much more computer than specified in the minimum requirements. In terms of speed, plan to pay particular attention to the speed of the CPU and the amount of RAM. For example, a small business using one server with Essentials Edition should consider purchasing a 2 GHz or faster ×64 (64-bit) processor with at least two cores (two logical processors).

A corporation or university that has large databases might consider running the Datacenter Edition on an SMP ×64 computer with fast multiple-core processors. The number of processors depends on the size of the databases and the frequency of performing large queries and reports. The corporation or university might start with two multiple-core processors, but with the option built into the computer (additional processor sockets) to easily add more in the future.

Another factor in terms of speed is the amount of RAM. More RAM usually equals a faster computer. The small business mentioned earlier might start with 16 GB of RAM. The corporation or university might consider 32–64 GB of RAM or more, again depending on the number of processors and the anticipated load from queries and reports, which can be considerable.

The amount of disk space is another important consideration. It doesn't take long to use up disk space, even in a small business. For a starter server, a small business might begin with a 1 TB or larger mirrored volume depending on the intended use. A mirrored volume is one hard drive with its data mirrored onto another identical drive for redundancy.

A large corporation or university might start with a **redundant array of inexpensive disks (RAID)**. This is an array of multiple hard drives designed to extend the life of disk drives and to prevent data loss from a hard disk failure. Each drive in the array might hold 1 TB or more of disk space. You learn more about mirrored volumes and RAID in Chapter 7, Configuring and Managing Data Storage.

Hardware Compatibility Testing Before any final decisions are made in selecting hardware, you should check the hardware for the Certified for Windows Server 2016 sticker or consult the **Windows Server Catalog**. The most up-to-date listing of compatible hardware (and software) is the Windows Server Catalog on Microsoft's website, which is at *www.windowsservercatalog.com* at this writing. Microsoft reviews all types of hardware and software to determine whether it will work with Windows Server editions and other Microsoft operating systems.

To avoid installation difficulties, it is recommended that you select hardware listed in the Windows Server Catalog or labeled with the Windows Server 2016 Certified logo. Most established computer manufacturers have products compatible with Windows Server 2016, but it's a good idea to check for compatibility before you buy. Cutting expenses when buying server hardware could prove to be costly later on if it results in unreliable equipment, difficult software installations, or not enough server resources for the need.

If you are upgrading a computer that has been used for a different operating system, such as one currently running Windows Server 2012, that computer might already be in the Windows Server Catalog, but it might still be necessary to upgrade the **basic input/output system (BIOS)**. The BIOS is a program on a read-only or flash memory chip that establishes basic communication with components such as the monitor and disk drives. Before you upgrade, contact the computer manufacturer or visit the manufacturer's website to determine if a BIOS upgrade is needed prior to installing Windows Server 2016. If an upgrade is needed, the manufacturer will provide an upgrade file and instructions about how to perform the upgrade.

Some steps in the activities in this book include bulleted questions for you to answer. Record your answers in a Microsoft Word document, in a course journal, in your class notes, or in the book margins for later personal reference or for your instructor to see. Additionally, for all of the activities in this chapter, you'll need an account with Administrator privileges. These activities can be completed on a standalone computer or on a virtual machine or computer, such as in Hyper-V.

Activity 2-1: Determining the BIOS Version of a Computer

Time Required: Approximately 10 minutes
Objective: Learn how to determine the BIOS version on a computer.

Description: Before you check with a computer manufacturer about which BIOS version on an older computer is compatible with Windows Server 2016, you will need to determine the BIOS version currently used on the computer. Also, before installing a new operating system on a new or older computer, it is always wise to have the most current BIOS installed on that computer. Some computers display the BIOS version at boot up. On nearly all computers, you can determine the BIOS version by entering the BIOS setup for the computer. This activity provides general instructions for determining the BIOS version.

1. Find out from your instructor or lab assistant how to access the computer's BIOS setup. On most computers, you access the BIOS setup screen by typing a specific key right after turning on the computer's power. For example, some computers use the F1, F2, or Del keys. Also, some computers display a brief message at boot up (before the operating system is loaded) that tells you what key sequence to use.
2. In some cases, the BIOS version number is displayed on the first setup screen. If it is not, follow the on-screen instructions to view or access the various BIOS setup menu(s) for the BIOS version information. You will often use the arrow keys on your keyboard to advance through the menus, or on some computers use the mouse. *Make absolutely certain that you do not change any of the parameters in the BIOS setup.*
   - What is the BIOS version?
3. Exit the BIOS setup without making any changes. On some computers, you can exit by pressing **Esc** and typing **No** to the query about saving your changes.

On many Windows systems, you can use the msinfo32.exe program to view system information, which includes the BIOS version. For example, in Windows 8.1 and 10, right-click Start, click Search, enter msinfo32, and press Enter. Ensure System Summary is selected in the left pane.

Determining Disk Partitioning Options

Knowing how you plan to partition your hard disks and on which partition you plan to install the operating system can make the Windows Server 2016 installation much smoother. Creating a partition is a process in which a hard disk section or a complete hard disk is prepared for use by an operating system. A disk can be formatted after it is partitioned. When you format a disk, this process divides the disk into small sections called tracks and sectors for the storage of files by a particular file system. During the installation, the Windows Server 2016 installation program will detect how your hard disk is currently partitioned (see Figure 2-1). The installation program will allow you to install the operating system on an existing partition or create a new one on which to install. Depending on how your hard disk is currently partitioned, you will be presented with options to put the operating system on an existing disk partition or on unallocated disk space. A *Load driver* option is also provided to enable you to load a driver for your disk drive, if you want to use a more recent driver or if some drives are not properly recognized by the installation program.

A good practice is to create at least two partitions on a server—one to hold the operating system and one to hold user and application data. Placing the operating system on its own partition has the advantage that the paging file, which you learn about in Chapter 3, Configuring the Windows Server 2016 Environment, can be placed on a partition other than the one housing the system files, yielding better system response. Also, having the data on a different partition can make the server more secure from some types of attacks and creates more flexibility for backup and redundancy measures.

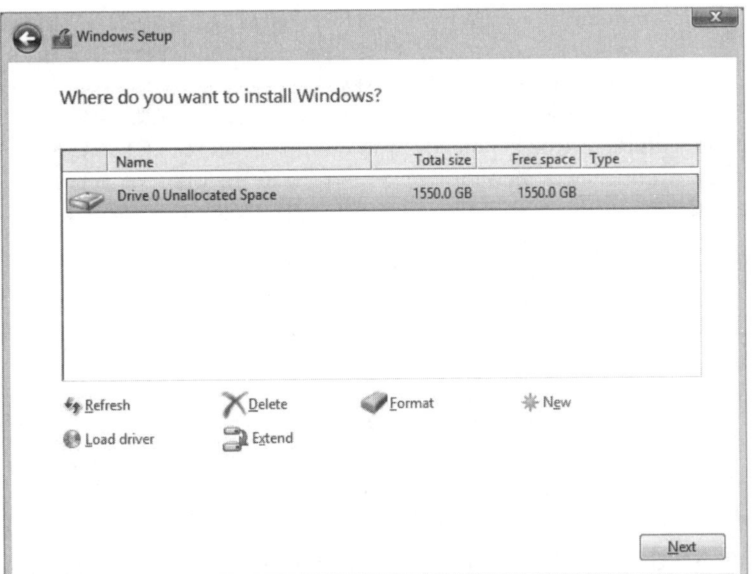

Figure 2-1 Installation program detecting existing partitions

After the installation is complete, you can use Server Manager or the Disk Management tool to create additional partitions, such as on any remaining unallocated disk space or on disks you add later. The Server Manager tool was introduced in Chapter 1 and is further explained in Chapter 3. Figure 2-2 shows the Disks tool opened from Server Manager in Windows Server 2016.

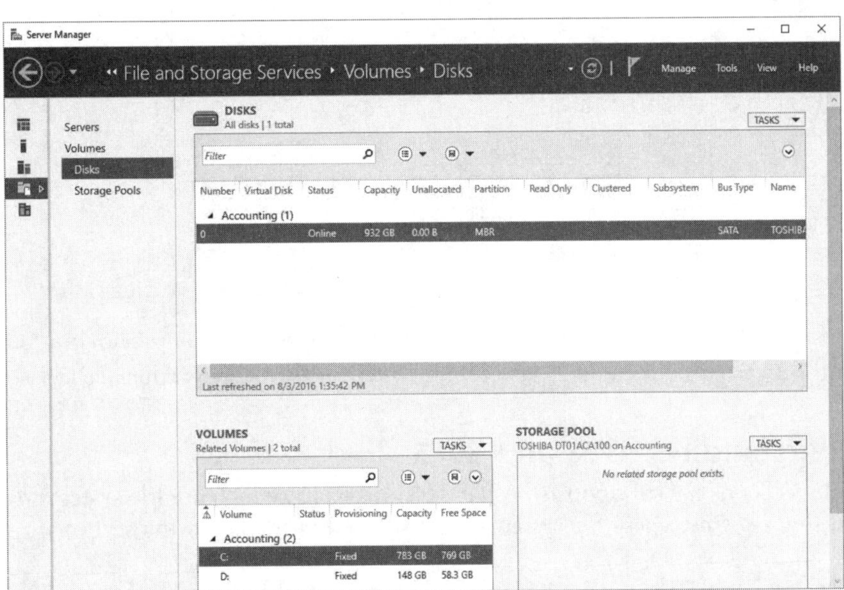

Figure 2-2 Using Server Manager to manage disks after an installation

Activity 2-2: Determining How an Existing Windows Server 2012 R2 Server Is Partitioned

Time Required: Approximately 15 minutes

Objective: Using the Disk Management tool, determine the space on disks in a Windows Server 2012 Release 2 (R2) server and how the disks are partitioned.

Description: If you are upgrading a Windows Server 2012 R2 server to Windows Server 2016, it is wise to check the available disk space and the partitioning before you start. This enables you to make plans about partitioning, including how to change existing partitions, before you begin the upgrade. You will need access to a computer running Windows Server 2012 R2 with an account that has Administrator privileges. If a Windows Server 2012 R2 server is not available, you can use the example steps in Windows Server 2016 for practice accessing Disk Manager to view its contents.

For Windows Server 2012 R2 or Windows Server 2016

1. In Windows Server 2012 R2, click **Start**, click **Administrative Tools**, and double-click **Computer Management**. In Windows Server 2016, right-click **Start** and click **Computer Management**.
2. Double-click **Storage** under the tree in the left pane, if the tools under Storage are not displayed.
3. Click **Disk Management** listed under Storage in the left pane. Notice the listing of partitions at the top of the middle pane (see Figure 2-3 as an example).
    - Record the drive letter assignments and the file systems in use on each partition, as well as the size of each partition.
4. Close the Computer Management tool.

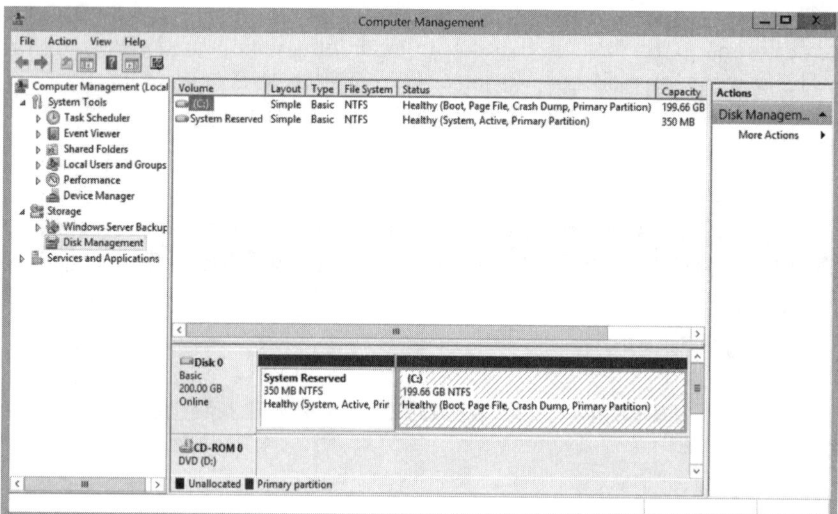

Figure 2-3 Sample disk partitioning in a Windows Server 2012 R2 server (running in a virtual machine)

Understanding NTFS and ReFS

Windows Server 2016 supports both NTFS and ReFS, which are file systems native to Microsoft operating systems. These file systems are discussed in the following sections.

New Technology File System The **New Technology File System (NTFS)** is the native Windows Server file system. Understanding NTFS before you start an installation is important so that you know its capabilities on your new server.

NTFS has been supported in Windows Server systems from when Windows NT Server was introduced in the early 1990s to Windows Server 2000, Server 2003, Server 2008/R2, and Server 2012/R2. Windows Server 2016 also uses NTFS, which includes the following traditional and upgraded NTFS features:

- Local security through file and folder permissions
- Compression

- Disk quotas
- Encryption
- Indexing
- POSIX.1 support
- Journaling
- Large volume capacity
- Hard links
- Self-healing
- File system cache in virtual machines automatically goes up or down as a virtual processor uses or frees memory

NTFS offers an important security advantage by providing folder- and file-level security. Permissions can be set on folders and individual files to protect resources from users accessing them from across the network or locally.

File compression is a process that significantly reduces the size of a file by techniques such as removing unused space within a file or using compression algorithms. Some files can be compressed by more than 40 percent, saving valuable disk space for other storage needs. This is particularly useful for files that are accessed infrequently. NTFS provides the ability to compress files as needed. File compression can be used on specified files after the server is installed. A disadvantage is that compressed files take a little longer to access because they must be decompressed when retrieved.

NTFS also supports disk quotas. Disk quotas allow an administrator to monitor disk space being consumed by users on the network and to control the amount of disk space being consumed on a per-user or per-group basis.

Data encryption is also included with NTFS. Folders and files can be encrypted so that only the designated user can view the contents, adding yet another level of security. For example, should someone remove a hard drive and place it in another system in an attempt to gain access to the data, they would be unable to view the contents of any folders and files that are encrypted.

Identity theft continues to grow as a problem, in part, because of unencrypted files on servers and other computers that have been stolen.

Indexing is used in conjunction with Active Directory to make file searching and retrieval faster. Indexing uses the Indexing Service, which creates a catalog of information about documents accessed through the Search option from Windows Explorer. Also, indexing and the Indexing Service can be replaced with the Windows Search Service for even faster searches in Windows Server 2016.

Windows Search Service is not automatically installed in Windows Server 2016. However, Windows Search Service is installed by default in Windows 7, 8/8.1, and 10. In Windows Server 2016, you can manually install Windows Search Service as a feature via Server Manager. You learn more about configuring a server, including server roles and features, in Chapter 3.

NTFS provides support for the **portable operating system interface (POSIX)**. POSIX is a set of standards designed to enable portability of applications from one computer system to another and has been used particularly for UNIX and Linux systems. NTFS follows the POSIX.1 standard, which includes case-sensitive filenames and the use of multiple filenames (called hard links). For example, the files Myfile.doc and MYFile.doc are considered different files (except when using Windows Explorer or the Command Prompt window).

Journaling by a file system means that it tracks changes to files and keeps a record of these changes in a separate log file. Journaling can be important, for example, when the computer crashes due to a power failure in the middle of updating or changing files. The logged journal information makes it possible to restore a file to its original condition prior to the power failure. Journaling enhances both the security and reliability of a system.

The storage needs for computers, and particularly for servers, are growing constantly. NTFS supports large disk volumes of up to 16 TB, which exceeds the 4 TB maximum volume capacity of Windows Server 2016 Standard and Datacenter Editions. (A volume is a portion of a storage area, such as a hard disk, that has been set up for one file system.) A volume often exists on a single partition, but this is not always the case, so partition and volume are not interchangeable terms (in some cases, a partition might not be recognized as a volume).

Windows NTFS supports the use of hard links. A **hard link** enables you to create one file and then establish links to that file in other folders, as though the file is in all of the folders. For example, an organization might have a document about its rules and regulations for employees. There might be a master copy in a Human Resources Department folder. Links to the master copy are placed in folders for each department in the organization so that employees from all departments can read the rules and regulations. The advantage of this approach is that when changes are made to the rules and regulations, they only need to be made to the master copy.

Self-healing disks is a feature of NTFS introduced in Windows Server 2008. Self-healing means that when software encounters a damaged disk area, NTFS can heal the area without having to take down the server. NTFS self-heals by generating a "worker thread" that repairs data from the damaged area. The data is not available to the software until the worker thread completes its work. The next time the software wants to access that data, it is available for use. Prior to Windows Server 2008, a damaged disk area meant that you had to take down the server and then bring it back up offline to users to run the *chkdsk* utility that rebuilt the data in the damaged area.

File system cache is an area designated in physical computer memory that is used in Windows operating systems to help speed up reading and writing to hard disk. The size of the allocated cache for NTFS operations can affect the speed of reading and writing, which in turn affects how long users have to wait on the server. Now in Hyper-V virtual machines, file system cache is dynamically allocated so that as memory is released by other applications or operating system processes, that memory is automatically used to increase the size of file system cache for faster read and write operations.

Resilient File System (ReFS) The **Resilient File System (ReFS)** was first offered with Windows 8 and Windows Server 2012, although it was acknowledged at the time as not fully developed to unseat NTFS as the file system of preference. The second generation version of ReFS (ReFS v2), which is available in Windows Server 2016, is still regarded with caution by many administrators. At this writing, Microsoft targets ReFS v2 primarily for use with data stores and storage spaces in Hyper-V—although its use is likely to be more broad-based as this file system matures.

One goal for ReFS has been to make it faster than NTFS, but at this writing there are still questions about performance. It is generally faster to create an ReFS volume than an NTFS volume. Further, ReFS can be faster than NTFS in read and write activities, but this increased speed is not consistent in different circumstances and types of loads.

In general, disk errors and file system corruption that occur in ReFS can be repaired more quickly than in NTFS. Also in Hyper-V, if there is frequent use of snapshots and new virtual disks are often created, ReFS provides more versatility than NTFS.

Upgrading to Windows Server 2016

Windows Server 2012 R2 can be upgraded to Windows Server 2016 if you are upgrading from compatible edition to compatible edition. For example, you can upgrade Windows Server 2012 R2 Standard Edition to Windows Server 2016 Standard or Datacenter Edition.

Even when you are upgrading using compatible editions, you might have other concerns, such as the service pack level implemented in Windows Server 2012 R2. A **service pack (SP)** is a major update for a Windows operating system and includes many updated and enhanced components and functions.

Importantly, when you upgrade to Windows Server 2016, you use a full version of the new operating system and not a special upgrade version sold at a reduced price. Table 2-1 provides the specifics about all upgrade paths from Windows Server 2012 and Server 2012 R2 to Windows Server 2016.

Table 2-1 Upgrade paths to Windows Server 2016

Windows Server 2012 and 2012 R2 Edition (with most recent service packs)	Windows Server 2016 Edition upgrade path
Windows Server 2012 R2, Standard Edition	Windows Server 2016, Standard Edition or Windows Server 2016, Datacenter Edition
Windows Server 2012 R2, Datacenter Edition	Windows Server 2016, Standard Edition or Windows Server 2016, Datacenter Edition
Windows Server 2012, Standard Edition	Windows Server 2016, Standard Edition or Windows Server 2016, Datacenter Edition
Windows Server 2012, Datacenter Edition	Windows Server 2016, Standard Edition or Windows Server 2016, Datacenter Edition

If you need to upgrade from Windows Server 2008 or Server 2008 R2, then first you must apply the most recent service pack to Windows Server 2008 or Server 2008 R2 and then upgrade to a compatible Windows Server 2012 Edition. After upgrading to Windows Server 2012, then you can upgrade to Windows Server 2016. Check out the expense, labor, and headaches involved before trying such an upgrade. As a starting place, consider the cost of converting client licenses. It is likely to be easier and cheaper to perform a clean (non-upgrade) installation of Windows Server 2016 and then individually install applications and data from original vendor application media and data backup media, such as DVDs, tapes, and cloud storage.

Planning User and Device Licensing

When you purchase Windows Server 2016, you also need to plan how many clients, including users and devices, will be accessing the server on the basis of the server edition. You also need to determine the number of processors or processor cores.

Access for a user or device is enabled through a **client access license (CAL)**. One CAL is a license for one client or device to access one or more Windows servers on a network. When Windows Server 2016 Standard or Datacenter Edition is installed in a virtual machine, users may have one virtual access per CAL.

In addition to CALs, licensing is done through processor cores, so that all physical processor cores on a server must be licensed. These licenses are available in two-core packs. For example, eight two-core license packs (16 core licenses) are required at minimum per one physical server. Further, each physical processor requires a minimum of eight core licenses.

The Standard and Datacenter Editions require both CALs and core-based licensing. The Essentials and Storage Server 2016 Editions use processor-based (number of processors) licensing and no CALs are required. The Multipoint Server Edition requires processor-based licensing, but no CALs. Users who upgrade from Windows Server 2012/R2 and who have processor-based licensing may qualify for core grants from Microsoft to help reduce the cost of upgrading.

Determining Domain or Workgroup Membership

During the installation process, you will need to determine the type of network access for which your computer will be configured. As you will recall from Chapter 1, a computer running Windows Server 2016 can be configured in a workgroup model or as a member of a domain.

You can specify a domain or workgroup configuration through the Server Manager window that is displayed when the computer reboots after the actual installation process is completed. This means the server can be booted and connected to the network without first having configured the workgroup or domain choice. By default, the initial installation configures a workgroup with the name Workgroup.

If you choose to add the computer to a domain, the following requirements should be met:

- You will need to provide the DNS name of the domain you want to join, for example, northwest.company.com.
- You must have an authorized user account in the domain you want to join.
- One domain controller (computer with Active Directory) and a DNS server must be online before you can join the domain.

If the server you are configuring is the first one in a proposed domain, configure the server in a workgroup. After the server is installed and started, you can install Active Directory and configure the first domain as you are installing Active Directory. Active Directory requires at least one active domain.

Choosing a Computer Name

When you install Windows Server 2016, the installation process assigns a randomly generated name for the server computer, such as WIN-9E7MT5EFTHG. The randomly assigned name is clumsy to type and doesn't tell users much about the server. It's easier on the users if you change the name to one that matches your organization's naming scheme or that says something about the purpose of the server.

Some organizations have a predetermined naming scheme for computers on their network. The scheme might be determined by a committee or by a group of administrators and is often one that represents the function of the server or that follows a particular theme. In some cases, the naming scheme for servers may simply follow a numbering system, such as Server01 or X210W01. In another example, a small bank might have servers named Accounts, Loans, and Databases. A college might use server names that reflect the names of specific divisions or departments, such as Business, Student-Services, Sciences, SocialSciences, English, and so on. A small college in the mountains might use a theme-based naming scheme that reflects the names of animals, including Bear, Marmot, Deer, Elk, and so on.

Microsoft's recommendations for creating a computer name include the following:

- The maximum length is 63 characters.
- Use shorter names up to 15 characters for easier typing.
- The computer should have a name that is different from any other computer name on the local network or in the domain.
- If no DNS server exists on the network, use only standard Internet characters, which include upper- and lowercase letters, numbers, and the hyphen (-) character, but do not use only numbers.
- If a DNS server is present on the network, use standard Internet characters plus additional characters such as $, %, &, *, and others.

If you create accounts using scripts instead of the Windows Server 2016 account creation utilities, including special characters in the account name, such as $, %, &, *, and so on could theoretically conflict with script commands. In this context it can be better to avoid using such characters.

Determining Whether to Install Nano Server, Server Core, or the Full GUI Version

Before you install Windows Server 2016, you'll need to consider the purpose for the server so you can determine whether to install Server Core, Nano Server, or the full GUI (graphical user interface) version. As you learned in Chapter 1, Server Core is designed to have a small footprint on a network, making it less vulnerable to Internet attackers. It is also for those who want to manage the server using command-line commands and scripts, without a GUI interface of windows, menus, icons, and other features. Although Server Core when introduced in Windows Server 2008 did not initially support .NET Framework or Windows PowerShell, Windows Server 2012/R2 and Windows Server 2016 come with these features by default. Some experienced server administrators prefer using the command line and writing server management scripts as in Server Core, because this environment offers direct control of the server. Also, scripts can automate many mundane management tasks, such as creating a group of user accounts.

Server Core is available only in the Windows Server 2016 Standard and Datacenter Editions. It is not available in the Essentials Edition because Essentials Edition hosts a small number of users, as in a small business—in a context in which the server administrators might be less experienced in using a command-line interface and writing scripts.

Another advantage of Server Core over the GUI installation is that Server Core uses less disk space for the system files, which is 4 GB. Because Server Core has fewer system services to run, it is easier to manage and uses less RAM than the GUI installation. If your server is intended for basic server functions such as DHCP, DNS, web services, virtual server (a Hyper-V host), or offering essential print and file services, then using Server Core can be a good option.

With a base image of 400 MB, Nano Server is used when you want an even smaller footprint than for Server Core. At this writing, many server administrators view Nano Server as particularly well suited for private, born-in-the-cloud applications and as a small-footprint server to house data fed to applications. Nano Server is also designed to fit into a server cluster environment. Additionally, Nano Server is well suited to be a virtual machine within a container on a Hyper-V virtual server. At this writing, besides lacking the capability for local sign-in, Nano Server also does not support as many server roles as Server Core, but Microsoft continues to add Nano Server roles through updates.

Server Core and Nano Server can be managed remotely using Windows PowerShell or GUI management tools such as Windows Remote Management and Windows Management Instrumentation.

The full GUI version of Windows Server 2016 offers many GUI management tools, including Server Manager. It also offers wizards to guide you through server configuration and management. New and experienced administrators like this type of environment for its ease of use and intuitive interface. Also, the full GUI version comes with features such as Microsoft Edge for Internet access, File Explorer for viewing files, graphical tools for monitoring the server and network, graphical search options, Start button options, installation and configuration wizards, menus, and many more applications. Other applications, such as Microsoft Office, can be installed in the full GUI version.

Here are some scenarios that could be considered for a Nano Server or Server Core installation, with your choice of one or the other based on how much footprint and functionality you want:

- Your organization is medium or large in size and wants to use one server to operate as a DHCP or combined DHCP and DNS server (see Chapter 1 for an introduction to DHCP and DNS and Chapter 8, Managing Windows Server 2016 Network Services).
- Your organization offers many shared folders to users for their work and the organization wants to centralize all of the shared folders on one computer, such as for distributed file sharing.
- The server contains only centralized databases accessed by users or is used as a data warehouse server for enabling fast reporting or lookup of data. The server holds critical files for the organization and needs to have the smallest attack surface with fewer services and fewer constant updates.

- The server is dedicated to one narrow task, such as frequently backing up important files so they can quickly be brought online for fail-safe protection or after a disaster.
- The server is a dedicated web server and you want to give it a small attack surface because it is accessed through the Internet.
- The server is used to offer private cloud-based applications to users.

Sample scenarios for installing the full GUI version are:

- Your organization is a small or medium-size business and does not plan to dedicate a server for a specific function, such as for DHCP.
- You prefer to work in a GUI environment for managing the server instead of at the command line.
- Your organization needs to have GUI-based software on the server, such as Microsoft Office.
- The server administrator is relatively new to Windows Server 2016 and wants to use wizards for guidance in configuring the server.
- The server is used by a small business in which the server administrator and the administrator's backup person are relatively novice at managing a server—because they have other responsibilities in the business.

In some earlier Windows Server versions, such as Windows Server 2012 and Windows Server 2012 R2 you could convert a GUI installation to Server Core and vice versa. At this writing, the options to convert back and forth are removed from Windows Server 2016.

Instructions for installing Nano Server are not included in this text, because Nano Server does not follow the normal installation setup and has more limited and specialized uses, such as implementing it in certain types of cloud environments.

Identifying Server Roles

The server role is the reason for having a server. Modern servers function in one or a combination of roles. One of the most basic roles is to serve files to users over a network. Another role is to offer printers and fax servers to network users. Servers are also used to offer a range of network services, with web services as the most visible and a DHCP server operating behind the scenes for smooth network operations.

Windows Server 2016 can function in many roles. In fact, this new version of the operating system offers more expanded, full-featured roles than in previous Windows Server systems. The next sections provide a brief review of the roles available at this writing.

New with Windows Server 2016 is that all of the roles listed in the next sections are available in Server Core as well as in the full GUI version. Previously, not all roles were supported in Server Core. Roles that can be used in Nano Server are noted in the following text, but keep in mind that Microsoft continues to add more Nano Server roles. Further, expect Microsoft to continue adding roles to the GUI, Server Core, and Nano Server options through updates or service packs.

Active Directory Certificate Services Role Active Directory (see Chapter 1 and Chapter 4, Introduction to Active Directory and Account Management) offers the ability to establish digital certificates for enhanced security. A **digital certificate** is a set of unique identification information that is typically put at the end of a file or that is associated with a computer communication. Its purpose is to show that the source of the file or communication is legitimate. A digital certificate is encrypted by the sender and decrypted by the receiver. The digital certificate ensures that the file or communication comes from an authentic source. The entity that issues the certificate is the certification authority, which in this case is Active Directory. Active Directory can issue certificates for computer users and computers that are managed within Active Directory. Active Directory can also be used to manage web security.

Along with digital certificates, the Active Directory Certificate Services role provides encryption to protect messages and documents sent with digital certificates. A new feature included in Windows Server 2016 is a module that can be used to enroll specific devices, such as a network printer, to use digital certificates. Another new feature is the inclusion of PowerShell cmdlets to use digital certificates for file backup and restore activities over a network. Windows Server 2016, additionally includes enhancements to **Trusted Platform Module (TPM)**, which enables use of a cryptoprocessor. A **cryptoprocessor** is a processor or chip that enables hardware to be protected through using cryptographic keys employing the TPM security specification. The enhancements apply to the use of smart cards and to enabling a broader range of devices to join a domain using TPM cryptographic keys. TPM is a security measure used by organizations requiring strong security, such as the Department of Defense. Servers often have a TPM chip as do some laptops built since 2006.

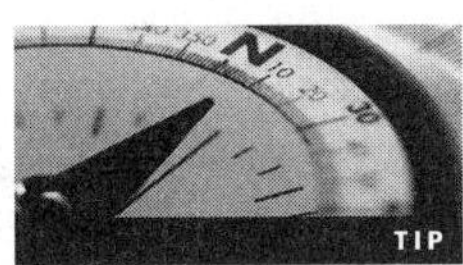

To determine if your server has a TPM chip, right-click Start, click Run, enter tpm.msc, and click OK. If you see *Compatible TPM cannot be found* in the TPM Management on Local Computer window, then either your computer does not have a TPM chip or the chip is not enabled in the computer's BIOS.

Four services are incorporated into the Active Directory Certificate Services role, as shown in Table 2-2.

Table 2-2 Active Directory certificate services

Service	Purpose
Certification Authority Web Enrollment	Enables requesting digital certificates for web communications, sets up smart card digital certificates, and can obtain lists of revoked certifications
Certification Authority	Used to set up the use of digital certificates for user accounts and computers
Microsoft Simple Certificate Enrollment Protocol	Enables routers and network devices to access digital certificates
Online Certificate Status Protocol (OCSP)	Enables detection of a revoked certificate without the need to access a revocation list

Active Directory Domain Services Role The Active Directory Domain Services (AD DS) role is central to implementing Active Directory and creating one or more domains. As you'll recall from Chapter 1, a domain is like a storehouse of computers, servers, user accounts, and other elements. A domain is a vital management tool for network resources and for determining who can access those resources. When you enable the Active Directory Domain Services role on a server, you can set up one or more domains. Also, the server becomes a domain controller, which houses a database of information about computers, users, and network resources (see Chapter 4).

If your network includes UNIX or Linux computers and you want to enable those computers to access a Windows Server 2016 server on your network, you'll need to install Active Directory Domain Services first.

When you install Active Directory Domain Services, you have access to two central services: Active Directory Domain Controller and Identity Management for UNIX.

Active Directory Domain Controller is the service that turns the Windows Server 2016 server into a domain controller. When users sign in to a Windows Server 2016 network, their computers first check in with a domain controller for permission to sign in. The domain controller also determines which resources a signed-in computer can access.

Identity Management for UNIX enables Windows and UNIX/Linux network clients to access shared directories on UNIX and Linux computers. **Shared directories** are directories on one or more computers that users on other computers can access through the network.

Identity Management for UNIX also enables passwords to be synchronized for Windows Server and UNIX/Linux access. When a user changes her password for a Windows user account, the password to access UNIX/Linux computer resources is changed at the same time.

Several new capabilities are added to the Active Directory Domain Services role in Windows Server 2016. One new feature is stronger privileged access protection to safeguard the server administrator while executing management tasks. And, if an intruder is suspected, there are new monitoring abilities to track the activities of an intruder who has accessed administrator capabilities. Further, the ability to join Azure Active Directory is enhanced to better administer and organize applications in the cloud versus local applications. Finally, the Active Directory Domain Services role can use Microsoft Passport. **Microsoft Passport** is a new authentication technique that replaces the use of passwords with a two-step authentication process that combines verifying a device is enrolled in the domain and that the device has a personal identification number. Windows 10 clients can use Microsoft Passport with a server running Windows Server 2016.

Active Directory Federation Services Role Active Directory Federation Services is used to manage security tokens and security services on a Windows Server 2016 web-based network. For example, consider a web server that is used by students at a college to obtain information about their grades, transcripts, tuition payments, and more. This server uses Active Directory Federation Services to issue security tokens that manage which applications and specific information a student can access. Students only access the programs and information that pertains to them, keeping other access restricted. The security tokens are used to manage access for browser clients and for web applications.

Active Directory Lightweight Directory Services Role Active Directory Lightweight Directory Services (AD LDS) is intended for servers that primarily manage applications for users. Some applications need to store configuration and/or critical data in a central database. This might be true, for example, of a customer service system application that is accessed by many different people in an organization. Another example is a student registration system in a college.

If Active Directory Domain Services are installed on the server that runs the application, it might be necessary to modify portions of Active Directory Domain Services to customize Active Directory for the database information needed by that application. Modifying Active Directory Domain Services can be complex and result in unexpected consequences if you make a mistake.

Active Directory Lightweight Directory Services offers an alternative to modifying Active Directory Domain Services for an application. AD LDS is a greatly reduced version of Active Directory Domain Services because it contains only those portions necessary for central configuration and data management required by applications, including directory replication and security services. It does not contain services for managing domains and domain resources, such as user accounts and computers. AD LDS is easier to modify for applications, and if you make a mistake in a modification, the result is not likely to affect how users access resources in a domain.

When you install AD LDS, you can use a wizard to create an "instance," which is an application directory. The new instance is separate from Active Directory Domain Services. This means that AD LDS can be installed on a server that either does or does not have Active Directory Domain Services installed.

Active Directory Rights Management Services Role The Active Directory Rights Management Services (AD RMS) role is for information protection. It uses security capabilities such as encryption, user authentication, and security certificates to help safeguard information. AD RMS works with word processors, spreadsheet, and other programs to build in an extra layer of protection so there are multiple ways to control how information is used and distributed. The extra layer of protection is in addition to the protection of files through security permissions and of a computer through a firewall.

Consider a situation in which a famous bakery of holiday cakes and breads has decided it wants to carefully protect the recipes so they do not go beyond the eyes of those bakers who must use them. Each recipe document can be protected through AD RMS so that it can only be seen by specific people who are on the local network. Also, the recipe document can be secured through AD RMS so that it cannot be copied, forwarded through email, printed, pasted, or generally reproduced in any way.

In another scenario, the president of a college sends out the college financial audit results to the dean of faculty and department heads. She wants this information kept confidential until she meets with the college trustees, and so she uses an email format enabled by AD RMS that prohibits forwarding, printing, copying, and editing her email after it is sent.

Device Health Attestation Service Role The Device Health Attestation Service (DHAS) role enables the server to assure that each server client meets a predetermined level of security before that client can gain access to server-managed resources. This is based on the idea that a server environment is only as secure as its least secure member. The client provides security information on its state of health, such as if it has secure booting or BitLocker file security, and that it uses TPM. This information is provided as an attested health statement. The server coordinates the requirements for the attested health statement and what level of shared resources is granted based on the attested health statement from the client.

DHCP Server Role Dynamic Host Configuration Protocol (DHCP, see Chapter 1) Server is a server role in which the server leases IP addresses to network clients. This service means that users do not have to configure their computer's IP address and other IP addressing information to access the network. The DHCP capability does the configuration automatically to avoid user configuration error and other addressing problems. This is important because no two computers can use the same IP address; they would be unable to communicate on a network. DHCP avoids this problem and ensures that all computers have an appropriate IP address for their network. The DHCP role can be used in Nano Server.

DNS Server Role As you learned in Chapter 1, the reason you don't have to memorize IP addresses to communicate on a network is because the server does the work for you. Domain Name System (DNS) maintains tables from which this service translates domain and computer names into IP addresses and vice versa. This role is available in Nano Server.

For easier administration, plan to implement both the Active Directory Domain Services and DNS roles so they can work together.

Fax Server Role Through the Fax Server role, you can manage all fax resources on a network. This service not only enables sending and receiving faxes but managing them as well. It enables configuring fax settings, producing reports about fax activities, and managing fax jobs.

File and Storage Services Role The File and Storage Services role has traditionally been the "bread and butter" for servers. This role is installed by default in the GUI and Server Core installations and is available to Nano Server. This role enables users to access and share files through one or more servers. For example, one of the services contained within the File and Storage Services role is for **Distributed File System (DFS)**. DFS enables folders shared from multiple computers to appear as though they exist in one centralized hierarchy of folders instead of on many different computers. For example, consider a network used by atmospheric science researchers. One server contains shared folders for weather research, and another server contains shared folders of geographical data. A third server has shared folders with maps, and a fourth server has shared folders with project information. Remembering which server houses which shared information can be a chore. With DFS, all of the shared folders still reside on different servers, but to the user it looks like all are on one server in one place.

This role also includes Services for Network File System (NFS) so that UNIX and Linux client computers can go to shared folders on Windows systems. For backward compatibility, the Windows Server 2016 File and Storage Services role enables file replication and indexing for Windows Server 2003, 2008/R2, and 2012/R2 services on a network that has these legacy systems along with Windows Server 2016 systems.

The storage portion of the File and Storage Services role is included so that you can manage server storage. Offering files to server users implies that there must be a place to store those files. Managing the storage of files is key to ensuring they are on secure and reliable media for ready access. File storage can be managed from Server Manager and from Windows PowerShell. Three examples of this role's storage functions in Windows Server 2016 include:

- *Storage Spaces* so that information can be located on storage that is readily available and that can be increased to meet the needs of file growth
- *Work Folders* (introduced in Windows Server 2012 R2) so that an organization's documents and data can be accessed by specific personal PCs and mobile devices from work folders stored and secured on the organization's servers
- *Data Deduplication* so that information is not duplicated in many places on a server, which enables conservation of storage media to reduce costs and confusion

Host Guardian Service Role The Host Guardian Service (HGS) is provided to ensure the "shielding" of virtual machines, particularly in the cloud. Shielding is used so that clients can be assured they can trust a virtual machine. A shielded virtual machine has security elements such as hard disk encryption enabled through a virtual TPM chip and restricted access to the virtual machine's memory or executable code. A shielded virtual machine is on what is called a "guarded host" running Hyper-V. HGS provides keys so that a guarded host can run a shielded virtual machine.

Hyper-V Role The Hyper-V role enables Windows Server 2016 to function as a virtual server (also see Chapter 1 and Appendix A, Windows Server 2016 Virtualization and Hyper-V). The virtual server role supports both 32-bit and 64-bit operating systems. However, the Hyper-V server itself must be an ×64 computer. Some of the advantages of using the Hyper-V role include:

- Lowers server costs by consolidating operating systems on less hardware
- Saves on computer room space and cooling costs because you use less hardware
- Provides the ability to have separate program development and test environments on the same hardware as production environments
- Provides a foundation for deploying cloud-based computing
- Increases disaster recovery options
- Enables network load balancing
- Supports Linux integration
- Enables the use of containers

Multipoint Services Role The Multipoint Services role enables multiple users to share one computer through connecting a keyboard, mouse, and monitor into a USB hub and connecting the USB hub to a USB port on a server. This capability was originally for use in classrooms, computer labs, and libraries. By including Multipoint Services as a role in Windows Server 2016, Microsoft is now also targeting these services for small and medium-sized businesses, such as a retail stores.

With Multipoint Services, each user has her own individual experience working with Windows. Multipoint Services technology is not used through remote desktop or remote access services, which enable one computer to connect to another, such as to run programs on the remote computer from a client computer. Instead, Multipoint Services does not require the user to have a fully equipped computer with a CPU—and the user has a Windows experience that is unique to that user's connection. Unlike remote desktop and remote access, which can be used from long distances over the Internet, Multipoint Services are intended for use among devices in close proximity, such as in a classroom that is connected to a LAN or a small sales floor in a store. For example, a foreign language classroom might have a server and each desk in the classroom have a keyboard, mouse, monitor, and USB hub to connect to the server. Each student can be using the same foreign language program lesson, a different lesson, or even different programs, while the teacher visits students at each desk to provide individual help. In a retail store, one employee might be looking up data in inventory while another employee at a different station is ordering an out-of-stock product for a customer.

Multipoint Services is a new role included with Windows Server 2016. In previous versions of Windows Server—since Windows Server 2008 R2—you had to obtain Multipoint Services as a separate product at extra cost.

Network Controller Role New to Windows Server 2016, the Network Controller role turns a NIC in the server into a central device that can mine the network for information to be used by one or more network management applications. Microsoft calls this making the NIC a "point of automation" for software used to manage network functions including network services setup, IP address management, network monitoring, assessing network topology, and network troubleshooting. These capabilities apply to virtual networks (such as private virtual networking and using virtual machines), to physical networks, and to networks that house computers used in clustering.

Medium and large organizations will find the Network Controller role particularly valuable to enable centralized management of their networks through automation software such as Microsoft's System Center.

Network Policy and Access Services Role A network is kept secure and healthy by having policies governing who can access it. The Network Policy and Access Services role offers services to:

- Set up and manage network policy by creating and using a Network Policy Server (NPS).
- Configure network policy from a single location rather than having to configure network policy on each network access server.
- Enable the use of secure wired and wireless authentication protocols so that unauthorized clients cannot access a network or receive an IP address via DHCP.
- Validate client health certificates to be sure all network client workstations are current on their security patches and other security conditions.

Microsoft uses the concept of a healthy network to mean one in which all of the computers on the network use prescribed security measures to avoid security problems. This includes creating security policies, maintaining security updates, using antivirus software, configuring a firewall, backing up data, and other measures.

In Windows Server 2012, Server 2012 R2, and Server 2016, the Network Policy and Access Services role no longer handles the Routing and Route Access Service, which was used for remote access by clients. This is now built into the Remote Access role.

Print and Document Services Role Managing network printing activities is a classic role for a server. The Print and Document Services role includes a service to make a Windows Server 2016 server a formal print server that manages print jobs and network printers from one place. Another service manages Internet printing, including sharing web-based printers. A third role is the Line Printer Daemon (LPD) service for managing printing activities for UNIX and Linux computers.

Remote Access Role Remote access enables clients to access network and server resources from anywhere the Internet is available. This includes DirectAccess, which means that a physician who needs to access data on a hospital network, can access it instantly through a safe Internet connection. A sales representative can access her company's services remotely and a professor can work from home, accessing the college's network via the Internet. Remote Access services also still support virtual private networks, which have traditionally been used for remote access.

Another feature of Remote Access services is to enable users to remotely access specific applications remotely. For example, a physician might access an application to be sure a new prescription does not conflict with other prescriptions a patient already uses.

Remote Desktop Services Role Beginning with Windows Server 2008 R2, Terminal Services are renamed Remote Desktop Services. Through this service, clients can use virtual machine and session-based desktops to access and run applications on a server. A *virtual machine desktop* is a remote connection to a virtual machine within a corporate network that is reflected in a virtual window on the client. A *session-based desktop* is an older model of remote computing through what was previously called a terminal server connection—a remote connection to a server in which the client responds as a terminal that does not have much computing power. A **terminal** is a device that consists of a monitor and keyboard that does not have a processor. Each connection in this second model is a session. A third feature of Remote Desktop Services is to serve up designated applications to a client computer.

Volume Activation Services Role Volume Activation Services can be used by business, government, and other organizations that purchase software in bulk for many clients. Such organizations can use Volume Activation Services along with Key Management Service to activate software used by server clients on a mass scale. The service also enables a server administrator to install operating systems on Hyper-V virtual machines so that the administrator does not have to manage server activation keys individually.

Web Server (IIS) Role The Web Server role enables Windows Server 2016 to provide an ever-expanding range of web services. The services are offered through Internet Information Services (IIS); these services turn Windows Server 2016 into a full-featured web server. When you enable the Web Server role, you enable the following general services: Web Server (IIS), IIS Manager, and web diagnostics tools. You can also add modules for specific web functions, such as FTP Publishing. Nano Server supports the Web Server (IIS) Role.

IIS Web Server services offer websites and full web communications through protocols such as **Hypertext Transfer Protocol (HTTP)**. HTTP is a protocol in the TCP/IP suite of protocols that is used to transport document and other data transmissions over networks and the Internet for access by web browsers.

The FTP publishing services enable uploading and downloading files from an FTP server over the Internet. **File Transfer Protocol (FTP)** is a TCP/IP application protocol that transfers files in bulk data streams and is commonly used on the Internet. An enhancement to FTP publishing services that is new with Windows Server 2012 through Windows Server 2016 is the ability to set FTP logon attempt limits to protect an FTP site from hackers.

The web management tools are for management of IIS Web Server, FTP publishing, and other web-related tasks, such as web scripts and remote management of a web server. There are also diagnostics tools to monitor web activity.

Windows Deployment Services Role When an organization purchases many new server computers at once or plans to do a widespread Windows server operating system upgrade, Windows Server 2016 can be installed on the computers through automated means via **Windows Deployment Services (WDS)**.

WDS enables an organization to purchase multiple computers without operating systems and then install Windows Server 2016 on all of the computers. This approach can save money and time because it enables the server administrator to be more productive. The following are some advantages of WDS:

- Lowers server operating system installation costs by automating the deployment of servers
- Enables servers to be deployed and configured in a consistent way

- Provides the ability to administer hundreds of servers on a mass scale with the help of scripts
- Takes advantage of network speed options for faster deployment

WDS is a good way to automate multiple client installations, such as for Windows 10, as well as server installations. You learn more about WDS later in this chapter.

Windows Server Essentials Experience Role Windows Server 2016 Essentials Edition offers some automated features that Standard and Datacenter Edition server administrators may want to use. Some of these features are:

- Easier centralization of data in one location
- Integration with online services provided by Microsoft, including Microsoft SharePoint, Office 365, and Exchange
- Management of mobile devices using Active Sync on the GUI Dashboard
- Simplified access to server and network health reports
- Convenient server and client data backup

Windows Server Update Services Role An effective way to keep a server and its network healthy is through quickly applying security patches and operating system fixes or additions, including service packs from Microsoft. Windows Server Update Services role provides a way to automate updating one, some, or all Windows servers and Windows clients on your network. One server can be designated as the **upstream server**, which regularly obtains the updates from Microsoft. The upstream server not only provides the updates to itself but it also provides them to all servers designated by the server administrator. In this way, when an operating system patch becomes available for a worrisome security issue, that patch is automatically made available for all servers to install.

Activity 2-3: Viewing Server Roles

Time Required: Approximately 15 minutes
Objective: Determine server roles already implemented and view all available server roles.

Description: When you work with a server, it can be important to know which server roles are implemented. In this activity, you use Server Manager to first check what server roles are implemented and then to view the server roles that can be installed. You will need to use an account that has Administrator privileges. (Also, if you don't have access to a computer running Windows Server 2016 at this point, you can complete this activity after you install Windows Server 2016 in Activity 2-4.)

1. If Server Manager is not open, click **Start** and click the **Server Manager** tile; or click **Start** and click **Server Manager** under the listing of applications that start with the letter S. You may need to wait for a minute or two for Server Manager to inventory server information.
2. Click **Local Server** in the left pane.
3. In the right pane, scroll to ROLES AND FEATURES.
4. Scroll down in the ROLES AND FEATURES box, noticing the installed roles and features (see Figure 2-4, which shows a newly installed server with the File and Storage Services role installed along with many features).
   - What roles are installed?
5. Click **Dashboard** in the left pane.
6. In the right pane, click **Add roles and features**.

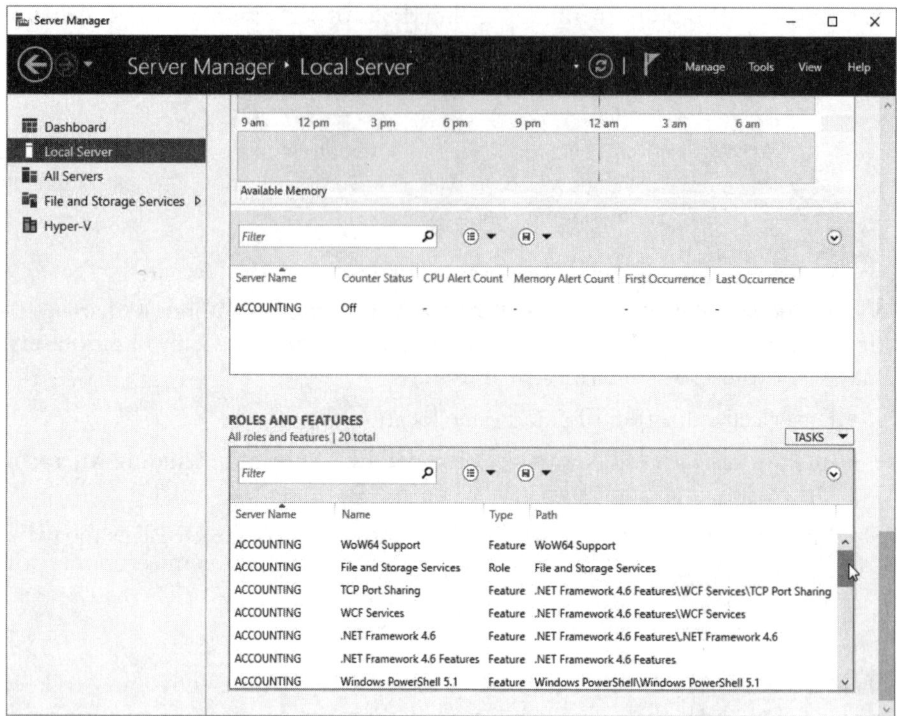

Figure 2-4 Viewing the installed roles and features

7. If you see the Before you begin window in the Add Roles and Features Wizard, click **Next.**
8. In the Select installation type window, ensure that **Role-based or feature-based installation** is selected. Click **Next.**
9. Be sure your server is selected in the Select destination server window. Click **Next.**
10. Scroll through the Roles box in the Select server roles window (see Figure 2-5). This is the window that enables you to install one or more of the roles available for the server. (The actual roles that are checked as installed already will depend on your particular server and how it is being used.)

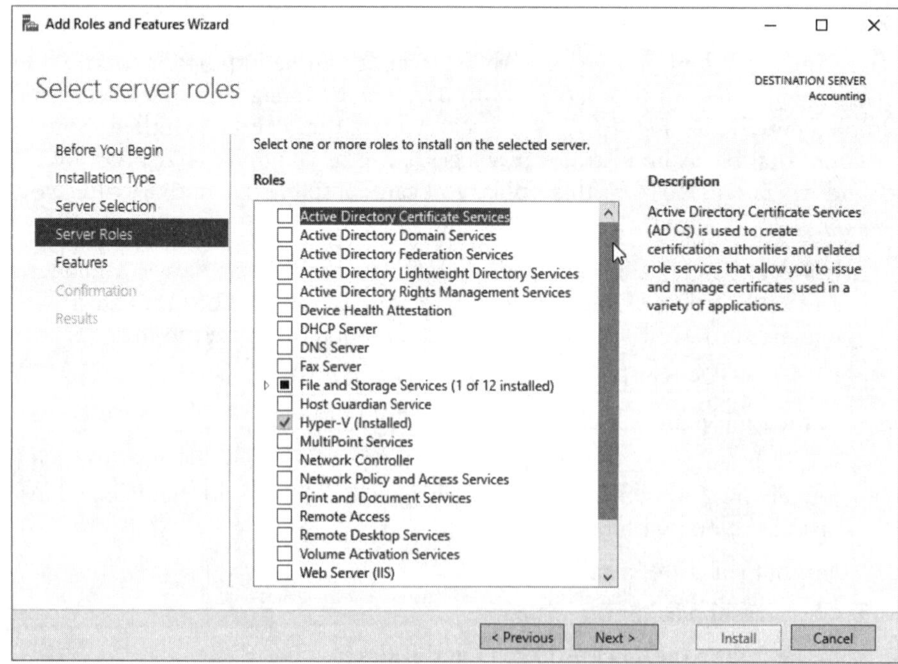

Figure 2-5 Viewing server roles that can be installed

11. Click **Cancel** to close the Select server roles window.
12. Close **Server Manager**.

Making Immediate Preparations

Just before you install Windows Server 2016, it is good practice to make some immediate preparations as follows:

- If you are upgrading an existing Windows Server 2012 or Server 2012 R2 system, back up the files before starting. Also consider testing the backup before you start to ensure you have working backup media for a restore. Besides backing up regular data and program files, back up the system configuration information by creating a USB recovery drive.
- Ensure that the NIC (or NICs if more than one are to be used), hard drives, RAID drives, DVD drive(s), USB port(s), and all other important hardware are preinstalled so that Windows Server 2016 can detect these devices.
- Disconnect or remove removable storage devices, particularly flash drives and DVDs, so they do not create possible problems during the installation.
- Disconnect any connection for communications with an uninterruptible power supply (UPS).
- Have on hand USB thumb drives or DVDs or other media with drivers for new peripherals, in case these are needed for configuring the peripherals during or after the installation.
- Use the test software disc or USB thumb drive that comes with the server to verify that the CPU, memory, disk drives, and other hardware are working properly.
- If you are installing Windows Server 2016 into a virtual machine, ensure there is adequate memory and disk storage on the parent virtual server hardware to support the installation and be certain that the virtual server software supports Windows Server 2016 as a guest operating system. Further, ensure that the computer has enough NICs to support the installation, particularly if the computer will support multiple virtual machines.

Overview of Windows Server 2016 Installation Methods

Once you have completed all the necessary preinstallation tasks, you are ready to install the operating system. The following sections outline the different installation methods available and step through a full installation of Windows Server 2016; you just need to decide on an installation method that best meets your needs. The method you choose depends on your specific situation. For example, if you are installing many servers, consider using Windows Deployment Services. The primary installation methods are as follows:

- DVD or USB thumb drive installation
- Upgrade from Windows Server 2012 or Server 2012 R2
- Installation for a virtual server using Hyper-V
- Windows Deployment Services

Each of the installation methods consists of techniques to boot the computer and enable you to load the installation files.

DVD or USB Thumb Drive Installation

To perform the DVD or USB thumb drive installation, your computer should be capable of booting from the DVD/optical drive or a USB drive, which is a capability of most modern computers. Also, you will need to know how to set up the computer's BIOS to boot from the optical or USB drive or how to tell the computer to boot from the optical or USB drive by pressing the appropriate key on the keyboard. For example, to start the installation from DVD:

1. Make sure the computer's BIOS is set to boot first from the optical drive (see Activity 2-1 to learn how to access the BIOS setup on a computer).

2. Insert the Windows Server 2016 installation DVD.
3. Power off the computer.
4. Turn on the computer, and if necessary press the key combination to boot from the optical drive.
5. Follow the instructions for installing Windows Server 2016 (see the section, Performing a DVD–based Installation).

Upgrading from Windows Server 2012/R2

If your computer is running Windows Server 2012 or Windows Server 2012 R2, you can perform an upgrade instead of doing a start-from-scratch installation. The benefit of performing an upgrade is that most of your settings, files, and applications are upgraded as well and do not need to be reinstalled. It's important to note that Windows Server 2016 is not purchased as an upgrade version, but instead you select to perform an upgrade after the installation starts. Also, check the information in Table 2-1 to ensure that you purchase the correct Windows Server 2016 edition for the edition of Windows Server 2012 or Server 2012 R2 that you plan to upgrade.

The general steps to begin an upgrade are similar to those for a DVD or USB thumb drive installation, but you select to perform an upgrade instead of a clean installation:

1. Make sure the computer's BIOS is set to boot first from the optical drive (see Activity 2-1 to learn how to access the BIOS setup on a computer).
2. Insert the Windows Server 2016 installation DVD.
3. Power off the computer.
4. Turn on the computer, and if necessary press the key combination to boot from the optical drive.
5. Follow the instructions for installing Windows Server 2016 (see the section, Performing a DVD–based Installation).
6. When you reach Step 11 in Activity 2-4, select *Upgrade: Install Windows and keep files, settings, and applications*. Follow the remaining steps to complete the installation.

If you see a message indicating the computer cannot run or upgrade this version of the operating system, this means you do not have the right Windows Server 2016 edition for the Windows Server 2012/R2 edition already on your computer or that you are trying to upgrade from a Windows Server version earlier than Windows Server 2012, such as Windows Server 2008.

Installation for a Virtual Server Using Hyper-V

Virtual servers are in common use, and Windows Server 2016 can be installed as a virtual server, such as in Microsoft Hyper-V. As you learned in Chapter 1, Hyper-V is included with the Standard and Datacenter Editions of Windows Server 2016. The actual installation steps of Windows Server 2016 as a virtual machine are nearly the same as those for a DVD or USB drive installation, but first you need to go through the steps to set up a virtual server. The following are the general steps for installing and using Hyper-V:

1. Windows Server 2016 Standard or Datacenter Edition must already be installed as a main server, such as by using the DVD installation method in Activity 2-4.
2. After Windows Server 2016 is installed, use Server Manager to install the Hyper-V server role (refer to Activity 2-3 to learn where to install roles). Follow the steps in the Add Roles and Features Wizard to install Hyper-V (and select to add all of the Hyper-V features). You'll need to reboot the computer after installing the Hyper-V role.
3. Start Hyper-V Manager by clicking Start and clicking Hyper-V Manager in the list of applications; or click Start, click the Windows Administrative Tools folder, and click Hyper-V Manager.
4. Click the server in the tree in the left pane, if it is not already selected.
5. Click the Action menu, point to New, and click Virtual Machine (see Figure 2-6) to start the New Virtual Machine Wizard.

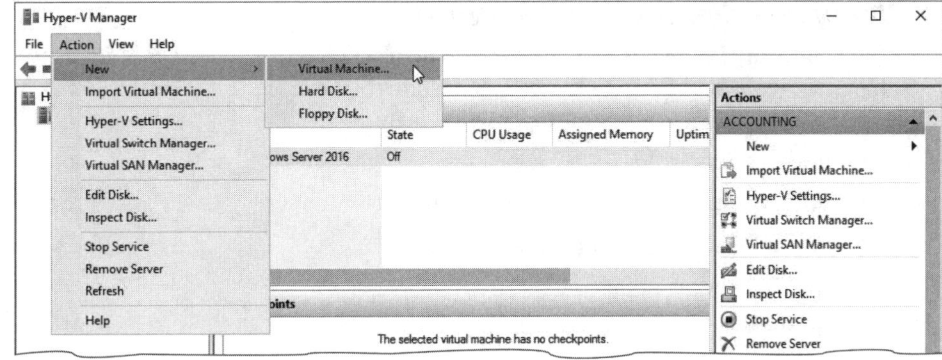

Figure 2-6 Creating a new virtual machine in Hyper-V Manager

6. If you see the Before You Begin dialog box, click Next.
7. In the Specify Name and Location window, enter the name for the virtual server, such as *Windows Server 2016* or *Windows Server 2016 Server_x* (where x equals 1 if this is the first virtual machine, 2 if it is the second virtual machine, and so on). Click Next.
8. In the Specify Generation window, select Generation 2 and click Next.
9. In the Assign Memory window, enter the amount of memory to be used for the virtual server in MB, such as 1024 to 2048 or higher (remember that the virtual server will be taking up memory from the main server host). Click Next.
10. In the Configure Networking window, select the way the server will be connected, such as by selecting the NIC it will use in the *Connection* box. Click Next.
11. Select the virtual hard disk option from the following:
    - Create a virtual hard disk (and provide the name, location, and size of the virtual hard disk)
    - Use an existing virtual hard disk
    - Attach a virtual hard disk later

    For this installation select Create a virtual hard disk.
12. Click Next.
13. Insert the Windows Server 2016 installation DVD (or USB thumb drive) or have an ISO image file already copied in a folder on the virtual server.
14. Select Install an operating system from a bootable image file and use the Browse button to provide the location of the Windows Server 2016 installation DVD, USB drive, or the ISO image file on the computer. In the Open window, click Open to use the file you selected. Click Next.
15. Click Finish.
16. If you don't see the connection window, double-click the name of the server in the middle pane. Click the Action menu and click Start.
17. Follow the steps for installing Windows Server 2016, starting at Step 3 in Activity 2-4.
18. After the Windows Server 2016 virtual machine is installed, you can configure it using Server Manager as in Activity 2-5.

You can shut down a virtual machine while in Hyper-V Manager by clicking that virtual machine at the top of the center pane, clicking the Action menu, and clicking Shut Down or Save (use Save to save the current virtual machine state but release CPU and memory resources). To start a virtual server in Hyper-V Manager, click the server in the center pane, click the Action menu, and click Start.

Windows Deployment Services

You've already learned that Windows Deployment Services or WDS is a role that can be installed in Windows Server 2016. This role is designed to enable the installation of multiple Windows server and workstation operating systems including:

- Windows Server 2016
- Windows Server 2012 and Server 2012 R2
- Windows Server 2008 and Server 2008 R2
- Windows Server 2003
- Windows 10
- Windows 8 or 8.1
- Windows 7

New to WDS in Windows Server 2016 is the ability to use Windows PowerShell cmdlets. Also, WDS in Windows Server 2016 adds driver provisioning to support more manufacturer's drivers.

When you use WDS, it's not necessary to stay at the computer during the operating system installation because it can be done unattended. WDS is not really new because it is based on redesigned programming code formerly used in Remote Installation Services from Windows Server 2003.

An installation DVD is not necessary for each computer because the installation files are sent over a network from the Windows Server 2016 Windows Deployment Services server. However, you do need to have licenses for all of the operating systems you install through WDS. You learn how to use WDS in the section of this chapter called Using Windows Deployment Services.

Performing a DVD-Based Installation

After you've gathered all your information, determined which options you will use to install Windows Server 2016, and made your immediate preparations, you can proceed with the installation. This section outlines the steps for a typical installation from DVD. The installation is performed by the Setup program on the DVD, which takes you through the installation process step-by-step.

The steps are similar if you use a bootable USB thumb drive with the Windows Server 2016 ISO installation file—but in instead of booting from the DVD you boot from a USB thumb drive.

Activity 2-4: Installing Windows Server 2016 from DVD

Time Required: Approximately 30–60 minutes (depending on the speed of your computer)
Objective: Install Windows Server 2016 from DVD.

Description: In this activity, you install Windows Server 2016. The installation steps provided here are for Windows Server 2016 Standard or Datacenter Edition. These steps are for an installation that is done from scratch and in which you install the full GUI version (Desktop Experience) of Windows Server 2016 and not a Server Core installation. You will need a Windows Server 2016 installation DVD. Also, make sure that you have the Product Key available, which is typically printed on a label on the jewel case or sleeve that houses the DVD. You'll need the Product Key to activate the server as described later in this chapter. Or you can obtain an evaluation version of Windows Server 2016 as a download from Microsoft at *www.microsoft.com*, which usually does not require a Product Key.

Have the computer already connected to a network with Internet access for the Windows Server 2016 installation, so that Windows Setup can obtain the latest updates as it installs the operating system (see Step 13 and Figure 2-11).

1. Follow Steps 1–5 in the section, DVD or USB Thumb Drive Installation, in which you ensure the BIOS is set to boot from the optical drive. Insert the Windows Server 2016 installation DVD, and boot the computer from the DVD.
2. If you see a box that indicates you have started an upgrade, and you want to perform a clean installation, click **No** (the selection that enables you to perform a clean installation).
3. The DVD might take a few moments to load. You may see a message that says Loading files along with a file loading progress bar.
4. When the Windows Setup window entitled, Windows Server 2016 appears, specify the language to install, such as **English (United States)**, in the *Language to install* drop-down box. In the Time and currency format box, make your selection, such as **English (United States)**. In the Keyboard or input method box, make your selection, such as **US** (see Figure 2-7). Click **Next.**

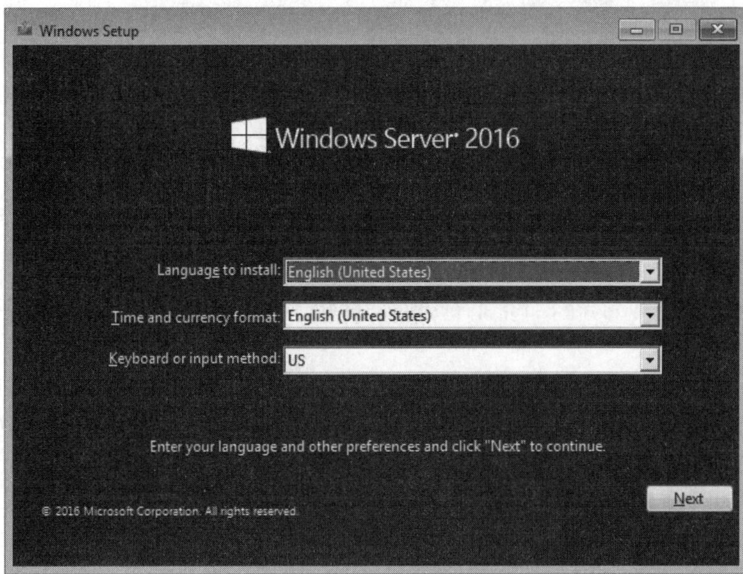

Figure 2-7 Specifying the language, time and currency format, and keyboard or input method

5. The next Windows Setup window enables you to commence the installation. Before you get started, notice there is a link for *Repair your computer*. The *Repair your computer* link is for after Windows Server 2016 is installed and a problem arises, such as when the computer won't boot after a power failure. You can use this link to repair problems with boot files (see Figure 2-8).
6. Click the **Install now** button as shown in Figure 2-8.
7. If you see the Activate Windows window, enter the product key and click **Next**; or if you don't have a product key because you are installing an evaluation version of Windows, click **I don't have a product key.**
8. In the next installation window to select the operating system you want to install, you can select one of the following under the Operating System column (this example installation is for a Windows Server 2016 Standard or Datacenter (Desktop Experience) installation using an evaluation copy):
   - Windows Server 2016 Standard
   - Windows Server 2016 Standard (Desktop Experience)
   - Windows Server 2016 Datacenter
   - Windows Server 2016 Datacenter (Desktop Experience)

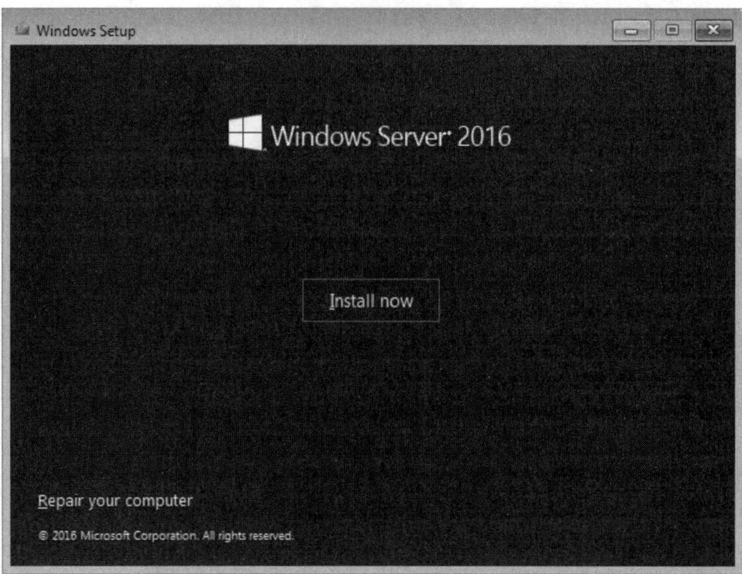

Figure 2-8 Starting the installation

If you do not select the option for Desktop Experience, this means that Server Core is installed, which does not include the GUI but enables you to manage Windows Server 2016 through Windows PowerShell. Also, if you are using an evaluation version, you will see choices with the word Evaluation, such as Windows Server 2016 Standard Evaluation.

Depending on your version, select Windows Server 2016 Standard (Desktop Experience) or Windows Server 2016 Datacenter (Desktop Experience) and click **Next**. (The examples in this book apply to Standard and Datacenter Editions, but select Datacenter Edition, if it is available for a more complete experience of Windows Server 2016 features.)

9. Read the license terms (see Figure 2-9), click the box for **I accept the license terms**, and click **Next**.
10. In the next window, you'll select (click) the type of installation you want to perform from the following options (see Figure 2-10):
    - Upgrade: Install Windows and keep files, settings, and applications
      The files, settings, and applications are moved to Windows with this option. This option is only available when a supported version of Windows is already running on the computer.
    - Custom: Install Windows only (advanced)
      The files, settings, and applications aren't moved to Windows with this option. If you want to make changes to partitions and drives, start the computer using the installation disc. We recommend backing up your files before you continue.

If you need help deciding when you do an installation for your organization, you can click *Help me decide* before you make a decision.

11. Click **Custom: Install Windows only (advanced)**.
12. The installation program displays disk partitions, including existing partitions and unallocated disk space (refer to Figure 2-1 earlier in the chapter). Select the disk partition or unallocated space you want to use. For example, click Drive 0 Unallocated Space on a new computer. (Note that the window displays an informational message at the bottom, if you highlight a partition that is too small or one that contains a non-NTFS partition.) Further, there are options shown at the bottom of the window to enable you to do the following:

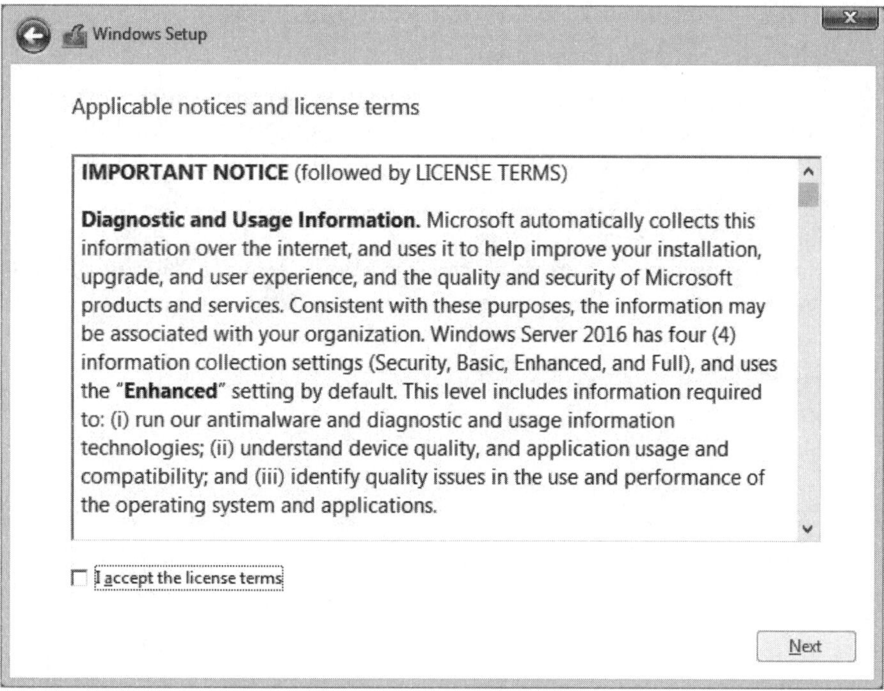

Figure 2-9 License terms window

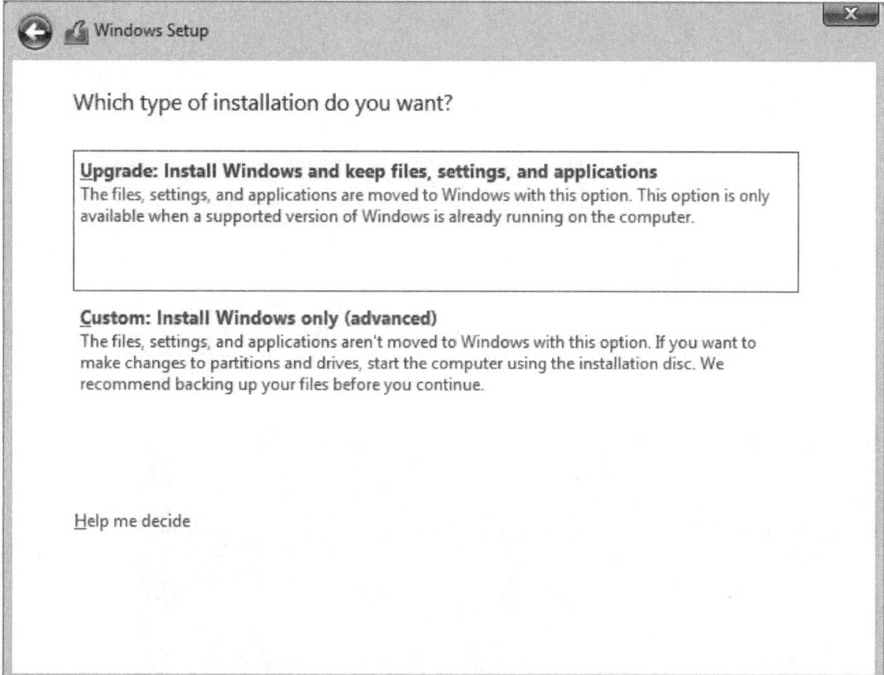

Figure 2-10 Selecting the installation type

- *Refresh* the window, after you have performed a task in the window, such as deleting a partition (one of the other options in the window)
- *Load driver* so you can install a more recent hard disk driver or a driver for a disk that is not properly recognized by Windows Server 2016.
- *Delete*, which enables you to delete an existing partition
- *Extend*, so that you can extend the size of an existing partition by adding unallocated space to it

- *Format*, which is used to format an existing partition
- *New* to create a new partition

For this installation, select a drive with unallocated space, such as **Drive 0 Unallocated Space** (be sure the drive you select has enough disk space to load and run Windows Server 2016, preferably at least 40 GB for a test server for learning or 150 GB or more for a production server). Click **Next** after you've made your selection.

13. The installation program begins installing Windows Server 2016. In the Installing Windows window, you'll see progress information about Copying Windows files, Getting files ready for installation, Installing features, Installing updates, and Finishing up; see Figure 2-11.

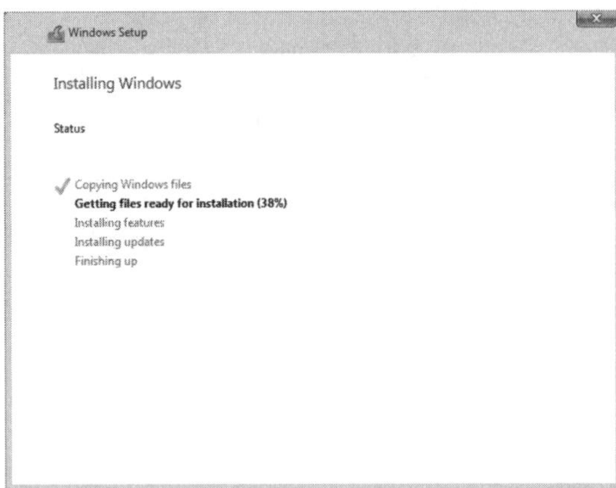

Figure 2-11 Installation progress

14. The installation program restarts the computer (or you can click **Restart now**). Let it boot from the hard drive.
15. You may see the message: Please wait while Windows sets up your computer. You'll also see Getting devices ready and Getting ready.
16. Next you'll see Restarting and then the system reboots again. Let it boot from the hard drive.
17. On the Customize settings screen (see Figure 2-12), enter a new password for the Administrator account and then enter the same password again to confirm the password. Click **Finish**.

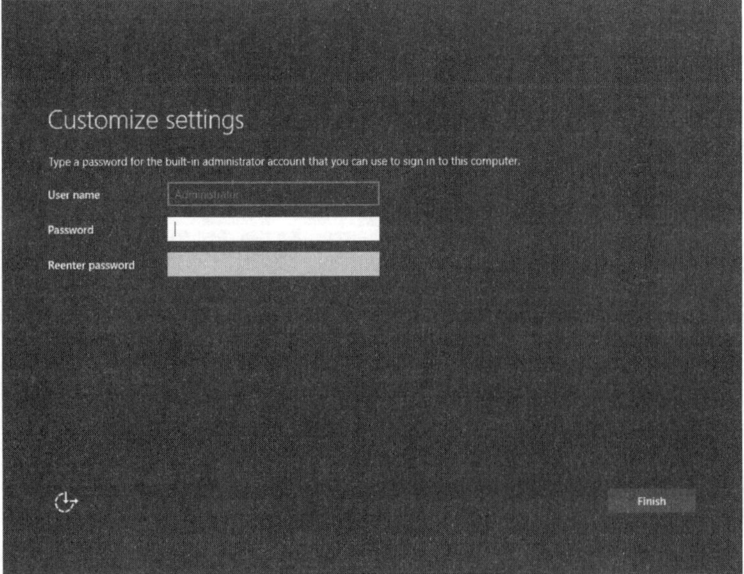

Figure 2-12 Providing a password for the Administrator account

If you enter a password that is not a strong password, you might see a message that the password cannot be updated because it does not meet strong password requirements, such as for length (over 7 characters), complexity (using letters, numbers, and extra characters, such as &), and history requirements. Click **OK** and enter a different password.

18. You'll see the message Finalizing your settings.
19. Press **Ctrl+Alt+Delete** to access the sign-in screen. (If you are installing into a Hyper-V virtual machine, in the Virtual Machine Connection window, click the **Action** menu and click **Ctrl+Alt+Delete.**)
20. On the Windows Server 2016 sign-in screen (see Figure 2-13), enter the Administrator account password that you created in Step 17. After you sign-in, Server Manager is automatically started so that you can begin configuring your server.

You may see the Networks panel on the right side of the screen that enables you to choose whether to find PCs and devices on an existing network. Click No for this installation, but keep in mind that this option is available, such as for a small business network.

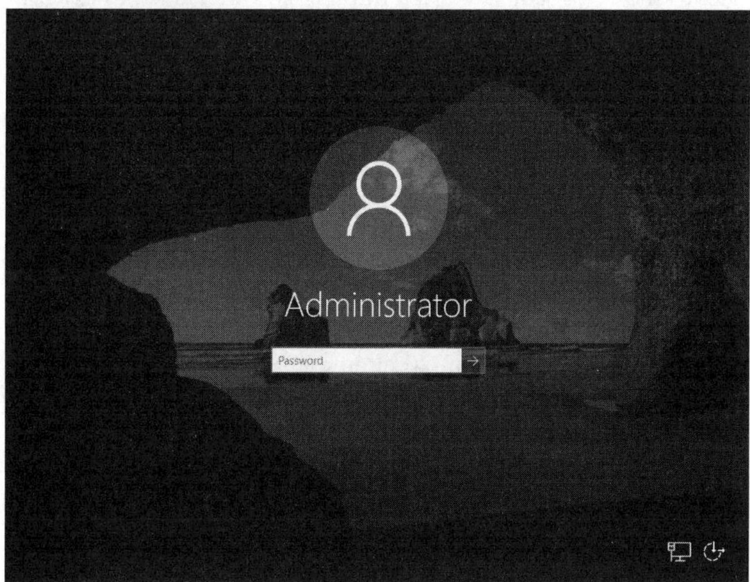

Figure 2-13 Sign-in screen for Windows Server 2016

21. Leave the computer signed in for the next activity (including if you are using Windows Server 2016 in Hyper-V).

Whenever you need to sign out or shut down from your Windows Server 2016 account or the Administrator account, right-click Start, point to Shut down or sign out, and click Sign out (or click Shut down to shut down the system, select a reason for the shut down, and click Continue). Alternatively, to sign out, click Start, click the Administrator symbol in the bottom left corner of the Start menu (above the Power and the Settings symbols), and click Sign out.

From this point on, if you sign out, you can sign back in to the Administrator account using the password you entered in Step 17. Press Ctrl+Alt+Delete to access the sign-in screen (or in a Hyper-V virtual machine click the Action menu and click Ctrl+Alt+Delete). The Administrator account has complete privileges to manage Windows Server 2016. Some administrators give their own account administrator privileges, as a security measure, so that they do not have to use the Administrator account very often.

Using Server Manager for the Initial Setup

You can use Server Manager to begin configuring the server through tasks such as:

- Establishing the server name, configuring the workgroup or domain name, setting up the firewall, configuring remote management and remote desktop, and configuring other properties.
- Configuring the time zone.
- Configuring IP addressing information
- Configuring server services and monitoring those services
- Installing and managing server roles and program features

You don't need to complete all of the tasks at this time, but you should complete some preliminary tasks right away, such as configuring basic information about the server. For example, you'll notice that the computer has been assigned a random name such as WIN-9E7MT5EFTHG in a workgroup called WORKGROUP. Also, the computer has been automatically set up to have an IP address automatically leased by DHCP. Typically, a server should have a static address that you assign or a static address assigned when you configure DHCP to give the server a permanent address.

Many server administrators check to be sure remote management is enabled so that they can remotely connect to the server console. Server administrators check to be certain that Windows Firewall is working or they disable Windows Firewall to set up other firewall software purchased for all servers in an organization. Another important initial step is to configure Windows Update to make certain that the latest updates are obtained and installed as a basic security measure.

If you already know some roles that the server is to perform or features you want to add, you can add those roles and features when you initially configure the server in Server Manager. (You'll learn more about configuring server roles and features in Chapter 3.)

Activity 2-5: Performing Initial Configuration Tasks Using Server Manager

Time Required: Approximately 15–20 minutes
Objective: Use Server Manager to start configuring Windows Server 2016.

Description: Now that you've installed Windows Server 2016, it's important to configure the server so that it has an appropriate name, is a member of a workgroup or domain, is regularly updated, and is secured through Windows Firewall. In this activity, you complete all of these tasks. The server should already be signed in to the Administrator account with the Server Manager window open. Also, you'll need a computer name and a domain or workgroup name. Additionally, your computer should be connected to a network so that you can verify the network configuration. For this activity, the network connection is Ethernet.

If you are at the server console and first need to sign back in, press **Ctrl+Alt+Delete**, enter your password, and click the **right-pointing arrow**. In Hyper-V in the Virtual Machine Connection window, if you need to sign back in, click the **Action menu**, click **Ctrl+Alt+Delete**, enter your password, and click the **right-pointing arrow**.

1. Ensure that the Server Manager window is open. If it is not, click **Start** and click the **Server Manager** tile, or click **Start** and click **Server Manager** in the listing of applications under the letter S. If the Server Manager window is not maximized, click the **Maximize** button in the top right side of the Server Manager title bar.
2. In the right pane of Server Manager, click **Configure this local server** (or you can click **Local Server** in the left pane).
3. In the right pane under PROPERTIES (see Figure 2-14), click the computer name just to the right of the Computer name label.

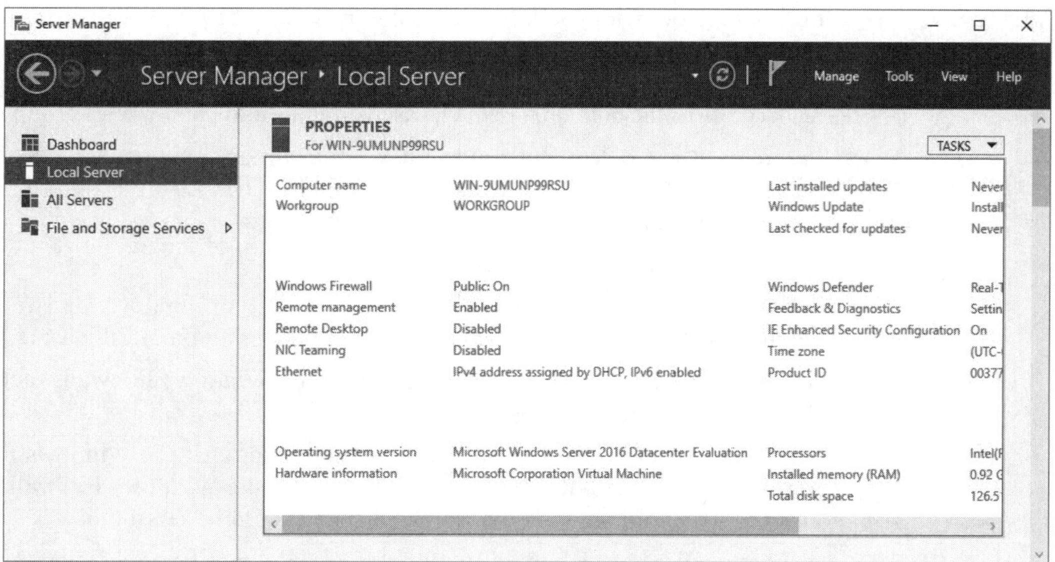

Figure 2-14 Using Server Manager for initial configuration tasks

4. In the System Properties dialog box, enter **Server** in the Computer description box and click the **Change** button (see Figure 2-15).

Figure 2-15 System Properties dialog box

5. On the Computer Name/Domain Changes dialog box, enter the new name for your server in the Computer name box.
6. Click the option button for **Domain** or **Workgroup** (depending on how your network is set up, but if you select domain then there should already be a domain set up on the network for the server to join). Enter the domain or workgroup name and click **OK**. (If you enter a domain name, Windows Server 2016 checks the network to verify there is such a domain; if it does

not find the domain, you'll see a warning box that the Active Directory Domain Controller for the domain could not be contacted. Click **OK**. Check to ensure you correctly spelled the domain name, correct the name and try again. Or if you spelled it correctly, you might not have access to the domain, in which case you'll need to enter a workgroup name for now.)

7. If you see a box welcoming you to the workgroup or domain, click **OK**. In the information box advising that you must restart the computer, click **OK** (but don't restart the computer yet). Click **Close** in the System Properties dialog box.
8. Click **Restart Later** in the information box.
9. In Server Manager under Properties, look to the right of Windows Update and notice that the default installation configuration says Install updates automatically using Windows Update.
10. In Server Manager, click the setting across from Windows Firewall, such as **Public: On** or **Private: On** (see Figure 2-14).
11. The Windows Firewall window enables you to configure the Windows Firewall (if you are not using other firewall software, in which case the Windows Firewall will likely be disabled). By default, the Windows Firewall state should be set to On.
    - What would you click in this window to allow a specific application to go through Windows Firewall?
12. Close the Windows Firewall window.
13. In Server Manager, click the parameter just to the right of Ethernet. (In Figure 2-14, this is **IPv4 address assigned by DHCP, IPv6 enabled**, because the server uses a wired connection and has already obtained an IP address from the local DHCP server.)
14. In the Network Connections Window, right-click **Ethernet** and click **Properties**. Double-click the IP version in use on your network, such as **Internet Protocol Version 4 (TCP/IPv4)**, as in Figure 2-16. The Properties dialog box can be configured in the same way as you did

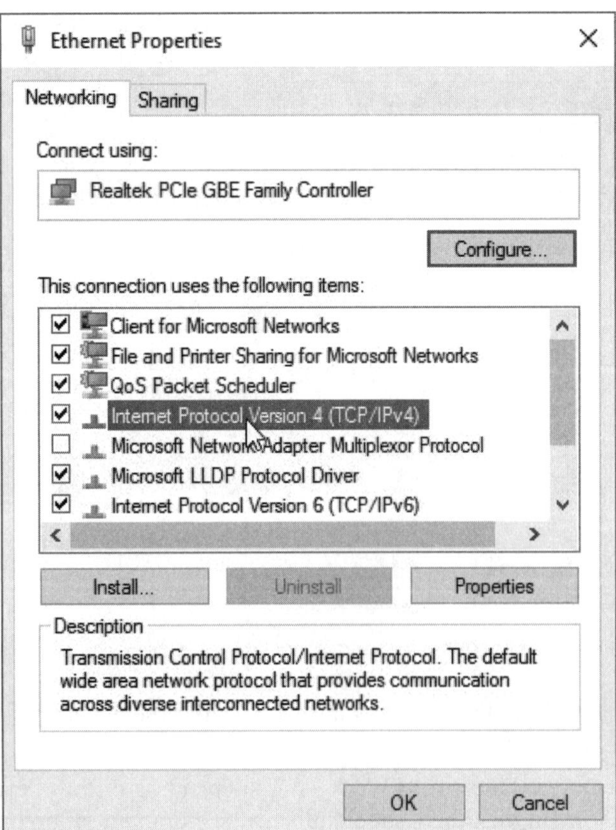

Figure 2-16 Configuring IP addressing

in Activity 1-7 in Chapter 1. If you want to configure a static IP address now, enter the IP address, subnet mask, and default gateway for this computer. Also, enter the IP address for the Preferred DNS server and the IP address for the Alternate DNS server (if there is one). Click **OK**. Click **OK** again in the Ethernet Properties dialog box. Close the Network Connections window.

15. Reboot the computer by right-clicking **Start**, pointing to **Shut down or sign out**, clicking **Restart**, selecting the reason to shut down (such as **Other Planned**), and clicking **Continue**.
16. Sign in to an account with administrator privileges and ensure that Server Manager opens.

Server Activation

After Windows Server 2016 is installed, it is necessary to activate your copy of the operating system. Microsoft uses activation to ensure the installed copy of the operating system is legitimate. Activation also enables Microsoft to be sure a single copy is not running on more than one computer. During the installation of Windows Server 2016, you may have found that there was no step for entering the product key. Instead, you need to enter the product key using Server Manager. When you enter the product key, your server contacts Microsoft to also activate the server. The product key is either on the installation DVD packaging or for OEM servers, it may be on a sticker with the server hardware.

You need to activate your copy of Windows Server 2016 before the short activation period expires, or else the server may frequently reboot or some normal functions of the operating system may be disabled. Windows Server 2016 can be activated through the Internet using Server Manager.

The general steps for activating Windows Server 2016 through Server Manager are as follows:

1. In Server Manager, click Local Server in the left pane.
2. Click the link for the product key just to the right of Product ID such as Not activated.
3. Enter the product key (see Figure 2-17).

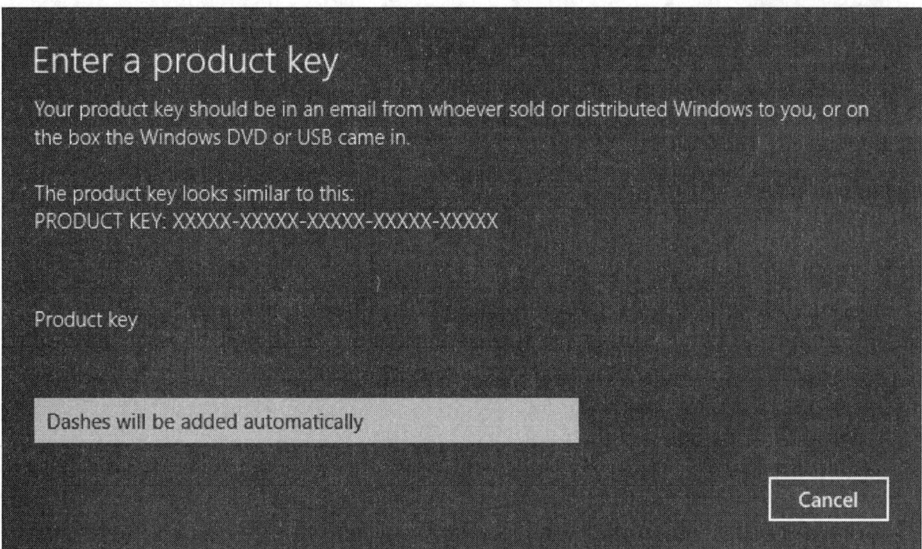

Figure 2-17 Enter a product key window for server activation

4. Click Activate.

Using Windows Deployment Services

Windows Deployment Services is an alternative to physically taking a DVD or USB thumb drive to each computer that needs to have Windows Server 2016 installed. This is a good alternative when there are many servers (or workstations if you are installing Windows 10) that need to be installed at once or over a specific time interval.

Windows Deployment Services is originally based on Windows Server 2003 Remote Installation Services (RIS). The upgraded code in Windows Deployment Services offers the following benefits:

- Installs Windows Server from Server 2003 through Server 2016
- Installs Windows desktop systems from Windows Vista to Windows 10
- Enhances performance
- Provides updated boot format
- Uses image-based installation techniques
- Can utilize multicasting for network efficiency
- Offers an enhanced presentation for choosing which operating system to install
- Supports cmdlets and scripting in Windows PowerShell, which is new with Windows Server 2012 R2 and Server 2016

Windows Deployment Services operate in a **Preboot Execution Environment (PXE)**. This means that the target computer on which to install the operating system already has software to be PXE-enabled. A PXE-enabled client can connect to the network and communicate with a server (or boot from the server) without first having to boot from an operating system on the client's hard disk. Some computers come with PXE capabilities. Microsoft uses Windows Preinstallation Environment (WinPE) to enable PXE on the client. Windows PE is a very stripped-down version of a Windows operating system.

New to Windows Server 2012, Server 2012 R2, and Server 2016 is WDS support for ARM clients. ARM, which is named after the ARM Holdings company, uses reduced instruction set computing (RISC) processors. The RISC processor design enables such computers to use less power and less expensive components and is targeted for mobile devices including smart phones and tablet PCs. Support for ARM devices is intended to enable Windows operating systems to run on a broader variety of mobile devices.

Installing and Configuring Windows Deployment Services

The first step is to install the Windows Deployment Services role on a computer that already has Windows Server 2016 installed. Before installing Windows Deployment Services, several requirements must be met:

- A DNS server already configured on the network
- A DHCP server already configured on the network
- Active Directory Domain Services already installed on a network server and the Windows Deployment Services server is part of the domain managed by Active Directory (the Deployment Services server can also house Active Directory)
- NTFS as the file system on the Windows Deployment Services server

You can install the Windows Deployment Services role from Server Manager as you learn in Activity 2-6.

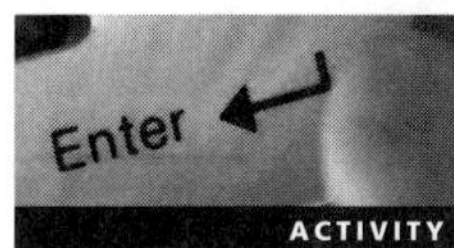

Activity 2-6: Installing and Configuring the Windows Deployment Services Role

2

Time Required: Approximately 15 minutes
Objective: Use Server Manager to install the Windows Deployment Services role.

Description: The first step in using Windows Deployment Services is to install this role on an existing Windows Server 2016 server. This activity shows you how to install the role. For practice, you install it on a standalone computer so that you do not need Active Directory installed in advance. Additionally, you will need to use the Administrator account and you'll need to know the location of the Windows image file to use.

1. Open Server Manager, if it is not already open.
2. Click **Dashboard**, if it is not already selected.
3. Click **Add roles and features**.
4. If you see the Before you begin window, click **Next**.
5. In the Select installation type window, ensure that **Role-based or feature-based installation** is selected and click **Next**.
6. In the Select destination server window, ensure that your local server is selected and click **Next**.
7. In the Select server roles window, click the box for **Windows Deployment Services** (refer back to Figure 2-5).
8. In the Add Roles and Features Wizard dialog box, make sure that the box is checked for *Include management tools (if applicable)*. Click **Add Features** to install the selected features.
9. Click **Next** in the Select server roles window.
10. Click **Next** in the Select features window.
11. In the WDS window, read the introductory information about Windows Deployment Services and click **Next**.
12. Ensure that both **Deployment Server** and **Transport Server** are selected as in Figure 2-18 and click **Next**.

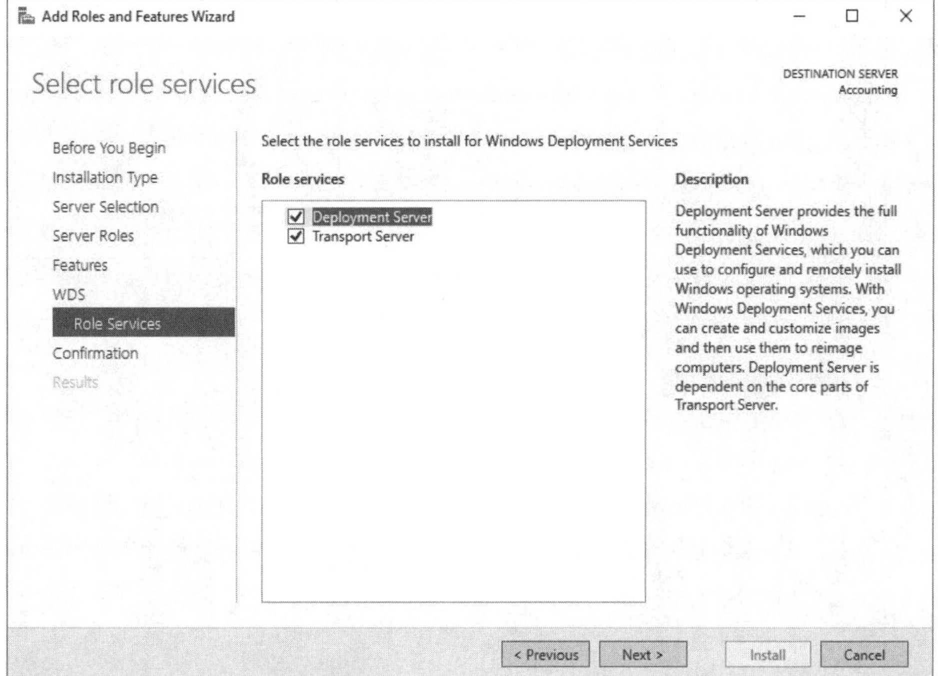

Figure 2-18 Selecting role services

13. Click **Install** in the Confirm installation selections window (see Figure 2-19). The installation will take a few moments.

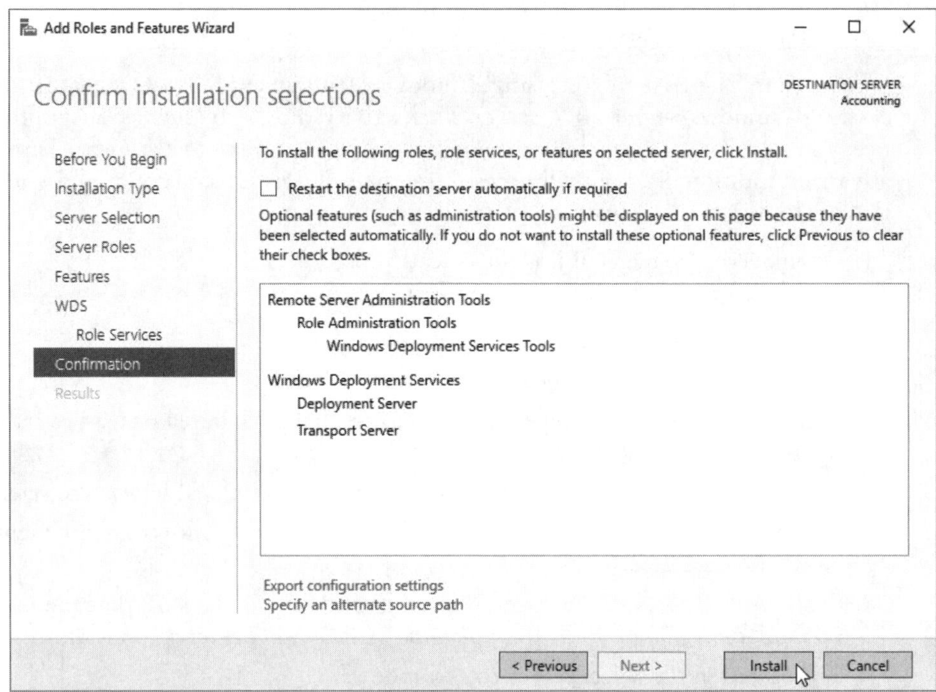

Figure 2-19 Confirm installation selections window

14. In the Installation progress window, make sure that you see the message: Installation succeeded on *servername* as in Figure 2-20. Click **Close.**

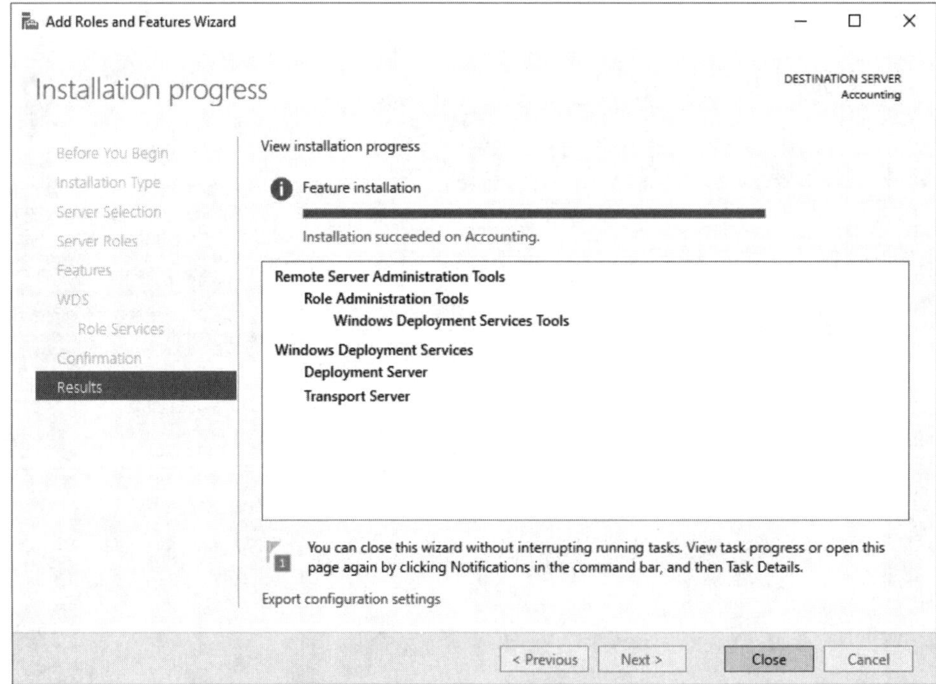

Figure 2-20 Installation progress window showing the installation succeeded

15. Close Server Manager.
16. Click **Start** and click the **Windows Administrative Tools** folder. If necessary, scroll to view Windows Deployment Services (see Figure 2-21).

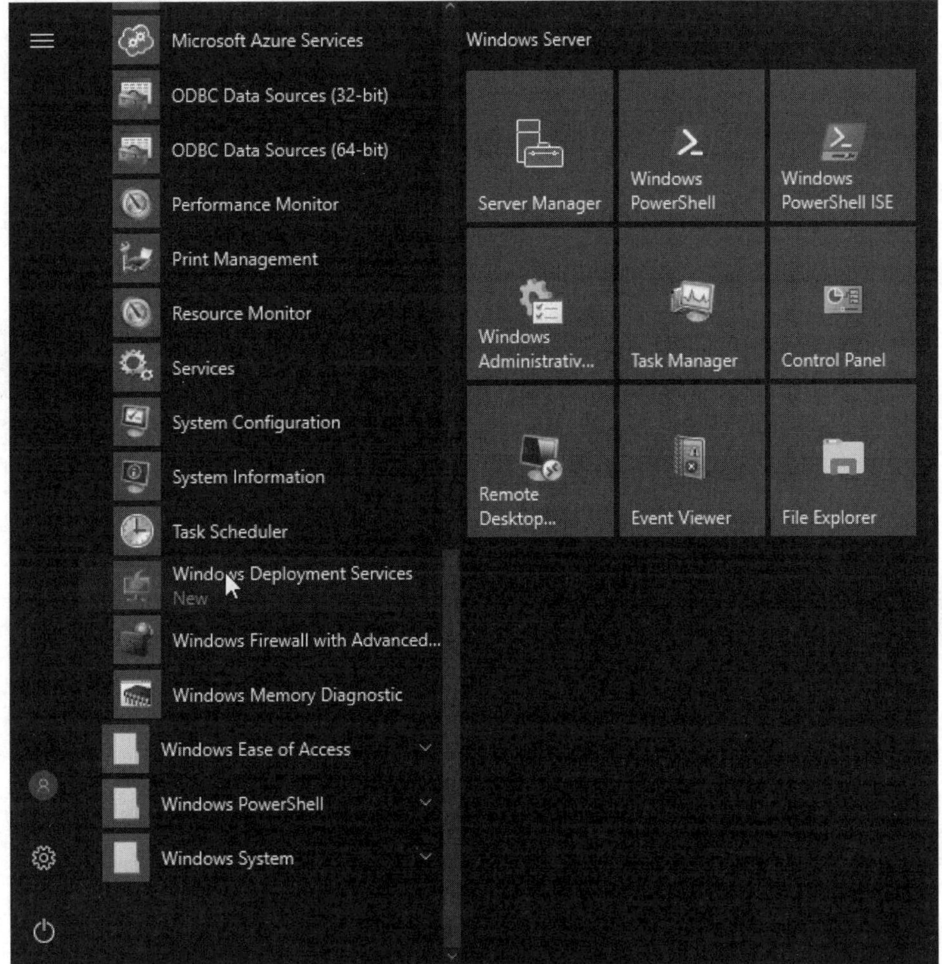

Figure 2-21 Administrative Tools listing from the Start menu

17. Click **Windows Deployment Services.**
18. In the left pane, click the right pointing arrow next to Servers to display the Windows Deployment Server's name.
19. Right-click the server's name and click **Configure Server** (see Figure 2-22).
20. Read the Before You Begin information and click **Next** in the Windows Deployment Services Configuration Wizard.
21. Ensure that **Standalone server** is selected and click **Next.** (It is more advantageous to select Integrated with Active Directory, but at this point you have not installed Active Directory. For practice you use the standalone server option in this activity.)
22. In the Remote Installation Folder Location window, leave the default selection, C:\RemoteInstall. This is a shared folder that will contain the operating system images to be installed on future servers. Click **Next** (see Figure 2-23).
23. If you see a warning about using the System Volume, click **Yes.** (In a production server environment, you would locate the remote installation folder on another volume, if one is available, instead of the system volume. Locating the folder on a different volume helps the server to run faster by reducing the competition for system volume resources.)

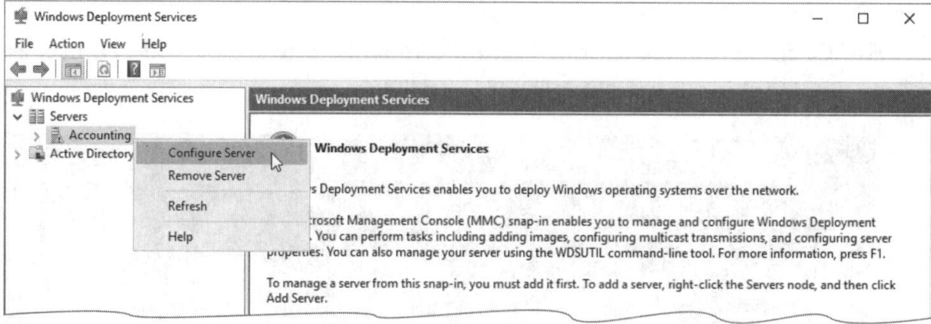

Figure 2-22 Selecting to configure the server

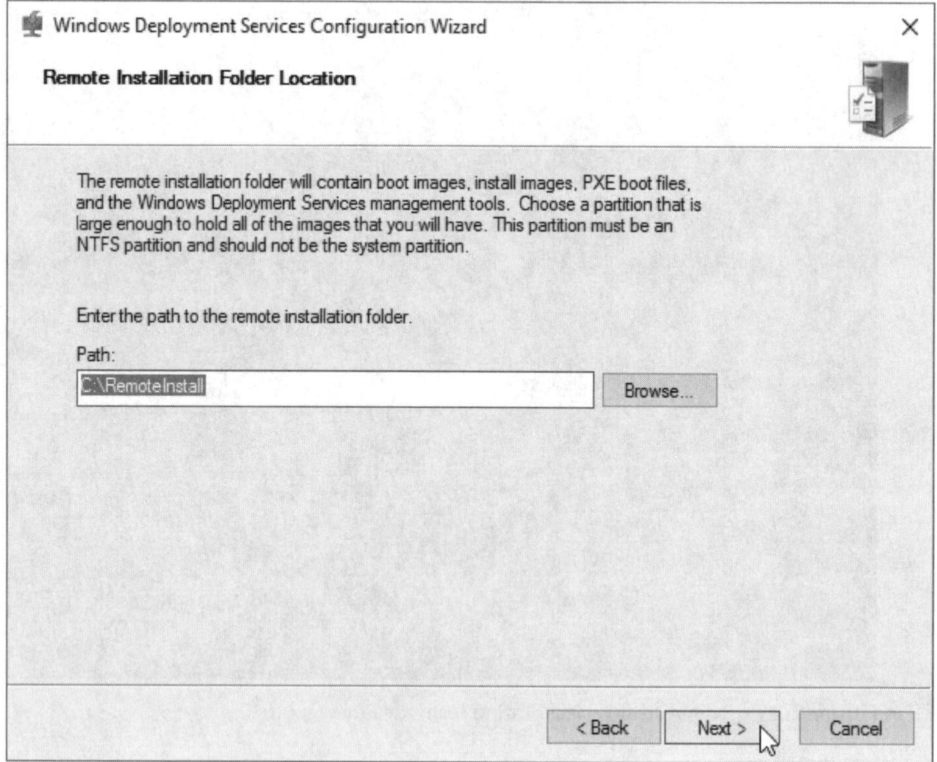

Figure 2-23 Specifying the remote installation folder location

24. If you see the Proxy DHCP Server window, use the default options and click **Next.**
25. Select **Respond to all client computers (known and unknown)** for the PXE setting to govern which computers can be used (see Figure 2-24). Click **Next.**
26. Click **Finish.**
27. In the left pane of the Windows Deployment Services window and under the server name in the tree, right-click **Install Images** (to add an image file from a DVD and click **Add Install Image**).
28. Insert the Windows Server 2016 installation DVD. (The operating system image used to deploy to other computers is from the installation DVD that you use, which can be an edition of Windows Server 2016 or Windows 10, for example.) Ensure that **Create an image group named** is selected and enter a name for the image group or leave the name as ImageGroup1. Click **Next.**

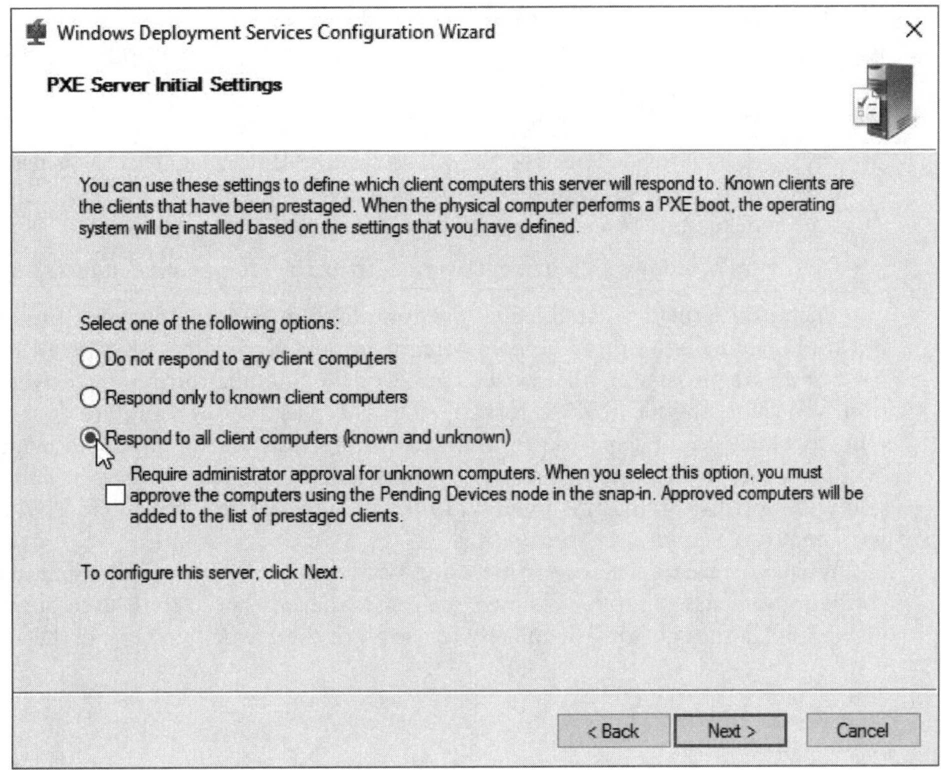

Figure 2-24 Configuring initial settings

29. Browse to the file location of the install.wim image file, such as *E:\sources*. Click **Open**.
30. In the Image File window of the Add Image Wizard, click **Next**.
31. If you see the Available Images window of the Add Image Wizard and there are multiple images from which to select, such as for the GUI and Server Core images for Standard and Datacenter Editions, check the boxes for the images you want to use. Click **Next**.
32. Review the summary of image selections and click **Next**.
33. Wait for the images to be loaded in the Task Progress window.
34. Click **Finish**.
35. Close the Windows Deployment Services window. Close the Administrative Tools window.

After you have installed and configured Windows Deployment Services, you can install Windows Server 2016 on a computer through the network. These are the general steps for installing the operating system:

1. Access the BIOS setup program on the client computer. Set the computer so it can do a PXE boot from the network. Save the changes and reboot.
2. When the computer boots, press the F12 key (or whichever key is specified on your computer to start the PXE boot).
3. At the boot menu, select to install the image for Windows Server 2016.
4. If necessary, specify the locale for the setup program.
5. If requested, provide a username and the associated password.
6. Follow the setup instructions to complete the installation.

Elements for an Unattended Installation

If you don't want to have to interactively respond when you use Windows Deployment Services, you can choose to perform an unattended installation. To set up for an unattended installation, it is necessary to do the following:

- Create the unattended answer file, which is in XML format. This file is used to answer questions that the setup program asks as it is installing Windows Server 2016, such as the time zone, edition to install, partition to use, and so on.
- Configure Windows Deployment Services to enable an unattended installation.

The answer file is created using **Windows System Image Manager (Windows SIM)**, which is a tool included with the Windows **Assessment and Deployment Kit (ADK)**. Windows SIM is used to create an answer file, revise an answer file, include third party drivers for an installation, and create the file in XML format. ADK contains a set of tools and documentation to help you customize use of a specific windows operating system. You have to download the ADK for Windows Server 2016 from Microsoft's website. Once on the website, at *www.microsoft.com*, you will most likely find the download file for the ADK at a download link, or you might try *www.microsoft.com/en-us/download.*

When you create the answer file using Windows SIM, you will likely need to set up several configuration passes. Table 2-3 shows the passes that may need to be used during an unattended installation, although you are unlikely to use all of these when you create the answer file.

Table 2-3 Configuration passes

Pass	Description
windowsPE	For the booting conditions, product key information (if needed), and elements related to the installation media
specialize	For special elements for the specific system or computer, such as network configuration or domain information
offlineServicing	For applying updates for the image file
auditSystem	If necessary, for steps to complete prior to when the user signs in—for audit mode
auditUser	If necessary, for steps to complete after the user signs in—for audit mode
generalize	Deletes specific system-related information, such as customized hardware settings not needed for the image file—only used when you use the sysprep /generalize command
oobeSystem	Installs settings prior to first sign-in.

The next task is to configure Windows Deployment Services to enable an unattended installation. The general steps for configuring Windows Deployment Services for this purpose are:

1. Click Start, click the Windows Administrative Tools folder, and click Windows Deployment Services.
2. In the left pane, click the right pointing arrow next to Servers to display the Windows Deployment Server.
3. Right-click the server and click Properties.
4. Click the Client tab.
5. Click Enable unattended installation, as shown in Figure 2-25.
6. Use the Browse buttons to specify desired computer architectures.
7. Click OK.
8. Close the Windows Deployment Services window.

2

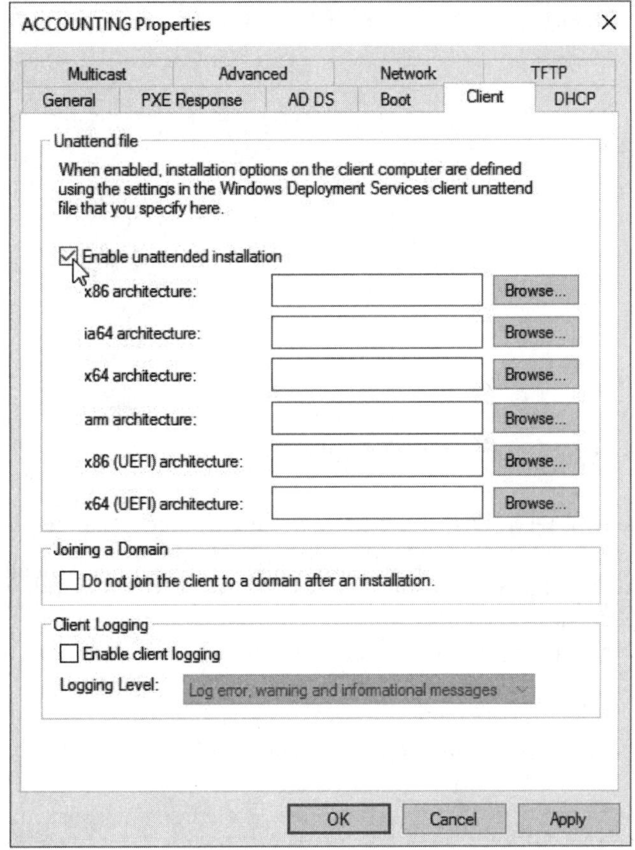

Figure 2-25 Configuring Windows Deployment Services for unattended installation

Installing Windows Server Core

The steps for installing Windows Server Core are nearly identical to the steps for a full installation, until you reach the end of the process when you need to sign in to the newly installed system. Here are the general steps for installing Windows Server Core:

1. Refer to Activity 2-4, Installing Windows Server 2016 from DVD and follow Steps 1–7.
2. In the step to select the operating system to install (Step 8 in Activity 2–4), select to install the Server Core Installation, such as Windows Server 2016 Standard or Windows Server 2016 Datacenter. Click Next.
3. Follow the same general tasks as in Steps 9–16 in Activity 2-4.
4. If necessary after the system reboots the second time, type Ctrl+Alt+Delete (or on a virtual machine, click the Action menu and click Ctrl+Alt+Delete) to unlock the command window. You may need to select OK to set a new password for the Administrator account.
5. Enter the new Administrator password and reenter it for verification. Press Enter.
6. When you see, *Your password has been changed*, ensure OK is selected and press Enter.
7. Your new system boots into a command-line window, as shown in Figure 2-26.

After Windows Server Core is installed, you can implement all or portions of the server roles that are listed in the section earlier in this chapter, Identifying Server Roles.

For some of these roles, not all role services can be installed as in the full GUI installation of Windows Server 2016. This is in keeping with the design concept of having a smaller attack surface to discourage attackers and malicious software. For example, the File and Storage Server

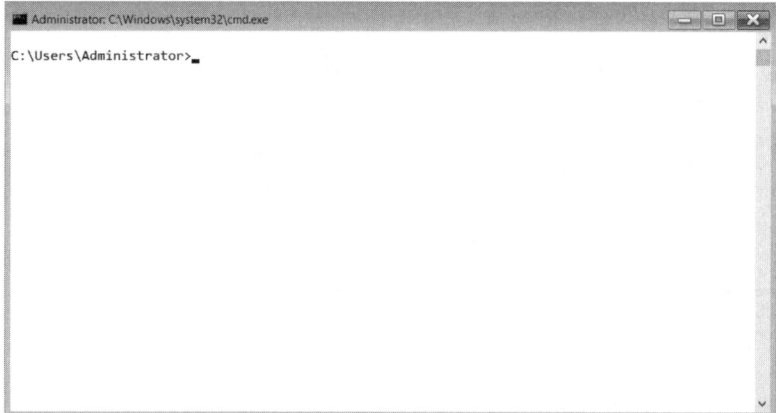

Figure 2-26 Windows Server 2016 Server Core command-line window

role includes basic file server, DFS (Distributed File System) Namespaces services, DFS Replication services, services for NFS (Network File System), work folder services, and storage services. Examples of the File and Storage Server role services not included are Windows Search Service and Windows Server 2003 File Services.

You can view the current configuration of the server by entering *sconfig* at the command line (see Figure 2-27). From this screen, you can configure some of the same elements as in Server Manager. For example, to join a domain or change the workgroup name, enter 1 and provide the domain or workgroup name. To change the computer name, enter 2 and provide the computer name.

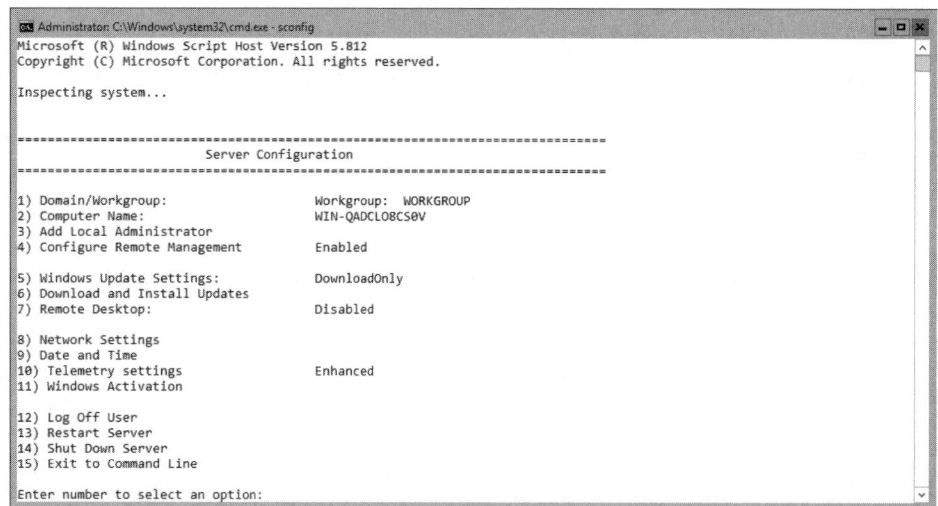

Figure 2-27 Configuration options when using *sconfig*

To access PowerShell, type *powershell* at the command prompt in the Server Core command-line window (refer to Figure 2-26). Now you see the command prompt *PS C:\Users\Administrator*, which means you can execute PowerShell cmdlets (the command line starts with PS to show you are in Windows PowerShell mode). For example, enter *Get-WindowsFeature* to view the roles and features that are available to install. To install a role from the PowerShell command line, enter *Add-WindowsFeature* plus the specific role. For example, to install the DNS Server role you would enter *Add-WindowsFeature DNS*. To install the Print and Documents Services role, you would enter *Add-Windows Feature Print-Services*. Not all features are automatically installed when you install a role, so you may need to specify certain features with the *Add-WindowsFeature* cmdlet, which you can do after you install the role (remember to use the *Get-WindowsFeature* command to review what is installed). Many other commands are available in Windows Server Core. At the command line, enter *help* to view a listing of commands. To learn more about a specific command, enter *help* plus the name of the command, such as *help start* to see the online documentation for the *start* command.

Besides the commands listed via *help*, there are a host of other commands for managing and using the server that are not listed. For example, to open a dialog box to set the time and date, enter *control timedate.cpl*. The *netsh* command enables you to view and configure network interfaces. To change the administrator account password, enter *net user administrator**. To activate the server, enter *slmgr.vbs -ato*. Use the *netdom join* command to join an existing domain on the network. Finally, use the *logoff* and *shutdown* commands to sign out an account or to shut down the computer.

For information about Server Core command-line commands, go to *http://technet.microsoft.com/en-us/library/cc754340.aspx*. For Windows PowerShell cmdlet help, visit *https://technet.microsoft.com/en-us/library/dd772285.aspx,* and for scripting help, visit *https://technet.microsoft.com/en-us/library/hh551144.aspx*.

Installing and Managing Service Packs

By the time you install an operating system, chances are there have already been reported problems and bugs with it. Service packs are designed to correct things such as security issues as well as problems affecting stability, performance, or the operation of features included with the operating system. Once you've installed the operating system, it is generally good practice to download and apply the latest service pack, if one is available, to fix any known issues and patch any security holes. You can obtain a service pack using Windows Update or by downloading the service pack from the Microsoft download website, which is for example at this writing, *www.microsoft.com/en-us/download* for US English speaking customers.

Installing a service pack is considered a major upgrade and should be given serious consideration because some of the operating system files will be replaced. There is always a chance that the upgrade will fail or new problems will be caused by installing the service pack. This is more of an issue for those servers that are already running on the network and being used by clients.

Use the following guidelines when installing the latest service packs for Windows Server 2016 (or any other Microsoft operating systems):

- Download the latest service pack from Microsoft's download site. The service pack is also usually available for order on DVD.
- Review the documentation that comes with the service pack. This will detail the installation procedures and alert you to any problems associated with installing the service pack.
- If the server is already in the production environment, be sure to perform a full backup before you do the service pack installation.
- If the server is already available to clients, schedule when the service pack will be installed because the server will need to be rebooted during the installation. This will alert clients to any downtime.
- Once the service pack is installed, document any problems that occurred and how you fixed them for future reference.

Many organizations have server downtime regularly scheduled for routine maintenance, backups, and installation of patches or service packs. In this way, users know in advance and can plan their work around the downtime.

Activity 2-7: Using Windows Update

Time Required: Approximately 10 minutes
Objective: Use Server Manager to start Windows Update.

Description: Plan to regularly update Windows Server 2016 to keep the operating system secure and to obtain the latest service pack when it becomes available. In this activity, you use Server Manager to access Windows Update and then check to see if there are updates waiting to be installed. The default setting for Windows Update is to automatically download updates, but to not install them until you initiate the installation. This is so that updating the operating system is not occurring automatically while users are active. In this way, you can install updates during a scheduled time when users are not on the server. For this activity, the server should already be connected to the Internet.

1. Open **Server Manager.**
2. Click **Local Server** in the left pane.
3. Ensure that you are connected to the Internet, such as viewing the information displayed for Ethernet, which will show the IP address plus *enabled* or will show that the address is obtained from DHCP.
4. Click the link to the right of Windows Update, which is **Download updates only, using Microsoft Update.**
5. In the Settings window under Update & security, check to see if there are updates waiting to be installed and if there are, click the **Install now** button (see Figure 2-28). (Alternatively, if there are no updates waiting to be installed, click the **Check for updates** button and then if updates are downloaded, click the **Install now** button.)

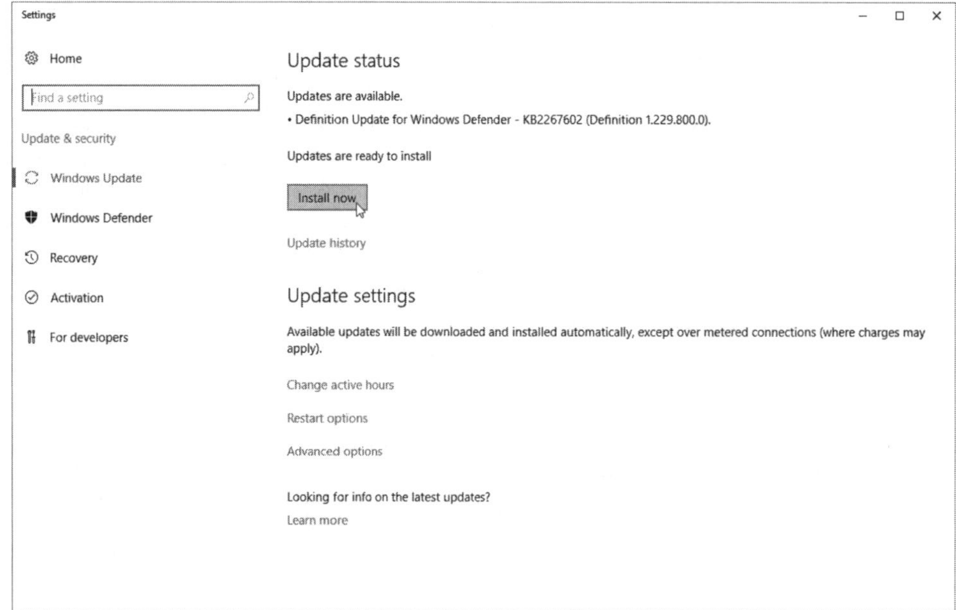

Figure 2-28 Installing updates

6. Close the Settings window.

Troubleshooting Installation Problems

With proper planning, many installation problems can be avoided, but even the most experienced installers can still experience difficulty. Following the preinstallation tasks outlined previously in this chapter can help to ensure a successful installation. Also keep the following points in mind to avoid problems:

- Ensure that the hardware has the Certified for Windows Server 2016 sticker or is in the Windows Server Catalog.
- Test all hardware before installing the operating system.
- Run the computer manufacturer's diagnostics before installing the operating system.
- Run a comprehensive test of the hard disk to ensure it is functioning properly.

Sometimes prevention is not enough and installation problems occur. Most problems are related to hardware drivers or to the actual hardware. For example, the computer might contain a hard drive, optical drive, network adapter, or display adapter that is newly marketed and not contained in the installation selection list. If Windows Server 2016 Setup does not contain the driver or it is not included on a disk with the hardware, it is necessary to contact the computer vendor for a new driver. Sometimes an adapter card, such as a network interface card or hard disk adapter, is loosened when the computer is moved and the card simply needs to be reseated.

If SCSI adapters are used, the SCSI cable might be loose or it might not be properly terminated. A network interface card or sound card driver might be needed because new models are often introduced to the market. Table 2-4 provides a list of common problems and steps to solve the problems.

Table 2-4 Troubleshooting a Windows Server 2016 installation

Problem description	Solution steps
Installation fails when connecting to the domain controller	Make sure you have previously created an account in the domain or have a user account with administrative privileges and provided the right domain name. Also, make sure the computer is connected to the network and that the domain controller (the server with Active Directory) and the DNS server are working.
Setup did not find any mass storage devices on the computer.	The most common cause is that Setup does not have a driver for a SCSI device or is detecting storage devices in the wrong order, such as the optical drive first. Click the *Load driver* link in the Where do you want to install Windows? window, and provide a driver for the mass storage device that will hold the operating system files.
	Check to make sure all adapters and controllers are working properly. Check power to all devices. Reseat adapters and controllers.
	For SCSI devices ensure: (1) The SCSI cabling is properly installed, (2) SCSI devices are terminated, (3) SCSI devices are correctly addressed, and (4) the BIOS correctly recognizes all SCSI adapters. Also, be sure the SCSI boot drive is addressed as 0. Check the manufacturer's recommendations for configuring SCSI adapters and hard disk drives. Try replacing the adapter before replacing the drive(s).
	For EIDE/SATA/ATA drives: (1) check the controller, (2) ensure file I/O and disk access are set to standard, and (3) ensure the system drive is the first device recognized by the controller.
	For IDE and ESDI drives: (1) check the cabling and controller, (2) check the drive setup in the BIOS for master/slave relationships, (3) ensure the drive is properly recognized in the BIOS.
Media errors	If you receive media errors when installing from DVD or a thumb drive, try installing from another optical drive or USB port. If the problem still persists, use another Windows Server 2016 installation DVD or thumb drive.
The system will not connect to the network.	Use Server Manager or Network and Sharing Center in Control Panel to ensure that networking is correctly configured. Check the network interface card to be certain it is working. Reseat or replace the card, if necessary. Use the diagnostic software provided with the card to test for problems. If this does not work, try a card from a different manufacturer, in case there is a hardware incompatibility.
The operating system will not install or will not start after installation.	Verify that the hardware you are using is supported by Windows Server 2016.
A STOP message appears during the installation.	Start the installation again. If the STOP message appears a second time, record the message and consult a Microsoft technician.
Computer locks up	Check the IRQ and I/O settings for conflicts among hardware components and cards (check the NIC and any specialized cards in particular).

Removing Windows Server 2016

At some point, it might be necessary to remove Windows Server 2016. For example, if your server is being replaced with a newer model, you might want to install a different operating system on the old server. Removing Windows Server 2016 is a relatively straightforward process where you format the partition on which it has been installed.

Before removing Windows Server 2016, be sure to back up any important data.

If you are installing another operating system, you are usually given an opportunity to format the hard drive for that operating system. Format the drive and install the other operating system. You can also use the FDISK and FORMAT utilities on a startup disk from an older Windows operating system to delete and format the partition. Another option is to use the FORMAT or DISKPART utilities from the Command Prompt screen. Once the partition has been formatted, you can install a new operating system.

Chapter Summary

- Before you install Windows Server 2016, complete the preinstallation tasks to help ensure the best result. These tasks include checking hardware requirements and compatibility, determining disk partitioning, understanding the implementation of NTFS, looking at upgrade options, planning the number of user licenses needed, deciding on domain or workgroup membership, determining the computer name, determining which version to install, and identifying the server roles.
- Windows Server 2016 has many server-based roles, from housing Active Directory functions to offering DNS or DHCP services to providing file and print services. In many cases, one server can have a combination of roles.
- Windows Server 2016 can be installed using any of several methods, which include DVD or thumb drive installation, upgrading from Windows Server 2012/R2, using Hyper-V for a virtual server, and Windows Deployment Services. Fortunately, the installation follows a logical step-by-step process that automates many activities, such as detection of hardware. Although you might need to troubleshoot a specific installation problem, the likelihood of having to deal with a problem is reduced in proportion to how well you have planned in advance.
- After Windows Server 2016 is installed, you can perform basic configuration activities using Server Manager. These tasks include providing computer information, configuring networking, naming the server, joining the server to a workgroup or domain, determining how to regularly update the server, installing server roles and features, and configuring a firewall.
- So that you can retain full use of Windows Server 2016, plan to activate the operating system immediately.
- If your organization is planning to install multiple servers or many Windows 10 computers, you can use Windows Deployment Services to save time and effort. Through using Windows Deployment Services, you can even perform installations unattended.
- An alternative to installing the GUI version of Windows Server 2016 is to install Server Core, which offers a lower profile on a network and can be managed through a command-line and Windows PowerShell interface. Installing Nano Server offers an even smaller profile than Server Core, and is particularly suited for cloud-based operations.
- Service packs and updates should be installed to fix any known problems with the operating system.

- If you run into installation problems, try the troubleshooting suggestions in Table 2-4.
- To remove Windows Server 2016, use the installation of another operating system to overwrite the Windows Server 2016 installation or use tools such as FDISK, FORMAT, and DISKPART.

Key Terms

Assessment and Deployment Kit (ADK) Tools and documentation targeted to help you use and customize a specific Windows operating system.

basic input/output system (BIOS) A program on a read-only or flash memory chip that establishes basic communication with components such as the monitor and disk drives. The advantage of a flash chip is that you can update the BIOS.

client access license (CAL) A license to enable a workstation to access a Windows server.

cryptoprocessor A processor that enables hardware to be protected through using cryptographic keys employing the Trusted Platform Module security specification. *See* Trusted Platform Module (TPM).

digital certificate A set of unique identification information that is typically put at the end of a file or that is associated with a computer communication. Its purpose is to show that the source of the file or communication is legitimate.

Distributed File System (DFS) A system that enables folders shared from multiple computers to appear as though they exist in one centralized hierarchy of folders instead of on many different computers.

file system cache An area designated in physical computer memory that is used in Windows operating systems to help speed up reading and writing to hard disk.

File Transfer Protocol (FTP) A TCP/IP application protocol that transfers files in bulk data streams and that is commonly used on the Internet.

hard link Enables you to create one file and then establish links to that file in other folders, as though the file is in all of the folders.

Hypertext Transfer Protocol (HTTP) A protocol in the TCP/IP suite of protocols that is used to transport Hypertext Markup Language (HTML) documents and other data transmissions over networks and the Internet for access by web-compliant browsers.

journaling The process of keeping chronological records of data or transactions so that if a system crashes without warning, the data or transactions can be reconstructed or backed out to avoid data loss or information that is not properly synchronized.

Microsoft Passport A new authentication technique that replaces the use of passwords with a two-step authentication process that combines verifying a device is enrolled in the domain and that the device has a personal identification number.

New Technology File System (NTFS) File system that is native to Windows Server systems and that supports features such as security, compression, disk quotas, encryption, self-healing from disk damage, and others.

portable operating system interface (POSIX) Standards set by the Institute of Electrical and Electronics Engineers (IEEE) for portability of applications.

Preboot Execution Environment (PXE) An environment in which a client computer has software or hardware to enable its network interface card to connect to the network and communicate with a server (or boot from the server) without having to first boot from an operating system on the client's hard disk.

redundant array of inexpensive (or independent) disks (RAID) A set of standards designed to extend the life of hard disk drives and to prevent data loss from a hard disk failure.

Resilient File System (ReFS) A Microsoft file system introduced with Windows 8 and Windows Server 2012 with the goal of better performance and faster repair of disk errors than NTFS. *See* New Technology File System.

service pack (SP) A major update for an operating system that includes fixes for known problems and provides product enhancements.

shared directory A directory on a networked computer that other computers on the network can access.

terminal A device that consists of a monitor and keyboard to communicate with host computers that run the programs. The terminal does not have a processor to use for running programs locally.

Trusted Platform Module (TPM) A security standard used through a microprocessor or cryptoprocessor, such as one built into a server. TPM enables hardware devices to be secured by cryptographic keys.

upstream server A server that has the Windows Server Update Services role installed and that is designated to obtain patches and service packs from Microsoft. Once it obtains the patches or service packs, it automatically makes them available to specific servers on the network.

Windows Deployment Services (WDS) Services in Windows Server 2016 that enable Windows Server 2016 and Windows 10 (and certain other Windows operating systems) to be installed on multiple computers using automated techniques.

Windows Server Catalog A list of computer hardware and software tested by Microsoft and determined to be compatible with a specific Windows Server operating system, such as Windows Server 2016.

Windows System Image Manager (Windows SIM) A tool in the Windows Server 2016 Assessment and Deployment Kit used to create and manage answer files for an unattended Windows operating system installation through Windows Deployment Services. *See* Assessment and Deployment Kit (ADK) and Windows Deployment Services (WDS).

Review Questions

1. Your colleague is trying to upgrade from Windows Server 2008, Datacenter Edition, to Windows Server 2016, Datacenter Edition, but the Setup program won't allow the upgrade. Which of the following is the problem?
   a. You must first install the most recent service pack in Windows Server 2008 and then upgrade to Windows Server 2012, Datacenter Edition.
   b. The Datacenter Edition had only a three-year license, and it has expired.
   c. Active Directory is set up on the network but needs to be configured to identify this computer as running Windows Server 2016 Datacenter Edition.
   d. The DNS server on the network must first be reconfigured to recognize Windows Server 2016.
2. Your IT director heard about a fast but inexpensive new computer and purchased it to be the new Windows Server 2016 server on the network. When you attempt to install Windows Server 2016, the operating system won't install because there seems to be a problem with the BIOS in the new computer. How might this dilemma have been avoided?
   a. The new computer should have been purchased with no BIOS, which is a requirement of Windows Server 2016.
   b. The new computer is too fast for Windows Server 2016 and should have been purchased with a CPU restrictor option.
   c. The IT director should have first had a system programmer make changes to the BIOS.
   d. The IT director should have first checked to see if the computer hardware and BIOS are certified for Windows Server 2016.
3. When you are at the Server Core command-prompt, you want to run a Windows PowerShell cmdlet. The command you type to go into Windows PowerShell is __________ and after you

type it the command line starts with the two characters _________ to show that you are in the Windows PowerShell mode.

4. Which of the following are roles that can be implemented in Windows Server 2016? (Choose all that apply.)
   a. Digital Review Services
   b. Active Directory Rights Management Services
   c. Active Directory Printer Spooling and Print Verification Services
   d. Network Policy and Access Services
5. You have installed Windows Deployment Services and configured it to be integrated with Active Directory, but the installation does not properly work. Which of the following might be the problem? (Choose all that apply.)
   a. No DHCP server is present on the network.
   b. Active Directory is not installed on a network server.
   c. Windows Deployment Services only works with IPv6, but your network is configured for IPv4.
   d. No File and Document Services server is present on the network.
6. The Accounting Department in your company, particularly the head accountant, is concerned that if there is a power failure, important accounting data may be lost on the department's new Windows Server 2016 server. Even though you regularly back up the server the concern is that it could go down when a backup has not been done. What feature(s) of NTFS in Windows Server 2016 can be used to help address this concern? (Choose all that apply.)
   a. Indexing
   b. Compression
   c. Disk quotas
   d. Journaling
7. The ability in NTFS to create one file and then set up links to that file in other folders is called a _________.
8. The _________ server role is used to manage security tokens and security services for a web-based network.
9. Your company plans to purchase and implement 21 new servers in the next few months and then add 10 more over the next year. You want to make a case for using Windows Deployment Services. Which of the following do you mention as you make the case? (Choose all that apply.)
   a. Lowers installation costs
   b. Enables consistent deployment and configuration
   c. Requires the purchase of only one server license, even after the servers are installed
   d. Enables the servers to be administered together through the help of scripts
10. You need to create an answer file for unattended installations of Windows Server 2016. Which of the following tools do you use and in what tool set is it found?
    a. Configuration Tasks window, which is found in the Administrative Tools menu
    b. Server Manager, which is automatically included with Windows Server 2016
    c. Windows System Image Manager, which is found in the Assessment and Deployment Kit
    d. Unattend File Maker, which is included with the Control Panel toolset
11. You have installed Server Core and want to change the name of the server as your first task. The command-prompt command you can use is _________.

12. Which of the following must you do shortly after installing Windows Server 2016 to keep the server functions enabled?
    a. Activate Windows Server 2016.
    b. Install the Server Control role.
    c. Click Start and click License Verification.
    d. Reenter the Product Key code when you register with Active Directory.
13. The __________ server role enables the use of work folders for PCs and mobile devices such as tablet PCs.
14. The latest service pack has some patches that you need for Windows Server 2016 security. Your assistant says the only way to get a service pack is to order a DVD from Microsoft. Is there a faster way to obtain the service pack? (Choose all that apply.)
    a. Purchase it on tape at an office supply retailer.
    b. Use Windows Update.
    c. Check Microsoft's website for a download of the service pack.
    d. Connect the computer to the Internet, insert the Windows Server 2016 installation DVD, reboot, and on the first setup screen, click *Obtain service pack*.
15. Which of the following are Windows Server 2016 installation methods? (Choose all that apply.)
    a. From streaming tape
    b. From Microsoft Surface Pro Installer
    c. From DVD
    d. Into a Hyper-V virtual machine
16. The __________ enables you to change the boot order on a computer prior to installing Windows Server 2016.
17. Your assistant is about to install the latest service pack for Windows Server 2016 on a production server. What is your advice before he starts? (Choose all that apply.)
    a. Put the server in fast mode to make the process go faster.
    b. Back up the server before starting.
    c. Use Server Manager to turn on Service Pack Enable.
    d. First take down the server and reboot it into Update Environment.
18. The Hyper-V role is installed using __________.
19. You are going to perform a Windows Server 2016 installation early in the morning before a meeting and decide to make yourself a checklist of things to do immediately before you start. Which of the following are on your checklist? (Choose all that apply.)
    a. Disconnect any flash drives.
    b. Have on-hand drivers for new peripherals in the computer.
    c. Use the test software disc that came with the computer to verify key hardware elements, such as the CPU.
    d. Ensure that all necessary hardware, such as the NIC, is preinstalled.
20. You are just taking over administration of a server running Windows Server 2016 Server Core and there is no current documentation to show which roles and features are loaded. What Windows PowerShell command enables you to determine these?
    a. Get-WindowsFeature
    b. View-WindowsRole
    c. Display-ServerApps
    d. List-Roles

Case Projects

This week you work with Gym Masters, a company that makes equipment for fitness centers and gyms. Gym Masters makes treadmills, stair steppers, cross trainers, exercise bikes, free weights, and stationary exercise devices. They supply fitness and recreation centers throughout the United States and Canada. Gym Masters has two locations, one in Chicago and one in Toronto. Both locations have computer centers currently filled with Windows Server 2008 servers. The Chicago location consists of an office building and a manufacturing building, both fully networked. The Toronto location has a single large building that houses offices and a manufacturing center. The Toronto building is also fully networked. All networks use IPv4 for communications.

The Chicago and Toronto locations have Windows 7 workstations. However, the Toronto location is to receive 24 new computers that will need to have Windows 10 installed.

In both locations, the servers are centralized in a controlled computer center environment. The Gym Masters management wants to upgrade the 22 servers in the Chicago location and the 18 servers in Toronto to Windows Server 2016. A combination of Standard, Enterprise, and Datacenter Edition servers must be upgraded. Also, the company is planning to add 12 new servers in Chicago and 14 new ones in Toronto. As is common in many organizations, the information technology (IT) staff are overworked and understaffed. Gym Masters has hired you through Aspen Consulting to coordinate and assist with the transition to Windows Server 2016.

Case Project 2-1: Advance Preparations

The IT managers from Chicago and Toronto have decided the first step is to form a transition committee to plan and track the progress of the server upgrades. The committee consists of both IT managers (from each location), two department heads from each location, the chief financial officer, the director of operations, a senior applications programmer, and a senior systems programmer.

During the kickoff meeting, you briefly mention a few advance preparation steps the committee needs to know about. In response, the committee asks you to create a full report or slide presentation of the steps that need to be considered in advance for Windows Server 2016 installations. In your report or slide show, present all of the steps appropriate to Gym Masters' situation.

Case Project 2-2: Server Roles

The committee has recently been discussing the functions of each server. They are not familiar with server roles, but they do know how specific servers are used. Some of the server functions they mention include:

- Providing a website
- Supporting mobile devices for accessing the server over the network
- Offering shared files on large scale
- Managing Active Directory functions for the domain
- Offering VPNs
- Coordinating printing
- Providing web-based applications to internal users

Create a short report for the committee that translates each of these functions into server roles offered through Windows Server 2016. Also, suggest some other roles that are likely necessary on the company's networks (*Hint:* Consider managing IP address assignments and translating computer names and IP addresses). Include a short explanation of each server role you mention.

Case Project 2-3: Initial Configuration

A Gym Masters system programmer has just installed the first Windows Server 2016 system and now needs to do an initial configuration of the server. Discuss which tool she can use for the initial configuration and briefly discuss the configuration tasks that should be performed at this point.

Case Project 2-4: Installing Multiple Servers

The Toronto IT Department wants to install Windows Server 2016 Standard Edition on all 14 new servers in its location. The servers have arrived, are unpacked, and have been tested. Also, the preliminary preparations have been completed. Now they want to install Standard Edition on a mass scale to complete this part of the project right away. What Windows Server 2016 capability enables them to do the mass installation quickly and efficiently? What general steps are involved in setting up this capability? Can the capability also be used to install Windows 10 on the 24 new client workstations arriving soon? Explain the answers to these questions in a memo to the IT manager in Toronto that you also copy to the transition committee.

chapter 3

Configuring the Windows Server 2016 Environment

After reading this chapter and completing the exercises, you will be able to:

- Use Server Manager to manage a server
- Install and remove server roles
- Use the Best Practices Analyzer on server roles
- Configure server hardware
- Use System File Checker and Sigverif to verify system files
- Configure the operating system, tune performance, and configure environment variables
- Understand and configure the Registry
- Use Windows PowerShell

A successful Windows Server 2016 installation is certainly the first step in preparing a server for prime time. The next step is to customize the server for your organization's needs. A server can be customized in hundreds of ways, including configuring server roles, hardware, software, and security. Fortunately, Windows Server 2016 has tools that make these tasks go smoothly. Some of the tools are time tested, such as Control Panel, whereas others are revised, such as Server Manager. All of the tools presented here help take the guesswork out of server management.

This chapter introduces the powerful Server Manager tool and expands on what you have learned about installing and managing server roles and features. Next, you use Control Panel and Device Manager and other tools to configure hardware and verify key files in Windows Server 2016. You also learn to tune the operating system for peak performance and to set up key functions such as startup and recovery. Because Windows Server 2016 relies on the Registry for vital system information, you learn the Registry's structure and how to configure it. Finally, you practice more with Windows PowerShell to manage one or more servers.

Using Server Manager

Server Manager consolidates administrative functions to make a server easier to manage. Other tools are still available, such as the individual tools listed on the Windows Administrative Tools menu and the Microsoft Management Console (MMC), which you learn about in Chapter 4, Introduction to Active Directory and Account Management. Server Manager, though, is both convenient and powerful for managing a server. It's also a good place to build on the initial configuration tasks you performed in Chapter 2, Installing Windows Server 2016.

Server Manager in the Windows Server 2016, Essentials Edition has some different features targeted for a more simplified introduction to server setup and management. The Server Manager functions you learn in this book relate to the Windows Server 2016 Standard and Datacenter Editions (without the Windows Server Essentials Experience role installed).

Whether you are a novice or an experienced server administrator, you'll find something to like about Server Manager. Server Manager provides a central place from which to manage many server functions from server roles and features to troubleshooting server problems. Server Manager typically has two main panels (see Figure 3-1). The left panel is in a tree format that has the following management areas:

- *Dashboard*—In the right pane, the Welcome tile in Dashboard provides options for adding roles and features, adding servers in a domain to manage from Server Manager on a single server, creating specific groups of servers in a domain that you can manage in the same way, and connecting the server to cloud services. The Welcome tile is intended to help you get started configuring the server and can be hidden once you no longer need it. Under the Welcome tile there are boxes for the Local Server, All Servers or specific server groups, and for each role that is installed. The boxes enable you to track information about a server, a server group, or a role such as error events, performance information, and other data. The boxes are color coded so you can see right away if there is a problem on a server. For example, if the diagnostics tracking service has stopped running on the local server, the box for the local server will be highlighted in red, and you can click the error source, such as Services to view the error (see Figure 3-2).
- *Local Server*—Shows boxes in the right pane for managing the local server. In Chapter 2 Activity 2-5, you already have used the Properties box (see Figure 3-3) to configure server properties including the server name, domain or workgroup, automatic updating, and the network connection. Below the Properties box is the Events box that shows problem information such as errors and warnings. Underneath the Events box is the Services box that displays information about server services, such as whether a service is stopped or running. Next is the **Best Practices Analyzer (BPA)**, which shows if server roles are set up

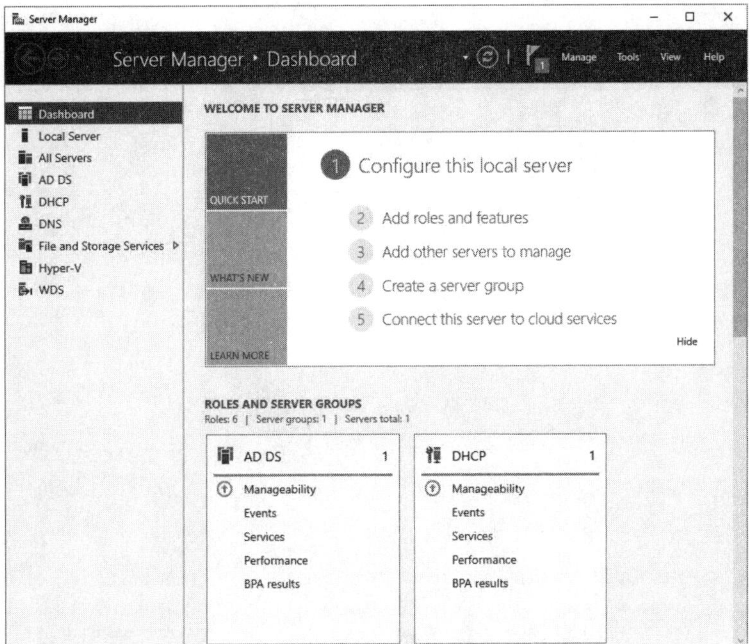

Figure 3-1 Server Manager with Dashboard selected in the left pane

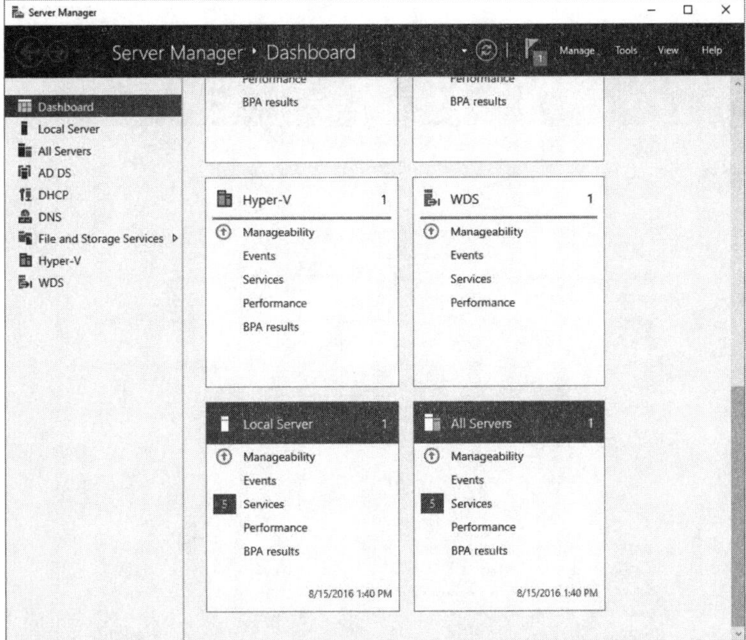

Figure 3-2 Dashboard showing error conditions on the Local Server and on All Servers

to follow the best practices defined by Microsoft. Below the BPA is the Performance box that shows information about the local server's CPU and memory use. Last is the Roles and Features box that shows which roles and features are installed. (See Figures 3-4 and 3-5 to view the boxes below the Properties box in Server Manager.)

- *All Servers*—Provides information about any server that is managed through Server Manager. In the right pane, you can click any server. For each server there are boxes for Events, Services, Best Practices Analyzer, Performance, and Roles and Features. These boxes provide the same information as described for Local Server.

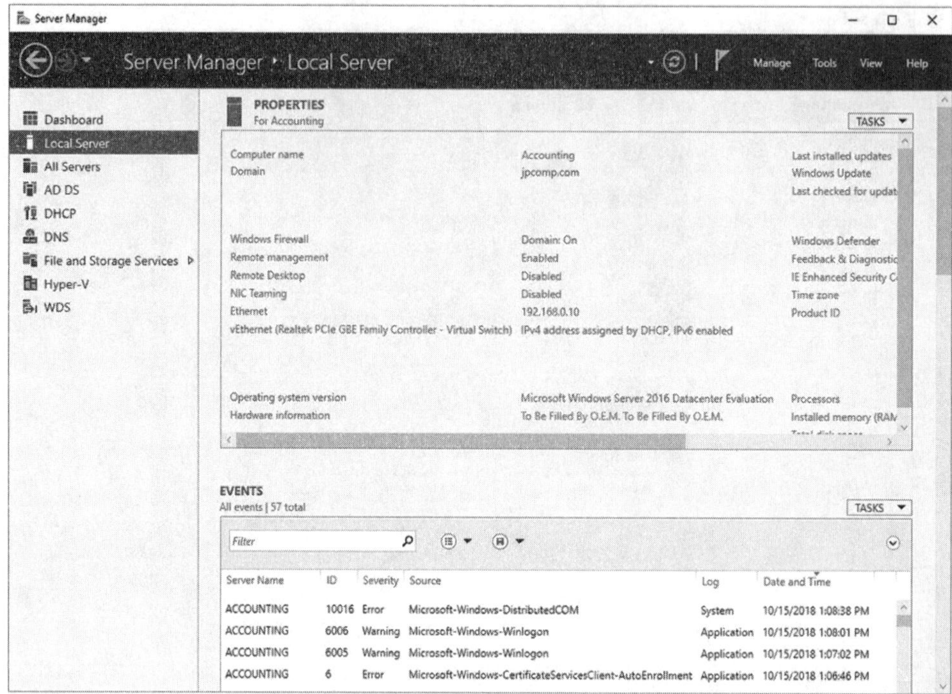

Figure 3-3 Server Manager showing the Properties box

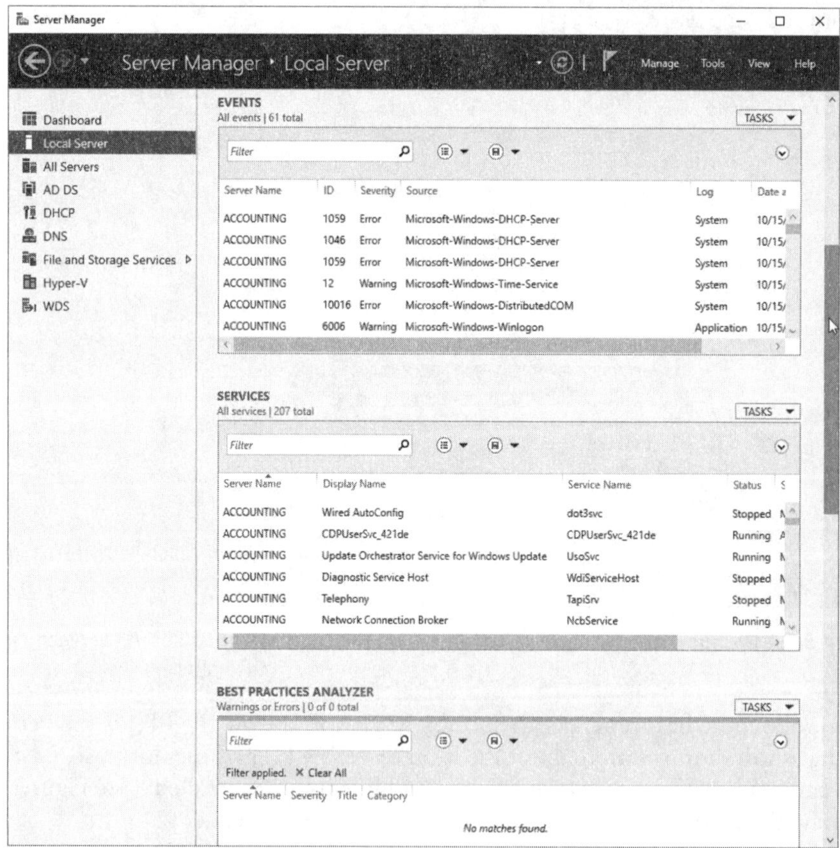

Figure 3-4 Server Manager showing the Events, Services, and Best Practices Analyzer boxes

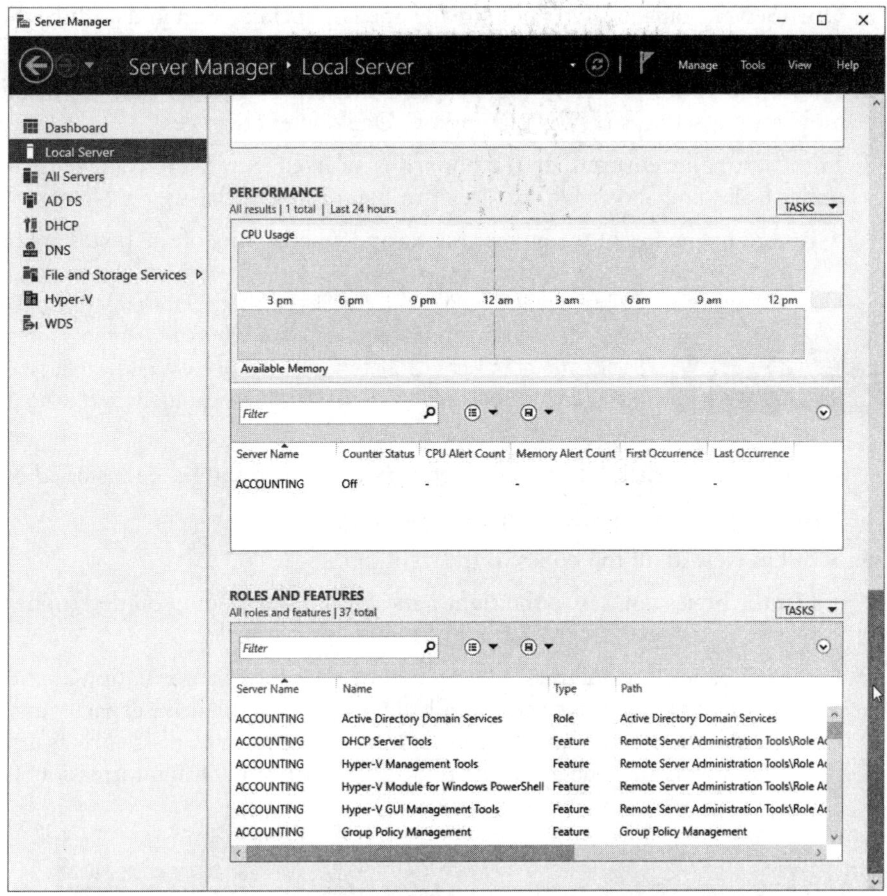

Figure 3-5 Server Manager showing the Performance and Roles and Features boxes

- *Server Role Listings*—Each server role that is installed is listed in the left pane, such as AD DS, DHCP, DNS, File and Storage Services, Hyper-V, and WDS as shown in Figure 3-5. When you select a server role in the left pane, you can then go to the right pane and select a server in the Servers box that has the role installed. Also, in the right pane under the Servers box there are boxes for Events, Services, Best Practices Analyzer, Performance, and Roles and Features.

Some steps in the activities in this book include bulleted questions for you to answer. Additionally, for all of the activities in this chapter, you'll need an account with Administrator privileges. These activities can be completed on a virtual machine or computer, such as in Hyper-V.

Activity 3-1: Getting to Know Server Manager

Time Required: Approximately 15 minutes
Objective: Get additional practice using Server Manager.

Description: Server Manager is a one-stop tool for managing a server. In this activity, you open Server Manager and survey its possibilities. This activity is just an introduction; you'll use Server Manager more in this chapter and in chapters that follow.

1. Open Server Manager, if it is not already open by clicking **Start** and clicking the **Server Manager** tile. (Or you can click **Start** and click **Server Manager** under the S application listings.)
2. Notice the options listed in the left pane, including the roles that are installed, such as File and Storage Services or WDS (Windows Deployment Services).
3. In the left pane, ensure that **Dashboard** is selected. Scroll the right pane to view the boxes under Roles and Server Groups (refer to Figures 3-1 and 3-2).
   - Record the names of the boxes you see and whether any of the boxes are highlighted in red.

If a box is highlighted in red, click the category of the error (there can be more than one), which is prefaced with a red box with a number inside, such as Services (refer to Figure 3-2), to see a Detail View window that provides information about the error. Close the Detail View window by clicking Cancel.

4. In the left pane, click **File and Storage Services**, which should be installed by default.
5. Ensure that **Servers** is selected in the left pane.
6. Scroll to view all of the boxes in the right pane.
   - List the boxes you see in the right pane. Also, how would you determine what role service is installed for the File and Storage Services role?
7. In the left pane click **Volumes**. The right pane now shows information about the drives on the server, such as if a drive is fixed (installed in the computer), drive capacity and free space, information about how drives are shared, and information about a disk, such as disk type and allocation. Click a volume, such as **C:** and notice the Shares and Disk information. (see Figure 3-6).

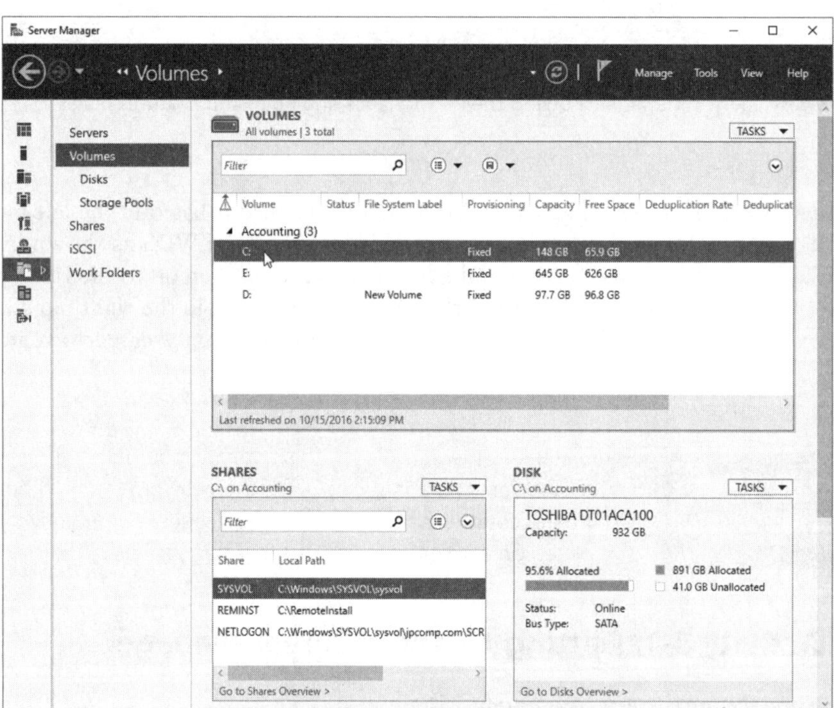

Figure 3-6 Viewing information about volumes

8. In the left pane, click **Disks** under Volumes and scroll the right pane, if necessary, to view additional disk information.
9. In the left pane, click **Storage Pools** under Volumes. Notice a server can have virtual disks (such as on a virtual machine) and physical disks set up for storage pools.

NOTE

A **storage pool** is storage capacity that can be set up from different physical and virtual disks to store specific information, such as inventory programs under development for a business. You learn more about storage pools in Chapter 7, Configuring and Managing Data Storage.

10. Under the title bar at the top of the Server Manager window, click **Manage** to view this menu's options. Notice that you can use this menu to add or remove roles and features, to add servers to manage from Server Manager, and to create server groups for managing servers for specific purposes, such as managing in one group all servers used for research or all servers used for marketing.
11. Click Server **Manager Properties** on the Manage menu.
    - In the Server Manager Properties dialog box, what selection can you make so that Server Manager is not started each time you sign in?
12. Click **Cancel** in the Server Manager Properties dialog box.
13. Click **Tools** under the title bar in the Server Manager window. This menu enables you to start any of the tools that are also available from clicking Start and clicking the Windows Administrative Tools folder. If, for example, you found that the Local Server box on Dashboard is highlighted in red as in Figure 3-2 because a service is not running, you can determine which service has stopped via Dashboard—and then you can click Services on the Tools menu to view all of a server's installed services and start the service that has stopped.
14. Finally, notice there is a Help option you can click under the title bar that enables you to access help for using Server Manager. Click **Help** to view the different options for obtaining help.
15. Click the **back arrow** as many times as needed at the top of the Server Manager window, so that you go back to the main Server Manager view that lists server roles in the left pane. Leave Server Manager open for the next activity.

Installing and Removing Server Roles

In Chapter 2, you learned about the many server roles that can be implemented in Windows Server 2016. You also learned how to install the Windows Deployment Services role. Installing the appropriate roles on a server is one of the first tasks after you complete the operating system installation and initial configuration. For most roles you install, there are also different role services you can choose to include or omit. Additionally, for some services associated with a role, you can select to install different portions or components of the services without installing all of the components.

Two common roles for a Windows Server 2016 server are those of a file and storage server and a print and document server, which are offered through the File and Storage Services and Print and Document Services roles. Both roles are commonly used in small- to medium-sized organizations. The File and Storage Services role is important for sharing files from the server or using the server to coordinate and simplify file sharing through Distributed File System (DFS).

In the Print and Document Services role, the Windows Server 2016 server can be used to manage network printing services and it can offer one or more network printers connected to the network through the server itself. You learn more about DFS in Chapter 5, Configuring, Managing, and Troubleshooting Resource Access, and about network printing in Chapter 6, Configuring Windows Server 2016 Printing. For now, we are simply focusing on the steps for installing and removing roles.

There are times when the role or roles of a server change. Consider, for example, an organization that has one server housing File and Storage Services, Print and Document Services, DHCP, and DNS. As the organization grows, it decides to dedicate that server to only the File and Storage and Print and Document Services roles and to add a new server for the DNS and DHCP roles.

Activity 3-2: Installing and Removing a Server Role

Time Required: Approximately 15 minutes

Objective: Install and then remove the Print and Document Services role in Windows Server 2016.

Description: Windows Server 2016 offers a wide range of roles on a server-based network. In this activity, you use Server Manager to install the Print and Document services role and then you practice removing this role. The activity is designed to give you additional experience (in addition to installing the WDS role in Activity 2-6 in Chapter 2) installing a server role and the opportunity to learn how to remove a role you have installed. (In Chapter 6, you'll learn more about the Print and Document services role as well as specific steps for configuring the services offered through this role.)

1. Ensure that Server Manager is open. If you need to open it, click **Start** and click the **Server Manager** tile.
2. Ensure **Dashboard** is selected in the left pane.
3. In the right pane, click **Add roles and features** under Welcome to Server Manager.
4. If you see the Before you begin window in the Add Roles and Features Wizard, click **Next.**
5. Make sure that **Role-based or feature-based installation** is selected in the Select installation type window. Click **Next.**
6. Ensure your computer is selected in the Server Pool box in the Select destination server window and click **Next.**
7. In the Select server roles window, check the box for **Print and Document Services.** If you see a dialog box to add features required for a role, such as remote server administration tools (see Figure 3-7), click **Add Features.**

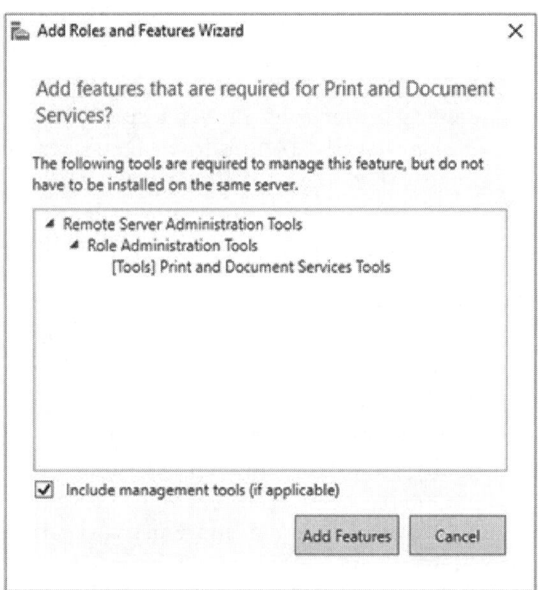

Figure 3-7 Adding features required for a role

8. Click **Next** in the Select server roles window.
9. Click **Next** in the Select features window.
10. In the Print and Document Services window, read the information about the Print and Document Services role and note that there is a link to learn about this role. Click **Next.**

11. In the Select role services window, make sure **Print Server** is selected (the default), and click **Next** (see Figure 3-8).

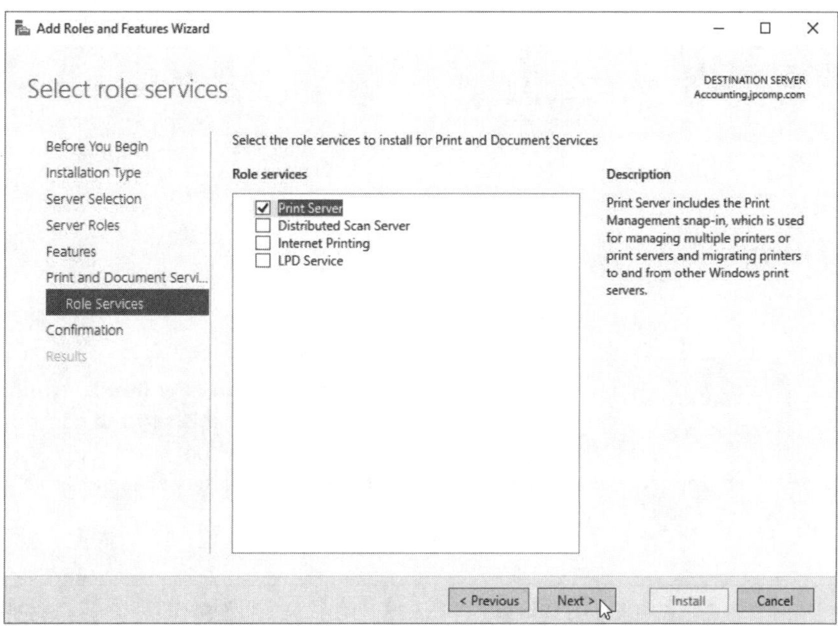

Figure 3-8 Selecting the Print Server role service to be installed as a role service

12. Click **Install** in the Confirm installation selections window.
13. Wait for a few minutes as the role is installed.
14. When the Installation progress window shows that the installation succeeded, click **Close**.
15. In the left pane of Server Manager, select **Print Services** and scroll through the right pane to view the boxes of information for this role.
    - What role and role service do you see in the Roles and Features box?
16. With Print Services still selected in the left pane, click **Manage** under the title bar in Server Manager. Click **Remove Roles and Features**.
17. If you see the Before you begin window in the Remove Roles and Features Wizard, click **Next**.
18. Ensure your computer is selected in the Server Pool box in the Select destination server window and click **Next**.
19. In the Remove server roles window, click the **Print and Document Services** check box and, if necessary, click **Remove Features** in the Remove Roles and Features Wizard dialog box.
20. Click **Next** in the Remove server roles window.
21. Click **Next** in the Remove features window.
22. Click **Remove** in the Confirm removal selections window (see Figure 3-9).
23. Wait a few minutes for the removal process to complete and then click **Close**.
24. Close Server Manager.

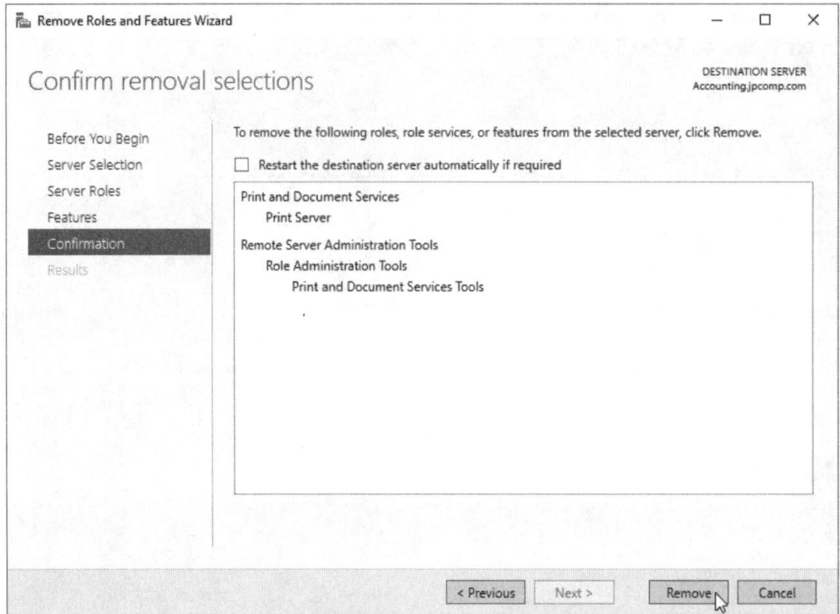

Figure 3-9 Removing role services associated with the Print and Document Services role

Using the Best Practices Analyzer (BPA) for Server Roles

Once you've installed a role and set it up, it is important to determine that you have followed the best practices for the establishment of the role. For example, is security properly set up for the role or is the role configured to fully perform the operations for which it is intended? You can run the BPA to determine if one or more roles are installed and configured to follow the guidelines recommended by Microsoft for sound implementation of a role. When problems are found, the analysis of each role yields a report that shows three levels of severity:

- *Information*—The role is in compliance, but a change is recommended. (For example, a server's NIC might have a valid IPv4 address temporarily leased by DHCP, but a static address is recommended.)
- *Warning*—The role complies under current operating conditions, but this may change if the operating conditions change. (For example, the Hyper-V role might become noncompliant if another virtual machine is added for which there is no available virtual disk space.)
- *Error*—The role does not meet best practices and problems can be expected.

The guidelines the BPA uses for analysis are as follows:

- *Configuration*—to ensure role settings are configured for best performance and to avoid conflicts
- *Predeployment*—to ensure that requirements for the role are properly installed or configured to follow optimal practices before the role is installed
- *Postdeployment*—to ensure services needed for the role are started and that the services and the role are running
- *Performance*—to ensure the role can perform the tasks for which it is intended on-time and adequately for the intended workload
- *BPA Prerequisites*—to ensure the role is set up in such a way (using features and settings) so that BPA can analyze the role (failure here is not the same as noncompliance, because it

simply could mean that a needed service is not started, there is a missing Registry element, there is an error in a Group Policy, etc.)

The general steps for running BPA are:

1. Open Server Manager.
2. Click Local Server in the left pane.
3. In the right pane, scroll to Best Practices Analyzer.
4. Click the down arrow for TASKS.
5. Click Start BPA Scan and wait for the scan to complete.
6. Read the results shown for the scan (see Figure 3-10 for a server with multiple roles).

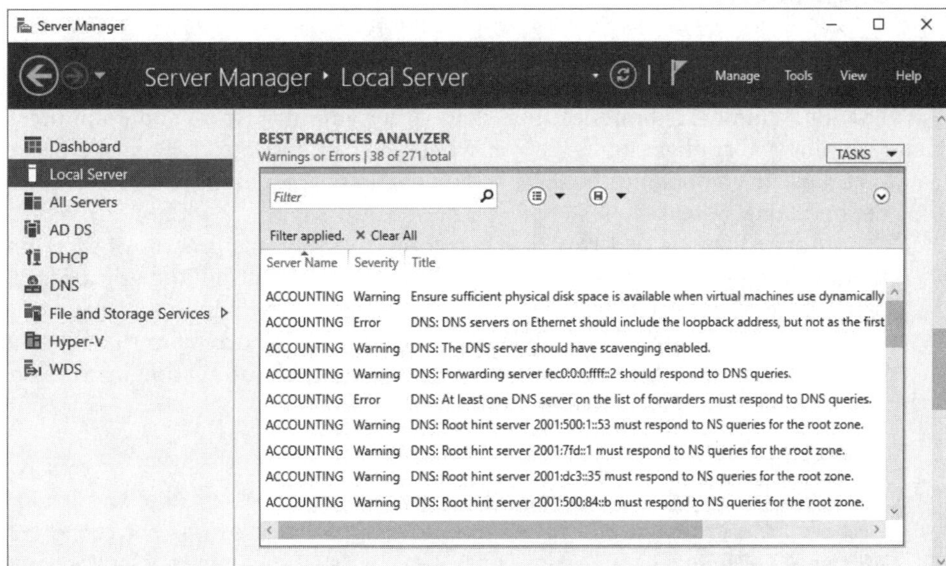

Figure 3-10 Results of BPA scan on a server with multiple roles installed

Configuring Server Hardware Devices

Sometimes you will need to replace existing hardware in a server due to failure of a component, or sometimes you'll need to upgrade the hardware. Additionally, you simply may be adding another component such as a second network adapter. Windows Server 2016 offers both Plug and Play services and the *Add a device* option to enable the installation of hardware. Hardware devices can include the following:

- Disk drives
- Disk controllers
- Network adapters
- Optical drives
- Keyboard
- Pointing devices
- Monitor

For those times when you add or replace hardware, you'll need to be familiar with how to install and configure new hardware on your server.

Plug and Play

One important capability in computer hardware and operating system software is the ability to automatically detect and configure newly installed hardware devices, such as a disk or tape drive. This is called **Plug and Play (PnP)**. For this capability to work, PnP must be:

- Built into the device
- Enabled in the target computer's BIOS
- Built into the computer operating system kernel

Microsoft developed PnP, which has now been supplemented by **Universal PnP (UPnP)**, an open standard that is used in all types of systems and that enables connectivity through networks and network protocols. UPnP supports server-based networking, wireless networking, peer-to-peer networking, and other networking services.

Modern hardware, including both computers and peripherals, almost universally supports PnP. PnP eliminates hours of time that server administrators and computer users once spent installing and configuring hardware. When you purchase a computer or a new device, make sure that it is PnP compatible and that the PnP compatibility conforms to the PnP capabilities used by the operating system.

Installing a Plug and Play device is a relatively simple process of attaching the device and then waiting for Windows Server 2016 to detect it and install the appropriate drivers. In some cases, once the device is installed you might need to configure its properties and settings. You may also need to download the latest driver for the device from the manufacturer's website. Keep in mind that you should review the manufacturer's installation instructions before attempting to connect the device to your computer.

Depending on your computer system, it might be necessary to power down before installing some types of devices. Also, even if it is not necessary to power down to install a device (such as one connected to a USB port), you still might have to restart your computer for Windows to detect the new device. Further, some computer manufacturers prefer that you use the CD/DVD they have supplied (or go to their website) to ensure the most recent driver or operating system software is installed, such as special options for configuring or troubleshooting the device.

Using Control Panel and the Devices and Printers Utility

If Windows Server 2016 does not automatically detect newly installed hardware, or if the device you are installing is non-Plug and Play, you can use the Devices and Printers utility to manually launch PnP or to manually install the device without PnP.

The Devices and Printers utility is used for the following tasks:

- Invoke the operating system to use PnP to detect new hardware.
- Install new non-PnP hardware and hardware drivers.
- Troubleshoot problems you might be having with existing hardware.

The Devices and Printers utility is started from Control Panel. Control Panel allows you to customize Windows Server 2016 for devices, network connectivity, display options, and many other functions.

Windows Server 2016 provides two Control Panel view options: Control Panel Home with the Category View and Control Panel with the Classic View consisting of large or small icons. The Category View groups functions under topical areas as follows (see Figure 3-11):

- System and Security
- Network and Internet

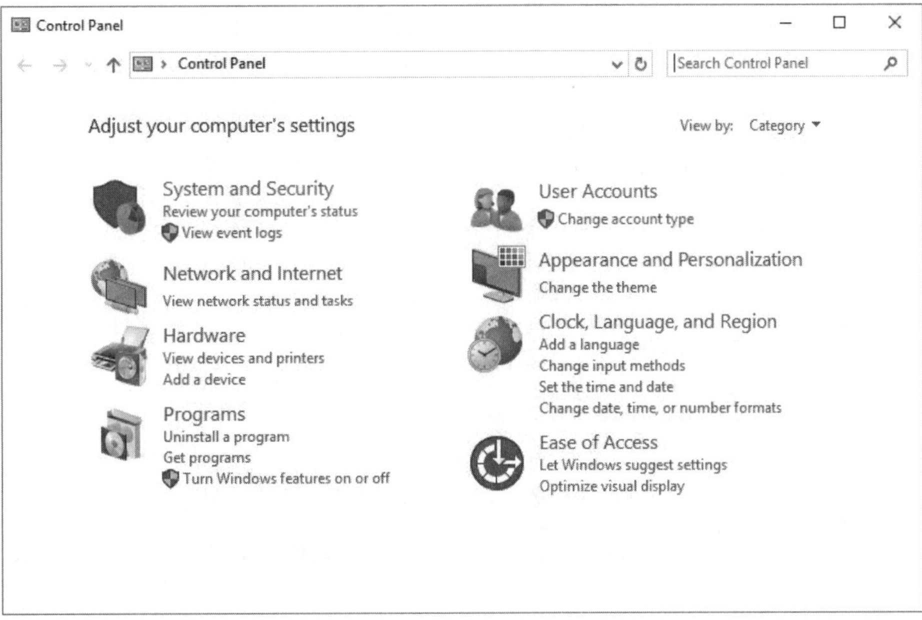

Figure 3-11 Category view in Control Panel

- Hardware
- Programs
- User Accounts
- Appearance and Personalization
- Clock, Language, and Region
- Ease of Access

Each topical area contains tools for configuring the server. For example, when you open System and Security, it displays tool selections for:

- Security and maintenance, including reviewing the server's security status and troubleshooting a hardware, software, or network problem
- Configuring Windows Firewall
- Configuring the system settings, including remote access
- Setting power options
- Accessing administrative tools for managing roles and other server tasks, as well as defragmenting, optimizing, and configuring server drives, viewing event logs, scheduling tasks, and creating a system health report

Classic View displays configuration tools as individual applets or icons, such as Administrative Tools, Device Manager, Devices and Printers, Network and Sharing Center, and so on. (Figure 3-12 shows Classic View with small icons.)

When you have hardware that does not start PnP services automatically or that you want to configure manually, open the Devices and Printers utility using the following steps:

1. Right-click Start and click Control Panel.
2. Set the View by option in the top right portion of the Control Panel window to Large icons or Small icons according to your preference.
3. Click Devices and Printers in Control Panel (refer to Figure 3-12).
4. Click *Add a device* in the Devices and Printers window (see Figure 3-13).

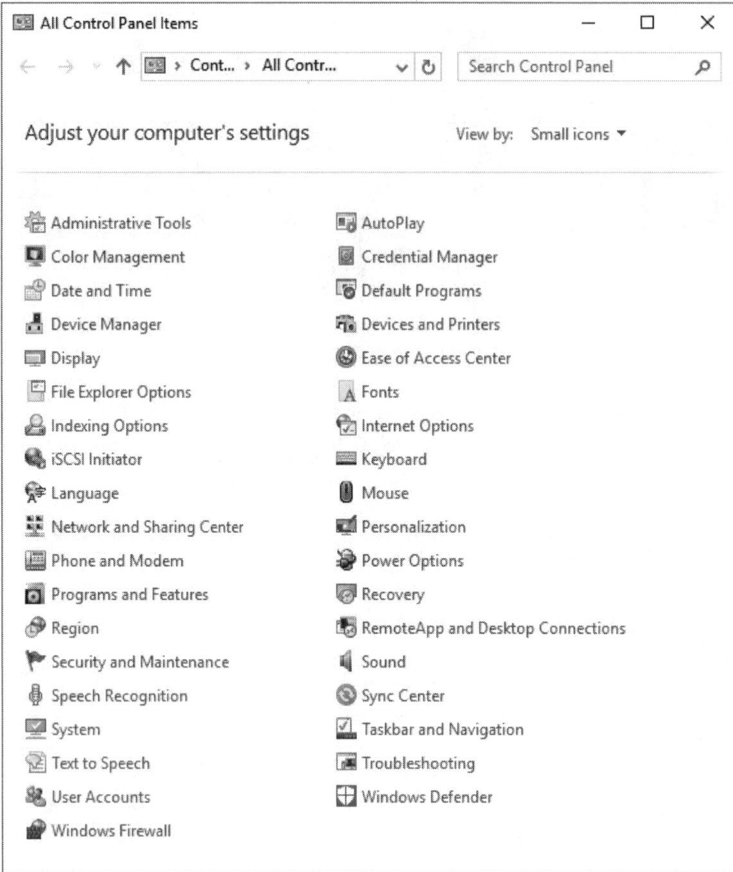

Figure 3-12 Classic view in Control Panel

Figure 3-13 Adding a device in the Devices and Printers utility

5. Allow the Devices and Printers Add a device utility to identify any devices that are not installed, select the device from the list, click Next, and complete the steps to install the device.

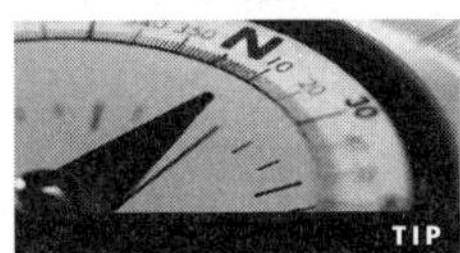

If you are installing hardware that is new to the market or that has new software drivers, it is often best to configure it manually so that you can use the software CD/DVD that comes with the hardware or the latest software driver files that you've obtained from the manufacturer's website.

3

Device Manager PnP and the Devices and Printers utility are very effective for automatically setting up hardware parameters, such as **resources**. A server's resources include the **interrupt request (IRQ) line** (which is a channel for communication with the CPU) and other elements such as the **I/O address** and reserved memory range. For example, a computer contains a limited number of IRQ lines, 01–15. The video display, each disk drive, USB ports, and the sound card each use a dedicated IRQ to communicate with the processor. Each component also needs reserved memory addresses for I/O operations. Resource conflicts can sometimes occur when a network adapter, a new SCSI device adapter, or some other hardware is automatically configured.

One approach to address the limited number of IRQ lines is the development of Advanced Programmable Interrupt Controllers (APICs), which offer more extensive interrupt management capabilities, including more IRQ line options. Intel provides this technology for symmetric multiprocessor (SMP) computers, for example.

You can use Device Manager to check for a resource conflict and to examine other properties associated with a device. Device Manager provides information about all hardware currently installed on your computer. It can also be used to:

- Verify if hardware installed on your computer is working properly.
- Update device drivers.
- Disable a device.
- Uninstall a device.
- Configure the settings for a device.

For example, consider a situation in which there is an IRQ line conflict between a network interface card (NIC) and a disk controller that you have just installed. The conflict is apparent because the NIC will no longer communicate with the network and you simultaneously have problems accessing a disk on the disk controller. The place to go to determine the problem and resolve it is Device Manager.

You can start Device Manager either from Control Panel (in various places) or from the Computer Management tool.

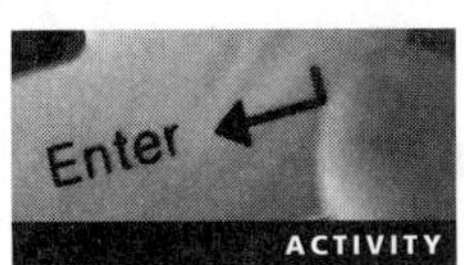

Activity 3-3: Resolving a Resource Conflict

Time Required: Approximately 10 minutes
Objective: Use Device Manager to resolve a resource conflict.

Description: Sometimes a resource conflict is subtle, such as a NIC locking up intermittently because it uses a portion of an I/O address range that is also used by another device. In this activity, you learn how to check for a resource conflict. Also, you see where to go to update or install a device driver, which is vital in case you have an outdated driver or the driver for a device is missing.

1. To start Device Manager from Control Panel, right-click **Start** and click **Control Panel**. From Control Panel Category View, click **Hardware** and click **Device Manager** under Devices and Printers; or from Classic View using either large or small icons, click the **Device Manager**

applet. Or, to start Device Manager from the Start button instead of Control Panel, right-click **Start** and click **Device Manager**.

2. Double-click **Network adapters**, as shown in Figure 3-14 (in this example, the figure shows both a physical network adapter and a virtual adapter used by Hyper-V).

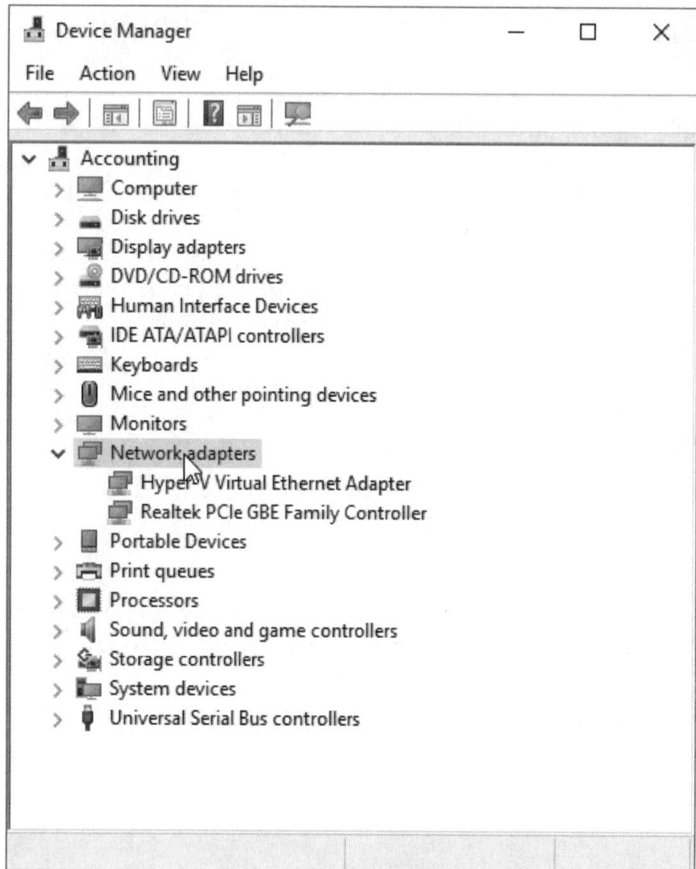

Figure 3-14 Double-clicking Network adapters in Device Manager

3. Right-click the adapter installed in your computer and then click **Properties**.
4. Notice that the Device status box reports whether the device is working properly. Keep this in mind as a troubleshooting tool for future use.
5. Observe the tabs that appear in the Properties dialog box for the device.
   - Check out each tab to see what it is for, and record your observations about the purpose of each tab.
6. Select the **Resources** tab and notice the resource settings that are used for the NIC.
   - What is the IRQ line used? Are any resource conflicts reported? How would you solve a resource conflict?
7. Select the **Driver** tab.
8. Click the **Driver Details** button. In the Driver File Details box, notice the information about the device driver, including the version and date associated with the version. If the device driver is missing, you'll be able to quickly determine that, too, from the Driver File Details box. Click **OK**.
9. Click the **Update Driver** button. There are two options in the Update Driver Software box. You can use the *Browse my computer for driver software* option to install a missing driver

from a download (or other) folder on the computer or from a CD/DVD or thumb drive. The *Search automatically for updated driver software* option will search your server and the Internet to see if there is a more recent driver than the one you have installed. Click **Cancel**.

10. Click **Cancel** on the Properties dialog box for the NIC.
11. Before you exit Device Manager, find out what resources are used by another device, such as the display adapter or a USB port with a thumb drive installed.
12. Close the Device Manager window and any other windows that are open, such as the Hardware window if you started from the Category View.

Driver Signing When you install a device such as a pointing device or a NIC, Windows Server 2016 checks to make sure that the driver for that device has been verified as secure. When a driver is verified, a unique digital signature is incorporated into it in a process called **driver signing.**

When Windows Server 2016 determines that a device driver is not signed, it gives you a warning, such as "Windows can't verify the publisher of this driver software." Another type of warning might indicate that the driver is altered. If you see such a warning, contact the manufacturer of the device to see if they can provide a signed driver.

Device drivers that are unsigned cannot be loaded into Windows Server 2016 (unless they are introduced by malware).

Using the System File Checker

If you copy an inappropriate file for a device—such as one that is unsigned, outdated, or from a different operating system—over a system or driver file, for example a .dll, .exe, or .sys file, Windows Server 2016 offers the System File Checker to scan system files for integrity. You can run this utility to scan all system files to verify integrity, to scan and replace files as needed, or to scan only certain files. When you opt to scan and replace, the System File Checker locates the original system file, which is stored in the Windows\System32 folder, and then copies it over the inappropriate or damaged file. The System File Checker can be manually run from the Command Prompt or Windows PowerShell window.

Using the System File Checker is one way to restore system files that have been corrupted because of a hardware power problem or a power failure.

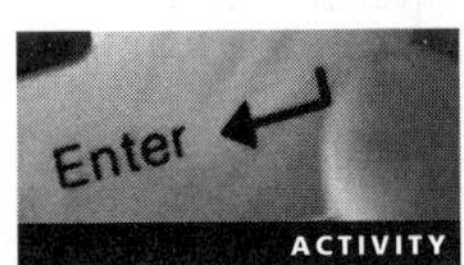

Activity 3-4: Manually Running the System File Checker

Time Required: Approximately 5 minutes to learn about the command options and 10–30 minutes to run the test

Objective: Use the System File Checker to verify system files.

Description: The System File Checker is an excellent tool for verifying your system files, particularly if you feel the system is not responding quite right or that a driver or system file has become corrupted. These problems might occur when there is a power failure on a system that is not on a battery backup or when the power filter for the system is not working properly to ensure quality power. This activity shows you how to start the System File Checker. Note that the best practice is to run the System File Checker only when there are no users on the system.

1. Right-click **Start** and click **Command Prompt (Admin)**.

You can also run the System File Checker in Windows PowerShell. To use Windows PowerShell, click **Start** and click the **Windows PowerShell** tile or click **Start**, click the **Windows PowerShell** folder, and click **Windows PowerShell**—and use the same steps that follow.

2. Type **sfc /?** at the prompt, and press **Enter** to view the switch options you can use to check and replace files.
   - What are the switch options? Which option or options would you use to perform a check of the files in the offline mode?
3. If you don't have permission from your instructor to run the System File Checker or if there are users on your system, close the Command Prompt or Windows PowerShell window at this point.

Remember that it is safest to have users off the system when you check files, and you might need to reboot before a replaced file goes into effect. In some cases, the checker might request that you insert the Windows Server 2016 DVD or thumb drive to obtain a file.

4. At the prompt, type **sfc /scannow** and press **Enter**.
5. The checker displays the results in the Command Prompt or Windows PowerShell window. (If the System File Checker finds a file that needs to be replaced, it prompts you.)
6. Leave the Command Prompt or Windows PowerShell window open for the next activity.

Using Sigverif to Verify System and Critical Files

Windows Server 2016 includes another tool, called **Sigverif**, which verifies system and critical files to determine if they have a signature. This tool only scans files and does not overwrite inappropriate files, enabling you to use the tool while users are signed in. After the scan is complete, the results are written to a log file, called sigverif.txt. If the tool finds a file without a signature that you believe needs to be replaced, you can replace the file when users are off the system.

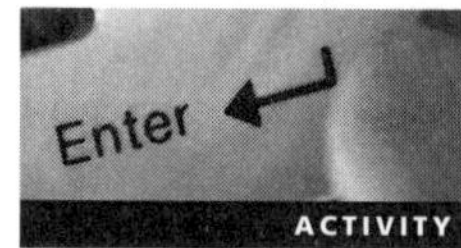

Activity 3-5: Verifying Critical Files for a Signature

Time Required: Approximately 15 minutes

Objective: Use Sigverif to find unsigned files.

Description: After you upgrade a server or if you bypass a driver signature warning, you can check Windows Server 2016 for driver files that are unsigned, which is a good security precaution. Further, you might experience a situation in which unsigned drivers interfere with the normal function of the server—a file that is missed even by the System File Checker. For example, you might install a new disk drive, install the drivers from the manufacturer's CD/DVD, and then find that some other peripheral is not working right because it shares a common .dll file. This activity shows you how to use the Sigverif tool to locate the unsigned files that might be the source of the problem and that should be replaced.

1. Open the **Command Prompt** window, if it is not open (or open **Windows PowerShell**).
2. Type **sigverif** at the prompt and press **Enter**.
3. Click the **Advanced** button in the File Signature Verification dialog box (see Figure 3-15). Notice the name of the log file that will contain the results of the scan, which is sigverif.txt by default.
4. Click **OK**.
5. Click **Start**. Figure 3-16 shows the summary results of a scan.
6. Click **OK** when the scan is completed and then click **Close**.
7. Click **File Explorer** (the file folder) in the taskbar to view files on the computer. In the left pane, browse to the drive on which the Windows folder is located, such as Local Disk (C:). Go to \Users\Public\Public Documents and double-click the **SIGVERIF** file.
8. Examine the Status column to see which files are signed or not signed (see Figure 3-17).
9. Close Notepad. Close the Public Documents window. Close the Command Prompt or Windows PowerShell window.

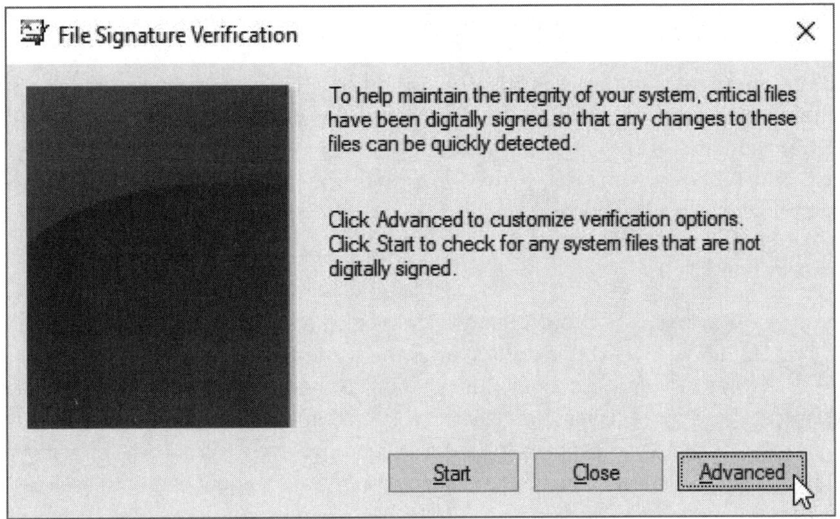

Figure 3-15 Selecting the Advanced button in the File Signature Verification dialog box

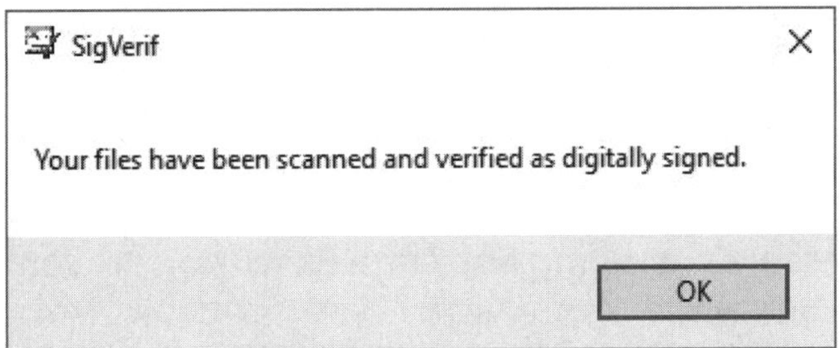

Figure 3-16 Scan results for file signature verification

SIGVERIF - Notepad

File Edit Format View Help

```
********************************


Microsoft Signature Verification

Log file generated on 10/16/2016 at 12:37 PM
OS Platform:  Windows (x64), Version:  10.0, Build: 14393, CSDVersion:
Scan Results:  Total Files: 61, Signed: 61, Unsigned: 0, Not Scanned: 0

File                Modified      Version          Status          Catalog          Signed By
------------------  ------------  -----------      ------------    -----------      ---------------
[c:\windows\system32]
sysfxui.dll         7/16/2016     2:5.1            Signed          Microsoft-Windows-SeMicrosoft Wind
vid.dll             9/15/2016     2:5.1            Signed          Package_2500_for_KB3Microsoft Wind
vmbuspiper.dll      9/27/2016     2:5.1            Signed          Microsoft-Hyper-V-OnMicrosoft Wind
wmalfxgfxdsp.dll    7/16/2016     2:5.1            Signed          Microsoft-Windows-SeMicrosoft Wind
wudfcoinstaller.dll 7/16/2016     2:5.1,2:5.2,2:6.0,2:Signed       Microsoft-Windows-SeMicrosoft Wind
[c:\windows\system32\drivers]
acpi.sys            7/16/2016     2:5.1            Signed          Package_761_for_KB31Microsoft Wind
basicdisplay.sys    7/16/2016     2:5.1            Signed          Microsoft-Windows-CoMicrosoft Wind
basicrender.sys     7/16/2016     2:5.1            Signed          Microsoft-Windows-CoMicrosoft Wind
cdrom.sys           7/16/2016     2:5.1            Signed          Microsoft-Windows-SeMicrosoft Wind
disk.sys            7/16/2016     2:5.1            Signed          Microsoft-Windows-SeMicrosoft Wind
drmk.sys            7/16/2016     2:5.1            Signed          Microsoft-Windows-SeMicrosoft Wind
drmkaud.sys         7/16/2016     2:5.1            Signed          Microsoft-Windows-SeMicrosoft Wind
hdaudbus.sys        7/16/2016     2:5.1            Signed          Microsoft-Windows-SeMicrosoft Wind
hdaudio.sys         7/16/2016     2:5.1            Signed          Microsoft-Windows-SeMicrosoft Wind
hecix64.sys         7/17/2012     None             Signed          heci.cat           Microsoft Wind
hidclass.sys        8/5/2016      2:5.1            Signed          Package_932_for_KB31Microsoft Wind
hidparse.sys        8/5/2016      2:5.1            Signed          Package_932_for_KB31Microsoft Wind
hidusb.sys          8/5/2016      2:5.1            Signed          Package_932_for_KB31Microsoft Wind
intelppm.sys        7/16/2016     2:5.1            Signed          Microsoft-Windows-SeMicrosoft Wind
kbdclass.sys        7/16/2016     2:5.1            Signed          Package_2563_for_KB3Microsoft Wind
kbdhid.sys          9/15/2016     2:5.1            Signed          Package_2563_for_KB3Microsoft Wind
kdnic.sys           7/16/2016     2:5.1            Signed          Microsoft-Windows-SeMicrosoft Wind
monitor.sys         7/16/2016     2:5.1,2:5.2,2:6.0,2:Signed       Microsoft-Windows-SeMicrosoft Wind
```

Figure 3-17 Viewing the Sigverif results file

Configuring the Operating System

After the operating system has been installed, it can be configured to optimize performance and meet very specific requirements. Using tools included with Windows Server 2016, you can configure elements of the operating system, such as performance options, environment variables, startup and recovery options, power options, and protocols. The following sections discuss important ways in which you can configure the operating system, focusing on configuration tools accessed from Control Panel.

The tips you learn in this section are important for setting up a server and remain important after the server is in production. All operating systems need periodic tuning to keep them running at their peak. Many of the activities you learn in this section should be performed or checked on a regular basis to keep a server tuned and to ensure that operational parameters that may have been changed are brought back into peak performance.

Configuring Performance Options

Windows Server 2016 enables you to configure and optimize your server for performance. You can configure basic areas of performance including:

- Processor scheduling and Data Execution Prevention
- Virtual memory
- File caching and flushing

Configuring Processor Scheduling and Data Execution Prevention

Processor scheduling allows you to configure how processor resources are allocated to programs. The default is set to Background services, which means that all programs running will receive equal amounts of processor time. The Programs setting refers to programs you are likely to be running at the server console, such as a backup program. Normally you will leave the default setting for Background services. Sometimes, though, you might need to give Programs most of the processor's resources, for instance when you determine that a disk drive is failing and you want to back up its contents as fast as possible using the Backup tool.

Another performance (and security) option that is good to know about is **Data Execution Prevention (DEP)**. When programs are running on the server, DEP monitors how they use memory to ensure they are not causing memory problems. This is intended to foil malware, such as computer viruses, Trojan horses, and worms. Malware sometimes works by trying to invade the memory space allocated to system functions. If DEP notices a program trying to use system memory space, it stops the program and notifies the system administrator.

Some types of applications might not work with DEP. For example, applications that use dynamic code generation ("in the moment" code), in which portions of the code are not flagged as executable, might not work with DEP. Another example is program code that runs exception handlers and other code requiring executable locations in memory.

Activity 3-6: Configuring Processor Scheduling and DEP

Time Required: Approximately 10 minutes
Objective: Learn where to set up processor scheduling and system memory protection.

Description: Sometimes it is important to temporarily reconfigure a server to function more like a workstation, so that applications in the foreground have the most resources. This is true, for example, if you need to perform an immediate backup to save vital data during a system emergency.

Also, it is important to use DEP to protect how system memory is used. In this activity, you learn where to set the system resources for processor scheduling and you learn to configure DEP.

1. Right-click **Start** and click **Control Panel.**
2. In the Control Panel or All Control Panel Items window, set **View by** to **Large icons** or **Small icons.**
3. Click **System.**
4. Click **Advanced system settings** in the left portion of the System window.
5. Click the **Advanced** tab in the System Properties window, if necessary.
6. In the Performance section of the System Properties window, click the **Settings** button.
7. On the Performance Options dialog box, click the **Advanced** tab. Notice the options that can be set under Processor scheduling, which are Programs and Background services.
8. Click the **Data Execution Prevention** tab. Ensure that *Turn on DEP for all programs and services except those I select* is enabled, as shown in Figure 3-18.

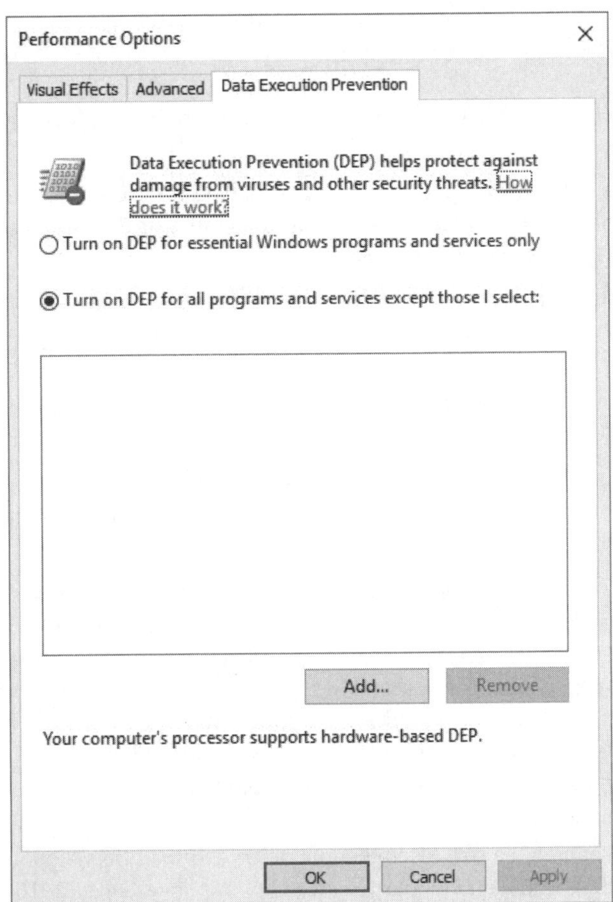

Figure 3-18 Configuring Data Execution Prevention

9. Click **OK** in the Performance Options dialog box.
10. Close the System Properties dialog box and the System window.

Configuring Virtual Memory **Virtual memory** is disk storage used to expand the capacity of the physical RAM installed in the computer. When the currently running programs and processes exceed the RAM, they treat disk space allocated for virtual memory just as if it were real memory. The disadvantage of this is that memory activities performed through virtual memory are not as fast as those performed in RAM (although disk access and data transfer speeds can be quite fast). Virtual memory works through a technique called **paging**, whereby blocks of information, called pages, are moved from RAM into virtual memory on disk. On a typical ×86 computer, data is paged in blocks of 4 KB. For example, if the system is not presently using a 7 KB block of code, it divides the code block between two pages, each 4 KB in size (part of one page will not be completely full). Next, both pages are moved to virtual memory on disk until needed. When the processor calls for that code block, the pages are moved back into RAM.

Although having a paging file is theoretically optional, it is recommended that you always have one configured. The paging file is not only important for server performance but also it is necessary for the creation of a crash dump file in the event of a server crash. To learn more, visit *support.microsoft.com/en-us/kb/2860880*.

Before virtual memory can be used, it must first be allocated for this purpose by tuning the operating system. The area of disk that is allocated for this purpose is called the **paging file**. A default amount of virtual memory is always established when Windows Server 2016 is installed, but the amount should be checked by the server administrator to ensure that it is not too large or too small.

The location of the paging file is also important. Some tips for placement of the paging file are:

- Server performance is better if the paging file is not placed on the boot partition (the one with the \Windows folder) of basic disks or the boot volume of dynamic disks (you'll learn more about the types of disks later in this book).
- If there are multiple disks, performance can be improved by placing a paging file on each disk (but avoid placing the paging file on the boot partition or volume that contains the system files in the \Windows folder).
- In a mirrored set or volume, place the paging file on the main disk, and not on the mirrored (backup) disk.
- Do not place the paging file on a stripe set, striped volume, stripe set with parity, or RAID-5 volume—because these are all disks specially set up to increase performance and fault tolerance (see Chapter 7).

When you tune the size of the paging file, two parameters must be set: initial size and maximum size. A general rule for configuring the initial size is to multiply the amount of installed RAM times 1.5. For a server with 12 GB of RAM, the initial paging file size should be at least 18 GB. Set the maximum size so it affords plenty of room for growth—such as twice the size of your initial paging file setting. For example, if your initial setting is 18 GB, then consider setting the maximum size to 36 GB. Windows Server 2016 always starts using the initial size and only expands the size of the paging file as additional space is needed.

The paging file size recommendation given here offers a good place to start. As you gain more experience with Windows Server 2016, you'll be interested in using Performance Monitor to study how a particular server uses paging and then set the paging file size on the basis of the monitoring statistics you obtain. You learn about Performance Monitor and monitoring paging activity in Chapter 11, Server and Network Monitoring.

The maximum paging file size on a 64-bit server computer is 256 terabytes.

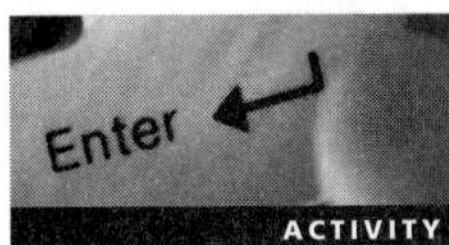

Activity 3-7: Configuring the Paging File

Time Required: Approximately 5 minutes
Objective: Learn where to configure the initial and maximum size of the paging file.

3

Description: One way to inexpensively improve the performance of a server is to adjust the size of the paging file. If a server seems to run a little slower than desired because the memory (RAM) is often used to the maximum, consider increasing the maximum paging file size. This activity shows you where to configure the paging file.

1. Right-click **Start** and click **Control Panel.**
2. If you're in the Control Panel Category View, click **System and Security**, and click **System.** If you're in the Large or Small icons (Classic) View, click **System.**
   - In the System window, look under the System section and record the amount of RAM in the computer.
3. Click **Advanced system settings.**
4. Click the **Advanced** tab, if it is not already selected.
5. In the Performance section, click the **Settings** button.
6. Click the **Advanced** tab in the Performance Options dialog box and then click the **Change** button under Virtual memory (see Figure 3-19).

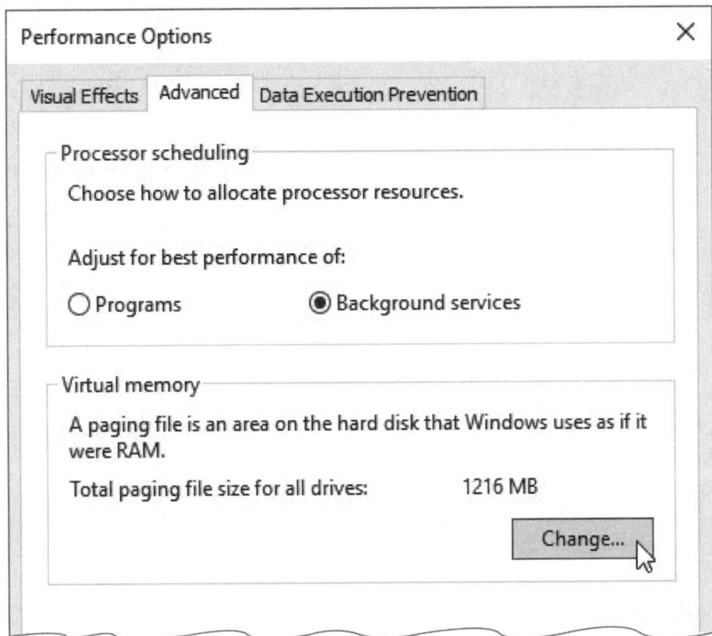

Figure 3-19 Selecting to change the virtual memory configuration

   - Record the current settings on your computer. Are the settings appropriate for the amount of memory in the computer? (It is likely that virtual memory is set at *Automatically manage paging file size for all drives* on a newly installed server. You can view the currently allocated space for virtual memory at the bottom of the Virtual Memory dialog box as shown in Figure 3-20. Also, notice the system calculates a recommended initial size for the paging file.)

7. Notice that if your computer is running slowly because of demands on RAM, you can turn off the automatic virtual memory configuration, which is the default setting, and set the parameters higher. You would do this by removing the check from **Automatically manage paging file size for all drives,** clicking **Custom size,** configuring the **Initial size** and **Maximum size** boxes, and clicking **Set.**

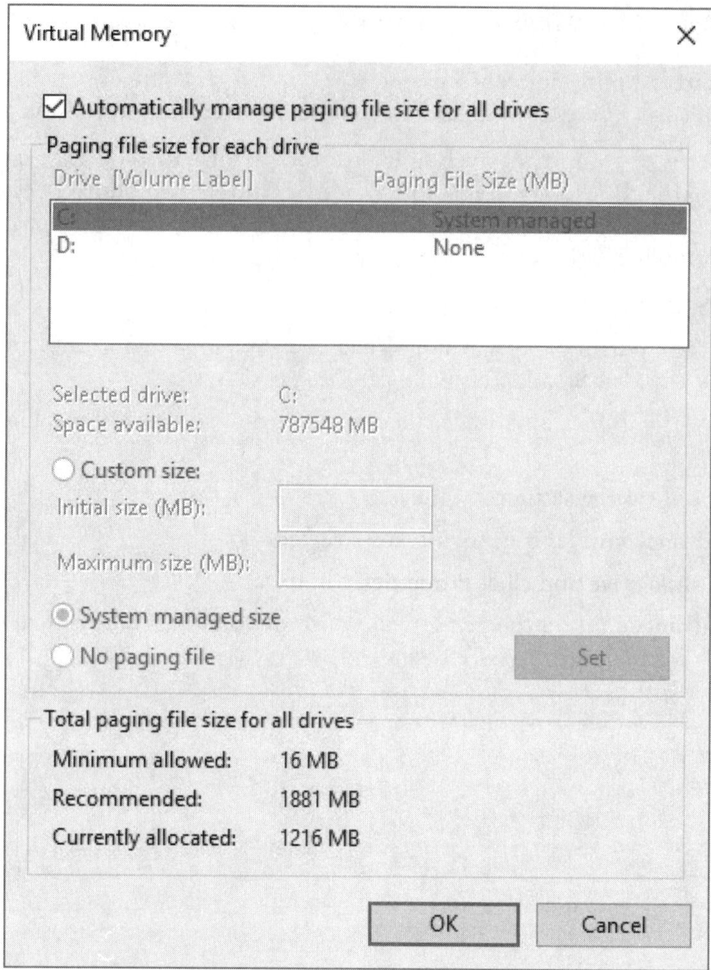

Figure 3-20 Configuring virtual memory

8. Click **Cancel** to leave the Virtual Memory dialog box, and then click **Cancel** to exit the Performance Options dialog box. Close the **System Properties** dialog box and close the System window.

If you change the virtual memory settings, the new settings do not go into effect until the server is rebooted.

Configuring File Caching Windows operating systems, including Windows Server 2016, cache file data for reading the data from a disk or writing it to disk. File caching is turned on by default and uses an area of RAM already established for file caching. File caching is controlled by the cache manager in Windows operating systems. Because file caching uses RAM, it can speed up the time it takes to read from or write to a disk.

After data is written to disk, the RAM used for that cached data is freed, via a process called flushing. On some server systems, administrators choose to turn off file caching and flushing, because this enables them to more easily hot swap a disk drive or controller, without using the Safety Remove Hardware notification icon, which warns that a device is in use.

When file caching is turned off, the server can seem slower to users particularly during times of heavy disk read and write operations. When flushing is turned off, there can be data loss when a disk drive is hot swapped while the server is in use.

In most cases, server performance is better and disk operations are safer when file caching and flushing are turned on. As you are working to tune a server, consider checking to be sure both capabilities are on. Additionally, you might check this at regular intervals if you work in a context where there are two or more server administrators, server operators, or system programmers who do work on the servers in an organization.

Activity 3-8: Configuring File Caching

Time Required: Approximately 5 minutes
Objective: Determine if file caching and flushing are turned on for a disk drive.

Description: In this activity, you determine if file caching and flushing are turned on for a particular disk drive. You will need to sign in using an account that has Administrator privileges.

1. Open **Server Manager**, if it is not open. In Server Manager, click **Tools**, click **Computer Management**, and click **Device Manager** in the tree in the left pane. (Alternatively, you can right-click **Start** and click **Device Manager**.)
2. Double-click **Disk drives** to display the available drives connected to the computer.
3. Right-click a disk drive and click **Properties**.
4. Click the **Policies** tab. Under Removal policy, ensure that **Better Performance (default)** is selected. Also, make sure that **Enable write caching on the device** is selected and that *Turn off Windows write-cache buffer flushing on the device* is not selected (see Figure 3-21). Note that if you are using a virtual disk, some of these options may not be available depending on your setup. Click **OK**.
5. Close any remaining open windows except for Server Manager.

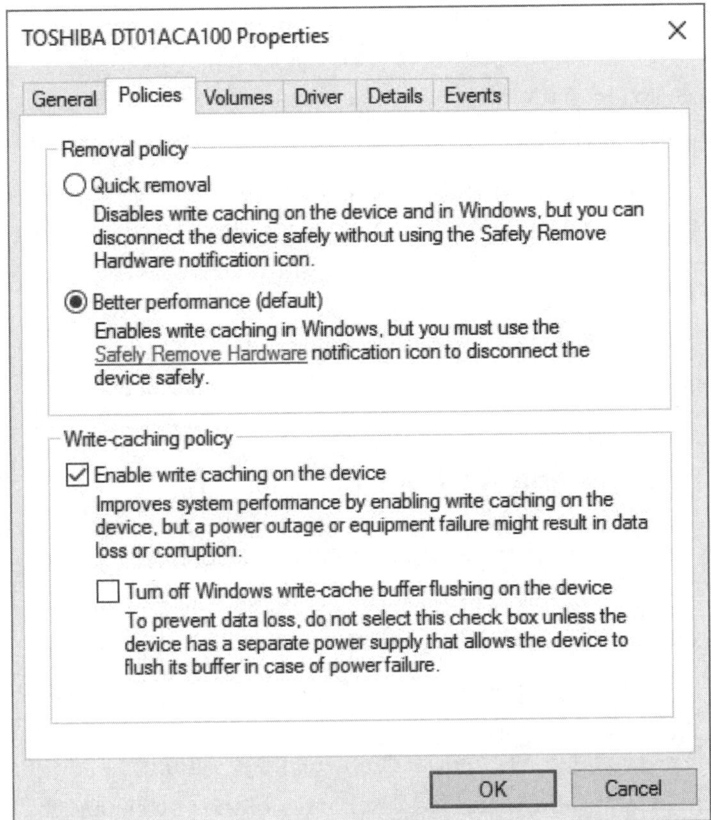

Figure 3-21 Configuring file caching and flushing

When write caching is enabled, it is possible to lose data after a power outage. For this reason, it is a good idea to have the server connected to an uninterruptible power supply (UPS).

Configuring Environment Variables

Environment variables are used to tell the operating system where to find certain programs and how to allocate memory to programs and to control different programs. Environment variables can be broken down into two categories: system environment variables and user environment variables. **System environment variables** are defined by the operating system and apply to any user signed in to the computer. Administrators can add new system environment variables or change the values of existing ones. **User environment variables** can be defined on a per-user basis, such as specifying the path where application files are stored.

Keep the following points in mind when you are working with environment variables:

- System environment variables are always set first.
- User environment variables are set next, overriding any conflicting system environment variables.

Activity 3-9: Configuring System and Environment Variables

Time Required: Approximately 5 minutes
Objective: Learn where to configure system and user environment variables.

Description: A newly installed Windows Server 2016 operating system has several system and user environment variables that are set up by default. In this activity, you learn where to configure the system and user environment variables and at the same time determine which ones are currently configured on your system.

1. Right-click **Start** and click **Control Panel**. If you are in the Category View, click **System and Security** and click **System**. If you are in the Large or Small icons (Classic) View, click **System**.
2. Click **Advanced system settings**.
3. Open the **Advanced** tab, if it is not already open.
4. Click **Environment Variables** to display a dialog box showing the environment variables.
   - Which user and system environment variables are defined already on your system? How would you add a new variable?
5. Click **Cancel** to close the Environment Variables dialog box.
6. Click **Cancel** to close the System Properties dialog box.
7. Leave the System window open for the next project (unless you cannot complete the project at this time).

Configuring Startup and Recovery

Windows Server 2016 enables you to configure parameters that dictate the startup sequence and how the system recovers from errors. You can configure the following system startup options:

- Which operating system to boot by default, if more than one operating system is installed
- How long to display a list of operating systems from which to boot
- How long to display a list of recovery options, if the computer needs to go into recovery mode after a system failure

In the event of a system failure, you can configure these options:

- Writing information to the system log (hard configured so you cannot change this)
- Whether to start automatically after a system failure
- How and where to write debugging information

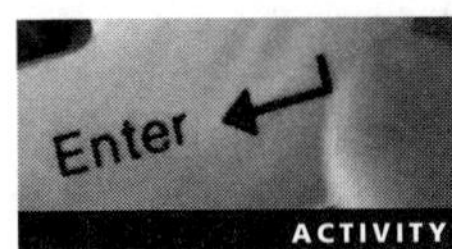

Activity 3-10: Configuring Startup and Recovery

Time Required: Approximately 5 minutes

Objective: Configure startup and recovery options.

Description: Soon after you install Windows Server 2016, it is important to customize the system startup and recovery options to match how your organization operates. This activity shows you how to configure these parameters on a non-dual-boot system so that the system does not automatically start up after a system failure. The advantage of not automatically restarting is that the system administrator has time to examine the system before it is rebooted. This is important, for example, when a disk drive is failing, so that the drive can be replaced before users resume work.

1. Open **Control Panel** into the **System** window if it is not already open.
2. Click **Advanced system settings.**
3. Open the **Advanced** tab, if necessary.
4. Find the Startup and Recovery section on the tab and click the **Settings** button in that section.
5. If necessary, set the **Time to display list of operating systems** parameter to **20** seconds (see Figure 3-22), so that you still have time to access recovery options when the system boots, but to reflect that you do not need time to select another operating system at boot up because this is not a dual-boot system.

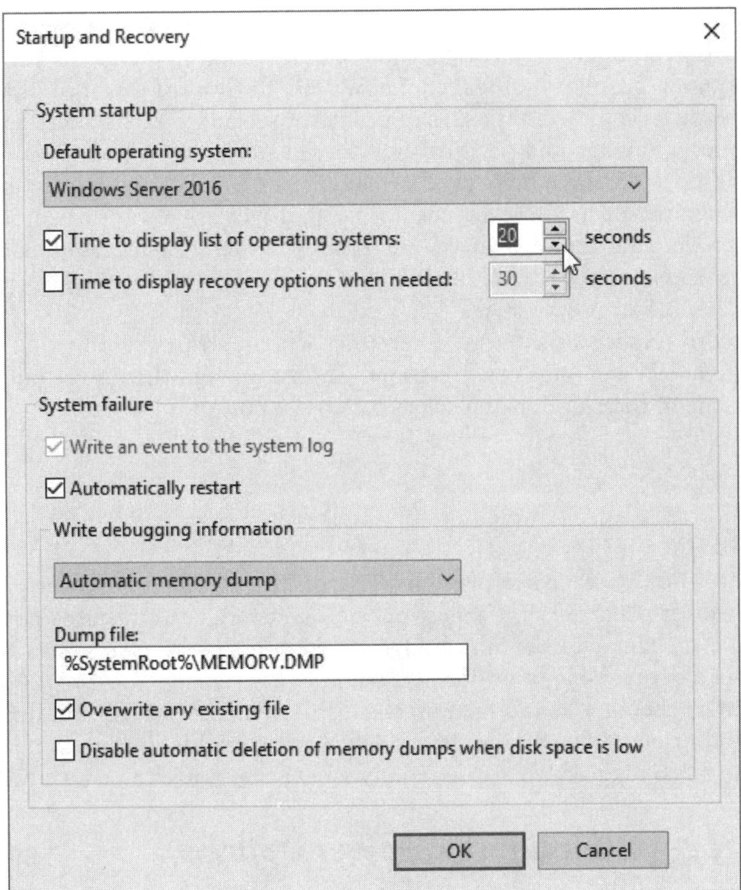

Figure 3-22 Configuring startup and recovery options

6. If **Automatically restart** is checked, remove the check mark (which means the system will not reboot after a failure until you do this manually).
7. Click **OK** in the Startup and Recovery dialog box.

8. Click **OK** in the System Properties dialog box.
9. From the System window, click the **back** (left pointing) **arrow** as many times as necessary under the title bar to go back to Control Panel.
10. Leave Control Panel open for the next activity.

Configuring Power Options

After you have installed Windows Server 2016, check the power management options to make sure that they are set appropriately for the computer and the way you are using the computer on the network. The Power Options that you can set are as follows:

- Select a power plan.
- Choose what the power button does.
- Create a power plan.
- Choose when to turn off the display.

If Windows Server 2016 is installed in a virtual machine, you might not see *Require a password on wakeup* or some other options.

Three power plans are already created: balanced, power saver, and high performance. Each plan consists of a combination of power options including how soon to turn off the display, whether to require a password on wakeup, how soon to turn off the hard disk, sleep/hibernate settings, USB settings, PCI card settings, and processor settings. The balanced setting offers equal emphasis to energy savings and performance. Power saver favors energy savings over performance, and high performance favors performance over energy savings. For example, with the balanced and high performance plans, the hard disk drives are never turned off. However, with the power saver plan, the hard disk drives are turned off after 20 minutes of inactivity. In another example, the processor activity state is set higher (more activity) for the high performance plan than it is for balanced or power saver.

The option to require a password determines whether a password is needed to access the system after it wakes up from sleep/hibernate. Choosing what the power button does enables you to specify one of three options for when the power button is pressed:

- Shut down
- Do nothing
- Hibernate

The option to create a power plan enables you to customize a power plan, if one of the three existing power plans does not meet your needs. Before customizing a power plan, keep in mind that you can change the default settings for the three power plans already created, and so creating a new power plan might not be necessary.

The option to choose when to turn off the display enables you to turn off the display after a specific period of inactivity, in minutes or hours, or to set the display to never turn off. This option can also be configured when you modify an existing power plan or create a new one.

Activity 3-11: Configuring Power Options

Time Required: Approximately 5 minutes
Objective: Configure the balanced power plan.

Description: Many server administrators have specific power options they want to set up. In this activity, you configure the balanced power plan to customize power options.

1. Open **Control Panel,** if it is not already open. If you are in the Control Panel Category View, click **System and Security.** If you are in the Large or Small icons (Classic) View, go to Step 2.
2. Click **Power Options.**
3. Notice the options on the left side of the window (see Figure 3-23) that enable you to *Choose what the power button does*, *Create a power plan*, and *Choose when to turn off the display*.

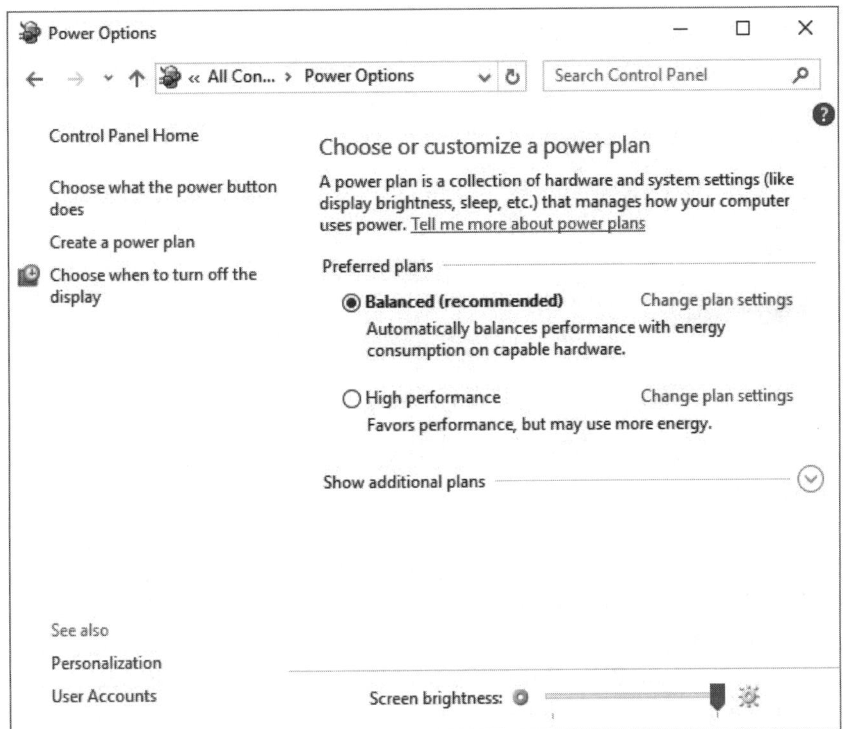

Figure 3-23 Power Options window

4. Click **Choose what the power button does** and ensure that **When I press the power button** is set to **Shut down.** If you had to make a change to the setting, click the **Save changes** button. If you didn't make any changes, click **Cancel.**
5. Click the **Balanced (recommended)** option button, if it is not already selected.
6. Click **Change plan settings** in the Balanced selection.
7. Click **Change advanced power settings** to see the Power Options Advanced settings tab, as shown in Figure 3-24 (if this is the first time you have accessed the Power Options dialog box, you might see the Setting parameter for *Turn off hard disk after* configured to *never*).
8. Ensure there is a minus sign in front of **Hard disk** and in front of **Turn off hard disk after** as shown in Figure 3-24.
9. Click **Setting** under *Turn off hard disk after* and configure the **Setting (Minutes)** box to **40.**
10. Click the **plus sign** in front of **USB settings** and the plus sign in front of **USB selective suspend setting.**
11. Click **Setting** and configure it to **Enabled,** if Enabled is not already selected.
12. Click the **plus sign** in front of **Display** and click the **plus sign** for **Turn off display after.**
13. Click **Setting** and configure the **Setting (Minutes)** box to **15.**
14. Click the **Apply** button and then click **OK.**

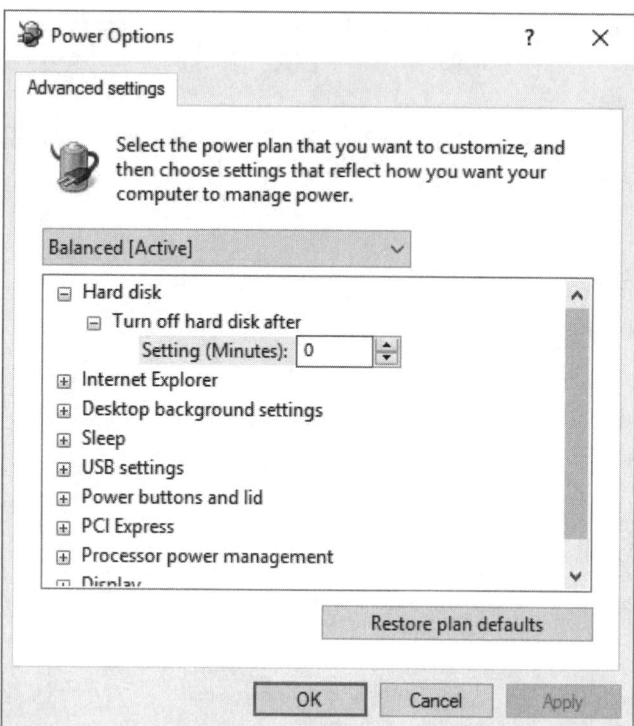

Figure 3-24 Power Options dialog box

15. In the Edit Plan Settings window, set **Turn off the display** to **15** minutes. Click **Save changes** in the Edit Plan Settings window.
16. Click the **back arrow** (left pointing arrow) under the title bar, as many times as necessary to go back to Control Panel. Leave Control Panel open for the next activity.

Installing a Protocol

Knowing how to install a protocol is a skill that is similar to knowing how to change a flat tire; you don't need it often but it is an important skill when you need it. Chapter 1, Introduction to Windows Server 2016, discussed static (manual) TCP/IP configuration. However, you might need to add other protocols to customize the server for your network. Control Panel enables you to install or uninstall protocols from the Network and Sharing Center. Two examples of protocols you might need to install are Hyper-V Extensible Virtual Switch Protocol and Reliable Multicast Protocol.

Hyper-V Extensible Virtual Switch Protocol is used when the Hyper-V role is installed in Windows Server 2016. When Windows Server 2016 is operating as a virtual server, Hyper-V Extensible Virtual Switch Protocol is used at the server's NIC (or NICs) to bind or associate the virtual network services to the NIC. Hyper-V Extensible Virtual Switch Protocol enables the use of a software virtual switch between the main operating system and the operating systems on virtual partitions. It also reduces the overhead in network communications when Hyper-V is installed.

If Hyper-V is in use and users find they cannot stay connected to a virtual server, the reason is often because Hyper-V Extensible Virtual Switch Protocol is not installed.

Reliable Multicast Protocol is used for multimedia transmissions, such as a combined voice and video transmission to provide user training to multiple people. In Chapter 1, you learned that in a multicast, the server sends one IP communication to multiple clients (see Figure 1-13 in

Chapter 1). For example, if five users are watching a training video at their PCs, the server can use multicasting to make one transmission that goes to all five at once, instead of sending five separate network transmissions. Multicasting can improve network efficiency on networks that provide multimedia transmissions. Reliable Multicast Protocol runs on top of IP and simplifies multicast communications because multicasting can be done even without routers to direct network traffic.

3

Activity 3-12: Installing a Protocol

Time Required: Approximately 10 minutes
Objective: Learn to install a protocol.

Description: Installing a protocol is not difficult, but it is important to know how to do this task.

1. Open **Control Panel,** if it's not already open. If you are in the Control Panel Category View, click **View network status and tasks** under Network and Internet. If you are in the Large or Small icons (Classic) View, click **Network and Sharing Center.**
2. Look for your connection in the upper right portion of the Network and Sharing Center window, such as *Connections: Ethernet*. Click the connection, such as **Ethernet** (see Figure 3-25).

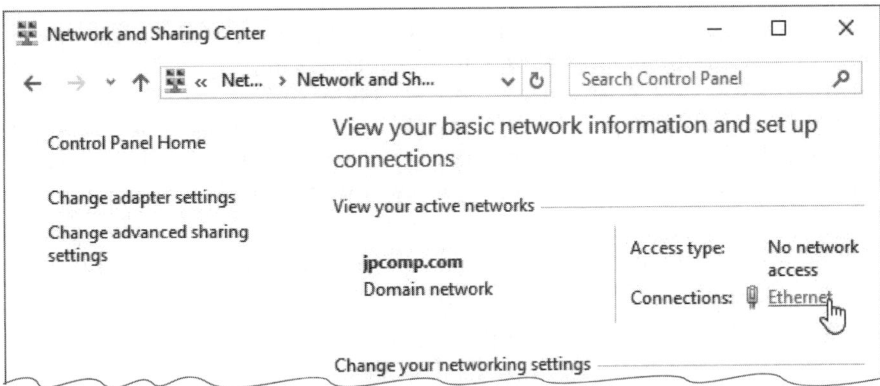

Figure 3-25 Selecting Ethernet in the Network and Sharing Center window

3. Click **Properties** in the Ethernet Status dialog box.
4. Click the **Install** button in the Ethernet Properties dialog box.
5. Double-click **Protocol** in the Select Network Feature Type dialog box (see Figure 3-26).

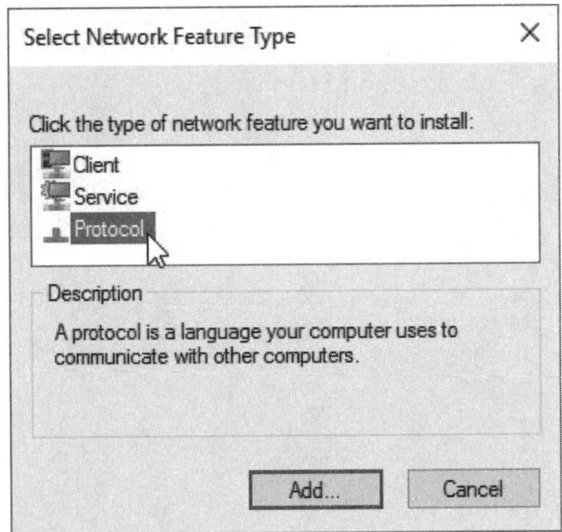

Figure 3-26 Selecting Protocol

6. Double-click **Reliable Multicast Protocol** (note that you can install any protocol at this time, but protocols already installed do not appear in the listing).
7. In the Ethernet Properties dialog box, notice that Reliable Multicast Protocol is now listed in the *This connection uses the following items* box. Also, notice that Hyper-V Extensible Virtual Switch Protocol should already be installed by default, but its box is likely not checked (it is not enabled) unless you are on a virtual machine using Hyper-V.
8. Close the Ethernet Properties dialog box and the Ethernet Status dialog box.
9. In the Network and Sharing Center window, click the **back arrow** under the title bar to go back to Control Panel.

You can use similar steps to install a service or client access for networking, such as Client for Microsoft Networks, which enables connecting to networks, and File and Printer Sharing for Microsoft Networks, which enables access to shared files, folders, and printers over the network. In Step 5, you would double-click Client or Service instead of Protocol.

Understanding the Windows Server 2016 Registry

The Windows Server 2016 Registry is a very complex database containing all information the operating system needs about the entire server. For example, the initialization files used by earlier versions of Windows operating systems, including the critical System.ini and Win.ini files, are contained in the Registry. Just as Active Directory can be the coordinating center for network services, the Registry is the coordinating center for a specific server. Without the Registry, Windows Server 2016 cannot function. Some examples of data contained in the Registry are as follows:

- Information about all hardware components, including the CPU, disk drives, network interface cards, optical drives, and more
- Information about Windows Server 2016 services that are installed, which services they depend on, and the order in which they are started
- Data about user profiles and Windows Server 2016 group policies
- Data on the last current and last known setup used to boot the computer
- Configuration information about all software in use
- Software licensing information
- Server Manager and Control Panel parameter configurations

In Windows Server 2016, the Registry Editor is launched from the Start button Run or Command prompt option as *regedit*. The same command can be used to start the Registry Editor in Windows PowerShell. The Registry Editor window is very straightforward, with common menu utilities such as File, Edit, View, Favorites, and Help (see Figure 3-27).

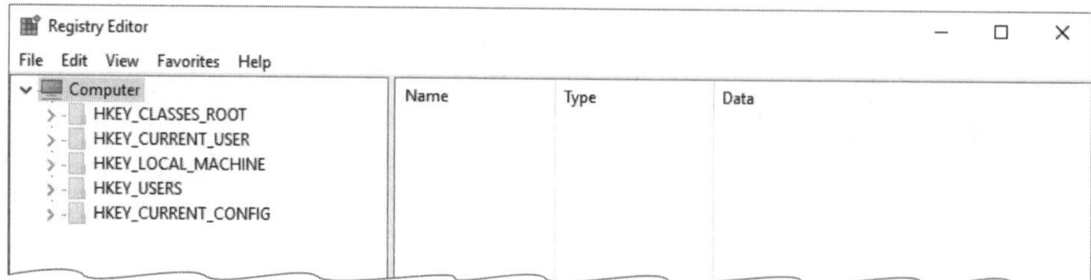

Figure 3-27 Registry Editor

Making incorrect changes to the Registry can have profound consequences for and possibly disable your operating system. Use the following precautions when working with the Registry:

- Establish a specific group of administrators who have privileges to open and modify the Registry. Take away Registry modification privileges from all others by controlling who can use the Registry Editor and .reg files.
- Only make changes to the Registry as a last resort, such as those changes recommended in a technical document from Microsoft. It is safer to use tools such as the Control Panel options or the Server Manager tool for changes to information in the Registry.
- Regularly back up the Registry as part of backing up the Windows Server 2016 Windows folder. Further, consider backing up the Registry prior to reconfiguring it through the Registry Editor.
- Never copy the Registry from one Windows-based system over the Registry of a different system, regardless of whether they use the same operating system or version, because each Registry and its contents is unique to the computer and operating system on which it resides. (This does not apply in situations where you create a replica Active Directory domain controller by using a removable hard drive, tape, or DVD backup of a domain controller to restore to a computer from scratch.)

The Registry folders and files are stored in two main places. System information for the Registry is stored in \Windows\System32\config, and information for user accounts is stored in \Users in hidden files within folders for specific user accounts.

Registry Contents

The Registry is hierarchical in structure (see Figure 3-28) and is made up of keys, subkeys, and entries:

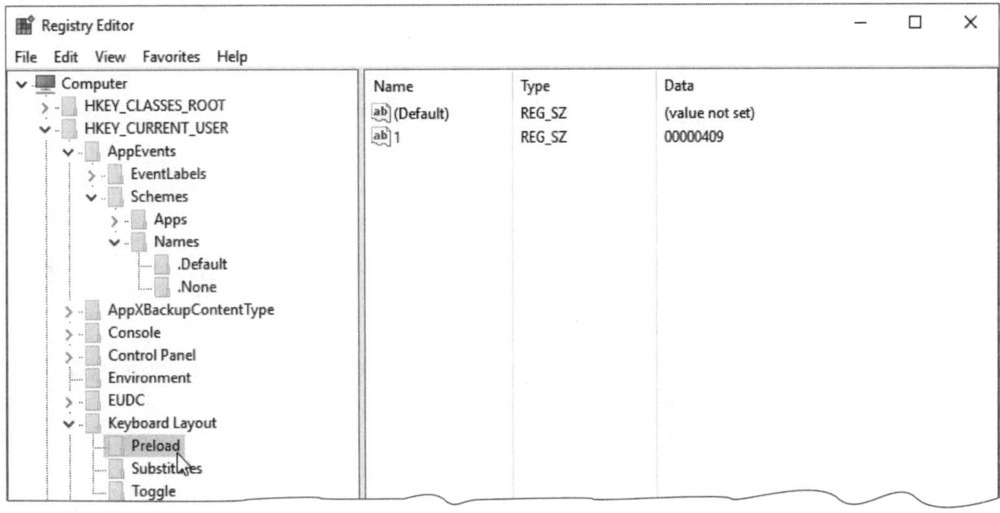

Figure 3-28 Hierarchical structure of the Registry

- *Key*—A folder that appears in the left pane of the Registry Editor and can contain subkeys and entries, for example, HKEY_CURRENT_USER.
- *Subkey*—A part of the Registry that is below a key. A subkey can contain entries or other subkeys.
- *Entry or value*—An item that appears in the details pane and is the lowest level in the Registry. An entry consists of an entry name, its data type, and its value.

A **Registry key** is a category or division of information within the Registry. A single key may contain one or more lower-level keys called **Registry subkeys**, just as a folder may contain several subfolders. A **Registry entry** is a data parameter associated with a software or hardware characteristic under a key (or subkey). A Registry entry consists of three parts—a name, the data type, and the configuration parameter. For example, in ErrorControl:REG_DWORD:0, ErrorControl is the name, REG_DWORD is the data type, and 0 is the parameter setting. In this Registry entry, the option to track errors is turned off if the parameter is 0, and error tracking is turned on if the value is 1. Registry entries can have different data formats: DWORD (32 bit) and QWORD (64 bit) are hexadecimal, string (including multi string and expandable string) contains text data, and binary is two hexadecimal values.

The Windows Server 2016 Registry is made up of five root keys:

- HKEY_LOCAL_MACHINE
- HKEY_CURRENT_USER
- HKEY_USERS
- HKEY_CLASSES_ROOT
- HKEY_CURRENT_CONFIG

A **root key**, also called a **subtree**, is a primary or highest level category of data contained in the Registry. It might be compared with a main folder, such as the \Windows folder, which is at the root level of folders. All root keys start with HKEY to show they are the highest level key.

HKEY_LOCAL_MACHINE

Information on every hardware component in the server is provided under the HKEY_LOCAL_MACHINE root key. This includes information about what drivers are loaded and their version levels, what IRQ (interrupt request) lines are used, setup configurations, the BIOS version, and more. Figure 3-29 shows the Registry contents, using the Registry Editor to view the HKEY_LOCAL_MACHINE root key information about video settings.

Under each root key are subkeys, which are BCD00000000, HARDWARE, SAM, SECURITY, SOFTWARE, and SYSTEM for the root key shown in Figure 3-29. Each subkey

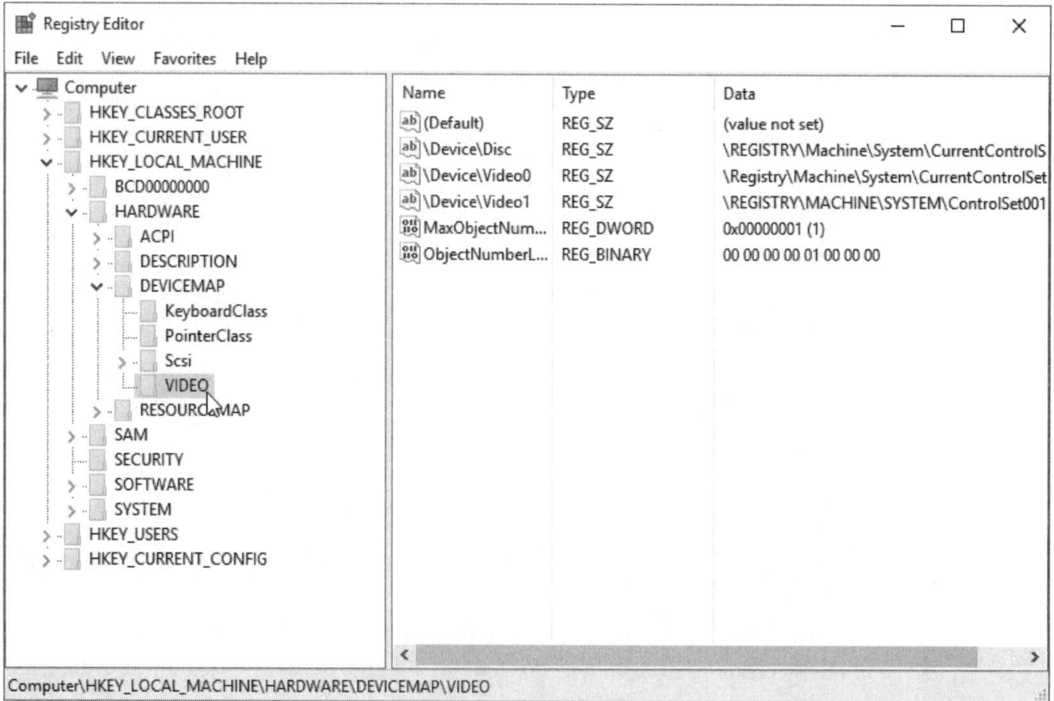

Figure 3-29 The HKEY_LOCAL_MACHINE root key containing hardware settings

may have subkeys under it, such as ACPI, DESCRIPTION, DEVICEMAP, and RESOURCEMAP under the HARDWARE subkey in Figure 3-29.

A few subkeys are stored as a set, called **hives**, because they hold related information. This is true for the SOFTWARE subkey, which holds information about installed software. You can make hardware configuration changes directly from the Registry, although this is not recommended (see the following Caution).

Although it is possible to make hardware configuration changes directly from the Registry, this is a dangerous undertaking because a wrong deletion might mean you cannot reboot your server into Windows Server 2016. It is better to use other options first, such as Control Panel. Make changes in the Registry only under the guidance of a Microsoft technical note or a Microsoft support person.

HKEY_CURRENT_USER

The HKEY_CURRENT_USER key contains information about the desktop setup for the account presently signed in to the server console, as opposed to the HKEY_USERS key, which contains profile settings for all users who have signed in to the server. It contains data on color combinations, font sizes and type, the keyboard layout, the taskbar, clock configuration, and nearly any setup action you have made on the desktop. For example, if you want to change the environment parameter governing where temporary files are stored for applications, you could do it from here. The new path is set by clicking the Environment subkey under the HKEY_CURRENT_USER root key and changing the path shown as the value in the right pane. The sounds associated with a given event can be set by clicking the path \HKEY_CURRENT_USER\AppEvents\EventLabels and then changing the sound value for a particular event, such as the event to close a window, which is a single value in the Close subkey (\HKEY_CURRENT_USER\AppEvents\EventLabels\Close).

Another example is to change the delay in the response of the keyboard. For example, click the following path: \HKEY_CURRENT_USER\Control Panel\Keyboard. If the KeyboardDelay data value is 0, this means there is minimum delay. You could slow down the response a little by setting the delay to 1. This has the same effect as going into Control Panel in Classic View (Large or Small icons), clicking Keyboard, and setting the Repeat delay slider bar one notch to the left of the Short setting. (This is just an example. Again it is strongly recommended that you rely on tools like Control Panel instead of making configuration changes in the Registry.)

HKEY_USERS

The HKEY_USERS root key contains profile information for each user who has signed in to the computer. Each profile is listed under this root key. Within each user profile is information identical to that viewed within the HKEY_CURRENT_USER root key. The profile used when you are signed in is one of the profiles stored under HKEY_USERS. You can make the same changes just examined by finding the subkey for your profile and making the changes here instead of under the HKEY_CURRENT_USER root key.

HKEY_CLASSES_ROOT

The HKEY_CLASSES_ROOT key holds data to associate file extensions with programs. This is a more extensive list than the one viewed under HKEY_CURRENT_USER. Associations exist for executable files, text files, graphics files, Clipboard files, audio files, and many more. These associations are used as defaults for all users who sign in to Windows Server 2016, whereas the associations in HKEY_CURRENT_USER and HKEY_USERS are those that have been customized for a given user profile.

HKEY_CURRENT_CONFIG

The last root key, HKEY_CURRENT_CONFIG, has information about the current hardware profile. It holds information about the monitor type, keyboard, mouse, and other hardware characteristics for the current profile. On most servers, there is only one default hardware profile set up. Two or more profiles could be used, but this is more common for a portable computer running Windows 10 that is used with and without a docking station. One profile would have the keyboard and monitor used when on the road, and another would have a larger keyboard and monitor used when the computer is docked.

Backing Up the Registry

Before you work on the Registry, it is important to have a backup of its contents, in case something goes wrong. An easy way to create a backup is to set a restore point. If the Registry is damaged after you work on it, you can go back to the restore point you created just before working on the Registry. You can create a restore point by using the Checkpoint-Computer cmdlet in PowerShell. In Chapter 12, System Reliability and Availability, you learn methods for going back to a restore point.

Activity 3-13: Using the Registry Editor

Time Required: Approximately 10 minutes
Objective: Practice backing up the Registry and using the Registry Editor to view the Registry contents.

Description: It is a good idea to have some experience with the Registry Editor before you make changes to the Registry, such as changes recommended through a Microsoft TechNet document. In this activity, you first create a restore point, so that if there is a problem while editing the Registry, you can go back to the restore point. Next, you use the Registry Editor to view where Control Panel settings are stored.

1. Open Windows PowerShell by clicking **Start** and clicking the **Windows PowerShell** tile. Alternatively, click **Start**, click the **Windows PowerShell** folder, and click **Windows PowerShell**. (Or if you want to use the Command Prompt window, right-click **Start**, click **Command Prompt (Admin)**, and type **powershell** at the prompt.)
2. At the prompt, type **Checkpoint-Computer -Description "Before editing Registry"** and press **Enter**. This command creates a restore point titled, Before editing Registry.
3. Type **regedit** at the prompt and press **Enter**.
4. In the tree in the left pane, double-click **HKEY_CURRENT_USER** and double-click **Control Panel**.
   - What Control Panel subkeys do you see?
5. Double-click **Accessibility**.
   - What subkeys are displayed?
6. Click **MouseKeys** to view the values set for that subkey?
   - What values do you see in the right pane?
7. Click two or three other subkeys to view their values.
8. Click a value and then click the **Edit** menu to view how to modify a value, delete a value, or add a new one.

Absolutely do not make any changes.

9. Close the Registry Editor.

Windows PowerShell

You've already gained some practice using Windows PowerShell to execute commands that have been traditionally available in the Command Prompt window. Windows PowerShell is well worth learning because it works in both the GUI and the Server Core installations of Windows Server 2016.

Windows PowerShell is a command-line interface or shell. As you learned in Chapter 1, a shell is a customized environment for executing commands and scripts. Two important features of Windows PowerShell are scripts and cmdlets. A script is a file of commands that is run when you run the script; cmdlets are specialized commands for completing common tasks in PowerShell. Windows PowerShell is particularly intended for situations in which there are multiple servers and it is more efficient to manage them using a consistent set of scripts. It is also ideal for managing servers that house user applications, particularly for situations where the applications need to be configured in the same way and regular updates are required.

You can create your own cmdlets for PowerShell. Visit *technet.microsoft.com/en-us/scriptcenter/dd772285.aspx* to learn more about existing cmdlets and creating new cmdlets. Another useful PowerShell resource that contains links to helpful articles and blogs is found at *technet.microsoft.com/en-us/library/bb978526.aspx*.

Some of the tasks you can complete using Windows PowerShell include the following:

- Manage files and folders.
- Manage network tasks.
- Manage fixed and removable storage.
- Configure printing services.
- Manage software applications and updates.
- Manage Remote Desktop Services.
- Manage server services and features.
- Manage web server services.
- Work with the Registry.

Windows PowerShell is installed by default for use in Windows Server 2016, so it is ready to use from the moment you finish installing the operating system.

Scores of cmdlet tools are available through Windows PowerShell. As you have already learned, Windows PowerShell also recognizes many traditional Command Prompt window commands. The following activity gives you more experience with PowerShell.

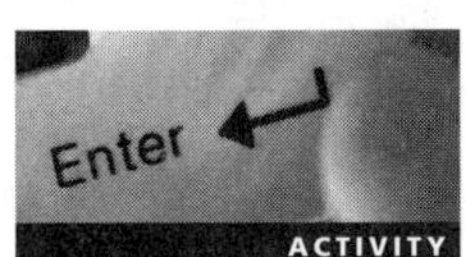

Activity 3-14: Using Windows PowerShell

Time Required: Approximately 15 minutes
Objective: Use traditional Command Prompt commands and cmdlets in Windows PowerShell.

Description: Learning how to use Windows PowerShell can be an important way to expand your server administration toolbox. In this activity, you take several traditional commands and cmdlets for a test drive.

1. Click **Start** and click the **Windows PowerShell** tile; or click **Start**, click the **Windows PowerShell** folder to open it, and click **Windows PowerShell**.
2. To view the files in the current folder, such as \Users\Administrator, one page at a time type the traditional command, **dir | more** and press **Enter**. Press the **Spacebar**, if necessary, to advance to additional screens.

3. To change to the \Users directory, enter **cd \users** and press **Enter**. Your Windows PowerShell window will look similar to Figure 3-30. (The default is light type on dark background; figures are shown here with dark type on light background for readability.)

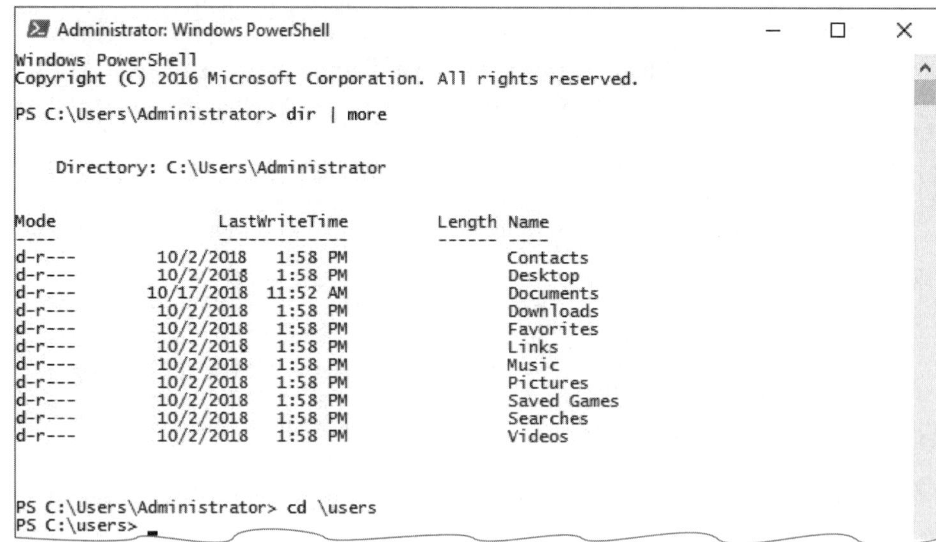

Figure 3-30 Using Windows PowerShell

4. View a listing of cmdlets. Type **Get-Command | more** and press **Enter**. You see the commands one screen at a time. Press the **Spacebar** to advance to the next screen, and repeat this step until you've viewed all of the screens. (Note that you can also press **q** to exit back to the command line, if you decide not to view all of the screens of commands.)
5. Press the **up arrow** and notice that the last command you entered is placed on the command line so that you can repeat the command. Press the **up arrow** again and you'll see the second to-last command you entered. Press **Enter** to run that command.
6. Type **Get-Process** and press **Enter** to view the processes running on the server.
7. Next, type **Get-Process | Where { $_.WS -gt 100MB }** and press **Enter**. (If no process is displayed change the command to use **20MB**.)
8. To stop a process you would type **Stop-Process -Name "*processname*"** (where *processname* is the name of a process you found in Step 7) and press **Enter**.
9. Type **Get-Service** and press **Enter** to view services that are running or are stopped. (Or you can enter **Get-Service | more** to display the services one screen at a time.)
10. You can view more about the main or core Windows PowerShell cmdlets. Type **Get-Help About_Core_Command** and press **Enter**. (If you are asked if you want to run Update-Help, type **Y** for yes and press **Enter**. Update-Help updates the help database when you are connected to the Internet. Wait for the update to complete.)
11. Also, you can view the online help about a specific cmdlet by typing *Get-Help* plus the cmdlet. For example, type **Get-Help Join-Path** and press **Enter**.
12. Close the Windows PowerShell window.

There is not enough room in the chapter to give you a full grounding in Windows PowerShell. This section is only meant to give you an idea of its capabilities. To fully appreciate Windows PowerShell, you will need to be familiar with writing scripts as well as the PowerShell cmdlets. For tutorials and more resources about Windows PowerShell, try the following websites:

- *social.technet.microsoft.com/wiki/contents/articles/4307.powershell-for-beginners.aspx* (for a list of PowerShell resources for beginners)
- *msdn.microsoft.com/en-us/powershell/scripting/getting-started/getting-started-with-windows-powershell* (for information about getting started with Windows PowerShell)
- *http://www.foxebook.net/mastering-powershell* (a free downloadable guide for mastering Windows PowerShell)
- *technet.microsoft.com/en-us/library/ee221100.aspx* (for the Windows PowerShell Owners Manual)

Chapter Summary

- Server Manager is a tool offered in Windows Server 2016 that helps centralize server management tasks. This tool enables you to install and remove roles, install and remove features, access diagnostic and reliability tools, configure server settings, and pool servers for easier management.
- After server roles are installed, you can use the Best Practices Analyzer (BPA) to ensure one or more roles are optimally configured and running.
- The Devices and Printers utility in Control Panel with the Add a device option enables the installation of hardware devices not properly detected by PnP.
- Device Manager is a tool you can access from Control Panel or the Computer Management tool to manage hardware.
- The System File Checker and Sigverif are tools for verifying system files.
- After Windows Server 2016 is installed, you can tune performance by configuring processor scheduling and Data Execution Prevention (DEP) use, virtual memory, and file caching and flushing.
- Environment variables are important to configure because they help the operating system to find specific programs, help programs to properly allocate memory, and help to control specific programs.
- To protect your system from complications due to power problems, configure startup and recovery options as well as power options.
- Knowing how to install a protocol is a skill that is similar to knowing how to change a flat tire; you don't need it often but it is important to know how when you need it. Use Control Panel to install or uninstall protocols.
- The Registry is a database that is at the foundation of Windows Server 2016. It's important to know the structure of Registry keys, subkeys, and values so you can carefully make Registry changes as might be called for in technical bulletins.
- Windows PowerShell is a command-line tool that enables a system administrator to manage a server using commands, cmdlets, and scripts.

Key Terms

Best Practices Analyzer (BPA) Analyzes the installed server roles to report if they are set up to conform to Microsoft's best practices for roles.

Data Execution Prevention (DEP) A security feature that monitors how programs use memory and stops programs that attempt to use memory allocated for system programs and processes. This is intended to foil viruses, Trojan horses, and worms that attempt to invade system memory.

driver signing A digital signature incorporated into driver and system files as a way to verify the files and to ensure that they are not inappropriately overwritten.

hive A set of related Registry keys and subkeys stored as a file.

Hyper-V Extensible Virtual Switch Protocol Used with the Hyper-V role at the server's network interface card(s) (NICs) to bind or associate the virtual network services to the NIC and enable the use of a virtual switch between the parent partition containing the main operating system, Windows Server 2016, and child partitions containing other operating systems.

interrupt request (IRQ) line A hardware line that a computer component, such as a disk drive or serial port, uses to communicate to the processor that it is ready to send or receive information. Intel-based computers have 16 IRQ lines, with 15 available for computer components to use.

I/O address The address in memory through which data is transferred between a computer component and the processor.

paging Moving blocks of information, called pages, from RAM to virtual memory (the paging file) on disk.

paging file Disk space, in the form of a file, for use when memory requirements exceed the available RAM.

Plug and Play (PnP) Ability of added computer hardware, such as an adapter or modem, to identify itself to the computer operating system for installation. PnP also refers to the Intel and Microsoft specifications for automatic device detection and installation. Many operating systems, such as Windows-based, Mac OS X, and UNIX/Linux, support PnP.

Registry entry A data parameter in the Registry stored as a value in hexadecimal, binary, or text format.

Registry key A category of information contained in the Windows Registry, such as hardware or software.

Registry subkey A key within a Registry key, similar to a subfolder under a folder.

Reliable Multicast Protocol Used on Windows-based networks to facilitate multicast transmissions for multimedia communications.

resource On a network, this refers to an object, such as a shared printer or shared directory, which can be accessed by users. On workstations as well as servers, a resource is an IRQ line, I/O address, or memory that is allocated to a computer component, such as a disk drive or communications port.

root key Also called a subtree, the highest category of data contained in the Registry. There are five root keys.

Sigverif A tool used to verify system and other critical files to determine if they have a signature.

storage pool Storage capacity that can be set up from different physical and virtual disks to store specific information, such as inventory programs under development for a business.

subtree Same as root key.

system environment variables Variables defined by the operating system and that apply to any user signed in to the computer.

Universal PnP (UPnP) A supplementation to PnP that enables automated configuration for devices connected through a network.

user environment variables Environment variables that are defined on a per-user basis.

virtual memory Disk storage allocated to link with physical RAM to temporarily hold data when there is not enough free RAM.

Review Questions

1. You have just taken over management of a server on which the previous server administrator has set up several server components including the hard drives to be hot swappable. However, you notice that server performance is slow and disk reading and

writing sometimes is delayed. What step can you take to improve the performance of the disk drives?

a. Check the disk controllers for a switch you can set for faster disk rotation.
b. Use the Control Panel Disk applet to double the disk transfer speed.
c. Allocate more RAM for disk transfers.
d. Ensure file caching and flushing are enabled for all disk drives.

2. Each time that you access files on a disk, the monitor blinks or goes blank for several seconds. What might be the source of the problem and possible solution?
   a. The disk and monitor are connected to the same controller, and you should use Control Panel to configure a hardware link bridge.
   b. This is called a "RAM pause" and you need to use Control Panel to allocate more RAM specifically for the data bus inside the computer.
   c. The disk controller should be replaced because it is an older generation controller that operates at the same frequency as the monitor
   d. There is an IRQ conflict, and you need to use Device Manager to resolve the problem.
3. As the server administrator for a hospital, you have received several notices about malware targeted at software applications used in hospitals. What server configuration step can you take to help protect applications from malware?
   a. Install the Malware role on the server.
   b. Ensure that Data Execution Prevention is turned on.
   c. Run the malware-protect cmdlet in Windows PowerShell.
   d. Install the Malware Block feature through Server Manager.
4. Another way to protect against malware is to ensure the system and other essential files have a signature. What tool enables you to verify files for a signature and what tool enables you to run this tool?
   a. Sigverif that is started through Windows PowerShell
   b. Signature Monitor that is started through Administrative Tools
   c. Fileverify that is started through the Command Prompt window
   d. Filesig that is started using Control Panel
5. Which of the following can be installed using the Add a device option? (Choose all that apply.)
   a. Optical drive
   b. Keyboard
   c. Monitor
   d. Disk drive
6. You've obtained a new driver from the Internet for your server's NIC. What tool enables you to install the driver?
   a. Driver icon in Control Panel
   b. Driver Updater
   c. Device Manager
   d. App Installer
7. You have noticed lately that your server is running very slowly, especially when switching between programs. You see that the C: partition is running low on space, limiting the size

of your paging file. You have a second partition, D: that has 100 GB of free space. How can you move the paging file from partition C: onto partition D:?

a. Use Device Manager to drag the paging file from partition C: to partition D:.

b. Configure it from the System window opened through Control Panel.

c. Move the Paging directory to partition D: via Device Manager.

d. Use the Paging file option in Control Panel and access the Size link in the Paging window.

8. A ________ variable is defined by the operating system and is applied to every user when signed in.

9. Your organization has consolidated servers through virtualization and now needs to remove the Windows Deployment Services server role from one of its servers. Which of the following tools enable you to remove a server role? (Choose all that apply.)

a. Control Panel>System

b. Control Panel>Server Roles

c. *role-delete* command in the Command Prompt window

d. Server Manager

10. The power supply in your server has just been replaced because of power problems. Your server boots, but now there is a message that a Windows directory file is corrupted. You can use ________ as a tool to check and then restore system files that have been corrupted.

11. ________ enables you to determine if a server role is set up to follow best practices.

12. Your server keyboard sometimes hesitates or seems like it is disconnecting from the computer. Which of the following tools enables you to run a quick check on whether the keyboard is working properly?

a. Device Manager

b. *sysconfig* command

c. Control Panel Check Components window

d. PnP

13. ________ Protocol is used to bind virtual network services on a virtual machine to the NIC.

14. The ________ cmdlet in Windows PowerShell is used to view which processes are running on a server.

15. Your server has a virus with elements of the virus embedded in the Registry. The virus checker has located these elements but cannot delete them. What tool can you use to delete these virus elements in the Registry?

a. *regedit*

b. *cd registry*

c. *sigverif*

d. *openedit*

16. You are working in PowerShell and receive a call that users cannot use the print services through the server. What command can you run to quickly determine services that are running or are stopped?

a. *core_services*

b. *services*

c. *get-service*

d. *dir services*

3

17. What option can you use in Server Manager to configure server properties, such as the computer name and the Ethernet connection, as well as view events, such as errors and warnings?
    a. Local Server in the left pane
    b. Server information menu
    c. WDS box in the default Server Manager window
    d. Analyze option on the Tools menu
18. Which of the following are Registry elements? (Choose all that apply.)
    a. OUs
    b. Keys
    c. Values
    d. Markers
19. The server you have just installed has 16 GB of RAM. What should the initial paging file size be set to when you manually configure it as a beginning tuning step before monitoring paging over time to fine tune it later?
    a. 1024 MB
    b. 2048 MB
    c. 8192 MB
    d. 24576 MB
20. Your company is working to save costs by conserving the power consumption of its servers. Which of the following default power plans should you select for Windows Server 2016 servers?
    a. High performance
    b. Miser
    c. Power saver
    d. Controlled consumption

Case Projects

Light Crafters is a small company that makes light fixtures for fluorescent, CFL, and LED lights. The company is installing two new Windows Server 2016 servers, one using Standard Edition and the other using Datacenter Edition. Both operating systems are freshly installed and now it's time to configure them. Light Crafters has hired you to consult with their IT staff about the installation and configuration of the servers. They recently had turnover in the IT staff, leaving only two personnel who formerly supported users with desktop computers.

Case Project 3-1: Server Manager Training

The two IT staff members responsible for the servers have heard about Server Manager and are requesting training in its use. Prepare a brief report or slide presentation for them, to cover the following:

- An overview of Server Manager's capabilities
- How to start Server Manager
- How to install roles and features

Case Project 3-2: Troubleshooting a NIC

As you are working, a network interface card (NIC) in one of the servers seems to be working erratically. Explain how you can:

- Test the NIC
- Determine if there is an IRQ conflict
- Determine the name of the driver used by the NIC

Case Project 3-3: Troubleshooting a Configuration Problem

As you are working on the Datacenter Edition server, you install a card to connect a set of RAID drives. After the card and drives are set up, you run the installation disc that accompanies the RAID drives and card. When you reboot the server, you get a message about problems with two .dll files. What has most likely happened and how can you fix it?

Case Project 3-4: Understanding the Registry

The Light Crafters IT staff has never worked with the Registry. Create a brief report or slide presentation for them to explain its contents. Also, they need to know how to access the tool used to edit the Registry.

Case Project 3-5: Following Microsoft Recommended Compliance for Server Roles

Light Crafters wants to be sure that all of the server roles on the two new servers are configured to be compliant with optimal operating practices as recommended by Microsoft, to reduce errors and to get off on the right footing for live operations. What tool can they use to achieve this goal and how is the tool started?

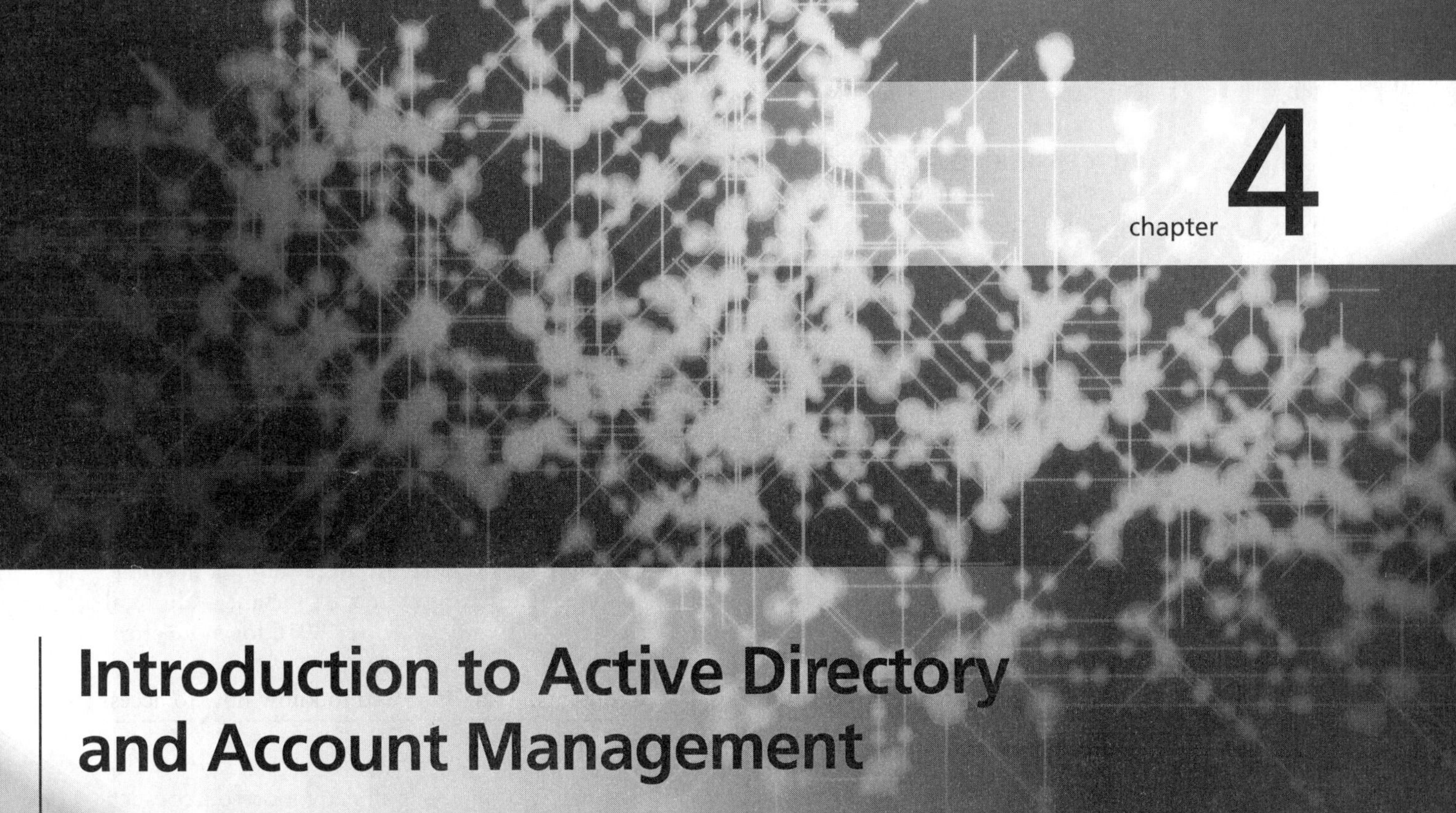

chapter 4

Introduction to Active Directory and Account Management

After reading this chapter and completing the exercises, you will be able to:

- Understand Active Directory basic concepts
- Install and configure Active Directory
- Implement Active Directory containers
- Understand Azure Active Directory
- Create and manage user accounts
- Configure and use security groups
- Understand user profiles
- Describe important additional features in Active Directory

Just as the central nervous system coordinates the activities of different parts of the human body, Active Directory coordinates servers, client computers, printers, shared files, and other resources in a Windows Server 2016 network. In addition to coordinating activities, Active Directory secures network resources. Active Directory accomplishes these tasks by providing a hierarchy of management elements that enable you to organize resources, control who accesses them, and advertise their existence—making the lives of users easier. Knowledge of Active Directory is invaluable to you as an administrator because it enables you to capably orchestrate your network.

In this chapter you learn the basics of Active Directory, including Active Directory elements such as the schema and global catalog. You also learn how to install Active Directory. Once Active Directory is installed, you learn how to set up and use containers, including forests, trees, domains, organizational units, and sites. You also become familiar with delegating control over containers to fit the management structure of your organization. You learn how Microsoft Azure Directory can be used for cloud-based implementations. Also, you learn to set up user accounts and security groups to manage access to resources. Finally, you review important additional Active Directory features that are new or relatively new to Windows Server 2016 for more effective management, such as Read-Only Domain Controllers.

Active Directory Basics

Active Directory is a **directory service** that houses information about all network resources such as servers, printers, user accounts, groups of user accounts, security policies, and other information. As a directory service, Active Directory (also referred to as Active Directory Domain Services or AD DS in this chapter) is responsible for providing a central listing of resources and ways to quickly find and access specific resources and for providing a way to manage network resources.

Windows Server 2016 uses Active Directory to manage accounts, groups, and many more network management services. Writable copies of information in Active Directory are contained in one or more **domain controllers (DCs)**, which are servers that have the AD DS server role installed. Servers on a network managed by Active Directory that do not have Active Directory installed are called **member servers** (and are not domain controllers).

Microsoft recommends that at least two DCs should be present in any organization using Active Directory. This ensures that if one DC goes down, the other is still available to service user account requests to sign in and access resources.

In Active Directory, a domain is a fundamental component or container that holds information about all network resources that are grouped within it—servers, printers, and other physical resources, users, and user groups. A domain usually is a higher-level representation of how a business, government, or school is organized, for example, reflecting a geographical location or major division of that organization. Every resource is called an **object** and is associated with a domain (see Figure 4-1). When you set up a new user account or a network printer, for instance, it becomes an object within a domain.

In Windows Server 2016, each DC is equal to every other DC in that it contains the full range of information that composes Active Directory. If information on one DC changes, such as the creation of an account, it is replicated to all other DCs in a process called **multimaster replication**. The advantage of this approach is that if one DC fails, Active Directory is fully intact on all other DCs, and there is no visible network interruption.

In Windows Server 2016, you can set replication of Active Directory information to occur at a preset interval instead of as soon as an update occurs. Also, you can determine how much of Active Directory is replicated each time it is copied from one DC to another. Active Directory is built to make replication efficient so that it transports as little as possible over a network, saving network resources. For example, Active Directory in Windows Server 2016 can:

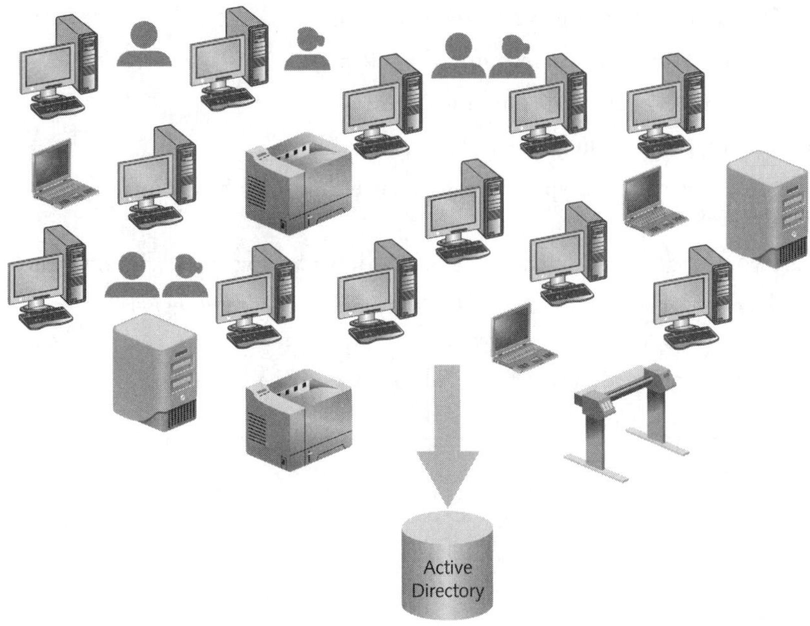

Figure 4-1 Active Directory domain objects include servers, workstations, printers, users, user groups, and other resources

- Replicate individual properties instead of entire accounts, which means that a single property can be changed without replicating information for the whole account.
- Replicate Active Directory on the basis of the speed of the network link, such as replicating more frequently over a local area network link than over a wide area network link.

Three general concepts are important as a starting place for understanding Active Directory: schema, global catalog, and namespace. These concepts are described in the next sections.

Some steps in the activities in this book include bulleted questions for you to answer. Additionally, for all of the activities in this chapter, you'll need an account with Administrator privileges. These activities can be completed on a virtual machine or computer, such as in Hyper-V.

Activity 4-1: Installing Active Directory

Time Required: Approximately 20–30 minutes
Objective: Install Active Directory.

Description: To make a Windows Server 2016 server a domain controller, you must install the Active Directory Domain Services role. In this activity, you learn how to install the role. You'll need to sign in to Windows Server 2016 as Administrator, and a DNS server should already be set up on your network. Before you begin, consult with your instructor about what domain name to use. Additionally, make sure that all other programs and windows are closed before you start (because the computer will reboot when you finish the installation).

For the activities in this book, use a domain name that will not be used beyond your test environment. Some instructors prefer to use *.test* in the domain name to show it is not intended for a production environment. The example in this activity uses *.com* but is intended only for the practice activities in this book.

1. Open **Server Manager**, if it is not already open.
2. Ensure that **Dashboard** is selected in the left pane.
3. In the right pane, click **Add roles and features**.
4. If you see the Before you begin window, click **Next**.
5. In the Select installation type window, ensure that **Role-based or feature-based installation** is selected. Click **Next**.
6. Be sure your server is selected in the Select destination server window. Click **Next**.
7. Click the box for **Active Directory Domain Services** (see Figure 4-2).
8. In the Add Roles and Features Wizard dialog box, notice the tools to be installed with the Active Directory installation. Click **Add Features** (see Figure 4-3).

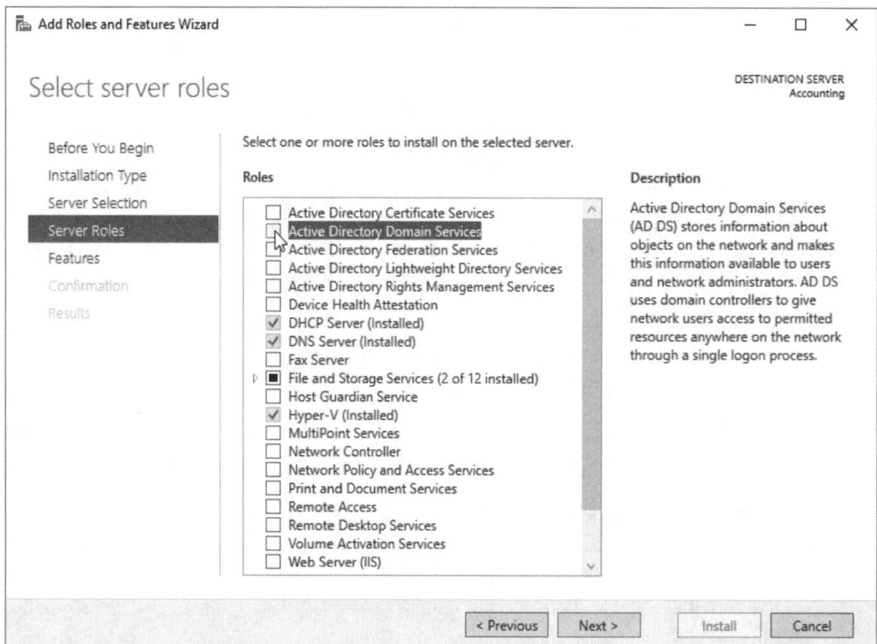

Figure 4-2 Selecting the Active Directory Domain Services role

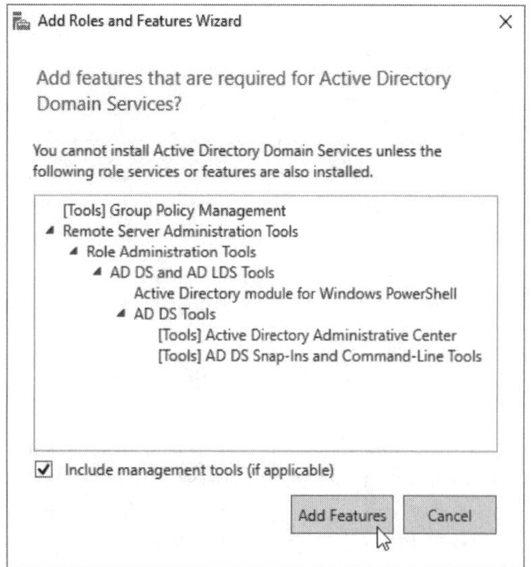

Figure 4-3 Add Roles and Features Wizard dialog box

9. Make sure the box for **Active Directory Domain Services** is checked and click **Next.**
10. Click **Next** in the Select features window.
11. Read the information about Active Directory Domain Services.
    - How many domain controllers are recommended as a minimum for a single domain?
12. Click **Next.**
13. In the Confirm installation selections window, click **Install.**
14. Wait a few minutes until the installation is completed.
15. Review the information in the Installation progress window, which also shows whether the installation succeeded (see Figure 4-4).

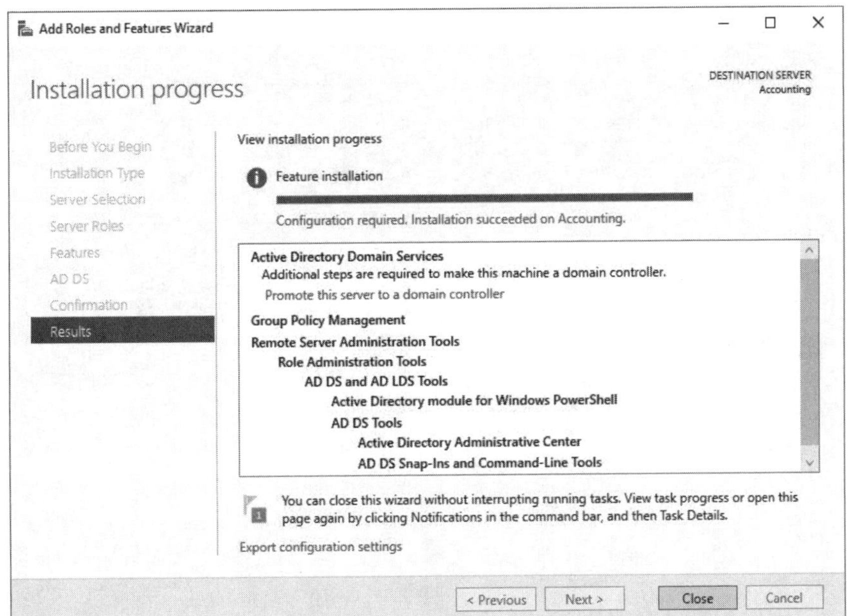

Figure 4-4 Active Directory installation results shown in the Installation progress window

16. Click **Close.**
17. After the Active Directory Domain Services role is installed, you need to promote the server to a domain controller and configure the AD DS role. Return to **Server Manager.** Notice there is an exclamation point inside a yellow caution symbol to the left of Manage just under the title bar in Server Manager. Click the **exclamation point** and then click **Promote this server to a domain controller** (see Figure 4-5). The Active Directory Domain Services Configuration Wizard opens.
18. Select **Add a new forest.** Enter a root domain name, such as *jpcomp.com* (where *jp* are your initials), and click **Next** (see Figure 4-6).
19. Click the **Forest functional level** drop-down list arrow. Notice that you can select from different forest functional levels: Windows Server 2008, Windows Server 2008 R2, Windows Server 2012, Windows Server 2012 R2, and Windows Server 2016. For this activity, select **Windows Server 2016,** unless your instructor specifies otherwise (you learn more about forest functional levels in the section, Forest). Ensure that the Domain functional level box also is selected for **Windows Server 2016.**
20. Enter a password for the Directory Services Restore Mode (DSRM), which is used to restore Active Directory, if needed. Confirm the password and click **Next.**

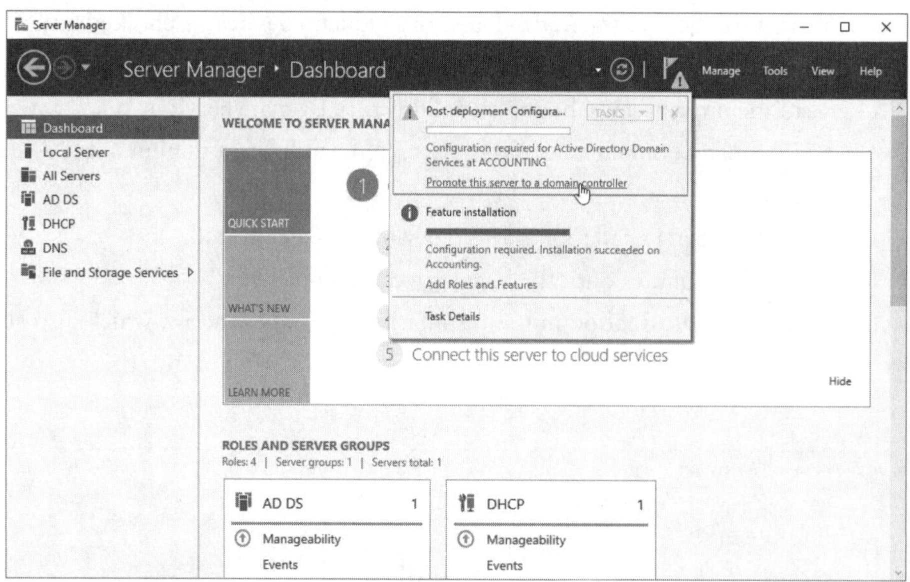

Figure 4-5 Configuring Active Directory Domain Services through Server Manager

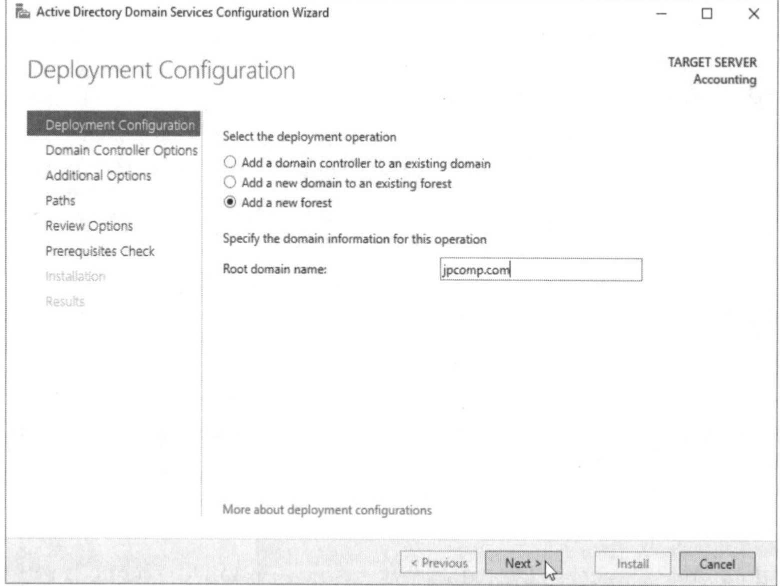

Figure 4-6 Adding a new forest and root domain

21. If you see a warning that *A delegation for this DNS server cannot be created because the authoritative parent zone cannot be found*, make a note to manually configure a delegation to the DNS server so this can be done by you or an instructor later. (You learn about configuring DNS in Chapter 8, Managing Windows Server 2016 Network Services.) If necessary, click **OK** in the DNS Options box (you may need to click the warning in the DNS Options window if it is in a yellow ribbon across the window and then click **OK** in the DNS Option box). Click **Next** in the DNS Options window.
22. In the Additional Options window, verify the NetBIOS name, such as JPCOMP and click **Next**.
23. In the Paths window leave the database, log files, and SYSVOL folder paths as the defaults.
    - Record the location of the database, log files, and SYSVOL folders.
24. Click **Next** in the Paths window.
25. Review the selections you have made (see Figure 4-7) and click **Next**.

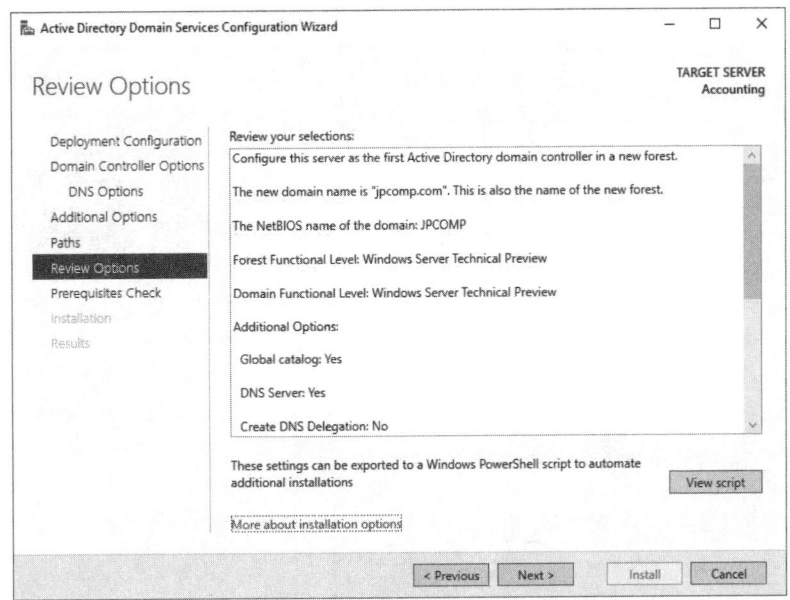

Figure 4-7 Reviewing the options selected for Active Directory Services configuration

26. The wizard performs a prerequisites check to verify your configuration for what Microsoft calls best practices. For example, if the server is not connected to a network, an error message is shown and the installation process is stopped until this is resolved. If the server does not have a static IP address, the prerequisites check shows a warning. Also, you may see a warning that the delegation for a DNS server cannot be created, if the DNS server installed is not fully configured. If you see warnings, you can continue to install Active Directory and make a note to fix problems associated with the warnings later, if necessary. If you see an error, you cannot continue with the Active Directory Domain Services installation until the error is corrected.
27. Click **Install**. It will take a few minutes for the installation process to complete. The Installation window will again review any warnings.
28. Click **Close** and wait for the computer to reboot.
29. Sign in after the computer has rebooted.

Schema

The Active Directory **schema** defines the objects and the information pertaining to those objects that can be stored in Active Directory. Each kind of object in Active Directory is defined through the schema, which is like a small database of information associated with that object, including the object class and its attributes. Schema information for objects in a domain is replicated on every DC. To help you understand a schema, consider the characteristics associated with a vehicle. First, there are different classes of vehicles, including automobiles, trucks, tractors, and motorcycles. Further, each class has a set of attributes. For automobiles, those attributes include engine, headlights, seats, steering wheel, dashboard, wheels, windshield, audio system, cup holder, and many others. Some of those attributes must be present in every automobile, such as an engine and wheels. Other attributes are optional—whether there is a CD player, Bluetooth communications, or heated seats, for instance.

A user account is one class of object in Active Directory that is defined through schema elements unique to that class. The user account class as a whole has the following schema characteristics (see Figure 4-8):

- A unique object name
- A **globally unique identifier** (GUID), which is a unique number associated with the object name

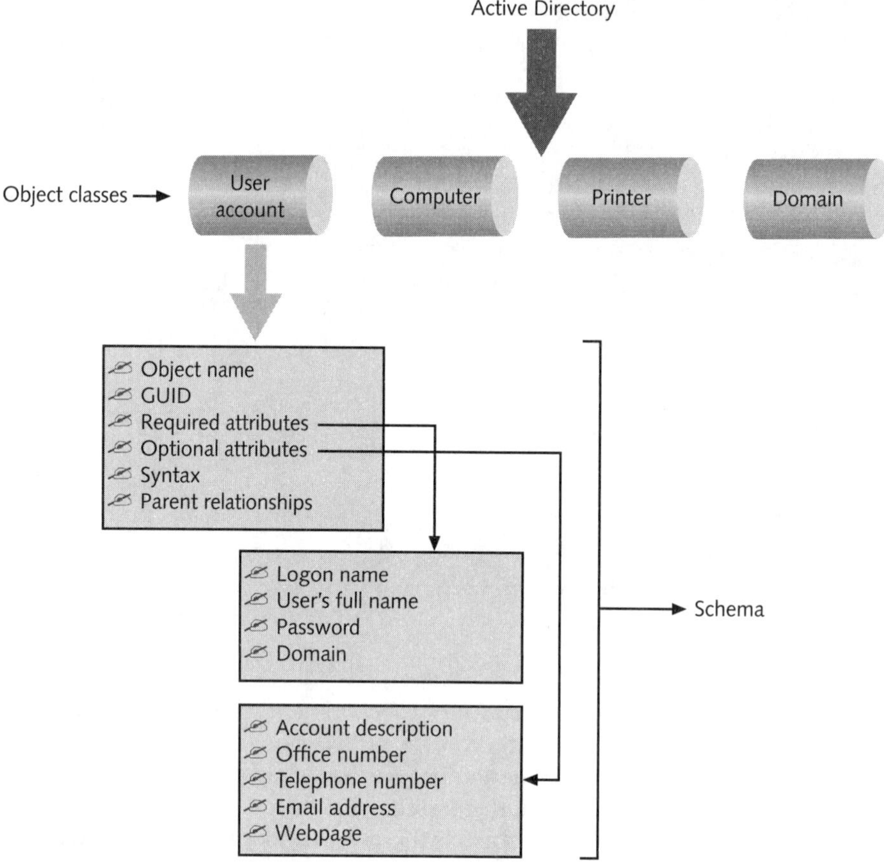

Figure 4-8 Sample schema information for user accounts

- Required attributes (those that must be defined with each object)
- Optional attributes (those that are optionally defined)
- A syntax (format) to determine how attributes are defined
- Pointers to parent entities, such as to a parent domain

Examples of required user account attributes that must be defined for each account are:

- Sign-in name
- User's full name
- Password
- Domain

Optional attributes for a user account include:

- Account description
- Account holder's office number or address
- Account holder's telephone number
- Account holder's email address
- Webpage

Providing an account description or specifying if the account holder has a webpage are examples of optional attributes that do not have to be completed when you create an account. In some instances, the attributes that are required and those that are optional can be influenced by the security policies that the server administrator sets in Active Directory for a class of objects (see Chapter 10, Securing Windows Server 2016 for more about security policies). This is true, for example, with account password restrictions because it is possible (but not recommended) for you to have a security policy that does not require account password restrictions.

Each attribute is automatically given a version number and date when it is created or changed. This information enables Active Directory to know when an attribute value, such as a password, is changed and update only that value on all DCs. When you install Windows Server 2016 for the first time on a network server, designating it as a domain controller, you also create several object classes automatically. The default object classes include domain, user account, group, shared drive, shared folder, computer, and printer.

Global Catalog

The **global catalog** stores information about every object within a forest (you learn more about forests later in this chapter). The first DC configured in a forest becomes the global catalog server. The global catalog server will store a full replica of every object within its own domain and a partial replica of each object within every domain in the forest. The partial replica for each object contains those attributes most commonly used to search for objects. The global catalog serves the following purposes:

- Serving as the central storehouse of key object information in a forest that has multiple domains
- Providing lookup and access to all resources in all domains
- Providing replication of key Active Directory elements
- Keeping a copy of the most-used attributes for each object for quick access

The global catalog server enables forest-wide searches of data. Because it contains attributes pertaining to every object within a forest, users can query this server to locate an object, as opposed to having to perform an extensive search. The global catalog server also can be used for network sign-ins. When a user signs in to the network, the global catalog server is contacted for universal group membership information pertaining to the user's account (universal groups are discussed in this chapter in the section, Implementing Universal Groups). In a Windows 2000 domain, if the global catalog was unavailable, the user could only sign in to the local computer. In Windows Server 2003 to Server 2016, if the global catalog is unavailable for group membership information, the user can sign in to the network with cached credentials.

Cached credential means that a record is kept in server cache if a user has successfully signed in previously. Thus, authentication when the user signs out and then signs in again can be performed by checking the cached credentials, instead of the global catalog. However, when a user is signing in for the first time and there is no cached credential for that user, if the global catalog is unavailable, access is provided only to the local computer.

By default, the first DC in the forest is automatically designated as the global catalog server. You have the option of configuring another DC to be a global catalog server as well as designating multiple DCs as global catalog servers.

There must be at least one global catalog server in a forest. Also, in most cases it makes sense to place one global catalog server in every site (you learn about sites in the section of this chapter called "Sites"). If you use email servers, such as for Microsoft Exchange, consider having one global catalog server for every four mailbox servers. Global catalog servers can create quite a lot of traffic, so configuring every DC to be a global catalog server is generally too much.

Namespace

Active Directory uses Domain Name System (DNS), which means there must be a DNS server on the network that Active Directory can access. As you learned in Chapter 1, Introduction to Windows Server 2016, DNS is a TCP/IP-based name service that converts computer and domain host names to dotted decimal addresses and vice versa, through a process called **name resolution**. A computer running Windows Server 2016 can be set up to act as a DNS server on a network. For example, when a Windows 10 client sends a TCP/IP-based request to connect to a specific server on the same network, such as a server named Research, a DNS server on the network can be used to translate Research into its dotted decimal address, 142.78.14.4.

A DNS server does more than provide name resolution. It also provides services such as registration of hosts, contains service (SRV) records to identify servers providing particular TCP/IP services, enables transfers of DNS information for redundancy, and provides other services. You learn more about DNS servers in Chapter 8, Managing Windows Server 2016 Network Services.

A **namespace** is a logical area on a network that contains directory services and named objects and that has the ability to perform name resolution. Active Directory depends on one or more DNS servers to resolve names in a designated logical DNS namespace. Within Active Directory is another namespace that contains named objects, such as accounts and printers, but which Active Directory coordinates with information in the DNS namespace. Both namespaces (DNS and Active Directory) can be on a single computer, such as a Windows Server 2016 server set up as a DC and a DNS server in a small network. Or, they can be distributed across several servers on a large network, which might have 2 servers set up as DNS servers and 22 servers set up as DCs.

Active Directory employs two kinds of namespaces: contiguous and disjointed. A **contiguous namespace** is one in which every child object contains the name of the parent object, such as in the example of the child object *msdn.microsoft.com* and its parent object *microsoft.com*. When the child name does not resemble the name of its parent object, this is called a **disjointed namespace**, such as when the parent for a university is *uni.edu* and a child is *bio.ethicsresearch.com*.

Containers in Active Directory

Active Directory has a treelike structure that is similar to the hierarchy of folders and subfolders in a directory structure. For example, in a directory structure, information is stored in a root folder, which is at the highest level. The root folder may contain several main folders, 15 or 20, for instance. Under each folder are subfolders, and within subfolders there can be more subfolders. Subfolders can have a nearly infinite depth, but typically do not go more than five or ten layers deep. Just as files are the basic elements that are grouped in a hierarchy of folders and subfolders, objects are the basic elements of Active Directory and are grouped in a hierarchy of larger containers. Also, just as the folder structure affects how you can set up security on a server, Active Directory structure affects how you can manage security in an enterprise. The hierarchical elements, or **containers**, of Active Directory include forests, trees, domains, organizational units (OUs), and sites (see Figure 4-9).

Forest

At the highest level in an Active Directory design is the **forest**. A forest consists of one or more Active Directory trees that are in a common relationship and that have the following characteristics:

- The trees can use a disjointed namespace.
- All trees use the same schema.
- All trees use the same global catalog.
- Domains enable administration of commonly associated objects, such as accounts and other resources, within a forest.
- Two-way transitive trusts (resources shared equally) are automatically configured between domains within a single forest.

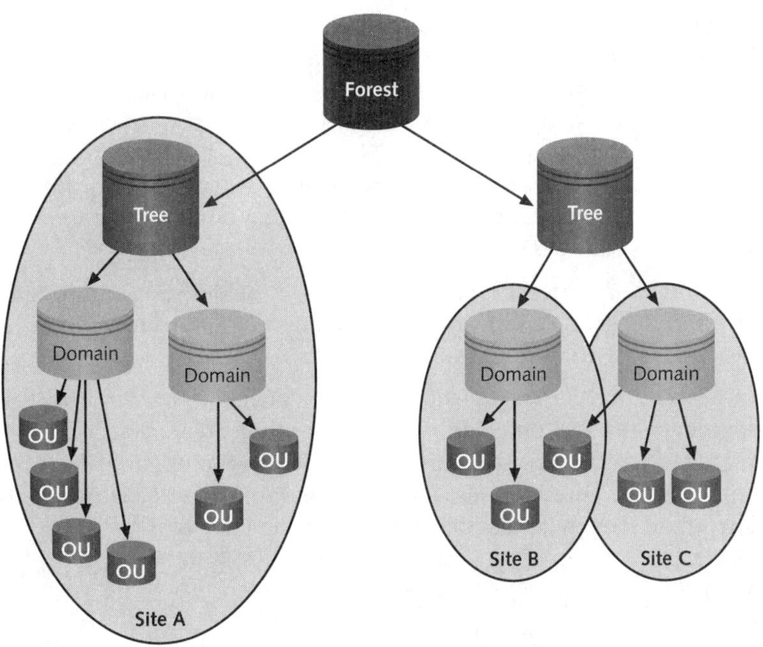

Figure 4-9 Active Directory hierarchical containers

A forest provides a means to relate trees that use a contiguous namespace in domains within each tree but that have disjointed namespaces in relationship to each other. Consider, for example, an international automotive parts company that is really a conglomerate of separate companies, each having a different brand name. The parent company is PartsPlus, located in Toronto. PartsPlus manufactures alternators, coils, and other electrical parts at plants in Toronto, Montreal, and Detroit and has a tree structure for domains that are part of partsplus.com. Another company owned by PartsPlus, Marty and Mike's (2m.com), makes radiators in two South Carolina cities, Florence and Greenville, and radiator fluid in Atlanta. A third member company, Chelos (chelos.com), makes engine parts and starters in Mexico City, Corsica, Monterrey, and Puebla, all in Mexico—and also has a manufacturing site in Valencia, Venezuela. In this situation, it makes sense to have a contiguous tree structure for each of the three related companies and to join the trees in a forest of disjointed namespaces, as shown in Figure 4-10.

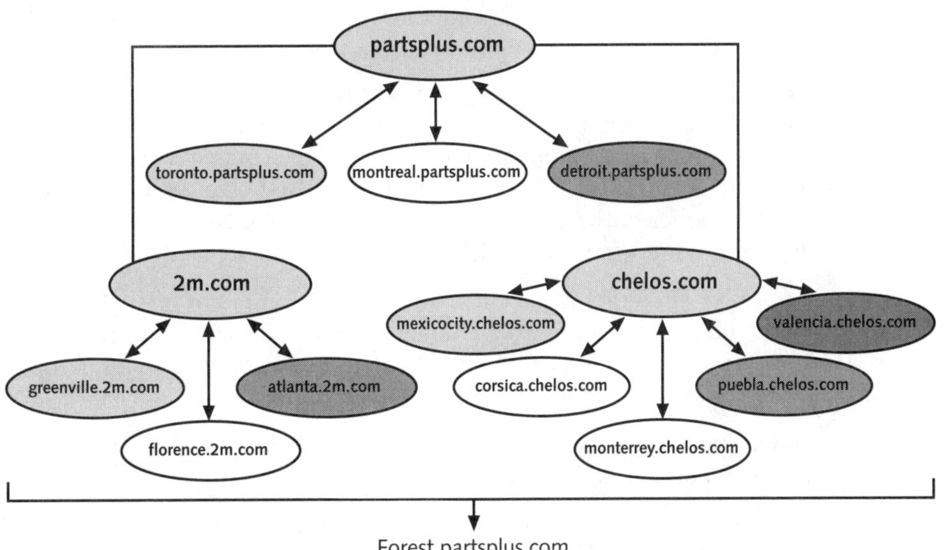

Figure 4-10 Forest partsplus.com

The advantage of joining trees into a forest is that all domains share the same schema and global catalog. A schema is set up in the root domain, which is partsplus.com in our example, and the root domain is home to the master schema server. At least one DC functions as a global catalog server, but in our example, it is likely that you would plan to have a global catalog server located at each geographic location.

Windows Server 2016 Active Directory recognizes several types of forest functional levels. The **forest functional level** refers to the Active Directory functions supported forest-wide. The functional levels are as follows:

- *Windows 2000 Native Forest Functional Level*—Provides support for basic AD capabilities including universal groups, security ID history, nesting of groups, and the ability to convert security groups to distribution groups and vice versa.
- *Windows Server 2003 Forest Functional Level*—Intended for Windows Server 2003 and above domain controllers only and enables more forest management functions, such as more options for creating trust relationships between forests, domain renaming, enhanced replication of Active Directory, last logon timestamp, and selective authentication. (You'll learn more about trust relationships in the next section.)
- *Windows Server 2008 Forest Functional Level*—Intended for forests containing Windows Server 2008 domain controllers and above. Besides the features in Server 2000 and Server 2003, Windows Server 2008 includes features such as support for Distributed File Replication (DFS) and other DFS enhancement support, expanded information for last sign-in for each user, Read-Only Domain Controllers, fine-grained password policies, and Personal Virtual Desktop support.
- *Windows Server 2008 R2 Forest Functional Level*—Intended for forests containing Windows Server 2008 R2 and above domain controllers. It includes all of the AD features of Windows Server 2008 plus newer features such as information about the sign in method used (such as for a card or the regular account sign-in method) and expanded DNS service capabilities.
- *Windows Server 2012 Forest Functional Level*—Intended for forests with Windows Server 2012 domain controllers and above. This forest functional level has new features such as key distribution center (KDC) support, which provides greater security for the exchange of encryption keys between client and server, when the client requests use of a specific server service. Also, this functional level expands on Kerberos security (see Chapter 10 for more information about Kerberos—Kerberos is a security system used for modern network communications encryption).
- *Windows Server 2012 R2 Forest Functional Level*—Intended for forests containing Windows Server 2012 R2 and above domain controllers. This functional level includes features for the new protected users security group (discussed later in this chapter), which was introduced with Windows Server 2012 R2. Other new features include enhanced authentication policies to control which client computers an account can use to access domain resources.
- *Windows Server 2016 Forest Functional Level*—Intended for forests containing only Windows Server 2016 domain controllers. This functional level includes new features such as new authentication capabilities when using AD FS (Active Directory Federation Services; see Chapter 2, Installing Windows Server 2016) and changes so that old Network Access Protection policies are no longer stored or supported. Network Access Protection is eliminated from Windows Server 2012 R2 and Windows Server 2016.

After Active Directory is installed, an organization might later change or upgrade domain controllers, such as upgrading to all Windows Server 2016 servers. In this situation, it makes sense to raise the forest functional level to match the server operating systems in use. The general steps for raising the forest functional level are as follows:

1. In Server Manager, click Tools and click Active Directory Domains and Trusts (or click Start, click the Windows Administrative Tools folder, and click Active Directory Domains and Trusts).
2. In the tree in the left pane, right-click Active Directory Domains and Trusts (*server and domain name*).
3. Click Raise Forest Functional Level (see Figure 4-11).

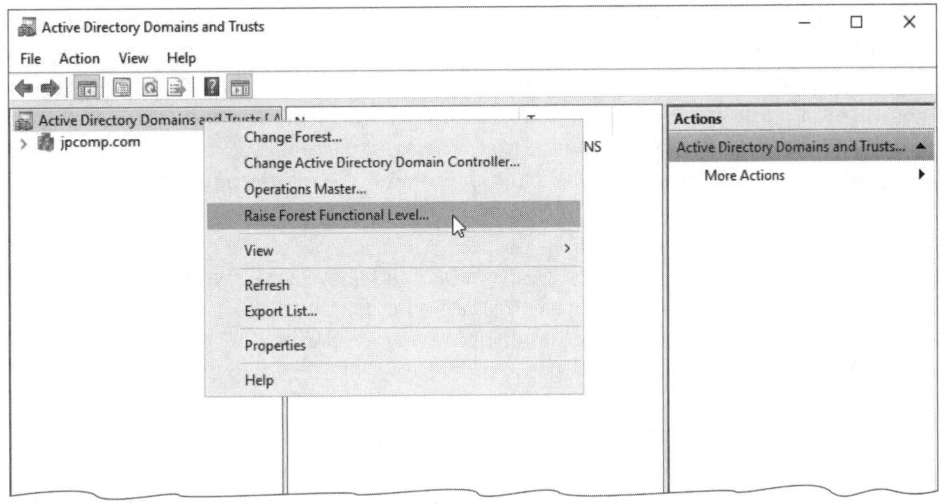

Figure 4-11 Raising the forest functional level

4. Select a functional level. (The options depend on which functional level is currently set. You cannot roll back to a lower functional level. If no options are displayed, this is because you are currently in the Windows Server 2016 forest functional level and all you can do is click OK and go to Step 8.)
5. Select the appropriate forest functional level and click Raise.
6. Read the message box and click OK.
7. Read the acknowledgement box and click OK.
8. Close the Active Directory Domains and Trusts window.

Tree

A **tree** contains one or more domains that are in a common relationship and has the following characteristics:

- Domains are represented in a contiguous namespace and can be in a hierarchy.
- Two-way trust relationships exist between parent domains and child domains, essentially creating a trust path.
- All domains in a single tree use the same schema for all types of common objects.
- All domains use the same global catalog.

The domains in a tree typically have a hierarchical structure, such as a root domain at the top and other domains under the root (similar to a parent-child relationship). Using tracksport.org as an example, tracksport.org might be the root domain and have four domains under the root to form one tree: east.tracksport.org, west.tracksport.org, north.tracksport.org, and south.tracksport.org, as shown in Figure 4-12. These domains use the contiguous namespace format in that the child domains each inherit a portion of their namespace from the parent domain.

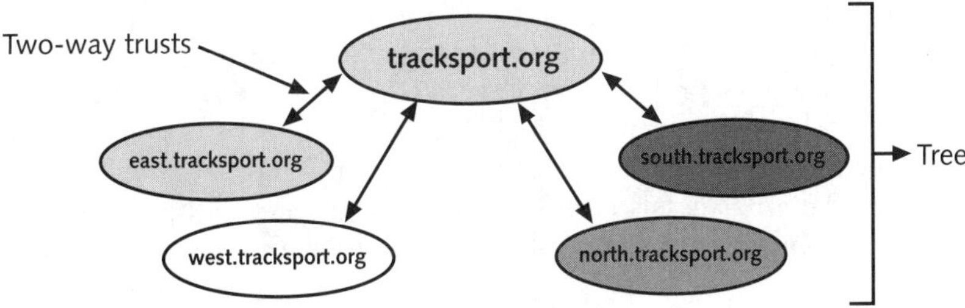

Figure 4-12 Tree with hierarchical domains

The domains within a tree are in what is called a **Kerberos transitive trust relationship**, which consists of **two-way trusts** between parent domains and child domains (see Figure 4-12). A **transitive trust** means that if A and B have a trust and B and C have a trust, A and C automatically have a trust as well. In a two-way trust, each domain is trusting and trusted. A trusted domain is one that is granted access to resources, whereas a trusting domain is the one granting access. In a two-way trust, members of each domain can have access to the resources of the other.

Windows Server 2003 and above server systems also have a forest trust. In a forest trust, a Kerberos transitive trust relationship exists between the root domains in Windows Server 2003 and above forests, resulting in trust relationships between all domains in the forests.

Because of the trust relationship between parent and child domains, any one domain can have access to the resources of all others. The security in the two-way trust relationships is based on Kerberos techniques, using a combination of protocol-based and encryption-based security techniques between clients and servers. A new domain joining a tree has an instant trust relationship with all other member domains through the trust relationship that is established with its parent domain, which makes all objects in the other domains available to the new one.

All domains within a single tree (as well as all trees in single forest) share the same schema defining all the object types that can be stored within Active Directory. Further, all domains in a tree also share the same global catalog and a portion of their namespace. In addition, a child domain contains part of the name of the parent domain.

Domain

Microsoft views a domain as a logical partition within an Active Directory forest. A domain is a grouping of objects that typically exists as a primary container within Active Directory. The basic functions of a domain are as follows:

- To provide an Active Directory "partition" in which to house objects, such as accounts and groups, that have a common relationship, particularly in terms of management and security
- To establish a set of information to be replicated from one DC to another
- To expedite management of a set of objects

When you use the server-based networking model described in Chapter 1 to verify users who sign in to the network, there is at least one domain. For example, if you are planning Active Directory for a small business of 34 employees who have workstations connected to a network that has one or two Windows Server 2016 servers, then one domain is sufficient for that business.

The domain functions as a partition within which to group all of the network resource objects consisting of servers, user accounts, shared printers, and shared folders and files.

In a midsized or large business, you might use more than one domain—for instance, when business units are separated by long distances and you want to limit the amount of DC replication over expensive wide area network links or to manage objects differently between locations, such as through different account or security policies. For example, consider a company that builds tractors in South Carolina and has a parts manufacturing division in Japan. Each site has a large enterprise network of Windows Server 2016 servers, and the sites are linked together in a wide area network by an expensive satellite connection. When you calculate the cost of replicating DCs over the satellite link, you cannot justify it in terms of the increased traffic that will delay other vital daily business communications. In this situation, it makes sense to create two separate domains, one for each site, as shown in Figure 4-13.

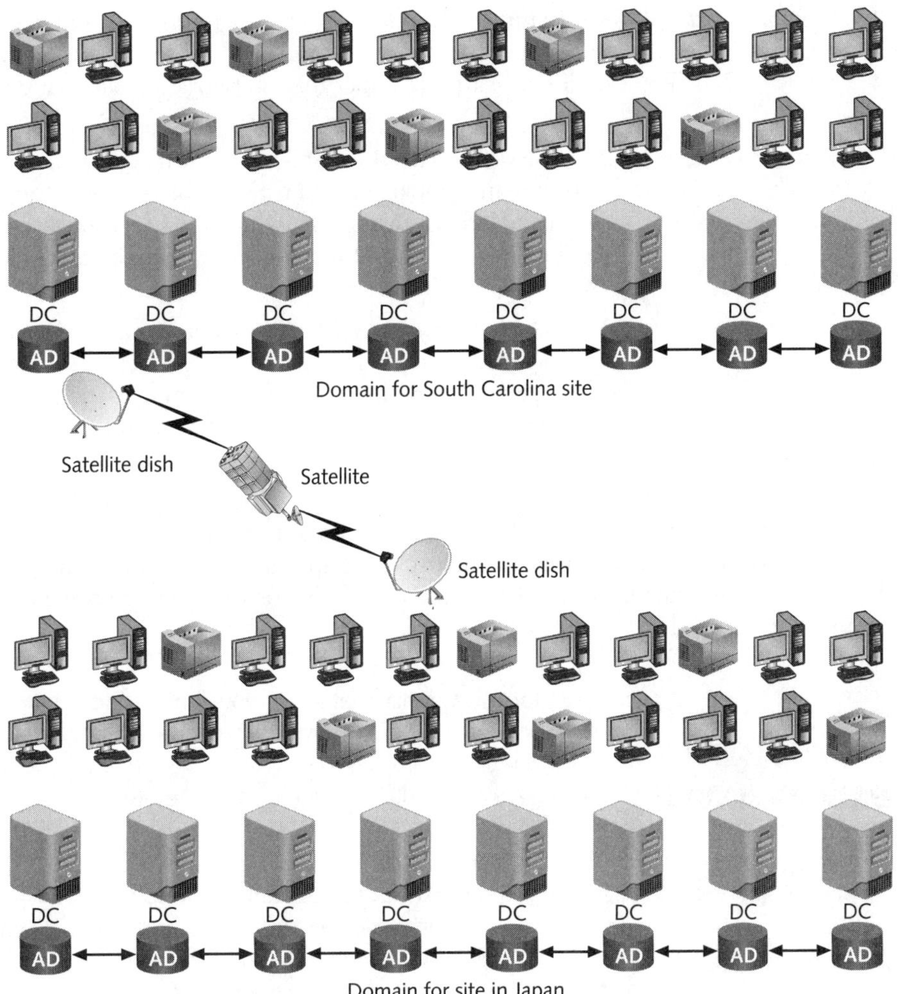

Figure 4-13 Using multiple domains

Windows Server 2016 Active Directory recognizes several **domain functional levels,** which refers to the Windows Server operating systems on domain controllers and the domain-specific functions they support. The domain functional levels are as follows:

- *Windows 2000 Native Domain Functional Level*—Provides Active Directory functions compatible with a network that has a combination of Windows 2000 Server through Windows Server 2016 domain controllers. This level supports universal groups, converting types of groups, and nesting groups (see the section in this chapter, "Security Group Management").
- *Windows Server 2003 Domain Functional Level*—Intended for a combination of Windows Server 2003 through Server 2016 domain controllers and enables more domain management functions, such as delegating management of Active Directory objects, time stamps for sign-ins, use of Authorization Manager policies in Active Directory, use of the Netdom.exe domain management tool, and other features not available in Windows 2000 Server domain controllers.
- *Windows Server 2008 Domain Functional Level*—Contains a combination of Windows Server 2008 through Server 2016 domain controllers and offers new features such as default incorporation of the Distributed File System (with better security), Advanced Encryption Standard (AES) security for Kerberos authentication, and enhanced user account password policies.

- *Windows Server 2008 R2 Domain Functional Level*—Contains a combination of Windows Server 2008 R2 through Server 2016 domain controllers and supports **Service Principal Name (SPN)**. SPN is an identification number for a network service that employs Kerberos security.
- *Windows Server 2012 Domain Functional Level*—Contains a combination of Windows Server 2012–Server 2016 domain controllers and offers **Flexible Authentication Secure Tunneling (FAST)**, also called **Kerberos armoring**, which creates a secure channel or tunnel between a client seeking authentication for a computer service and the server providing secure access keys for secure communications.
- *Windows Server 2012 R2 Domain Functional Level*—Contains a combination of Windows Server 2012 R2 through Server 2016 domain controllers and includes new cipher suites for Kerberos security. A cipher suite is a combination of different encryption techniques and encryption key programs for authenticating clients and services on a network.
- *Windows Server 2016 Domain Functional Level*—Intended for a domain that contains only Windows Server 2016 domain controllers. Windows Server 2016 adds even more authentication features to secure client and server communications. As mentioned for the Windows Server 2016 forest functional level, it is also important to remember that the Windows Server 2016 domain functional level does not support Network Access Protection, which is available in earlier Windows Server versions.

As is true for forest functional levels, you cannot go back to an earlier domain functional level. For example, if you are at the Windows Server 2016 domain functional level, you cannot go back to the Windows Server 2012 R2 or Windows 2008 domain functional levels.

For both forest and domain functional levels, use the highest level possible so that you can take advantage of the most AD features. For example, if you know your forest or domain will only house Windows Server 2016 servers, then use the Windows Server 2016 functional level. However, if the forest or domain will house, for example, Windows Server 2016 and Windows Server 2008 R2 servers, then use the Windows Server 2008 R2 functional level. The bottom line is that you must set the functional level to the lowest version of Windows Server to be in the forest or domain. If you need the additional functions in a level that is higher, then consider upgrading the appropriate servers.

Activity 4-2: Managing Domains

Time Required: Approximately 10 minutes
Objective: Learn where to manage domains and domain trust relationships.

Description: After Active Directory is installed, you might need to customize the properties of a domain or its trust relationships. In this activity, you learn about the tool used to manage domains and trust relationships.

1. Open **Server Manager**, if it is not open, click **Tools**, and click **Active Directory Domains and Trusts.**
2. In the left pane, right-click the domain you created in the last project (or an existing domain).
3. Click **Properties.**
4. Click each of the **General, Trusts,** and **Managed By** tabs to view their contents (see Figure 4-14).
   - Make notes about their contents.
5. Click **Cancel.**

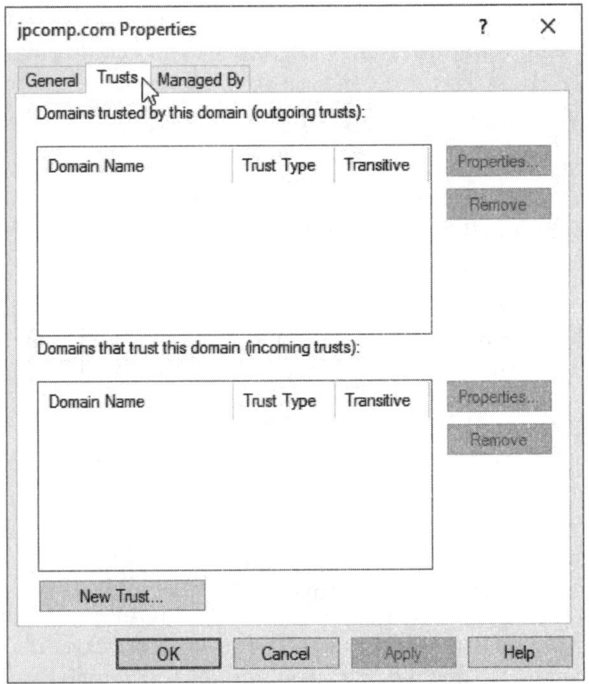

Figure 4-14 Viewing the Trusts tab

6. Right-click the domain again and click **Raise Domain Functional Level.** Notice that if you are currently at the Windows Server 2008 domain functional level, for example, you can raise to any of the levels for Windows Server 2008 R2, Windows Server 2012, Windows Server 2012 R2, or Windows Server 2016. If you are currently at the Windows Server 2012 domain functional level, you can raise to either the Windows Server 2012 R2 or Windows Server 2016 level. If you are at the Windows Server 2016 functional level, there are no options to implement a different functional level. You can only raise to a higher functional level; you cannot go back to a lower level. Depending on the options available to you, click either **Cancel** or **Close.**
7. Close the Active Directory Domains and Trusts window.

Organizational Unit

An **organizational unit** (**OU**) offers a way to achieve more flexibility in managing the resources associated with a business unit, department, or division than is possible through domain administration alone. An OU is a grouping of related objects within a domain, similar to the idea of having subfolders within a folder. OUs can be used to reflect the structure of the organization without having to completely restructure the domain(s) when that structure changes.

OUs allow the grouping of objects so that they can be administered using the same group policies, such as security and desktop setup. OUs also make it possible for server administration to be delegated or decentralized. For example, in a software company in which the employees are divided into 15 project teams, the user accounts, shared folders, shared printers, and other shared resources of each team can be defined as objects in separate OUs. There would be one domain for the entire company and 15 OUs within that domain, all defined in Active Directory. With this arrangement, folder objects can be defined to specific OUs for security, and the management of user accounts, account setup policies, and file and folder permissions (access privileges) can be delegated to each group leader (OU administrator).

OUs can be nested within OUs, as subfolders are nested in subfolders, so that you can create them several layers deep. In the grocery chain example, you might have one OU under the Retail OU for the Accounting Department, an OU under the Accounting OU for the Accounts Receivable Group, and an OU under Accounts Receivable for the cashiers—creating four layers of OUs. The problem with this approach is that creating OUs many layers deep can get as confusing as creating subfolders several layers deep. It is confusing for the server administrator to track layered OUs, and it is laborious for Active Directory to search through each layer.

When you plan to create OUs, keep three concerns in mind:

- Microsoft recommends that you limit OUs to 10 levels or fewer.
- Active Directory works more efficiently (using less CPU resources) when OUs are set up horizontally instead of vertically. Using the grocery chain example, it is more efficient to create the Accounting, Accounts Receivable, and Cashier OUs directly under the Retail OU, resulting in two levels instead of four.
- The creation of OUs involves more processing resources because each request through an OU (for example, to determine permissions on a folder) requires CPU time. When that request must go several layers deep through nested OUs, even more CPU time is needed.

Activity 4-3: Managing OUs

Time Required: Approximately 10 minutes

Objective: Create an OU and delegate control over it.

Description: One advantage of an OU is that it enables a server administrator to delegate some server management tasks, such as managing user accounts. For example, some organizations prefer to have OUs that reflect the department structure. In this way, user accounts for a particular department are created within an OU, and a department administrator who has authority over an OU can create and manage user accounts for her or his department within the OU. In this activity, you learn how to create an OU and delegate authority for account management within that OU.

1. In **Server Manager**, click **Tools**, and click **Active Directory Users and Computers.**
2. Right-click the top domain in the tree in the left pane, such as *jpcomp.com*, point to **New**, and click **Organizational Unit.**
3. Enter **SalesOU** and your initials, such as *SalesOUJP* (see Figure 4-15). Click **OK.**

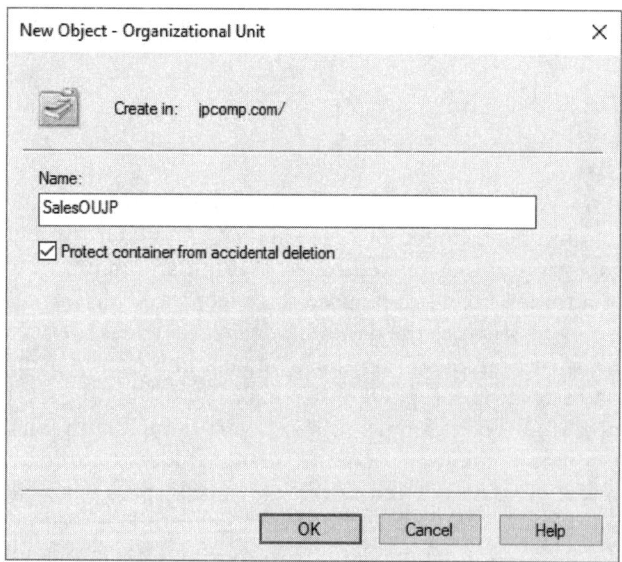

Figure 4-15 Creating an OU

4. Click the **arrow** in front of the domain in the left pane so that you can see the OU you created listed under the domain.
5. Right-click the OU, such as ***SalesOUJP***.
   - What options are available on the menu?

6. Click **Delegate Control.**
7. Click **Next** when the Delegation of Control Wizard starts.
8. Click **Add.**
9. Click the **Advanced** button.
10. Click **Find Now.**
11. Because you have not yet defined user accounts, click **Administrator** for this activity. Notice that names with a single head icon represent accounts and names with a double head icon represent groups of accounts. Click **OK.**
12. Click **OK** in the Select Users, Computers, or Groups dialog box.
13. Click **Next** in the Delegation of Control Wizard.
14. Click the box for **Create, delete, and manage user accounts,** as shown in Figure 4-16.

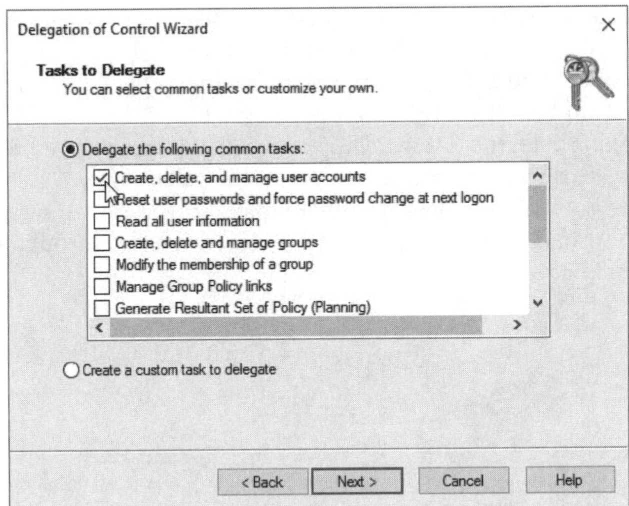

Figure 4-16 Delegating tasks for an OU

15. Click **Next.**
16. Review the tasks that you have completed and then click **Finish.**
17. Close the Active Directory Users and Computers window.

In addition to delegating control of an OU, it is possible to delegate control of a domain. Some large organizations, for example, have different server administrators manage different domains. You can delegate control over a domain by right-clicking the domain in the Active Directory Users and Computers window and clicking Delegate Control. Then, follow the instructions in the Delegation of Control Wizard.

Site

A **site** is a TCP/IP-based concept (container) within Active Directory that is linked to IP subnets and has the following functions:

- Reflects one or more interconnected subnets, usually having good network connectivity
- Reflects the physical aspect of the network
- Is used for DC replication
- Is used to enable a client to access the DC that is physically closest
- Is composed of only two types of objects, servers and configuration objects

Sites are based on connectivity and replication functions. You might think of sites as a way of grouping Active Directory objects by physical location so Active Directory can identify the fastest communications paths between clients and servers and between DCs. The physical representation of the network to Active Directory is accomplished by defining subnets that are interconnected. For this reason, one site may be contained within a single OU or a single domain, or a site may span multiple OUs and domains, depending on how subnets are set up. The most typical boundary for a site consists of the local area network topology and subnet boundaries rather than the OU and domain boundaries.

There are two important reasons to define a site. First, by defining site locations based on IP subnets, you enable a client to access network servers using the most efficient physical route. In the PartsPlus example (discussed in the Forest section), it is faster for a client in Toronto to be authenticated by a Toronto global catalog server than for the client to go through Detroit or Mexico City. Second, DC replication is most efficient when Active Directory has information about which DCs are in which locations.

Within a site, each DC replicates forest, tree, domain, and OU naming structures, configuration naming elements, such as computers and printers, and schema information. One advantage of creating a site is that it sets up redundant paths between DCs so that if one path is down, there is a second path that can be used for replication. This redundancy is in a logical ring format, which means that replication goes from DC to DC around a ring until each DC is replicated. If a DC is down along the main route, then Active Directory uses site information to send replication information in the opposite direction around the ring. Whenever a new DC is added or an old one removed, Active Directory reconfigures the ring to make sure there are two replication paths available from each DC. Also, between sites, replication is coordinated through one server, called a bridgehead server, located at each site (see Figure 4-17).

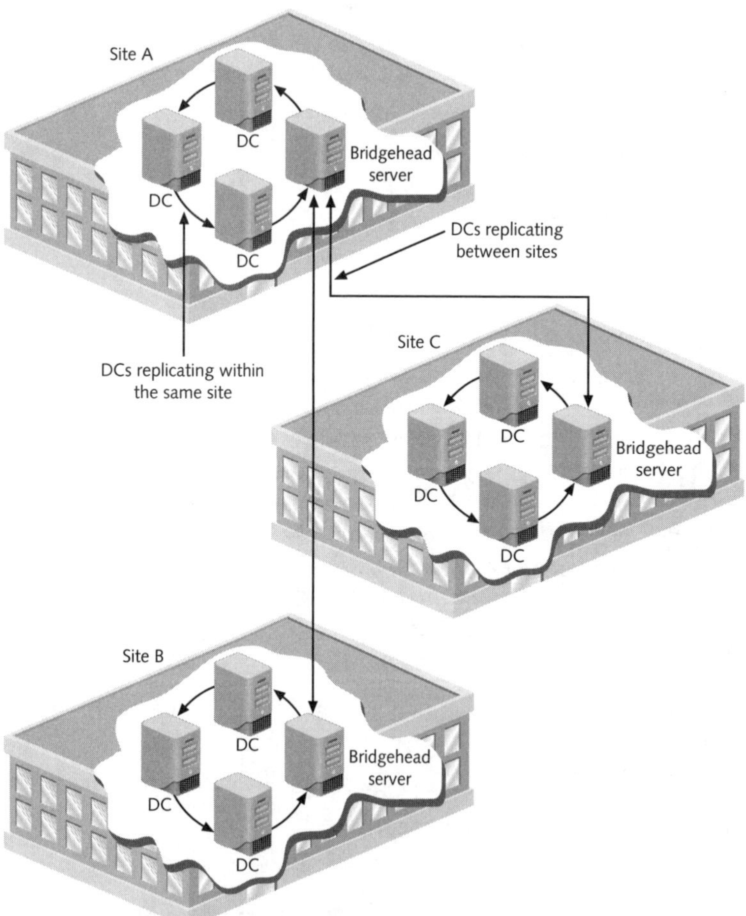

Figure 4-17 DCs replicating within and between sites

When you replicate between sites, the replication occurs only between two bridgehead servers. The **bridgehead server** is a DC that is designated to have the role of exchanging replication information. Only one bridgehead server is set up per site, so the network traffic per site is kept to a minimum. Otherwise, having multiple DCs replicating with partners across sites could take up considerable bandwidth.

Consider a state university network that might take advantage of sites. The university has three domains—students.uni.edu, faculty.uni.edu, and staffadmin.uni.edu—organized into a single tree. Also, the university has three campuses in different cities. The domains span each campus location. Thus students.uni.edu contains accounts and printers on DCs at all locations, for example. Each domain contains OUs that are appropriate to that domain. For instance, students.uni.edu has an OU for students at each campus—for a total of three OUs all at the same level. The campuses are relatively large with 7000 students, 10,000 students, and 18,000 students and have networks that are physically divided into subnets. In this situation, you can designate each campus network as a site in Active Directory, which enables it to find the fastest routes for traffic that is on-campus and for traffic that goes between campuses. For example, when a student signs in to students.uni.edu, Active Directory can help that student find the nearest DC and avoid the chance that the sign-in authentication is performed over a wide area network link at a different campus location. Another advantage is that the DC replication for each domain between sites (over wide area network links) can be set to occur less frequently than replication within a site.

Active Directory Guidelines

Planning the Active Directory structure of forests, trees, domains, OUs, and sites is a potentially complex process. The following guidelines summarize the most important aspects of the Active Directory planning process that you have learned in the previous sections for the forest, tree, domain, OU, and site containers:

- Above all, keep Active Directory as simple as possible and plan its structure before you implement it.
- Implement the least number of domains possible, with one domain being the ideal and building from there.
- Implement only one domain on most small networks.
- When you are planning for an organization that is likely to reorganize in the future, use OUs to reflect the organization's structure.
- Create only the number of OUs that are absolutely necessary.
- Do not build an Active Directory with more than 10 levels of OUs (optimally, no more than one or two levels).
- Use domains as partitions in forests to demarcate commonly associated accounts and resources governed by group and security policies.
- Implement multiple trees and forests only as necessary.
- Use sites in situations where there are multiple IP subnets and multiple geographic locations, as a means to improve sign-in and DC replication performance.

Azure Active Directory

Microsoft Azure Active Directory is an Active Directory service that an organization can use for online cloud applications, such as Office 365. Office 365 consists of office and productivity applications including Word (word processing), Excel (spreadsheets), PowerPoint (slide presentations), Outlook (email), Publisher (publishable documents), and OneNote (multiuser information gathering and collaboration). An organization can choose to subscribe to Office 365 for its users in the Microsoft cloud. **Cloud computing** involves providing a host of scalable web-based applications and services (including storage) over the Internet or a private network that are used by clients through web browsers and downloadable apps.

Microsoft Azure Active Directory provides user authorization and identity management for organizations that subscribe to Microsoft cloud services. For instance, when an organization subscribes to Office 365 for the organization's users to access, Microsoft Azure Active Directory is automatically used in the cloud to manage resources and user access to the resources in the cloud.

An organization can use Microsoft Azure Active Directory without having Active Directory installed on its own premises. For example, a small office of five architects might use Windows Server 2016 and share information through one or more workgroups and no domain—hence no Active Directory installation. This small office can subscribe to Office 365 and other Microsoft cloud applications and simply rely on Microsoft Azure Active Directory, which is used automatically when the architects sign up to be Office 365 in-the-cloud subscribers.

An organization that is larger, such as a law office of 28 attorneys and employees or a university of 15,000 students and employees, can implement Active Directory through one or more domains. In these contexts, the attorneys' office or university can set up to coordinate use of Active Directory on their premises with Microsoft Azure Active Directory in the Microsoft cloud. In this way, the organization's on-premises Active Directory can act as the local authority for providing authorization to the cloud applications and cloud storage. The on-premises users and groups are shared via the local on-premises Active Directory installation with Microsoft Azure Active Directory (see Figure 4-18).

The specifics of subscribing to Office 365 and other Microsoft cloud applications, as well as setting up synchronization between the on-premises Active Directory and Microsoft Azure

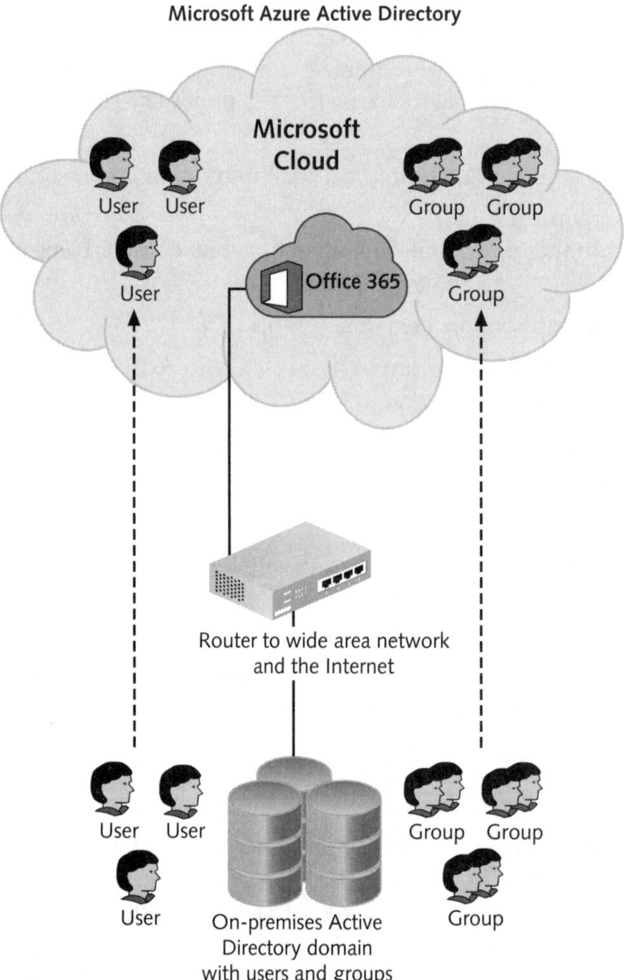

Figure 4-18 Using the on-premises Active Directory synchronized with Microsoft Azure Active Directory to access Office 365 in the cloud

Active Directory in the cloud, are beyond the scope of this book. However, Microsoft makes this process easy for you. All you really need to do is to go to the Microsoft Azure website, *azure.microsoft.com* and subscribe; or try out Azure for free.

User Account Management

Once Active Directory is installed and configured, you enable users to access network servers and resources through user accounts. Several accounts might be set up by default, depending on which Windows components you install, but including two primary accounts: Administrator and Guest (Guest is disabled as a security measure).

Accounts can be set up in two general environments:

- Accounts that are set up through a stand-alone server that does not have Active Directory installed
- Accounts that are set up in a domain when Active Directory is installed

When accounts are created in the domain through Active Directory, then those accounts can be used to access any server or resource in the domain.

Creating Accounts When Active Directory Is Not Installed

New accounts are created by first installing the Local Users and Groups MMC snap-in for stand-alone servers that do not use Active Directory. The general steps for creating a local user account on a server that is not a DC are as follows:

This example and the hands-on activities that appear later in this chapter use the Microsoft Management Console (MMC) so that you have the opportunity to become familiar with the MMC. The MMC uses snap-ins for specific server administration tools. The advantage of using the MMC is that you can customize which snap-ins are installed to match the way you work. Customized MMCs can be saved so that you can use them over and over, always with the option to further customize a specific MMC for your needs.

1. Right-click Start, click Run, enter mmc in the Open box, and click OK (see Figure 4-19). If you see the User Account Control box, click Yes to allow the app to make changes to your PC.

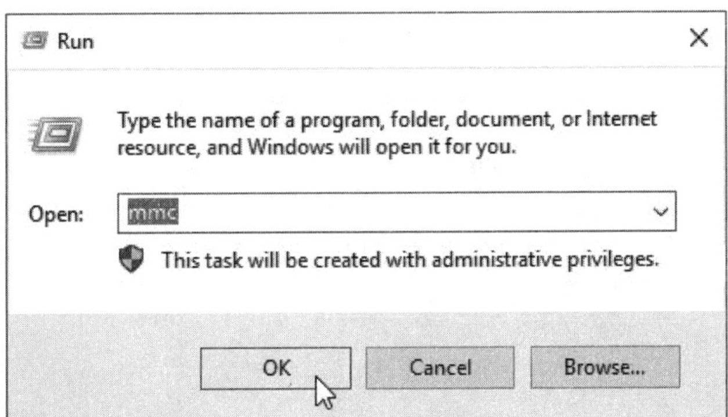

Figure 4-19 Entering *mmc* in the Open box

2. Click the File menu, and click Add/Remove Snap-in.
3. Under Available snap-ins, find and click Local Users and Groups, as shown in Figure 4-20.

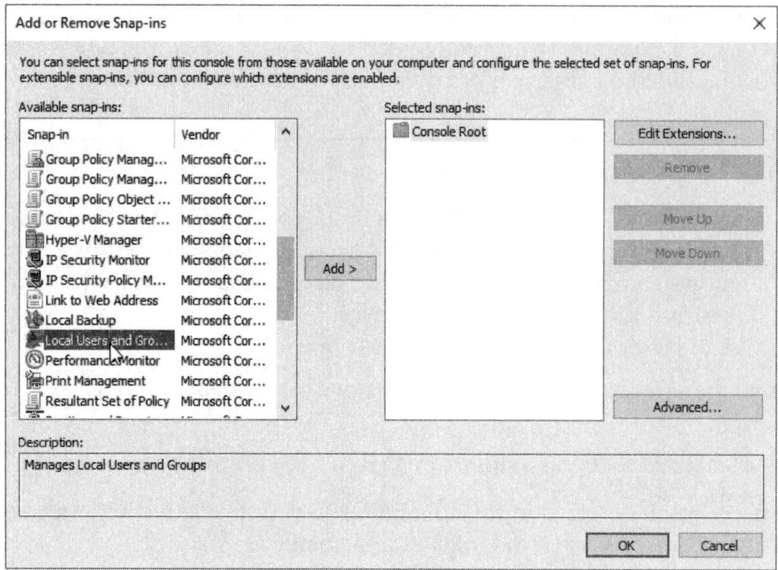

Figure 4-20 Selecting the Local Users and Groups mmc snap-in

4. Click the Add button to make this a selected snap-in.
5. In the Choose Target Machine dialog box, leave Local computer (the computer on which this console is running) selected and click Finish.
6. Click OK. Expand the console window, if necessary.
7. Double-click Local Users and Groups (Local) in the tree in the left pane.
8. Click the Users folder in the tree and then click the Action menu.
9. Click New User and complete the information to create the user account, as shown in Figure 4-21.

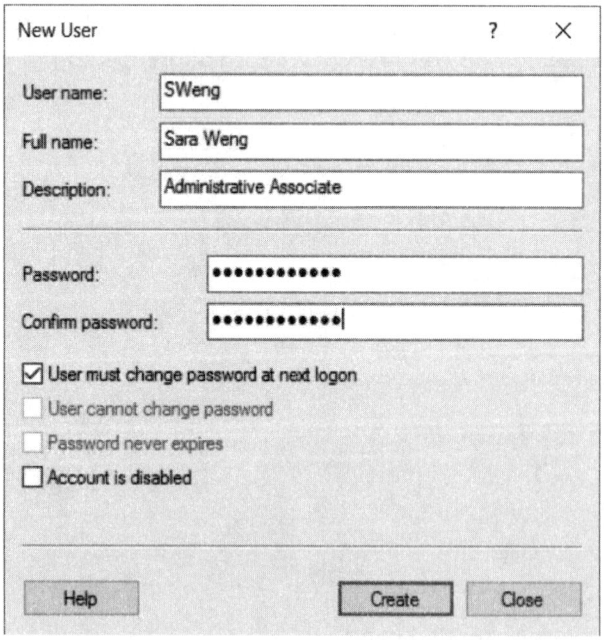

New User
User name: SWeng
Full name: Sara Weng
Description: Administrative Associate
Password: ●●●●●●●●●●●●
Confirm password: ●●●●●●●●●●●●
User must change password at next logon
User cannot change password
Password never expires
Account is disabled
Help
Create
Close

Figure 4-21 Providing New User information for a user account on a stand-alone server

Symbols that cannot be used in an account name in Windows Server 2016 are [ ] ; : < > = , + / \ | . Also, each account name must be unique, so that there are no duplicates. Finally, when you specify a password, it needs to meet the password policy requirements on the local computer. The password requirements include a minimum password length, complexity, and whether the password has been used recently (password history). You learn about setting up password requirements in Chapter 10.

10. Click Create. If you see a warning message that the password does not meet the password requirements, click OK and enter a new password that does meet the requirements, such as one that is over six characters long and that contains a combination of uppercase and lowercase letters, symbols, and numbers.
11. Create another account, or click Close if you're finished creating accounts.
12. Notice the new account you created under the Name column in the Console1 window. Close the MMC (Console1 window) and click Yes to save the console settings. Enter a name for the console, such as Manage Accounts, click Desktop in the left portion of the dialog box, and click Save.

The console will now appear as an icon on your desktop. This is true when you save a customized MMC regardless of whether Active Directory is installed.

Creating Accounts When Active Directory Is Installed

When Active Directory is installed and the server is a domain controller, use the Active Directory Users and Computers tool either from the Windows Administrative Tools folder on the Start menu, from Tools in Server Manager, or as an MMC snap-in. You create each new account by entering account information and password controls.

If you are using Active Directory and are working on a DC, Windows Server 2016 will not allow you to install the Local Users and Groups snap-in, because you must use the Active Directory Users and Computers snap-in instead.

Activity 4-4: Creating User Accounts in Active Directory

Time Required: Approximately 15 minutes
Objective: Learn how to create a user account in Active Directory.

Description: Management and access to resources through Active Directory begins through user accounts. In this activity, you learn how to set up a new account.

1. Right-click **Start**, click **Run**, type **mmc** in the Open box, and click **OK**. Maximize the console window, if necessary. Click the **File** menu and click **Add/Remove Snap-in**. Under the Available snap-ins, click **Active Directory Users and Computers** and click **Add**. Click **OK**.
2. In the left pane, click the **right pointing arrow** in front of **Active Directory Users and Computers**, if necessary, to display the elements under it. Click the **right pointing arrow** in front of the domain name, such as *jpcomp.com*, to display the folders and OUs under it (see Figure 22).
3. Click the **Users** folder in the left pane and then in the middle pane, view the user accounts (with one head icons) and groups (with two head icons) already created.
   - Are any accounts already created? What groups are shown along with the accounts?
4. Click the **Action** menu or right-click **Users** in the left pane, point to New, and click User.

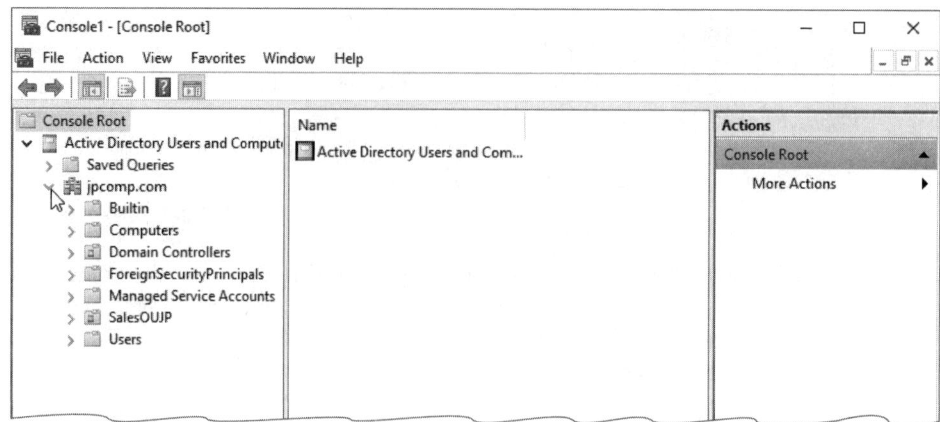

Figure 4-22 Viewing the OUs and folders under the domain

5. Type your first name in the First name box, type your middle initial (no period), and type your last name with the word "Test" appended to it in the Last name box (for example, KozlowskiTest). Enter your initials with Test appended to them in the User logon name box (for example, AKTest), as shown in Figure 4-23.
   - What options are automatically completed for you?

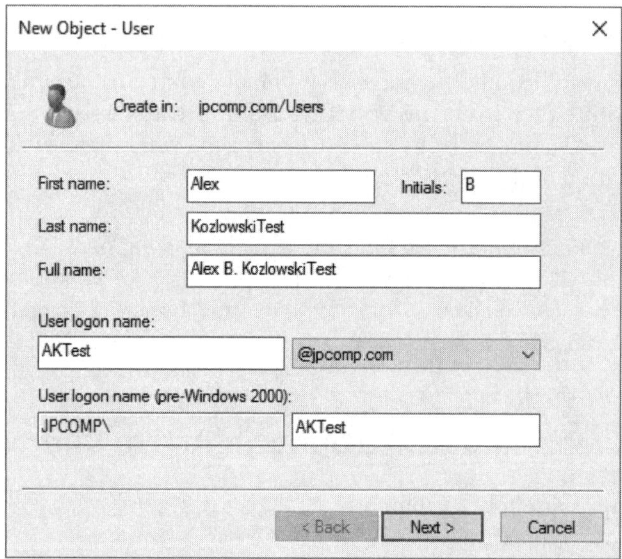

Figure 4-23 Creating a user account

Many organizations follow a user account naming scheme. For example, some organizations prefer to use account names that consist of the first name initial and the user's last name. Others prefer to use the last name followed by the first name initial. Still others prefer to use a name that matches the job title. The advantage of using last name first is that reports of users' logon names can be printed in alphabetical order. Also, it is easier to find a particular user's account by last name. The advantage of using the job title is that the user account can continue to be used by a new employee after the old employee leaves.

6. Click **Next**.

7. Enter a password and enter the password confirmation. Ensure the box is checked for **User must change password at next logon**. This option forces users to enter a new password the first time they sign in, so that the account creator will not know their password. The other options include:
   - *User cannot change password*, which means that only the account administrator can change the user's password
   - *Password never expires*, which is used in situations in which an account must always be accessed, such as when a program accesses an account to run a special process
   - *Account is disabled*, which provides a way to prevent access to an account without deleting it

The Windows Server 2016 default password requirements are enabled when you create an account. A password must be seven characters or longer and cannot contain the account name or portions of the user's full name (beyond two characters of the name). Also, a minimum of three of the following four rules apply: includes numbers, includes uppercase letters, includes lowercase letters, includes characters such as $, #, and !.

8. Click **Next.**
9. Verify the information you have entered and click **Finish.**
10. To continue configuring the account, in the middle pane, double-click the account you just created, such as **KozlowskiTest** (alternatively, you can right-click the account and click **Properties**).
11. Notice the tabs that are displayed for the account properties.
12. Click the **General** tab, if it is not already displayed, and enter a description of the account, such as **Test account.**
13. Click the **Account** tab to view the information you can enter on it.
14. Click the tabs you have not yet viewed to find out what information can be configured through each one.
15. Click **OK.**
16. Leave the console window open for the next activity.

If you need to close the MMC after a project in this chapter, close it and click Yes to save the console settings. Enter a name for the console, such as Manage Accounts, click Desktop to save it on the desktop for fast access, and click Save. You can later quickly open the console you saved by clicking its icon on the desktop. Of course, you can also go to the Windows Administrative Tools folder on the Start menu as in previous activities and click Active Directory Users and Computers—or open it from the Server Manager Tools menu.

The following is a brief summary of the account properties that can be set by right-clicking an account and clicking Properties in the Active Directory Users and Computers window (see Figure 4-24).

- *General Tab*—Enables you to enter or modify personal information about the account holder that includes the first name, last name, and name as it is displayed in the console, description of the user or account, office location, telephone number, email address, and webpage. There are also buttons to enter additional telephone numbers and webpage addresses for the account holder.

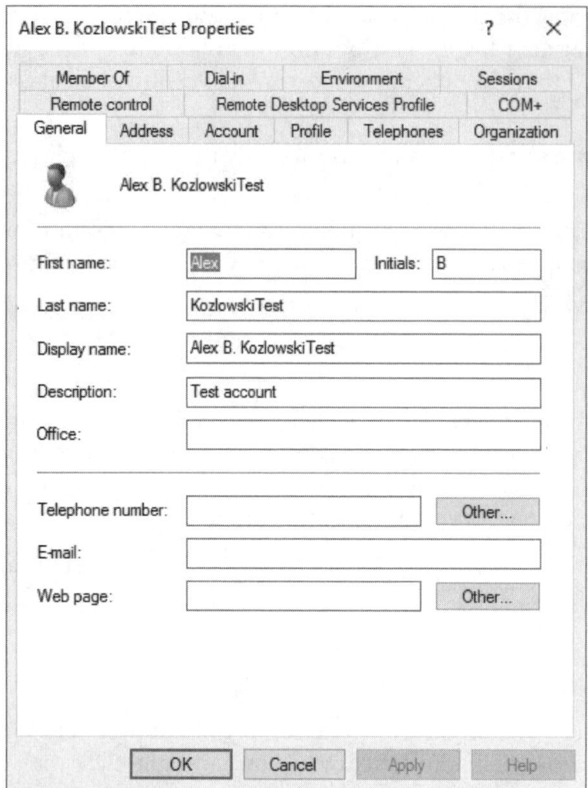

Figure 4-24 User account properties

- *Address Tab*—Provides information about the account holder's street address, post office box, city, state or province, postal code, and country or region.
- *Account Tab*—Provides information about the logon name, domain name, and account options, such as requiring the user to change her or his password at next logon, and account expiration date, if one applies. A Logon Hours button on this tab enables you to set up an account so that the user only signs in to the domain at designated times, such as only from 8:00 AM to 7:00 PM Monday through Friday. Also, the Log On To button enables you to limit from which computer a user can sign in to the server or domain.
- *Profile Tab*—Enables you to associate a particular profile with a user or set of users, such as a common desktop (profiles are discussed later in this chapter). This tab also is used to associate a logon script and a home folder (directory) with an account. A logon script is a file of commands that are executed at logon, and a home folder is disk space on a particular server given to a user to store his or her files.

You can use the %username% variable to automatically create a user's home folder with her or his logon name. For example, to automatically create a home folder for the user JRyan, simply enter the universal naming convention name and the variable (\\servername\sharename\%username%).

- *Telephones Tab*—Enables you to associate specific types of telephone contact numbers for an account holder, which include one or more numbers for home, pager, mobile, fax, and IP phones.
- *Organization Tab*—Provides a place to enter the account holder's title, department, company name, and the name of the person who manages the account holder.

- *Remote Control Tab*—Enables you to set up remote control parameters for a client who uses Remote Desktop Services. The remote control capability enables you to view and manipulate the client session while it is active, in order to troubleshoot problems.
- *Remote Desktop Services Profile Tab*—Enables you to set up a user profile for a client who uses Remote Desktop Services.
- *COM+ Tab*—Specifies the COM+ partition set of which the user is a member.
- *Member Of Tab*—Enables you to add the account to an existing group of users that has the same security and access requirements (you'll learn more about groups later in this chapter). The tab also is used to remove the account from a group.
- *Dial-In Tab*—Permits you to control remote access from dial-in modems or from virtual private networks (VPNs).
- *Environment Tab*—Enables you to configure the startup environment for clients who access one or more servers using Remote Desktop Services (for running programs on the server).
- *Sessions Tab*—Enables you to configure session parameters for a client using Remote Desktop Services, such as a session time limit, a limit on how long a session can be idle, what to do when a connection is broken, and how to reconnect.

The information on some of these tabs can be extra work to maintain, such as when telephone numbers and office locations change. Keep this in mind as you enter information, so that you don't introduce more work than is necessary or required by your organization.

Disabling, Enabling, and Renaming Accounts

When a user takes a leave of absence, you have the option to disable his or her account. Your organization might also have the practice of disabling accounts when someone leaves and then later renaming and enabling the account for that person's replacement (this is easier than deleting the account and creating a new one).

Activity 4-5: Disabling, Renaming, and Enabling an Account

Time Required: Approximately 5 minutes
Objective: Practice disabling, renaming, and then enabling an account.

Description: In this activity, you learn how to disable an account, rename the account, and then enable that account.

1. Access the MMC console window for **Active Directory Users and Computers**, or if it is closed, open it.
2. Browse to find the account, such as the one for *Alex B. KozlowskiTest*, you created in Activity 4-4 under the Users folder within the domain that you created.
3. Right-click the account and click **Disable Account**, as shown in Figure 4-25.
4. Click **OK** when you see the informational dialog box that verifies you have disabled the account. The account icon will have a down arrow inside a white circle to show that it is disabled. No one can use the account until you enable it.
5. To rename the account, right-click it and click **Rename** (see Figure 4-25). Enter a new name, such as *Martin SanchezTest*, and then press **Enter**.
6. When you see the Rename User dialog box, change the First name and the Last name boxes to reflect the new name. Change the User logon name, such as to *MSTest*. Click **OK**.
7. Make sure the account is now listed as *Martin SanchezTest* in the Users folder.

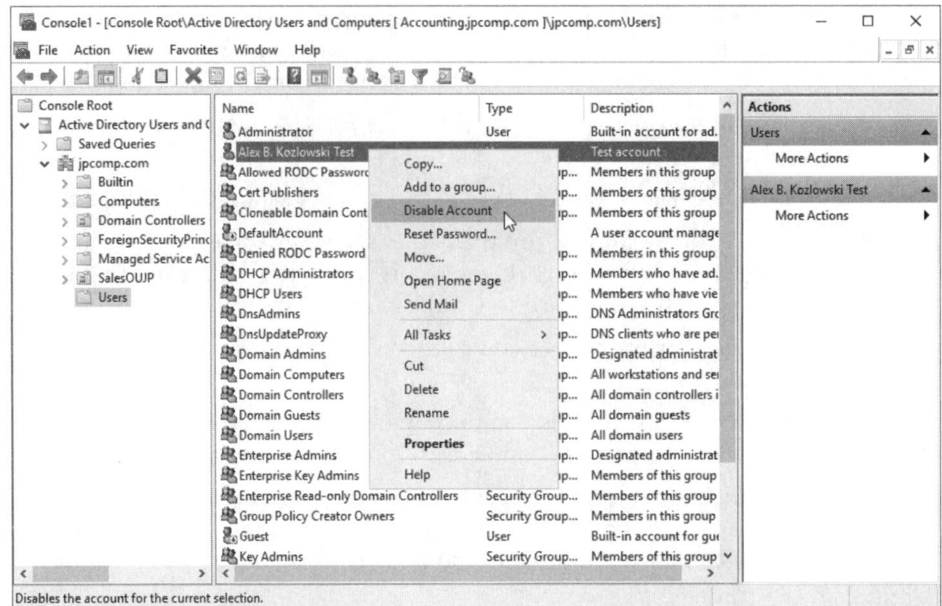

Figure 4-25 Disabling an account

8. Right-click the account you renamed and click **Enable Account.** Click **OK.**
   - What happens to the display of the account in the Users folder?
9. Leave the MMC console window for Active Directory Users and Computers window open for the next activity.

Moving an Account

When an employee moves from one department to another, for example, from the Payroll Department to the budget office, you might need to move that person's account from one container to another—between OUs, for example.

Activity 4-6: Moving an Account

Time Required: Approximately 5 minutes
Objective: Practice moving an account.

Description: If your organization uses OUs to reflect different departments, then you might need to move accounts between OUs as people are transferred to different departments. In this activity, you move the account you renamed in Activity 4-5 to the OU that you created in Activity 4-3.

1. Access the MMC console window for **Active Directory Users and Computers,** or if it is closed, open it.
2. Right-click the account you renamed, such as *Martin SanchezTest.*
3. Click **Move** (refer to Figure 4-25).
4. In the Move dialog box, find the OU that you created in Activity 4-3, such as *SalesOUJP*, and click it (see Figure 4-26). Click **OK.**
5. In the tree of the left pane, click the OU to which you moved the account and verify that the account is moved (see the middle pane).
6. Leave the Active Directory Users and Computers MMC console window open for the next activity.

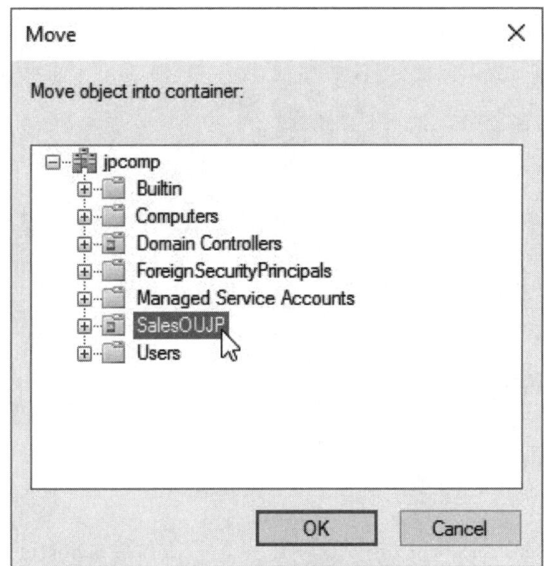

Figure 4-26 Moving an account

Resetting a Password

Sometimes users change their passwords or go several weeks without logging on—and forget their passwords. You do not have the option to look up a password, but you can reset it for the user. For organizations that have accounts that manage sensitive information, particularly financial information, it is advisable to have specific guidelines that govern the circumstances under which an account password is reset. For example, an organization might require that the account holder physically visit his or her account manager, rather than placing a telephone call—because there is no way to absolutely verify the authenticity of the request by telephone.

Accounts that handle financial information are typically audited by independent financial auditors. These auditors might require that you keep records of each time a password is reset, so that the auditors can examine them along with other financial information.

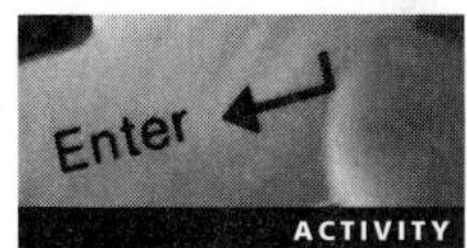

Activity 4-7: Changing an Account's Password

Time Required: Approximately 5 minutes
Objective: Practice changing an account's password.

Description: One of the most common account management tasks is resetting passwords. In this activity, you learn how to reset the password for a user.

1. Access the MMC console window for **Active Directory Users and Computers**, or open it if it is closed.
2. Open the OU that you created in Activity 4-3, if it is not already open, so that you can see the account you created and renamed.
3. Right-click the account for which you want to reset the password, such as *Martin SanchezTest*.
4. Click **Reset Password** (refer to Figure 4-25).
5. Enter the new password and then confirm it.
6. Ensure that the box is checked for **User must change password at next logon** (see Figure 4-27). Checking this box enables you to force the user to change the password

Figure 4-27 Resetting a password

you set, so that you will not know the new password, which is a best practice endorsed by Microsoft and often a requirement of financial auditors who scrutinize networks that handle financial information.

Notice in Figure 4-27 that you can also unlock an account that has been locked. You might need to unlock an account when a user has unsuccessfully tried to sign in too many times and the account goes into a locked status for a prespecified interval.

7. Click **OK** in the Reset Password dialog box. Click **OK** in the information message box.
8. Leave the MMC console window for Active Directory Users and Computers open for the next activity.

Deleting an Account

Plan to practice good account management by deleting accounts that are no longer in use. If you don't, the number of dormant accounts might grow into a confused tangle of accounts, and you expose your company to security risks. When you delete an account, its globally unique identifier (GUID) is also deleted and will not be reused even if you create another account using the same name.

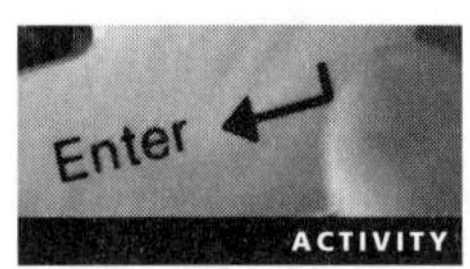

Activity 4-8: Deleting an Account

Time Required: Approximately 5 minutes
Objective: Practice deleting an account.

Description: In this project, you delete the account that you renamed in Activity 4-5.

1. Access the MMC console window for **Active Directory Users and Computers**, or open it if it is closed.
2. Open the OU that you created in Activity 4-3, if it is not already open, so that you can see the account you created and renamed.
3. Right-click the account you want to delete, such as *Martin SanchezTest*, and click **Delete** (refer to Figure 4-25).
4. Click **Yes** to verify that you want to delete this account.
5. Leave the MMC console window for Active Directory Users and Computers open for the next activity.

Security Group Management

One of the best ways to manage accounts is by grouping accounts that have similar characteristics, such as those that are in a single department, in a specific project group, or that access the same folders and printers. The group management concept saves time by eliminating repetitive steps in managing user and resource access.

In Active Directory, the use of groups focuses on the concept of **scope of influence** (**scope**), which is the reach of a group for gaining access to resources in Active Directory. When Active Directory is not implemented, the scope of a group is limited to the stand-alone server, and only local groups are created. In contrast, the implementation of Active Directory increases the scope from a local server or domain to all domains in a forest. The types of groups and their associated scopes are as follows:

- *Local*—Used on stand-alone servers that are not part of a domain; scope of this type of group does not go beyond the local server on which it is defined
- *Domain Local*—Used when there is a single domain or to manage resources in a particular domain so that global and universal groups can access those resources
- *Global*—Used to manage group accounts from the same domain so that those accounts can access resources in the same and in other domains
- *Universal*—Used to provide access to resources in any domain within a forest

All of these groups can be used for security or distribution groups. **Security groups** are used to enable access to resources on a stand-alone server or in Active Directory. **Distribution groups** are used for email or telephone lists, to provide quick, mass distribution of information. In this section, the focus is on security groups.

Implementing Local Groups

A **local security group** is used to manage resources on a stand-alone computer that is not part of a domain and on member servers in a domain (non-DCs). For example, you might use a local group in a small office situation with only 5, 15, or 30 users. Consider an office of mineral resource consultants in which there are 18 user accounts on the server. Four of these accounts are used by the founding partners of the consulting firm, who manage employee hiring, payroll, schedules, and general accounting. Seven accounts are for consultants who specialize in coal-bed methane extraction, and the seven remaining accounts belong to consultants who work with oil extraction. In this situation, the company might decide not to install Active Directory and divide these accounts into three local groups. One group would be called Managers and consist of the four founding partners. Another group would be called CBM for the coal-bed methane consultants, and the third group would be called Oil and be used for the oil consultants. Each group would be given different security access based on the resources at the server, which would include access to folders and to printers.

You create local groups by using the Local Users and Groups MMC snap-in.

Implementing Domain Local Groups

A **domain local security group** is used when Active Directory is deployed. This type of group is typically used to manage resources in a domain and to give global groups from the same and other domains access to those resources. As shown in Table 4-1, a domain local group can contain user accounts, global groups, and universal groups.

The scope of a domain local group is the domain in which the group exists, but you can convert a domain local group to a universal group as long as the domain local group does not contain any other domain local groups. Also, to convert any group, the domain must be in the Windows Server 2003 or above domain functional level.

Table 4-1 Membership capabilities of a domain local group

Active Directory objects that can be members of a domain local group	Active Directory objects that a domain local group can join as a member
User accounts in the same domain	Access control (security) lists for objects in the same domain, such as permissions to access a folder, shared folder, or printer
Domain local groups in the same domain	Domain local groups in the same domain
Global groups in any domain in a tree or forest (as long as there are transitive or two-way trust relationships maintained)	
Universal groups in any domain in a tree or forest (as long as there are transitive or two-way trust relationships maintained)	

Although a domain local group can contain any combination of accounts, global, and universal groups, the typical purpose of a domain local group is to provide access to resources, which means that you grant access to servers, folders, shared folders, and printers to a domain local group. Under most circumstances, you should plan to put domain local groups in access control lists only, and the members of domain local groups should be mainly global groups. An **access control list (ACL)** is a list of security descriptors (privileges) that have been set up for a particular object, such as a shared folder or shared printer. Generally, a domain local group does not contain accounts, because account management is more efficient when you handle it through global groups. Examples of using domain local groups with global groups are presented in the next section.

You'll learn more about how ACLs are configured as you learn about permissions in Chapter 5, Configuring, Managing, and Troubleshooting Resource Access.

Implementing Global Groups

A **global security group** is intended to contain user accounts from a single domain and can also be set up as a member of a domain local group in the same or another domain. This capability gives global groups a broader scope than domain local groups, because their members can access resources in other domains. A global group can contain user accounts and other global groups from the domain in which it was created.

Nesting global groups to reflect the structure of OUs means that global groups can be layered. For example, your organization might consist of an OU for management, an OU under the management OU for the Finance Department, and an OU under the Finance Department for the Budget office—resulting in three levels of OUs. Also, you might have a global group composed of the accounts of vice presidents in the management OU, a global group of accounts for supervisors in the Finance Department OU, and a global group of all members of the Budget office in the budget OU. The global group membership can be set up to reflect the structure of OUs, as shown in Figure 4-28.

Plan nesting of global groups carefully. You can convert a global group to a universal group at a later time, but only if it is not a member of another global group.

A global group can be converted to a universal group as long as it is not nested in another global group or in a universal group. In the example shown in Figure 4-28, the Finance and Budget global groups cannot be converted to universal groups because they already are members of the Managers and Finance groups, respectively.

A typical use for a global group is to build it with accounts that need access to resources in the same or in another domain and then to make the global group in one domain a member of

*Managers global group (top-level global group)
- Amber Richards
- Joe Scarpelli
- Kathy Brown
- Sam Rameriz
- **Finance global group (second-level global group)
  - Martin LeDuc
  - Sarah Humphrey
  - Heather Shultz
  - Sam Weisenberg
  - Jason Lew
  - ***Budget global group (third-level global group)
    - Michele Gomez
    - Kristin Beck
    - Chris Doyle

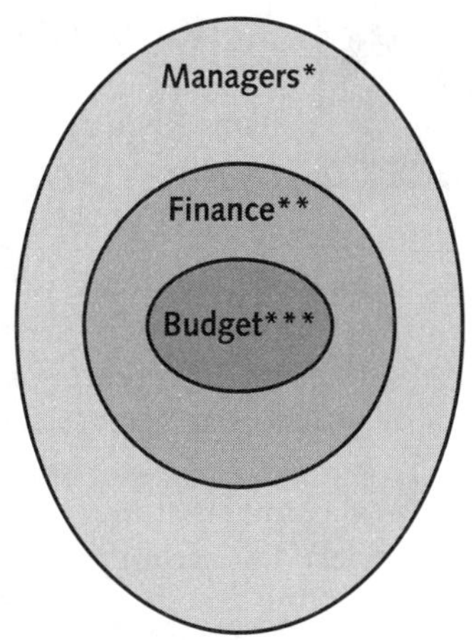

Figure 4-28 Nested global groups

a domain local group in the same or another domain. This model enables you to manage user accounts and their access to resources through one or more global groups, while reducing the complexity of managing accounts.

For example, consider a college that has a domain for students, a domain for faculty and staff, and a domain for research organizations that are associated with the college. The college's executive council, consisting of the college president and vice presidents, needs access to resources in all three domains. One way to enable the executive council to have access is to create a domain local group called LocalExec in each domain that provides the appropriate access to folders, files, and other resources. Next, create a GlobalExec global group in the faculty and staff domain that has the president's and vice presidents' user accounts as members (see Figure 4-29). These steps enable you to manage security for all of their accounts at one time from one global group. If the president or a vice president leaves to take another job, you simply delete (or disable) that person's account from the global group and later add an account (or rename and enable the old account) for her or his replacement. You also can manage access to resources in each domain one time through each domain local group, resulting in much less management work. If a new printer is added to a domain, for example, you can give the domain local group full privileges to the printer.

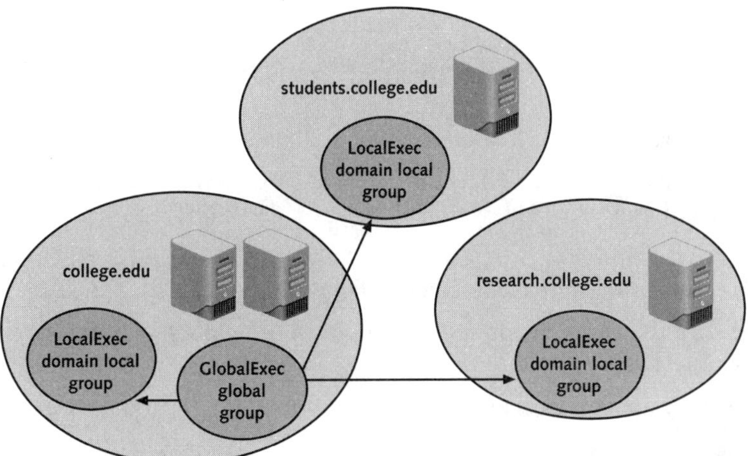

Figure 4-29 Managing security through domain local and global security groups

When the Active Directory structure becomes complex enough in a large organization so that many domains, trees, and forests are in use, global groups are used as members of universal groups to manage accounts, as described in the next section, Implementing Universal Groups.

Activity 4-9: Creating Domain Local and Global Security Groups

Time Required: Approximately 15 minutes
Objective: Create a domain local and a global security group and make the global group a member of the domain local group.

Description: In this activity, assume that you have been asked to set up groups to manage access for the managers in an Active Directory that has four domains. You will practice beginning the setup by creating a domain local group that will be used to manage resources and a global group of accounts. Last, you will add the global group to the domain local group. To complete the activity, you will first need an environment in which Active Directory is installed and two accounts that are already set up by your instructor (or that you create in advance). You'll also need to have an account that has Administrator privileges.

1. Access the MMC console window for **Active Directory Users and Computers** that you have been using, or click it's icon on the desktop, if you have saved it to the desktop. Alternatively, you can use the **Tools** menu in Server Manager to open **Active Directory Users and Computers**.
2. In the tree in the left pane, display the contents under the domain, such as *jpcomp.com*.
3. Click **Users** in the tree.
4. Click the **Action** menu, point to **New**, and click **Group**.
   - What defaults are already selected in the New Object–Group dialog box?
5. In the Group name box, enter **DomainMgrs** plus your initials, for example, *DomainMgrsJP*.
6. Click **Domain local** under Group scope, and click **Security** (if it is not already selected) under Group type.
7. Click **OK** and then look for the group you just created in the right pane within the Users folder.
8. Click the **Create a new group in the current container** icon on the button bar (with two heads).
9. In the Group name box, type **GlobalMgrs** plus your initials, for example, GlobalMgrsJP.
10. Ensure **Global** is selected under Group scope and that **Security** is selected under Group type.
11. Click **OK** and then look for the group you just created in the right pane.
12. Double-click the global group you created.
13. Click the **Members** tab. Notice that no members are currently associated with this group.
14. Click the **Add** button.
15. Click the **Advanced** button in the Select Users, Contacts, Computers, Service Accounts, or Groups dialog box.
16. Click **Find Now**.
17. Click the first user provided by your instructor, press and hold down the **CTRL** key and click the second user provided by your instructor. Click **OK** (see Figure 4-30).
18. Make sure that the users you selected are shown in the Select Users, Contacts, Computers, Service Accounts, or Groups dialog box. Click **OK**.
19. Again, be sure that both accounts are shown in the global group's Properties box on the Members tab. Click **OK**.
20. Double-click the domain local group, such as *DomainMgrsJP*, and then click the **Members** tab.
    - What members are shown?
21. Click **Add**.
22. Click **Advanced** in the Select Users, Contacts, Computers, Service Accounts, or Groups dialog box.
23. Click **Find Now**.
24. Locate the global group you created, such as *GlobalMgrsJP*. Click that global group and click **OK**.

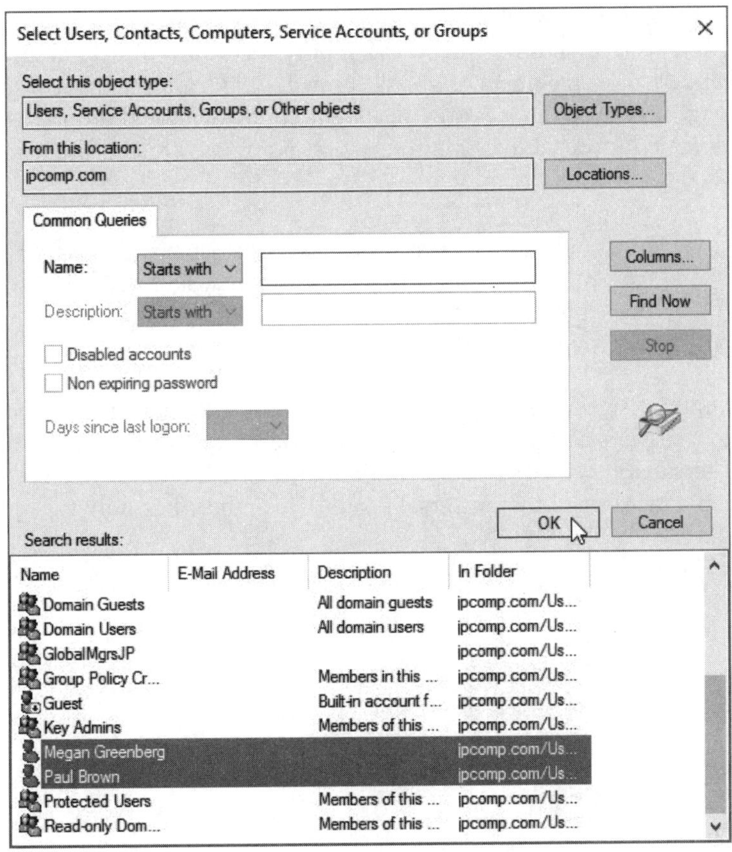

Figure 4-30 Adding user accounts as global group members

25. Verify that the global group is displayed in the Select Users, Contacts, Computers, Service Accounts, or Groups dialog box, and then click **OK**.
26. Make sure the global group is listed under Members on the Members tab. Click **OK**.
27. Close the MMC console window and click **Yes** to save the console settings, if you have not done this previously. If you are saving the settings, click **Desktop** in the left portion of the dialog box. Enter a name for the console, such as *Manage Accounts*, and click **Save**.

Implementing Universal Groups

In an Active Directory context in which there are multiple hierarchies of domains, trees, and forests, **universal security groups** provide a means to span domains and trees. Universal group membership can include user accounts from any domain, global groups from any domain, and other universal groups from any domain.

Universal groups are offered to provide an easy means to access any resource in a tree or among trees in a forest. If you carefully plan the use of universal groups, then you can manage security for single accounts with a minimum of effort. Planning is done in relation to the scope of access required for a group of accounts. Here are some guidelines to help simplify how you plan to use groups:

- Use global groups to hold accounts as members—and keep the nesting of global groups to a minimum (or do not use nesting) to avoid confusion. Give accounts access to resources by making the global groups to which they belong members of domain local groups or universal groups or both.
- Use domain local groups to provide access to resources in a specific domain. Avoid placing accounts in domain local groups—but do make domain local groups members of access control lists for specific resources in the domain, such as shared folders and printers.

- Use universal groups to provide extensive access to resources, particularly when Active Directory contains trees and forests, or to simplify access when there are multiple domains. Make universal groups members of access control lists for objects in any domain, tree, or forest. Manage user account access by placing accounts in global groups and joining global groups to domain local or universal groups, depending on which is most appropriate to the scope required for access.

If you attempt to create a new universal group but find that the radio button in the Create New Object — (Group) dialog box is deactivated, this means that the domain is set up in Windows 2000 domain functional level and you must convert the domain to a higher domain functional level.

In the example of setting up access for the executive council in a college that has three domains, an alternative is to create one universal group that has access to all resources in the three domains—create one global group containing the president and vice presidents and make that global group a member of the universal group. This model has only two groups to manage, as shown in Figure 4-31.

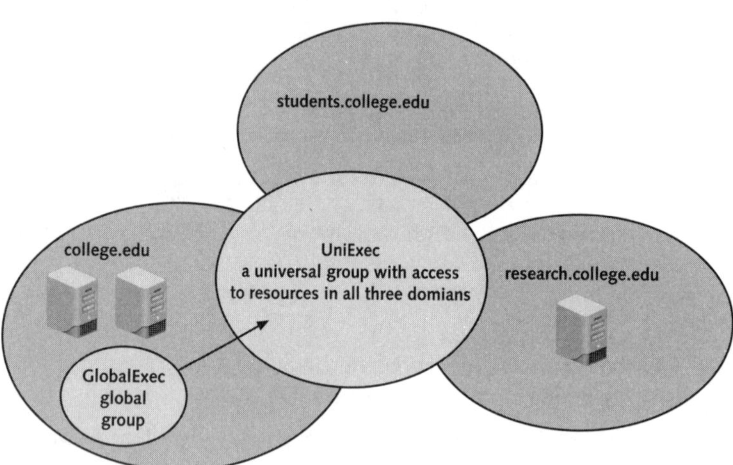

Figure 4-31 Managing security through universal and global groups

Properties of Groups

All of the groups that you can create in Windows Server 2016 have a set of properties that can be configured. As you probably noticed in Activity 4-9, you can configure the properties of a specific group by double-clicking that group in the Local Users and Groups tool for a standalone (nondomain) or member server, or in the Active Directory Users and Computers tool for DC servers in a domain. The properties are configured using the following tabs:

- *General*—Used to enter a description of the group, change the scope and type of group, and provide email addresses for a distribution group
- *Members*—Used to add members to a group, such as adding user accounts to a global group, and enables members to be removed
- *Member Of*—Used to make the group a member of another group or to remove the group's membership
- *Managed By*—Used to establish an account or group that will manage the group, if the manager is other than the server administrator; also, the location, telephone number, and fax number of the manager can be provided

Implementing User Profiles

Client access to Windows Server 2016 can be customized through user profiles. A **local user profile** is automatically created at the local computer when you sign in with an account for the first time, and the profile can be modified to consist of desktop settings that are customized for one or more clients who sign in locally.

User profiles provide the following advantages:

- Multiple users can use the same computer and maintain their own customized settings. When users sign in, they receive their own personalized settings that were saved when they last signed out.
- Profiles can be stored on a network server so they are available to users regardless of the computer they use to sign in.
- Profiles can be made mandatory so users have the same settings each time they sign in. When a user signs in, she can modify the settings but the changes are never saved when the user signs out.

Profiles are used in Microsoft operating systems to provide a consistent working environment for one or more users. A local user profile is a particular desktop setup that always starts in the same way and is stored on the local computer. A **roaming profile** is a desktop setup that starts in the same way from any computer used to access an account, including remote connections from home or on the road. In a network environment where users are moving between computers, a roaming profile is ideal so the users' settings are available from any computer.

For example, if there are two server administrators and two backup operators who primarily run backups, you might create one profile for the administrators and a different one for the backup operators. That can be useful if each type of account needs to have certain program icons, startup programs, or some other prearranged desktop settings. Also, a user profile can be set up on a server so it is downloaded to the client workstation each time a specific account is signed in. This roaming profile enables a user to start off with the same desktop setup, no matter which computer she or he uses. In some circumstances, you need to set up profiles so that certain users cannot change their profiles. This is done by creating a **mandatory user profile** in which the user does not have permission to update the folder containing his profile. A mandatory user profile overrides the user's locally stored profile if it has been changed from the version stored on the server. This means that when a user signs in, he can make changes to the profile and customize it, but when the user signs out, the changes are not saved. To make a server profile (either local or roaming) mandatory, you can rename the user's Ntuser.dat file to Ntuser.man. A specific user's profile can be placed under the /User/*Accountname* folder in Windows Server 2016, for instance.

One way to set up a profile is to first set up a generic account on the server or use the Guest account as a model with the desired desktop configuration, including desktop icons, shortcut folders, and programs in the Startup folder to start when the client workstation starts. Then copy the Ntuser.dat file for that account to the \Users\Default folder in Windows Server 2016. This step makes that profile the default for new users. You can also create a profile to use as a roaming profile for specific users. To create the roaming profile, set up a generic account and customize the desktop. For example, you might create an account called BUDGET for users in the budget office and customize the desktop, Start menu, and network and printer connections. After you create that account, set up those users to access that profile by opening the Profile tab in each user's account properties (see Figure 4-32) and entering the path to that profile.

You can also use the System window to copy profiles from one location to another. You can access the System window by right-clicking Start and clicking System or open the System applet in the Control Panel Classic View. To copy a profile through the System applet use these general steps:

1. Right-click Start and click System.
2. Click Advanced system settings

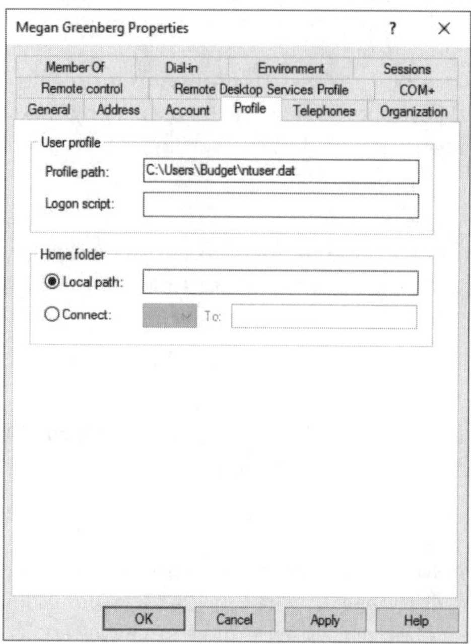

Figure 4-32 Setting a roaming profile in an account's properties

3. Select the Advanced tab, if necessary.
4. Click the Settings button for User Profiles.
5. Select a profile and use the Copy To button to copy the profile to a user's account location.

User profiles are discussed here so that you are aware of them. However, creating the equivalent of user profiles can be accomplished more effectively by instead creating group policies for specific security groups of users. Creating group policies is a more powerful and versatile way to customize how specific user accounts access and use server resources. You learn how to create and use group policies in Chapter 10.

Important Features in Windows Server 2016 Active Directory

Windows Server 2016 Active Directory offers many features. Five important or new features that deserve particular mention are:

- Restart capability
- Read-Only domain controller
- Cloning domain controllers
- Fine-grained password policy enhancements
- Protected users global group

Restart Capability

Beginning with Windows Server 2008, there is a way to stop Active Directory Domain Services without taking down the computer. After your work is done on Active Directory, you simply restart Active Directory Domain Services. The general steps to stop and restart Active Directory Domain Services are as follows:

1. Open Server Manager and click Tools.
2. Click Component Services.
3. In the left pane in the tree, click Services.

4. Click Active Directory Domain Services in the middle pane.
5. Click *Stop the service*, as shown in Figure 4-33.

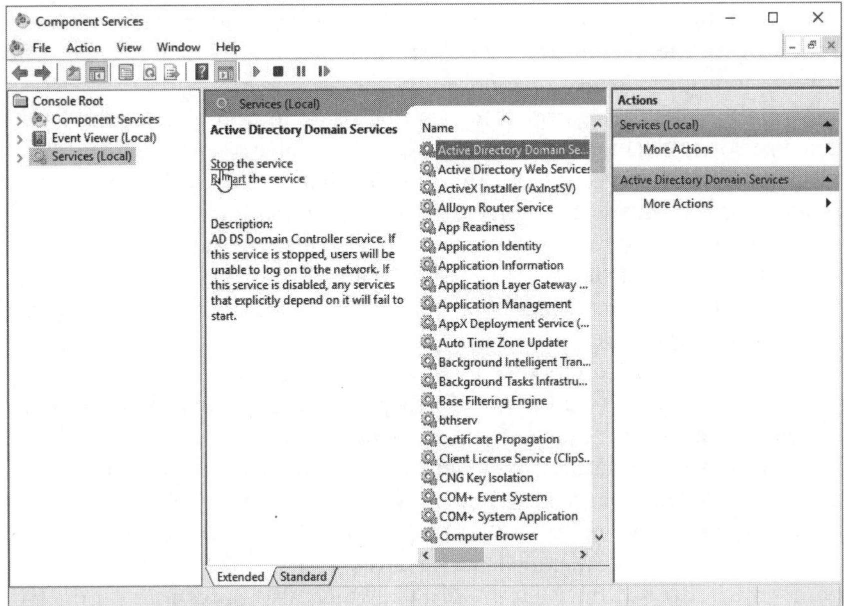

Figure 4-33 Stopping Active Directory Domain Services

6. Click Yes to confirm the other services that will be stopped along with Active Directory Domain Services.
7. Complete your work on Active Directory.
8. Go back into the Component Services window and repeat Steps 3 and 4, if necessary.
9. Click *Start the service* (the other services that were stopped in Step 6 will restart also).
10. Close the Component Services window.

Read-Only Domain Controller

In Windows Server 2008, one of the most anticipated updates to Active Directory was the implementation of the Read-Only Domain Controller. As you learned earlier in this chapter, normal DCs replicate information to one another. If a new account is created or a password is changed, this information is replicated to all DCs on a network. A **Read-Only Domain Controller (RODC)** is different in that you cannot use it to update information in Active Directory and it does not replicate to regular DCs. If a company uses Distributed File System (DFS, see Chapter 2), shared files in DFS are only updated to the RODC, but the RODC cannot update DFS files to the entire network.

An RODC can still function as a Key Distribution Center for the Kerberos authentication method that is the default authentication in Windows Server 2016 (see Chapter 10 to learn about Kerberos). It acts as a Key Distribution Center contacting a DC (all DCs are Key Distribution Centers) when a user first requests to sign in. The user's account credentials are then loaded into cache (memory) on the RODC so the credentials can be verified from the RODC for future sign-ins by that user.

An RODC can only function as a Key Distribution Center for user credentials if you first configure the Password Replication Policy in Active Directory to allow it. You learn about configuring policies in Chapter 10.

At this point, you're probably wondering why this is an important addition to Active Directory. The purpose of having an RODC is for better security at branch locations, where physical security measures might not be as strong as at a central office. Take, for example, a national investment company that invests in mutual funds, stocks, and other securities for its clients. The company has a home office in Chicago and branch offices throughout the United States. Each branch office has a server that is configured as an RODC. Some branch offices keep the server in a locked room, but some have only open office locations and the server is not physically secured from theft. Also, there is no trained server administrator at each branch office, only a regular employee who is given general responsibility for the server.

In this example, the central office can delegate authority over the RODC to a relatively untrained person at the branch office, who would not have access to change Active Directory at the local RODC in any significant way. Additionally, that employee could make no changes to Active Directory that would affect the entire company. If an unauthorized person, such as a night cleaning person, attempts to create an account or make a change to Active Directory, he can't do it. He also can't upload a bogus or virus-infected file via DFS to all DCs on the network. This protects the entire network from Active Directory intrusions coming from a less secure branch office and also reduces the risk of spreading viruses. If the branch office server is stolen, the thieves only have access to the Key Distribution Center credentials stored in the RODC's cache, and not the credentials of everyone in the company. In the event of a theft, the account credentials of users at one branch are much easier to change on a moment's notice than the credentials for all users in the company.

In the past, some organizations chose not to have DCs at branch offices, even though this makes sign-in credential authentication slower because it has to go over a busy wide area network (WAN) connection to a central office DC. Also, access to shared files through DFS is slower for the same reason. With Windows Server 2016 Active Directory, the security concerns of these companies are addressed by using an RODC, which also raises user productivity through faster network access.

Another advantage of having an RODC at the branch site is that it can be configured as a DNS server. This means DNS translations can be performed locally, which reduces WAN traffic and provides users with faster response.

To further enhance the security on an RODC, you can combine it with BitLocker Drive Encryption, which enables data encryption and protected data deletion in Windows Server 2016 data volumes, including Active Directory data. With this protection enabled, even if your server is stolen, thieves won't be able to get much valuable information from it. You learn about BitLocker Drive Encryption in Chapter 10.

Cloning Domain Controllers

Windows Server 2012 R2 introduces the ability to clone domain controllers. This capability is especially targeted for easier deployment of multiple domain controllers in an environment with multiple virtual machines.

Cloning cuts down on the steps required to create additional virtual domain controllers. The server administrator can configure Active Directory and then create a copy of the virtual domain controller. Additional steps can be handled by running PowerShell cmdlets and using a PowerShell script to define configuration parameters.

Fine-Grained Password Policy Enhancements

Fine-grained password policies mean that different security groups can have different password policies. For example, a group of researchers in an engineering company might need very secure password policies, such as for passwords over 10 characters in length and that must be changed every 2 weeks. In contrast, employees in a customer services group might not require as strict security with passwords only over 6 characters and that are changed only once every 3 months.

Windows Server 2008 introduced the ability to have fine-grained passwords. Prior to Windows Server 2008, one set of password policies covered all users. Windows Server 2012 R2 adds needed improvements for administering fine-grained passwords, which was a complex process in Windows Server 2008. Windows Server 2012 R2 introduces the ability to use the Active Directory Administrative Center for managing password setting objects in the Active Directory schema. These capabilities make server access even more secure, and they help reduce errors made by server administrators when working with fine-grained passwords.

Protected Users Global Group

Windows Server 2012 R2 and Server 2016 offer the new protected users global group as a way to provide very strong security for members of this group. The **protected users global group** enforces strict locked-in security and protection measures that cannot be reconfigured. The only way to change the security for a member of this group is to remove the member from the group. User accounts, computers, printers, and servers can be members of the group. Due to the enforced security restrictions, only computers running Windows 8.1 or higher or Windows Server 2012 R2 or higher can be member computers.

For example, consider a jet engine manufacturer that is developing a revolutionary new technology. The company wants to ensure that the technology does not fall into the hands of industrial spies or foreign governments. As one security measure, this company might place all user accounts and the server itself in the protected users global group.

Some of the security restrictions that apply to the protected user global group include:

- Group members cannot use weaker forms of authentication, such as NTLM, CredSSP, or digest authentication.
- The Kerberos Ticket Granting Ticket's lifetime is limited to 4 hours, which means the group member must be authenticated every 4 hours.
- For members of the protected users global group, connections to systems that do not utilize this global group may not succeed.
- Only higher-level encryption methods compatible with Kerberos security, such as Advanced Encryption Standard (AES) can be used. For example, Data Encryption Standard (DES) security, which is compatible with Kerberos cannot be used because it is less secure. (You learn more about Kerberos, AES, and DES in Chapter 10.)

Chapter Summary

- Active Directory (or AD DS) is a directory service to house information about network resources including servers, computers, user accounts, printers, and management and security policies. AD DS is like a central management center for a Windows Server network.
- Servers housing Active Directory are called domain controllers (DCs), and the same Active Directory information is replicated to every DC.
- The most basic component of Active Directory is an object. Each object is defined through an information set called a schema.
- The global catalog stores information about every object, replicates key Active Directory elements, and is used to authenticate user accounts when they sign in.
- A namespace consists of using the Domain Name System for resolving computer and domain names to IP addresses and vice versa. Named objects in Active Directory also exist in a namespace. Active Directory requires a Domain Name System server to help with the management of network resources.
- Active Directory is a hierarchy of logical containers: forests, trees, domains, and organizational units. Forests are the highest-level containers; organizational units are the lowest level. Another important container is the site, which is created out of IP subnets.
- You can delegate management of many Active Directory containers to specific types of administrators to match the structure of your organization.
- User accounts enable individual users to access specific resources, such as folders and files. You can customize account properties as well as manage accounts to disable, enable, rename, move, and delete them. Another common management function is to change user account passwords.
- On a stand-alone or member server, you can create local security groups to help manage user accounts. When Active Directory is installed, you can use domain local, global, and universal security groups for managing access to resources through accounts.

- User profiles are tools for customizing accounts, such as customizing desktop and other user features. However, managing user desktop, application, and resource elements is more effective through configuring group policies.
- The ability to stop and restart Active Directory without taking down a DC is an important capability to know when it is necessary to work on Active Directory and you don't want users accessing it while you work.
- The implementation of Read-Only Domain Controllers (RODCs) is another important feature for using and securing Active Directory in branch office and remote locations.
- The work of setting up multiple virtual machines as domain controllers can go faster and with fewer errors by using the ability to clone domain controllers.
- Fine-grained password policies give an organization more capabilities to customize password policies for different security groups of users. The process of setting up fine-grained passwords is made easier through administrative tools, such as the Active Directory Administrative Center.
- The protected users global group is newly available to create strict locked-in security measures that apply to all members of the group, such as user accounts, client computers, servers, printers, and other members. Use this global security group for situations that require high security.

Key Terms

access control list (ACL) A list of all security descriptors that have been set up for a particular object, such as for a shared folder or a shared printer.

bridgehead server A domain controller at each Active Directory site with access to a site network link, which is designated as the DC to exchange replication information. There is only one bridgehead server per site. *See* site.

cloud computing Providing a host of scalable web-based applications and services (including cloud storage) over the Internet or a private network that are used by clients through web browsers and downloadable apps.

container An Active Directory object that houses other objects, such as a tree that houses domains or a domain that houses organizational units.

contiguous namespace A namespace in which every child object has a portion of its name from its parent object.

directory service A large container (database) of information about network data and resources, such as computers, printers, user accounts, and user groups, that enables management and fast access to those resources.

disjointed namespace A namespace in which the child object name does not resemble the parent object name.

distribution group A list of users that enables one email message to be sent to all users on the list. A distribution group is not used for security and thus cannot appear in an access control list (ACL).

domain controller (DC) A Windows 2000 Server or above server that contains a full copy of the Active Directory information, is used to add a new object to Active Directory, and replicates all changes made to it so the changes are updated on every DC in the same domain.

domain functional level Refers to the Windows Server operating systems on domain controllers and the domain-specific functions they support. Depending on the functional level, one, two, or all of the following operating systems are supported: Windows 2000 Server, Windows Server 2003, Windows Server 2008/R2, Windows Server 2012/R2, and Windows Server 2016.

domain local security group A group that is used to manage resources—shared folders and printers, for example—in its home domain and that is primarily used to give global groups access to those resources.

fine-grained password policies Used so that different security groups can have different password policies.

Flexible Authentication Secure Tunneling (FAST) Used in Kerberos security to establish a secure channel or communications tunnel between a client seeking authentication for access to a computer service and the server providing access keys for secure communications. Also called Kerberos armoring.

forest A grouping of Active Directory trees that each have contiguous namespaces within their own domain structure but that have disjointed namespaces between trees. The trees and their domains use the same schema and global catalog.

forest functional level A forest-wide setting that refers to the types of domain controllers in a forest, which can be any combination of Windows 2000 Server, Windows Server 2003, Windows Server 2008/R2, Windows Server 2012/R2, or Windows Server 2016. The level also reflects the types of Active Directory services and functions supported.

global catalog A repository for all objects and the most frequently used attributes for each object in all domains. Each forest has a single global catalog that can be replicated onto multiple servers.

global security group A group that typically contains user accounts from its home domain and that is a member of domain local groups in the same or other domains, so as to give that global group's member accounts access to the resources defined to the domain local groups.

globally unique identifier (GUID) A unique number, up to 16 characters long, that is associated with an Active Directory object.

Kerberos armoring *See* Flexible Authentication Secure Tunneling (FAST).

Kerberos transitive trust relationship A set of two-way trusts between two or more domains (or forests in a forest trust) in which Kerberos security is used.

local security group A group of user accounts that is used to manage resources on a standalone computer.

local user profile A desktop setup that is associated with one or more accounts to determine what startup programs are used, additional desktop icons, and other customizations. A user profile is local to the computer in which it is stored.

mandatory user profile A user profile set up by the server administrator that is loaded from the server to the client each time the user logs on; changes that the user makes to the profile are not saved.

member server A server on an Active Directory managed network that is not installed to have Active Directory.

Microsoft Azure Active Directory An Active Directory service that an organization can use for online cloud applications, such as Office 365. Microsoft Azure Active Directory is a directory service that provides user authorization and identity management for organizations that subscribe to Microsoft cloud services.

multimaster replication Windows Server 2016 networks can have multiple servers called DCs that store Active Directory information and replicate it to each other. Because each DC acts as a master, replication does not stop when one DC is down and updates to Active Directory continue, for example, when creating a new account.

name resolution A process used to translate a computer's logical or host name into a network address, such as to a dotted decimal address associated with a computer—and vice versa.

namespace A logical area on a network that contains directory services and named objects and that has the ability to perform name resolution.

object A network resource, such as a server or a user account, that has distinct attributes or properties, is defined in a domain, and exists in Active Directory.

organizational unit (OU) A grouping of objects within a domain that provides a means to establish specific policies for governing those objects and that enables object management to be delegated.

protected users global group A global group that is created by default and enforces strict locked-in security that cannot be reconfigured.

Read-Only Domain Controller (RODC) A domain controller that houses Active Directory information but cannot be updated, such as to create a new account. This specialized domain controller receives updates from regular DCs but does not replicate to any DCs because it is read-only by design. *See* domain controller (DC).

roaming profile Desktop settings that are associated with an account so that the same settings are employed no matter which computer is used to access the account (the profile is downloaded to the client from a server).

schema Elements used in the definition of each object contained in Active Directory, including the object class and its attributes.

scope of influence (scope) The reach of a type of group, such as access to resources in a single domain or access to all resources in all domains in a forest (see domain local, global, and universal security groups). (Another meaning for the term *scope* is the beginning through ending IP addresses defined in a DHCP server for use by DHCP clients; see Chapter 8).

security group Used to assign a group of users permission to access network resources.

Service Principal Name (SPN) An identification number for a network service that employs Kerberos security.

site An option in Active Directory to interconnect IP subnets so that the server can determine the fastest route to connect clients for authentication and to connect DCs for replication of Active Directory. Site information also enables Active Directory to create redundant routes for DC replication.

transitive trust A trust relationship between two or more domains in a tree, in which each domain has access to objects in the others.

tree Related domains that use a contiguous namespace, share the same schema, and have two-way transitive trust relationships.

two-way trust A domain relationship in which both domains are trusted and trusting, enabling one to have access to objects in the other.

universal security group A group that is used to provide access to resources in any domain within a forest. A common implementation is to make global groups that contain accounts members of a universal group that has access to resources.

Review Questions

1. Your company has four departments: Marketing and Sales, Manufacturing, Product Research, and Business. Which of the following Active Directory container design plans might you use to best manage the user accounts and network access needs of each department?
   a. Create four trees.
   b. Create four parent domains in one site.
   c. Create four OUs in one domain.
   d. Create four trees and map them to four domains.
2. Using the example in Question 1, what Active Directory capability can you use to establish different account lockout policies for each of the four departments?
   a. Fine-grained password policies
   b. Lightweight group policies
   c. Password distribution groups
   d. Shadow password files
3. Your colleague has installed Active Directory Domain Services as a server role, but he has discovered that Active Directory cannot be used at this point. What next step must he take to get Active Directory ready for use?
   a. He must create a domain local group for Active Directory administrators.
   b. He must create a universal distribution group and make Active Directory a member.
   c. He must perform initial configuration to promote the server housing the Active Directory Domain Services role to a domain controller.
   d. He must initialize the Active Directory Changes and Use log.
4. You receive a message that Active Directory Domain Services has experienced an error and the Active Directory Domain Services service must be stopped and restarted. Which of the following tools can you use? (Choose all that apply.)

a. Component Services
b. Active Directory Domain Services Configuration Wizard
c. Device Manager
d. Active Directory Users and Computers

5. Which of the following server operating systems can be used when the domains in Windows Server 2016 Active Directory are set at the Windows Server 2012 domain functional level? (Choose all that apply.)
   a. Windows Server 2003 with Server 2008 Domain Services installed
   b. Windows Server 2008
   c. Windows Server 2012 R2
   d. Windows Server 2016

6. Domains in a tree are in a ___ relationship.
7. What tool can you use to manage fine-grained password policies?
   a. Active Directory Users and Computers
   b. Active Directory Administrative Center
   c. Password Administrator
   d. Security Configuration tool
8. A ___ is a unique number associated with each object in AD DS.
9. Your school has a parent object named straton.edu and the child object names stratonalum.org and studentarts.org. What kind of namespace is this?
   a. Disjointed
   b. Distributed
   c. Contiguous
   d. Coordinated
10. Your company's management has decided that the accounts in all OUs should be set up and managed by the Information Technology Department's security specialist. As the AD DS administrator, how can you best give this capability to the security specialist?
    a. Give her Full Control rights to AD DS.
    b. Make her user account a member of the AD DS Admins local security group.
    c. Use the delegate control feature to give her control of all OUs that contain user accounts.
    d. Give her Accounts Management permissions in AD DS.
11. A local security group is used on a ________ server.
12. Which of the following are actions performed by the global catalog? (Choose all that apply.)
    a. Provides lookup and access to all resources in all domains
    b. Caches IP addresses for all computers in a forest for faster sign-in
    c. Stores shared DFS folders and files for centralized shared file access
    d. Authenticates users when they sign in
13. You work for a bank that has five branch offices and one to two servers are located at each branch office. For best security, what kind of domain controller should be used at each branch office?
    a. An Active Directory Branch Controller
    b. A domain controller with Active Directory Federation Services installed as a role
    c. A Protected Security Domain Controller
    d. A Read-Only Domain Controller

14. You are creating a special user profile for all members of the inventory control unit in your business. After you create the profile, what tool can you use to copy it to all of the user accounts in the inventory control unit?
    a. Active Directory Users and Computers
    b. System applet in Control Panel
    c. Server Manager
    d. MMC Profiles snap-in
15. Which of the following is true about all trees in a forest? (Choose all that apply.)
    a. They all use the same schema.
    b. They all use the same OUs.
    c. They all use the same global catalog.
    d. They all use the same groups.
16. The list of security descriptors associated with a user account in Active Directory is called a(n) ________.
17. A site reflects interconnected ___ and is used for DC ___.
18. You manage the servers for your city government. You've installed a new Windows Server 2016 server and one of your first tasks is to configure user accounts for the police patrol division. All of the police officers will have the same security configuration on their user accounts. Which of the following is a good practice for managing the security on these user accounts?
    a. Create a separate forest to hold the accounts.
    b. Create a global security group and make all of the user accounts members.
    c. Establish a new domain to hold the accounts and provide extra security.
    d. Ensure all of the properties associated with these accounts are identical.
19. To reset a password, you use the ___ tool.
20. Which of the following are required attributes for a user account? (Choose all that apply.)
    a. Domain
    b. User's full name
    c. Password
    d. Logon name

Case Projects

Advanced Sounds makes audio systems for home entertainment centers, computers, industry, and motor vehicles. Over the past 10 years, this company has pioneered new technologies in audio systems, which have spurred rapid growth. The company has one large office, research, and manufacturing complex in New York City. This complex is divided into the following divisions: Business, Research and Development, Manufacturing, and Distribution. Parts manufacturing centers are located in Quebec City and in Montreal. Advanced Sounds also has seven outlet stores in New York City, four outlets in Quebec City, and two in Montreal. Each outlet store has a WAN connection to the central office computer center in New York City.

Advanced Sounds is engaging in a full upgrade of its Windows Server 2008 R2 network to Windows Server 2016. The upgrade includes using Windows Server 2016 Active Directory. Advanced Sounds has pioneered many technological innovations and is very concerned about keeping its network and computer systems secure. Their Information Technology (IT) Department hires you to help them implement Windows Server 2016 Active Directory.

Case Project 4-1: Active Directory Installation Planning

Advanced Sounds IT Department has formed a small installation planning committee consisting of the IT server operations manager, two system programmers, the current Active Directory administrator, and you. After the first meeting, they have asked you to prepare a small report to address the following questions:

- What tools are used in Windows Server 2016 to install Active Directory?
- What information is needed for the initial installation involving these tools?
- What special considerations exist in terms of having both Windows Server 2008 R2 and Windows Server 2016 servers as DCs?

Case Project 4-2: Active Directory Design

Due to a political decision several years ago, there is only one forest and domain for this company. Given what you know about the company's basic structure, how many forests, trees, and domains do you recommend? Do you recommend any sites? Note that there are four IP subnets at the New York City complex and two IP subnets at each of the Quebec City and Montreal locations. Create a report and if you have access to drawing software, create a diagram of your proposed design.

Case Project 4-3: Creating OUs

Until now, user accounts have been stored in only three OUs in the single domain. There is currently one OU for each of the New York City, Quebec City, and Montreal locations. The Advanced Sounds installation planning committee has decided to adopt your Active Directory structure proposed in Case Project 4-2, and now they want to also create OUs for each division in the company and place these under the domains that you have proposed. Further, the committee wants to have a computer technical specialist in each division to manage its OU and the user accounts under it. To help accomplish this, the committee asks you to create an instructional document that shows how to create an OU and delegate authority.

Case Project 4-4: Installing Servers at the Outlet Stores

All of the outlet stores have grown and have their own networks with 10 or more workstations. In the past, these stores have not had network connectivity to the home complex. However, this has created many problems due to extra paperwork and outdated handling of data. The installation committee would like to install WAN links to each outlet store and place servers in them. For efficiency, they would like to have the servers installed with Active Directory. Create a short report of your recommendations for installing a server at these outlet stores and include the reasoning behind your recommendations.

chapter 5

Configuring, Managing, and Troubleshooting Resource Access

After reading this chapter and completing the exercises, you will be able to:

- Set up security for folders and files
- Configure shared folders and shared folder security
- Troubleshoot security conflicts
- Implement work folders
- Install and set up the Distributed File System
- Configure disk quotas

Resource sharing is a bread-and-butter function for a Windows Server 2016 network because it empowers users to be productive. The most frequently used resources on a server are folders and files, which include written documents, spreadsheets, data files and databases, and multimedia files. Some of these resources need to be kept secure because they contain sensitive information. Other resources are to be shared with limited groups to far-reaching audiences. Windows Server 2016 can securely protect folders and files or open them up to wide-scale sharing, depending on the need.

You begin this chapter by learning how to use attributes and permissions to manage who accesses folders and files. You learn how to use the Encrypting File System to guard important resources and how to customize access through advanced permissions and ownership. You also learn how to create an audit trail for historical data about who has accessed information. You explore the steps for configuring information to be shared over the network by Windows and UNIX/Linux computers; and you publish shared folders in Active Directory. You learn about and configure work folders to accommodate devices that users may bring from home, including laptops and tablet PCs. You additionally find out how to install and set up the Distributed File System for coordinating and backing up a system of shared information. Finally, you examine how to avoid overloaded disks by setting up disk quotas.

Managing Folder and File Security

Creating users and groups are the initial steps for sharing resources, such as folders, files, and printers. The next steps are to create access control lists (ACLs) to secure these objects and then to set them up for sharing. As you learned in Chapter 4, Introduction to Active Directory and Account Management, an ACL is a list of privileges given to an account or security group granting access to an object, such as a shared folder or shared printer.

Windows Server 2016 uses two types of ACLs: discretionary and system control. A **discretionary ACL (DACL)** is an ACL that is configured by a server administrator or owner of an object. For example, the server administrator can configure who can access a company-wide shared folder containing personnel policies. Additionally, the human resources director may have her own folder of confidential information on the server that she makes available only to members of the Human Resources Department. Because she owns the folder, she can configure the folder's ACL to permit access only to members of her department.

A **system control ACL (SACL)** contains information used to audit the access to an object. For example, a soft drink company decides to audit files that contain the secret recipes for their products. By configuring an SACL for each file containing a recipe, the company monitors who has successfully viewed the file's contents and who has tried to view the contents but failed because of DACL restrictions. When an SACL is not configured, this means an object is not audited. The server administrator and object owners can configure DACLs and SACLs.

Good security practices mean using DACLs and SACLs to protect the resources on your Windows Server 2016 network. The ACL-based object security techniques that you learn in the next sections include the following DACL and SACL controls for folders and files:

- Attributes
- Permissions
- Auditing
- Ownership

Configuring Folder and File Attributes

Use of **attributes** is retained in the NT file system (NTFS) from its predecessor File Allocation Table (FAT) file system. Attributes are stored as header information with each folder and file, along with other characteristics including volume label, designation as a subfolder, date of creation, and time of creation.

Two basic attributes remain in NTFS that are still compatible with FAT in older Windows operating systems: read-only and hidden. Both of these attributes are accessed from the General tab when you right-click a folder or file and click Properties, such as from File Explorer.

When you check read-only for a folder, the folder is read-only but not the files in the folder. This means the folder cannot be deleted by using the *del* (delete) command from the Command Prompt or PowerShell windows (even though the folder attribute says "Only applies to files in folder"). When a file is checked as read-only, it also cannot be deleted from the Command Prompt or PowerShell windows. However, you can delete a file or folder with the read-only attribute using File Explorer. This discrepancy and the popularity of PowerShell make use of the read-only attribute less attractive.

Most Windows Server 2016 server administrators ignore the read-only attribute box and set the equivalent protection in permissions instead, because the read-only permissions apply to the folder and can be inherited by its files.

Folders and files can be marked as hidden to prevent users from viewing their contents, which is a carryover from MS-DOS operating systems. The hidden attribute can be defeated by using File Explorer, when the user displays the ribbon (click the Expand the ribbon down-arrow under the title bar), clicks the View tab, and clicks Hidden items (see Figure 5-1).

The read-only and hidden attributes are on the General tab in an NTFS folder's or file's properties dialog box. In addition to these attributes, NTFS offers advanced or extended attributes, which are accessed by clicking the General tab's Advanced button (see Figure 5-2).

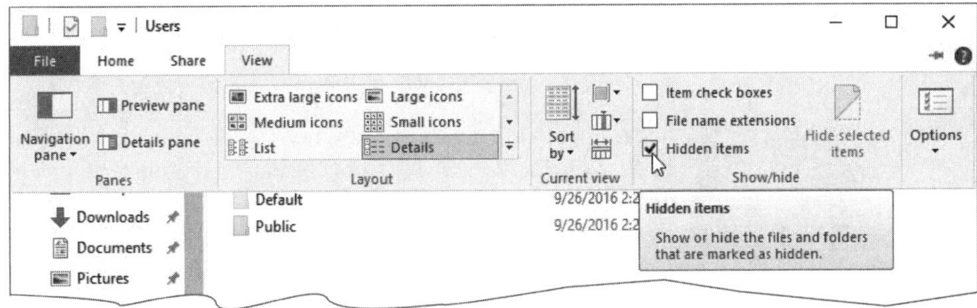

Figure 5-1 Selecting to view hidden files in the File Explorer ribbon

The advanced attributes are archive, index, compress, and encrypt. When you make a change to an attribute in the Advanced Attributes dialog box in a folder's properties, you see a message box with the option to apply that change to only the folder and the files in that folder or to apply the change to the folder, its files, and all subfolders and files within the folder. After the message box appears, make your selection about how to apply the change and click OK (as in Activity 5-1).

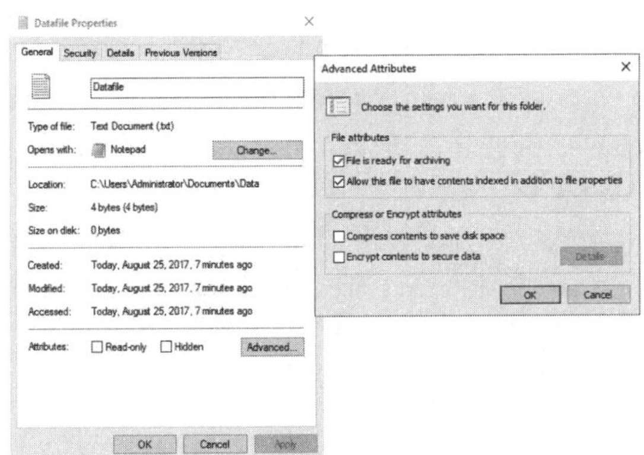

Figure 5-2 Attributes of a folder on an NTFS formatted disk

Archive Attribute The archive attribute (Folder or File is ready for archiving; see Figure 5-2) is checked to indicate that the folder or file needs to be backed up because it is new or changed. Most network administrators ignore the folder archive attribute, but instead rely on it for files. Files, but not folders, are automatically flagged to archive when they are changed. File server backup systems can be set to detect files with the archive attribute to ensure those files are backed up. The backup system ensures each file is saved following the same folder or subfolder scheme as on the server.

Index Attribute vs. Windows Search Service The index attribute and accompanying Indexing Service are legacy features for continuity with earlier operating systems, such as Windows Server 2003 and Windows 2000 Server. The NTFS index attribute (Allow this file to have contents indexed in addition to the file properties; see Figure 5-2) is used to index the folder and file contents so that file name, text, creation or modification date, author, and other properties can be quickly searched in Windows Server 2016. The index attribute marks a folder's contents or a specific file to be indexed through the Indexing Service. The Indexing Service creates a catalog of documents to be tracked and searched.

Windows Server 2016 offers a newer, faster search service called the Windows Search Service. This service is meant to replace using the index attribute and the Indexing Service, and it is recommended that you use this replacement—you can't use both the Windows Search Service and the Indexing Service at the same time. When you use Windows Search Service, you'll be impressed by its speed compared with the old Indexing Service.

To use the Windows Search Service, the File and Storage Services role must be installed (see Chapter 3, Configuring the Windows Server 2016 Environment) and the Windows Search Service must be selected as a feature.

Some steps in the activities in this book include bulleted questions for you to answer. Additionally, for all of the activities in this chapter, you'll need an account with Administrator privileges. These activities can be completed on a virtual machine or computer, such as in Hyper-V.

Activity 5-1: Installing Windows Search Service

Time Required: Approximately 10 minutes
Objective: Install Windows Search Service for faster folder and file searches.

Description: Having Windows Search Service installed on a server can save time and energy for server administrators and operators in an organization. In this activity, you install the Windows Search Service feature, which complements the File and Storage Services role. The File and Storage Services role should already be installed, which is the default when you install Windows Server 2016.

1. Open **Server Manager**, if it is not open.
2. Click **Manage** under the title bar in Server Manager and click **Add Roles and Features.**
3. If you see the Before you begin window in the Add Roles and Features Wizard, click **Next.**
4. Ensure **Role-based or feature-based installation** is selected in the Select installation type window and click **Next.**
5. Ensure your server is selected in the Select destination server window and click **Next.**
6. Ensure that **File and Storage Services (*x* of 12 installed)** is already marked as installed and click **Next** (where the *x* stands for the number of role services installed).
7. In the Select features window, scroll to and then click **Windows Search Service** (see Figure 5-3). Click **Next.**

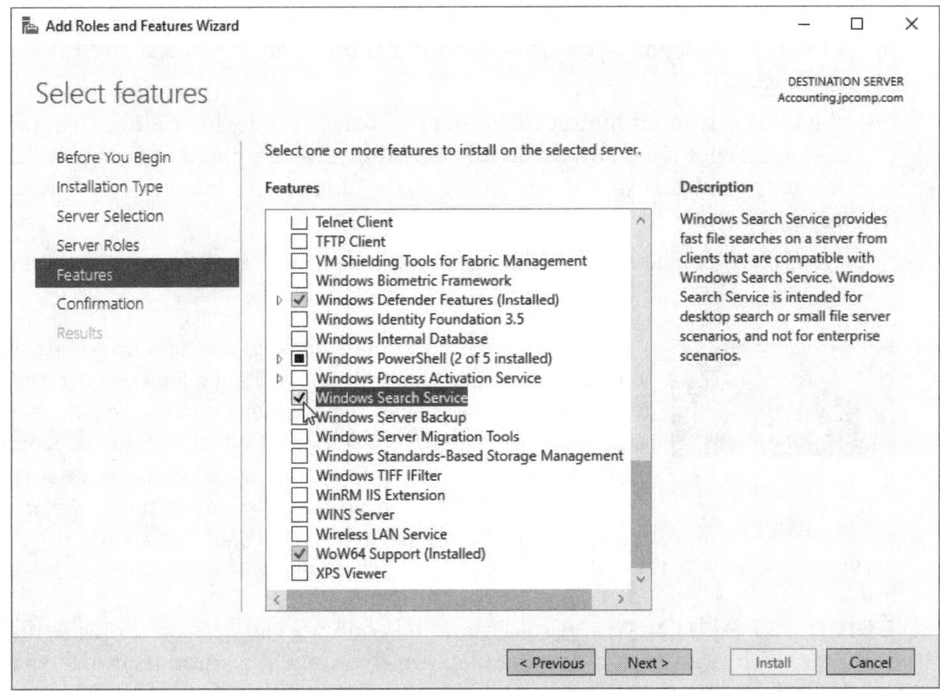

Figure 5-3 Installing the Windows Search Service

8. Click **Install** in the Confirm installation selections window.
9. Ensure that the installation succeeded and click **Close** in the Installation progress window.
10. Make sure that the Windows Search service is started by clicking **Tools** in Server Manager and clicking **Services.**
11. In the Services Window, double-click **Windows Search** under the Name column.
12. In the Windows Search Properties (Local Computer) dialog box, ensure that the **Startup type** is set to **Automatic**. Click **Apply.**
13. Click **Start** in the Windows Search Properties (Local Computer) dialog box.
14. Wait for the Service Control box to show the service is started. Click **OK** in the Windows Search Properties (Local computer) dialog box.
15. Close the Services window.

Once Windows Search Service is installed and started, Windows Server 2016 automatically creates an index of files. The indexed files include files in the Documents folder for an account, email files, photos, multimedia files, and any files that are commonly accessed. Some files that are not conducive to searches, such as system files, are not flagged for indexing by default (although you can configure them to be indexed). These files are excluded by default to help reduce the size of the index catalog as a way to keep searches as fast as possible.

Whenever you open a window, such as File Explorer, that has a Search box with a magnifying glass icon, you can use that box to perform a fast search using the Windows Search Service. Also, when a Windows 10 client searches for a file on Windows Server 2016, the Windows Search Service is used. Having fast client searches alone is a compelling reason for installing the Windows Search Service in Windows Server 2016. This makes users more productive and reduces time using the network that connects to a server.

You can maintain the Windows Search Service through Control Panel as follows:

1. Right-click Start and click Control Panel.
2. In the Large or Small icons view, click Indexing Options.

3. To select a new folder or volume to index (or stop indexing a folder or volume), click the Modify button, and select or deselect the appropriate volume(s) and folders (see Figure 5-4) and click OK.
4. Click the Advanced button to configure advanced indexing options from the Index Settings and File Types tabs. For example, you can index encrypted files, rebuild the index, change where the index is stored, or select certain file types to index. Click OK after making your selections.
5. Close the Indexing Options dialog box and Control Panel when you are finished.

If your searches are slow or not working, you can stop and restart the service. To do this, open Server Manager, click the Tools menu, click Computer Management, click Services and Applications in the tree, double-click Services in the middle pane, scroll to see if Windows Search is stopped. Even if the service is running, it may need to be stopped and restarted. To reset the service, first click to select it, then click *Restart the service*; or click *Stop the service* to fully stop it and then click *Start the service*.

Compress Attribute A folder and its contents can be stored on the disk in compressed format, which is an option that enables you to reduce the amount of disk space used for files, particularly in situations in which disk space is limited or for folders that are accessed infrequently, such as those used to store accounting data from a previous fiscal year. Compression saves space and you can work on compressed files in the same way as on uncompressed files. The disadvantage of compressed files is increased CPU overhead to open the files and to copy them. On a busy server, this might be an important consideration.

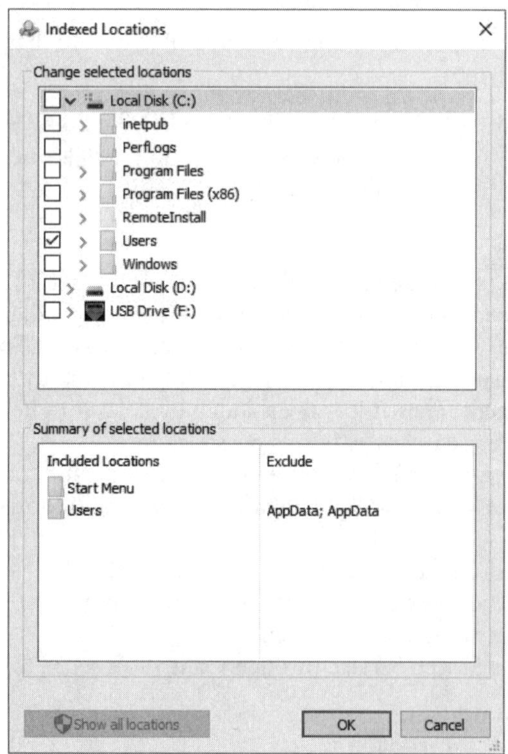

Figure 5-4 Configuring the locations to index

In general the best practices for using the compress attribute include the following tips:

- Busy servers that experience high-volume write or execute operations are poor candidates for the use of compression, which can tax the CPU and slow server performance.
- Servers that are rarely busy or that primarily have read traffic are acceptable candidates for file compression.
- Files that are rarely accessed or that are archived on the server can be candidates for compression.
- User home folders on a server typically have high levels of read and write activity and generally should not be compressed.

When you compress a folder, you have the option to compress the folder, its subfolders, and files in the folder. Also, when you add new files to a folder marked with the compress attribute, the new files are compressed automatically. By default, compressed files and folders are displayed in colored font, such as blue. If they are not displayed in color, you can turn on this feature using the following steps:

1. Right-click Start and click Control Panel.
2. In the Control Panel Category view, click Appearance and Personalization, and click File Explorer Options. Or in the Large icons or Small icons view, click File Explorer Options.
3. Click the View tab.
4. If necessary, click Show encrypted or compressed NTFS files in color.
5. Click OK in the File Explorer Options dialog box and close the Control Panel window.

If you are concerned about security and want to use the encrypt attribute, do not compress files because compressed files cannot be encrypted.

Encrypt Attribute The NTFS encrypt attribute protects folders and files so that only user accounts with the corresponding encryption or recovery key are able to read the file. As a server administrator, you might use this option to protect certain system files or new software files that you are not yet ready to release for general use. In an organization with sensitive file contents, encryption can be an essential security measure. It's also good business practice to encrypt stored files vital to a business strategy or containing company secrets. (Using BitLocker Drive Encryption is another way to protect files; see Chapter 10, Securing Windows Server 2016.)

An encrypted folder or file uses the Microsoft **Encrypting File System (EFS)**, which sets up a unique, private encryption key associated with the user account that encrypted the folder or file. The file is protected from network intruders and in situations in which a server or hard drive is stolen. EFS uses both symmetric and asymmetric encryption techniques. The symmetric portion uses a single key to encrypt the file or folder. In the asymmetric portion, two encryption keys are used to protect the key for encrypting the file or folder. Because the asymmetric portion is connected to a user account, the account should have a strong password to help ensure that attackers can't guess it easily.

File encryption and decryption involve some CPU overhead, which might be a consideration on a busy server.

When you view them in File Explorer, encrypted folders and files are displayed in color by default (but not the same color as compressed files), such as green. If they are not in color, you can configure the File Explorer Options to show them in color, using the same steps as for compressed files.

For the sake of security and disaster recovery, backing up EFS keys is as important as backing up EFS files. If EFS keys are not backed up, you have no access to EFS files when they are restored after a recovery. To make sure the keys are backed up, ensure that you back up the full OS, not just the EFS files. You can also back up EFS keys using the Certificates MMC snap-in and exporting the keys to removable media, such as a CD/DVD or thumb drive, for each account that uses EFS. Once you are in the Certificates MMC, expand the Personal folder in the tree and click Certificates. In the middle pane, right-click the user account, point to All Tasks, click Export, and follow the steps in the Certificate Export Wizard.

When you move an encrypted file to another NTFS folder on the same computer, that file remains encrypted, even if you rename it. No prompt is given to retain the Encrypt attribute when you move the file. The same holds true for copying the file to a different Windows Server 2016 server as long as it is formatted for NTFS (in which case it is decrypted, transferred, and then encrypted again). If you move the file to an older technology FAT or FAT32 partition, the file is decrypted. It is also decrypted if you move the file to a USB drive formatted for FAT/FAT32.

If you are the owner or have appropriate permissions, you can decrypt a folder or file by using File Explorer (click the File Explorer icon in the taskbar) to remove the Encrypt attribute and then apply the change. Folders and files can also be encrypted or decrypted by using the *cipher* command in the Command Prompt or PowerShell window (type *cipher /?* to view the command's switch options).

The best practices for using EFS as recommended by Microsoft include the following:

- Move files for encryption into specifically designated folders flagged for encryption. This is easier than managing encrypted files that are scattered in different locations. When a user needs to ensure a file is encrypted, she only needs to move that file to the designated folder location, to make sure it is encrypted.
- It is safer for an application to work on a file in an encrypted folder rather than to work on a file that is individually encrypted and not in an encrypted folder. When working on the individually encrypted file, the application may not ensure the saved result is encrypted. In contrast, if the file is in an encrypted folder, it will stay encrypted after it is saved by the application.
- Workstation users and server administrators should consider encrypting the My Documents or Documents folders on their systems (*\Users\accountname\My Documents* or (*\Users\accountname\Documents*).
- Users and server administrators should frequently export certificates and private keys to portable media and store the media in a secure place.

Activity 5-2: Encrypting Files

Time Required: Approximately 10 minutes
Objective: Encrypt files in a folder.

Description: The news media have reported on cases about theft in organizations in which a computer's drive has been stolen because of its valuable contents, such as business secrets or information crucial to national security. One way to provide security in these situations is to use the Encrypting File System to protect files. In this activity, you practice encrypting the contents of a folder.

1. Use File Explorer to create a new folder. For example, click the **File Explorer** icon in the taskbar, click a local drive, such as *Local Disk C:*, navigate to the Documents folder in your account or in the Administrator account, such as **\Users\Administrator\Documents**. Right-click an open area, click **New**, click **Folder**, and enter a folder name that is a combination of your first initial and last name, such as *JRyan*, and press **Enter**. Find a file to copy into the folder, such as a text-based document or another file already in the root of drive C. To copy the file, right-click it and click **Copy**. Open the new folder you created, right-click in an open area, and click **Paste** to copy the file into the new folder.

2. Right-click your new folder, such as *JRyan*, and click **Properties**. Make sure that the **General** tab is displayed, and if it is not, then click it.
   - What attributes are already checked?
3. Click the **Advanced** button.
   - Which attributes are already checked in the Advanced Attributes dialog box?
4. Check **Encrypt contents to secure data**, and then click **OK**.
5. Click **Apply**.
6. Be certain that **Apply changes to this folder, subfolders and files** is selected, and click **OK**.
   - Make a note of how you would verify that the file you copied into the folder is now encrypted. How would you decrypt the entire folder contents?
7. Click **OK** again to exit the Properties dialog box. Move the pointer to a blank area and click so that your folder is no longer highlighted. Now notice that the folder name appears in green (as long as *Show encrypted or compressed NTFS files in color* has previously been configured in File Explorer Options via Control Panel).
8. Decrypt the folder so that you can use it for another activity.
9. Close the folder's Properties dialog box and leave open File Explorer for the next activity.

Configuring Folder and File Permissions

Permissions control access to an object, such as a folder or file. For example, when you configure a folder so that a domain local group has access to only read the contents of that folder, you are configuring permissions. At the same time, you are configuring that folder's discretionary access control list (DACL) of security descriptors.

Use the Edit button on the folder properties Security tab to change which groups and users have permissions to a folder. To add a group, for example, click the Edit button, as shown in Figure 5-5. Activity 5-3 enables you to configure permissions and add a group. (As you learn shortly, in some cases you must remove inherited permissions before you can make changes.)

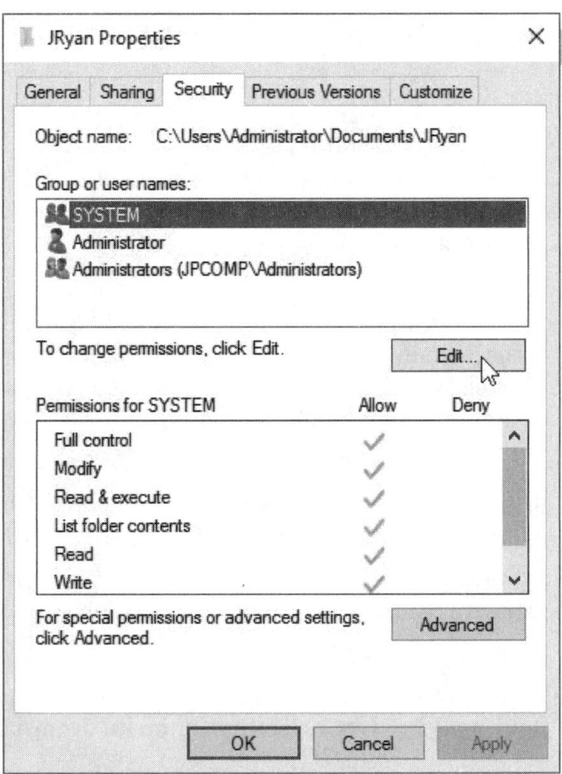

Figure 5-5 Configuring folder permissions

Table 5-1 lists the folder and file permissions supported by NTFS.

Table 5-1 NTFS folder and file permissions

Permission	Description	Applies to
Full control	Can read, add, delete, execute, and modify files, change permissions and attributes, and take ownership	Folders and files
Modify	Can read, add, delete, execute, and modify files; cannot delete subfolders and their file contents, change permissions, or take ownership	Folders and files
Read and execute	Implies the capabilities of both List folder contents and Read (traverse folders, view file contents, view attributes and permissions, and execute files)	Folders and files
List folder contents	Can list (traverse) files in the folder or switch to a subfolder, view folder attributes and permissions, and execute files, but cannot view file contents	Folders only
Read	Can view file contents, view folder attributes and permissions, but cannot traverse folders or execute files	Folders and files
Write	Can create files, write data to files, append data to files, create folders, delete files (but not subfolders and their files), and modify folder and file attributes	Folders and files
Advanced permissions	Advanced permissions apply (see Table 5-2)	Folders and files

If none of the Allow or Deny boxes are checked, then the associated group or user has no access to the folder. Also, when a new folder or file is created, it typically inherits permissions from the parent folder or from the root. Finally, if the Deny box is checked, this overrides any other access. For instance, if an account in a group has Allow checked for a specific permission but the group to which the account belongs has Deny checked, Deny prevails, even for the account with Allow checked.

Activity 5-3: Configuring Folder Permissions

Time Required: Approximately 10 minutes
Objective: Configure permissions on a folder so that users can modify its contents.

Description: Some organizations employ a group of server operators who perform the day-to-day management of servers. Assume that you need to create a Utilities folder for the server operators so that they can place new utilities in the folder, plus list the folder's contents and execute utilities out of that folder.

1. Open **File Explorer** (click its icon in the taskbar), if it is not already open. In the Documents folder of your account or of the Administrator account (see Step 1 of Activity 5-2), create a folder called Test plus your initials, such as *TestJR*. Inside the folder you just created, create a subfolder called Utilities plus your initials, such as *UtilitiesJR*.
2. Right-click the new Utilities folder, click **Properties,** and then click the **Security** tab.
   - What users and groups already have permissions to access the folder? Click each group and user to determine what permissions they have and record your results.
3. Click the **Edit** button. Click each group and user again, and notice that some boxes are checked and deactivated because they represent inherited permissions.
4. Click the **Add** button.
5. Click the **Advanced** button in the Select Users, Computers, Service Accounts, or Groups dialog box. Click **Find Now.** Double-click **Server Operators** in the list at the bottom of the box (see Figure 5-6). Click **OK.**

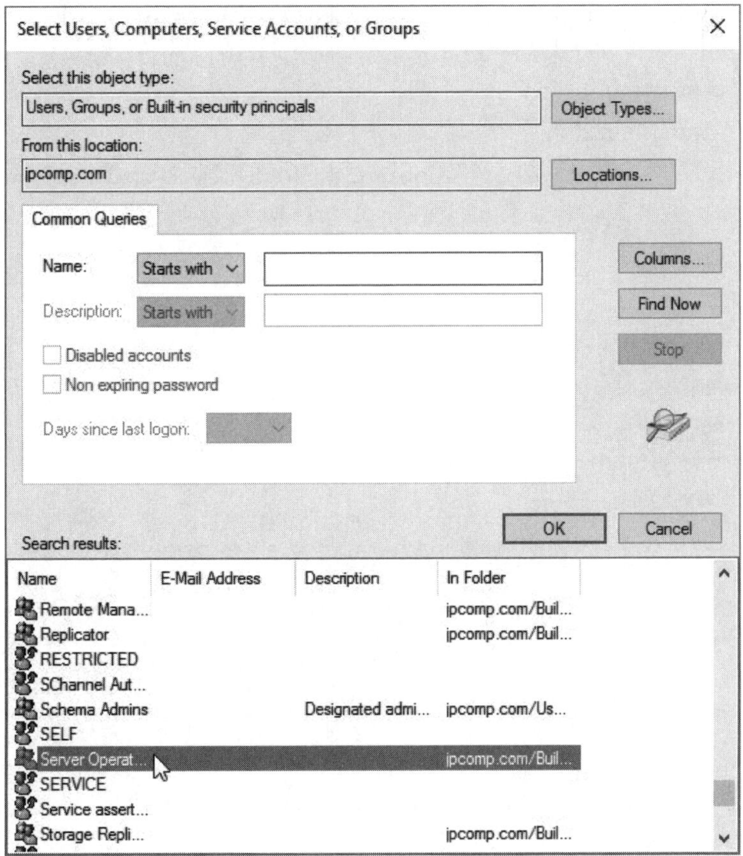

Figure 5-6 Selecting the Server Operators group

6. In the Permissions dialog box, ensure that **Server Operators** is selected.
   - What permission do the Server Operators have by default?
7. Click the **Allow** box for **Modify**.
8. Click **OK** in the folder's Permissions dialog box and click **OK** in the Properties dialog box.
9. Leave open File Explorer (the window with the folder containing the Utilities folder you have been working on) for the next activity, unless you need to stop working now.

As you noticed in Step 3 of Activity 5-3, some of the Allow boxes for permissions are checked and deactivated (refer to Figure 5-5). These are **inherited permissions**, which means that the same permissions on a parent object, such as the root folder in this case, apply to the child objects such as files and subfolders within the parent folder. If you want to change inherited permissions that cause Allow or Deny boxes to be deactivated (and checked), you can do this by removing the inherited permissions.

Activity 5-4: Removing Inherited Permissions

Time Required: Approximately 10 minutes
Objective: Remove inherited permissions on a folder.

Description: Often you want to remove inherited permissions for specific situations. In this activity, you learn how to turn off inherited permissions, so that permissions can be changed or even so that a specific group can be removed from accessing a folder. In this activity, you use the Utilities folder that you created earlier.

1. Use **File Explorer** to display the Utilities folder that you created in the last activity. Right-click the folder, and click **Properties**.
2. Click the **Security** tab.
3. Click the **Advanced** button.
4. Review the groups that have permissions for the folder. Click the **Disable inheritance** button (see Figure 5-7).

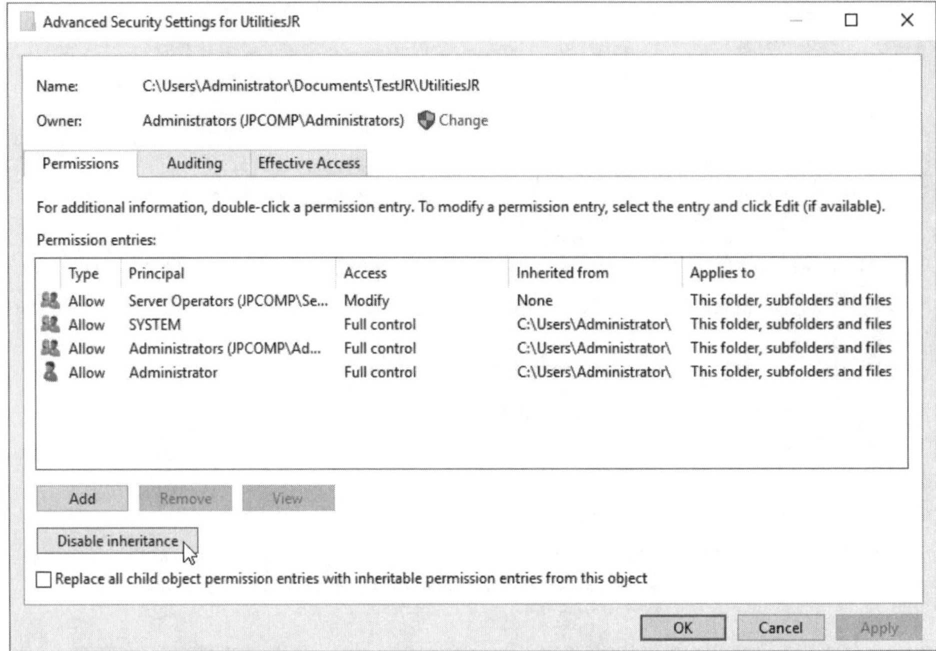

Figure 5-7 Disabling inheritance

5. Notice that you can select to convert inherited permissions to specific permissions for the folder or you can select to remove all inherited permissions. Click **Remove all inherited permissions from this object.**
6. In the Advanced Security Settings window, you'll now see that all other groups and user accounts with permissions have been removed, except for the Server Operators group that you configured manually and that does not use inherited permissions. Click **Cancel.**
7. In the folder Properties dialog box, notice that because you canceled the operation in Step 6, the default inherited groups are still listed.
8. Click **OK** in the folder's Properties dialog box.
9. Leave File Explorer open for the next activity, unless you need to stop working now.

If you need to customize permissions, you have the option to set up advanced permissions for a particular group or user. Figure 5-8 illustrates the advanced permissions that you can set up, and Table 5-2 explains each of the advanced permissions.

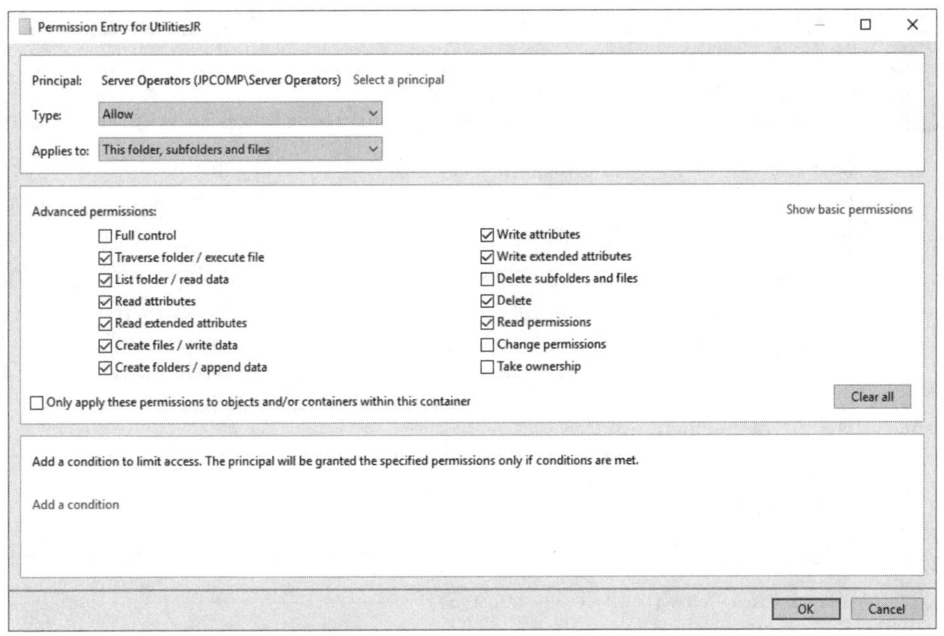

Figure 5-8 Advanced permissions

Table 5-2 NTFS folder and file advanced permissions

Permission	Description	Applies to
Full control	Can read, add, delete, execute, and modify files, plus change permissions and attributes, and take ownership	Folders and files
Traverse folder/execute file	Can list the contents of a folder and run program files in that folder	Folders and files
List folder/read data	Can list the contents of folders and subfolders and read the contents of files	Folders and files
Read attributes	Can view folder and file attributes (read-only and hidden)	Folders and files
Read extended attributes	Enables the viewing of extended attributes (archive, index, compress, and encrypt)	Folders and files
Create files/write data	Can add new files to a folder and modify, append to, or write over file contents	Folders and files
Create folders/append data	Can add new folders and add new data at the end of files, but otherwise cannot delete, write over, or modify data	Folders and files
Write attributes	Can add or remove the read-only and hidden attributes	Folders and files
Write extended attributes	Can add or remove the archive, index, compress, and encrypt attributes	Folders and files
Delete subfolders and files	Can delete subfolders and files (the following Delete permission is not required)	Folders and files
Delete	Can delete the specific subfolder or file to which this permission is attached	Folders and files
Read permissions	Can view the permissions (ACL information) associated with a folder or file (but does not imply you can change them)	Folders and files
Change permissions	Can change the permissions associated with a folder or file	Folders and files
Take ownership	Can take ownership of the folder or file (read permissions and change permissions automatically accompany this permission)	Folders and files

Activity 5-5: Configuring Advanced Permissions

Time Required: Approximately 15 minutes

Objective: Configure advanced permissions for a folder to grant a group expanded access.

Description: Sometimes the regular NTFS permissions do not enable you to create exactly the type of access you want on a folder. In this activity, you set up advanced permissions on a new folder for use by all users in your organization.

1. Using **File Explorer**, create a new folder (under the \Users*Youraccount*\Documents folder or in another location specified by your instructor, such as for the Administrator account) called Documentation plus your initials, such as *DocumentationJR*.
2. Right-click the new folder, and click **Properties**.
3. Click the **Security** tab.
4. Click **Edit**.
5. Click **Add**.
6. Click **Advanced** in the Select Users, Computers, Service Accounts, or Groups dialog box.
7. Click **Find Now** (refer to Figure 5-6).
8. Double-click the **Domain Users** group under *Search results*.
9. Click **OK** in the Select Users, Computers, Service Accounts, or Groups dialog box.
10. Click **OK** in the Permissions dialog box.
11. Ensure that **Domain Users** is selected under *Group or user names* in the Properties dialog box.
12. Click the **Advanced** button.
13. Select **Domain Users** under *Permission entries* in the Advanced Security Settings window, and click the **Edit** button.
14. Click **Show advanced permissions** in the Permission Entry window (see Figure 5-9).
    - Record the permissions that are selected by default for the Domain Users group.

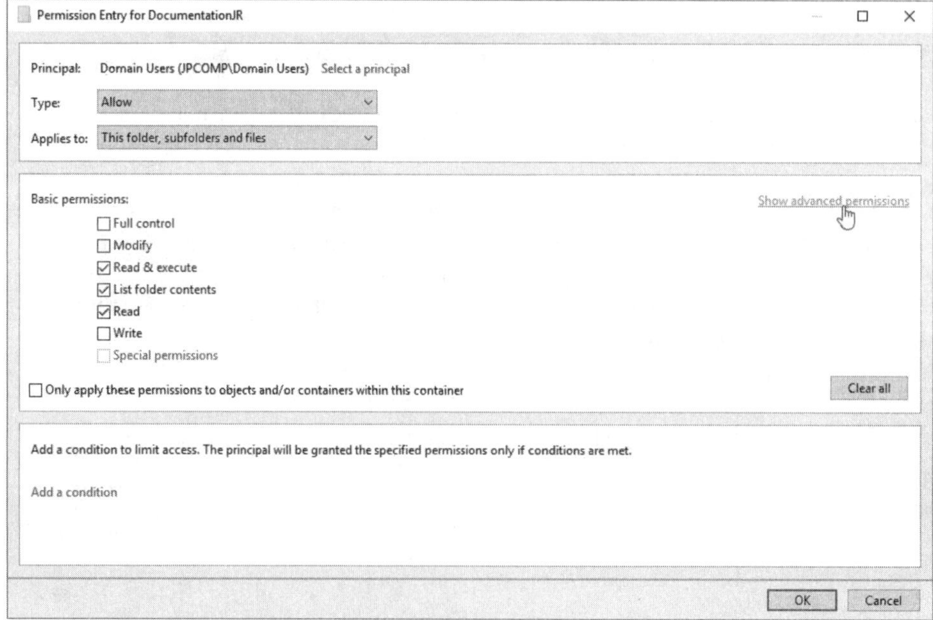

Figure 5-9 Clicking Show advanced permissions

15. Click the **Allow** box for each of the following advanced permissions entries: **Create files/write data, Create folders/append data, Delete subfolders and files**, and **Delete.**
16. Click the box for **Only apply these permissions to objects and/or containers within this container.**
17. Click **OK** in the Permission Entry window.
18. Click **OK** in the Advanced Security Settings window.
19. Click **OK** in the Properties dialog box.
20. Leave File Explorer open for the next activity (unless you need to stop working).

Microsoft provides best practice guidelines for setting permissions as follows:

- Protect the \Windows folder that contains operating system files on Windows Server 2016 servers and its subfolders from general users through allowing limited access, such as Read & execute and List folder contents or by just using the special permission to Traverse folder / execute file, but give the Administrators group Full control access.
- Protect server utility folders, such as for backup software and network management, with access permissions only for the Administrators, Server Operators, and Backup Operators groups.
- Protect software application folders with Read & execute and Write to enable users to run applications and write temporary files.
- Create publicly used folders to have Modify access, so users have broad access except to Take ownership, Change permissions, and Delete subfolders and files.
- Provide users Full control of their own home folders.
- Remove unnecessary access groups from confidential folders, as in those used for personal mail, for sensitive files, or for software development projects. (This can help protect members of unnecessary groups from suspicion, as well as meet requirements from system auditors.)
- Use Deny sparingly, for special circumstances only. For example, the Marketing group in your business contains all employees in the Marketing department, including the interns. This group has modify permissions to the Campaign folder, but the two interns in the department should not have access to the folder. Configure the folder permissions so that both intern's user accounts have Deny set for Modify. Also, the Marketing director has Full control permissions for the Campaign folder, but he or she should not be able to take ownership. In the folder's permissions, flag his or her account in the advanced permissions to deny Take ownership.

Always err on the side of too much security. It is easier, in terms of human relations, to give users permissions later than it is to take away permissions.

When removing groups and users from confidential folders, make sure you do not remove all access. Remember to keep administrator access (but have audit controls on such folders to protect the administrators from questions about accessing confidential material). Avoid using Deny on any object for the Administrators group or account, unless required by the financial auditors or company policy.

Configuring Folder and File Auditing

Accessing folders and files can be tracked by setting up **auditing**, which in Windows Server 2016 enables you to track activity on a folder or file, such as read or write activity. Some organizations choose to implement auditing on folders and files that involve financially sensitive information, such as those involving accounting and payroll. Other organizations monitor access to see which users access information, such as a folder containing files of employee guidelines and announcements, to determine if it is being used. Windows Server 2016 NTFS folders and files enable you to audit a combination of any or all of the activities listed as advanced permissions in Table 5-2. When you set up auditing, the options for each type of access are to track successful and failed attempts.

For example, consider a situation in which your organization's financial auditors specify that all accounting files in the Accounting folder must create an "audit trail" for each time a person who has access changes the contents of a file in the folder. Further, the financial auditors might want to verify that only groups that have access to write to files are those in the Accounting and Administrators groups. You would set up auditing by configuring the folder's security to audit each successful type of write event, such as Create files / write data and Create folders / append data. For extra information, you might track permission, attribute, and ownership changes by monitoring successful attempts to Write attributes, Write extended attributes, Change permissions, and Take ownership. Audited events are recorded in the Windows Server 2016 Security log that is accessed from Event Viewer. You learn to use the Event Viewer in Chapter 11, Server and Network Monitoring.

Activity 5-6: Auditing a Folder

Time Required: Approximately 20 minutes

Objective: Configure auditing on a folder to monitor how it is accessed and who is making changes to the folder.

Description: Now that you have created the Documentation folder, you decide to monitor how people are using the folder as well as the frequency of use. To do this, you set up auditing on that folder. To start, you must first enable auditing through a Group Policy in Active Directory, which is a one-time setup (you learn more about configuring group policies in Chapter 10, Securing Windows Server 2016). Once auditing is enabled, you can audit many types of objects, including specific folders. After you enable auditing, you configure the Documentation folder you created so that activity in the Documentation folder can be audited.

To enable auditing in Active Directory:

1. Right-click **Start** and click **Run**, enter **mmc** in the Run box, and click **OK**.
2. Click **File** and click **Add/Remove Snap-in.**
3. Click the **Group Policy Management Editor** (the second Group Policy option under available snap-ins) and click **Add.**
4. In the Select Group Policy Object dialog box, click the **Browse** button.
5. In the Browse for a Group Policy Object dialog box, click **Default Domain Policy** and click **OK.**
6. Click **Finish** in the Select Group Policy Object dialog box.
7. Click **OK** in the Add or Remove Snap-ins dialog box.
8. In the left pane, click the **right pointing arrow** in front of Default Domain Policy [*computername.domainname*] to display the items under it.
9. In the left pane, click the **right pointing arrow** in front of **Computer Configuration.**
10. Double-click the **Policies** folder in the left pane.
11. Double-click **Windows Settings** in the left pane.
12. Double-click **Security Settings** in the left pane.
13. Double-click **Local Policies** in the left pane.
14. Double-click **Audit Policy** in the left pane.
15. In the middle pane, notice the audit policies you can enable.
    - What would you select to audit logons? What would you select to audit account management activity, such as account creation and changing a password for a user?
16. In the middle pane, double-click **Audit directory service access** (see Figure 5-10).

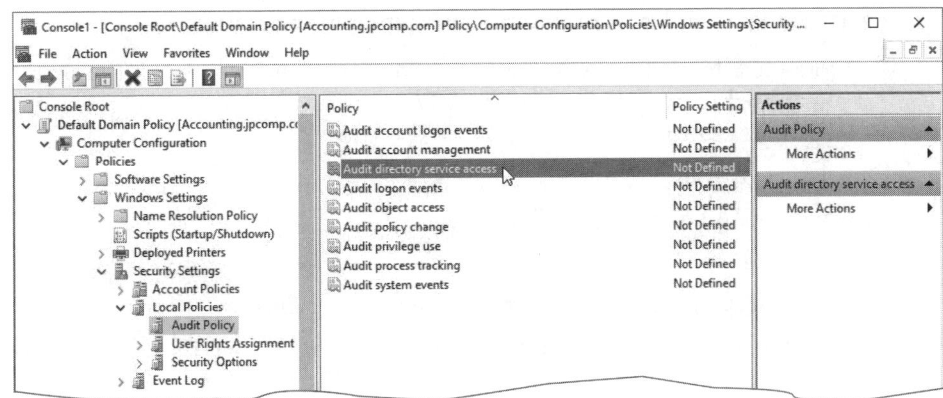

Figure 5-10 Selecting Audit directory service access

17. Click **Define these policy settings.** Next click **Success** and click **Failure** (to audit successful completion of an action and failure of an action; see Figure 5-11). Click **OK.** Notice the right portion of the middle pane shows you have configured Success, Failure for this option.
18. In the middle pane, double-click **Audit object access.**
19. Click **Define these policy settings.** Next click **Success** and click **Failure.** Click **OK.**
20. Close the Console1 MMC window. Click **Yes,** provide a name for the console, such as **Default Domain Policies,** click **Desktop** to save it on the desktop, and click **Save.**

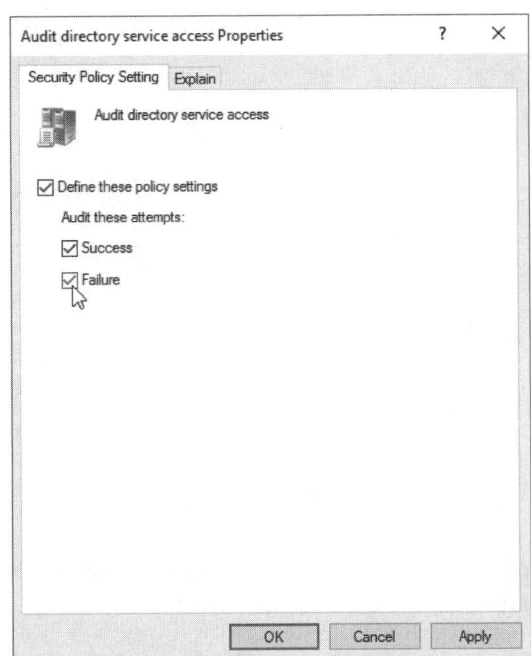

Figure 5-11 Configuring policy settings

You can audit activity on many Active Directory objects, such as accounts, folders, OUs, and other elements of Active Directory. The reason for tracking Active Directory changes is that many organizations now include this as part of their written security policy. Also, financial and computer system auditors expect this kind of tracking information. Active Directory is central to many Windows Server networks, and tracking changes to it is a sound security practice. In terms of best practices, the key is to have an auditing policy as part of your organization's security policy.

To configure auditing for the Documentation folder:

1. From the **File Explorer** window you have been using, right-click the Documentation folder you created in Activity 5-5, and click **Properties**.
2. Click the **Security** tab.
3. Click the **Advanced** button.
4. Click the **Auditing** tab (see Figure 5-12).
5. Click **Add**.
6. Click **Select a principal** at the top of the Auditing Entry window.
7. Click the **Advanced** button in the Select User, Computer, Service Account, or Group dialog box.

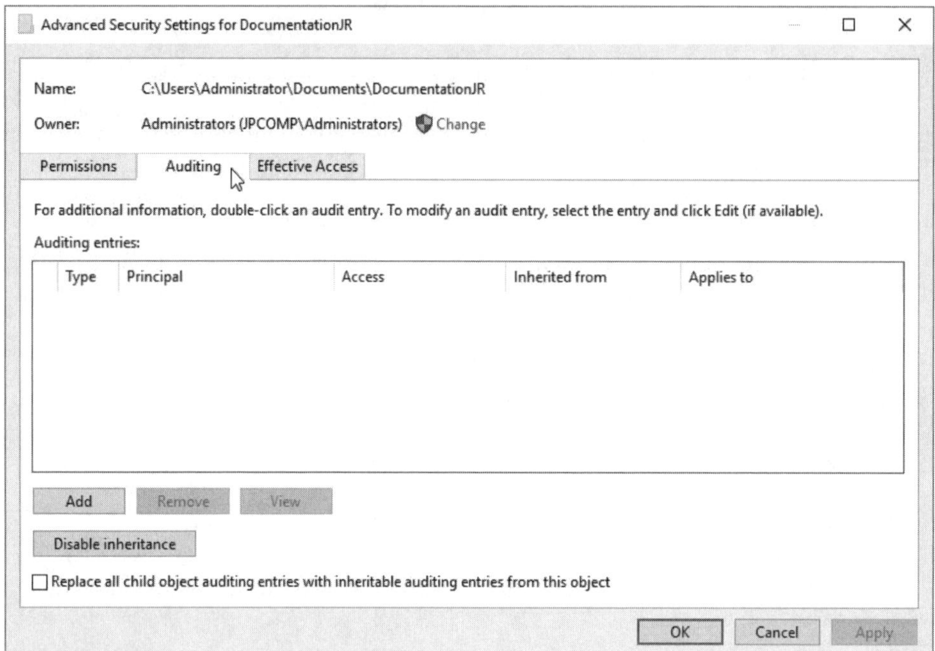

Figure 5-12 Selecting the Auditing tab

8. Click **Find Now**.
9. Double-click the **Everyone** group. (This group includes all network and authenticated users.)
10. Click **OK**.
11. Notice the permissions granted to the group. Click the **down arrow** for the Type box, and select **All** to audit both successful and failed access activities.
12. Click **OK**.
13. Click **OK** in the Advanced Security Settings dialog box.
14. Click **OK** in the Properties dialog box.
15. Close any open windows.

Be cautious about how much you choose to audit on a server. The more you audit, the more you will fill the Security log, requiring constant maintenance of the log. Also, with too much auditing configured, you can tie up a server's resources so they can't be used on the actual business of the server. These are additional reasons to have a written security policy, so you are clear about what needs to be audited.

You can view the contents of the Security log, which tracks auditing events, by opening Server Manager, clicking Tools, clicking Event Viewer, double-clicking Windows Logs in the left pane, and clicking Security in the left pane. You learn more about how to use Event Viewer logs in Chapter 12, Managing System Reliability and Availability.

Configuring Folder and File Ownership

With permissions and auditing set up, you might want to verify the **ownership** of a folder. Folders are first owned by the account that creates them, such as the Administrator account. Folder owners have the ability to change permissions for the folders they create. Also, ownership can be transferred only by having the Take ownership advanced permission or Full control permission (which includes Take ownership). These permissions enable a user to take control of a folder or file and become its owner. Taking ownership enables a shift of control from one account to another. The Administrators group always has the right to take control of any folder, regardless of the permissions, particularly because there are instances in which the server administrator needs to take ownership of a folder, such as when someone leaves an organization. The general steps you use to take ownership of a folder, using your account with Administrator privileges, are as follows:

1. Right-click the folder for which you want to take ownership, and click Properties.
2. Click the Security tab.
3. Click the Advanced button.
4. Click Change in the top of the Advanced Security Settings window and to the right of owner (refer to Figure 5-7).
5. Click the Advanced button in the Select User, Computer, Service Account, or Group box.
6. Click Find Now.
7. Click the new owner (see Figure 5-13) and click OK.

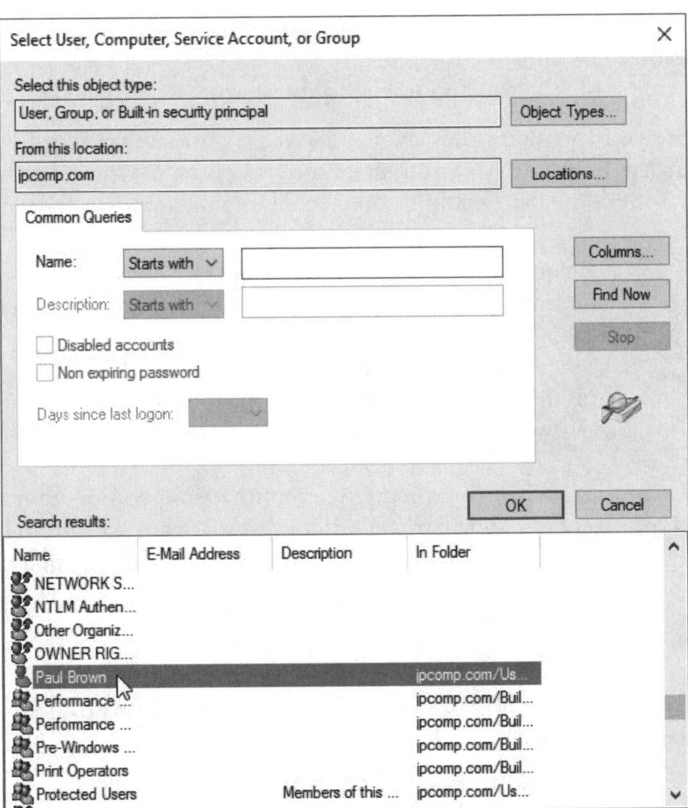

Figure 5-13 Selecting a new owner

8. Click OK in the Select User, Computer, Service Account, or Group box.
9. Click OK in the Advanced Security Settings window for the folder.
10. Click OK in the folder's Properties dialog box.
11. Close any other open windows.

Configuring Shared Folders and Shared Folder Permissions

Along with establishing folder permissions, auditing, and ownership, a folder can be set up as a shared folder for users to access over the network. Configuring a shared folder includes features so that the person configuring a share is more aware of security options. For example, when you select to share a folder, you go into the File Sharing dialog box, which has a format to encourage selecting specific users with which to share a folder (although you can still select to share with other users or groups).

Sharing a folder or file consists of first enabling sharing. The next step is to configure sharing for specific folders or files by specifying the user accounts or groups (or both) that have access and the permission they can use for the access. Configuring a share can be accomplished through managing a folder's or file's sharing through its individual properties. An additional way to configure sharing is through Server Manager.

Enabling Sharing

The first step for sharing a folder or file over the network is to make sure folder/file and printer sharing are turned on. Also, **network discovery**, which is the ability to view other network computers and devices, can be turned on. You only need to do this once, but it is necessary for users to be able to access the server's shared file/folder and printer resources. As you learn in Activity 5-7, you can do this from the Network window.

Activity 5-7: Enabling File and Folder Sharing

Time Required: Approximately 5 minutes
Objective: Turn on file sharing and public folder sharing as well as network discovery.

Description: Before you can share files over a network, ensure that Windows Server 2016 is enabled for file sharing. In this activity, you make sure that both network discovery and file sharing are turned on. Your computer should be connected to a network for this activity.

Even though you follow the steps to turn on network discovery and save your changes, Windows Server 2016 might not actually implement your changes. Before configuring network discovery, open Server Manager, click Tools, and click Services. Make sure that each of the following services are set to start automatically and that they are started: DNS Client, Function Discovery Resource Publication, SSDP Discovery, and UPnP Device Host.

1. In the right side of the taskbar, find the **network connection icon** in the tray. Right-click the icon and click **Open Network and Sharing Center**. (Alternatively, you can right-click **Start**, click **Control Panel**, use the **Large icons** or **Small icons** view, and click **Network and Sharing Center**.)
2. In the left side of the Network and Sharing Center window, click **Change advanced sharing settings**.
3. In the Advanced sharing settings window, notice that the current profile is Domain for a server that is a DC in a domain. The arrow for **Domain (current profile)** should be pointing up, and if it is not, click the **down arrow** to view the configuration options.
4. Ensure that **Turn on network discovery** is selected.
5. Next, ensure that **Turn on file and printer sharing** is selected (see Figure 5-14).

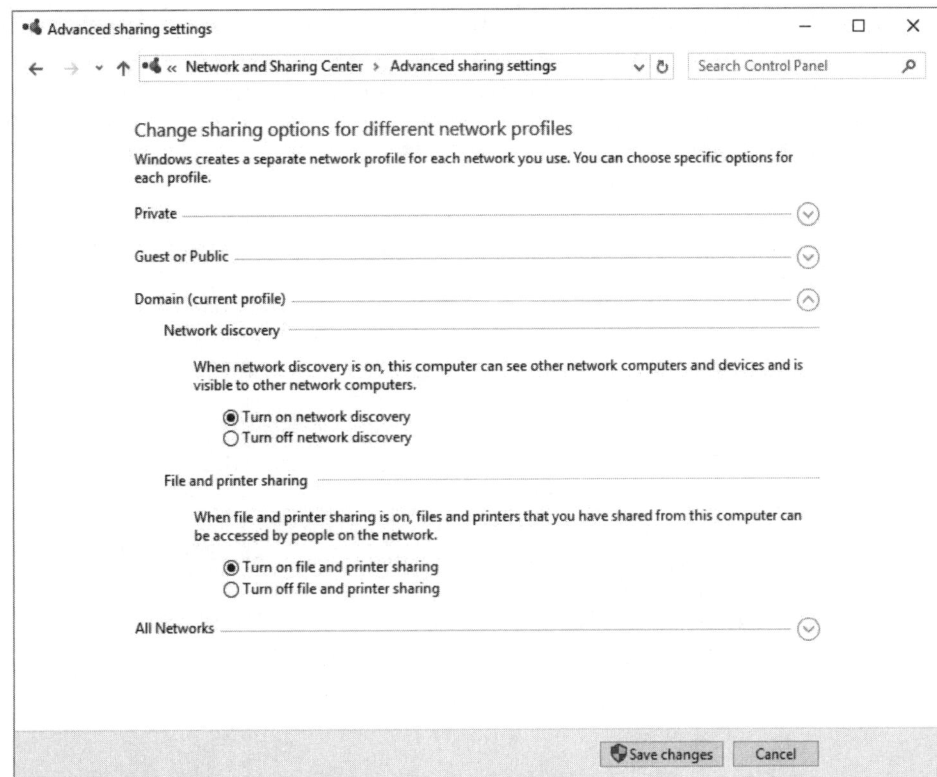

Figure 5-14 Configuring network discovery and file and printer sharing for the domain

6. Click the **down arrow** for **All Networks.**
7. Click **Turn on sharing so anyone with network access can read and write files in the Public folders.** This enables network clients to access the Public folders in Windows Server 2016 over the network to read or copy files.
8. Click **Save changes.**
9. Close the Network and Sharing Center window and any other open windows.

The Public folders are similar to the same folders in other Windows operating systems including Public Documents, Public Downloads, Public Music, Public Pictures, and Public Videos. Public folders offer a convenient way to share files over a network. You simply drag the files you want to share into the appropriate Public folder. By default, Public folders cannot be accessed by network clients unless you configure to share them. You can find these folders in \Users\Public.

Network discovery must be enabled so that clients can find and access a shared folder. If you try to turn on network discovery but it goes back to the off state, configure the Firewall exceptions to allow this type of network access. Click the Windows Firewall link in the Network and Sharing Center, click Allow an app or feature through Windows Firewall, review the listing under Allowed apps and features, and ensure features such as Network Discovery and Netlogon Service are allowed for Domain (and also Private or Public, if applicable). The Windows Firewall also needs to be configured in terms of inbound and outbound rules. You learn more about Windows Firewall in Chapter 10.

Configuring Folder/File Sharing Through the Folder/File Properties

The basic **share permissions** for a folder or file can be set by configuring sharing using the File Sharing window (see Figure 5-15) and a folder's or file's Sharing tab in its Properties dialog box. You can configure both sharing permissions and advanced sharing properties. When you configure sharing using the advanced sharing options, the share permissions also include Full control and Change. The share permissions are:

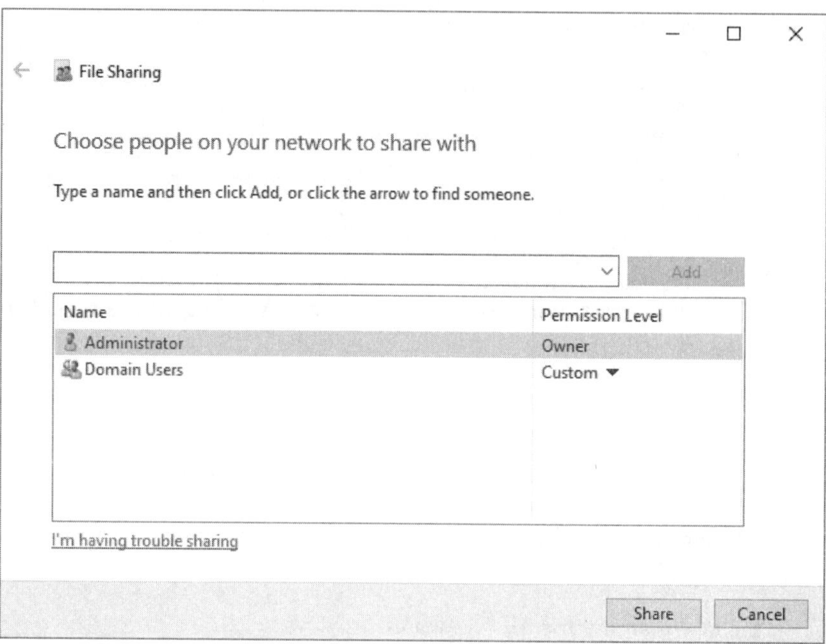

Figure 5-15 File Sharing window

- *Read*—Permits groups or users to read and execute files, but they cannot add or delete files and folders and cannot modify files
- *Write*—Enables groups or users to modify the contents of files
- *Change or Contribute* (advanced permission)—Enables groups and users to read, execute, and add files, but they can only modify and delete files provided by them
- *Custom*—Means advanced permissions already apply on this folder or file
- *Full control* (advanced share permission)—Permits groups or users to read, execute, add, delete, and modify files, and to create and delete subfolders and manage share permissions
- *Owner*—Assigned to the owner of the folder, such as the folder's creator, and enables the owner to read, execute, add, delete, and modify files in the shared folder as well as create and delete subfolders and manage the share permissions

NTFS permissions and share permissions are cumulative. The bottom line is that a user or group has access based on the lowest common denominator. For example, if you have Full control share permissions to a folder, but regular NTFS permissions give you no access to the same folder, then you have no access. A practice used by many server administrators and supported by Microsoft is to keep permission granting simple. First rather than using Deny, just don't include users and groups in the security for a folder or file who should not have access. For users and groups who need access to a shared folder, give them Full control or Change share permissions and then restrict their access through setting regular NTFS permissions—thus controlling access through one mechanism, the NTFS permissions.

Advanced sharing is configured using the Advanced Sharing button on the Sharing tab of a folder's or file's Properties box. Before setting the share permissions, first make sure you have selected the appropriate groups and users, such as by specifying the Everyone, Domain Users, or Users groups for a publicly accessed folder. Select to share the folder or file and then use the Permissions dialog box to set up additional groups and users to have access to a shared folder.

When configuring Advanced Sharing, you can click the Caching button to make the contents of a shared folder available offline. This step enables you to set up a folder so that it can be accessed by a client even when the client computer is not connected to the network, such as when the network connection is lost or when a user disconnects a laptop computer to take home. Offline in this situation means that the folder is cached on the client computer's hard drive for continued access after losing the network connection and that the folder location remains unchanged in File Explorer. When the network connection is resumed, any offline files that have been modified can be synchronized with the network versions of the files. If two or more users attempt to synchronize a file, they have the option of choosing whose version to use or of saving both versions. A folder can be cached in three ways:

- *Only the files and programs that users specify will be available offline*—Files and programs are cached only per the user's request per each document (the default option).
- *No files or programs from the shared folder are available offline*—Files and programs are not cached on the computer's hard drive.
- *All files and programs that users open from the shared folder are automatically available offline*—Files and programs are cached without user intervention, which means that all files in the folder which are opened by the client or which are executed by the client are cached automatically.

When you share a folder, an option is provided to hide that shared folder so that it does not appear on a browser list, as in the Network window in Windows 10 or Server 2016. To hide a share, place the $ sign just after its name. For instance, if the *Share name* text box contains the share name Budget, you can hide the share by entering Budget$. (This is an actual example of what one university does to discourage general scanning of a folder containing budget worksheets. However, department accounting technicians who know of the folder's existence can map it to help with budget planning.)

Besides hiding a shared folder using the $ sign, you can instead enable access-based enumeration. **Access-based enumeration** permits the user to view only folders and files for which they have permissions. At minimum the user must have Read permission or the equivalent to view the folder or file. You can enable access-based enumeration when you configure a shared folder using Server Manager (see Activity 5-9) or by later configuring the settings via Server Manager in a shared folder's properties. Many server administrators consider access-based enumeration a better practice than using the $ sign.

When you right-click a folder to view its properties, the Share with option on the shortcut menu might be missing or you might not see the Sharing tab in the Properties dialog box. You can troubleshoot this problem by making sure that the Server service is started, and even if it is, you can restart it in case the service is hung (make sure no users are on if you restart it). To start or restart the Server service, open Server Manager, click Tools, click Component Services, click Services (local) in the left pane, click Server in the middle pane. Click Start or Restart in the middle pane.

Activity 5-8: Configuring a Shared Folder

Time Required: Approximately 15 minutes
Objective: Configure a shared folder, share permissions, and offline access.

Description: As a server administrator, one of the most important tasks you perform is to enable folder sharing. In this activity, you configure a folder to be shared over the network.

1. Use File Explorer (click the **File Explorer** icon in the taskbar) to locate the Documentation folder you created in Activity 5-5, such as *DocumentationJR*.
2. Right-click the folder, point to **Share with**, and click **Specific people** to see the File Sharing window (see Figure 5-15).
3. Click the **down arrow** next to the Add button and click **Find people.**
4. Click the **Advanced** button in the Select Users or Groups dialog box.
5. Click **Find Now**.
6. Double-click the DomainMgrs group you created in Activity 4-9 in Chapter 4, such as *DomainMgrsJP* (DomainMgrs with your initials). Click **OK.**
7. Click the **down arrow** for the Permission Level for the DomainMgrs group and click **Read/Write.**
8. Click the **Share** button at the bottom of the File Sharing window.
9. The File Sharing window indicates the folder is shared and enables you to email the link for the shared folder or to copy the link into a program (see Figure 5-16). Click **Done.**

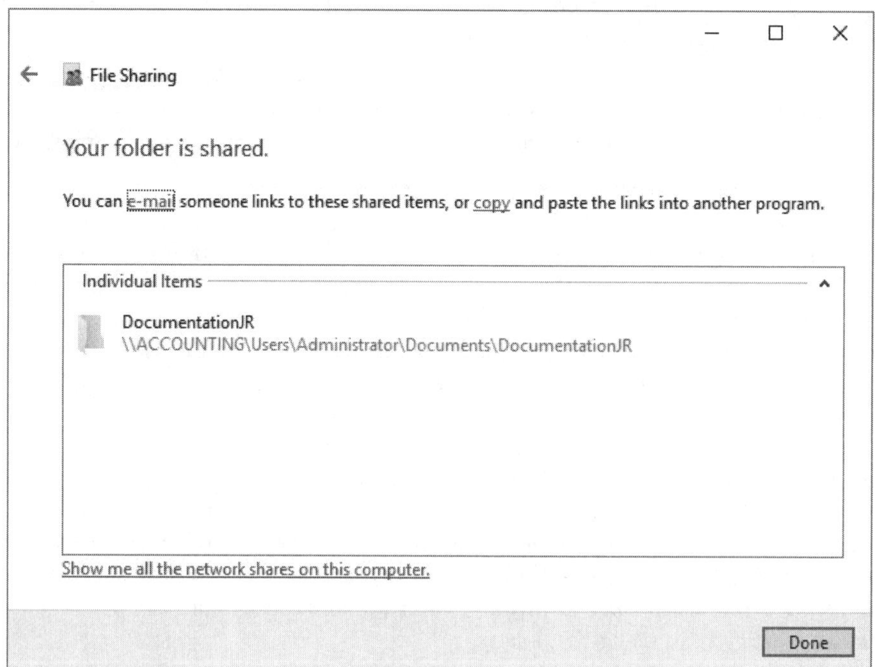

Figure 5-16 Options to email the link of a shared folder or to copy it into a program

10. In File Explorer, right-click the folder you just shared and click **Properties.**
11. Click the **Sharing** tab.
12. Click the **Share** button.
    - What window is now displayed? How would you remove a user or group from those sharing the folder?
13. Click **Cancel.**

14. Click the **Advanced Sharing** button in the Properties dialog box.
15. In the Advanced Sharing dialog box, click the box for **Share this folder**. Notice that the Share name is the same name as the shared folder (see Figure 5-17).
    - How can you change the name of the share? How can you set the limit of users who can access the share at the same time?

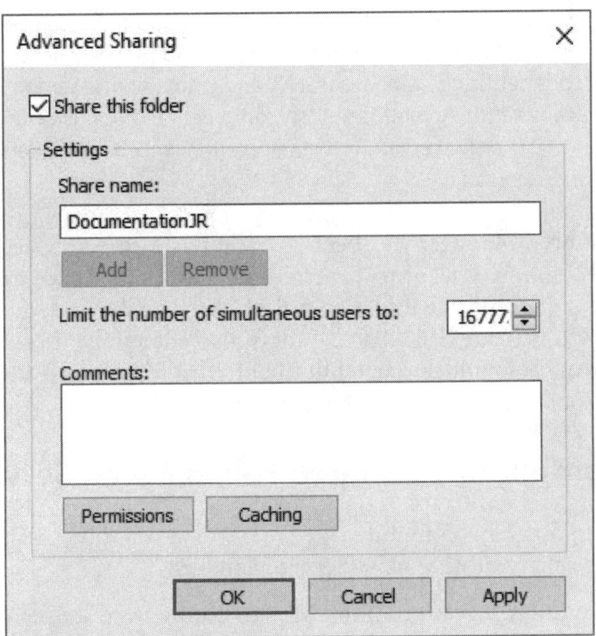

Figure 5-17 Advanced Sharing dialog box

16. Click the **Permissions** button in the Advanced Sharing dialog box. Notice that the permissions are now displayed as Full control, Change (same as Contribute), and Read. Also, you can select the Allow or Deny boxes for any of the permissions. Further, you can add or remove users and groups. Click **Cancel**.
17. In the Advanced Sharing dialog box, click **Caching**.
18. To configure full offline use, click **All files and programs that users open from the shared folder are automatically available offline**. Notice that *Optimized for performance* is enabled by default. Click **OK**.
19. Click **OK** in the Advanced Sharing dialog box.
20. Click **Close** in the Properties for the folder dialog box. Close File Explorer.

Client computers can now access the shared folder through the network, such as through the Network window available from Windows Explorer in older versions of Windows or File Explorer in Windows 8.1 and Server 2012 R2 and later versions.

Configuring Sharing Through Server Manager

Another way to configure folder and file permissions and share permissions is by using Server Manager. This method is popular with server administrators because Server Manager offers an interface for managing permissions and shares from one tool. Also, there are more easily accessed options for share management, such as configuring the protocol to use for sharing and establishing folder quotas. By default, file sharing uses the **Server Message Block (SMB) protocol**. SMB protocol, which was originally designed by IBM, enables an operating system to offer shared files, folders, printers, serial ports, and other port communications on a network. Through the years, SMB has been continually enhanced by Microsoft to offer new features, particularly for virtualization. Another file and folder sharing protocol that can be used is **Network File System (NFS) protocol**, which is used for file and folder sharing on UNIX and Linux systems and, when installed on a Windows system share, enables it to be accessed by UNIX and Linux computers.

Rather than using NFS to access a shared resource on a Windows-based server, many UNIX and Linux users employ Samba. Samba is free open-source software that enables a UNIX or Linux computer to use SMB protocol to access shared Windows resources. So before you set up to use NFS, consider using Samba on UNIX and Linux clients. Samba for Mac is also available for Apple Macintosh computers running Mac OS X before version 10.9 or Mavericks. Newer Apple Macintosh computers use SMB version 3.x by default.

When File Server Resource Manager has been installed as a role service, you can also set folder quotas. For example, you may want to control how much disk space can be allocated to a shared folder, so that users don't fill the folder so full of files that the folder occupies too much disk space. Besides helping to manage disk space, quotas also encourage users to delete old files so that they don't run out of their folder space allotment. You learn more about quotas in the section, Configuring Disk Quotas, later in this chapter.

Activity 5-9: Configuring a Shared Folder Using Server Manager

Time Required: Approximately 15 minutes
Objective: Configure a shared folder from Server Manager.

Description: A popular way for a server administrator to configure a shared folder is by using Server Manager. In this activity, you first use Server Manager to install the File Server Resource Manager to enable the use of folder quotas. Next, you use Server Manager to configure a shared folder. The File and Storage Services role should already be installed on the server, which is done by default when you install the operating system.

1. Open **Server Manager**, if it is not open.
2. Click **Manage** near the top of the Server Manager window and click **Add Roles and Features.**
3. Click **Next**, if you see the Before you begin window.
4. Ensure **Role-based or feature-based installation** is selected and click **Next.**
5. In the Select destination server window make sure your server is selected and click **Next.**
6. Ensure that **File and Storage Services** is already marked as installed. Click the **right-pointing arrow** in front of **File and Storage Services.** Click the **right-pointing arrow** in front of **File and iSCSI Services** to view the options under it (see Figure 5-18).
7. Check the box for **File Server Resource Manager.** (If File Server Resource Manager is already installed, click **Cancel** and go to Step 13.)
8. If you see the Add Roles and Features Wizard to add additional features, click **Add Features.**
9. Click **Next** in the Select server roles window.
10. Click **Next** in the Select features window.
11. Click **Install** in the Confirm installation selections window.
12. Make sure the installation was successful and then click **Close** in the Installation progress window.
13. In the left pane of Server Manager, click **File and Storage Services.**
14. Click **Shares** in the left pane.
15. In the middle pane, notice the Documentation folder that you configured in Activity 5-8 is listed under SHARES.

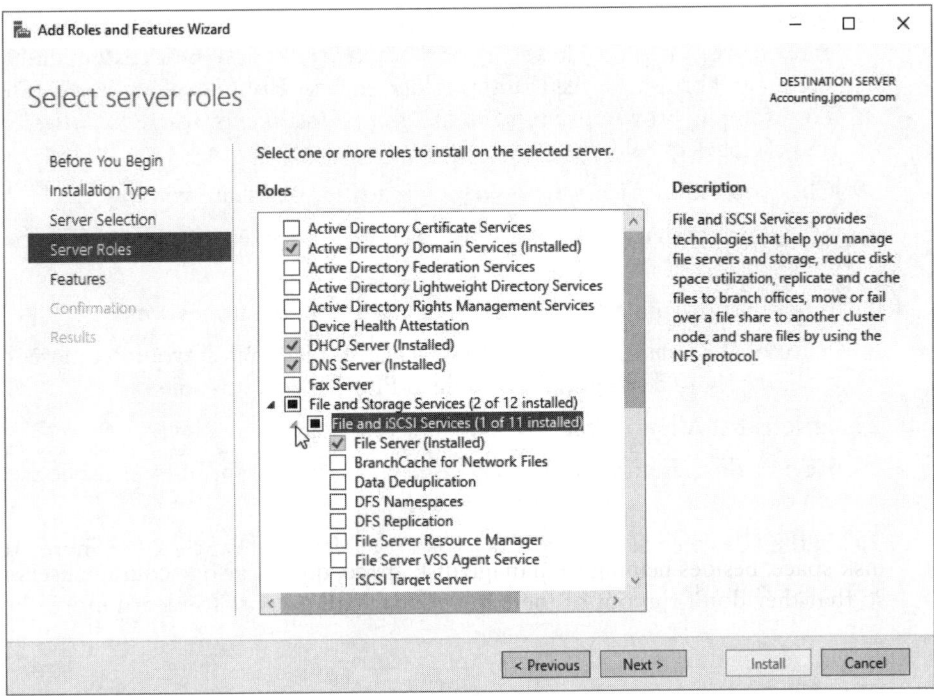

Figure 5-18 Installing File Server Resource Manager

16. In the middle pane, click the **down arrow** for **TASKS**. Click **New Share**.
17. In the Select the profile for this share window, select **SMB Share – Advanced** (see Figure 5-19). The profiles are methods established for guiding you through creating shares, presenting options for simple to more advanced situations. Notice that the right pane provides a description of this profile. Click **Next**.

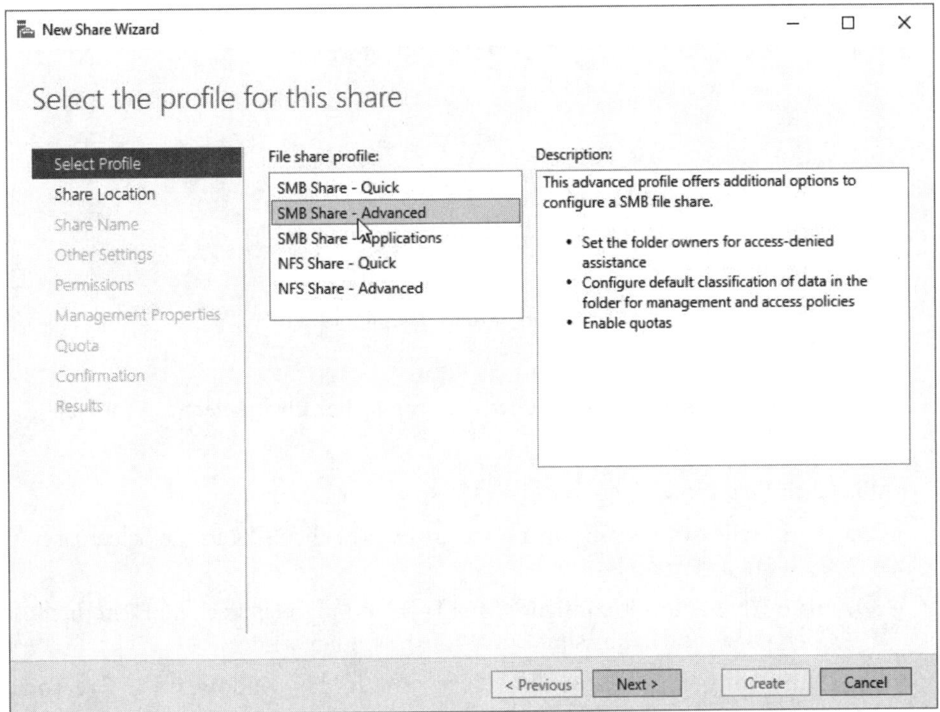

Figure 5-19 Selecting the file share profile

18. In the Select the server and path for this share window, notice that you can select to share an entire drive, if needed. However, for this activity, select **Type a custom path**. Click the **Browse** button and browse to the Utilities folder, such as *UtilitiesJR* that you created in Activity 5-3. For example, browse to *users/administrator/documents/TestJR/UtilitiesJR*. Click the folder and click **Select Folder.**
19. Click **Next** in the Select the server and path for this share window.
20. In the Specify share name window, leave the share name of the folder as the default and click **Next.**
21. Notice the options available in the Configure share settings window.
    - Record the options from which to select. Which option would you use to permit users to view only folders and files for which they have permissions?
22. Ensure that **Allow caching of share** is selected and click **Next.**
23. Review the permissions already configured in the Specify permissions to control access window. Click **Customize permissions.**
24. In the Advanced Security Settings for the folder window, click the **Share** tab.
25. Click **Add** (see Figure 5-20).

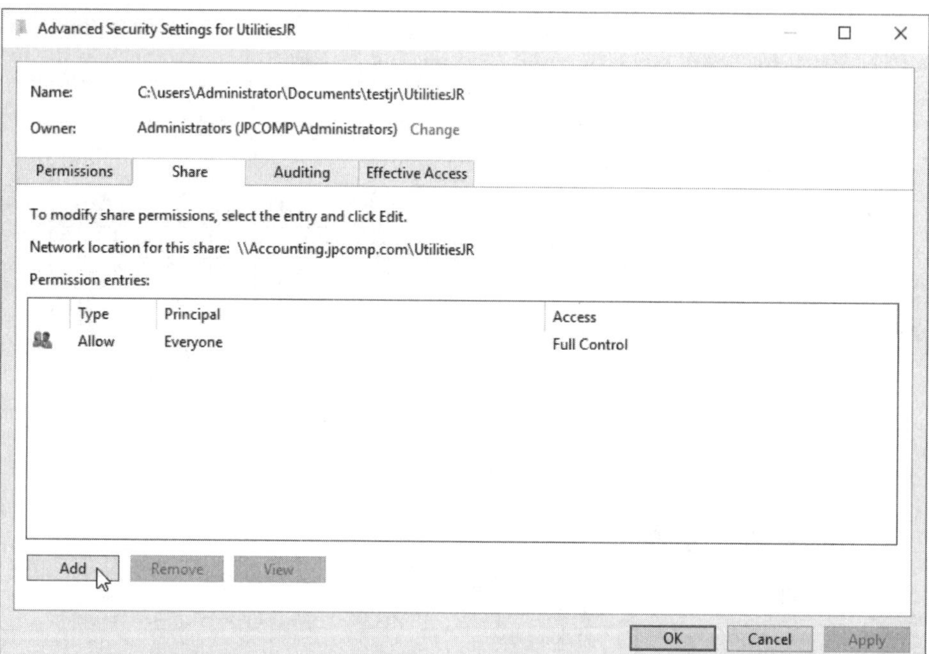

Figure 5-20 Adding a user or group to the share permissions

26. In the Permissions Entry window for the folder, click **Select a principal.**
27. Click **Advanced.**
28. Click **Find Now.**
29. Double-click the **Server Operators** group and click **OK** in the Select User, Computer, Service Account, or Group box.
30. Ensure that **Allow** is configured for Type and place a check mark in the box for **Full Control.** Click **OK** in the Permission Entry for the folder window.
31. In the Advanced Security Settings for the folder window, if the **Everyone** group is shown, click it and click **Remove.**

32. Click the **Permissions** tab. Click **Server Operators** and click **Edit.** In the Permission Entry for the folder window, be sure that **Full control** is selected for the Allow Type. This step ensures that both the folder permissions and the share permissions are the same. Click **OK.**
33. Click **OK** in the Advanced Security Settings for the folder window.
34. In the New Share Wizard window, click **Next.**
35. In the Specify folder management properties window, check the boxes for **User Files** and **Application Files** (as you will recall the folder is for server operators to use to run utilities).
36. Click **Next.**
37. In the Apply a quota to a folder or volume window, notice there is an informational note at the bottom of the window that says *A quota is already applied to the folder that will be shared.* Click **Next.**
38. In the Confirm selections window, review your choices and click **Create.**
39. Click **Close** in the View results window (see Figure 5-21).

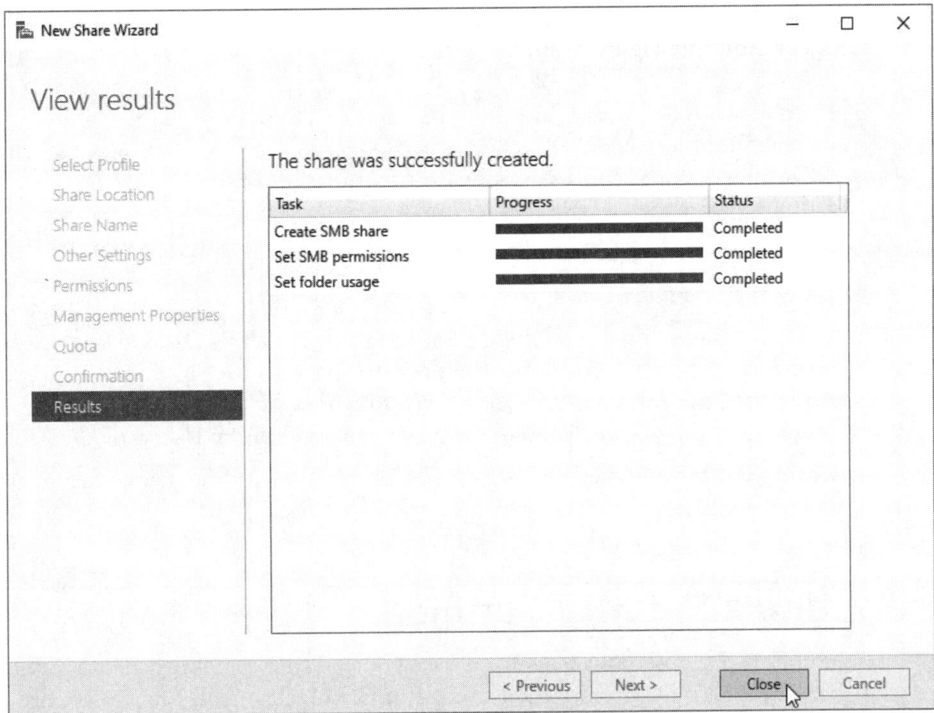

Figure 5-21 View results window

40. In Server Manager, confirm that your new share is shown under SHARES.
41. Click the **back arrow** twice near the top of Server Manager, to return to the main window. Leave Server Manager open for the next activity.

Publishing a Shared Folder in Active Directory

One reason for having Active Directory is to enable certain objects to be "published" so that users can find and access them quickly. To **publish** an object means to make it available for users to access when they view Active Directory contents. For example, a shared folder or a shared printer can be published in Active Directory for clients to access. Publishing an object also makes it easier to find when a user searches for that object, such as by using the Network window from Windows Explorer and File Explorer on Windows clients. Once an object is published, information associated with it is replicated in copies of Active Directory that are kept when multiple domain controllers are present on a network, enabling a published object to be accessed even when one domain controller is down.

Active Directory search capabilities are automatically built into all modern Windows operating systems, including Windows 10 and Server 2016.

When you publish an object, you can publish it to be shared for domain-wide access or to be shared and managed through an organizational unit (OU). A shared folder, for example, might be used only by a department in a company. If you publish the shared folder in that department's OU, then the accounts (users) that manage that OU can also manage the shared folder and how it is accessed.

Activity 5-10: Publishing a Shared Folder

Time Required: Approximately 5 minutes
Objective: Publish a shared folder in Active Directory.

Description: In this activity, you learn how to use the Active Directory Users and Computers tool to publish the shared Documentation folder you configured in Activity 5-8.

1. Open **Server Manager**, if it is not open.
2. Click **Tools** and click **Active Directory Users and Computers**.
3. If necessary, click the **right arrow** in front of the domain name in the left pane to see the items under the domain. Right-click the **Users** folder in the tree (or you could right-click an OU at this point to control administration of the published folder from an OU by delegating authority over the OU). Point to **New**.
   - What are two objects that you can publish using this menu?
4. Click **Shared Folder.**
5. Enter the name for the published shared folder, such as *DocumentationJR* (the folder you created in Activity 5-5). Enter the network path to the share, such as *\\servername\Users\Administrator\Documents\ DocumentationJR*. Click **OK**. Notice that the shared folder is now one of the objects listed in the right pane within the Users (or OU) folder.
6. Close the Active Directory Users and Computers window. Leave Server Manager open for the next activity.

Troubleshooting a Security Conflict

Sometimes you will set up access for a user but find that the user does not actually have the type of access you set up. Consider the example of Cleo Jackson, an English professor who maintains a shared subfolder called Assignments for his students from the account CJackson. Assignments is a subfolder under the parent folder English, which contains folders used by all English professors. CJackson needs to update files, copy in new files, and delete files. As Administrator, you have granted CJackson Modify access permissions to Assignments. However, you omitted the step of reviewing the groups to which CJackson belongs, such as the Paper group, which consists of Cleo Jackson and the student newspaper staff. The Paper group has been denied all access to the English folder and all of its subfolders. When Cleo Jackson attempts to copy a file to the Assignments folder, he receives an access denied message.

To troubleshoot the problem, you should review the folder permissions and share permissions for the CJackson account and for all of the groups to which CJackson belongs. In this case, because the Paper group is denied access, CJackson is also denied. The easiest solution is to remove CJackson from the Paper group and perhaps create a group of English professors, such as Eng-Profs, who all have access to the same resources as the Paper group.

Windows Server 2016 offers the Effective Access tab in the properties of a folder or file as a tool to help troubleshoot permissions conflicts. To access this tab, right-click a folder or file, click Properties, click the Security tab, click the Advanced button, and click the Effective Access tab. Using the Effective Access tab, you can view the effective permissions assigned to a user or group. The calculation will take into account group membership as well as permission inheritance. After the calculation is complete, a user's or group's effective permissions are indicated with a check mark beside them.

When you troubleshoot permissions, also take into account what happens when a folder or files in a folder are copied or moved. When a file is copied, the original file remains intact and a copy is made in another folder. Moving a file causes it to be deleted from the original location and placed in a different folder on the same or on a different volume. Copying and moving works the same for a folder, but the entire folder contents (files and subfolders) is copied or moved. When a file or folder is created, copied, or moved, the file and folder permissions can be affected in the following ways (depending on how inheritance is set up in the target location):

- A newly created file inherits the permissions already set up in a folder.
- A file that is copied from one folder to another on the same volume inherits the permissions of the folder to which it is copied.
- A file or folder that is moved from one folder to another on the same volume takes with it the permissions it had in the original folder. For example, if the original folder had Read permissions for the Users domain local group and the folder to which it is transplanted has Modify permissions for Users, that file (or folder) will still only have Read permissions.
- A file or folder that is moved or copied to a folder on a different volume inherits the permissions of the folder to which it is moved or copied.
- A file or folder that is moved or copied from an NTFS volume to a folder in a FAT or FAT32 volume (including USB drives formatted for FAT/FAT32), such as on an older Windows Server 2003 server, is not protected by NTFS permissions, but it does inherit share permissions if they are assigned to the FAT/FAT32 folder.
- A file or folder that is moved or copied from a FAT volume to a folder in an NTFS volume inherits the permissions already assigned in the NTFS folder.

Activity 5-11: Troubleshooting Permissions

Time Required: Approximately 10 minutes
Objective: View the effective access for a folder.

Description: The Effective Access tab in a folder's properties is an excellent place to start when you are troubleshooting a security conflict, such as when you think someone should be able to access a folder, but the system prevents them from accessing it. In this activity, you use the Effective Access tab to view the effective access for the Administrators group on the Documentation folder you have been configuring.

1. Find the Documentation folder that you created in Activity 5-5, such as *DocumentationJR*, via File Explorer.
2. Right-click the folder and click **Properties**.
3. Click the **Security** tab.
4. Click the **Advanced** button.
5. Click the **Effective Access** tab.
6. Click the link for **Select a user**.
7. In the Select User, Computer, Service Account, or Group dialog box, click **Advanced**, click **Find Now**, and double-click the **Administrators** group. Click **OK**.
8. Click the **View effective access** button in the window for Advanced Security Settings for the folder and, if necessary, scroll through the Effective access box (see Figure 5-22).
9. Click the **Select a user** link.
10. Click **Advanced**, click **Find Now**, and double-click the **Everyone** group. Click **OK**.

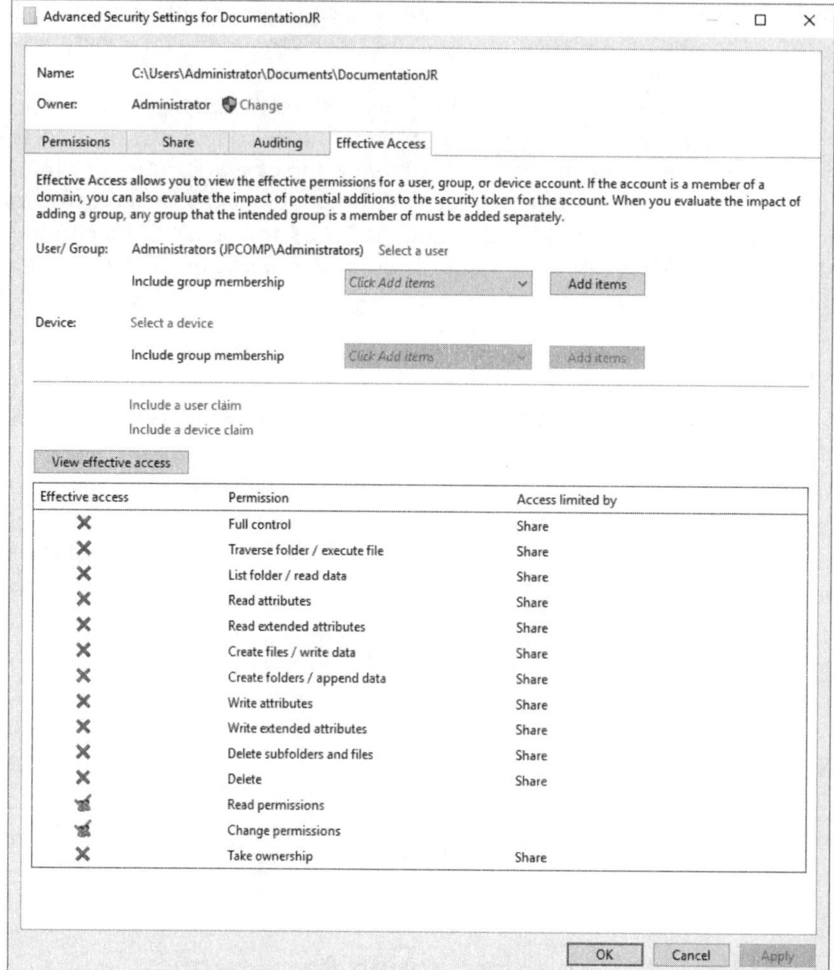

Figure 5-22 Viewing effective access for the Administrators group

11. Click the **View effective access** button.
    - What is the effective access for the Everyone group?
12. Click **OK** in the Advanced Security Settings for the folder window and close the folder Properties window.

Using Work Folders

Work folders are employed so that users can access and synchronize folders used in work environments through employing all types of devices, mobile and stationary, such as tablet PCs, laptops, and stationary PCs. Work folders are designed to accommodate the bring-your-own-device (BYOD) environment common to many places of work, such as where a user brings her own iPad to work on documents. User folders are stored on a server in a master folder called a **sync share**, a name used because folders and files can be automatically synchronized between the user's mobile or stationary device and the contents in the sync share folder.

To accommodate BYOD, work folders enable a business to centralize storage of work documents, while maintaining control of access and use of these documents. For the employee, such documents can be synchronized between the server and a mobile device, enabling employees to work from home or while on the road—to facilitate the employees' individual needs for mobility.

Security is another advantage. Work folders are subject to NTFS permissions and share permissions. Further, a Group Policy can be set up on the server to ensure that mobile and stationary devices must use screen locking with a password and must encrypt files. It's important to remember that the business owns the files and needs to set permissions and take other security precautions to protect its business interests.

Work folders were introduced in Windows Server 2012 R2 and are enhanced in Windows Server 2016. At this writing, they are supported in Windows 10, Windows 8.1, Windows RT 8.1 (for mobile devices), Windows 7 and 8 (when the application files are downloaded and installed) and in Apple iOS 8 or above on an iPad.

Because work folders are compatible with offline files, both can be set up on the same server, if needed. However, a more likely scenario is to use work folders as a replacement for offline files. Which you use depends on the needs and design of your network environment, including whether your organization uses BYOD. Offline files are accessed away from the main network through a virtual private network or remote access. Work folders are accessed away from the main network via direct Internet using server certificates. Thus, your decision about whether to use work folders or offline folders should be influenced by the capabilities you decide to establish on your network. Further, work folders can be run on a virtual machine in a Windows Azure cloud (contact Microsoft cloud services for more information).

To use work folders, install the Work Folders role service in the File and Storage Services role and then configure Work Folders in Server Manager. The following are the general steps for setting up Work Folders.

1. Open Server Manager, if necessary.
2. Click Manage near the top of the Server Manager window and click Add Roles and Features.
3. Click Next, if you see the Before you begin window.
4. Ensure Role-based or feature-based installation is selected and click Next.
5. In the Select destination server window, make sure your server is selected and click Next.
6. Ensure that File and Storage Services is already marked as installed. Click the right-pointing arrow in front of File and Storage Services. Click the right-pointing arrow in front of File and iSCSI Services to view the options under it (refer to Figure 5-18).
7. If necessary, scroll the Roles box and click the box for Work Folders.
8. If you see the Add Roles and Features Wizard to add additional roles and features, click Add Features.
9. Click Next in the Select server roles window.
10. Click Next in the Select features window.
11. Click Install in the Confirm installation selections window.
12. Click Close in the Installation progress window.
13. In the left pane of Server Manager, click File and Storage Services.
14. In the left pane, click Work Folders and click the link: *To create a sync share for Work Folders, start the New Sync Share Wizard* (see Figure 5-23).

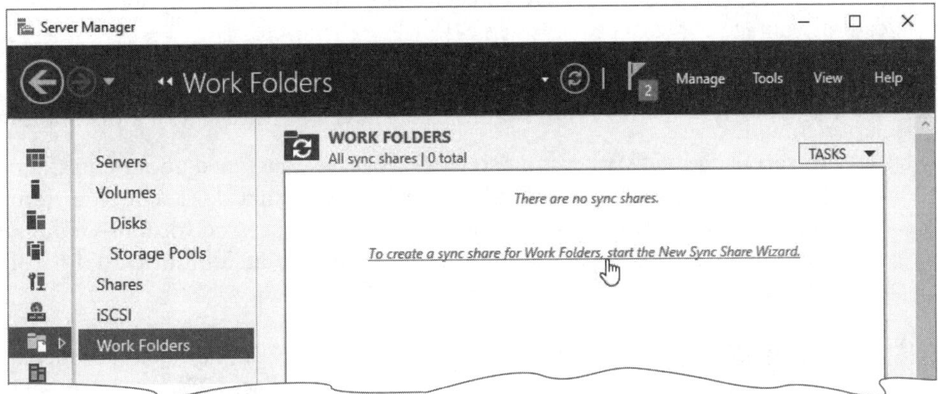

Figure 5-23 Starting the Sync Share Wizard to configure work folders

15. Use the New Sync Share Wizard to guide you through the steps for setting up work folders.

Implementing a Distributed File System

The **Distributed File System (DFS)** enables you to simplify access to the shared folders on a network by setting up folders to appear as though they are accessed from only one place. If the network, for example, has eight Windows Server 2016 servers that make a variety of shared folders available to network users, DFS can be set up so that users do not have to know what server offers which shared folder. All of the folders can be set up to appear as though they are on one server and under one broad folder structure. DFS also makes managing folder access easier for server administrators. After the DFS role is installed, DFS is configured using the DFS Management tool started from Server Manager, in the Windows Administrative Tools folder (click Start and click the Windows Administrative Tools folder) or from the DFS Management MMC snap-in.

If DFS is used in a domain, then shared folder contents can be replicated to one or more DCs or member servers, which means that if the original server goes offline then its shared folders are still available to users through the replica servers. Also, from the server administrator's perspective, he or she can update software in a shared folder without having to make the folder temporarily inaccessible during the update. DFS offers the following advantages:

- Shared folders can be set up so that they appear in one hierarchy of folders, enabling users to save time when searching for information.
- NTFS access permissions fully apply to DFS on NTFS-formatted volumes.
- Fault tolerance is an option by replicating shared folders on multiple servers resulting in uninterrupted access for users.
- Access to shared folders can be distributed across many servers, resulting in the ability to perform **load balancing**, so that one server does not experience more load than others.
- Access is improved to resources for web-based Internet and intranet sites.
- Vital shared folders on multiple computers can be backed up from one set of master folders.

In addition to enabling users to be more productive, server administrators are also immediately more productive because DFS reduces the number of calls to server administrators asking where to find a particular resource.

DFS Replication

Another advantage of DFS in a domain is that folders can be replicated automatically or manually through **DFS Replication**, which is a role service you can install within the File and Storage Services role. When you install DFS functionality, plan to install DFS Replication. DFS Replication can be used so that shared folders are replicated on two or more servers (called targets). Each time the contents of a DFS folder are changed, DFS Replication goes into action. Shared folders in DFS are copied to each designated target computer, which yields two significant advantages:

- Important information is not lost when a disk drive on one server fails.
- Users always have access to shared folders even in the event of a disk failure.

For server and network administrators who are concerned about extra network traffic, DFS Replication uses remote differential compression, so that data sent to different servers on the local network and across network sites is sent in compressed format—reducing the use of network bandwidth. Also, DFS and DFS Replication can be administrated through GUI tools or through PowerShell cmdlets.

Beginning with Windows Server 2012 R2, new DFS implementations cannot use the older File Replication Services (FRS). DFS Replication is used instead.

DFS Models

The two models for implementing DFS are stand-alone and domain-based. The stand-alone DFS model offers more limited capabilities than the domain-based model. In the **stand-alone DFS model**, no Active Directory implementation is available to help manage the shared folders, and this model provides only a single or flat-level share, which means that the main DFS shared folder does not contain a hierarchy of other shared folders. Also, the stand-alone model does not have DFS folders that are linked to other computers through a DFS container that has a main root and a deep, multilevel hierarchical structure.

The **domain-based DFS model** has more features than the stand-alone approach. Most important, the domain-based model takes full advantage of Active Directory and is available only to servers and clients that are members of a domain. The domain-based model enables a deep, root-based, hierarchical arrangement of shared folders that is published in Active Directory. DFS shared folders in the domain-based model are replicated for fault tolerance and load balancing, whereas the stand-alone DFS model does not implement these features.

DFS Topology

The hierarchical structure of DFS in the domain-based model is called the **DFS topology**. The three elements to the DFS topology are namespace root, folder, and replication group.

A **namespace root** is a main container (top-level folder) in Active Directory that holds links to shared folders that can be accessed from the root. The server that maintains the namespace root is called the namespace server. When a network client views the shared folders under the namespace root, all of the folders appear as though they are in one main folder on the same computer, which is the Windows Server 2016 server containing the namespace root—even though the folders might actually reside on many different computers in the domain. Consider, for example, a plant biology research group that has shared folders on four different servers. Those folders can be associated with a namespace root so that all of the folders appear as though they are available from one place, with the namespace BioResearch, through the published information in Active Directory. Importantly, the namespace can also exist on more than one computer to distribute the access load and increase availability of the shared information.

Use care in providing the name for the root, so that the name is easily recognizable by users. In the domain-based DFS model, one recommendation from Microsoft is to use the domain name for the root. Another recommendation is to use Public or to use *domainname*\Public.

After the namespace root is created, it is populated by shared folders for users to access. Folders are established in a level hierarchy and appear to be in one server location, although they can be on many servers.

A **replication group** is a set of shared folders that is replicated or copied to one or more servers in a domain. In the plant biology example, the replica set would consist of all shared folders under the DFS namespace root that are designated to be replicated to other network servers. Part of this process means that links are established to each server that participates in the replication. Another part of the process is to set up synchronization so that replication takes place among all servers at a specified interval, such as every 15 minutes.

Installing DFS

DFS is installed as a role service within the File and Storage Services role. Although the File and Storage Services role is installed by default when you install Windows Server 2016, the elements needed for a domain-based DFS system with namespaces and DFS replication are not automatically installed. Use Server Manager to install DFS namespaces and DFS Replication.

Activity 5-12: Installing DFS Namespaces and DFS Replication

Time Required: Approximately 15 minutes
Objective: Install the role services DFS Namespaces and DFS Replication.

Description: To set up domain-based DFS, you'll need to install DFS Namespaces and DFS Replication as role services within the File and Storage Services role. In this activity, you install both role services using Server Manager.

1. Open **Server Manager,** if it is not open.
2. Click **Manage** near the top of the Server Manager window and click **Add Roles and Features.**
3. Click **Next,** if you see the Before you begin window.
4. Ensure **Role-based or feature-based installation** is selected and click **Next.**
5. In the Select destination server window, make sure your server is selected and click **Next.**
6. Ensure that File and Storage Services is already marked as installed. Click the **right-pointing arrow** in front of **File and Storage Services.** If necessary, click the **right-pointing arrow** in front of **File and iSCSI Services** to view the options under it (refer to Figure 5-18).
7. Click the checkbox for **DFS Replication.** If you see the Add Roles and Features Wizard box, click **Add Features.**
8. Click the checkbox for **DFS Namespaces.** Click **Next** in the Select server roles window.
9. Click **Next** in the Select features window.
10. Click **Install** in the Confirm installation selections window.
11. Make sure the installation succeeded and then click **Close** in the Installation progress window.
12. Leave Server Manager open for the next activity.

Now that you've installed DFS Namespaces and DFS Replication, the next step is to configure a namespace root as in Activity 5-13.

Activity 5-13: Creating a Namespace Root

Time Required: Approximately 10 minutes
Objective: Configure a namespace root.

Description: Creating a namespace root is an important configuration step for DFS. In this activity, you create a new namespace root. Don't worry whether a namespace root already exists, because you use the same steps to install the first namespace root and additional ones. Have in mind a name for the namespace, such as Data plus your initials.

Before you start, ensure that Windows Firewall is configured to allow the necessary applications. Right-click the Start button, click Control Panel, set View by to Large icons or Small icons, click Windows Firewall, click Allow an app or feature through Windows Firewall, ensure that the boxes for DFS Management, DFS Replication, and Distributed Transaction Coordinator are checked, click OK, and close the Windows Firewall window.

1. If necessary, open **Server Manager.** Click **Tools** in Server Manager and click **DFS Management.** (Alternatively, you can use the DFS Management MMC snap-in.)
2. In the DFS Management window, click the **Action** menu at the top of the window or right-click **Namespaces** in the tree.
3. Click **New Namespace** (see Figure 5-24) to start the New Namespace Wizard.
4. Enter the name of the server to hold the namespace (the name of the server you are using) or use the **Browse** button to locate the server, and click **Next.**

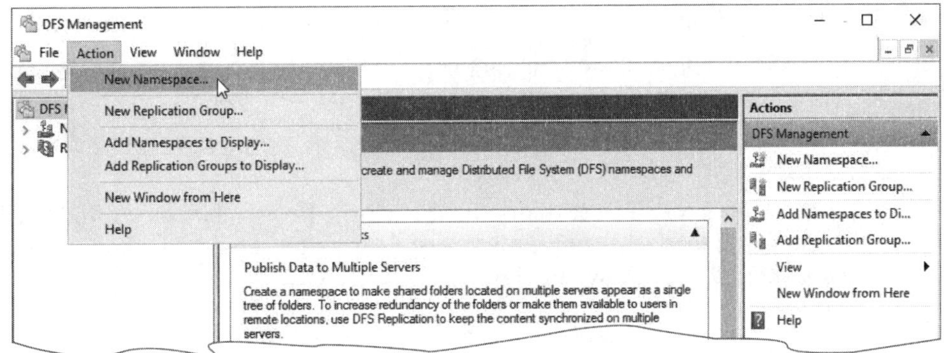

Figure 5-24 Creating a new namespace in the DFS Management window

5. Enter the namespace name, such as *DataJR* (Data + your initials) and click **Next**.
6. Leave **Domain-based namespace** as the default selection. If Enable Windows Server 2008 mode is selected, remove the checkmark from its box. Click **Next**.
7. In the Review Settings and Create Namespace window, click **Create**.
8. Click **Close**.
9. Leave the DFS Management window open for the next activity.

Managing a Domain-Based Namespace Root System

After the namespace root system is set up, several tasks are involved in managing the namespace root. These tasks can include:

- Creating a folder in a namespace
- Delegating management
- Tuning a namespace
- Deleting a namespace root
- Using DFS replication

Each of these tasks is described in the following sections.

Creating a Folder in a Namespace After the namespace root is created, the next step is to add folders and folder targets. A folder is simply a shared folder that you add to (or link to) the namespace root. However, you cannot add a folder that already contains other DFS folders under it.

You can also create folder targets. A **folder target** is a path in the Universal Naming Convention (UNC) format, such as to a shared folder or to a different DFS path—for example, a namespace for another folder (including a shared folder you have created outside of DFS). **Universal Naming Convention (UNC)** is a naming convention that designates network servers, computers, and shared resources. The format for a UNC name is, for example, \\servername\namespace\folder\file.

Clients who access the namespace can see a list of folder targets ordered in a hierarchy. The hierarchy is called the target priority, which the DFS administrator can configure.

Activity 5-14: Adding a Folder and Folder Target in DFS

Time Required: Approximately 5 minutes
Objective: Add a folder in DFS.

Description: In this activity, you add a folder under the DFS namespace root you have created.

1. Open the **DFS Management** tool if it is not already open.
2. Click the **right-pointing arrow** in front of Namespaces in the left pane to see your new namespace listed. Right-click the namespace you created in the tree under Namespaces.

3. Click **New Folder**.
4. In the New Folder dialog box, enter **Documentation** plus your initials as the name of the new folder, such as *DocumentationJR*.
5. Click the **Add** button to add the path to the Documentation folder you set up as a shared folder in Activity 5-5.
6. In the Add Folder Target dialog box, click the **Browse** button to find the Documentation folder you shared and double-click the folder, and it should now appear in the *Path to folder target* text box, as shown in Figure 5-25. Click **OK**.

Figure 5-25 Add Folder Target box

7. Notice that the folder target you configured now appears in the *Folder targets* box. Click **OK** in the New Folder dialog box. You'll see the new folder listed under the namespace in the tree (click the right-pointing arrow in front of the namespace name).
8. Close the DFS Management tool and close any open windows.

Delegating Management You can delegate management of a DFS namespace so that the day-to-day activities can be managed by an assistant or by another person who oversees the management of the DFS shared folders. Delegating management simply involves right-clicking the namespace in the DFS Management tool and clicking Delegate Management Permissions. Even if you are the main person to manage the DFS shared folders, it is still a good idea to have a backup person who is trained to work with the namespace root while you are out of the office.

Tuning a Namespace After you configure a DFS namespace, you can tune it to match the needs of your organization. The tuning options include the following:

- *Configure the order for referrals*—When a client accesses the namespace domain controller, she receives a list of targets in a specified order. This is called a referral. Targets on the same Active Directory site are listed before those on remote sites. To configure the order of referrals via the DFS Management tool, right-click the namespace root, click Properties, and click the Referrals tab (see Figure 5-26). The possible ordering methods are: Random order, Lowest cost, and Exclude targets outside of the client's site. Lowest cost refers to accessing the DFS server that is closest or on the least-cost network link.
- *Configure cache duration for a namespace*—A client can cache in memory a referral so that the referral is faster to access on later attempts. The cache duration is configured in seconds, with 300 seconds as the default. You can reconfigure the cache duration from the Referrals tab in the properties of the namespace root (see Figure 5-26).
- *Configure cache duration for a folder*—You can also configure the cache duration for a folder, such as one you access often. To do this, right-click the folder in the DFS Management tool and click the Referrals tab. The default setting for a folder is 1,800 seconds.
- *Configure namespace polling*—If more than one namespace server exists, the servers check or poll other namespace servers in case there are changes to the namespace, such as the addition of a folder or target folder. In this way, all namespace servers stay current when

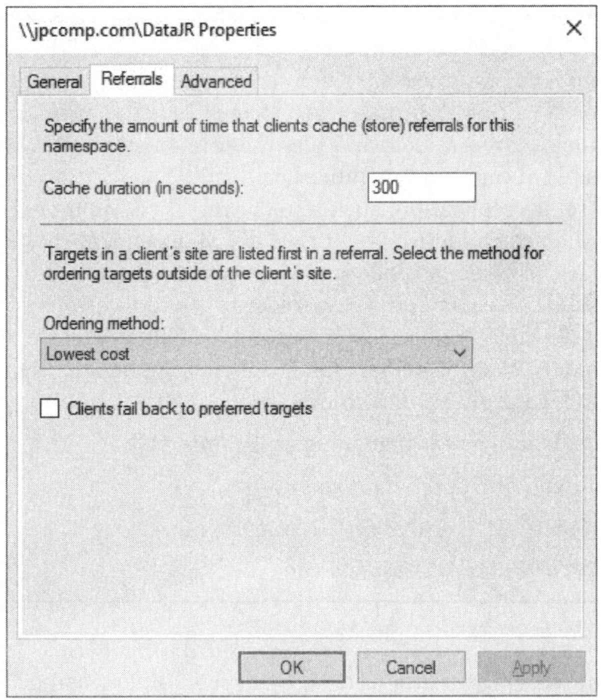

Figure 5-26 Configuring the order for referrals

there are changes. You can tune the poll method. One method is to optimize for consistency, which means that the namespace servers poll the primary domain controller for each change. Another option is to optimize for scalability. This means a namespace server polls its nearest namespace controller for any changes. The polling method is changed by right-clicking the namespace root in the DFS Management tool, clicking Properties, and clicking the Advanced tab.

- *Configure folder targets as enabled or disabled*—You can configure a folder target so that it is enabled or disabled. You might disable a folder target, for example, while you are working on the folder or adding many new files and then enable it when you are done. To do this from the DFS Management tool, click the folder with folder targets in the tree, ensuring that the Folder Targets tab is displayed in the middle pane. Right-click the folder in the middle pane and click Disable Folder Target (this option toggles between Disable and Enable). When you are ready to enable it, right-click the folder in the middle pane and click Enable Folder Target.

Deleting a Namespace Root If you find there is no longer a need to have a namespace root, you can delete it. You might do this, for example, because the namespace root was for a special project that is now finished. You can delete the namespace root via the DFS Management tool by right-clicking the namespace root in the left pane and clicking Delete.

If you want to leave the namespace intact for a while, but not displayed for users to see, you can right-click the namespace root in the left pane of the DFS Management tool and click Remove Namespace from Display.

Using DFS Replication DFS folders in a namespace root can be replicated on servers other than the one that contains the master folders (which is called the primary member). The replication capability is what enables you to provide fault tolerance and to create load balancing. On a network in which there are multiple servers, replication can prove to be a vital service to provide uninterrupted access for users, in case the computer with the master folder is inaccessible.

Load balancing also is vital as a way to provide users with faster service and better network performance by enabling them to access the nearest server containing the DFS shared folders.

To configure replication, you first must have defined two or more folder targets. Also, you need to decide which server is to be the primary group member. The primary group member should be the server containing shared folders and files that are most current. Other servers that you replicate to are called replication group members.

When you are ready to set up replication, click a folder under the namespace root in the tree of the DFS Management tool. In the middle pane of the DFS Management tool, click the Replication tab, click Replicate Folder Wizard, and follow the instructions presented in the wizard. After a replication group is established, you can add a new folder to the replication group by expanding Replication in the tree, right-clicking a replication group, and clicking New Replicated Folders to start the New Replicated Folders Wizard. Replication is handled by the DFS Replication service.

Recent improvements to DFS replication include:

- New Windows PowerShell cmdlets for managing replication tasks
- New resources for rebuilding corrupted databases
- Improved ability to automatically recover after a power failure

Configuring Disk Quotas

One reason why setting up shared folders and DFS shared folders using NTFS-formatted volumes works well is that NTFS offers the ability to establish **disk quotas**. Using disk quotas has the following advantages:

- Preventing users from filling the disk capacity
- Encouraging users to help manage disk space by deleting old files when they receive a warning that their quota limit is approaching
- Tracking disk capacity needs on a per-user basis for future planning
- Providing server administrators with information about when users are nearing or have reached their quota limits

In Activity 5-9, you installed the File Server Resource Manager to enable using disk quotas and a quota was automatically applied to the shared folder you were configuring. Another way to manage quotas and to directly configure quota templates is to use the File Server Resource Manager administrative tool, which can be started from Server Manager, from the Windows Administrative Tools folder via the Start button or as an MMC snap-in. Activity 5-15 shows you how to access File Server Resource Manager and configure disk quotas.

Activity 5-15: Configuring Disk Quotas

Time Required: Approximately 10 minutes
Objective: Use File Server Resource Manager to configure quotas.

Description: In this activity, you use File Server Resource Manager to manage disk quotas and disk quota templates.

1. Open **Server Manager**, if it is closed.
2. Click **Tools** and click **File Server Resource Manager**.
3. In the left pane, click the **right-pointing arrow** for **Quota Management**, to view the items under it.
4. Double-click **Quotas** in the left pane.
5. In the middle pane, notice the 500 MB quota that was set up automatically for the shared Utilities folder you were configuring in Activity 5-9. This folder has a soft quota, which means that users receive a warning when they exceed the quota, but they are still able to exceed it. This is in contrast to a hard quota, which does not permit the user to go over the quota.

6. Click **Action** under the title bar in the File Server Resource Manager window, and click **Create Quota.**
7. In the Create Quota dialog box, use the **Browse** button to find the path to the Documentation folder you have been working on earlier, such as *\Documents\DocumentationJR*. Click **OK** in the Browse For Folder box.
8. Make sure that **Create quota on path** is selected in the Create Quota dialog box.
9. Ensure that **Derive properties from the quota template (recommended)** is selected.
10. Click the **down arrow** in the box to set the quota limit. Click **200 MB Limit Reports to User,** so that the quota for the Documentation folder is 200 MB with usage reports produced. Your selections should be similar to those in Figure 5-27.

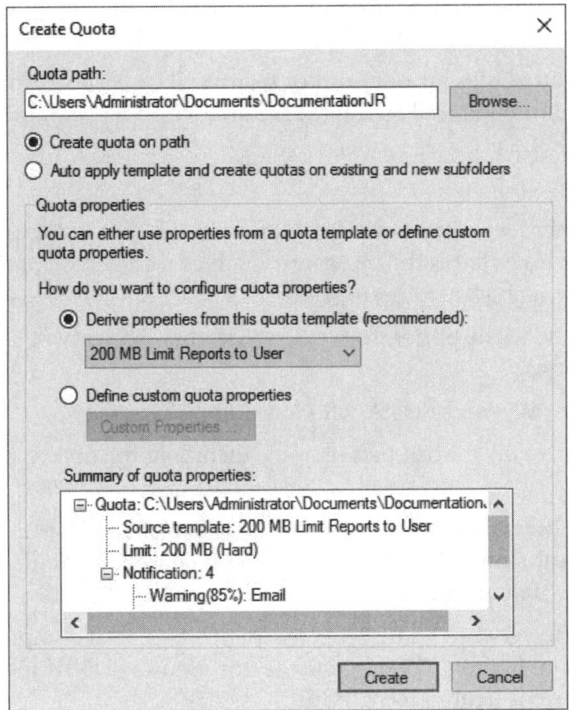

Figure 5-27 Configuring a quota

11. Scroll through the Summary of quota properties to confirm the properties associated with this quota setting. Click **Create.**
12. Verify that the new quota appears in the middle pane under *Source Template: 200 MB Limit Reports to User* in the File Server Resource Manager window.
13. In the left pane, click **Quota Templates.**
14. In the middle pane, review the quota templates already available.
15. In the middle pane, double-click the **100 MB Limit** template.
16. Review the settings for this template as shown in the Quota Template Properties for 100 MB Limit dialog box. Click **Cancel.**
17. Right-click **Quota Templates** in the left pane and click **Create Quota Template.**
18. Notice the settings you can configure for a new template.
    - Record the settings you can configure.
19. Click **Cancel.**
20. Close File Server Resource Manager and close Server Manager.

Be careful that you don't set general disk quotas too low, such as on an entire drive or on a system or applications folder—because this could restrict activities for the administrator and others. For example, if general quotas are set too low, Server Manager cannot inventory information for roles and features because it needs disk space in a temporary folder for its work. Further, print jobs might not print because they need temporary space to prepare and send a print job to the printer.

Chapter Summary

- Windows Server 2016 uses discretionary access control lists for managing access to resources.
- NTFS uses folder and file attributes for one level of security. The basic attributes are read-only and hidden. Extended or enhanced attributes are archive, index, compress, and encrypt.
- When you use the encrypt attribute, this employs the Microsoft Encrypting File System to protect files and folders.
- Permissions provide another level of security for files and folders. The types of permissions depend on the type of resource that is to be secured, such as a folder, file, printer, or other resource. Groups and users are granted permissions.
- Advanced permissions provide the option to further customize security at a more granular level than basic permissions.
- Folder and file auditing enable you to track who has accessed resources.
- Folder and file owners have Full control permissions, including the ability to change permissions.
- Folders can be shared for users to access over a network, and shared folder security is configured through share permissions. After a folder has been shared, it can be published in Active Directory for better management.
- Files can be shared over the network using SMB for Windows-based computers and UNIX or Linux computers that run Samba. When Samba is not used for UNIX or Linux access to shared files, sharing can be configured using NFS.
- Use the Effective Access capability to troubleshoot a security conflict.
- Users who need access to folders and files when they are not connected to the network can have access through making resources available offline. Another way to make folders and files available in this way is to configure work folders. The advantage of work folders is that they are compatible with BYOD in the workplace.
- The Distributed File System (DFS) enables you to set up shared folders that are easier for users to access and can be replicated for backup and load distribution.
- Use disk quotas to manage the resources put on a server disk volume so you do not prematurely or unexpectedly run out of disk space.

Key Terms

access-based enumeration When enabled, permits the user to view only shared folders and files for which they have permissions.

attribute A characteristic associated with a folder or file used to help manage access.

auditing In Windows Server 2016, a security capability that tracks activity on an object, such as reading, writing, creating, or deleting a file in a folder.

DFS Replication A role service you can install within the File and Storage Services role, so that shared folders offered through DFS are backed up to protect against data loss, such as through hardware failure, and to provide redundancy. *See* Distributed File System (DFS).

DFS topology Applies to a domain-based DFS model and encompasses the DFS namespace root, shared folders, and replication folders.

discretionary ACL (DACL) An access control list that manages access to an object, such as a folder, and that is configured by a server administrator or owner of the object.

disk quota Allocating a specific amount of disk space to a user or application with the ability to ensure that the user or application cannot use more disk space than is specified in the allocation.

Distributed File System (DFS) A system that enables folders shared from multiple computers to appear as though they exist in one centralized hierarchy of folders instead of on many different computers.

domain-based DFS model A DFS model that uses Active Directory and is available only to servers and workstations that are members of a particular domain. The domain-based model enables a deep, root-based, hierarchical arrangement of shared folders that is published in Active Directory. DFS shared folders in the domain-based model can be replicated for fault tolerance and load balancing.

Encrypting File System (EFS) Set by an attribute of NTFS, this Microsoft file system enables a user to encrypt the contents of a folder or a file so that it can only be accessed via private key code by the user who encrypted it. EFS adheres to the Data Encryption Standard's expanded version for data protection.

folder target A path in the Universal Naming Convention (UNC) format, such as to a DFS shared folder or to a different DFS path.

inherited permissions Permissions of a parent object that also apply to child objects of the parent, such as to subfolders within a folder.

load balancing On a single server, distributing resources across multiple server disk drives and paths for better server response; and on multiple network servers, distributing resources across two or more servers for better server and network performance.

namespace root The main Active Directory container that holds DFS links to shared folders in a domain.

network discovery The ability to view other network computers and devices.

Network File System (NFS) protocol A file transfer protocol common to UNIX and Linux systems that transfers information in record streams instead of in bulk file streams.

ownership Having the privilege to change permissions and to fully manipulate an object. The account that creates an object, such as a folder or printer, initially has ownership.

permissions In Windows Server 2016, privileges to access and manipulate resource objects, such as folders and printers; for example, the privilege to read a file or to create a new file.

publish Making an object, such as a printer or shared folder, available for users to access when they view Active Directory contents and so that the data associated with the object can be replicated.

replication group A grouping of shared folders in a DFS namespace root that are replicated or copied to all servers that participate in DFS replication. When changes are made to DFS shared folders, all of the participating servers are automatically or manually synchronized so that they have the same copy.

Server Message Block (SMB) protocol Used by default on Microsoft systems, enables an operating system to offer shared files, folders, printers, serial ports, and other shared elements on a network.

share permissions Permissions that apply to a particular object that is shared over a network, such as a shared folder or printer.

stand-alone DFS model A DFS model in which no Active Directory implementation is available to help manage the shared folders. This model provides only a single or flat-level share.

sync share A server folder that holds work files for mobile and stationary devices. *See* work folders.

system control ACL (SACL) An access control list that contains settings to audit the access to an object, such as a folder.

Universal Naming Convention (UNC) A naming convention that designates network servers, computers, and shared resources. The format for a UNC name is, for example, \\servername\namespace\folder\file.

work folders A feature of the File and Storage Services role that enables users to access and synchronize work folders through using all types of devices, mobile and stationary, such as tablet PCs, laptops, and stationary PCs. Work folders are designed to accommodate the bring-your-own-device (BYOD) environment common to many places of work.

Review Questions

1. Your company writes software for voting machines and needs to ensure that the software and documentation is carefully protected on its servers. Last week, one of the servers was stolen from its machine room, but fortunately that server did not contain sensitive voting machine files. What folder and file security can your company use to protect its information in the future, so that even if a server is stolen its files cannot be accessed?
   a. Microsoft Encrypting File System
   b. the Verify permission
   c. scramble key authentication for folders and files
   d. Microsoft Distributed Security
2. A fellow programmer has set up a shared folder of programs he is working on, but the problem is that several users have discovered the folder and have been trying out the programs. What steps can the programmer take to ensure that only he can view and access the folder? (Choose all that apply.)
   a. Use permissions to secure the shared folder.
   b. Remove all attributes to the shared folder.
   c. Place a dollar sign after the name of the shared folder to hide it.
   d. Create a logon list for the shared folder.
3. Your company has salespeople who use Apple iPad tablet computers for travel. These salespeople need a way to use company files offline while traveling and then to synchronize the files on a server when they return. What Windows Server 2016 capability meets this need?
   a. synchronization clipboard
   b. work folders
   c. travel syncing
   d. dynamic folders
4. The water resources group in your organization asked you to create a shared folder to hold research data. Ten people are in the group; two of them cannot access the file but the other eight can. What can you do to easily determine why two people cannot access it?
   a. Check every group on the server to determine its members.
   b. Re-create the accounts for the two users.
   c. Use the Security Configuration Wizard to create new security.
   d. Check the effective access for that folder.
5. You attempt to set folder quotas on a shared folder you are configuring through Server Manager, but this feature is not enabled. What can you do to enable using folder quotas? (Choose all that apply.)
   a. Enable folder sizing.
   b. Set up quota recognition in network discovery.

c. Install File Server Resource Manager as a role service.

d. Turn on folder reciprocation.

6. A folder's owner has _________ permissions.

7. Which of the following are ACL-based object security techniques available in Windows Server 2016? (Choose all that apply.)

   a. Ownership

   b. Duration

   c. Attributes

   d. Auditing

8. An Apple Macintosh running Sierra (macOS 10.12) can share files with Windows Server 2016 using the _________ protocol.

9. A first step in configuring Distributed File System is to install which of the following File and Storage Services role services? (Choose all that apply.)

   a. DFS File Share Tracker

   b. DFS Replication

   c. DFS Load Balancer

   d. DFS Namespaces

10. The Computer Advisory Committee in your company has been concerned that users store many files on the servers but aren't good about deleting old files. This has resulted in less free space on the servers' disks. What solution do you propose?

    a. Only store files on member computers and not DCs.

    b. Configure the file space attribute on user folders.

    c. Use DFS to allocate limited space for users.

    d. Set up disk quotas for user accounts.

11. What are the two DFS models?

12. When you move a file from the Spreadsheets folder to the Corp Documents folder on a Windows Server 2016 server, what happens to the permissions on the file?

    a. The moved file takes the permissions of the Corp Documents folder.

    b. The moved file takes on the same permissions as a newly created file.

    c. The moved file takes with it the permission it had in the Spreadsheets folder.

    d. The moved file is only accessible by its owner and the server administrator, until new permissions are assigned.

13. Several of your DFS clients complain that it can take some time to access a DFS shared folder, even though they just recently accessed it. They are expecting faster response. What can you do?

    a. Tune the cache duration for the folder.

    b. Disable polling.

    c. Limit the size of shared folders in DFS.

    d. Configure a DFS site link.

14. You have a series of older files that you don't access often, but you do need them occasionally. Some of these folders take up large quantities of disk space. What NTFS feature can you use to reduce the disk space they occupy?

    a. Use the virtual indexing attribute.

    b. Use the compress attribute.

c. Use the zip permission.
d. Use the size control permission.

15. Which of the following is required to configure DFS Replication? (Choose all that apply.)
    a. Transfer ownership of all shared folders to the server administrator.
    b. Publish the DFS shared folders in Active Directory.
    c. Determine which server is the primary group member.
    d. Define two or more folder targets.
16. If Sara Weng belongs to one group that has modify permissions to the Research folder and to another group that only has read permissions to the Research folder, what access does she have?
    a. read
    b. modify
    c. contingent modify
    d. no access, because the system locks her out until the permissions conflict is fixed.
17. Before you can share a folder through Windows Server 2016, you must first _________.
18. Which of the following can you accomplish using the DFS Management tool? (Choose all that apply.)
    a. Create a namespace root.
    b. Delegate management over a namespace root.
    c. Create a folder in a namespace root.
    d. Tune a namespace root.
19. A set of shared folders copied in DFS to one or more servers is called a __________.
20. You are attempting to configure auditing for a folder, but you don't see the Auditing tab. Which of the following is likely to be the problem?
    a. You haven't enabled auditing as a Group Policy.
    b. You haven't installed the Auditing Service as a server role.
    c. You haven't installed the Auditing feature through Server Manager.
    d. You haven't established a quota in the folder.

Case Projects

Rocky Mountain College in Colorado is a fast-growing community college. It offers typical college programs and combines these with special classes for certificate and 2-year programs such as fisheries management, wildlife studies and management, mountain geology, and ski and snowboard technologies. The college is located in the foothills below Rocky Mountain National Park and is both a residential and commuter campus.

The college's Information Technology Department manages the servers used for academic and administrative computing. Some departments, such as Engineering Studies, Computer Science, and English, have servers located in the departments, with some administrative server tasks delegated to each department's computer specialist. The Engineering Studies Department uses Macintosh and Linux client computers. The college's Development Department also uses Macintosh computers. All academic and administrative servers are in the process of being upgraded from Windows Server 2012 to Windows Server 2016. Active Directory is installed and used for the servers. The college has 10 walk-in computer labs for students and faculty. Also, many faculty and students use laptop computers and iPads that they want to connect to the college computer network. The IT Department has hired you to consult on improving use of the servers and to advise on the upgrades.

Case Project 5-1: Security Conflict

The English Department maintains a Minutes folder, which contains minutes of department meetings and is accessed by the department chair, English Department faculty, and the staff. After the English Department's computer specialist upgrades the department's server to Windows Server 2016 and configures folders, the English Department chair and faculty can no longer access the Minutes folder. What tool do you suggest to solve this problem? Outline the general steps for using the tool.

Case Project 5-2: Planning Folder Permissions

Up to this point, the college has used a relatively unplanned approach to folder permissions, sometimes using the default permissions on newly created folders. Now they have created a new committee to review security on the servers, and the committee is working to develop a specific policy for setting up NTFS folder permissions and share permissions. They have asked for your recommendations on the following types of folders:

- The \Windows folder (which is not shared)
- Software application folders (which are not shared)
- Home folders for faculty and staff (which are not shared)
- Folders containing the college's financial accounting databases (which are not shared and are used only by members of the Administrative Business Department)
- A shared folder containing electronic pages from the faculty and staff handbook (which is shared for faculty and staff use only)
- Shared folders used by instructors to provide students with class information and assignments

If slide presentation software is available to you, such as PowerPoint, consider giving your response as a slide presentation.

Case Project 5-3: Using DFS

Each Windows Server 2016 server contains shared folders that are accessed by students, faculty, and staff. The problem is that many users are still very confused about which folders are on which servers. As a result, they waste a lot of time trying to find the specific shared folder that they need. The college asks you to help them develop a way to make the folders easier to find and access. Create a report that explains how DFS works and how it can be of value in their situation. Design a very general DFS folder structure that they might implement. For example, you might base the folder structure on academic and administrative departments in the college.

Consider preparing a slide presentation, if you have this software available, such as PowerPoint.

Case Project 5-4: Accommodating Shared Access to the Macintosh and Linux Clients

The Engineering Studies and Development departments want to access shared folders on the Windows Server 2016 servers. What Windows Server 2016 and client options are available to enable sharing with these clients?

chapter 6

Configuring Windows Server 2016 Printing

After reading this chapter and completing the exercises, you will be able to:

- Understand how Windows Server 2016 printing works on a network and on the Internet
- Understand and apply the Print and Document Services role
- Use the XPS Print Path
- Use the Print Management tool to configure network printing resources
- Install local and shared printers
- Configure printer properties
- Configure a network or Internet printer
- Manage print jobs
- Troubleshoot common printing problems

If you have ever needed to print a file but didn't have access to a printer or found your printer not working, then you know how important printing can be. It's something people take for granted until the printer is down or not available. Networks and servers have helped to revolutionize printing by enabling shared printers. Sharing printers can save dollars, because not everyone needs a printer physically connected to his or her computer. Sharing printers also can save time by ensuring there is a group of printers that are reliably set up and available.

In this chapter, you learn how printing works in Windows Server 2016, including network and Internet printing. You learn how to build print services through the Print and Document Services role. As a server administrator, you learn how to use the Print Management tool to configure and coordinate local and network printing functions on a server, which includes installing local, network, and Internet printers. You set up a shared printer and configure security for that printer. With your printer set up, you learn to manage print jobs and print queues. Finally, you learn how to troubleshoot a range of printing problems.

An Overview of Windows Server 2016 Printing

The network printing process on Windows Server 2016 networks begins when a client decides to print a file, either on a printer locally connected to the client's computer (a **local print device**), on a shared network printer (a **network print device**), or through Internet printing (a type of network print device). A shared network printer can be connected to a workstation sharing a printer, a printer attached to a server, or a printer with its own built-in print server device. The workstation or application that initially generates the print job is the network **print client**, and the Windows Server 2016 computer or network printer with a built-in print server device offering the printer share is the network **print server**. A **print job** is a document or items to be printed.

In this chapter, the focus is on Windows Server 2016 acting as the main print server. In this role, the Windows Server 2016 print server can be used to manage shared printers directly connected to the server or other servers, a printer connected to a network workstation, or a wired or wireless printer connected to the network and having its own built-in print server card.

A shared network printer device is an object, like a folder, that is made available to network users for print services. When the printout goes to a printer share, it is temporarily spooled in specially designated disk storage or memory and held until it is sent to be printed. **Spooling** frees the server CPU to handle other processing requests in addition to print requests.

When its turn comes, the print file is sent to the printer (formally called the print device) along with formatting instructions. A **printer driver** that holds configuration information for the given printer provides the formatting instructions. The formatting and configuration information includes instructions to reset the printer before starting, information about printing fonts, and special printer control codes.

The printer driver resides on the computer offering the printer services (for local and network print jobs) and also can reside on the workstation client sending the print job. For example, when you send a print job to be printed on a Windows Server 2016 print share, your printout is formatted using the printer driver at your workstation and then further interpreted by print services software on the Windows Server 2016 print server. The printer driver is either contained on the Windows Server 2016 installation media or obtained from the printer manufacturer.

How Network Printing Works

In technical terms, both the network print client and the network print server run specific processes to deliver a print job to a printer. The following steps outline the printing process:

1. The first stage in the process is when the software application at the client generates a print file.
2. As it creates the print file, the application communicates with the Windows **graphics device interface (GDI)**. The GDI integrates information about the print file—such as word-processing codes for fonts, colors, and embedded graphics objects—with information

obtained from the printer driver installed at the client for the target printer, in a process that Microsoft calls rendering.

3. When the GDI is finished, the print file is formatted with control codes to implement the special graphics, font, and color characteristics of the file. At the same time, the software application places the print file in the client's spooler by writing the file, called the **spool file**, to a subfolder used for spooling. In the Windows environment, a **spooler** is a group of DLLs, information files, and programs that process print jobs for printing.

Large print files cannot be processed if there is inadequate disk space on which to store spooled files. Make sure clients and the server have sufficient disk space to handle the largest print requests, particularly for huge graphics and color files that are targeted for a color printer or plotter. Also, ensure that any disk quotas you have set allow enough room for print spooling.

4. The remote print provider at the client makes a remote procedure call to the network print server to which the print file is targeted, such as a Windows Server 2016 server. If the print server is responding and ready to accept the print file, the remote printer transmits that file from the client's spooler folder to the Server service on Windows Server 2016.
5. The network print server uses four processes to receive and process a print file: router, print provider, print processor, and print monitor. The router, print provider, and print processor all are pieces of the network print server's spooler.
6. Once it is contacted by the remote print provider on the print client, the Server service calls its router, the Print Spooler service. The router directs the print file to the print provider, which stores it in a spool file until it can be sent to the printer.
7. While the file is spooled, the print provider works with the print processor to ensure that the file is formatted to use the right data type, such as TEXT or RAW.
8. When the spool file is fully formatted for transmission to the printer, the print monitor pulls it from the spooler's disk storage and sends it off to the printer.

Some steps in the activities in this book include bulleted questions for you to answer. Additionally, for all of the activities in this chapter, you'll need an account with Administrator privileges. These activities can be completed on a virtual machine or computer, such as in Hyper-V.

Activity 6-1: Print Spooler Service

Time Required: Approximately 5 minutes
Objective: Learn about the Print Spooler service and the services upon which it depends.

Description: The Print Spooler service works in conjunction with the Remote Procedure Call service to help make Windows Server 2016 printing possible. In this activity, you use the Services tool to view the Print Spooler service as well as services upon which it depends.

1. Open **Server Manager**, if it is not open.
2. Click **Tools** and click **Services**.
3. If necessary, click **Services** in the left pane.
4. Scroll the right pane in the Services window to find the Print Spooler service. Click **Print Spooler**. Notice the description of the Print Spooler service, as shown in Figure 6-1.

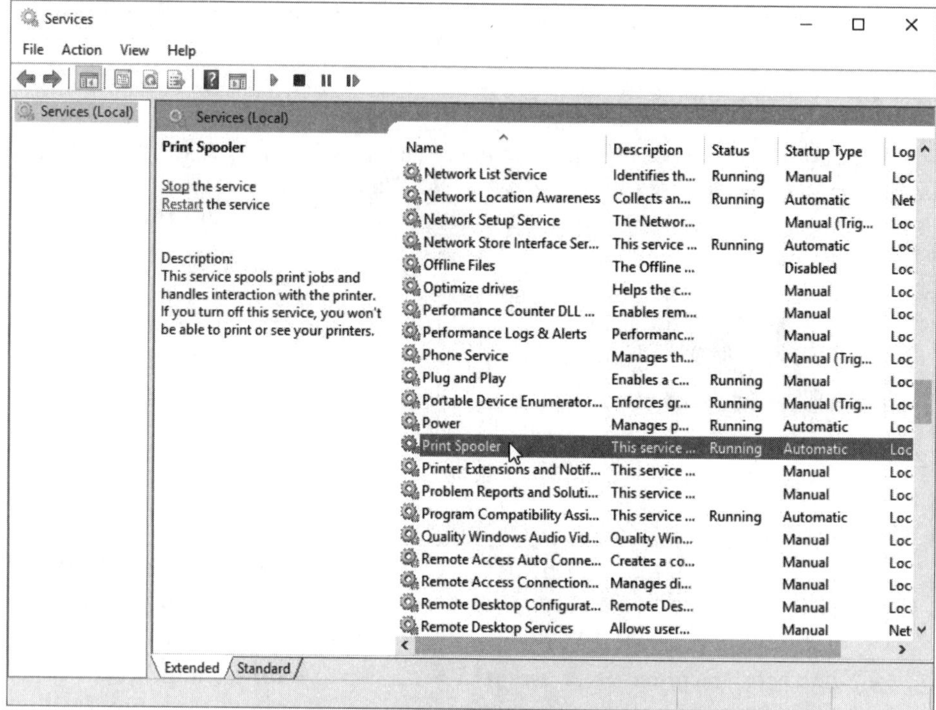

Figure 6-1 Viewing the description of the Print Spooler Service

5. Double-click **Print Spooler** to view its properties.
6. Click the **Dependencies** tab.
   - What service(s) depend on the Print Spooler service? On what service(s) does the Print Spooler depend?
7. Click **Cancel** in the Print Spooler Properties (Local Computer) dialog box.
8. Close the Services window. Leave Server Manager open for the next activity.

How Internet Printing Works

When a Windows client, such as Windows 8/8.1 or Windows 10, wants to process a print job through the Internet, the client must have **Internet Printing Client** installed. Further, Internet Printing Client should be installed in Windows Server 2016, so that client and server can communicate using a common protocol for printing. Additionally, Windows Server 2016 can be configured to act as a web-based print server by having the following elements:

- *Internet Printing Client*—for communicating using Internet Printing Protocol
- *Print and Document Services role with the Internet Printing role service installed*—for incorporating web-based print management and printing sharing
- *Web Server role (IIS; Internet Information Services)*—for enabling printing services in a web server environment

When a print job is processed over the Internet or an intranet, the client connects to the Windows Server 2016 web server using a web browser such as Microsoft Internet Explorer. The print process on the client is nearly the same as for network printing, with a couple of exceptions. One exception is that the browser, instead of a software application such as Microsoft Word, sends the print file to the GDI. Another exception is that the remote print provider at the client makes a remote procedure call to IIS on the Windows Server 2016 server. The remote procedure call is made through the TCP/IP-based Hypertext Transfer Protocol (HTTP), which transports another protocol, called the **Internet Printing Protocol (IPP)**. IPP is facilitated through the Internet Printing Client on the client requesting the print job and the Windows Server 2016 server. The IPP encapsulates the remote procedure call and print process information and is transported in HTTP just as a human passenger is transported inside a bus along a highway. IIS sends the IPP encapsulated information to its HTTP print server. The HTTP print server works with the regular Windows Server 2016 spooler services—the print provider, print processor, and print monitor processes—to prepare the print file for transmission to the target printer.

For the sake of security, server clients using the Internet printing capability through IPP should use a web browser that has strong security. If you use a Microsoft web browser, consider using Microsoft Edge rather than Internet Explorer. Microsoft Edge comes with more modern security, in part because new security measures do not have to be compatible with older program coding, as exists in Internet Explorer. Also, if you use Microsoft Edge, configure the advanced settings to employ the SmartScreen Filter.

In Activity 6-2, you learn how to install Internet Printing Client in Windows Server 2016. After the activity, you learn the general steps for installing Internet Printing Client in Windows 8/8.1 and Windows 10. Next, in the section, The Print and Document Services Role, you learn how to install the Internet Printing role service. Installing a web server is a more advanced topic, which you learn in Chapter 8, Managing Windows Server 2016 Network Services.

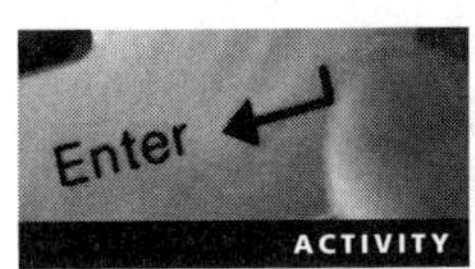

Activity 6-2: Installing the Internet Printing Client

Time Required: Approximately 5 minutes
Objective: Install the Internet Printing Client in Windows Server 2016 so that it can communicate using IPP.

Description: Windows Server 2016 comes with the Internet Printing Client that enables clients connecting to Windows Server 2016 to use Internet printing services through IPP. In this activity, you install the Internet Printing Client in Windows Server 2016.

1. Open **Server Manager**, if necessary.
2. Click **Manage** and click **Add Roles and Features.**
3. If you see the Before you begin window, click **Next.**
4. Ensure **Role-based or feature-based installation** is selected and click **Next.**
5. Be sure your server is selected in the Select destination server window and click **Next.**
6. Click **Next** in the Select server roles window.
7. Click **Internet Printing** client in the Select features window (see Figure 6-2) and click **Next.**
8. Click **Install** in the Confirm installation selections window.
9. Click **Close.**
10. Leave Server Manager open for the next activity.

Internet Printing Client is installed by default in modern Windows clients, such as Windows 8/8.1 and Windows 10. To make sure it is installed in Windows 8/8.1 and Windows 10:

1. Right-click Start and click Programs and Features.
2. Click *Turn Windows features on or off.*
3. Scroll to find Print and Document Services. Click the plus sign or right-pointing arrow to expand to see the elements underneath Print and Document Services.
4. Ensure there is a checkmark in the box for Internet Printing Client (see Figure 6-3).
5. Click OK in the Windows Features dialog box.
6. Close the Programs and Features window.

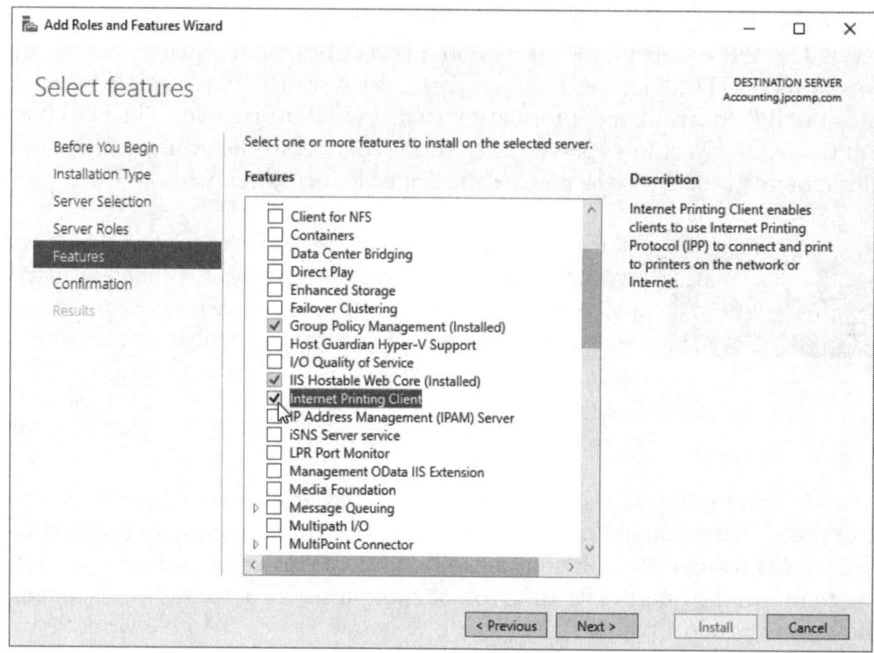

Figure 6-2 Installing Internet Printing Client in Windows Server 2016

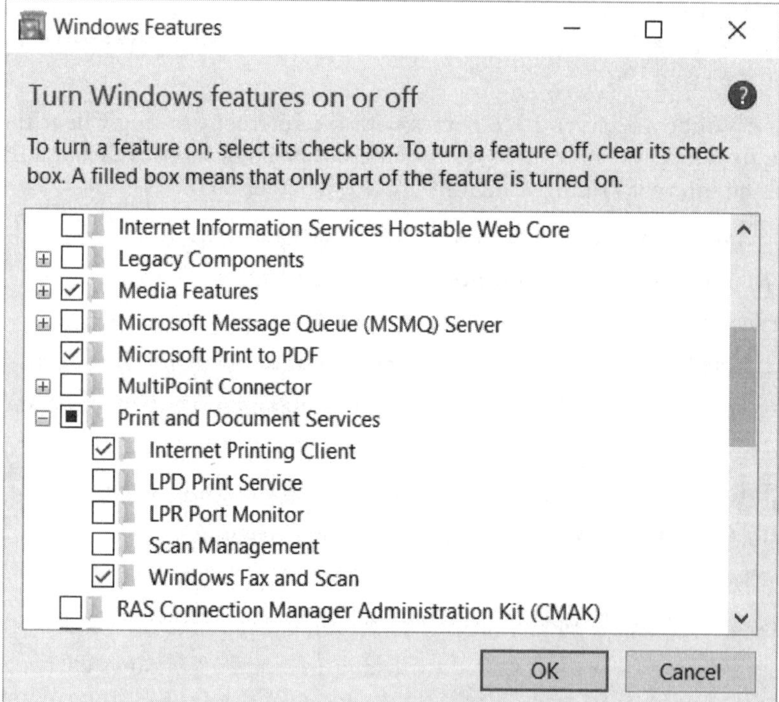

Figure 6-3 Configuring Internet Printing Client in Windows 10

The Print and Document Services Role

To take full advantage of Windows Server 2016 to manage shared printers for one location, it is necessary to have the Print and Document Services role installed. The Print and Document Services role enables you to set up Windows Server 2016 as a print server from which to coordinate and manage network and Internet printing functions. Another advantage of the Print and

Document Services role is that you can configure a Group Policy for standardized management of printer resources (you learn about Group Policy in Chapter 10, Securing Windows Server 2016).

The Print and Document Services role enables you to use the Print Management tool to manage shared printers (see the section in this chapter, Using the Print Management Tool). It also enables you to track printing events through a log you can view using the Event Viewer.

With the Print and Document Services role installed, you can use the following role services within the role:

- *Print Server*—Turns the server into a print server and installs the Print Management tool. This role service also creates an exception in the Windows Firewall to permit file and printer sharing.
- *Distributed Scan Server*—Enables Windows Server 2016 to receive scanned documents from network scanners and to deliver the scans to designated server clients. This role service also includes the Scan Management tool for setting up network scanning and for managing network scanners.
- *Internet Printing*—Creates a website through IIS (Web Server must also be installed as a server role) for Internet printing, for managing print jobs, and for connecting to shared printers using IPP through Internet Printing Client.
- *LPD Service*—Line Printer Daemon (LPD) enables UNIX and Linux computers to print to shared printers managed through Windows Server 2016. This installs and uses the TCP/IP Print Server service, and when installed it configures the Windows Firewall to allow the TCP communications port (port 515) for network spooler communications to be used for print processing between the client and the server.

Activity 6-3: Installing the Print and Document Services Role

Time Required: Approximately 15 minutes
Objective: Install the Print and Document Services Role.

Description: In this activity, you install the Print and Document Services role along with the Print Server role service.

In Chapter 3, Configuring the Windows Server 2016 Environment, you installed and then removed the Print and Documents Services role in Activity 3-2. If you chose not to remove the Print and Document Services role in that activity, then you can omit this activity as long as the Print and Document Services role is still installed on your server.

1. Open **Server Manager**, if it is closed.
2. Click **Manage** and click **Add Roles and Features.**
3. If you see the Before you begin window, click **Next.**
4. Ensure **Role-based or feature-based installation** is selected and click **Next.**
5. Be sure your server is selected in the Select destination server window and click **Next.**
6. In the Select server roles window, check the box for **Print and Document Services.** If you see a dialog box to add features required for a role, such as remote server administration tools, click **Add Features.**
7. Click **Next** in the Select server roles window.
8. Click **Next** in the Select features window.
9. In the Print and Document Services window, read the information about the Print and Document Services role and note that there is a link to learn about this role. Click **Next.**
10. In the Select role services window, make sure **Print Server** is selected (the default), and click **Next** (see Figure 6-4).

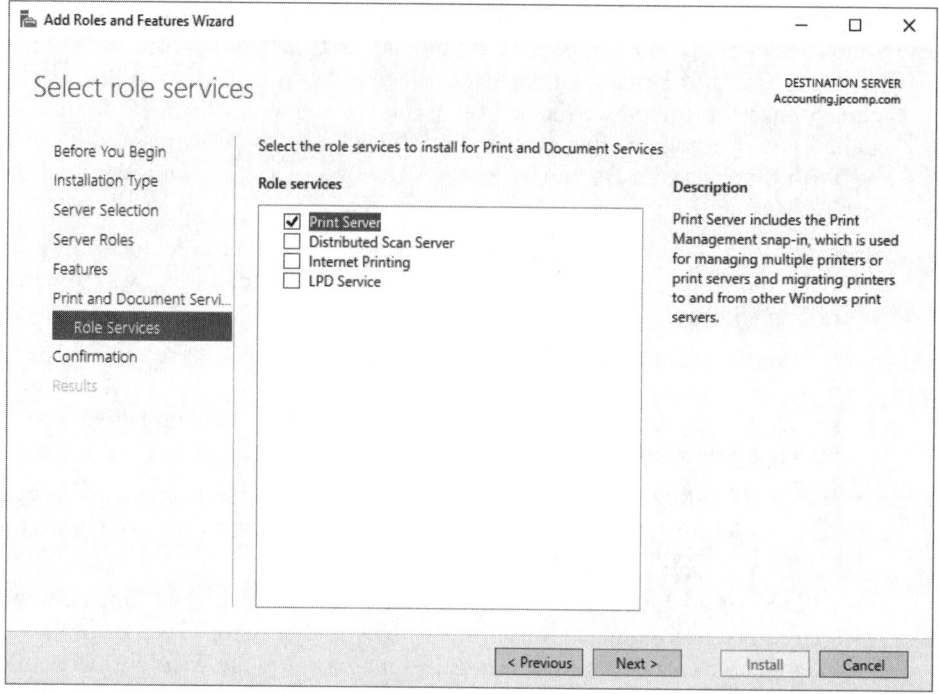

Figure 6-4 Selecting the Print Server role service

11. Click **Install** in the Confirm installation selections window.
12. Wait for a few minutes as the role is installed.
13. When the Installation progress window shows that the installation succeeded, click **Close.**
14. In the left pane of Server Manager, select **Print Services** and scroll through the right pane to view the boxes of information for this role. Notice that the Roles and Features box shows that Print Server is installed as a role service.
15. Click the **back arrow** near the top left of the window in Server Manager to go back to the main display. Leave Server Manager open for the next activity.

Using the XPS Print Path

Windows Server 2016 printing comes with support for **XML Paper Specification (XPS)**. XPS is an advanced way of printing documents for multiple purposes, including viewing electronic pages and printing pages in a polished format. XPS is a concept similar to using PDF files. When you print to this option, the document can be opened to view in XPS document format, which is an electronic view of the document as though it has been printed.

The XPS print path in Windows Server 2016 is offered as an alternative to the GDI print path used by conventional documents. The XPS print path offers these enhancements to printing:

- Customized print path for documents using XPS
- Advanced color support for sophisticated color printers
- Faster performance for printouts generated by .NET Framework applications
- Full WYSIWYG (What You See Is What You Get, which means documents viewed in the creation/editing stage are rendered in a similar format in a printout)

The XPS drive path uses the XPSDrv Driver Model. This driver can print to an XPS-enabled printer or a file. It brings more efficiency to print spooling by eliminating intermediate spool files for formatting and by using smaller spool files in final printing. One technique it uses to produce smaller spool files is Zip compression. Smaller spool files means less network traffic and faster network transmission from print server to printer.

Windows Server 2016 has XPS services built into the Print and Document Services role. Additionally, you can install the XPS Viewer as a feature through the Add Roles and Features Wizard you have been using to install roles, role services, and features. The **XPS Viewer** enables you to view a file saved in the XPS format. You can also view an XPS file in Microsoft Word.

The XPS Viewer and XPS Services are installed by default in Windows 8/8.1 and 10. If they are not working for some reason, the general steps to configure them are:

1. Right-click Start.
2. Click Programs and Features.
3. Click *Turn Windows features on or off* in the Programs and Features window.
4. Make certain that the checkboxes for XPS Services and XPS Viewer are selected in the Windows Features dialog box. Click OK.
5. Close the Programs and Features window.

The Devices and Printers Utility

The Windows Server 2016 Devices and Printers utility (see Figure 6-5) is one tool you can use to configure printing resources. This utility enables you to set up a printer directly connected to a server, set up a network printer, and set up a printer through Bluetooth. After a printer is set up, you can install a new printer driver, configure printer security, set a default printer for the server, and access a window for managing print jobs.

The Devices and Printers utility is started from Control Panel by using the following steps:

1. Right-click Start.
2. Click Control Panel.
3. In the Large icons or Small icons (Classic) View, click Devices and Printers. Or in the Category view, click View devices and printers under Hardware.

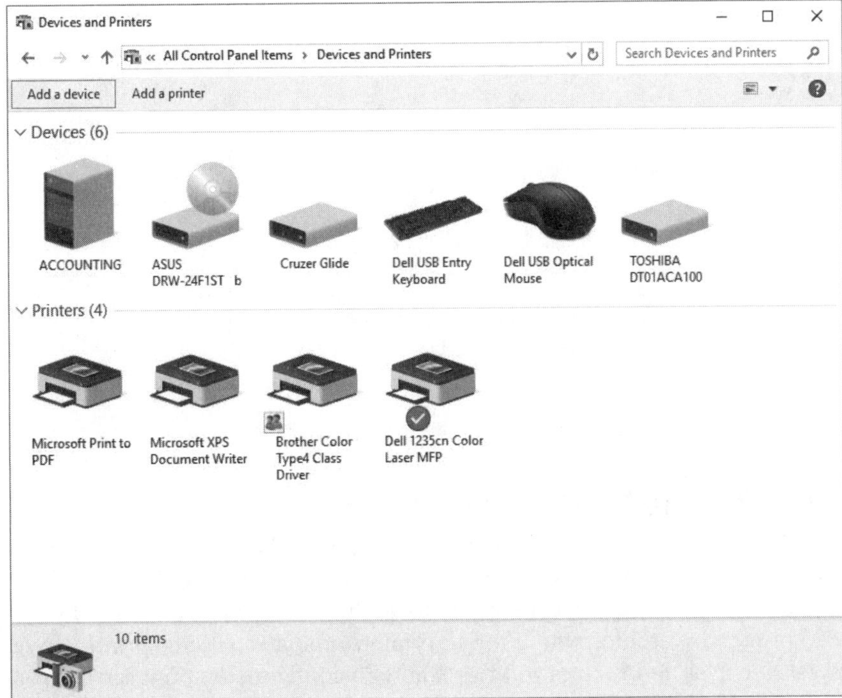

Figure 6-5 Devices and Printers utility

An alternate way to set up and manage printers in Windows Server 2016 is to use the Print Management tool that is installed through the Print and Document Services role. The next sections focus on using the Print Management tool, because it is tailored for server administrators with more functionality than the Devices and Printers utility. You use the Print Management tool to configure and manage printing resources on a Windows Server 2016 computer that is functioning as a full-featured print server.

Using the Print Management Tool

The Print Management tool (also available as an MMC snap-in) centralizes local and shared printer control in one place, enabling printer administrators and operators to manage the print functions of some or all of the shared printers on a network. This tool offers the capabilities of the Devices and Printers Utility and adds more management options. You can use the tool to install and configure local and network printers. It configures printer properties, sharing, and security.

Because printers can be a labor-intensive part of managing a network, the Windows Server 2016 Print Management tool is a welcome utility. For example, if a remote printer is offline or paused, you can use the Print Management tool to identify which printer has the problem. If you receive a call that a printer seems overloaded with print jobs, you can verify the number of jobs in that printer's queue and change the priority of jobs as needed. You can open this tool from the Server Manager Tools menu, from the MMC, and from the Start button by clicking the Windows Administrative Tools folder and Print Management. Figure 6-6 shows the Print Management tool.

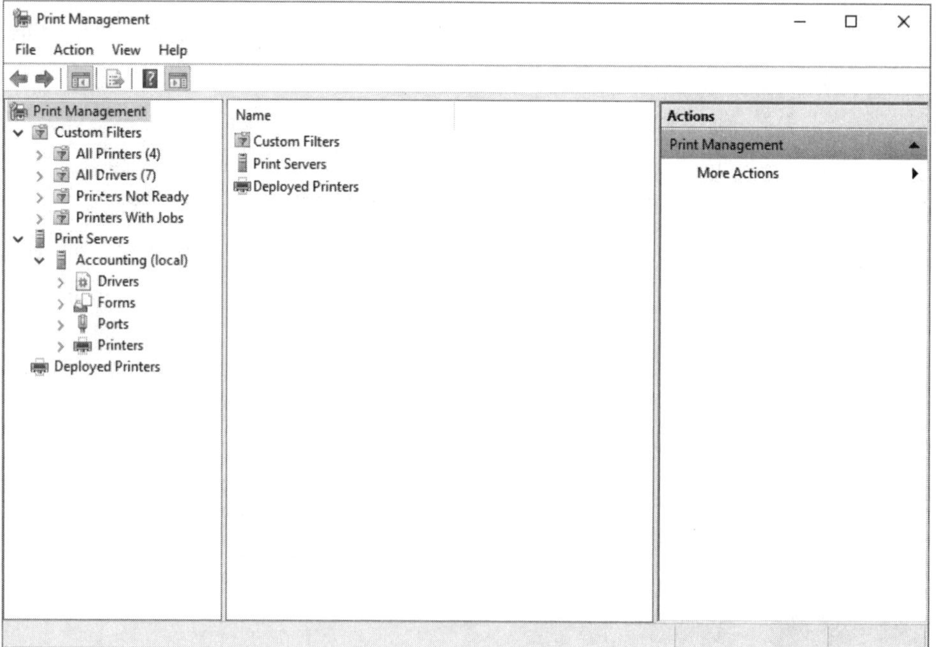

Figure 6-6 Print Management tool

Configuring the Print Server Properties

A good place to start setting up printing capabilities in the Print Management tool is to configure the print server properties in Windows Server 2016. You can set up the forms to use, configure print spooler properties, configure security to apply to all printers managed by the print server, view installed printer driver information for all printers, update a specific printer driver, and accomplish other tasks. Activity 6-4 enables you to see how to configure the print server properties.

Activity 6-4: Configuring the Print Server Properties

Time Required: Approximately 10 minutes
Objective: Configure the print server properties from the Print Management tool.

Description: In this activity, you open the Print Management tool and configure the print server properties.

1. If necessary, open **Server Manager.**
2. Click **Tools** and click **Print Management.**
3. In the left pane, click the **right-pointing arrow** in front of Print Servers to view the available print services, including your server.
4. Right-click your server, such as *Accounting (local)* and click **Properties** (see Figure 6-7).
5. Five tabs are shown in the Print Server Properties dialog box: Forms, Ports, Drivers, Security, and Advanced. Click each tab to view its configuration options.
6. If it is not selected, click the **Advanced** tab.
   - What spooler management options are already selected? What is the folder and its path where spooler files can be written?

6

On Windows Server 2016 servers configured in the role of print server, there can be periods of high I/O associated with handling print jobs, thus interfering with overall server performance. Microsoft recommends moving the folder used for spooling from the drive that houses the operating system to a different drive. You can do that by changing the folder path on the Advanced tab.

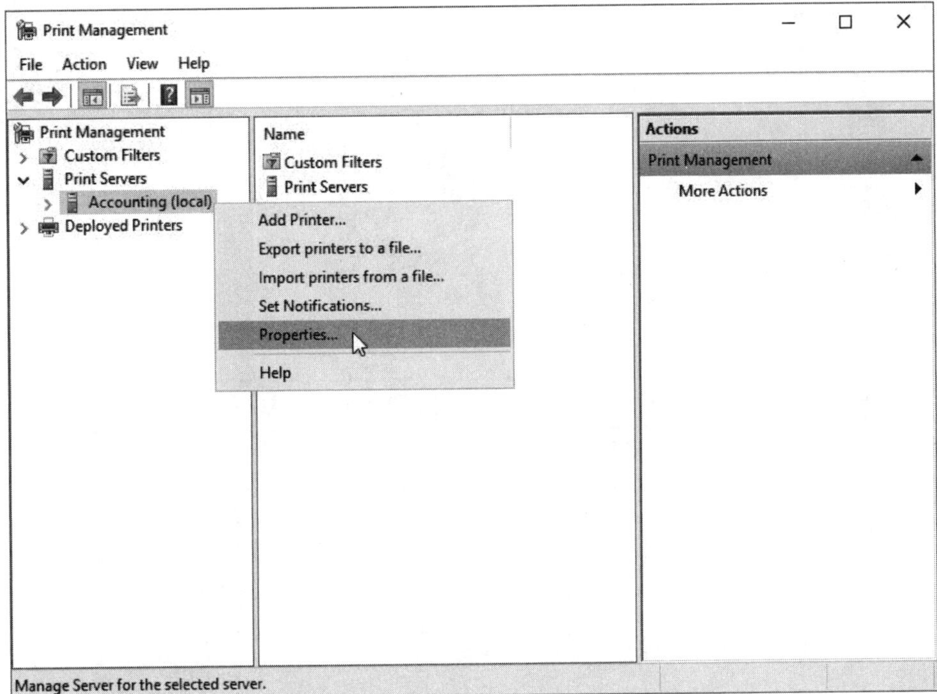

Figure 6-7 Accessing the print server properties

7. Click the **Security** tab. Notice the groups and users who have security access.
   - What default permissions are granted to the Everyone group (you'll learn more about permissions in the section, Configuring Security).
8. Click **Cancel**.
9. Leave the Print Management window open for the next activity.

Installing Local and Shared Printers

On a Microsoft network, any server or workstation running Windows Server 2016 or 2012/R2, Windows 10, Windows 8/8.1, or Windows 7 can host a shared printer for others to use through the network. In Windows Server 2016, you can configure a printer that is attached to the server computer as a local printer and then enable it as a shared printer. You can also configure a network printer, such as one wirelessly connected to the network, as a shared printer managed through a Windows Server 2016 print server. Figure 6-8 is a simplified representation of how shared printers are connected to a network, including printers connected to a server or through a built-in wireless print server card.

If you are setting up a computer as a print server, make sure it has sufficient RAM to process the documents and sufficient disk space to store the spooled documents.

The steps for installing a local printer in Windows Server 2016 depend on the type of printer you are adding. If you are installing a Plug and Play compatible printer, Windows Server 2016 will automatically detect and install the new hardware. If the printer is not automatically detected, you can use the Network Printer Installation Wizard to install it. Printers that are added using the Network Printer Installation Wizard are shared by default.

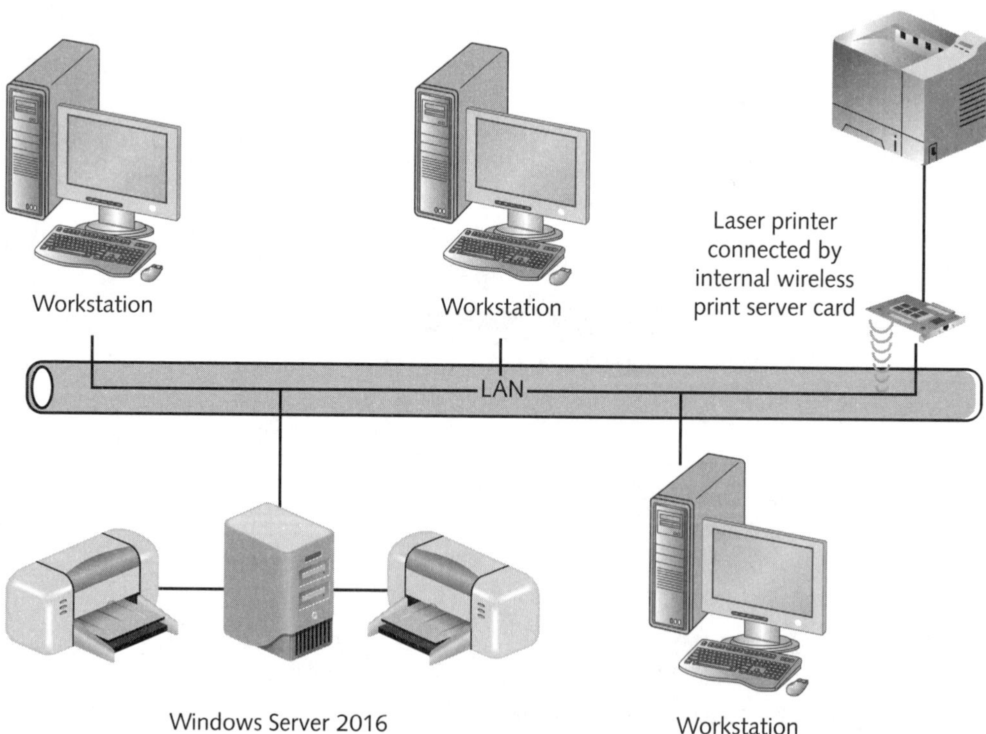

Figure 6-8 Shared network printers

Activity 6-5: Installing a Printer

Time Required: Approximately 15 minutes
Objective: Install a printer using the Network Printer Installation Wizard.

Description: In this activity, you install a printer using the Network Printer Installation Wizard. This activity does not require a printer to be attached to the computer, because you practice a manual configuration without automatic detection.

1. Open the **Print Management** window, if it is not already open. Or, to open it from Server Manager, click **Tools** and click **Print Management**.
2. In the left pane, use the **right-pointing arrow**, if necessary to ensure you can view the server name under Print Servers.
3. In the left pane, right-click the server name under Print Servers and click **Add Printer** (refer to Figure 6-7).
4. Notice the options to install a local or a network printer (see Figure 6-9). A local printer is one that is physically attached to the computer through a port, and a network printer is one that is connected to a different computer or to a dedicated print server device (wireless or cabled to the network) and that is shared over the network. For this activity, click **Add a new printer using an existing port.**
5. Click the **down arrow** that shows LPT1: (Printer Port) as the default.
   - What options are available?
6. For practice, use the default selection for the printer port (port to which the printer is connected), such as LPT1: (Printer Port), and click **Next.**
7. Ensure that **Install a new driver** is selected and click **Next.**
8. For the Manufacturer, select **Brother** (the default), and for the Printer, select **Brother Color Leg Type 1 Class Driver** (or select a manufacturer and printer of your choice). If you selected the defaults, notice that the driver is digitally signed. Digital signing offers some security that the driver is authentically written by the manufacturer. Click **Next.**

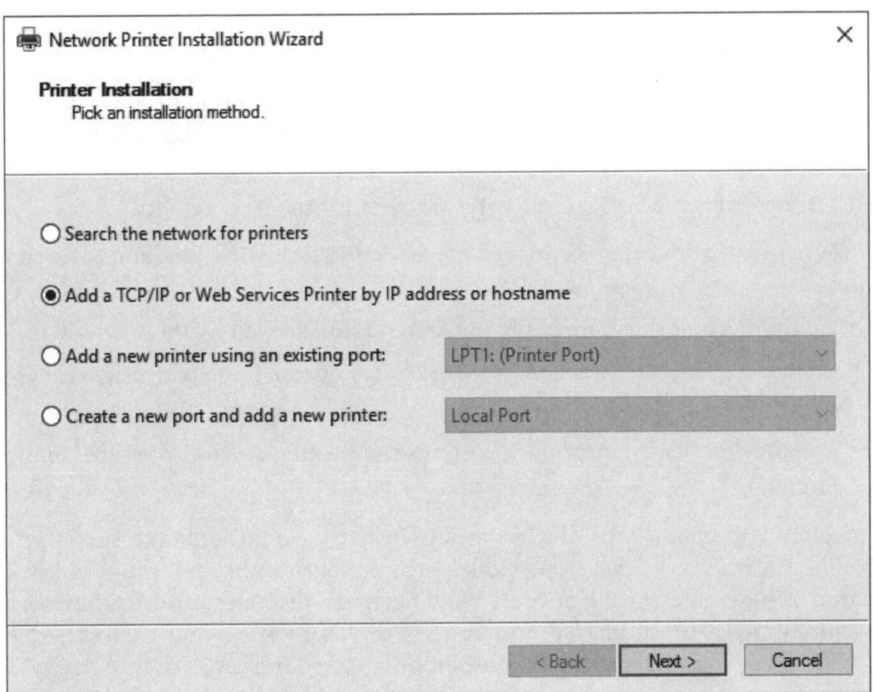

Figure 6-9 Printer installation options

9. In the Printer Name and Sharing Settings dialog box, ensure that there is a check in the box for **Share this printer**, which is the default. In the *Share Name* text box, enter **Office Printer** plus your initials, such as **Office Printer JR**. This is the name that users on the network will see. In the *Location* text box, enter a theoretical room number, such as **Room 10.** Also, enter a comment, such as **Shared color printer** (see Figure 6-10). Click **Next.**

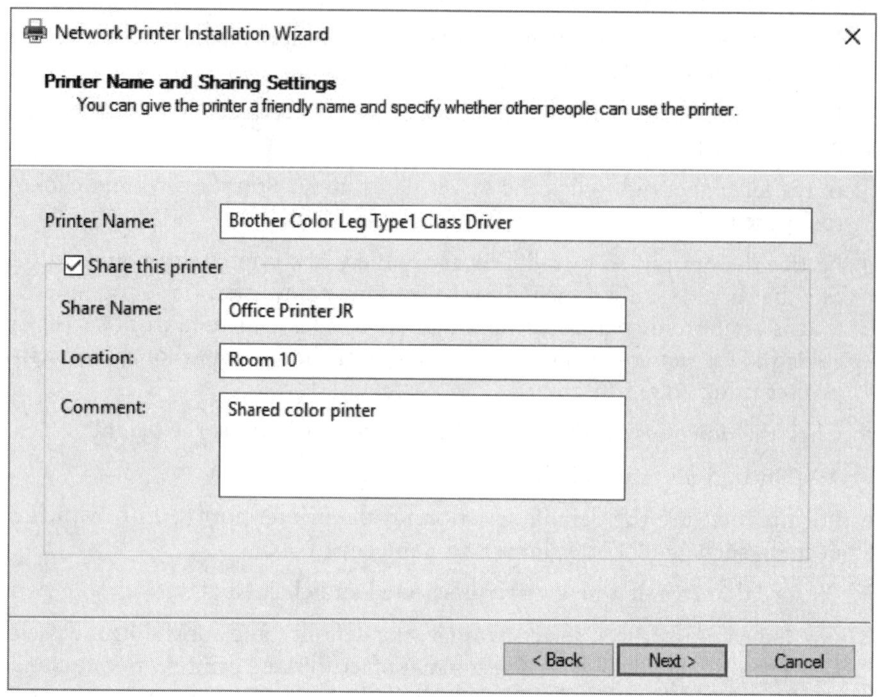

Figure 6-10 Configuring printer share information

10. Review the information for the printer and click **Next.**
11. Ensure that the Status shows the driver and printer installations succeeded. Notice that you could now print a test page as a way to test your installation. You can also choose to add another printer. Click **Finish.**
12. Leave the Print Management window open for the next activity.

When you add a shared printer, consider the following guidelines when choosing a share name:

- Compose names that are easily understood and spelled by those who will use the printer.
- Include a room number, floor, or workstation name to help identify where the printer is located.
- Include descriptive information about the printer, such as the type, manufacturer, or model.

After you install a printer on a network to be shared, make sure that network printer sharing is turned on. This step enables printer sharing through the Windows Firewall so that shared printers appear when users view network resources and so that communications are permitted between the shared printers and the users who want to access them. In Chapter 5, Configuring, Managing, and Troubleshooting Resource Access, in Activity 5-7, you used the Network and Sharing Center to turn on file and printer sharing. Review those steps to make sure both are enabled.

Configuring Printer Properties

The setup information that you specify while stepping through the Network Printer Installation Wizard can be modified and further tuned by accessing the Properties dialog box for a printer. Printer properties are accessible from the Print Management tool by right-clicking a printer and clicking Properties. You can manage the following functions associated with a printer from the tabs in the Properties dialog box:

- General printer information
- Printer sharing
- Printer port setup
- Printer availability and advanced spooling options
- Security
- Device settings
- Special characteristics of a specific printer, such as color management for a color printer

The specific properties depend on the printer, printer manufacturer, and the printer driver available from the manufacturer.

General Printer Specifications

The title bar and top portion of the General tab in a printer's Properties dialog box show the name of the printer driver or just the name of the printer (see Figure 6-11). The Location and Comment boxes are used to store special notes about the printer that can help distinguish it from other printers, particularly for the sake of users if the printer is shared on the network. The printer model name is shown below the Comment box, and below the name is an area that describes features of the printer, such as its color capability and resolution. The Preferences button is used to specify additional information such as the default paper size, layout (portrait or landscape) paper source, print resizing options, and more. Also, the Print Test Page button enables you to print a test page as a way to verify that the printer is working.

Activity 6-6: Viewing Printing Preferences

Time Required: Approximately 10 minutes
Objective: Determine the default setup for printing preferences on a printer.

Description: After you install a printer, it is a good idea to verify the printing preferences to make certain they match the intended use of the printer. In this activity, you view the printing preferences for the printer you installed in Activity 6-5.

1. Ensure the **Print Management** tool is open.
2. In the left pane, use the **right-pointing arrow** to expand the elements under the print server so that you see Printers listed (refer to Figure 6-6). Click **Printers** in the left pane to view the installed printers in the middle pane.
3. In the middle pane, right-click the printer you installed in Activity 6-5, such as **Brother Color Leg Type 1 Class Driver**. Click **Properties**.
4. Make sure the **General** tab is displayed. Click the **Preferences** button near the bottom of the dialog box.
   - What tabs are shown? What are the options on the tabs that can be configured?
5. Click **Cancel**. Leave the Properties dialog box for the printer open for Activity 6-8 (the Properties dialog box is not used in Activity 6-7 because that activity uses a different tool).

Brother Color Leg Type1 Class Driver Properties

General | Sharing | Ports | Advanced | Color Management | Security | Device Settings

Brother Color Leg Type1 Class Driver

Location: Room 10

Comment: Shared color pinter

Model: Brother Color Leg Type1 Class Driver

Features

Color: Yes

Double-sided: No

Staple: No

Speed: Unknown

Maximum resolution: 600 dpi

Paper available: Letter

Preferences... | Print Test Page

OK | Cancel | Apply

Figure 6-11 General tab for a printer's properties

Sharing Printers

The Sharing tab is used to enable or disable a printer for sharing as well as to specify the name of the share (see Figure 6-12). When you enable sharing, be sure to provide a share name and check the box for *List in the directory* to publish the printer through Active Directory.

When you publish a printer, Windows 7, 8/8.1, and 10 clients as well as other client operating systems that have the Directory Service Client software installed can easily find it using the Search function. However, before printers can be published, there must be a domain Group Policy in Active Directory to enable publishing a printer in the domain.

Another way to publish a printer in Active Directory is to open the Active Directory Users and Computers tool, right-click the domain (or an OU in the domain), point to New, click Printer, and enter the UNC (Universal Naming Convention) path to the shared printer.

The option to *Render print jobs on client computers* shown in Figure 6-12 means that the print job is first prepared by software on the client and submitted to the spooler on the client (which is the default setting).

The Additional Drivers button on a printer's properties Sharing tab is used to add new types of clients. For example, if the server is an ×64 computer, you might add drivers for ×86 clients. When you check these boxes, the appropriate printer drivers are installed so users can automatically download them when they connect to the Windows Server 2016 print server for the first time. You might need the Windows Server 2016 installation media to install the drivers. In some cases, as in Figure 6-12, such additional drivers are not available for a printer, and so the Additional Drivers button is deactivated.

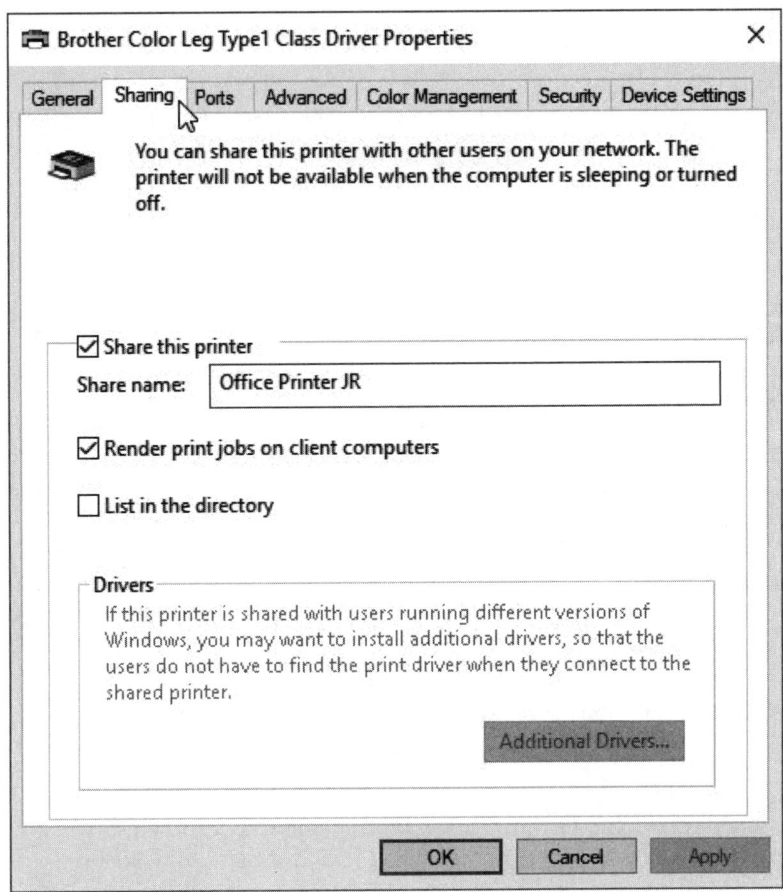

Figure 6-12 Sharing tab

6

Client computers check the printer driver each time they connect to the printer. If the driver on a client is not current, the driver will automatically be updated. Alternatively, Windows Server 2016 enables use of **Point and Print** with the v4 driver model. v4 print drivers are available through Windows Update. With v4 drivers at the updated client, the driver for a specific print device is not necessarily needed for printer sharing. This means the Windows Server 2016 print server does not have to distribute specific drivers to clients updated with v4 printer drivers.

Activity 6-7: Configuring the Domain Group Policy to Enable Publishing a Printer

Time Required: Approximately 10 minutes
Objective: Learn how to enable printer publishing in the domain's Group Policy.

Description: Publishing a printer for domain-wide access must be enabled in a domain's Group Policy within Active Directory. In this activity, you make certain that the domain's Group Policy for publishing printers is enabled.

1. Open **Server Manager,** if it is not open.
2. Click **Tools** and click **Group Policy Management.**
3. In the left pane, use the **right-pointing arrows** to expand **Domains** and your specific domain, so that you see **Default Domain Policy** as in Figure 6-13.
4. Right-click **Default Domain Policy** and click **Edit.**

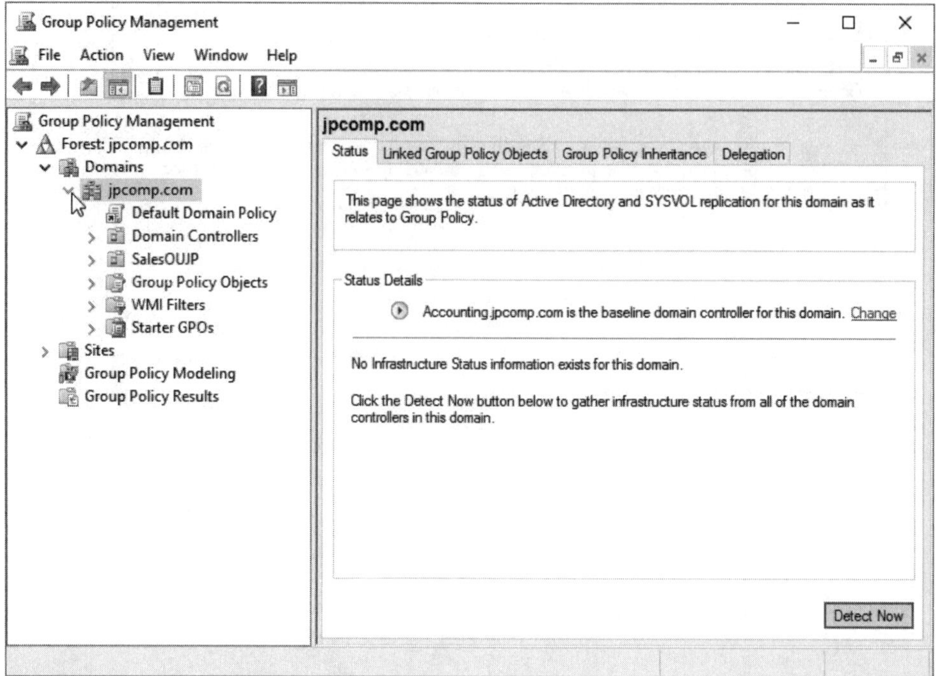

Figure 6-13 Accessing the Default Domain Policy

5. In the left pane of the Group Policy Management Editor window, as necessary, use the **right-pointing arrows** to display the elements under these folders: **Computer Configuration, Policies,** and **Administrative Templates.**
6. In the left pane, click the **Printers** folder under Administrative Templates (see Figure 6-14).

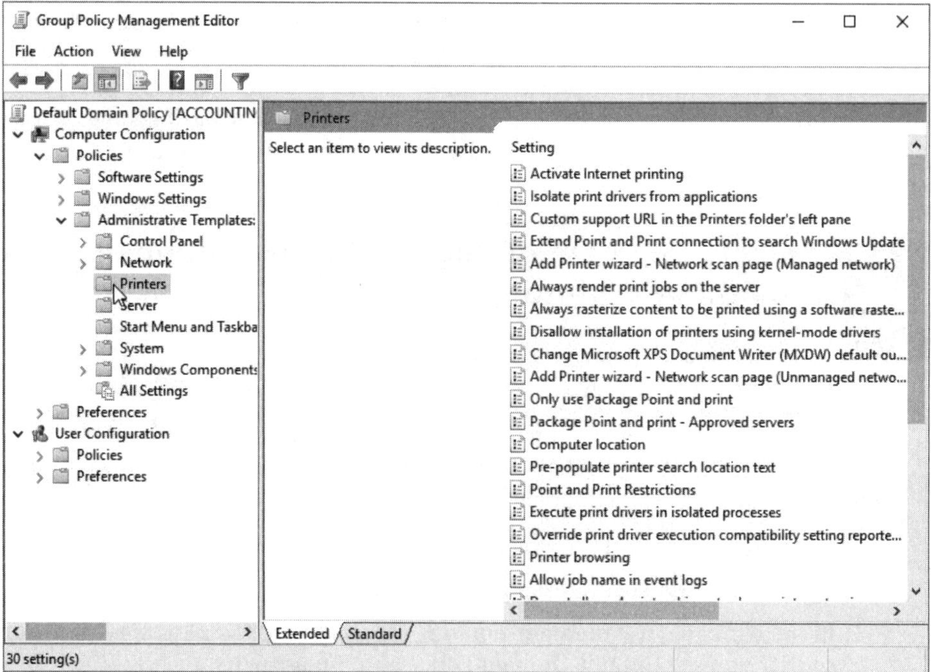

Figure 6-14 Selecting Printers

7. If necessary, click the **Standard** tab at the bottom of the middle pane for better viewing of the settings that can be configured.
8. Scroll through the right pane and notice the policies that can be configured.
9. In the right pane, double-click **Allow printers to be published.**
   - How is this policy currently configured?
10. Make sure **Enabled** is selected.
11. Click **OK**.
12. In addition to enabling printer publishing, you might want to enable the ability for browsing master servers to include published printers, as users browse for network printers when installing them through their operating system's version of the Network Printer Installation Wizard. To enable printer browsing, double-click **Printer browsing**, select **Enabled** (if it is not already selected), and click **OK**.
13. Review the middle pane of the Group Policy Management Editor window to ensure your changes have been made, as shown in Figure 6-15.
14. Close the **Group Policy Management Editor** window. Close the **Group Policy Management** window.

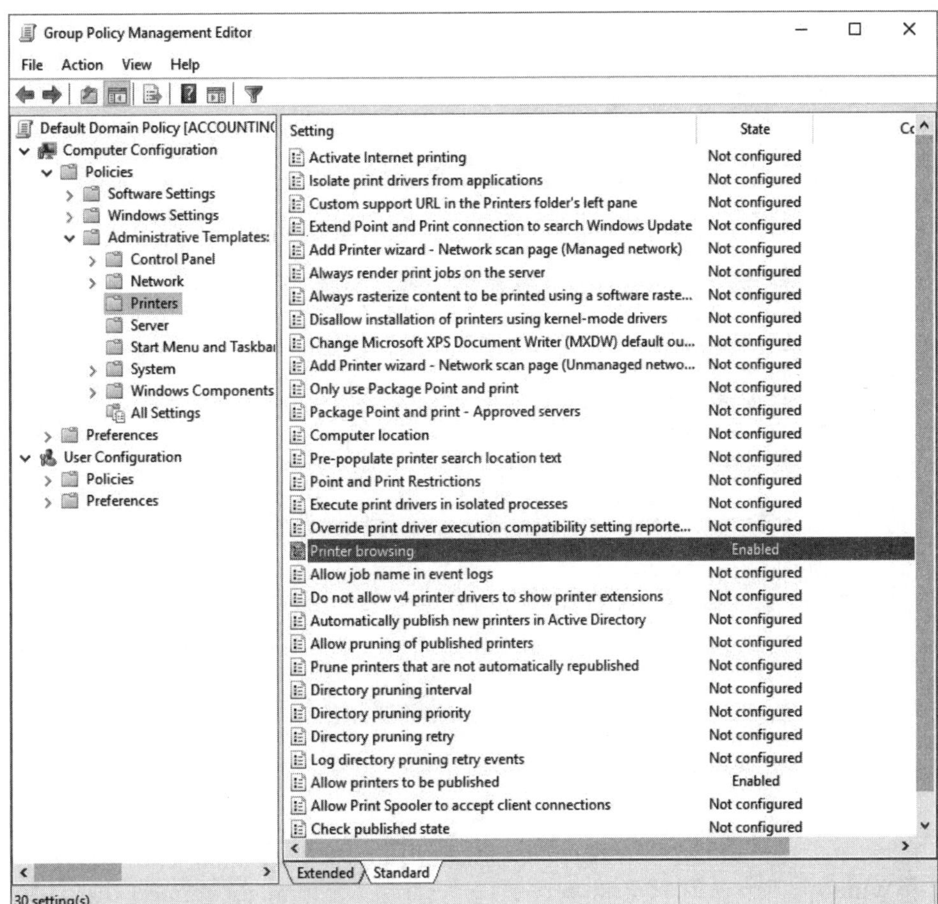

Figure 6-15 Ensuring the State column shows enabled

Setting this Group Policy has the benefit that when a client installs a printer driver from the print server, there is no prompting at the client for administrative credentials to install the driver.

Port Specifications

The Ports tab has options to specify which server port, such as LPT1 or COM1, is used for the printer and options to set up bidirectional printing and printer pooling (see Figure 6-16). **Bidirectional printing** is used with printers that have bidirectional capability. A bidirectional printer can engage in two-way communications with the print server and with software applications. These allow the printer driver to determine how much memory is installed in the printer, or other print capabilities. The printer also might be equipped with the ability to communicate that it is out of paper in a particular drawer or that it has a paper jam.

Before you connect a cabled printer, consult the manual to determine whether the printer is bidirectional. If so, the printer may require a special bidirectional cable labeled as an IEEE 1284 cable, and the printer port might need to be designated as bidirectional in the computer's BIOS setup program. Check both of these contingencies if you have a bidirectional printer, but the bidirectional box is deactivated on the Ports tab as in Figure 6-16.

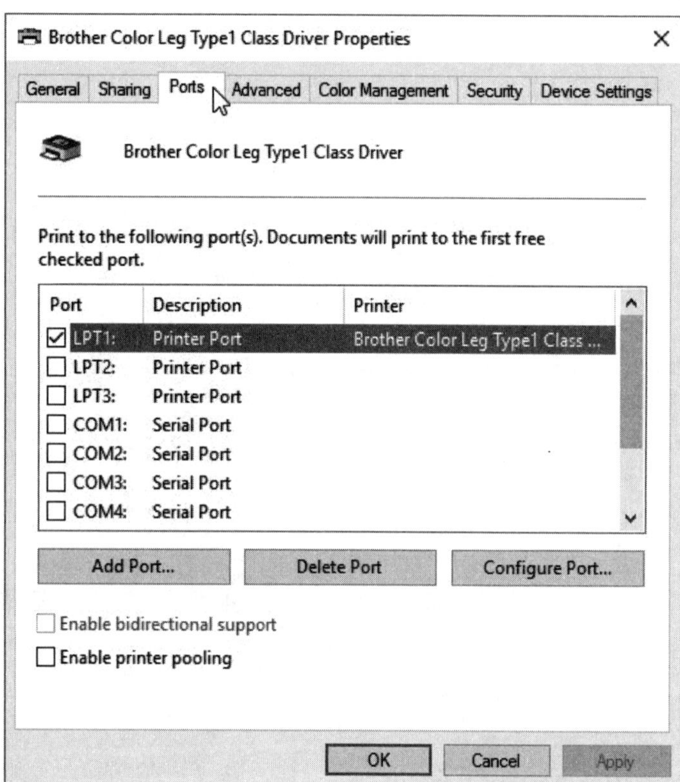

Figure 6-16 Ports tab

Printer pooling involves configuring two or more identical printers connected to one Windows Server 2016 print server. For example, you might connect three identical laser printers (except for port access) to three USB ports on a Windows Server 2016 server. On the Ports tab, check the Enable printer pooling box, and then check all of the ports to which printers are attached, such as USB001, USB002, and USB003, for example.

All of the printers in a pool must be identical so that they use the same printer driver and handle print files in the same way. The advantage of having a printer pool is that the Windows Server 2016 print monitor can send print files to any of the three printers (or however many you set up). If two of the printers are busy, it can send an incoming file to the third printer.

Printer pooling can significantly increase the print volume in a busy office, without the need to configure network printing for different kinds of printers.

It is wise to locate pooled printers in close physical proximity, because users are not able to tell to which pooled printer a print job may be sent.

The Add Port button enables you to add a new port, such as a new print monitor or a fax port. Click this button if you need to configure print monitors for specialized printing needs. The default options are shown in Figure 6-17 and described next.

- *Local Port*—The Local Port print monitor handles print jobs sent to a local physical port on the server or to a virtual port, such as an LPT, COM, or USB port. It also sends print jobs to a file, if you specify FILE as the port. When a print job is sent to FILE, a prompt appears to supply a file name. XPS users have an option to print to XPS using the XPS print path.

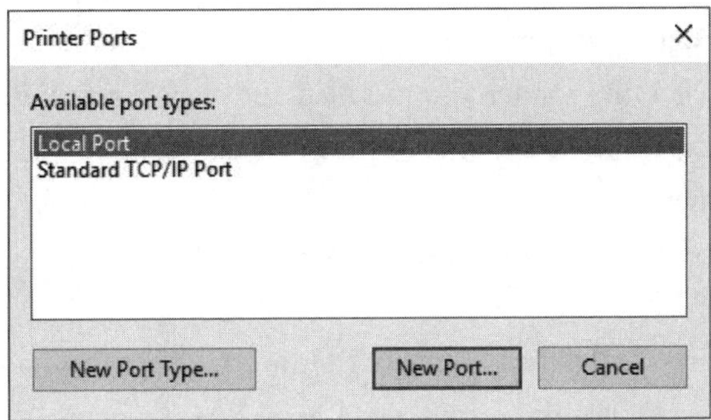

Figure 6-17 Port options

- *Standard TCP/IP Port*—This print monitor is used for TCP/IP-based printers that are connected to the network through wired or wireless printers with built-in print server cards. A TCP/IP address is shown on the Ports tab as the IP address of the printer. Alternatively, if the printer supports **Web Services for Devices (WSD)** technology, it will be listed as WSD on the Ports tab. WSD devices include web services and can use protocol-based messaging to inform clients of their capabilities. WSD additionally uses Web Services Discovery (WS-Discovery) so that the port monitor in an operating system can repeatedly discover a printer and its IP address. Web services can also be used to obtain configuration information about a printer that is needed for managing a print job, for example. Windows treats a WSD port as a combination of network printer and software-based port similar to a USB virtual printer port.

When you connect a USB printer locally, Windows creates a virtual printer port, such as USB001 or USB002. This is a local port, but it is not a physical port, like LPT1 or COM1. Instead, it is a software-based port, created by the operating system interfaced with the printer so that the printer has a unique channel of communication with the computer. The first USB-connected printer on a Windows computer is usually USB001 and the second USB printer is USB002.

The Delete Port button on the Ports tab is used to remove a port option from the list of ports. The Configure Port button is used to tune the configuration parameters that are appropriate to the type of port. On an LPT port, click the Configure Port button to check the port timeout setting. This setting is the amount of time the server will continue to try sending a print file to a printer while the printer is not responding. The default setting is normally 90 seconds. Consider increasing the setting to 120 seconds or more if you are installing a printer to handle large print files, such as files for combined graphics and color printing. On a COM port, the Configure Port button is used to set the serial port speed in bits per second, data bits, parity, stop bits, and flow control.

Activity 6-8: Configuring Printer Pooling

Time Required: Approximately 10 minutes
Objective: Learn how to configure printer pooling.

Description: Printer pooling can enable users in a busy office to be more productive, so they are not waiting on printouts. In this activity, you practice configuring printer pooling (you do not need an additional printer for this activity, but you would, of course, in an actual office situation).

1. The **Print Management** window should still be open from Activity 6-6; if not, open it. If you still have the printer Properties dialog box open from Activity 6-6, go to Step 4; or if the dialog box is not open go to Step 2 after you have opened the Print Management window.
2. In the left pane, select **Printers**, if it is not selected.
3. In the middle pane, right-click the printer you installed and click **Properties**.
4. In the Properties dialog box for the printer, click the **Ports** tab (refer to Figure 6-16).
5. Click **Enable printer pooling**.
6. Click **COM3** or another port that is not in use.
7. Click **Apply**.
   - How has that port's printer assignment changed? How could you print a test page?
8. Leave the Properties dialog box for the printer open for the next activity.

Activity 6-9: Transferring Print Jobs

Time Required: Approximately 15 minutes
Objective: Learn how to transfer print jobs from a malfunctioning printer.

Description: Assume that you have a small network in which a printer is connected to the server, the printer has failed, but an identical printer shared by a workstation on the network is working. You practice configuring the print monitor associated with the Local Port option and, at the same time, learn how to transfer print jobs to another printer. Besides the printer you have already installed, you will need an additional printer on the network that is shared, such as a printer connected to another computer. Obtain from your instructor the name of a workstation or server that has a shared printer.

1. Make sure the **Ports** tab is still displayed from Activity 6-8.
2. Click the **Add Port** button.
   - What port types are available?
3. Click **Local Port** and click the **New Port** button (do not click the New Port Type button). Enter the UNC name of the workstation and printer provided by your instructor, such as **\\ Lab1\HPLaser** and click **OK**.

If your server has two printers connected, you can also enter the server name and the name of the other printer.

4. Click **Close**.
   - Is the new port added to the list of ports? What is the Port name and description?
5. Click **Close**.
6. Leave the Print Management window open for the next activity.

Printer Scheduling and Advanced Options

The Advanced tab allows you to have a printer available at all times or to limit the time to a range of hours (see Figure 6-18). To have a printer available at all times, click *Always available*; to limit printer use to only certain times, click *Available from* and enter the range of times when the printer can be used, such as from 8:00 AM to 10:00 PM.

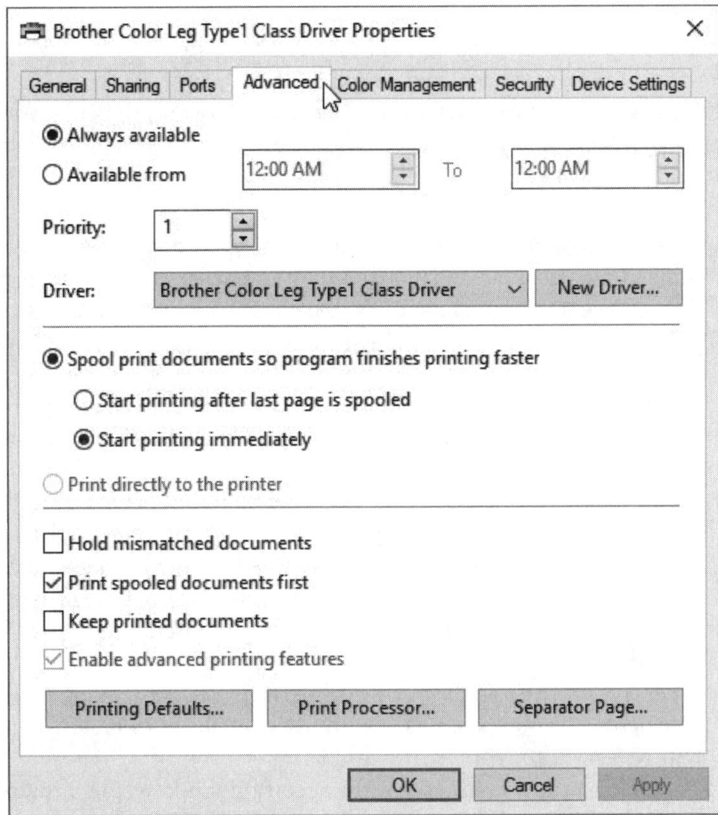

Figure 6-18 Advanced tab

You can set the priority higher to give a particular printer or printer pool priority over other printers attached to the server, which applies only if there are two or more installed printers. The priority can be set from 1 to 99. For example, if the server is managing several printer shares, one may be set for higher priority because it prints payroll checks or is used by the company president.

Printer scheduling can be useful when there is one print device and two printer objects (shares) for that printer. One object can be set up for immediate printing, and the other can be used for long print jobs that are not immediately needed. The object for the longer jobs that can wait might be set up so those print jobs are scheduled to print between 6:00 PM and midnight. Another way to handle the longer jobs is to pause that printer object and resume printing when the printer has a light load, such as at noon or during slow times of the day.

The Advanced tab provides the option to use spooled printing or to bypass the spooler and send print files directly to the printer. It works best to spool print jobs so they are printed on a first-come, first-served basis and to enable background printing so the CPU can work on other tasks. Printing directly to the printer is not recommended, unless there is an emergency need to focus all resources on a specific printout. Print spooling also helps ensure that jobs are printed together, so a long Word document is not interrupted by a one-page print job. Without spooling, such an interruption can occur if the one-page job is ready to print at the time the Word job is pausing to read the disk. The spool option is selected by default, with the instruction to start printing before all the pages are spooled. This is an appropriate option in a small office in which most print files are not resource-intensive and there is infrequent contention for printers, reducing the odds of intermixing printouts.

If a busy office has a problem with pages intermixing from printouts, click the option to *Start printing after last page is spooled*.

The *Hold mismatched documents* option causes the system to compare the setup of the printer with the setup in the document. For example, if the printer is set up in a print share as a laser printer but the document is formatted for a plotter, the print job is placed on hold. The job does not print until the document is released by the user, such as a member of the Print Operators or Server Operators group, or an administrator.

The *Hold mismatched documents* option is a good way to save paper in a heterogeneous situation, such as a student lab, where users have very different formatted print jobs. One mismatch situation can use hundreds of pages printing one character per page.

The option to *Print spooled documents first* enables jobs that have completed spooling to be printed, no matter what their priority. In high-volume printing situations, this speeds the process by reducing the wait for long print jobs to spool.

The *Keep printed documents* option retains documents in the spooler after they have printed, which enables the network administrator to re-create a printout damaged by a printer jam or other problem. For example, if a large number of paychecks are printing and a printer problem strikes in the middle of the printout, this critical option makes it possible to reprint the damaged checks. However, this option should be accompanied by a maintenance schedule to delete documents no longer needed.

The *Enable advanced printing features* option permits you to make use of special features associated with a particular printer, such as the ability to print booklets or to vary the order in which pages are printed—back to front, for example.

The Printing Defaults button enables you to specify default settings for print jobs, unless they are overridden by control codes in the print file. These can include the print layout, page print order (front to back), and paper source, depending on the printer.

Use the Print Processor button to specify one of the print processors and data types, for example, using the WinPrint print processor (the default) and the EMF data type for Windows-based clients. The **data type** is the way in which information is formatted in a print file. Data types include the following:

- *RAW*—A print file formatted as the **RAW** data type is often used for files sent from legacy Windows operating systems and from UNIX and Linux clients. It is also the default setting for a PostScript printer. A RAW print file is intended to be printed by the Windows 10 Server print server with no additional formatting.
- *RAW (FF appended)*—In this data type, the FF is a form-feed code placed at the end of the print file. Some non-Windows and very old 16-bit Windows software do not place a form feed at the end of a print file. The form feed is used to make sure the last page of the file is printed.
- *RAW (FF auto)*—In this data type, the print processor checks the print file for a form feed as the last character set, before appending a form feed at the end. If a form feed is already present, it does not add anything to the file.

- *NT EMF (different versions)*—Modern Windows operating system clients, such as Windows 10, use the **enhanced metafile (EMF)** data type. This data type is created when a print file is prepared by the GDI at the client. EMF print files offer a distinct advantage in Windows operating system environments because they are very portable from computer to computer.
- *TEXT*—The **TEXT** data type is used for printing text files formatted according to the ANSI standard that uses values between 0 and 255 to represent characters, numbers, and symbols. You would use the TEXT data type for printing many types of print files from very old Windows operating systems, such as text files printed from old word processors or MS-DOS text editors. It can also be used for printing WordPad files that are in text format (WordPad can be handy for creating scripts used by PowerShell or on Linux systems).
- *XPS2GDI*—This data type converts XPS documents to GDI (graphics device interface) for GDI compatible printers.

A **PostScript (PS) printer** is one that has special firmware or cartridges to print using a page-description language (PDL). Most non-PostScript laser printers use a version of the **Printer Control Language (PCL)**, which was developed by Hewlett-Packard.

The Separator Page button is used to place a blank page at the beginning of each printed document. This helps designate the end of one printout and the beginning of another, so that printouts do not get mixed together, or so that someone does not take the wrong printout in a medium-size or large office setting in which many people share the same printer. Another advantage to using a separator page is that it sends control codes to the printer to make sure that special formatting set for the last printout is reset prior to the next one. In small offices, a separator page might not be needed, because print formatting might not vary, and users can quickly identify their own printouts. Windows Server 2016 has four separator page files from which to choose, located in the \Windows\System32 folder:

- *Pcl.sep*—Used to print a Printer Control Language (PCL) separator page on a printer that handles PCL and PostScript
- *Pscript.sep*—Used to print a PostScript separator page on a printer that handles PCL and PostScript
- *Sysprint.sep*—Used with PostScript-only printers and prints a separator page at the beginning of each document
- *Sysprtj.sep*—Used in the same way as Sysprint.sep, but for documents printed in the Japanese language

Separator pages can also be customized. See the website *technet.microsoft.com/en-us/library/jj149734.aspx*. Although this website is for Windows Server 2012, it also works for Windows Server 2016.

Consider the cost of paper before you set up separator pages. If you set up a separator page for each document and each user also specifies a banner page from the client, the resulting paper costs quickly mount in an office. For example, depending on the setup, one or more extra pages will print per document, turning a one-page original document into two, three, or more printed pages. Many offices sharing a printer simply decide to forgo separator and banner pages, because each person usually knows what she or he printed.

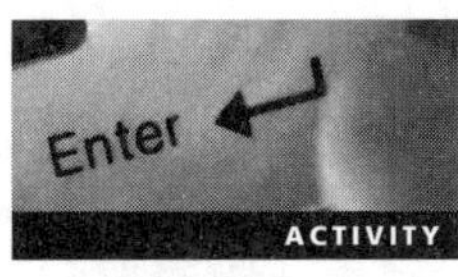

Activity 6-10: Changing Data Types

Time Required: Approximately 10 minutes

Objective: Learn how to change the data type when printing problems occur.

Description: In this activity, you practice changing the data type to accommodate UNIX and Linux clients that print to a printer connected to Windows Server 2016. Assume you have been experiencing garbled printouts using the TEXT setup and a problem with getting the first page to print. To solve the problem, you change the data type to RAW with FF appended.

1. Open the **Print Management** tool, if it is closed.
2. If necessary, click **Printers** in the left pane and in the middle pane, right-click the printer you installed. Click **Properties.**
3. Select the **Advanced** tab and click the **Print Processor** button.
   - What print processors and data types are listed?
4. Click **winprint** (if it is not already selected) and click **RAW [FF appended]**.
5. Click **OK.**
6. Leave the Properties dialog box for the printer open for the next activity.

Configuring Security

As an object, a shared printer can be set up to use security features such as share permissions, auditing, and ownership. To configure security for a printer, you must have Manage printers permissions for that printer. Use the Security tab to set up printer share permissions (see Figure 6-19).

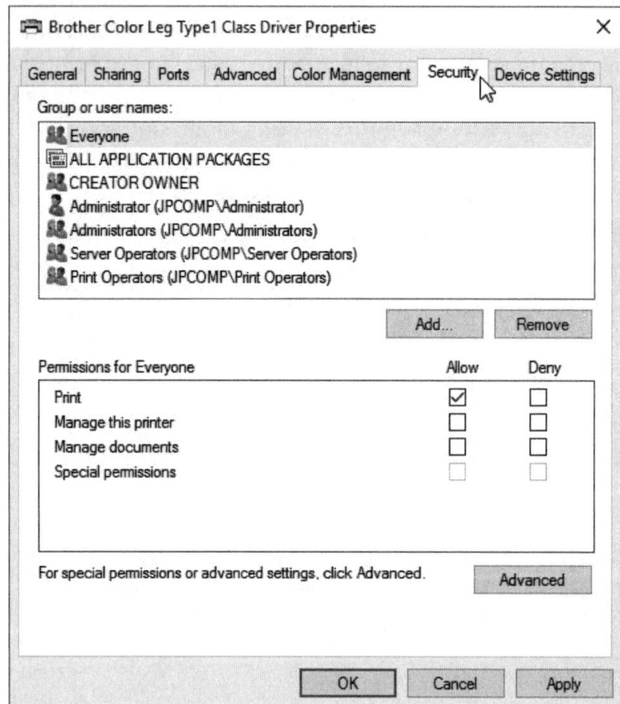

Figure 6-19 Security tab

Once a printer is shared, the default permissions are as follows:

- *Everyone group*—Print
- *ALL APPLICATION PACKAGES*—Print and Manage documents
- *CREATOR OWNER*—Manage documents
- *Administrator account*—Print, Manage this printer, and Manage documents
- *Administrators, Server Operators, Print Operators groups*—Print, Manage this printer, and Manage documents

Click an existing group to modify its permissions, and use the Add button to add new groups or the Remove button to delete a group from accessing the printer. Table 6-1 lists the printer share permissions that can be set.

Table 6-1 Printer share permissions

Share permission	Access capability
Print	Users can connect to the shared printer, send print jobs, and manage their own print requests (such as to pause, restart, resume, or cancel a print job)
Manage documents	Users can connect to the shared printer, send print jobs, and manage any print job sent (including jobs sent by other users)
Manage this printer	Users have complete access to a printer share, including the ability to change permissions, turn off sharing, configure printer properties, and delete the share
Advanced permissions (same as special permissions)	Similar to configuring special permissions for a folder, special permissions can be set up for a printer from the Advanced tab

By clicking the Advanced button on the Security tab, you can:

- Set up advanced or special printer permissions for a specific group or user (use the Permissions tab, select the user or group, click Edit, click Show advanced permissions).
- Add or remove a group or user for security access or denial (use the Permissions tab).
- Set up printer auditing (use the Auditing tab).
- Take ownership of a printer (use the Take ownership advanced permission configured from the Permissions tab).
- View the effective access for a user or group (use the Effective Access tab).

Advanced or special access permissions enable you to fine-tune shared printer permissions, for instance to configure a group that has Print permissions so that group can perform all functions except taking ownership.

Any user account or group can be set up for auditing, by clicking the Auditing tab and the Add button. Before you set up printer auditing, make sure that there is a Group Policy or default domain security policy that enables object auditing on the basis of successful and failed activity attempts (refer to Activity 5-6 in Chapter 5). For a shared printer, you can track successful or failed attempts to:

- Print jobs.
- Manage the printer.
- Manage documents.
- Read printer share permissions.
- Change printer share permissions.
- Take ownership of the printer.

Activity 6-11: Configuring Printer Security

Time Required: Approximately 10 minutes
Objective: Learn how to set up security on a shared printer.

Description: Configuring security is very important on a shared printer, so that you can control who has access and ensure the productivity of the printer's users. In this activity, you remove the Everyone group from access to a printer and provide access to the domain local group that you created in Chapter 4, Introduction to Active Directory and Account Management. You also set up auditing of failed printing attempts for the domain local group you created.

1. Access the printer **Properties** dialog box still open from Activity 6-10.
2. Click the **Security** tab.
   - What security is set up already?
3. Click the **Everyone** group and click **Remove**. Notice that the *Group or user names* box is updated to reflect the change.
4. Click the **Add** button.
5. In the Select Users, Computers, Service Accounts, or Groups dialog box, click the **Advanced** button, click **Find Now**, double-click the domain local group you created in Chapter 4, such as DomainMgrsJP, and click **OK**.
   - What permissions are given to this group by default?
6. Click the **Advanced** button.
7. In the Advanced Security Settings dialog box for the printer, click the **Auditing** tab.
8. Click **Add**.
9. In the Auditing Entry window for the printer, click the link for **Select a principal**.
10. In the Select User, Computer, Service Account, or Group dialog box, click the **Advanced** button, click **Find Now**, double-click the domain local group you created in Chapter 4, such as DomainMgrsJP, and click **OK**.
11. In the Auditing Entry window for the printer, click the **down arrow** in the Type box and select **Fail** to track failed print attempts (see Figure 6-20). Click **OK**. Notice that your auditing configuration now appears on the Auditing tab for the Advanced Security Settings window for the printer.
12. Click **OK**.
    - If there is a message that auditing is not turned on as a Group Policy, how would you turn it on?
13. Click **OK** in the Properties dialog box for the printer.
14. Leave the Print Management tool open for the next activity.

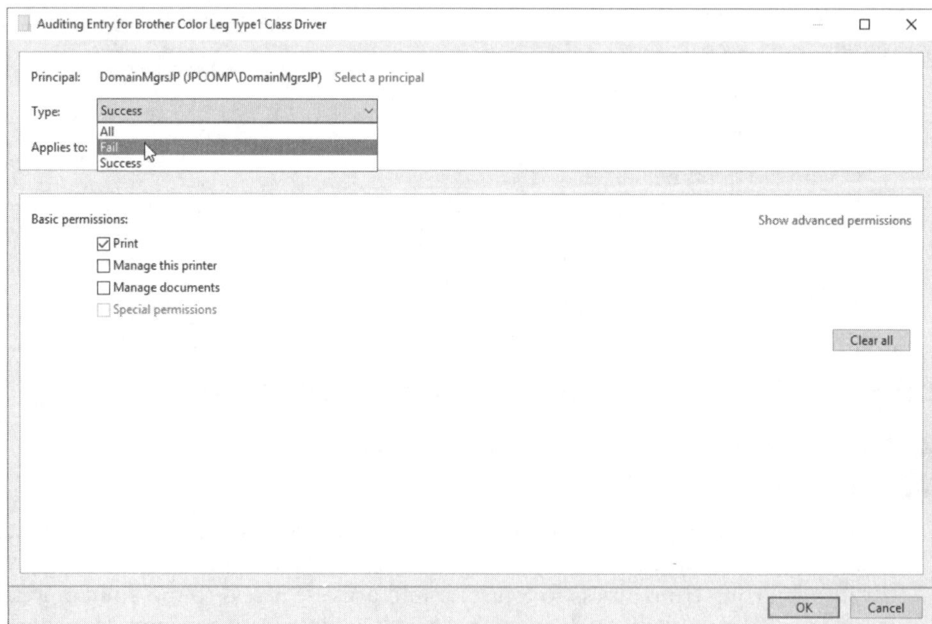

Figure 6-20 Configuring printer auditing

Configuring Device Settings

The Device Settings tab enables you to specify printer settings that are specific to the printer you have installed, such as printer trays, memory, paper size, fonts, duplexing, and installable options (see Figure 6-21). For example, in many cases if you have a multiple-tray printer you will leave the paper tray assignment on Auto Select (not shown in Figure 6-21 but available on some printers) and let the software application at the client specify the printer tray. However, if your organization uses special forms such as paychecks, you can specify use of a designated paper tray when checks are printing.

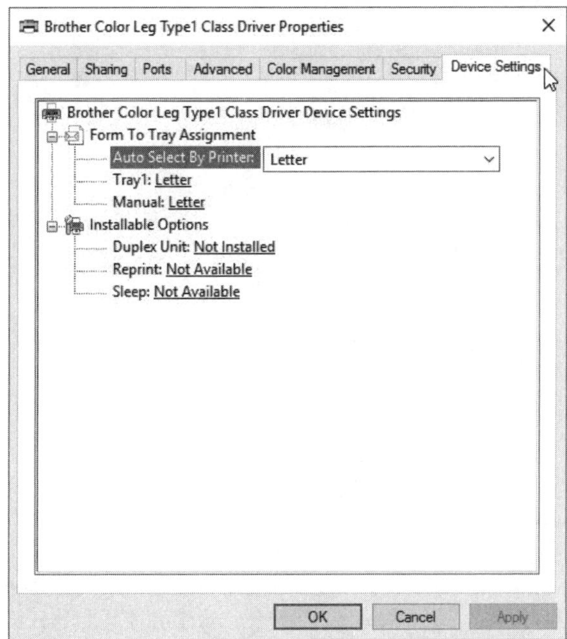

Figure 6-21 Device Settings tab

The printer memory is usually automatically detected in bidirectional printers, but if it is not, you can specify the amount of memory in the Printer Memory option under Installable Options. In the client operating system, such as Windows 10, the workstation printer setup also can have information about how much memory is installed in a shared printer.

Make sure the memory reported in the device settings matches the memory installed in the printer, because this enables the Windows Server 2016 print server to offload more work to the printer, improving the speed at which print jobs are completed as well as server performance. Most other settings are better left to the software at the client end to handle. For example, a client printing in Microsoft Word can specify font and paper tray instructions inside the document and by using the Printer Setup.

Configuring a Nonlocal Printer or an Internet Printer

There are times when you want to enable a Windows Server 2016 server to connect to a printer that is not directly connected to one of its ports, for example, a printer shared from a workstation, another server, the Internet or an intranet, or one that is connected to the network through its own internal print server card. You can connect to a network printer by using the Network Printer Installation Wizard and following these general steps:

1. Open the Print Management tool, if it is not already open.
2. Right-click Printers in the left pane under the server name and click Add Printer.

3. Click Search the network for printers and click Next. (Or if you know the TCP/IP address of the printer use the *Add a TCP/IP or Web Services Printer by IP address or hostname* option.)
4. Find the printer you want to add in the Network Printer Search box (see Figure 6-22) and click Next.

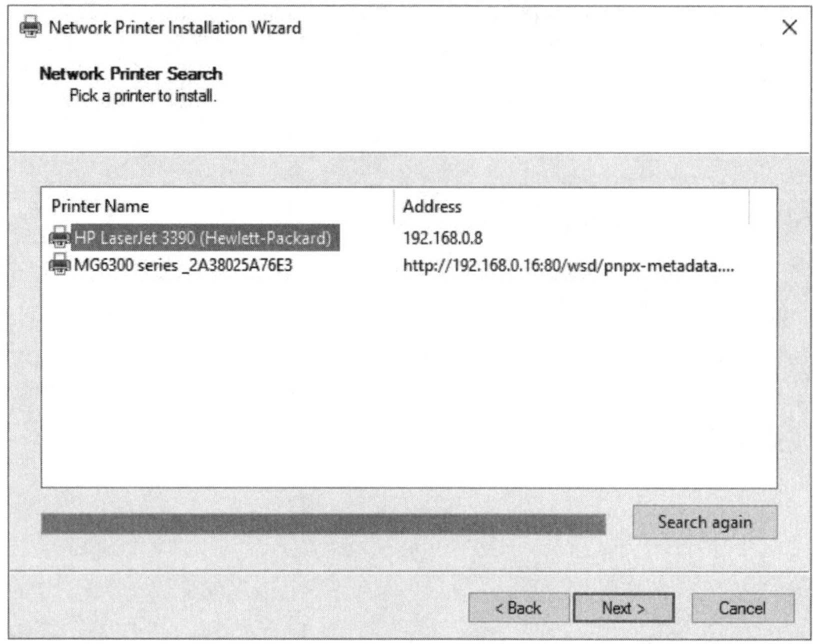

Figure 6-22 Network Printer Search results

5. In the Printer Name and Sharing Settings box, ensure that Share this printer is selected. Provide the Share Name, Location, and Comment information. Click Next.
6. Review the information in the Printer Found box. Click Next.
7. Click Finish.
8. Ensure that the printer appears in the middle pane of the Print Management tool (with Printers selected in the left pane, first).

When the remote printer is installed on a domain controller, you can change the properties of the shared printer you just installed, even if the printer is connected to a host computer and you are not logged onto that computer. This means you can manage any remote shared network printer, even though it is not connected to a physical port on the server. You can manage the remote printer's properties from the Print Management tool, just as you have done for a local printer using the activities in this chapter. This capability is very useful when you manage a large network with network printers located in distant buildings. If you need to change the print processor used by a shared printer that is a block away, you can do so without leaving your office.

Managing Print Jobs

In the time after a print job is sent and before it is fully transmitted to the printer, several options are available for managing that job. Users with print permissions can print and manage their own jobs. Also, members of the Printer Operators, Server Operators, and Administrators groups can manage the jobs of others through the Manage documents and Manage the printer permissions. To manage printed documents as administrator, use the Print Management tool. Users can manage their own documents before the documents are sent to the server's print spooler by opening the printer icon in the tray on the right side of the taskbar in Windows 7, 8/8.1, and 10. For the server administrator, open the Print Management tool, select Printers in the left pane under the server name, right-click a printer in the middle pane, and click Open Printer Queue.

Users with Print permissions can:

- Send print jobs to the printer.
- Pause, resume, and restart their own print jobs.
- Cancel their own print jobs.

Print Operators, Server Operators, and other groups having Manage documents permissions can:

- Send print jobs to the printer.
- Pause, resume, and restart any user's print jobs.
- Cancel any user's print jobs.

Administrators, Print Operators, Server Operators, and any other groups having Manage this printer permissions can do all of the same things as those with Manage documents permissions, but they also can pause and restart the printer and change the properties of the printer. For example, in terms of changing properties, those with Manage this printer permissions can start and stop sharing, configure printer properties, take ownership, change permissions, and set the default printer for the Windows Server 2016 server.

Controlling the Status of Printing

In Windows Server 2016, printer control and setup information for a particular printer is associated with that printer's properties and the printer's print queue. For example, if you have two printers installed, HPLaser_Rm20 and InkJet_Rm8, a set of properties and printer control information via the printer's print queue applies for each printer. For example, if you want to pause a print job for the HPLaser_Rm20 printer, open the Print Management tool, right-click the HPLaser_Rm20 printer, and click Open Printer Queue to access options for managing the print job while it is still in the print queue.

Sometimes you need to pause a printer to fix a problem, for example, to reattach a loose cable or to power the printer off and on to reset it. You can pause printing to that printer in two ways. One way is to right-click the printer in the middle pane of the Print Management tool and click Pause Printing. To restart the printer, right-click it and click Resume Printing. Alternatively, open the printer's print queue window, click Printer, and click the Pause Printing option so there is a check mark beside it (see Figure 6-23) when you open the Printer menu again. Remember that you need to uncheck Pause Printing before print jobs can continue printing.

The Pause Printing capability is particularly important if a user sends an improperly formatted document to the printer, such as a PostScript-formatted document to a non-PostScript printer. If you do not have *Hold mismatched documents* enabled, the printer might print tens or hundreds of pages with a single control code on each page. By pausing printing, you have time to identify and delete the document before too much paper is used.

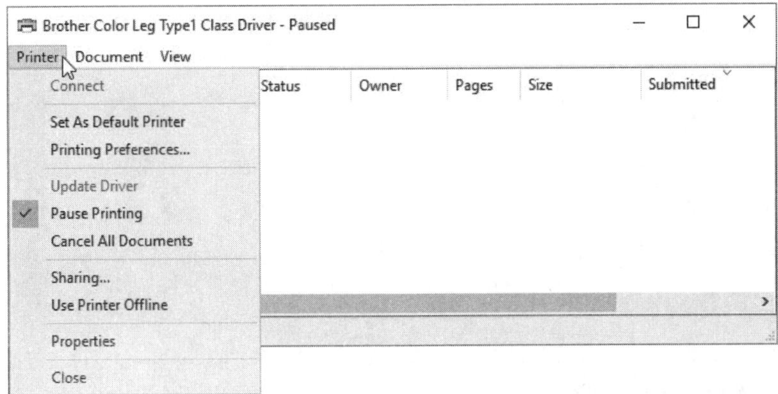

Figure 6-23 Pausing a printer

Controlling Specific Print Jobs

You can pause, resume, restart, or view the properties of one or more documents in the print queue of a printer. A **print queue** is like a stack of print jobs, with the first job submitted at the top of the stack and the last job submitted at the bottom, and all of the jobs waiting to be sent from the spooler to the printer.

In Windows Server 2016, to pause a print job, open the print queue window for the printer. The window shows a list of jobs to be printed, the status of each job, the owner, the number of pages to be printed, the size of the print file, and when the print job was submitted. Click the document you want to pause, click the Document menu, and then click Pause. The print job will stop printing (if some of it has not already been sent to the printer) until you highlight the document and click Resume or Restart on the Document menu. Resume starts printing at the point in the document where the printing was paused. Restart prints from the beginning of the document. You also can use the Document menu to cancel a print job. First click the job in the status window, click the Document menu, and click Cancel.

Depending on the amount of memory in your printer, a print job might not stop printing right away after you cancel it.

Jobs print in the order they are received, unless the administrator changes their priority. Jobs come in with a priority of 1 but can be assigned a priority as high as 99. For example, if you work for a university, the president might need to quickly print a last-minute report before going to a meeting with the trustees. You can give the president a 99 priority by clicking her print job in the window listing the print jobs. Next, click the Document menu, click Properties, and access the General tab. The Priority box is in the middle of the General tab. Move the slider from Lowest (1) to Highest (99) as in Figure 6-24, depending on your requirements, and click OK.

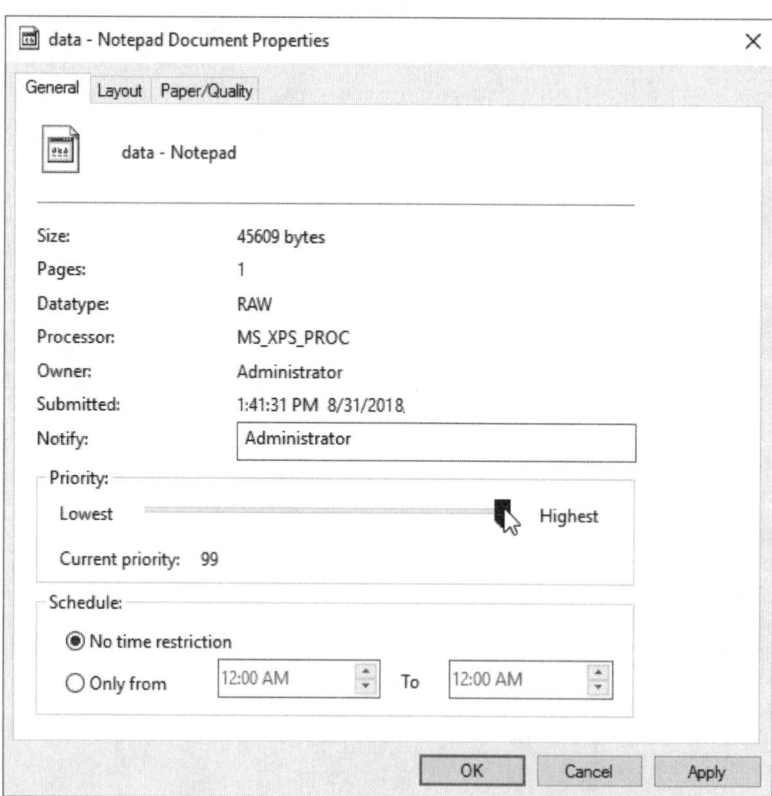

Figure 6-24 Adjusting the printing priority

You also can use the General tab to set a time for selected jobs to print on a printer. For example, if the server is very busy during the day, you can ease the load by setting jobs to print at a certain time of day, such as from noon to 1:00 PM. The General tab also provides basic information about the file, such as the size, owner, data type used, print processor used, and when the job was submitted.

Activity 6-12: Pausing a Printer and Canceling a Document

Time Required: Approximately 10 minutes
Objective: Learn how to pause a printer and then cancel a document in a printer's print queue window.

Description: Assume that your office has a printer that is printing sheet after sheet of garbled text. This activity enables you to pause printing to that printer until you can cancel the print job.

1. Open the **Print Management** tool, if it is not still open.
2. Click **Printers** in the left pane under the server name, if Printers is not already selected.
3. Right-click the printer you installed in Activity 6-5 and click **Open Printer Queue**.
4. Click **Printer** and click **Pause Printing**.
   - Has the title bar of the printer's window changed, and if so how?
5. Create a document using a word processor or Notepad that contains only one or two words, such as **Test**. (To use Notepad, click **Start**, click the **Windows Accessories** folder, and click **Notepad**.) Print the document to the printer that you have paused. (In Notepad, click **File**, click **Print**, ensure the correct printer is selected, and click **Print**.) Close the document you created and do not save it.
6. When the document appears in the printer window, click it.
7. Click **Document** and leave the menu open.
   - What options are available to you to control a print job?
8. Move your pointer to a blank area and click it to close the Document menu.
9. Double-click the document you sent to the print queue.
   - How would you reset the priority of this print job?
10. Click **Cancel** to close the Properties dialog box for the document.
11. Right-click the document that you sent to the printer and click **Cancel**. Click **Yes** to cancel the document.
12. Click **Printer** and click **Pause Printing** to remove the check.
13. Close the window you have been using to manage print jobs and close the Print Management tool.

A similar print queue management tool is available to Windows clients and is displayed in the taskbar (or by clicking the up arrow in the right side of the taskbar) after a client selects to print a document and until the document is sent off from the client (which can be too fast to manage when there are only one or two printed documents) to the print server. Windows Server 2016 print clients can manage their own documents from this window, including selecting a default printer to use for their print jobs.

Troubleshooting Common Printing Problems

As a server administrator, you are likely to get a call from users who cannot get printouts on a specific printer. In this circumstance, use the Print Management tool to quickly check the status of a printer to see if it is offline or paused—in which case the solution may be as simple as turning on a printer or resuming a paused printer. To check a printer's status:

1. Open the Print Management tool.
2. Click Printers in the left pane under the server.
3. View the Queue Status column in the middle pane. For example, Figure 6-25 shows one printer that is paused and another printer that is offline. The offline printer is perhaps just turned off or needs to be rebooted because its print server card needs to be reinitiated due to a recent power brownout.

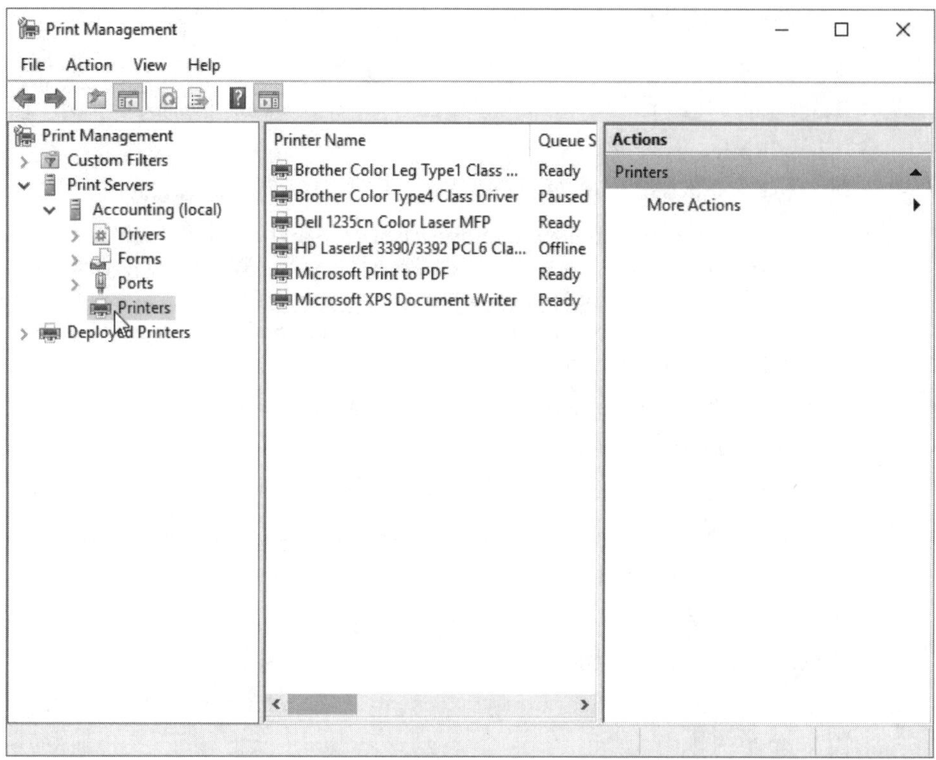

Figure 6-25 Checking the status for printers

A typical printing problem can occur when the Windows Server 2016 Print Spooler service experiences a temporary difficulty, gets out of synchronization, or hangs. Because the spooler contains several complex pieces and is central to printing functions, it is a possible source of printer problems. The result is that print jobs are not processed until the problem is solved. If a print job is not going through and you determine that one or more printers are not paused and that the cable or wireless connection is good, then stop and restart the Print Spooler service by using the following general steps:

1. Open Server Manager, click Tools, and click Services.
2. Scroll to find the Print Spooler service and then double-click this service.
3. Check the status to determine if the Print Spooler service is running, and make sure that it is set to start automatically. If you need to start the service, click Start. If you need to set the service to start automatically, set this option in the Startup type box. To stop and restart the service, click Stop and then click Start. Make sure that the service status is Running and that the startup type is Automatic. Click OK.

4. Because the Print Spooler service is dependent on the Remote Procedure Call (RPC) service, check to make sure that the Remote Procedure Call service is also started and set to start automatically. (The Print Spooler is also dependent on the HTTP Service, but you won't see it listed, because you can't manage it in this way.) Further, make sure that the Server service is working.
5. Close the Services window.

Warn users before you stop and restart the Print Spooler service, because queued print jobs will be deleted.

Several other common problems and their solutions are summarized in Table 6-2.

6

Table 6-2 Troubleshooting printing problems

Network printing problem	Solutions
Only one character prints per page	If only one workstation experiences this problem, reinstall the printer driver on that workstation. If all workstations are experiencing the problem, first turn off the printer, wait 30 seconds, and turn on the printer. If this doesn't work, reinstall the printer and printer driver at the computer or print server offering the printer share (such as by using the Print Management tool). Check the print monitor and data type setup.
Some users get a no-access message when trying to access the printer share	Check the share permissions. Make certain the clients belong to a group for which at least Print permission has been granted and that none of the groups to which these users belong are denied Print permission. The fast way to check this is by using the effective access capability from the Security tab of that printer's properties.
Printer control codes are on the printout	Sometimes this is caused by the formatting of a previous printout; all you need to do is turn the printer off, wait for 30 seconds, and turn it back on. This action resets the printer. If only one client workstation experiences the problem, reinstall the printer driver on that workstation. Also, make sure the software generating the printout is installed correctly. If all workstations are experiencing the problem, reinstall the printer and printer driver at the computer or print server offering the printer share (such as by using the Printer Management tool on the server). Make sure the share is set up for all operating systems that access it, that the correct print monitor is installed, and that the appropriate data type is used.
A print job shows it is printing, the printer looks fine, but nothing is printing	Check for a problem with the print job at the top of the print queue for that printer. If it shows the job is printing but nothing is happening, delete the print job because it might be hung (and resubmit the print job). Next, try deleting additional print jobs at the top of the queue, in case more than one job is hung. As a last resort, try stopping and restarting the Print Spooler service (warn users first).
Some clients find that the ending pages are not printed for large print jobs	Check the disk space on the server or client workstation in which the job is spooled. It might not have enough space to fully spool all jobs.

(continued)

Table 6-2 Troubleshooting printing problems (continued)

Network printing problem	Solutions
On some long print jobs, pages from other print jobs are found in the printout	Set the printer's properties so that the printer starts printing only after all pages are spooled. To do this, right-click the printer in the Print Management tool, click Properties, click the Advanced tab, select *Spool print documents so program finishes printing faster* and select *Start printing after last page is spooled*, and click OK.
Extra separator pages are printed or print jobs seem to get stuck in the printer for all users	Check the print processor in use by accessing the Properties dialog box for the printer, click the Advanced tab, click the Print Processor button, and check the print processor in use. Also check the data type. If the problem continues, try a different data type.
Clients send documents that print garbage on hundreds of pages before anyone can stop the printing	Have the spooler automatically hold print jobs that contain the wrong printer setup information. To do this, access the Properties dialog box for the printer, click the Advanced tab, check the box for *Hold mismatched documents*, and click OK.
No documents are printing from the printer	Look for warning lights on the printer indicating a printer jam. If you see them, clear the printer jam. Turn off the printer, wait 30 seconds, and restart the printer. Also, check the printer's connection to a computer or the network (both ends). For a cabled printer, unplug the cable connection and plug it back in. For a wireless printer connection, again see if turning the printer off and then back on helps.

Chapter Summary

- Windows Server 2016 printing uses the graphics device interface (GDI) to integrate print file information with the printer driver. It also involves using the spooler and spool files for printing via the Print Spooler services.
- Internet printing enables users to print files through an Internet connection using HTTP and Internet Printing Protocol (IPP). The Internet Printing Client is used by Windows clients and Windows Server 2016 to facilitate IPP communications through a web-based print server.
- Windows Server 2016 can be a full-featured print server through the use of the Print and Document Services role.
- Windows Server 2016 supports using XML Paper Specification (XPS) for polished print documents.
- The Devices and Printers utility is one way to set up local and Network printing.
- The Windows Server 2016 Print Management tool is popular among server administrators for managing print server resources. The Print Management tool consolidates printer control and management features in one place, for convenient administration. This tool enables you to configure print server properties, install a printer, manage printer sharing, and configure individual printer properties.
- The properties of an installed printer enable you to configure printer sharing, printer port setup, scheduling, security, and specialized device settings.
- Through the Network Printer Installation Wizard, that can be started from the Print Management tool, you can install a local, network, or Internet printer.
- Printers are configured with permissions to control who can use or manage specific printers.
- Managing a printer and its printer queue involves actions such as pausing and resuming printing and setting the default printer. Specific print jobs can be canceled, paused, started,

and resumed. Also, each print job has associated properties, such as the priority setting for the print job.

- Printer problems can occur at any time. In many cases, you have several actions to try to solve printer problems. Some approaches are as simple as turning the printer off and back on. Others are more complex, such as reinstalling a printer driver or restarting the Print Spooler service.

Key Terms

bidirectional printing Ability of a printer to conduct two-way communication between the printer and the computer, such as to provide out-of-paper information; also, bidirectional printing supports Plug and Play and enables an operating system to query a printer about its capabilities.

data type Way in which information is formatted in a print file.

enhanced metafile (EMF) A data type for printing used by modern Windows operating systems, such as Windows 10 and Windows Server 2016. EMF print files offer a distinct advantage in Windows operating system environments because they are very portable from computer to computer.

graphics device interface (GDI) An interface on a Windows network print client that works with a local software application, such as Microsoft Word, and a local printer driver to format a file to be sent to a local printer or a network print server.

Internet Printing Client A software plug-in to enable handling Internet printing through IPP and HTTP Internet communications. *See* Internet Printing Protocol (IPP).

Internet Printing Protocol (IPP) A protocol that is encapsulated in HTTP and that is used to print files over the Internet.

local print device A printer, such as a laser printer, physically attached to a port on the local computer.

network print device A printing device, such as a laser printer, connected to a print server through a network.

Point and Print Implements the v4 driver model, so that a print server does not have to provide clients with printer drivers for specific models of printers.

PostScript (PS) printer A printer that has special firmware or cartridges to print using a page-description language (PDL).

print client Client computer or application that generates a print job.

print job A document or items to be printed.

print queue A stack or lineup of print jobs, with the first job submitted at the top of the stack and the last job submitted at the bottom, and all of the jobs waiting to be sent from the spooler to the printer. On a Windows Server 2016 print server, the priority of a print job can be changed so that a job that is not at the top of the queue can be printed right away.

print server Network computer or server device that connects printers to the network for sharing and that receives and processes print requests from print clients.

Printer Control Language (PCL) A printer language used by non-PostScript Hewlett-Packard and compatible laser printers.

printer driver Contains device-specific information that Windows Server 2016 requires to control a particular print device, implementing customized printer control codes, font, and style information so that documents are converted into a printer-specific language.

printer pooling Linking two or more identical printers with one printer setup or printer share.

RAW A data type often used for printing UNIX and Linux print files and legacy Windows operating system print files.

spool file A print file written to disk until it can be transmitted to a printer.

spooler In the Windows environment, a group of DLLs, information files, and programs that process print jobs for printing.

spooling A process working in the background to enable several print files to go to a single printer. Each file is placed in temporary storage until its turn comes to be printed.

TEXT A data type used for printing text files formatted using the ANSI standard that employs values between 0 and 255 to represent characters, numbers, and symbols.

Web Services for Devices (WSD) A technology in which devices, such as printers, can use web-based services to inform clients of their capabilities.

XML Paper Specification (XPS) An advanced way of printing documents for multiple purposes, including viewing electronic pages and printing pages in a polished format.

XPS Viewer Enables you to view a file saved in the XPS format.

Review Questions

1. One of the users on your network has called to report that a shared printer on your Windows Server 2016 print server is not printing. Which of the following can you use to check the status of the printer?
   a. Status button on the Control Panel Device Status Report
   b. Queue Status column for printers in the Print Management tool
   c. Actions column in the Print Management tool
   d. Status bar in the Shared Printer tool in Control Panel
2. You have a printer that is primarily used to handle large graphics print files. When you configure the port for this printer, which of the following port timeout settings should you use?
   a. 10 seconds
   b. 40 seconds
   c. 75 seconds
   d. 120 seconds
3. You own an architectural firm that has two plotters and four laser printers. Your paper costs are very high because people often send print jobs intended for a plotter to a laser printer and vice versa. These errors typically result in page after page of printing with strange characters, wasting money and time. What can you do to address this problem?
   a. Use smaller spooling files.
   b. Configure the printers to hold mismatched documents.
   c. Configure printers to print spooled documents after nonspooled documents.
   d. Enable the advanced printing features in the properties of all of the printers.
4. __________ is the protocol used by Windows Server 2016 and Windows clients for Internet printing.
5. Your company's programmers use one shared printer to print out lines of program code for analysis. They complain that often when they retrieve a printout, ending pages from the last printout or the beginning pages of the next printout are mixed in. This is because many of the printed pages appear very similar at first glance and it's hard to know where one printout ends and the next begins. What do you propose as a solution?
   a. Set up the grayscale colors in the printer's properties so that one printout is printed lighter and the next is printed darker, the next lighter, and so on.
   b. Configure a different spooler for each programmer to use.

c. Configure the printer properties to use a separator page.

d. Use a different print processor for each programmer.

6. By default, the Everyone group has ________ permissions when a printer is set up for sharing.

7. Which of the following Print and Document Services role services enables printing for UNIX and Linux clients?

   a. LPD Service

   b. Linux Print Enabler

   c. Shared Print Service

   d. Distributed Scan Server Service

8. Users can access a shared printer in Active Directory when you ________ the printer.

9. Which of the following are advantages of a Web Services for Devices port setup for a printer? (Choose all that apply.)

   a. WS-Discovery so that the port monitor in an operating system can repeatedly discover the printer

   b. WS-Speed so that printer port speed can be up to 1 MB per second

   c. ability for web services to obtain configuration information about the printer

   d. reverse flow control at the printer port

10. Your associate has configured five shared printers so that print files are sent directly to the printer and printing is done in the foreground. However, when the printers are busy, this slows down the CPU on the server managing the print jobs. What should be done to address this problem?

   a. Deactivate one of the printers because a Windows Server 2016 print server is only intended to manage four printers maximum.

   b. In the printers' properties, configure printing to cycle CPU use.

   c. Configure the printers to use zipped spool files.

   d. Configure every printer to spool the print jobs and to print in the background.

11. Briefly explain the purpose of the graphics device interface (GDI).

12. Which of the following are characteristics of a USB001 port when you connect a USB printer locally to a Windows Server 2016 server? (Choose all that apply.)

   a. The data type for the printer must be set to RAW (FF appended).

   b. This is a software port and not a true physical port.

   c. The first USB printer connected to the computer is usually designated as USB001.

   d. The USB printer must use only page-description language through the printer port.

13. Which of the following can you accomplish using the Print Management tool? (Choose all that apply.)

   a. Consolidate Windows Server 2016 print servers and printers in one place for management.

   b. Find out how many jobs are in the print queue of a printer.

   c. Set up to use special forms for printing.

   d. Reconfigure printer ports used with printers.

14. You have set up a shared printer on a Windows Server 2016 server. Also, you have given Mat Chen's user account Manage documents permission so that Mat can delete the print jobs of any user. However, when Mat tries to delete someone else's print job, he doesn't

have permission. Mat is a member of two global groups, Supervisors and Marketing. Also, the Supervisors group is a member of the Managers domain local group, and the Marketing group is a member of the Business domain local group. Which of the following might be a problem?

a. Global groups cannot be given printer permissions and so they are automatically denied use of printers.

b. The Business domain local group is denied Manage documents permission on that printer.

c. One of the domain local groups to which Mat belongs must be given Print permissions to that printer.

d. The Supervisors global group must also be a member of the Business domain local group.

15. You have purchased a printer that has the capability to print in duplex mode so that users can print on both sides of a sheet of paper. However, when users try to use this capability when they send a print job, documents are still printed on only one side. Which of the following might be the problem?

a. The print timeout is set too low in the printer's properties Advanced tab, which does not allow enough time for duplexing.

b. No printer driver is installed for the printer, and Windows Server 2016 is using the Generic Print Mode Driver.

c. The duplex button is not turned to on in the Printers window.

d. The duplex mode needs to be enabled on the Device Settings tab in the printer's properties.

16. From where can you stop and restart the Print Spooler service?

a. Control Panel Services applet in the Large icons or Small icons (Classic) view

b. Spooler MMC snap-in

c. General tab in the Properties dialog box for the printer designated as the default printer

d. Services tool started from Server Manager

17. The Print Spooler service depends on the ________ and __________ services.

18. Your committee has created a 290-page report for management and you decide to print one copy initially. You send the copy to the printer and then remember that you might not have made a correction to the footer material that prints at the bottom of each page. You pause the printout to check. After you determine all is OK, you decide to continue printing. Which of the following options should you use from the Document menu on the printer window for the print queue for that printer to continue from where you left off?

a. Continue

b. Resume

c. Restart

d. Rerun

19. The data type that is typically used for the winprint print processor for modern Windows shared printer clients is __________.

20. Your department head is in a hurry to print his report for the managers meeting that starts in 20 minutes, but the printer he uses is currently backed up with 32 print jobs that might take more than 20 minutes to print. You are the print server administrator. How can you help your department head?

a. Delete the 32 print jobs and send a message to users to resubmit them.

b. Pause the printer and then use the Pause option to print a single document by ID number while the other documents are paused.

c. Open that printer's print queue window and drag the print job to the top of the print queue.

d. Open that printer's print queue window and change the priority of the print job to 99 in that print job's properties.

Case Projects

Capital Financial Advantage offers accounting and other financial and legal services for small businesses. This firm consists of 28 accountants, one attorney, two bookkeepers, and 20 support staff including two computer support persons. They have been in the process of upgrading their two servers from Windows Server 2012 to Windows Server 2016. Windows Server 2016 is now installed on both servers, but there are continuing configuration tasks as they modernize how they use the servers.

Because computer users in the firm have aging printers, the firm is also upgrading printers and working to centralize printers and printing functions. Their goal is to have more consistency among printers and to reduce printer support time spent by the computer support staff. In terms of client computers, about half of the users have Windows 7 and the other half have Windows 10. The firm has been upgrading users to Windows 10 gradually to ensure that the support staff is not further overloaded. Capital Financial Advantage has hired you through Aspen Consulting to consult on the server upgrade process and now they are relying on you to help with the printer upgrades.

Case Project 6-1: Installing a Print Server

After a history of nearly anyone configuring and reconfiguring printers throughout the firm, the management has decided to centralize coordination of five new centrally located printers in the hands of the two computer support staff. The computer support staff wants to turn one of the servers into a print server from which to manage the five new printers. Create a short report that describes the basic steps for installing a Windows Server 2016 print server. In your report, also discuss two tools that can be used to set up and manage printers that the support staff will be able to use with the print server.

If you have access to slide presentation software, consider making your report as a slide presentation and also add your answers for Case Project 6-2 to the slide presentation.

Case Project 6-2: Configuring Printer Security

The computer support staff is not sure what permissions should be configured on each printer for themselves and what permissions to configure for the users of the printers. They ask you to create a short report that explains:

- What permissions to use for the computer support people
- What permissions to give to average users of the printers
- How to set up permissions on shared printers

Case Project 6-3: Configuring Printers for Special Needs

As you are working with the computer support staff, they have some questions about specific printing needs for the firm. Their questions are the following:

- During tax season, there is a need to print out completed limited partnership and corporate tax returns in bulk after most of the staff has gone home by 9:00 PM. Each tax return can involve many pages of forms. Is there a way to set up a printer to print these tax returns after 9:00 PM?

- How can a printer be stopped from printing while it is being maintained?
- Is there a way to retain print files, such as completed tax returns, so that they can be reprinted? And if so, how are they deleted when no longer needed?

Case Project 6-4: Using the Print Management Tool

The computer support staff wants to learn more about the Windows Server 2016 Print Management tool and has questions for you about how to do certain tasks. Create a short report explaining how to use this tool to:

- Install a network printer.
- Pause a printer.
- View the driver files for a printer.
- Determine which printers are currently printing jobs.

chapter 7

Configuring and Managing Data Storage

After reading this chapter and completing the exercises, you will be able to:

- Understand storage options for Windows Server 2016
- Use the Disk Management tool to configure and manage storage
- Explain and configure RAID disk storage fault tolerance
- Use Storage Spaces for disk storage and fault tolerance
- Understand Multipath I/O
- Back up and recover disks, folders, and files

Storing information on a computer is important to users, so server administrators spend considerable time ensuring the integrity of disk drives. Everyone who uses a computer sleeps better when they know that disk storage is set up properly, carefully managed, and regularly backed up. With good disk management practices comes the assurance that data is there when you need it and that your work can continue even when a disk drive fails.

This chapter begins by explaining disk storage options in Windows Server 2016, including the use of basic and dynamic disks. You learn how to set up different disk configurations, starting with simple volumes and advancing to more complex disk configurations. You learn to configure and manage disks using the Disk Management tool. For times when you encounter disk problems, you learn to use the Disk Optimizer and the tools for finding and fixing disk problems. Next, you learn about using RAID alternatives to help ensure high availability of data, even when a disk fails. You also learn to use Storage Spaces for powerful flexibility in implementing different storage media combinations, while still applying RAID-like redundancy. Finally, you learn how to back up and recover data on storage media.

Windows Server 2016 Storage Options

Windows Server 2016 supports two essential disk storage types: basic disks and dynamic disks. A **basic disk** is one that uses traditional disk management techniques and contains primary partitions, extended partitions, and logical drives. A **dynamic disk** is one that does not use traditional partitioning. Dynamic disk architecture provides more flexibility than basic disks so there is virtually no restriction on the number of volumes that can be on one disk. Both types of data storage are discussed in the next sections.

Basic Disks

Because a basic disk uses traditional disk management techniques, it is partitioned and formatted and can be set up to employ disk sets. **Partitioning** is a process that allocates a group of tracks and sectors to be used by a particular file system, such as NTFS. **Formatting** is a process that creates a table containing file and folder information for a specific file system in a partition. Formatting also creates a root directory (folder) and a volume label.

Another concept important to introduce is volume. A **volume** is a logical designation of disk storage that is created out of one or more physical disks. It is partitioned and formatted with one file system, such as NTFS. A volume can also be identified to users through a unique drive letter, such as C:. One volume contains at least one partition, but can encompass more than one partition.

The terms *volume* and *partition* are sometimes used interchangeably, but this is not technically accurate, in part because a volume may consist of more than one partition. Also, a volume is a logical designation and a partition is a physical designation. For example, you might have a server that houses two operating systems, Windows Server 2016 and Linux. When you are in Windows Server 2016, this operating system recognizes the NTFS-formatted partition as a volume with a drive letter (a logical designation)—but it only recognizes the Linux file system portion of a disk as a partition (physical designation) it cannot access. However, because a volume often has one formatted partition on a physical disk, volume and partition are sometimes mistakenly said to be the same thing.

Basic disks recognize primary and extended partitions, which are discussed in the next section. Basic disks also can be configured for any of three RAID levels: disk striping (RAID level 0), disk mirroring (RAID level 1), and disk striping with parity (RAID level 5). **RAID (redundant array of inexpensive** [or **independent**] **disks)** is a set of standards for lengthening disk life and preventing data loss. Disk **striping** is the ability to spread data over multiple disks or volumes. For example, part of a large file may be written to one disk and part to another. The goal is to spread disk activity equally across all disks, preventing wear from being focused on a single disk in a set. Perhaps more importantly, with striping disk performance is improved because the content can be written across multiple disks faster than to a single disk. **Disk mirroring** is the practice of creating a mirror image of all data on an original disk, so that the data is fully copied or mirrored to a backup disk. The sole purpose of the backup disk is to go into live production if the original disk fails.

When you install Windows Server 2016, the existing disks are configured as basic disks by default. Any disks that are added later are automatically configured as basic disks. Also, if you upgrade Windows Server 2012 with basic disks to Windows Server 2016, the basic disks remain.

MBR and GPT Support When a drive is initialized, a partition method must be selected. The choices include Master Boot Record or Globally Unique Identifier Partition Table. With the Master Boot Record method, a **Master Boot Record (MBR)** and a **partition table** are created at the beginning track and sectors on the disk. The MBR is located in the first sector and track of the hard disk and has startup information about partitions and how to access the disk. The partition table contains information about each partition created, such as the type of partition on MBR disks, size, and location. Also, the partition table provides information to the computer about which partition to access first. As you learn in the next section, Primary and Extended Partitions on MBR Disks, the MBR limits the number of partitions per disk.

Globally Unique Identifier (GUID) Partition Table or GPT is a newer way to partition disks, without imposing the same type of limits on the number of partitions as with MBR. GPT is one element of the **Unified Extensible Firmware Interface (UEFI)** approach that is offered by the Unified EFI Forum. UEFI is an alternative to using BIOS firmware (see Chapter 2, Installing Windows Server 2016). Some computers that you work on might have UEFI instead of the traditional BIOS firmware, and along with UEFI they will have GPT disks. GPT disks can also be used in computers that use BIOS firmware.

UEFI was initiated by Intel for new-generation computers. You can find out more about it at *www.uefi.org* and *www.uefi.org/faq*.

Instead of storing partition information in an MBR and a partition table at the beginning of the disk, GPT disks store partition information in each partition using main and backup tables. Also, each partition is identified by a different GUID or reference number. One reason why GPT disks have been developed is that GPT disk partitions can be very large, with size limited by the operating system rather than by the actual physical limit of the GPT disk. In Windows Server 2016 systems, a GPT partition can theoretically be up to 18 exabytes, which is considerably larger than the 2 terabyte limit of a traditional MBR disk in Windows Server 2016. Also, in Windows Server 2016, a GPT disk can hold up to 128 partitions (a limit imposed by the operating system). In Windows Server 2016, you can convert an MBR disk to GPT and vice versa. You might convert an MBR disk, for example, if it is GPT compatible, very large in size, and you want to have many basic disk partitions, such as 10, 20, or more. You can also convert a GPT disk to MBR, which you might consider if you have other MBR disks you want to use with it.

Converting from MBR to GPT or from GPT to MBR is destructive to data. Before converting in either direction, back up the data on the volume. After the conversion is done, you'll need to recreate the volume and then restore the data from your backup.

The general steps for converting an MBR disk to GPT are as follows:

1. Back up any data on the MBR disk before you do the conversion (see the section, Disk Backup, later in this chapter).
2. Right-click Start and click Disk Management. (Alternatively, you can access the Disk Management tool as an MMC snap-in or click Start, click Windows Administrative Tools, click Computer Management, if necessary expand Storage under the tree in the left pane, and click Disk Management in the left pane.)

3. Use the Disk Management tool to delete any volumes on the MBR disk. To do this, right-click each volume and click Delete Volume.
4. In the Disk Management tool, right-click the disk to convert, such as Disk 1, and click Convert to GPT Disk.
5. Recreate volumes and restore the data backed up in Step 1.

The steps for converting a GPT disk to MBR are as follows:

1. Back up the data on the disk prior to the conversion.
2. Open the Disk Management tool, click each volume on the GPT disk, and click Delete Volume.
3. Right-click the GPT disk, such as Disk 1, and click Convert to MBR Disk.
4. Recreate the necessary partitions and restore the data backed up in Step 1.

Primary and Extended Partitions on MBR Disks An MBR disk partition can be set up as primary or extended. A basic disk usually contains at least one primary partition (although it is possible, but not very practical, to create only an extended partition) and can contain up to a maximum of four partitions per disk. A **primary partition** is one from which you can boot an operating system, such as Windows Server 2016. Or a primary partition can simply hold files in a different file system format.

For the system to boot, one primary partition on the primary drive must be marked as active, and only one primary partition can be active at a given time. When you boot from a primary partition, it contains the operating system startup files in a location at the beginning of the partition. The **active partition** is the partition where your computer will look for the hardware-specific files to start the operating system (system partition).

An **extended partition** is created from space that is not yet partitioned. The purpose of an extended partition is to enable you to exceed the four-partition limit of a basic disk. Only one extended partition can exist on a single basic disk. An extended partition is not actually formatted and assigned a drive letter. Once an extended partition is created, it is further divided into logical drives. The logical drives are then formatted and assigned drive letters. Figure 7-1 illustrates two disks in a server. Disk 0 has four partitions, including the active partition, and Disk 1 has two regular partitions and one extended partition.

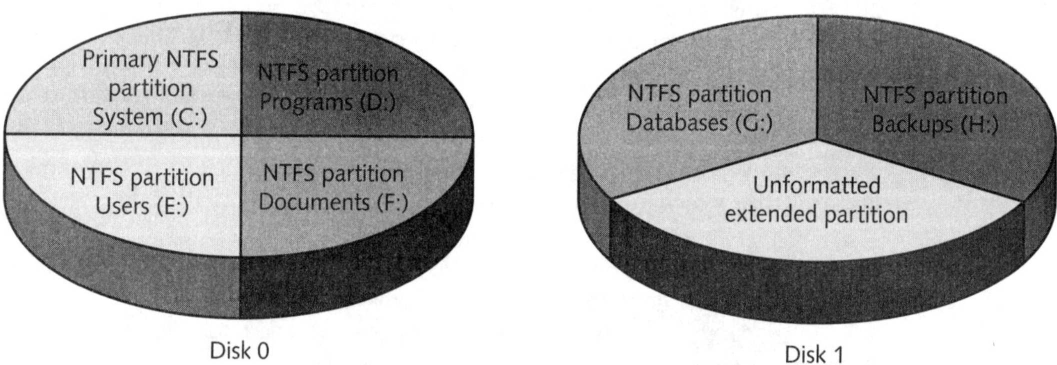

Figure 7-1 Partitions on two disk drives

A computer with multiple partitions boots from the partition that is designated as the active partition, which must also be the system partition containing the startup files. To determine which partition is designated as active, look for the "(System)" designation in the Disk Management tool pane that gives information about the disk's size and file system.

Two other references to partitioning used by Microsoft are important to understand. The **system partition** is the partition that contains the hardware-specific files needed to load the operating system. The **boot partition** is the partition that contains the operating system files located in the \Windows folder. The system partition has to be on a primary partition, but the boot partition can be installed on either a primary or extended partition.

Some steps in the activities in this book include bulleted questions for you to answer. Additionally, for all of the activities in this chapter, you'll need an account with Administrator privileges. These activities can be completed on a virtual machine or computer, such as in Hyper-V.

7

Activity 7-1: Viewing the Active Partition

Time Required: Approximately 10 minutes
Objective: Verify which partition is marked as active.

Description: In this activity, you use the Computer Management window to access the Disk Management tool and verify which is the active partition, along with other information about the disks on your system. Also, you learn how to mark a partition as active.

1. Right-click **Start** and click **Disk Management.**
2. Notice the listing of partitions (see Figure 7-2). The Disk Management tool also shows installed disks as well as removable media, and the tool shows if a disk is online.
    - What is the disk type for each of your partitions? Also, look under the Status column. Which partition is marked as active? Which are shown as the Boot and System partitions?
3. Find a partition that is not the system partition and **right-click** it (do not click in the area that says Disk 0 or Disk 1, but do click in the area labeled as (C:) or (D:), for example).
4. Notice the Mark Partition as Active option on the menu (see Figure 7-3). This is the option you would click to mark a partition as active. (Do not mark the partition active in this practice session, unless your instructor gives you permission.)
5. Leave the Disk Management window open for the next activity.

Volume and Stripe Sets Under Windows NT 4.0, you could create multidisk volumes known as volume sets and stripe sets. A **volume set** consists of two or more partitions that are combined to look like one volume with a single drive letter. A **stripe set** is two or more disks that are combined like a volume set but that are striped for RAID level 0 or RAID level 5 (RAID is discussed later in this chapter). Windows Server 2016 provides backward compatibility with basic disk volume and stripe sets that have previously been created through legacy Windows Server systems. However, you should plan to convert basic disks to dynamic disks in order to implement any new multidisk volumes.

Dynamic Disks

A dynamic disk does not use traditional partitioning, which makes it possible to set up a large number of volumes on one disk and provides the ability to extend volumes onto

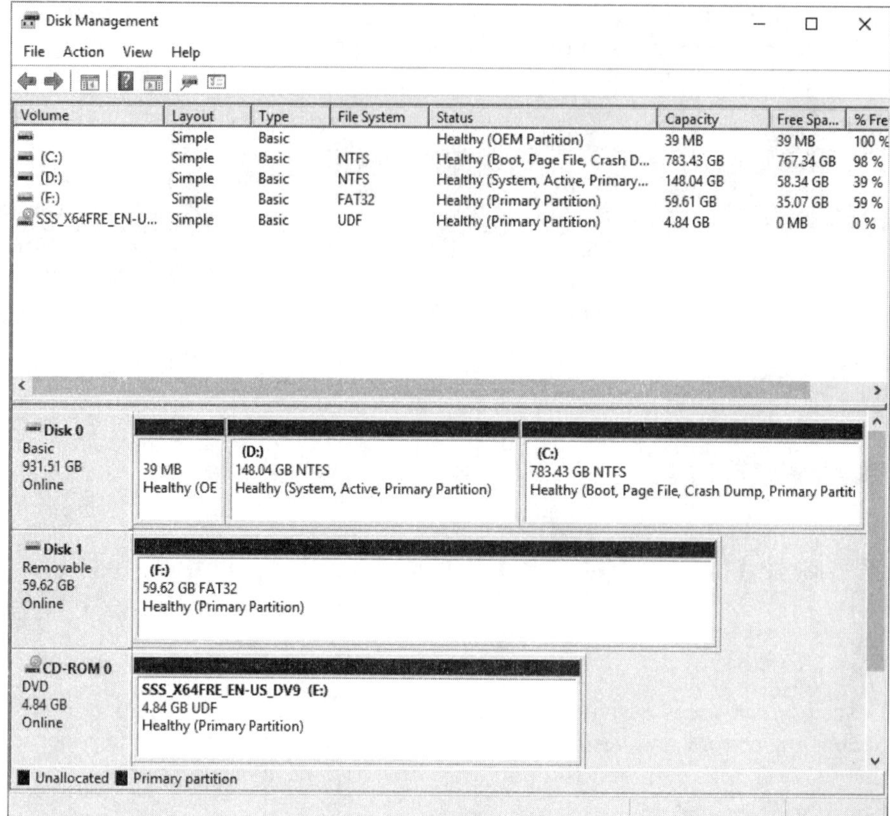

Figure 7-2 Viewing disk information in the Disk Management tool

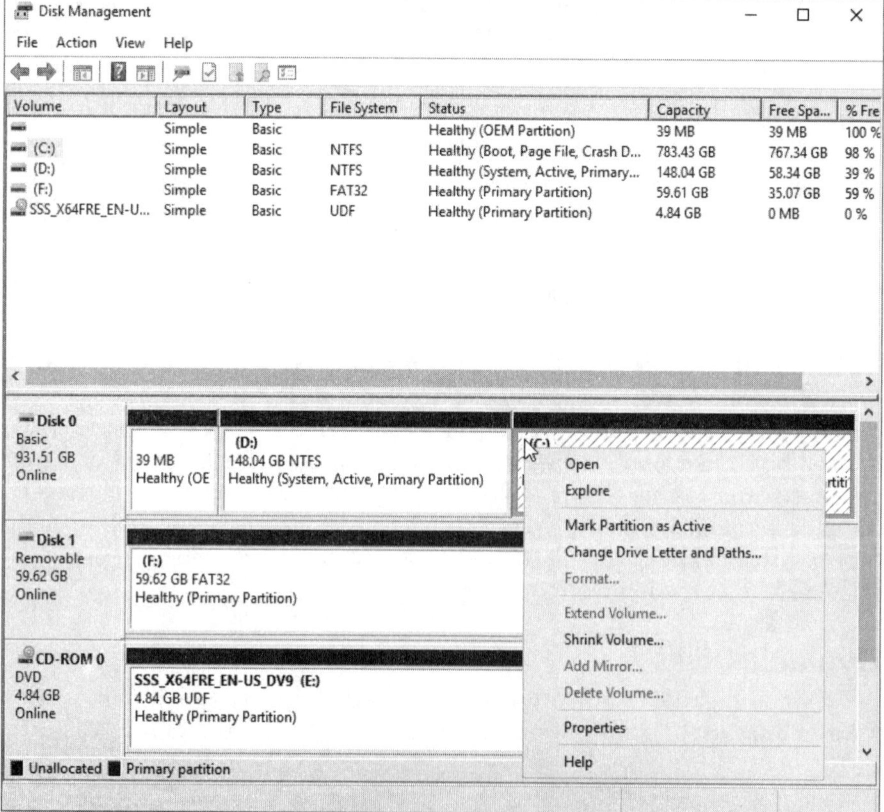

Figure 7-3 Menu options

additional physical disks. The number of disks that can be incorporated into one spanned volume is limited to 32. In addition to volume extensions and spanned volumes, dynamic disks support RAID levels 0, 1, and 5. Dynamic disks can be formatted for NTFS. Also, dynamic disks can be reactivated should they go offline because they have been powered down or disconnected.

If you plan to have a multi-boot computer, which means there are two or more operating systems from which to boot, you will need to implement basic disks and not dynamic disks.

When you upgrade from a Windows Server 2012/R2 system with basic disks or when you install Windows Server 2016 from scratch, you end up with basic disks. Consider converting basic disks to dynamic disks after you install Windows Server 2016 so that you can take advantage of the richer set of options associated with dynamic disks. The five types of dynamic disk configurations are simple volumes, spanned volumes, mirrored volumes, striped volumes, and RAID-5 volumes. The functional concepts of these disk configurations are similar to those used in early Windows Server systems, but the Windows Server 2016 dynamic disks have better disk management options and do not use partitioning. For example, the dynamic disk equivalent of a simple or regular basic disk is a simple dynamic disk volume, and the equivalent of a basic disk stripe set is called striped volumes.

On dynamic disks, instead of using the basic disk terminology of boot partition and system partition, the volume that contains the \Windows folder of system files is called the **boot volume**, and the volume that contains the files used to boot the computer is called the **system volume**.

In the next sections, you learn more about simple, spanned, and striped volumes. Later, in the section titled, Introduction to Fault Tolerance, you learn about dynamic disk mirrored volumes and RAID-5 volumes, plus additional information about using striped volumes.

Simple Volume A **simple volume** is a portion of a disk or an entire disk that is set up as a dynamic disk. If you do not allocate all of a disk as a simple volume, you have the option to later take all or a portion of the unallocated space and add it to an existing simple volume, which is called extending the volume. A simple volume can be extended onto multiple sections of the same disk (up to 32 sections). A simple volume does not provide fault tolerance because it cannot be set up for any RAID level (see the section, Introduction to Fault Tolerance, later in the chapter).

Spanned Volume A **spanned volume** is stored on 2 to 32 dynamic disks that are treated as one volume. For example, you might create a spanned volume if you have four separate small hard disks or if you have several small free portions of disk space scattered throughout the server's disk drives. You might have 600 MB of free space on one drive, 750 MB on another, and 424 MB on a third. All of these free areas can be combined into a single 1774 MB spanned volume with its own drive letter, with the advantage that you reduce the number of drive letters needed to make use of the space. Another difference between spanned volumes and striped volumes is that spanned volumes are filled with data sequentially.

Another way to combine multiple disks is to use storage pools. Creating storage pools is discussed later in this chapter in the section, Storage Pools.

As you add new disks, the spanned volume can be extended to include each disk. The advantage of creating spanned volumes is the ability to more easily manage several small disk drives or to maximize the use of scattered pockets of disk space across several disks.

The disadvantage of using a spanned volume is that if one disk fails, the entire volume is inaccessible. Also, if a portion of a spanned volume is deleted, the entire disk set is deleted. For these reasons, avoid placing mission-critical data and applications on a spanned volume.

Striped Volume **Striped volumes** are often referred to as RAID-0. An important advantage of striping is that it increases disk performance. Contention among disks is equalized and data is accessed faster for both reads and writes than when it is on a single drive, because Windows Server 2016 can write to all drives at the same time (if the disk controller also has this capability). Additionally, striping disks in a volume can extend the life of hard disk drives by spreading data equally over two or more drives. Spreading the data divides the drive load so that one drive is not working more than any other.

In Windows Server 2016, striping requires at least two disks and can be performed over as many as 32. The total of striped disks is called a striped volume. Equal portions of data are written in 64 KB blocks in rows or stripes on each disk. For example, consider that you have set up striping across five hard disks and are working with a 720 KB data file. The first 64 KB portion of the file is written to disk 1, the next 64 KB portion is written to disk 2, the third portion is written to disk 3, and so on. After 320 KB are spread in the first data row across disks 1 through 5, the next 320 KB are written in 64 KB blocks in the second row across the disks. Finally, 64 KB will be written to the third row on disk 1 and 16 KB in the third row on disk 2 (see Figure 7-4).

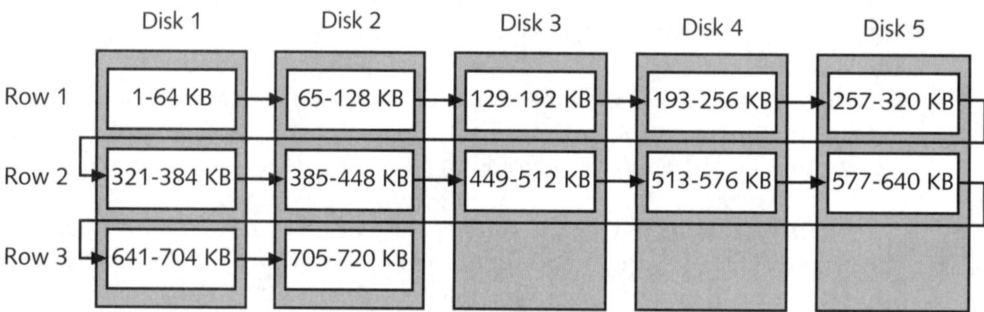

Figure 7-4 Disks in a striped volume

Because of its high performance, striping is useful for volumes that store large databases or for data replication from one volume to another. Striping is not a benefit when most of the data files on a server are very small, such as under 64 KB.

Data can be lost when one or more disks in the striped volume fail because the system has no automated way to rebuild data. If you use striping to increase disk performance for a critical database, consider frequently backing up that database (backups are discussed later in this chapter).

You also can create mirrored volumes and RAID-5 volumes on a dynamic disk for fault tolerance. Fault-tolerant volumes are covered later in this chapter.

Shrinking a Volume Windows Server 2016 comes with the ability to shrink a basic or dynamic disk volume. Shrinking a volume enables you to create a new partition when one is needed and you don't have extra disks. For example, you might need a partition for a new database as a way to better secure, manage, and back up that database. Another example is to create a new partition for an additional server system, such as Linux, that you install as a virtual server in Hyper-V.

When you shrink a volume, Windows Server 2016 starts from the end of that volume and works its way back through contiguous space to create unallocated disk space. You can specify the amount of space to recover. If files on the space are being recovered, Windows Server 2016 moves those files to the original partition so the move is transparent to the user. If the shrinking process encounters a file that cannot be moved, it stops shrinking at that point. Examples of files that cannot be moved include the paging file and shadow backup files.

If you need to recover more space but cannot because of the paging file, you can move the paging file to another volume (see Chapter 3, Configuring the Windows Server 2016 Environment). Also, disks that have a high number of bad clusters cannot be shrunk.

The general steps for shrinking a volume are as follows:

1. Open the Disk Management tool or snap-in.
2. Right-click the blue bar above the volume you want to shrink.
3. Click Shrink Volume.
4. Specify the amount of space you need for the unallocated space in the box, *Enter the amount of space to shrink in MB* (see Figure 7-5).

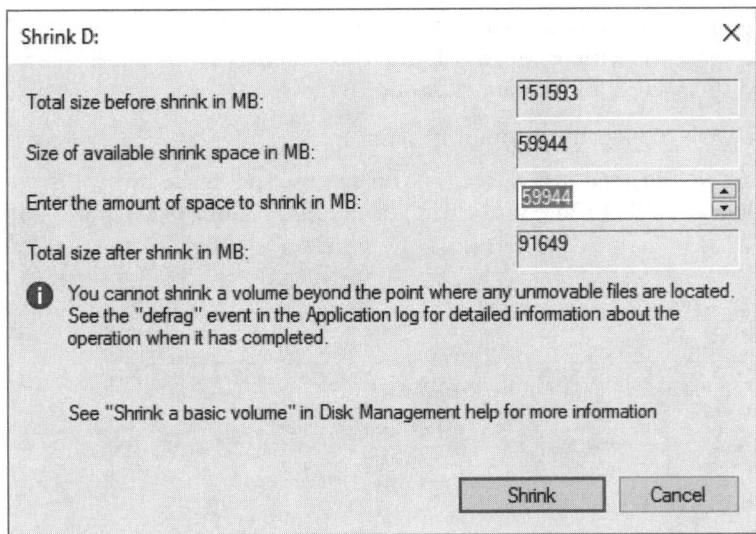

Figure 7-5 Shrinking a volume

5. Click Shrink.
6. After a few minutes, you'll see the newly unallocated space in the Disk Management tool.

Disk Management

Disk Management tasks can be performed using the Disk Management tool. This tool provides a central location for viewing disk information and performing tasks such as creating and deleting partitions and volumes. The following sections introduce you to the different tasks you can perform using the Disk Management tool: creating a partition and simple volume, converting to dynamic disks, and mounting a drive. Also in the next sections, you learn how to manage and troubleshoot disks using the Disk Optimizer, Disk Check, and *chkdsk* tools.

Creating a Partition and Simple Volume

When you partition a disk, leave 1 MB or more of the disk space free. This is the amount of workspace that Windows Server 2016 needs to convert a basic disk to a dynamic disk, in case you want to upgrade later.

Partitions operate as separate storage units on a hard disk. This allows you to better organize your data and make better use of your hard disk space. For example, you can create one partition on which to install the operating system and another partition for user data. The most elementary way to create a partition is to take unallocated disk space and use the New Simple Volume Wizard to create a simple volume. In this process, you can specify the size of the volume, whether or not to format the volume, the file system (NTFS), and a volume label.

In terms of configuring your server, it's always a good idea to keep the operating system on a partition separate from user data. This way, if you need to reinstall the operating system, all your data still remains intact (unless you format the partition the data is stored on during the reinstall).

Activity 7-2: Creating a Simple Volume

Time Required: Approximately 10–30 minutes
Objective: Create a new partition from unpartitioned disk space.

Description: This activity enables you to create a new partition. You'll need access to a server that has some amount of unpartitioned disk space or free space. If a server is not available with unpartitioned space, remember the location of this activity so you can refer to these steps before partitioning disk space in a live work situation.

1. Open the **Disk Management** tool if it is not open.
2. If you have unallocated disk space (or you can use free space if there is no unallocated disk space), right-click that space and click **New Simple Volume** (see Figure 7-6).

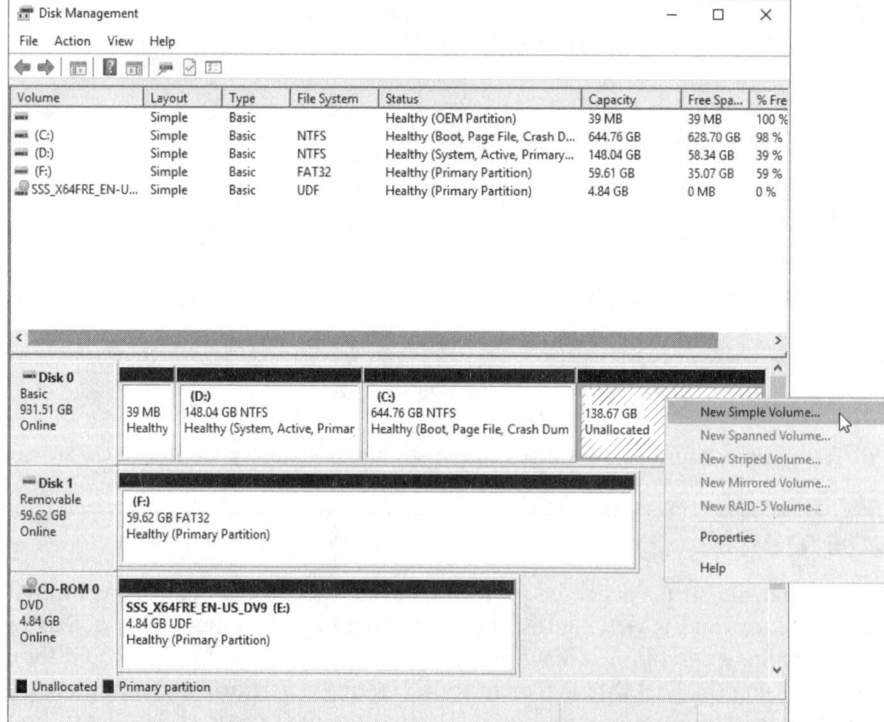

Figure 7-6 Creating a new simple volume

3. Click **Next** in the New Simple Volume Wizard.
4. For *Simple volume size in MB*, enter an appropriate size for the volume you are creating or use the default entry (see Figure 7-7).

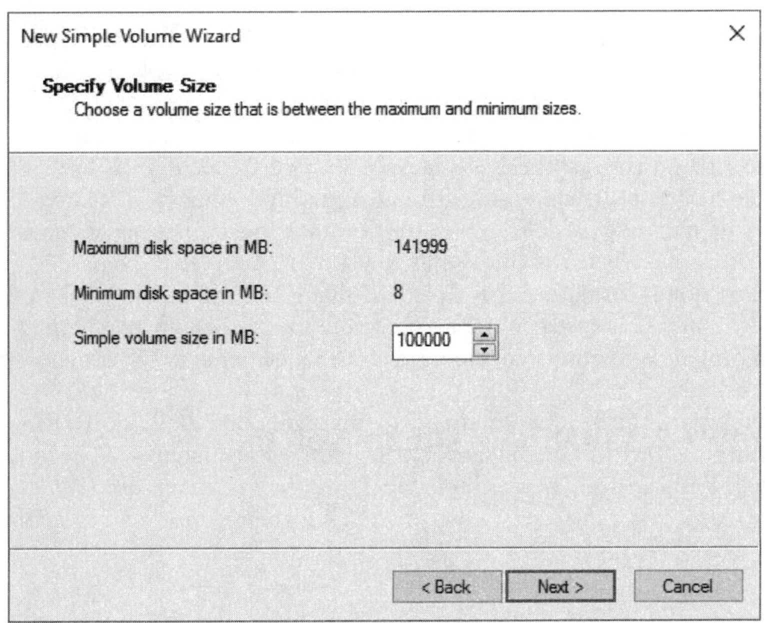

Figure 7-7 Configuring the simple volume size

5. Click **Next.**
6. Use the default drive letter, such as G, and click **Next.** (If you see a message that the drive letter is already mapped, change the current mapping or go back and select a different drive letter.)
7. In the Format Partition dialog box, the default is to format the volume using NTFS and use the Default allocation unit size. You can also specify a volume label (see Figure 7-8). Additionally, you have the option to perform a quick format, which is not advised because this doesn't check the integrity of the partition. Another option is to compress folders and files by default. Click **Next.**

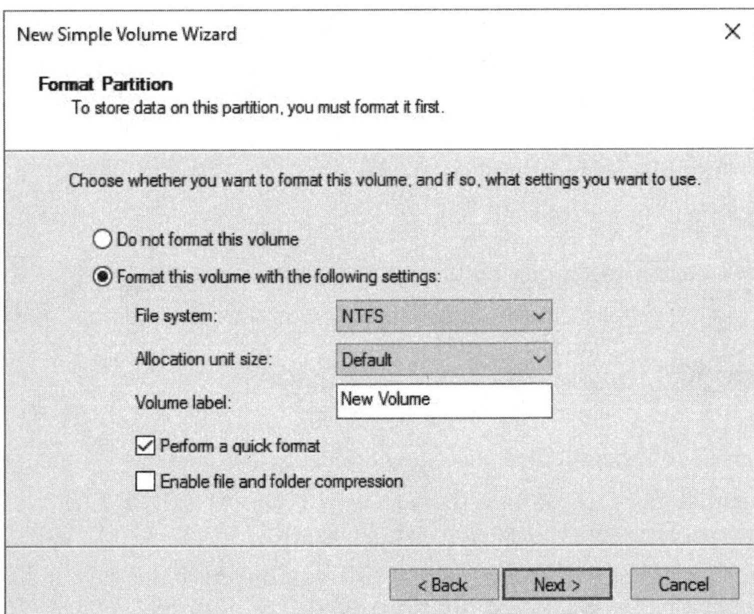

Figure 7-8 Configuring the formatting options

8. Review the selections you have made and click **Finish.** (It may take a few minutes to create the new simple volume. The Disk Management tool displays its progress, such as formatting as it is working.)
9. Leave the Disk Management window open for the next activity.

You can also delete a partition using the Disk Management tool. To delete a partition, right-click the partition you want to delete. The partition will have a dark gray border and shading to indicate that you have selected it. Click Delete Volume on the menu. The Disk Management tool gives you a warning that data will be lost. Click Yes to continue the delete process.

When you step through the New Simple Volume Wizard, you have the option of not formatting the partition. If you do not format a partition when it is created, it still needs to be formatted before it can be used. You may, for example, format it later with a different operating system, such as Linux, when you install Linux as a virtual server in Hyper-V.

Once a partition is formatted, it is called a volume and can be assigned a drive letter. Assigning a drive letter makes it easier to refer to the volume, for example, assigning it drive letter G:. You can also provide a customized volume label to reflect what is contained in the volume (refer to Figure 7-8).

To format a partition that is not already formatted, open the Disk Management tool, right-click the partition to be formatted, and click Format (refer to Figure 7-3, only the Format option will be active). You can specify a volume label, the file system to use (NTFS), and the allocation unit size. Also, you can select to use the quick format option and to enable file and folder compression.

Converting a Partitioned Basic Disk to a Dynamic Disk Converting a simple basic disk to a dynamic disk is accomplished from the Disk Management tool. When you convert from a basic to dynamic disk, the process does not damage data in any way, but you must be certain that 1 MB or more of free space is available on the basic disk before you convert it.

Activity 7-3: Converting a Basic Disk

Time Required: Approximately 10 minutes
Objective: Convert a simple basic disk to a dynamic disk.

Description: In this activity, you convert a simple basic disk, such as the one you created in Activity 7-2, to a dynamic disk. Before you start, make sure you have permission from your instructor to convert the disk. If you do not have permission to convert the disk, click Cancel at Step 5.

1. Open the **Disk Management** tool if it is closed.
2. Right-click the disk you want to convert.

Make sure that you right-click the disk, for example, Disk 0, and not the volume, for example, (C:), or else the upgrade option will not be displayed.

3. Click **Convert to Dynamic Disk**, as shown in Figure 7-9.
4. Make sure that the correct disk is selected, such as Disk 0 or Disk 1 (check all that apply), in the Convert to Dynamic Disk dialog box. Click **OK**.
5. Verify the disk or disks to convert in the Disks to Convert dialog box and click **Convert**. Or, if you do not have permission to convert the disk, click **Cancel**.

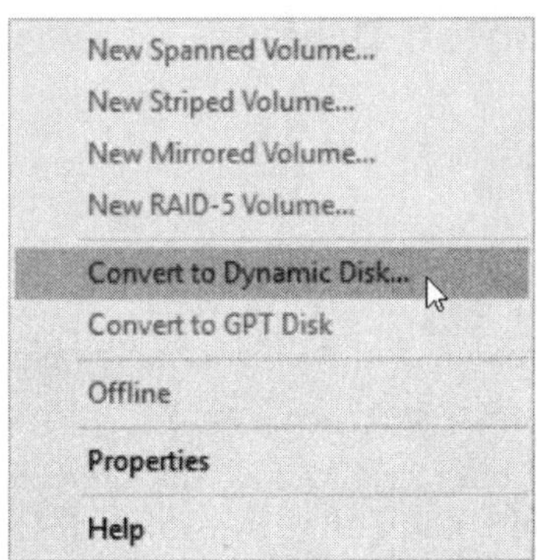

Figure 7-9 Converting to a dynamic disk

7

6. Click **Yes** in the Disk Management information box.
7. If necessary, click **Yes** to acknowledge that the file systems on the disk will be dismounted.
8. Notice under the Type column that the basic disk has now been converted to a dynamic disk.
9. Leave the Disk Management window open for the next activity.

In some circumstances, you might need to change a dynamic disk back to a basic disk, such as when you want to implement a dual-boot setup with an operating system that doesn't support dynamic disks or when you want to remove Windows Server 2016 from the computer so that a different operating system can be loaded. Before reverting back to a basic disk, the disk must be empty—so data must be backed up or moved to another disk. A dynamic disk can be converted back to a basic disk by using the following general steps:

1. Back up all data on the dynamic disk volume before you start.
2. Delete all of the dynamic disk volumes on the disk, using the Disk Management tool, by right-clicking the volume, such as (D:), and clicking Delete Volume. Then click Yes in the Delete simple volume dialog box and click Yes again.
3. The disk should convert back to a basic disk automatically.

Mounting a Drive Windows Server 2016 enables you to mount a drive as an alternative to giving it a drive letter. A **mounted drive** is one that appears as a folder and is accessed through a path like any other folder. You can mount a basic or dynamic disk drive, an optical drive, or a removable drive. Only an empty folder on a volume formatted for NTFS can be used for mounting a drive. Once a drive is mounted, other drives can be added to the same folder to appear as one drive. There are several reasons for using mounted drives. The most apparent reason is that Windows operating systems are limited to 26 drive letters, and mounting drives enables you to reduce the number of drive letters in use because they are not associated with letters. Another reason for creating a mounted drive is for user home directories that are stored on the server. A **home directory** or **home folder** is a server folder that is associated with a user's account and that is a designated workspace for the user to store files. (Microsoft sometimes uses the term *home directory* instead of home folder for consistency with terminology used by legacy server systems.) As server administrator, you might allocate one drive for all user home directories and mount that drive in a folder called Users. The path to the drive might be C:\Home or C:\Users Data. In another situation, you might have a database that you want to manage as a mounted drive so that it is easier for users to access. Also, by mounting the drive, you can set up special backups for that database by simply backing up its folder.

Activity 7-4: Configuring a Mounted Drive

Time Required: Approximately 10–15 minutes
Objective: Learn how to set up a mounted drive.

Description: This activity enables you to create a mounted volume. In the first series of steps, you create a folder on an NTFS-formatted volume or disk that will hold the mounted drive. After those steps, you mount the drive into the folder. You will need an available disk drive to mount into the folder (or stop at Step 9).

1. Click the **File Explorer** (folder) icon in the taskbar or right-click **Start** and click **File Explorer**. In the left pane of File Explorer, click a main volume that is formatted for NTFS, such as *Local Disk C:*. (Alternatively, in the Disk Management window, click the drive, such as *(C:)*, under Volume and then click the Explore icon [a folder opening] under the menu bar.)
2. In the right pane of File Explorer (where the folders are listed), right-click a blank area, point to **New**, and click **Folder**. Enter your initials appended to Mount for the folder name, such as *MountJR*. Press **Enter**. Leave the window open.
3. Access the **Disk Management** tool.
4. Right-click the disk drive, such as *D:*, that you want to mount into the folder and click **Change Drive Letter and Paths.**
5. If necessary, click the existing drive letter for the drive, such as *D:*, in the Name box and click the **Add** button.
6. Ensure **Mount in the following empty NTFS folder** (the default) is selected.
7. Click the **Browse** button and navigate to the folder you created, then click that folder, such as *MountJR*.
8. Click **OK** in the Browse for Drive Path dialog box.
9. Click **OK** in the Add Drive Letter or Path dialog box as in Figure 7-10 (or click **Cancel** if you do not want to complete mounting the drive).

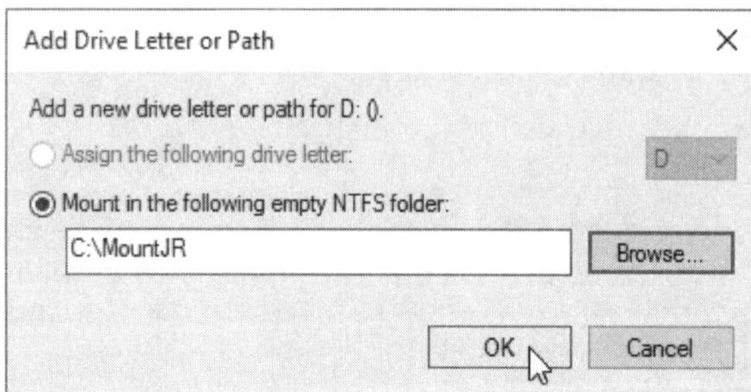

Figure 7-10 Add Drive Letter or Path box

10. Go back to the File Explorer window containing the folder you created, such as the Local Disk (C:) window. Find the mounted volume you created.
    - What icon is used to represent the mounted volume?
11. Right-click the mounted volume and click **Properties**.
    - What tabs are available? What is entered for *Type* on the General tab?
12. Close the mounted volume's properties dialog box and close the File Explorer window, such as Local Disk (C:). Leave the Disk Management window open.

Managing Disks

Once you have your physical disks partitioned and formatted, they are ready to be used as storage mediums. To ensure system performance, the disks must still be maintained. Windows Server 2016 includes several tools, such as Disk Optimizer, Disk Check, and *chkdsk*, that can be used to diagnose disk problems and maintain disk performance.

Using Disk Optimizer

When you save a file to a disk, Windows Server 2016 saves the file to the first area of available space. The file might not be saved to a contiguous area of free space and the disk gradually becomes **fragmented**, particularly as more and more files are created and deleted. When your computer attempts to access the file, it might have to be read from different areas on a disk, slowing access time and creating disk wear. The process of **defragmenting** locates fragmented folders and files and moves them to a location on the physical disk so they are in contiguous order.

On a busy server, drives should be defragmented every week to two weeks. On less busy servers, defragment the drives at least once a month. However, solid state drives (described in the section, Storage Spaces) should not be defragmented using the Disk Optimizer, because they use a different storage technology and defragmentation decreases their performance and longevity. If your solid state drives support it, instead use the TRIM function. Windows 10 supports TRIM/UNMAP, including for VHDX files for Hyper-V storage.

7

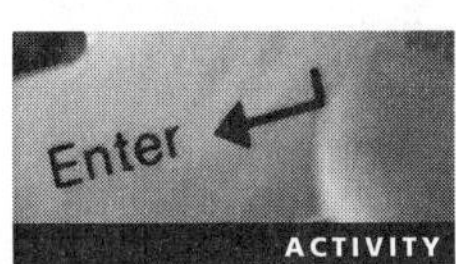

Activity 7-5: Using the Disk Optimizer

Time Required: Approximately 15 minutes
Objective: Practice using the Disk Optimizer.

Description: One of the best ways to keep your server running quickly is to defragment its disk drives. This activity enables you to use the Windows Server 2016 Optimize tool to defragment a disk.

1. If necessary, open the **Disk Management** tool.
2. Click a drive under Volume, such as *C:*. Click the **Properties** icon under the menu bar. (Alternatively, you can right-click the drive and click **Properties**.)
3. Click the **Tools** tab in the Properties dialog box for the drive.
4. Click the **Optimize** button.
5. In the Optimize Dives window, click **Change settings** (see Figure 7-11).
   - What is the default optimization schedule? What frequencies can you select?
6. Click **Cancel** in the Optimize Drives box.
7. In the Optimize Drives window, ensure a drive is selected, such as *(C:)*, and click **Analyze**. After a disk is analyzed, you'll see the amount of fragmentation under the Current status column for the drive (refer to Figure 7-11).
8. Click the **Optimize** button (do this for practice, even if your disk does not need to be defragmented at this time). Observe the Current status column to watch the progress for the disk you have selected.
9. Close the Optimize Drives window. Leave open the Properties window for the drive to use in the next activity.

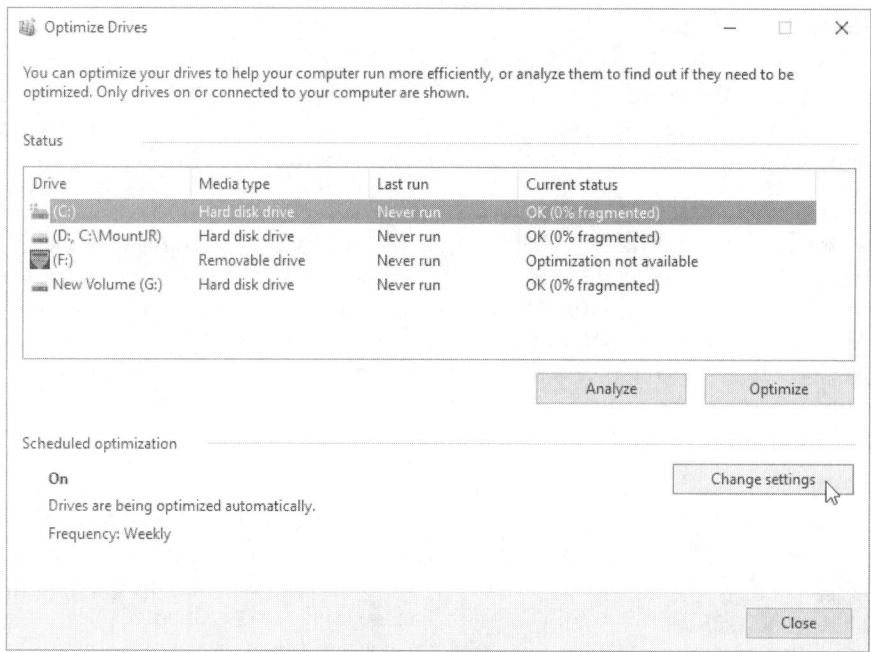

Figure 7-11 Accessing settings for drive optimization

Using Disk Check The Disk Check tool allows you to scan your disk for bad sectors and file system errors. This tool is meant for use when no users need to access the files on the disk you want to check because the disk is made unavailable during the scan for problems. The Disk Check tool is started from the Properties dialog box for a disk as you learn in Activity 7-6.

Activity 7-6: Using Disk Check

Time Required: Depends on the size of the disk and number of files (10 to over 40 minutes)
Objective: Learn how to use Disk Check.

Description: In this activity, you practice using the Disk Check utility to scan your disk. If you are using a multiple disk system, ask your instructor which disk to scan. Also, if you have a large disk with many files, you might want to stop at Step 6 because the disk check can take a long time. When you do this activity, you really defer Disk Check to run the next time you boot the server.

1. Use the Properties dialog box that you left open from the last activity, or reopen it by following Steps 1–3 from Activity 7-5. Ensure you are on the **Tools** tab.
2. Click the **Check** button.
3. If you see the *You don't need to scan this drive box*, click **Scan drive** anyway for this activity (see Figure 7-12). Wait for the scan to complete. If the process finds errors, it lets you choose whether to fix them.

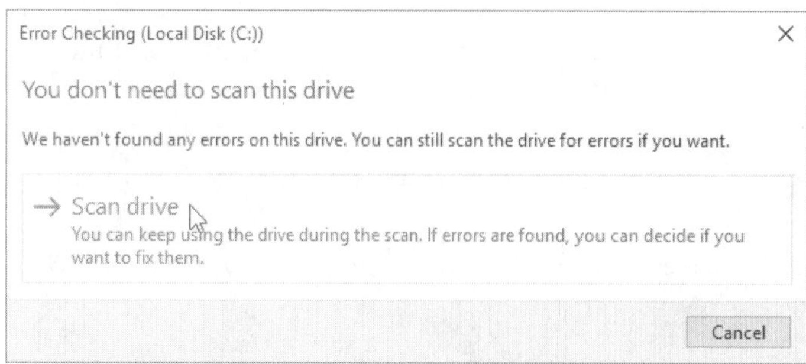

Figure 7-12 Selecting to scan a drive

4. The Error Checking box for the drive will show whether any errors were found and corrected. Notice that you can click the Show Details link to go to Event Viewer to see specific information about what the scan found. Click **Close.**
5. Click **OK** in the Properties dialog box for the disk.
6. Close the Disk Management window.

Using *chkdsk* You can also check your disk for errors by running the *chkdsk* utility from the PowerShell or Command Prompt window. *chkdsk* also starts automatically when you boot Windows Server 2016, and the boot process detects file allocation table or file corruption, such as in the system files. In NTFS, *chkdsk* checks files, folders, indexes, security descriptors, user files, sectors, and disk allocation units. Table 7-1 summarizes commonly used switches for the *chkdsk* command. To view all of the switches in the online documentation, enter at the command prompt *chkdsk /?*.

7

Table 7-1 *chkdsk* switch and parameter options

Switch/Parameter	Purpose
[*volume*] (such as C:)	Specifies that *chkdsk* only check the designated volume
[filename] (such as *.dll)	Enables a check of the specified file or files only
/scan	Scans the disk while it is online
/spotfix	Enables *chkdsk* to go directly to a corrupted spot identified earlier by the Spot Verifier service and just fix that spot, thus saving time
/c	Uses an abbreviated check of the folder structure
/f	Instructs *chkdsk* to fix errors that it finds
/i	Uses an abbreviated check of indexes
/L:*size*	Enables you to specify the size of the log file created by the disk check
/r	Searches for bad sectors, fixes problems, and recovers information (when not possible, use the Recover command on separate files)
/x	Dismounts or locks a volume before starting

Allow plenty of time for *chkdsk* to run on large disk systems, such as for disks over 500 GB. If you have multiple disks, you might want to stagger running *chkdsk* on different disks for each week. Also, the presence of some bad sectors is normal. Many disks have a few bad sectors that are marked by the manufacturer during the low-level format and on which data cannot be written.

When *chkdsk* finds lost allocation units or chains, it prompts you with the Yes or No question: *Convert lost chains to files?*. Answer Yes to the question so that you can save the lost information to files. The files that *chkdsk* creates for each lost chain are labeled File*xxx*.chk and can be edited with a text editor to determine their contents.

Microsoft now offers Spot Verifier, which is a service that is triggered whenever the operating system receives a report of a bad disk area, such as from trouble reading or writing to a particular location. Spot Verifier runs in the background to check disk integrity and has little effect on performance. When it finds a disk spot that needs to be repaired, it records the disk location in an event log. As you check the log to determine if there are spots that need to be repaired, you can take the disk offline and run *chkdsk /spotfix*. The */spotfix* option causes *chkdsk* to go to the reported damaged spots only and fix them in rapid time. The result is negligible downtime compared to running a full *chkdsk* scan and repair with one or more disks offline, which can keep a system down for a long time.

Activity 7-7: Using *chkdsk* from PowerShell

Time Required: Depends on the size of the disk and number of files (10 to over 40 minutes)
Objective: Learn how to use *chkdsk* from Windows PowerShell.

Description: You run the *chkdsk* command-line utility to examine a disk for errors.

1. Click **Start** and click the **Windows PowerShell** tile. Alternatively, you can click **Start,** click the **Windows PowerShell** folder, and click **Windows PowerShell.**
2. Type **chkdsk** and press **Enter.** Figure 7-13 shows the sample results of this tool.
   - What happens when you run *chkdsk* without the */f* option?

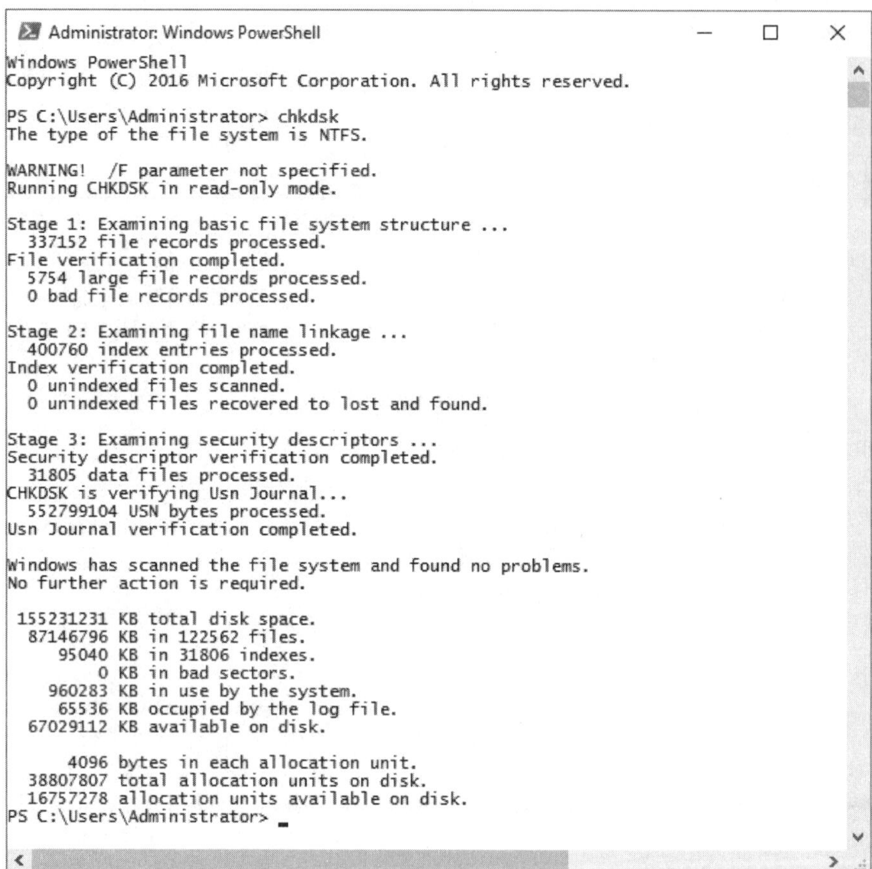

Figure 7-13 *chkdsk* results

3. Close the Windows PowerShell window.

Another option in PowerShell is to use the cmdlet, Repair-Volume. This cmdlet is used to perform volume repairs. It has options to scan a volume while disks are online and create a report of bad areas, to take a volume offline and scan and repair bad areas, and to take a volume offline briefly to only spot fix bad areas found by a previous online scan.

Introduction to Fault Tolerance

Fault tolerance is the ability of a system to gracefully recover from hardware or software failure. Servers often store critical data that must have high availability. Windows Server 2016 provides a level of fault tolerance through software-level RAID. Using storage pools is another way to achieve fault tolerance, which is discussed later in the section, Storage Pools.

RAID is not meant as a replacement for performing regular backups of data, but it increases the availability of disk storage. For example, if a hard disk fails and you have not implemented fault tolerance, any data stored on that disk is lost and unavailable until the drive is replaced and data is restored from backup. With fault tolerance, data is written to more than one drive so in the event one drive fails, data can still be accessed from one of the remaining drives.

RAID Volumes

Because hard disk drives are prone to failure, one of the best data security measures is to plan for disk redundancy in servers and host computers. This is accomplished in three ways: by performing regular backups, by installing RAID drives, and by using storage pools.

RAID is a set of standards for lengthening disk life, preventing data loss, and enabling relatively uninterrupted access to data. There are six basic levels of RAID (other RAID levels exist beyond the basic levels), beginning with the use of disk striping.

The six basic RAID levels are as follows:

- *RAID level 0*—Striping with no other redundancy features (such as no parity or mirroring) is RAID level 0. Striping is used to extend disk life and improve performance. Data access on striped volumes is fast because of the way the data is divided into blocks that are quickly accessed through multiple disk reads and data paths. A significant disadvantage to using level 0 striping is that if one disk fails, you can expect a large data loss on all volumes. Windows Server 2016 supports RAID level 0, using 2 to 32 disks in a set. In Windows Server 2016, this is called striped volumes, as you learned earlier in this chapter. The useable capacity is 100 percent.
- *RAID level 1*—This level employs simple disk mirroring and provides a means to duplicate the operating system files in the event of a disk failure. Disk mirroring is a fault-tolerance method that prevents data loss by duplicating data from a main disk to a backup disk (see Figure 7-14). **Disk duplexing** is the same as disk mirroring, with the exception that it places the backup disk on a different controller or adapter than is used by the main disk (see Figure 7-15). Windows Server 2016 supports level 1, but includes disk duplexing as well as mirroring. The useable capacity of RAID level 1 is 50 percent. If three or more volumes will be mirrored or duplexed, this solution is more expensive than the other RAID levels. On modern operating systems including Windows Server 2016, data is written simultaneously (if supported by the disk controller) on both disks for the sake of performance (instead of writing on the primary disk and then on the mirrored disk). Some server administrators consider disk mirroring and disk duplexing to offer one of the best guarantees of data recovery when a disk failure occurs.

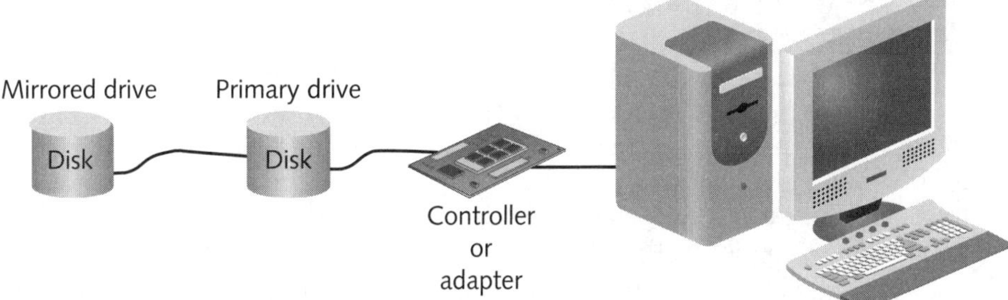

Figure 7-14 Disk mirroring

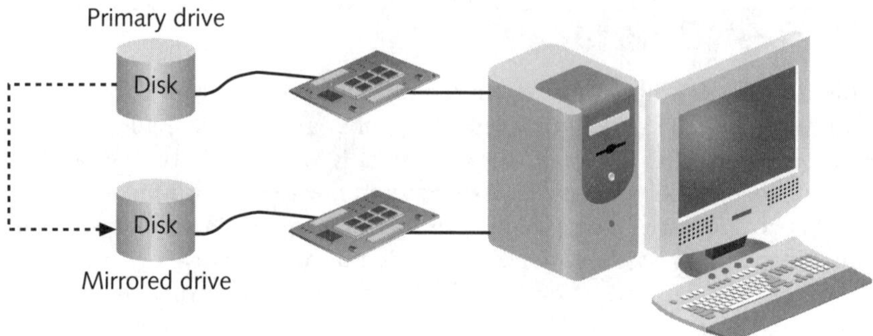

Figure 7-15 Disk duplexing

- *RAID level 2*—This uses an array of disks whereby the data is striped across all disks in the array (also called bit-level striping). Also, in this method, all disks store error-correction information that enables the array to reconstruct data from a failed disk. The advantages of level 2 are that disk wear is reduced and data can be reconstructed if a disk fails.
- *RAID level 3*—Like level 2, RAID level 3 uses disk striping and stores error-correcting information, but the information is only written to one disk in the array. If that disk fails, the array cannot rebuild its contents. This is also called byte-level striping because each byte is written sequentially on a different disk.
- *RAID level 4*—This level stripes data and stores error-correcting information on all drives, in a manner similar to level 2. An added feature is its ability to perform checksum verification. The checksum is a sum of bits in a file. When a file is re-created after a disk failure, the checksum previously stored for that file is checked against the actual file after it is reconstructed. If the two do not match, you will know that the file might be corrupted. Windows Server 2016 does not support RAID levels 2 through 4.
- *RAID level 5*—Level 5 combines the best features of RAID, including striping, error correction, and checksum verification. Windows Server 2016 supports level 5, calling it "stripe set with parity on basic disks" or a RAID-5 volume (for dynamic disks), depending on the disk architecture. Whereas level 4 stores checksum data on only one disk, level 5 spreads both error-correction and checksum data over all of the disks, so there is no single point of failure. This level uses more memory than other RAID levels, with at least 16 MB recommended as additional memory for system functions. In addition, level 5 requires at least three disks in the RAID array. Recovery from a failed disk provides roughly the same guarantee as with disk mirroring but takes longer with level 5. RAID 5 can recover from a single disk failure. However, if more than one drive in the array fails, all data is lost and must be restored from backup.

None of these RAID techniques mean that you no longer have to do backups. A solid backup, for example, is the only way to recover an important file or set of files that are inadvertently deleted.

Windows Server 2016 supports RAID levels 0, 1, and 5 for disk fault tolerance (each of these levels is discussed further in the sections that follow), with levels 1 and 5 recommended. RAID level 0 is not recommended in many situations because it does not really provide fault tolerance, except to help extend the life of disks while providing relatively fast access. When you decide upon using RAID level 1 or RAID level 5, consider the following:

- The boot and system files can be placed on RAID level 1, but not on RAID level 5. Thus, if you use RAID level 5, these files must be on a separate disk or a separate RAID level 1 disk set.
- RAID level 1 uses two hard disks, and RAID level 5 uses from 3 to 32.

- RAID level 1 is more expensive to implement than RAID level 5, when you consider the cost on the basis of each megabyte of storage. Keep in mind that in RAID level 1, half of your total disk space is used for redundancy, whereas that value is one-third (for three disks) or less (for more disks) for RAID level 5. The amount of RAID level 5 used for parity is 1/*n* where *n* is the number of disk drives in the array.
- RAID level 5 requires more memory than RAID level 1.
- Depending on the disk controller, in Windows Server 2016 disk read access is faster in RAID level 1 and RAID level 5 than is write access, with read access for RAID level 1 identical to that of a disk that does not have RAID.
- Because RAID level 5 involves more disks and because the read/write heads can acquire data simultaneously across striped volumes, it has much faster read access than RAID level 1.

RAID levels 0, 1, and 5 are used most commonly in server operating systems because they address most disk fault-tolerance needs. These RAID levels are also used in Storage Spaces as you learn later in this chapter.

Using a Striped Volume (RAID-0)

As you learned earlier in this chapter, the reasons for using a RAID level 0 or a striped volume in Windows Server 2016 are to:

- Reduce the wear on multiple disk drives by equally spreading the load.
- Increase disk performance compared with other methods for configuring dynamic disk volumes.

Although striped volumes do not provide fault tolerance, other than to extend the life of the disks, they are acceptable for use in some situations. Microsoft notes that one of the best uses of RAID 0 is the storage of temporary data. Consider, for example, an organization that maintains a "data warehouse" in which the vital data is stored and updated on a large server or mainframe, and a copy is downloaded at regular intervals to a server housing the data warehouse. The purpose of the data on the server is to create reports and to provide fast lookup of certain kinds of data, without slowing down the server or mainframe. In this instance, the goal is to provide the fastest possible access to the data and not fault tolerance, because the original data and primary data services are on the mainframe. For this application, you might create a striped volume on the server used for the data warehouse, because it yields the fastest data access.

To create a striped volume, right-click the unallocated space for the volume and click New Striped Volume. Only dynamic disks can be striped volumes.

Using a Mirrored Volume (RAID-1)

Disk mirroring involves creating a shadow copy of data on a backup disk and is RAID level 1. Only dynamic disks can be set up as a **mirrored volume** in Windows Server 2016. It is one of the most guaranteed forms of disk fault tolerance because the data on a failed drive is still available on the mirrored drive (with a short downtime to make the mirrored drive accessible). Also, disk read performance is the same as reading data from any single disk drive. Depending on the hardware and system configuration, in some cases there can be a slight performance degradation for disk writes, but this is likely to go unnoticed. However, a disk write in mirroring is normally faster than writing to disk when you use RAID-5. A mirrored volume cannot be striped and requires two dynamic disks.

A mirrored volume is particularly well suited for situations in which data is mission-critical and must not be lost under any circumstances, such as customer files at a bank. It also is valuable for situations in which computer systems must not be down for long, such as for medical applications or in 24-hour manufacturing. Microsoft recommends using RAID level 1 for operating system and log files. The increased expense of having duplicate disks is offset by the assurance that data will not be lost and that the system will quickly be back online after a disk failure.

The Windows Server 2016 system and boot volumes can be in a mirrored volume, but they cannot be in a striped or RAID-5 volume.

A mirrored volume is created through the Disk Management tool. To create the volume, right-click unallocated space on one disk and click New Mirrored Volume.

Using a RAID-5 Volume

Fault tolerance is better for a RAID-5 volume than for a simple striped volume. A **RAID-5 volume** requires a minimum of three disk drives. Parity information is distributed on each disk so that if one disk fails, the information on that disk can be reconstructed. The parity used by Microsoft is Boolean (true/false, one/zero) logic, with information about the data contained in each row of 64 KB data blocks on the striped disks. Using the example of storing a 720 KB file across five disks, one 64 KB parity block is written on each disk. The first parity block is always written in row 1 of disk 1, the second is in row 2 of disk 2, and so on, as illustrated in Figure 7-16 (compare this figure with Figure 7-4 for a striped volume).

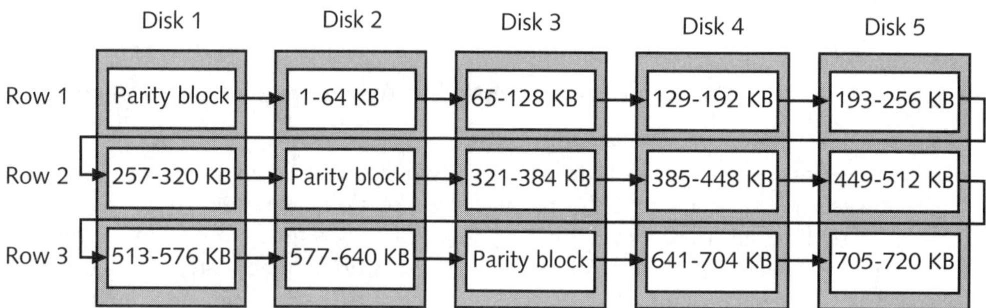

Figure 7-16 Disks in a RAID-5 volume

When you set up a RAID-5 volume, the performance is not as fast as with a striped volume because it takes longer to write the data and calculate the parity block for each row. However, accessing data through disk reads is as fast as a striped volume. RAID-5 is a viable fault-tolerance choice for user data, shared data, and mission-critical data and for applications when full mirroring is not feasible due to the expense. It works well with disk arrays that are compatible with RAID-5. A RAID-5 volume is particularly useful in a client/server system that uses a separate database for queries and creating reports because disk read performance is fast for obtaining data. In applications such as a customer service database that is constantly updated with new orders, disk read performance will be slower than with striping without parity.

If you create a RAID-5 volume, keep in mind that it uses 16 MB or more of RAM because RAID-5 uses more memory than mirroring or simple striping. Also, RAID-5 takes up disk space for the parity information.

The amount of storage space used is based on the formula $1/n$ where n is the number of physical disks in the volume. For example, with four disks, the amount of space taken for parity information is one-fourth of the total space of all disk drives in the volume. This means you get more usable disk storage if there are more disks in the volume. A set of eight 500 GB disks yields more usable storage than a set of four 1 TB disks in RAID-5.

Use the Disk Management tool to create a RAID-5 volume. To start, right-click the unallocated or free space on a disk that is to be part of the volume, then click New RAID-5 Volume. RAID-5 can only be configured on dynamic disks.

Software RAID vs. Hardware RAID

Two approaches to RAID can be implemented on a server: software RAID and hardware RAID. Software RAID implements fault tolerance through the server's operating system, such as using RAID levels 0, 1, or 5 through the Windows Server 2016 Disk Management tool. Hardware RAID is implemented through the server hardware and is independent of the operating system. Many manufacturers implement hardware RAID on the adapter, such as a SCSI adapter, to which the disk drives are connected. The RAID logic is contained in a chip on the adapter. Also, a battery is often connected to the chip to ensure that the chip never loses power and has fault tolerance to retain the RAID setup even when a power outage occurs. Hardware RAID is more expensive than software RAID but offers many advantages over software RAID:

- Faster read and write response (although there are exceptions depending on the capabilities of the adapter or controller)
- The ability to place boot and system files on different RAID levels, such as RAID levels 1 and 5
- The ability to "hot-swap" a failed disk with one that works or is new, thus replacing the disk without shutting down the server (this option can vary by manufacturer)
- More setup options to retrieve damaged data and to combine different RAID levels within one array of disks, such as mirroring two disks using RAID level 1 and setting up five disks for RAID level 5 in a seven disk array (the RAID options depend on what the manufacturer offers)

The vast majority of RAID implementations, particularly in medium and large organizations, use hardware RAID rather than software RAID—in part because hardware RAID provides more options. Also, when you purchase hardware RAID, pay particular attention to the capabilities of the adapter or controller. These capabilities affect the actual read and write performance. Storage Spaces, described next, is a technology that offers RAID-like capabilities while mixing different storage media and provides an additional popular direction for server storage.

Storage Spaces

Storage Spaces is a Windows Server 2016 technology that enables you to form groupings of physical disks and free disk space to manage together as individual virtual disks. Each grouping is a storage pool that gathers together physical disks to appear to an application or a user as one virtual disk. The concept of Storage Spaces is to give the server administrator versatile ways to use different kinds of physical disks, while having the ability to apply RAID-based fault tolerance capabilities.

The kinds of physical disks that can be combined and used within a storage pool include:

- **Serial Advanced Technology Attachment (SATA)**—A high-speed serial interface technology for hard disks
- **Solid state drive (SSD)**—A fast storage technology based on using semiconductors for storage, similar to flash drives
- **Non-volatile Memory Express (NVMe)**—A communications protocol and interface created for SSD to enable much faster data access and to reduce data latency
- *Universal Serial Bus*—An SSD or regular hard drive attached through a USB port

- **Small Computer System Interface (SCSI)**—A 32- or 64-bit computer adapter that transports data between one or more attached devices, such as hard disks, and the computer, using parallel communications technology
- **Internet SCSI (iSCSI)**—A Storage Area Network (SAN) grouping of storage devices, which forms a subnet that uses SCSI drives and communicates employing TCP/IP network communications
- **Serial Attached SCSI (SAS)**—An update to parallel SCSI that uses serial communications and does not require terminators as with the older parallel SCSI technology

A virtual disk that is formed out of a storage pool can, at this writing, be one of three resiliency types (fault tolerance capabilities):

- *Simple*—Similar to RAID level 0 using stripe sets without parity. As is true for RAID level 0, this storage pool resiliency type is used primarily to achieve faster disk reads and writes. Disk failure means you lose your data. This resiliency type might be used for data you can afford to lose, such as temporary files used in a data warehouse for querying database information.
- *Mirror*—Similar in concept to RAID level 1 for disk mirroring or duplexing. This resiliency type stripes data onto several volumes, while creating additional copies of the data for fault tolerance. You must have two or more disks. This resiliency type requires the use of more disk space on which to create additional data copies, but it is relatively high performance. Microsoft recommends including some solid state drives (SSDs) in the mix of physical disks in the pool to achieve additional performance.

Three-way mirroring can also be configured if you have five or more physical disks. In three-way mirroring a particular file is stored on three drives.

- *Parity*—Similar to RAID level 5 using striping with parity. Requiring at least three disks, this resiliency type offers redundancy, but with lower disk write performance than the other forms of resiliency. You might use this type for the same situations as for regular RAID level 5, including databases, applications, and others. Microsoft also recommends this resiliency type for archiving data, streaming data, and situations that maximize data workloads.

Storage Spaces have several advantages. For example, when there is a failure in a mirror or parity resiliency type, the system can automatically repair the disk failure by using a hot space placed in the pool for this purpose or by implementing unused space on physical disk in the pool. Or, if the failure is due to a bad area on a disk, the system can automatically make an error correction, such as by finding another disk area that is not damaged.

An important advantage of Storage Spaces is that when a disk fails in a storage pool, there is no noticeable delay in performance. Storage Spaces uses parallelized repair, which means the remaining functioning disks take over the data that was on the failed disk, automatically spreading the load over all the disks. In a RAID array, there is more downtime as the data is rebuilt on a designated spare disk placed in the array.

Windows Server 2012 R2 introduced a new capability called *tiered storage places*. This capability means that two tiers can be established: slow and fast. The slow tier consists of SATA drives that are intended for high capacity storage, such as data files for applications. The fast tier consists of SSD drives that offer faster performance than SATA. The fast tier is intended to hold information that is frequently accessed. The Storage Spaces system monitors data activity to determine which data is accessed frequently and which is not. Frequently accessed data is automatically routed to the fast tier while less frequently accessed data is routed to the slow tier. In some cases, files are recognized by the server administrator to always be on the fast tier, such as spreadsheets used by the company owner. These files can be manually placed in the fast tier by the server administrator in a process called pinning.

Within a storage pool, you can decide how to allocate disk space using one of the following provisioning methods:

- *thin*—You can allocate more space than is required for the current amount of data, but the system only uses the actual space it needs enabling the actual size to grow with the data.
- *fixed*—You allocate a given amount of space for the data, which means if the data grows to require more space you have to add more disks.

A new storage pool is created through Server Manager. Because many readers will not have a system to learn on that has at least one unused disk, the general steps for creating a storage pool are provided rather than using a hands-on activity:

1. Open Server Manager, such as by clicking Start and clicking the Server Manager tile, or clicking Start and clicking Server Manager.
2. In the left pane, click File and Storage Services.
3. Click Storage Pools.
4. In the right pane, click the down arrow for TASKS near the top of the right pane for the Storage Pools box and click New Storage Pool.
5. Click Next in the Before you begin screen of the New Storage Pool Wizard.
6. In the Specify a storage pool name and subsystem window, enter the name for the pool and a description. Click Next. (Note that the Next button will be deactivated if there are no groups of available disks to use.)
7. In the Select physical disks for the storage pool window, select the physical disks to be in the pool. Notice that in the Allocation column for each disk you can set the options: Automatic, Hot Spare, and Manual. The default is Automatic. Automatic and manual disk selections should not be used in the same pool. In many cases, the best idea is to use automatic because it creates a good distribution between usable disks and disks employed as hot spares. Click Next.
8. In the Confirm selections window, review your selections and click Create.
9. In the View results window, click Close.

Storage Spaces Direct

A Storage Spaces feature that is new to Windows Server 2016 is Storage Spaces Direct. **Storage Spaces Direct** is software-defined storage and is intended to make storage more versatile through making it easier to add storage as needed, to access storage, and to use new storage capabilities. **Software-defined storage (SDS)** refers to managing data storage with software that is independent of the actual storage hardware. For example, software-defined storage might employ ways to duplicate data or pool storage that are not built into the hardware, but are enabled through software that manages the hardware.

In the case of Storage Spaces Direct, local storage hardware devices are grouped into storage nodes. The storage can be any combination of the hardware storage technologies previously listed for storage pools, such as SATA drives, SATA solid state drives, NVMe solid state devices, and so on. Storage Spaces Direct uses Server Message Block version 3 protocol for rapid communication between storage nodes. **Server Message Block version 3 (SMBv3)** is the same protocol that Windows operating systems use natively for sharing folders and files on a network.

Chapter 5, Configuring, Managing, and Troubleshooting Resource Access, discusses SMB in the section, Configuring Sharing Through Server Manager.

Storage Spaces Direct is particularly targeted for use with virtual machines operating through Hyper-V and for clustered virtual machines. At this writing, one cluster can have up to

240 disks and up to 12 nodes within Storage Spaces Direct. Also, there are two ways to deploy Storage Spaces Direct:

- Hyper-converged—In this deployment, Hyper-V clustered servers and their storage are on the same hardware (an approach more common to smaller operations).
- Disaggregated—With this deployment, the Hyper-V clusters of servers and the Storage Spaces Direct storage components (storage servers) exist on different hardware (a technique used by larger operations).

Multipath Input/Output

Even though you have RAID or a SAN (or both), you still do not have complete fault tolerance if a server has just one path to reach the disks in your storage setup, such as having one adapter and one cable to a RAID array. One approach already discussed for establishing redundant paths is to use disk duplexing. Another approach in Windows Server 2016 is to use Multipath I/O.

Multipath I/O provides a means to establish multiple paths between a server and its disk storage. The first step in this process is to create the multiple paths between the storage and the server or servers, depending on the type of disk storage setup you are using. For example, on a server with one RAID array, establishing multiple paths would be connecting two cables and adapter cards between the RAID array and the server. For a SAN, creating multiple paths might involve establishing two or more network paths through two or more network switches or routers to the SAN.

Once the multiple paths are physically set up, the next step is to install Multipath I/O, which is a feature installed through Server Manager using the Add Roles and Features Wizard (see Figure 7-17).

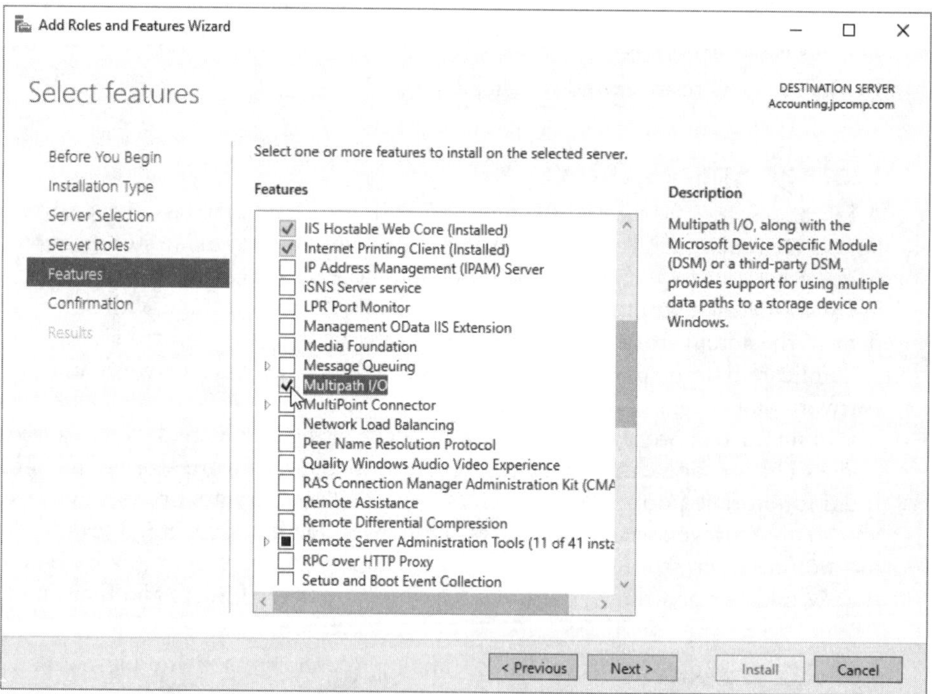

Figure 7-17 Installing the Multipath I/O feature

When you install Multipath I/O, you also install the **Device Specific Module** (**DSM**), which is compatible with the following disk storage array controller technologies:

- *Asymmetric logical unit access (ALUA),* which provides multiple ports to arrays and different levels of access per port

- *Active/Active controller model,* which means that the contents of one controller's cache is shadowed to another controller in an array, creating a backup path to the array

Windows Server 2016 DSM enables you to choose between the following configuration models:

- *Dynamic Least Queue Depth*—This tracks current traffic on all paths and transmits the newest traffic to the least busy path.
- *Failback*—This sends current traffic to disks on a path that is preselected as the main path to use. If that path is down, then an alternate path is used.
- *Failover*—This uses a main path and secondary paths. The main path is used unless it is down. Next, the secondary path marked with the highest priority is used, and so on. All secondary paths are ranked in terms of priority.
- *Round Robin*—Each functional path is used in a round-robin order, such as path 1 first, path 2 next, and so on.
- *Round Robin with a subset of paths*—Sets of primary paths and secondary paths are established. Each primary path is used in round-robin order. If all of the primary paths are down, then the secondary paths are used in round-robin order.
- *Weighted Path*—Each path is given a priority. For example, if there are five paths, then the path to use first is designated as 1, and the path weighted as 2 is used next in priority if the path weighted as 1 is down. If the paths weighted as 1, 2, and 3 are down, then the path weighted as 4 is used, and so on.

Disk Backup

Using Storage Spaces resiliency or traditional RAID are two of the ways that you can provide fault tolerance for your server's hard disks. Storage Spaces has options for recovering from more than a single disk failure. Most software implementations of RAID can only recover from single disk failure. However, even with these technologies there is no substitute for performing regular, scheduled backups. One of the best ways to make sure you do not lose valuable information is to fully back up that information on a regular basis, using backup media such as DVDs, installed hard drives, removable hard drives, network drives, and other drive options. These backups can be performed from a server on the network, for example.

Performing backups from a backup device installed on the server has several advantages:

- No extra load is produced on the network from traffic caused by transferring files over the network.
- Equipping each server with its own backup capability gives you a way to perform backups on a multiple-server network, even if a backup device fails on one of the servers. Backups can be performed from backup media on one of the other servers.
- Backing up from backup media on a server enables you to back up key operating system files and settings for that server, including the Registry and boot files.

The advantages of performing a network backup are that backup jobs can be stored on a single backup media and one administrator can be responsible for backing up multiple servers. The main disadvantages are the increase in network traffic. Also, you need to make sure you periodically back up operating system and boot files as well as the Registry.

Windows Server Backup

Windows Server 2016 comes with the Windows Server Backup tool. To use this tool, you need to install it using Server Manager. The Windows Server Backup tool offers the ability to back up all server files or files that have changed. It is particularly targeted for use by new server administrators, small to medium organizations, and server administrators who like to use a tool specifically designed to work for Windows Server 2016.

The Windows Server Backup tool in Windows Server 2016 contains the following features:

- It offers both full and incremental backups.
- It has the ability to use **Volume Shadow Copy Service** (**VSS**), which is created to make stable images of files and folders on servers based on the point in time when the image is made. It also includes facilities so that programmers can write applications to enhance backing up application pieces and data created by those applications, such as SQL Server database applications and Microsoft Exchange Server for email.
- It offers reliable data restoration.
- It provides information about how much space is needed on the target medium for a particular backup.
- It offers the *wbadmin* command-line tool for server administrators who prefer command-line control of backups.
- It has full support to back up to optical media, such as DVDs.

Microsoft lists the following considerations for using the Windows Server Backup tool:

- The Windows Server Backup tool only backs up NTFS volumes and not FAT volumes.
- Windows Server Backup does not back up to tape.
- Windows Server Backup cannot restore backups made from pre-Windows Server 2008 operating systems that use Ntbackup.exe, such as archived financial records. You can, however, download Ntbackup.exe from Microsoft's website (at this writing found at *http://www.microsoft.com/en-us/download/details.aspx?id=4220*) and run it in Windows Server 2016 to restore files from backups made from pre-Windows Server 2008 server systems.

If you download the tool, do not try to use Ntbackup.exe to make backups from your Windows Server 2016 server. Also, many organizations store old financial records made on systems and media no longer used or supported by newer computers that have replaced older technologies—so they have no way to read old archived information. Before reaching this dilemma in your organization, plan to convert old backup media so the contents can be used with newer systems.

The first step in using Windows Server Backup is to install it as a feature, as shown in Activity 7-8.

Activity 7-8: Installing the Windows Server Backup Tool

Time Required: Approximately 10 minutes
Objective: Install the Windows Server Backup tool.

Description: Performing regular backups is a critical task for ensuring your organization's working environment. Even if you lose a disk drive or inadvertently delete an important folder, you still have your important information if you have it backed up. You probably won't need to restore from backups often, but when you need to, there is no better feeling than having sound backups. In this activity, you install the Windows Server Backup tool that some server administrators prefer using for backups, because it is native to Windows Server.

1. Open **Server Manager**, if it isn't already open.
2. Click **Manage** and then click **Add Roles and Features.**
3. If you see the Before you begin window, click **Next.**
4. In the Select installation type window, ensure that **Role-based or feature–based installation** is selected and click **Next.**
5. Make sure your server is selected in the Select destination server window and click **Next.**
6. Click **Next** in the Select server roles window.

7. Click the box for **Windows Server Backup** in the Select features window (see Figure 7-18). Click **Next.**

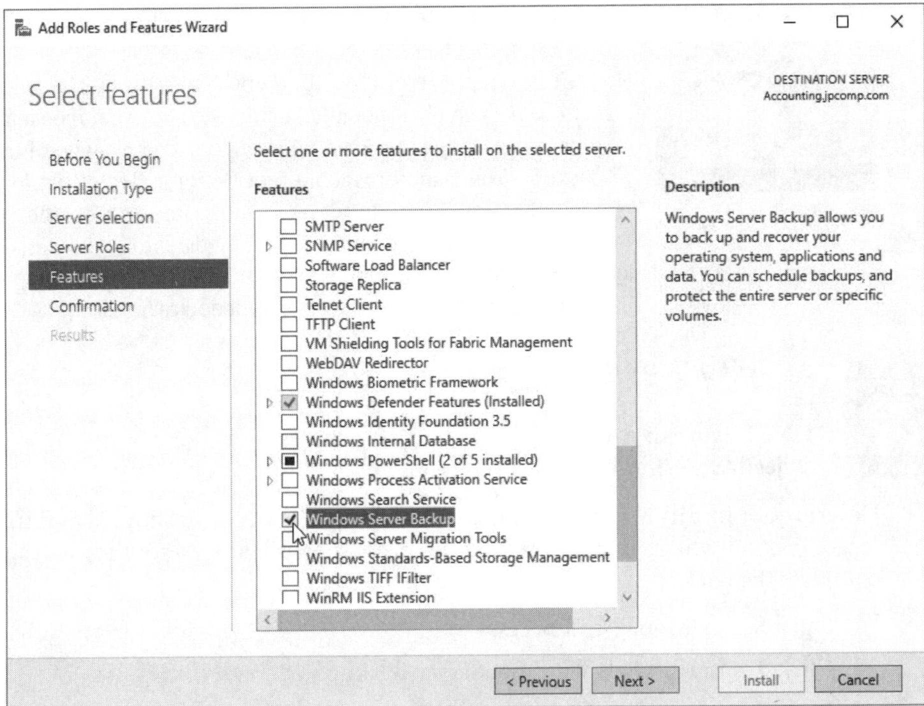

Figure 7-18 Installing the Windows Server Backup feature

8. In the Confirm installation selections window, click **Install.**
9. In the Installation progress window, make sure the installation succeeded and then click **Close.**
10. Leave Server Manager open for the next activity.

Backup Options

The three types of backups that can be performed using the Windows Server Backup tool are:

- Full backup
- Incremental backup
- Custom backup

A **full backup** is a backup of an entire system, including all system files, programs, and data files. The full backup changes each file's archive attribute to show that it has been backed up. As you will recall from Chapter 5, each NTFS folder or file has an archive attribute that can be set to show whether that folder or file has been backed up since the last change to it. A full backup is performed the first time you back up a server, and afterwards once a night, once a week, or at a regular interval depending on the number of files on your server and your organization's particular needs. You can configure a schedule in Windows Server Backup to regularly perform a full backup.

An **incremental backup** only backs up files that are new or that have been updated. The Windows Server 2016 incremental option backs up only files that have the archive attribute marked. When it backs up a file, the incremental backup removes the archive attribute to show that the file has been backed up. Using incremental backups enables you to save time backing up a server when there are large numbers of files to back up. Many files don't change on a server and so don't have to be backed up every time. Your organization might, for example, perform a full backup once a week, such as at the end of the work week or on Saturdays. On all other work days, it might perform incremental backups.

A **custom backup** enables you to configure a file-by-file backup so that you back up only a specific drive, folder, or subfolder, for example. You can also choose to back up operating system data and information. Further, you can create a binary or image backup that backs up the entire system in binary format (which doesn't allow for restoring a specific folder or drive).

No matter what size organization you have, develop a solid backup plan. Your backup plan should take into account what media to use and whether to use full, incremental, custom, or a combination of these types of backups. The plan also should provide for a safe offsite location for storage of selected backup media as a disaster recovery measure—and the plan should include the rotation of media into and out of the offsite location. Additionally, it should address when to schedule backups, who performs the backups, and a means to periodically test the backups.

Activity 7-9: Backing Up a Server

Time Required: Approximately 10 to 30 minutes
Objective: Perform a Custom backup.

Description: In this activity, you practice starting a custom backup. You don't need an actual target disk on which to store the backup, because you'll stop before instructing the program to complete the backup.

1. Open **Server Manager**, if necessary.
2. Click **Tools** and click **Windows Server Backup**.
3. In the left pane, click **Local Backup**, if it is not selected. Wait a moment, if necessary for the tool to read your files.
4. Click **Action** in the menu bar in the top left portion of the window and click **Backup Once**.
5. In the Backup Options window, **Different options** should be selected by default, as in Figure 7-19. Click **Next**.

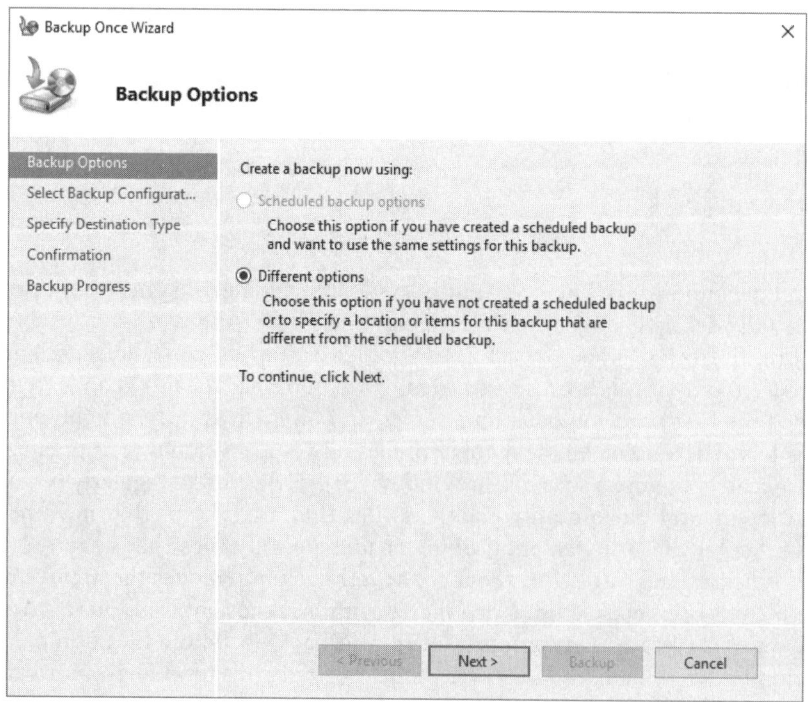

Figure 7-19 Backup Options window

6. In the Select Backup Configuration window, notice that you can do a Full server backup or a Custom backup. Select **Custom** and click **Next**.
7. In the Select Items for Backup window, click **Add Items** (see Figure 7-20).

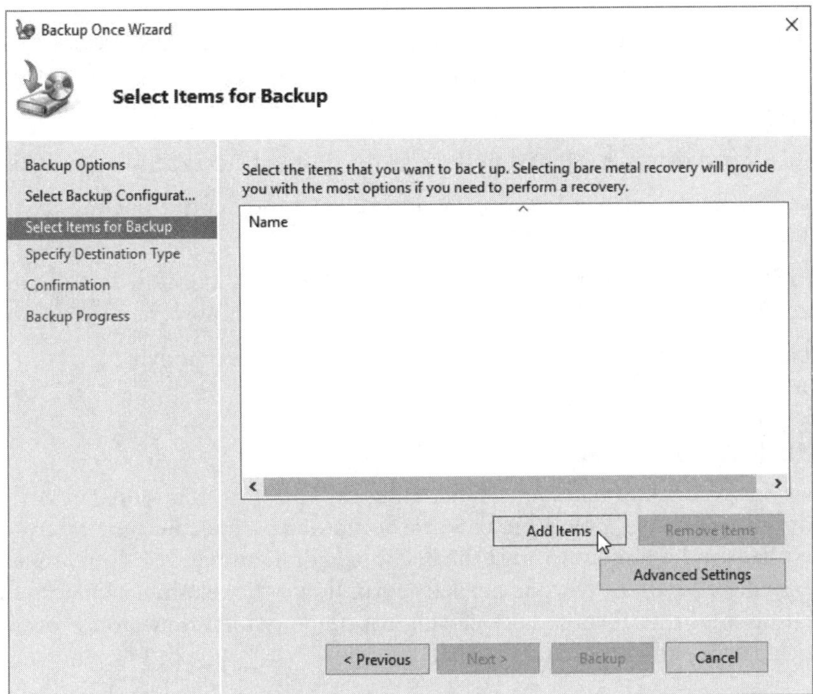

Figure 7-20 Select Items for Backup window

8. In the Select Items window, you'll see items such as the following from which to select:
   - *Bare metal recovery*—This creates a binary image of the operating system and all files that can be used for a full restore, sort of like taking a full snapshot of the system as it exists in the moment of the backup. Keep in mind that to assure a successful restore from a binary image backup, you will need a machine that is as identical as possible to the original, including the same computer configuration, manufacturer, and BIOS.

A binary backup does not give you the option to restore specific folders or files. It's all or none, either you restore everything or you don't do the restore at all.

   - *System state*—This saves system state data including the operating system and boot files, plus extra components and information that reflect the currently configured state of the server depending on what roles and features are installed (you learn more about system state data in Chapter 12, Managing System Reliability and Availability).
   - *Hyper*-V—This backs up virtual server information associated with Hyper-V virtual machines.
   - *System Reserved*—This backs up information on Boot and Recovery volumes as well as system volume information (if you have a recovery volume configured).
   - *Individual disks attached to the server*—This backs up specific disks, such as Local disk (C:), with the option to select particular folders and subfolders.

9. In the Select Items window, click the **plus sign** in front of **Local disk** (**C:**), making sure you do not place a checkmark in its box at this time.
   - How would you back up only the Users folder?
10. In the Select Items window, click the **minus sign** in front of **Local disk** (**C:**).
11. Place a checkmark in the boxes for **System state** and **Local disk** (**C:**). Click **OK**.
12. In the Select Items for Backup window, click **Advanced Settings**. Notice that you can configure settings for a VSS backup. Click **Cancel**.
13. Click **Next** in the Select Items for Backup window.
14. Ensure **Local drives** is selected in the Specify Destination Type window. Click **Next**.
15. In the Select Backup Destination window, leave the default backup destination and click **Next**.
16. In the Confirmation window, notice your selections for Local disk (C:) and System state are listed. Click **Cancel** so that you discontinue your backup practice at this point.
17. Leave the Windows Server Backup tool open for the next activity.

Scheduling Backups

Windows Server Backup includes a scheduling capability so that you can have the server automatically start backups after regular work hours or at a specific time of day. This means that you don't have to be present to start the backups. For example, you could schedule full backups to start at 9:00 PM after everyone has left work. In another example, an accounting office in an organization might perform a daily closing routine in which they stop processing by 4:20 PM and back up accounting files at 4:30 PM.

The scheduling process requires a target disk to back up to, such as a removable hard drive.

The following general steps illustrate how to create and schedule a backup:

1. Open the Windows Server Backup tool.
2. Click Action and click Backup Schedule.
3. Click Next in the Getting Started window of the Backup Schedule Wizard.
4. Select the type of backup, Full server (recommended) or Custom (see Figure 7-21). Click Next. If you select the Custom backup, click the Add Items button and choose which volumes to back up. Click OK in the Select Items window and then click Next in the Select Items for Backup window. (If you have a FAT volume configured, you'll see a warning that FAT is an unsupported file system and cannot be backed up. Click OK to continue.)
5. In the Specify Backup Time window, if you choose to back up once a day, specify the time to start the backup (see Figure 7-22). (If you selected Custom backup in Step 4, you will also see a listing for Select Items for Backup in the left pane.) If you choose more than once a day, specify the times to schedule the backup. Click Next.
6. Select the destination for the backup. Note that the Windows Server Backup tool will format the disk if it is not formatted for the backup. Click Next. (Depending on the destination you select, you may see another window, such as the Select Destination Volume window, if you selected to back up to a volume.)
7. Review your selections and click Finish.

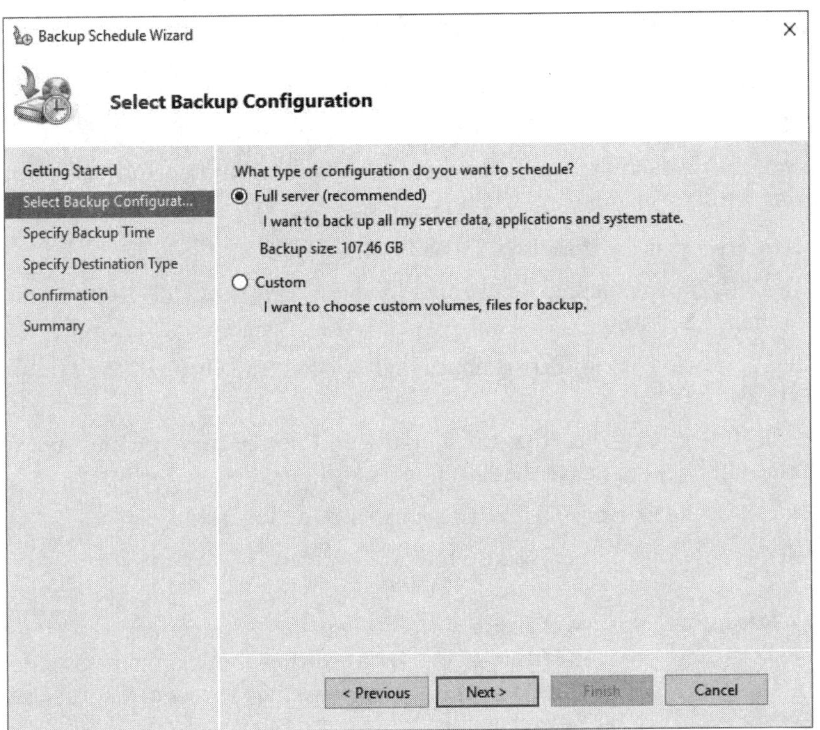

Figure 7-21 Selecting the backup configuration

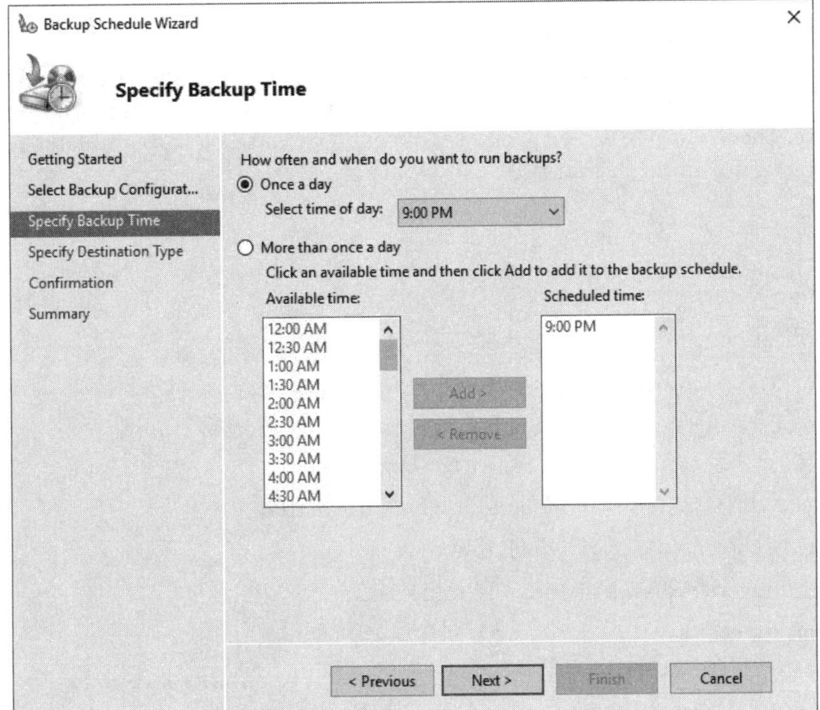

Figure 7-22 Configuring the backup time

Configuring Backup Performance

Configuring the backup performance options enables you to specify the speed of the backup and whether to perform a full backup or incremental backup. The default is to perform full backups; however, to save time on your backups, you might prefer to use incremental backups or a combination of full and incremental, depending on the volume.

Activity 7-10: Configuring Backup Performance

Time Required: Approximately 5 minutes
Objective: Configure backup performance.

Description: In this activity, you learn how to set up backup performance options, such as for configuring a full or incremental backup.

1. If necessary, open the **Windows Server Backup** tool.
2. Ensure that **Local Backup** is selected in the left pane. Click **Action** and click **Configure Performance Settings.**
3. In the Optimize Backup Performance dialog box, read through each option that is offered. Select **Custom.**
4. For Local disk (C:), click the **down arrow** and notice that you can specify Full backup or Incremental backup. Leave the selection as **Full backup.**
5. Click **OK** in the Optimize Backup Performance dialog box.
6. Close the Windows Server Backup tool.

As part of a disaster recovery plan, it is important to store a copy of a backup off-site or to have a scheduled rotation of backup media to be stored off-site. This is a good precaution in case of fire, flooding, or some other natural disaster. Many organizations are now fulfilling this need by using off-site backup services or software or by using cloud services from a vendor.

Performing a Recovery

Use the Windows Server Backup tool to perform a recovery from network connected, local, or removable media. The Recovery Wizard in the Windows Server Backup utility steps you through a restore. The Windows Server Backup tool enables you to backup and later recover any of the following (if it is in the backup):

- Files
- Folders
- Volumes
- Applications and application data
- The backup catalog (of information in the backup)
- The operating system (to the same computer or to another computer using identical hardware)

Before you start, determine the following information:

- Date of the backup from which to recover
- Type of recovery, such as files and folders or applications
- What to recover
- Where to recover, such as in the original location or another location

To start a recovery first insert, attach, or connect via the network the media with the backup files. Open the Windows Server Backup tool, ensure that Local Backup is selected in the left pane, click Action, click Recover, and follow the steps as presented in the Recovery Wizard (which will vary depending on what you are recovering). Figure 7-23 shows the Getting Started window in the Recovery Wizard.

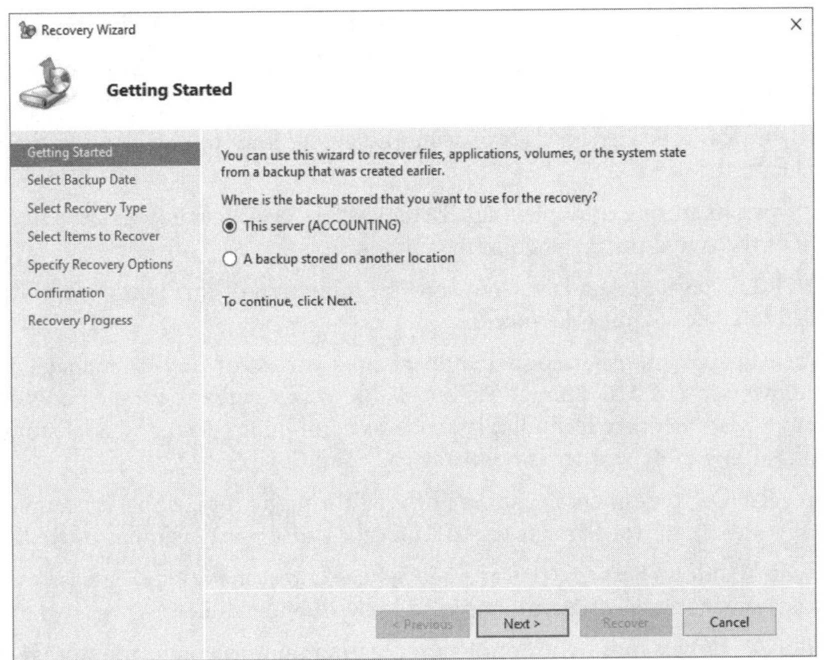

Figure 7-23 Recovery Wizard

Chapter 12, Managing System Reliability and Availability, explains backing up and using system state data for recovering the operating system.

Many organizations have found that they thought they had good backups, but when the time came to use them, there were problems—such as that the backups were configured incorrectly and didn't contain all of the needed data. Don't let this happen to you. Periodically test your backups, such as on a spare nonproduction server. Make sure you are in reality backing up what you believe you are backing up. Also, by testing the backup, you are getting training in doing a restore so that you are prepared for the real situation.

Chapter Summary

- Windows Server 2016 uses basic and dynamic disks. Basic disks are backward compatible with earlier Windows server and workstation operating systems. Dynamic disks offer more flexibility for configuration.
- Dynamic disks can be configured as simple, spanned, striped, mirrored, and RAID-5 volumes.
- If you need to recover space from a basic or dynamic disk, you can shrink the disk so that the recovered space can be configured as a separate volume.
- The Disk Management tool enables you to configure basic and dynamic disks. It performs disk configurations from simple volumes to RAID-5. You can also use it to convert a basic disk to a dynamic disk or vice versa.
- For optimum disk performance, plan to set up a schedule to regularly defragment disks on a server.

- Use the Disk Check and *chkdsk* tools to find and repair disk problems.
- RAID provides fault tolerance for hard disks. Windows Server 2016 supports RAID levels 0, 1, and 5.
- RAID level 0 is disk striping. It provides no actual fault tolerance other than to help extend the life of the disks.
- With disk mirroring or duplexing (RAID level 1), the same data is written to a partition on each of the two disks included in the mirror.
- With RAID level 5, data is written across a minimum of three disks. Parity information is added to achieve fault tolerance.
- Storage Spaces is a technology that opens up a variety of ways to manage disk storage in Windows Server 2016. Storage Spaces enables you to create storage pools containing different types of storage technologies, such as combining SATA and SSD storage in the same pool. Adding more storage is relatively easy and flexible.
- Three RAID-like resiliency types are offered through Storage Spaces: simple (similar to RAID level 0), mirror (similar to RAID level 1), and parity (similar to RAID level 5).
- New to Windows Server 2016, Storage Spaces Direct makes it even easier to add and access storage spaces and is especially targeted for virtual machines.
- Multipath I/O extends your options for creating fault tolerance for storage through using redundant paths.
- Windows Server Backup offers features to schedule backups, perform full, custom, or incremental backups, and recover data from backups.

Key Terms

active partition The partition from which a computer boots.

basic disk In Windows Server 2016, a partitioned disk that can have up to four partitions and that uses logical drive designations. This type of disk is backward compatible with previous versions of Windows client and server operating systems and MS-DOS and supports multi-boot with other operating systems.

boot partition Partition on basic disks that holds the Windows Server 2016 \Windows folder containing the system files.

boot volume Volume on dynamic disks that holds the \Windows folder of system files.

custom backup Enables you to configure backups differently for each volume, using either a full backup or an incremental backup.

defragmenting A software process that rearranges data to fill in the empty spaces that develop on disks and makes data easier to obtain.

Device Specific Module (DSM) A software interface between the Multipath I/O capability in Windows Server 2016 and the hard disk hardware.

disk duplexing A fault-tolerance method similar to disk mirroring in that it prevents data loss by duplicating data from a main disk to a backup disk, but disk duplexing places the backup disk on a different controller or adapter than is used by the main disk.

disk mirroring A fault-tolerance method that prevents data loss by duplicating data from a main disk to a backup disk. Some operating systems also refer to this as disk shadowing.

dynamic disk In Windows Server 2016, a disk that does not use traditional partitioning, which means that there is no restriction to the number of volumes that can be set up on one disk or to the ability to extend volumes onto additional physical disks. Dynamic disks are compatible with Windows Server 2016 back through Windows 2000 Server.

extended partition A partition that is created from unpartitioned free disk space and is linked to a primary partition in order to increase the available disk space.

fault tolerance Techniques that employ hardware and software to provide assurance against equipment failures, computer service interruptions, and data loss.

formatting A process that prepares a hard disk partition for a specific file system.

fragmented Having files spread throughout a disk with empty pockets of space between files; a normal and gradual process in the functioning of an operating system, addressed by using a defragmentation utility.

full backup A backup of an entire system, including all system files, programs, and data files.

Globally Unique Identifier (GUID) Partition Table (GPT) A method for partitioning disks that allows for theoretically unlimited partitions and use of larger disks. In Windows Server 2016, the maximum number of partitions on a GPT disk is 128, and the maximum partition size is up to 18 exabytes.

home directory or home folder A server folder that is associated with a user's account and that is a designated workspace for the user to store files.

incremental backup Backs up only files that are new or that have been updated.

Internet Small Computer System Interface (iSCSI) A high-speed technology used in SANs that employs TCP/IP communications and SCSI disk drives. *See* Storage Area Network (SAN).

Master Boot Record (MBR) Data created in the first sector of a disk, containing startup information and information about disk partitions.

mirrored volume Two dynamic disks that are set up for RAID level 1 so that data on one disk is stored on a redundant disk.

mounted drive A physical disk, CD/DVD, removable drive, or other drive that appears as a folder and that is accessed through a path like any other folder.

Multipath I/O A set of drivers in Windows Server 2016 that can be used with device and network architecture to set up multiple paths between a server and its disk storage to achieve fault tolerance.

Non-volatile Memory Express (NVMe) A communications protocol and interface created for SSD to enable much faster data access and to reduce data latency.

parallelized repair A process in Storage Spaces that causes the data on a failed disk to be automatically spread over all of the remaining functioning disks.

partition table Table containing information about each partition on a disk, such as the type of partition, size, and location. Also, the partition table provides information to the computer about how to access the disk.

partitioning Allocating a group of tracks and sectors on a disk to be used by a particular file system, such as NTFS.

primary partition Partition or portion of a hard disk that is bootable.

RAID (redundant array of inexpensive [or independent] disks) A set of standards designed to extend the life of hard disk drives and to prevent data loss from a hard disk failure.

RAID-5 volume Three or more dynamic disks that use RAID level 5 fault tolerance through disk striping and creating parity blocks for data recovery.

Serial Advanced Technology Attachment (SATA) A high-speed serial interface technology for hard disks.

Serial Attached SCSI (SAS) An update to parallel SCSI that uses serial communications and does not require terminators as with the older parallel SCSI technology.

Server Message Block version 3 (SMBv3) Version 3 of the SMB protocol native to Windows operating systems that is used for sharing folders and files on a network as well as for communications between nodes in Storage Spaces Direct.

simple volume A portion of a disk or an entire disk that is set up as a dynamic disk.

Small Computer System Interface (SCSI) A 32- or 64-bit computer adapter that transports data between one or more attached devices, such as hard disks, and the computer using parallel communications technology.

software-defined storage (SDS) Managing data storage with software that is independent of the actual storage hardware.

solid state drive (SSD) A fast storage technology based on using semiconductors for storage, similar to flash drives.

spanned volume Two or more Windows Server dynamic disks that are combined to appear as one disk.

Storage Area Network (SAN) A grouping of storage devices that forms a subnet. The storage devices are available to any server on the main network and appear to the user as though they are attached to the server they are accessing.

storage pool Used in Storage Spaces, a grouping of physical disks and disk space to be managed by a Windows Server 2016 server as a virtual disk.

Storage Spaces A Windows Server 2016 technology that enables multiple physical disks to be formed into individual storage pools. *See* storage pool.

Storage Spaces Direct Software-defined storage that is intended to make storage more versatile through making it easier to add storage as needed, to access storage, and to use new storage capabilities. *See* Storage Spaces.

stripe set Two or more basic disks set up so that files are spread in blocks across the disks.

striped volume Two or more dynamic disks that use striping so that files are spread in blocks across the disks.

striping A data storage method that breaks up data files across all volumes of a disk set to minimize wear on a single volume.

system partition Partition on basic disks that contains boot files.

system volume Volume on dynamic disks that is used to boot the computer.

tiered storage places In Storage Spaces, the ability to have slow tiers (slow disk technology, such as SATA) for less frequently accessed data and fast tiers (faster disk technology, such as SSD) for more frequently accessed data.

Unified Extensible Firmware Interface (UEFI) A firmware alternative to BIOS that includes the use of GPT disks. *See* Globally Unique Identifier (GUID) Partition Table (GPT).

virtual disk As used in Storage Spaces, a grouping of different kinds of physical disks, also known as a storage pool, that are combined on a server to appear to the user or to an application as one disk. *See* storage pool and Storage Spaces.

volume A logical designation of one or more physical disks partitioned and formatted with one file system. One volume can be composed of one or more partitions. In Windows Server 2016, a volume can be a basic disk partition that has been formatted for a particular file system, a primary partition, a volume set, an extended volume, a stripe set, a stripe set with parity, or a mirror set. A volume can also be a dynamic disk that is set up as a simple volume, spanned volume, striped volume, RAID-5 volume, or mirrored volume.

volume set Two or more formatted basic disk partitions (volumes) that are combined to look like one volume with a single drive letter.

Volume Shadow Copy Service (VSS) Backup service used in Windows Server 2016 to create stable images of files and folders on servers based on the point in time when the image is made.

Review Questions

1. When you partition and format a disk, the process creates a table containing file and folder information for the file system. Which of the following are tables supported by Windows Server 2016 formatted for NTFS? (Choose all that apply.)
   a. Globally Unique Identifier Partition Table
   b. Sector Extending Partition Table
   c. Extensible Unique Block Partition Table
   d. Master Boot Record with partition table

2. The __________ partition or volume contains the operating system files, such as the files in the \Windows folder.
3. Which of the following can be configured when your server is using dynamic disks? (Choose all that apply.)
   a. Simple volume
   b. Spare volume
   c. Striped volume
   d. Spanned volume
4. Your server has a 1 TB volume that is only one-fifth used. You would like to recover the unused portion of this volume as unallocated disk space. What process can you use?
   a. You'll have to back up the volume, repartition it, and then restore the files to one of the partitions.
   b. Use opaque formatting to recover the unused space.
   c. Shrink the volume.
   d. Use the partition tool to create an unused pool.
5. You are consulting for a company that has been performing full backups every night for its Windows Server 2016 servers. A problem they have been experiencing is that the backups are taking longer and longer. What is your recommendation for this company?
   a. Perform the full backups in zip mode, which cuts the backup time in half.
   b. Use a custom backup that enables you to use a combination of full and incremental backups.
   c. Use a copy backup, which copies every other folder each time it runs.
   d. Purchase disk drives with smaller spindles for faster rotation.
6. Dynamic disks support RAID levels __________, __________, and __________.
7. Your business needs to have storage that is quickly accessed for customer service representatives who work the phones and storage for high capacity use, such as for data and application files used internally by company employees. Which of the following solutions do you recommend?
   a. A storage pool that uses SSD and SATA disks using tiered storage places
   b. Basic disks configured as spanned disks
   c. Dynamic disks configured with data optimization
   d. A RAID array containing small disks that provide fast access while achieving high capacity storage
8. Traditional RAID level 5 requires a minimum of __________ hard disks.
9. As the IT director for a large investment company, you are always looking for ways to build in better fault tolerance for your computer systems and versatile disk handling. As you consider your present hard disk storage situation, you have a large iSCSI SAN connected to the main network through a high-speed switch. You also have Solid State Drives and SAS drives built into individual computers. Which of the following technologies gives you the most versatility for this kind of storage, while allowing you to have redundancy?
   a. Traditional RAID level 1
   b. Serial RAID
   c. Dynamic disk
   d. Storage Spaces

10. Which of the following can you restore from the Windows Server Backup tool? (Choose all that apply.)
    a. Subfolders
    b. Volumes
    c. Folders
    d. The operating system
11. How much free space must you have on a basic disk to convert it to a dynamic disk?
12. Your company uses RAID arrays to help ensure the most uptime for access to its data. Each RAID array can be connected using two cables for extra redundancy. What Windows Server 2016 capability do you need to install to take advantage of the two-cable connectivity?
    a. Disk mirroring
    b. RAID duplexing
    c. Multipath I/O
    d. Storage switching
13. You have spent the morning archiving old files to DVDs and then deleting those files as a way to get back some disk space. Also, you've recovered some archived financial files to prepare for the auditor's visit. After you finish, you notice that the server seems to run slower. What should you do?
    a. Start the Optimize tool to defrag your disks.
    b. Perform a full backup. Reformat the disk and then perform a recovery from your backup.
    c. Use the Disk Check tool to retrieve contiguous disk space.
    d. Use Device Manager to perform a disk verification.
14. Windows Server 2016 has automatically identified some damaged disk areas on your organization's server. Which of the following tools should you run to fix these damaged areas (with users off your system)?
    a. Disk Check
    b. Disk Clean
    c. *chkdsk /i*
    d. *chkdsk /spotfix*
15. Your new IT colleague is trying to determine the location of a mounted drive on the server because he is not sure what a mounted drive is. Which of the following do you tell him?
    a. A mounted drive is always a DVD mounted in the DVD drive.
    b. A mounted drive is located in a folder.
    c. Because Windows Server 2016 does not support floppy drives, a mounted drive is always drive A.
    d. A mounted drive is always a drive used by UNIX and Linux clients for sharing folders and files on Windows Server 2016 and is designated as drive U.
16. When you use software RAID level 5, recognize that you must have __________ additional memory for system functions related to RAID.
17. Briefly explain the concept of a spanned volume.
18. You want to use three-way mirroring in a storage pool. What is the minimum number of disks that you must have?
    a. 2
    b. 3
    c. 4
    d. 5

19. Explain disk duplexing.
20. You have configured a RAID-5 volume using five 750 GB disks. How much disk space is actually available for storage of folders and files?
    a. 1875 GB
    b. 2812.5 GB
    c. 3000 GB
    d. 3750 GB

Case Projects

Fresh Recipes started over 50 years ago producing different varieties of soups. Today the company is a well-recognized brand name that offers soups, chili, stews, and other canned foods. Fresh Recipes is divided into the following departments: Business, Research and Recipes, Canning, Distribution, and IT. The company has over 450 employees and is employee owned. Two employees from each department make up the Management Council, which additionally includes the company president, vice president, operations manager, and the managers of each department.

Five Windows Server 2016 servers are located in the Business Department. The Research and Recipes Department has three Windows Server 2016 servers at its location. The Canning and Distribution departments have four Windows Server 2016 servers each, including servers that are used to control machinery. The IT Department has three servers. The company makes extensive use of databases, and each department has at least one Datacenter Edition server to house its databases.

The IT Department has been working with the Management Council on storage capacity issues because many of the company's servers will soon need more disk storage. The IT Department has retained you through Aspen Consulting to help with storage setup and planning issues.

Case Project 7-1: Planning for Basic or Dynamic Disks

The company has always used basic disks in the form of stripe sets even as the servers have been upgraded through the years to Windows Server 2016 (historically they started with Windows NT 4.0 Server). They like the speed of the stripe sets, but now want to investigate if there are advantages to using dynamic disks. The IT Department asks you to create a report or slide presentation that addresses the following:

- Advantages of dynamic disks
- Sample steps for converting from basic to dynamic disks

Case Project 7-2: Fault Tolerance for the Canning Department

The Canning Department uses one server to run the canning conveyor machinery, which operates 24 hours a day. The server has some built-in fault tolerance, such as two network interface cards and battery backup for its power supply. However, no fault tolerance is provided for the single hard drive in the server, which is configured as a basic disk. Fault tolerance is important for this server because the company loses over $15,000 an hour when the conveyor machinery is down. Create a short report with your recommendations for fault tolerance, including general guidelines for setting it up.

Case Project 7-3: Planning Disk Storage for the Databases

The databases used by the Datacenter Edition servers are experiencing rapid growth in terms of use and size. Many of the databases are now used across departments. These databases are considered by the Management Council to be one of the company's best strategic assets. The Management Council wants to consolidate physical management of the databases and the Datacenter Edition servers in the IT Department's computer room as a way to secure them in one place. Also, they want to consolidate the disk storage used for these databases and provide for fault tolerance. Create a report or slide show for the Management Council with your recommendations, including the advantages of what you recommend.

Case Project 7-4: Changing the Backups to Accommodate Growth

Because they have used basic disk stripe sets, the server administrators at Fresh Recipes have been performing nightly full backups for years. They have also chosen to manually start the backups. Now that the company has grown and the amount of data to back up has increased, the backups are taking much longer, which is causing the server administrators to put in extra hours. Create a short report with some suggestions for changing how they do backups to correspond with the company's growth.

chapter 8

Managing Windows Server 2016 Network Services

After reading this chapter and completing the exercises, you will be able to:

- Install, configure, and troubleshoot DNS
- Create a DNS implementation plan
- Install, configure, and troubleshoot DHCP
- Install the IP Address Management tool
- Configure NIC teaming
- Install, configure, and troubleshoot Microsoft Internet Information Services

When users communicate through a network, a variety of activities go on behind the scenes. Many of these activities involve managing IP communications. Users don't want to have to remember IP addresses of a server or another user; it's easier to remember a name of a user or server. Users don't want the responsibility of configuring their own IP addresses. Also, network administrators don't want users configuring their IP addresses, because mistakes can mean network chaos. Fortunately, services such as Domain Name System and Dynamic Host Configuration Protocol have automated network IP communications and removed a large burden from users and network administrators.

Accessing websites is another aspect of network communications. Microsoft offers Internet Information Services as website software for Windows Server 2016 servers. Internet Information Services turns Windows Server 2016 into a multifeatured web server and comes with versatile management tools.

This chapter gives you a foundation for understanding both Domain Name System and Dynamic Host Configuration Protocol. You learn how to install, configure, and troubleshoot these services for automated IP communications. You also learn about the IP Address Management tool, and you learn how to implement NIC teaming for faster network response and redundancy. At the end of the chapter, you learn to install and manage Internet Information Services to round out your network communications expertise.

Implementing Microsoft DNS

As you learned in Chapter 1, Introduction to Windows Server 2016, Domain Name System (DNS) is a TCP/IP application protocol that enables a DNS server to resolve (translate) domain and computer names to IP addresses or IP addresses to domain and computer names. For example, your server might have the name Banker and be in the domain *bankingcorp.com*. Also, its address might be 198.51.100.10. When a request is placed by another computer to contact Banker in the domain *bankingcorp.com*, DNS resolves this name to the IP address 198.51.100.10 so network communications can use this IP address.

DNS servers provide the DNS namespace for an enterprise (see Chapter 4, Introduction to Active Directory and Account Management), which includes resolving computer names and IP addresses as well as many other services.

Microsoft recommends that a DNS server has an IP address that is static, which means it is manually configured or given a permanent lease in DHCP (you learn more about DHCP later in this chapter). Also, before installing DNS on a server when Active Directory is in use on a network, make sure that the server is a DC (see Chapter 4; if your server is to be the first DC on the network, you'll need to install DNS along with the Active Directory Domain Services role on the server and promote the server to be a domain controller).

One of the requirements for using Active Directory on a Windows Server 2016 network is to have a DNS server on the network. When you set up a Windows Server 2016 network, if no DNS servers have been implemented, plan to use Windows Server 2016 DNS, because it is most compatible with Active Directory. Non-Microsoft DNS servers can be used, but then it is necessary to make sure they are compatible with Active Directory. Also, non-Microsoft versions of DNS do not offer the DNS replication advantages through Active Directory.

In the following sections, you learn how to install DNS, how to set up zones and services in DNS, and about DNS replication.

Installing DNS Services

DNS is installed as a server role in Windows Server 2016. After you install DNS, you'll need to configure elements in DNS such as zones, as described in the next sections. For optimal results in using DNS, develop a DNS implementation plan (see the section, Creating a DNS Implementation Plan) before you set up DNS in a production environment. Also, if you want to use Active Directory on a network, plan to install DNS at the time you install Active Directory.

Some steps in the activities in this book include bulleted questions for you to answer. Additionally, for all of the activities in this chapter, you'll need an account with Administrator privileges. These activities can be completed on a virtual machine or computer, such as in Hyper-V.

Activity 8-1: Installing DNS

Time Required: Approximately 10 minutes
Objective: Learn how to install DNS.

8

Description: DNS works behind the scenes to help automate network access. In this activity, you use Server Manager to install the DNS role.

If DNS has been installed previously to enable you to install Active Directory, you can remove it now without removing Active Directory (as long as you are on a nonproduction server in a practice environment). To remove it, open Server Manager, click Manage, click Remove Roles and Features, click Next twice, remove the checkmark from the DNS Server box, click Remove Features, click Next twice, click Remove, and click Close. Restart the server. Also, leaving Active Directory installed is advised so that when you create zones, you can specify to store the zones in Active Directory for replication, as you'll see in Activity 8-2.

1. Open **Server Manager**, if it is not already open.
2. Click **Manage** and click **Add Roles and Features**.
3. If you see the Before you begin window, click **Next**.
4. In the Select installation type window, ensure that **Role-based or feature-based installation** is selected. Click **Next**.
5. Be sure your server is selected in the Select destination server window. Click **Next**.
6. Click the check box for **DNS Server**.
7. In the Add Roles and Features Wizard, click **Add Features** (to install the DNS management tool).
8. Click **Next** in the Select server roles window, which should now have a checkmark in the box for DNS Server (see Figure 8-1).
9. Click **Next** in the Select features window.
10. Read the information about the DNS Server role (see Figure 8-2). Click **Next**.
11. Click **Install** in the Confirm installation selections window.
12. Once you verify the installation is successful, click **Close** in the Installation progress window. Leave Server Manager open for the next activity.

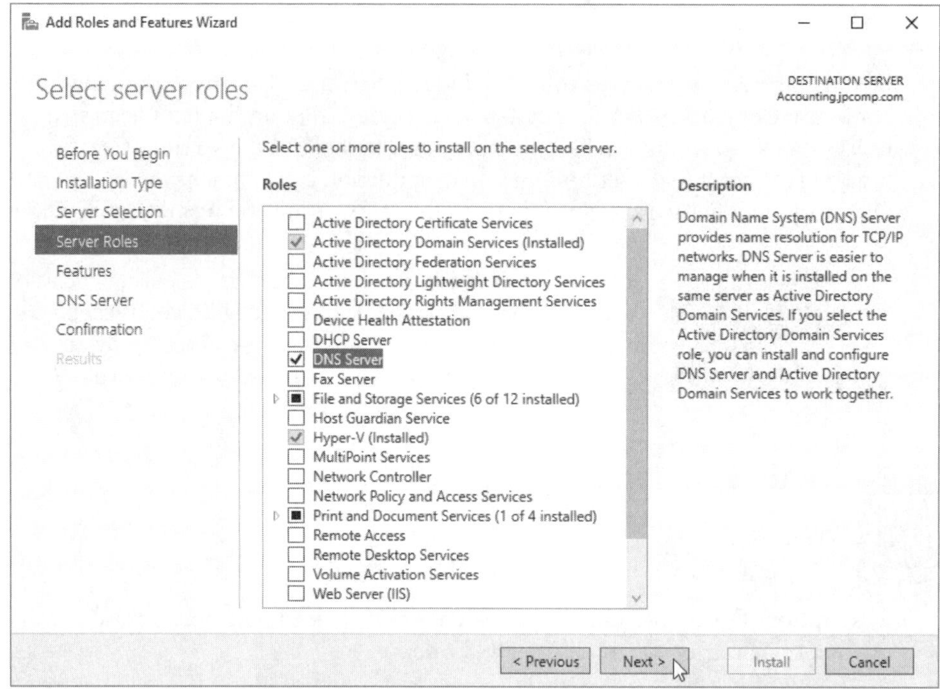

Figure 8-1 Installing the DNS Server role

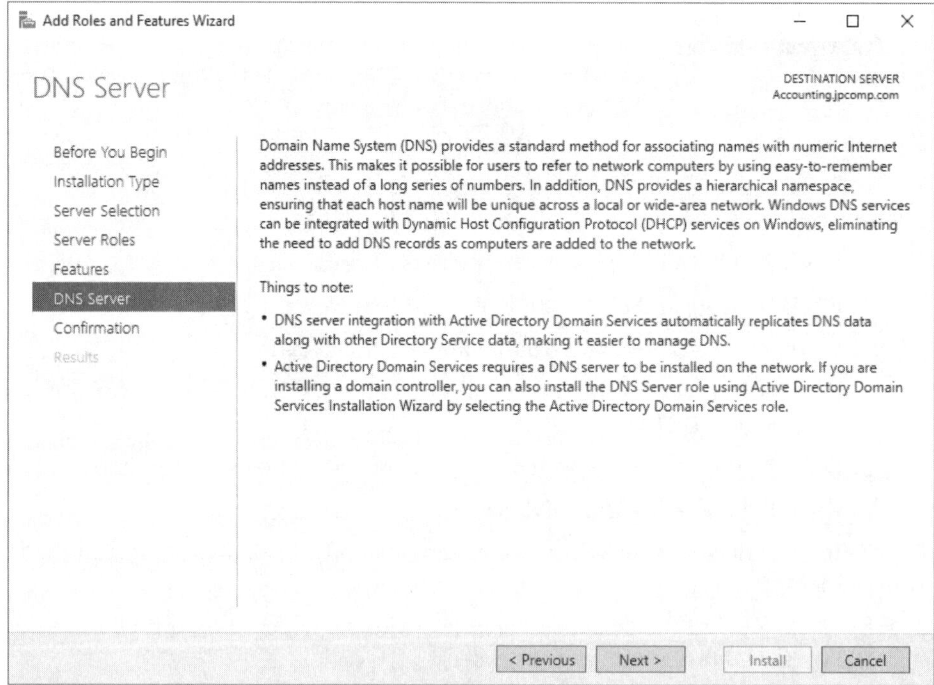

Figure 8-2 Information window for the DNS Server role

DNS Zones

DNS name resolution is enabled through the use of tables of information that link computer names and IP addresses. The tables are associated with partitions in a DNS server that are called **zones** and that contain resource records. Each zone houses tables, called the zone file or zone database, of different types of resource records, such as records that link a computer name to an IP address.

The zone that links computer names to IP addresses is called the **forward lookup zone,** which holds host name records called address records. Each IP-based server and client should have a host record so that it can be found through DNS. For example, if the DNS server name is Accounting, with the IPv4 address 198.51.100.10, then the forward lookup zone maps Accounting to 198.51.100.10. In IPv4, a host record is called a **host address (A) resource record.** IPv6 consists of a 128-bit address (instead of the 32-bit address used with IPv4). An IPv6 record is called an **IPv6 host address (AAAA) resource record.** When you install DNS on a domain controller (DC) in a domain, a forward lookup zone is automatically created for the domain with the DNS server's address record already entered. You must enter the records of other hosts or configure Dynamic Host Configuration Protocol (DHCP) to automatically update the DNS forward lookup zone each time it leases an IP address (you learn more about DHCP in the section of this chapter, Implementing Microsoft DHCP).

Depending on the domain structure and Internet connectivity, a DNS server can have several forward lookup zones, but there should be at least one for the parent domain, such as *jpcomp.com*. Another zone, called the **reverse lookup zone,** holds the **pointer (PTR) resource record,** which contains the IP address-to-host name. The reverse lookup zone is not used as commonly as the forward lookup zone but can be important to create for those instances when a network communication requires associating an IP address to a computer name, such as for monitoring a network using IP address information. Because it is less commonly used, the reverse lookup zone is not automatically configured when DNS is installed. If you anticipate that there will be users who access your network off-site, such as over the Internet, however, plan to implement information in a reverse lookup zone. Table 8-1 summarizes the commonly used resource records in DNS.

8

Table 8-1 DNS resource records

Resource record	Description
Host (A) or (AAAA)	Links a computer or network host name to its IPv4 or IPv6 address
Canonical name (CNAME)	Links an alias to a computer name; sometimes also called common name
Load sharing	Used to spread the load of DNS lookup requests among multiple DNS servers as a way to provide faster resolution for clients and better network response
Mail exchanger (MX)	Provides the IP addresses for Simple Mail Transfer Protocol (SMTP) servers that can accept email for users in a domain
Name server (NS)	Provides information in response to queries about secondary DNS servers for an authoritative server (described later in this section) and information about off-site primary servers that are not authoritative for the domain
Pointer record (PTR)	Associates an IP address to a computer or network host name
Service (SRV) locator	Associates a particular TCP/IP service to a server along with the domain of the server and its protocol
Start of authority (SOA)	Is the first record in a zone and also indicates if this server is authoritative for the current zone
Windows Internet Naming Service (WINS)	Used to forward a lookup request for a NetBIOS name to a Windows Internet Naming Service (retained for pre-Windows 2000 legacy computers, such as early Windows servers that use NetBIOS computer names) server when the host name cannot be found in DNS
Windows Internet Naming Service Reverse (WINS-R)	Used to forward a reverse lookup (IP address to computer name) request to a WINS server

Activity 8-2: Creating a Reverse Lookup Zone

Time Required: Approximately 10 minutes
Objective: Learn how to create a reverse lookup zone.

Description: If you plan to use a reverse lookup zone, create it before DNS forward lookup zone records are created. The reason for this is that when a DNS forward lookup zone record is created, either manually or through dynamic updating, an associated reverse lookup zone PTR record can be created automatically. You create a reverse lookup zone in this activity, and in Activity 8-3 you create a forward lookup zone.

1. Open **Server Manager,** if it is not open.
2. Click **Tools** and click **DNS.**
3. If necessary, in the left pane of DNS Manager click the **right-pointing arrow** in front of your server's name to expand the elements under it (if you don't see the arrow, click the server's name in the left pane first).
4. In the left pane, click **Reverse Lookup Zones** and notice the Add a New Zone display in the right pane. Right-click **Reverse Lookup Zones** in the left pane and click **New Zone** (see Figure 8-3).

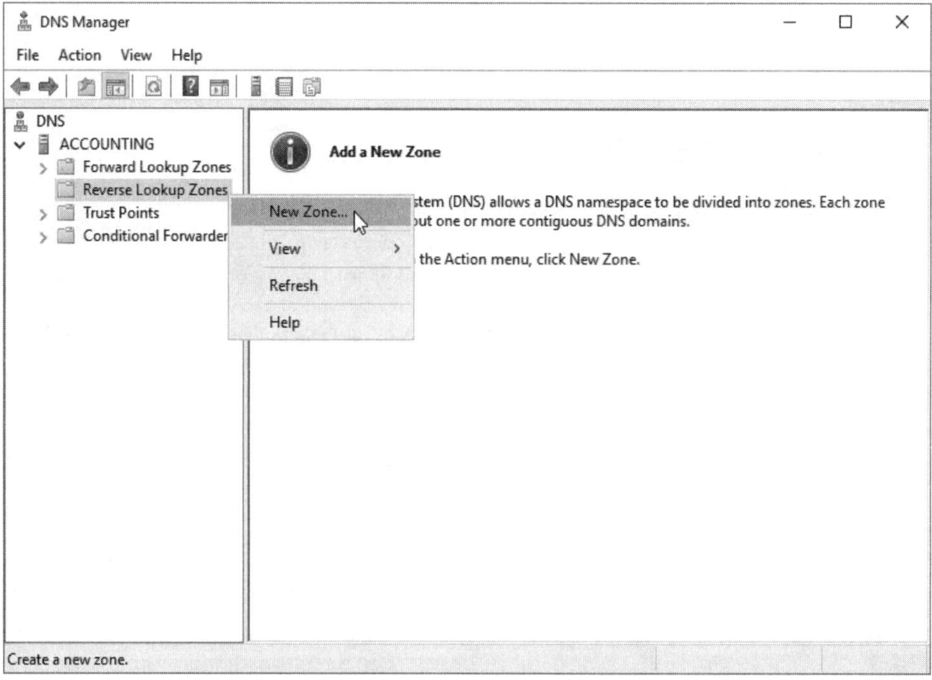

Figure 8-3 Creating a new reverse lookup zone

5. Click **Next** after the New Zone Wizard starts.
6. Notice the zone options that are available (see Figure 8-4) and then ensure that **Primary zone** is selected. Also, ensure the box is checked for **Store the zone in Active Directory (available only if DNS server is a writeable domain controller).** This last option enables the DNS server contents to be replicated to other DNS servers on the network (you learn more about this later in the chapter).

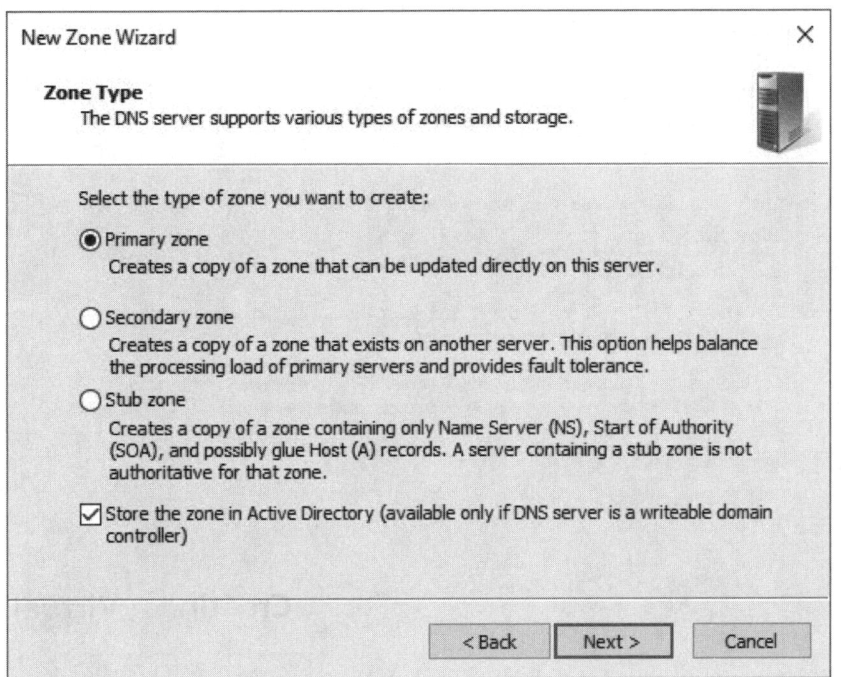

Figure 8-4 Configuring the zone type

When you select the option to Store the zone in Active Directory (available only if DNS server is a writeable domain controller), this means that you are creating an Active Directory Integrated zone, so that the zone data is stored in Active Directory. The benefit is that zone data is replicated when Active Directory is replicated and such zones are afforded Active Directory security. Zone data is also replicated to all new domain controllers.

7. Click **Next.**
8. In the Active Directory Zone Replication Scope window, you can select how the DNS server is replicated through Active Directory. Make sure that **To all DNS servers running on domain controllers in the domain: *domainname*** is selected.
   - What other options are available?
9. Click **Next.**
10. In the next window, you can select whether to create the reverse lookup zone for IPv4 or IPv6. For this activity click (if necessary) **IPv4 Reverse Lookup Zone.** Click **Next.**
11. Enter the network ID of the reverse lookup zone (which is the first two or three octets that identify the network, depending on the subnet mask that you use). This information is used to build the "in-addr.arpa" reverse lookup zone name. For example, if your zone network address is 192.168 then the in-addr.arpa reverse lookup zone is named 168.192.in-addr.arpa. The wizard automatically builds the in-addr.arpa name format when you enter the network address (see Figure 8-5). Click **Next.**

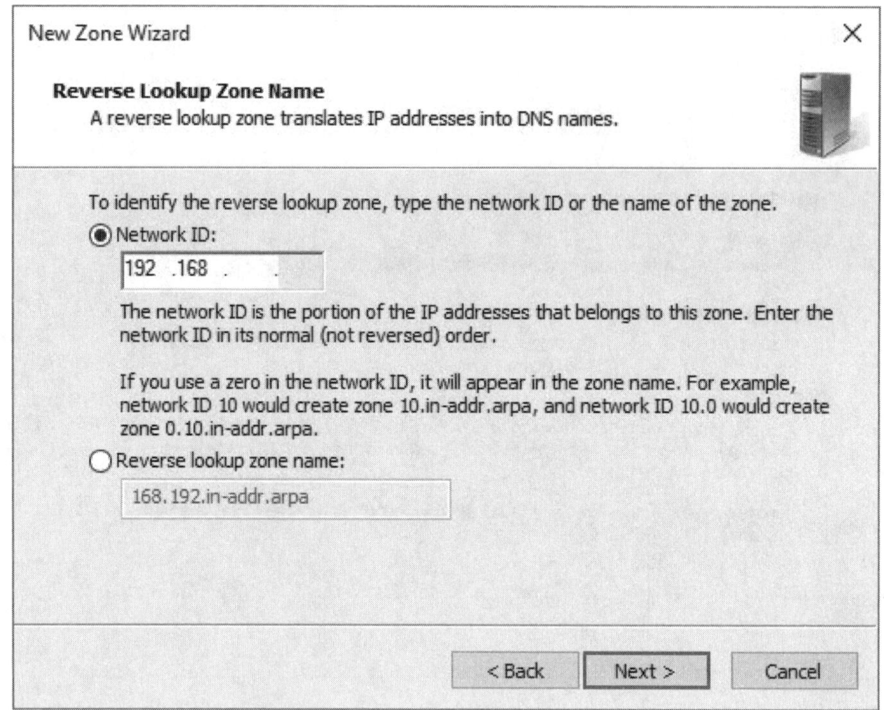

Figure 8-5 Configuring the reverse lookup zone name

12. Configure the security of updates made through DHCP by making sure that **Allow only secure dynamic updates (recommended for Active Directory)** is selected.
    - What other options are available and which option is least secure?
13. Click **Next**.
14. Review the information you have entered and click **Finish**. You should see the new reverse lookup zone displayed in the right pane.
15. Leave DNS Manager open for the next activity. Also, leave Server Manager open for later use.

Activity 8-3: Manually Creating DNS Host Address A Resource Records

Time Required: Approximately 15 minutes
Objective: Create a Host Address A Resource Record.

Description: In this activity, you learn how to configure a Host Address A Resource Record in a forward lookup zone. Obtain the name of a host computer and its IP address from your instructor.

1. Open **DNS** Manager, if it is not still open.
2. Double-click **Forward Lookup Zones** in the tree under the server's name.
3. Double-click the domain name, such as *jpcomp.com* (see Figure 8-6). Notice there is already a Host (A) record for your server in the right pane.

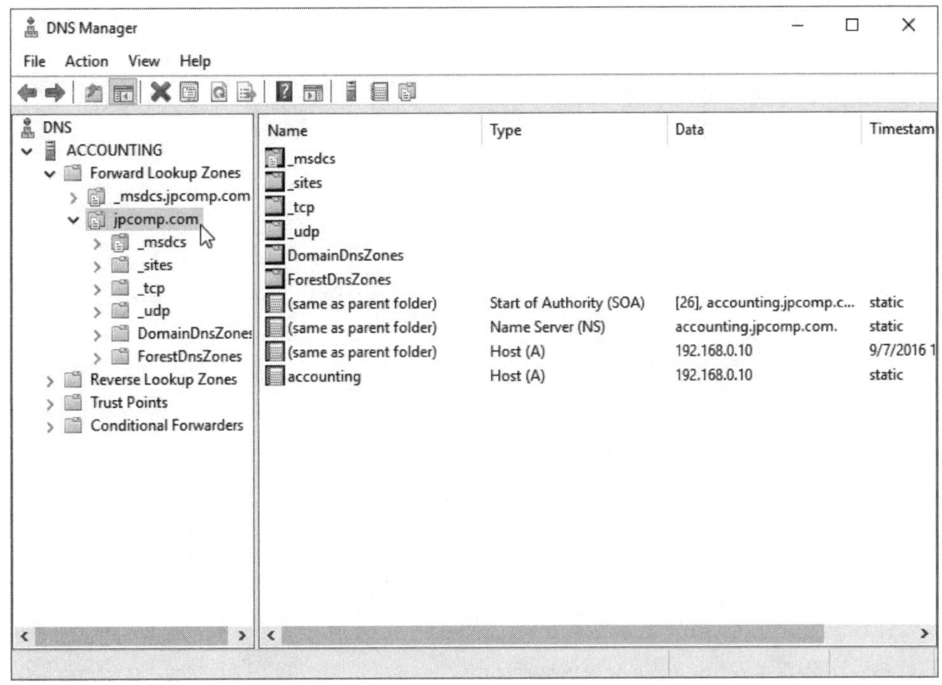

Figure 8-6 Opening the DNS tree

4. Click the **Action** menu.
   - What are the options in this menu?
5. Click **New Host (A or AAAA)**.
6. Enter the name of the host computer, such as **Computer1**, and its IP address, such as **192.168.0.40** in the New Host dialog box.
7. Check the box to **Create associated pointer (PTR)** record (note that the reverse lookup zone must be created first, as in Activity 8-2).
8. Check the box to **Allow any authenticated user to update DNS records with the same owner name** (for computers running Windows 8.1, Windows 10, or Windows Server 2016, for example, that can update in coordination with DHCP; this option also ensures security, because it associates an ACL with the record).
9. Click **Add Host** (see Figure 8-7).
10. Click **OK** when you see the message box that your host record was successfully created.
11. Click **Done**.
12. Leave DNS Manager open for the next activity.

Using the DNS Dynamic Update Protocol

Microsoft DNS is also called **Dynamic DNS (DDNS)**, which is a modern form of DNS that enables client computers and DHCP servers to automatically register IP addresses. The **DNS dynamic update protocol** enables information in a DNS server to be automatically updated in coordination with DHCP. Using the DNS dynamic update protocol can save network

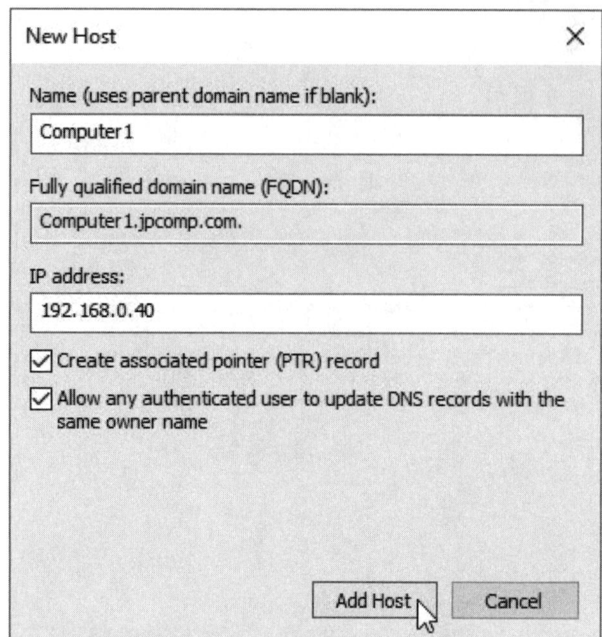

Figure 8-7 Configuring a new host record

administrators a great deal of time, because they no longer have to manually register each new workstation or to register a workstation each time its IP lease is up and a new IP address is issued. After you configure DNS, always make sure that it is configured to use the DNS dynamic update protocol.

Activity 8-4: Verifying the DNS Dynamic Update Configuration

Time Required: Approximately 5 minutes
Objective: Verify that DNS is configured to be dynamically updated using the DNS dynamic update protocol.

Description: In this activity, you make certain that dynamic DNS updating is properly configured. This step is important in two respects. One is to ensure that the workload for the DNS server administrator is reduced and the other is to be sure security is set on dynamic updating.

1. Open **DNS** Manager, if it is not still open.
2. In the left pane under Forward Lookup Zones (expand the tree, if necessary), right-click the domain, such as *jpcomp.com*, and click **Properties**.
3. Make sure that the **General** tab is displayed. In the *Data is stored in Active Directory* section of the dialog box, verify the setting for *Dynamic updates*. The best practice, as shown in Figure 8-8, is for this parameter to be configured as *Secure only*, so that an ACL is associated with a host record (only an authorized client can perform an update). Click the down arrow in the list box to view the other options.
   - What are the other options?
4. Click **OK** in the Properties dialog box for the domain.
5. Close the DNS management tool.

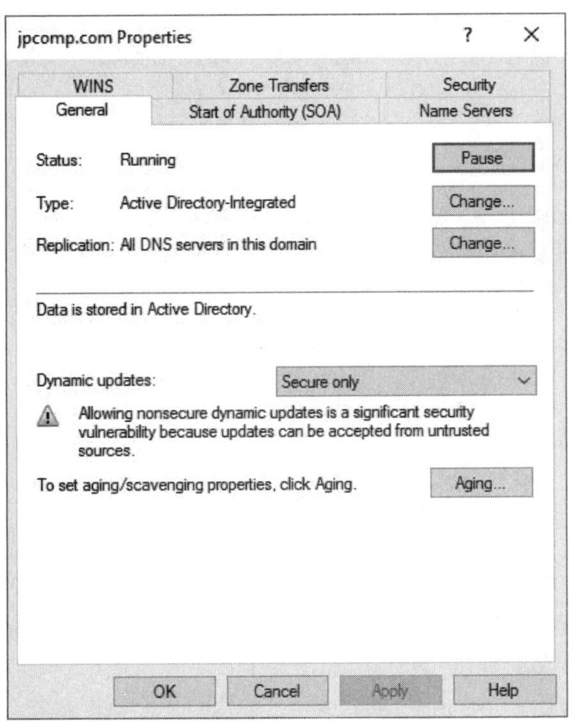

Figure 8-8 Dynamic updates configuration

Keep in mind that the DHCP server must also be configured to perform automatic DNS registration, as you will learn in Activity 8-9.

DNS Replication

DNS servers on a network fall into two broad categories: primary and secondary. A **primary DNS server** is the DNS server that is the main administrative server for a zone and thus is also the *authoritative* server for that zone. For example, when you first create a forward lookup zone on a DNS server for the york.com domain, you create an SOA resource record that identifies that DNS server as authoritative for the domain. This means that all changes to the zone, the creation of address (A) resource records, new SRV resource records, and so on must be made on that DNS server.

You have the option to create one or more backup DNS servers, called **secondary DNS servers**, for a primary DNS server. A secondary DNS server contains a read-only copy of the primary DNS server's zone database, but is not used for administration (is not authoritative). It obtains that copy through a zone transfer over the network. The three vital services performed by secondary DNS servers are:

- To make sure that there is a copy of the primary DNS server's data, in case the primary server fails.
- To enable DNS load balancing (via the load sharing resource records) among a primary DNS server and its secondary servers. Load balancing means that if the DNS primary server is busy performing a name resolution, a different request for a name resolution that is received at the same time can be fielded by a secondary DNS server for faster response to users.
- To reduce congestion in one part of the network by spreading secondary servers to different geographic locations and to different Active Directory sites, yielding faster network response.

One DNS server can be authoritative for multiple domains because it can have multiple zones. Also, because one server can have multiple zones, a single DNS server can be a secondary server for more than one primary server. Plus, one DNS server can be a primary server for one zone and a secondary server for another zone.

If you use Active Directory and have two or more DCs, plan to set up Microsoft DNS services on at least two of the DCs, because the multimaster replication model (see Chapter 4) enables you to replicate DNS information on each DC. The advantage of replicating DNS information is that if one DC that hosts DNS services fails, another DC is available to provide uninterrupted DNS services for the network. This is especially critical on a network that provides Internet access and web-based email services. Whenever you create a zone, as you practiced in Activity 8-2, select the option to *Store the zone in Active Directory (available only if DNS server is a writeable domain controller)* as shown in Figure 8-4, which enables you to take advantage of multimaster replication.

Stub Zone

A **stub zone** has only the bare necessities for DNS functions, which are copies of the following:

- SOA record zone
- Name server (NS) records to identify authoritative servers
- A record for name servers that are authoritative

One common use for a stub zone is to help quickly resolve computer names between two different namespaces by enabling clients in one namespace to instantly find an authoritative server in a different namespace. For example, when two companies with different namespaces such as compA.com and compB.com merge, creating stub zones on DNS servers in each namespace can help clients in one namespace quickly find an authoritative DNS server in the other namespace. This is faster and creates less network traffic than if the client has to query a root name server (one of just a few master servers that look up namespaces) on the Internet, for example. Also, because stub zones are so small, replicating them between DNS servers within a namespace creates negligible network traffic.

You can create a stub zone using the same steps as when you create a primary or secondary zone. The general steps for creating a stub zone are:

1. Open DNS Manager.
2. Right-click the server name in the left pane.
3. Click New Zone to start the New Zone Wizard.
4. Click Next.
5. Click Stub zone (refer to Figure 8-4) and click Next.
6. Follow the guided steps in the New Zone Wizard.

Additional DNS Server Roles

DNS servers can play several specialized roles in addition to or other than those of authoritative/primary or secondary DNS server. For instance, when there are multiple sites (see Chapter 4) or when there is Internet connectivity, it is common to designate one DNS server to forward name resolution requests to a specific remote DNS server. One example of how forwarding works is a set of state community colleges that operate under a community college commission. Each college maintains DNS servers for resolution of addresses within its own namespace. Each college also has designated one on-site DNS server to automatically forward name resolution requests involving another college or the commission. For a name resolution request that involves finding a server at the community college commission, the DNS forwarder server on the college network forwards the resolution request to a DNS server on the commission's network (see Figure 8-9). For example, if a professor at one college needs to access a shared folder offered by a professor at another college, the DNS forwarder server at the first college transfers the resolution request to a DNS server at the other college.

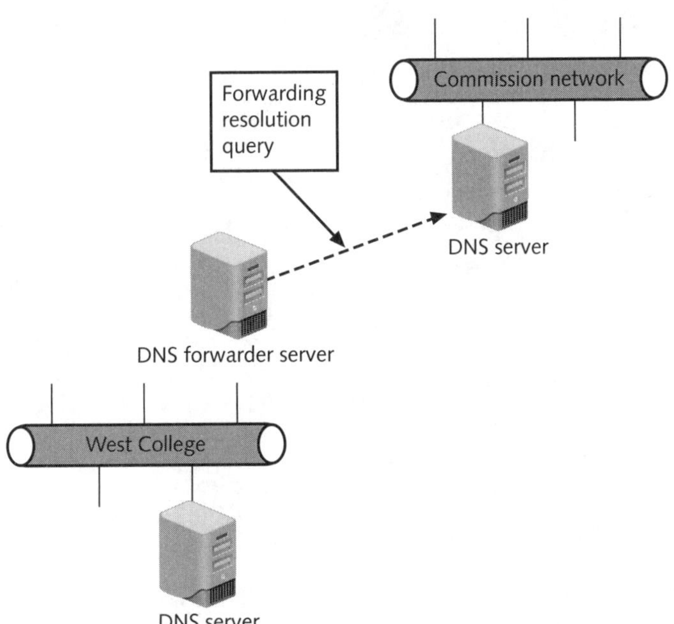

Figure 8-9 DNS forwarder server

When one DNS server is set up as the forwarder, then all other DNS servers that have queries to send to an off-site DNS server send those queries to the single DNS forwarder server. By designating only one DNS forwarder server, you ensure that only one server is sending queries over a site link, instead of having multiple servers sending queries and creating extra traffic over the site link.

DNS forwarding can be set up so that if the DNS server that receives the forwarded request cannot resolve the name, then the server that originally forwarded the request attempts to resolve it. This is called *nonexclusive forwarding*. When DNS forwarding is set so that only the DNS server receiving the request attempts resolution (and not the server that forwarded the request), this is called *exclusive forwarding*. In exclusive forwarding, the DNS server that initially forwards the request is called a *slave DNS server*.

Windows Server 2016 supports the use of root hints, which are similar to forwarders. On a DNS server, a **root hint** is a resource record to enable a DNS server to quickly find an authoritative DNS server in a zone that is not on the DNS server and is used in particular to find an authoritative DNS server on the Internet. When a DNS server receives a query for a domain it does not recognize, it can use the root hint to find that domain on the Internet.

When you configure a DNS server, there are about 15 root hints configured automatically for well-known top-level Internet domains (see Figure 8-10).

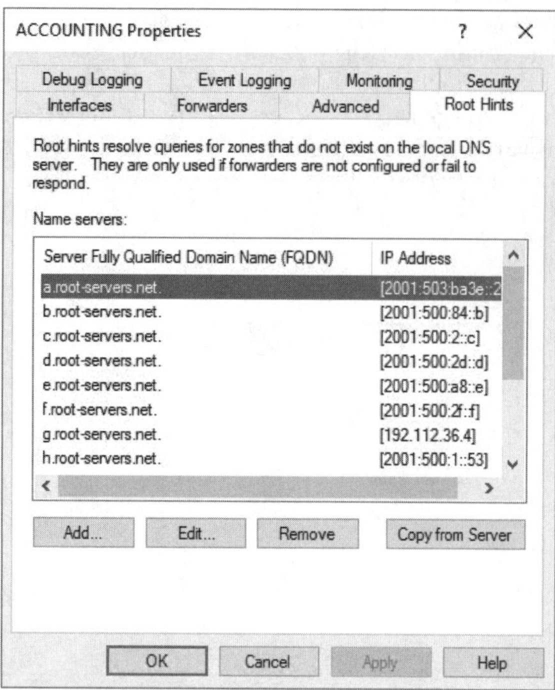

Figure 8-10 Sample pre-configured root hints

It is important for a network to have Internet access prior to configuring a root hint; otherwise, the more root hints you have the more response overhead you create for DNS referrals.

The general steps for configuring forwarders or root hints are as follows:

1. Open DNS Manager.
2. Right-click the server name under DNS in the tree in the left pane.
3. Click Properties.
4. To configure a forwarder in the server Properties dialog box, click the Forwarders tab, click the Edit button (see Figure 8-11), and enter the IP address of the forwarder in the box titled, *IP addresses of forwarding servers*. When you are finished entering the address, click OK in the Edit Forwarders dialog box.
5. To configure a root hint, click the Root Hints tab in the server Properties dialog box (refer to Figure 8-10). Click the Add button and complete the information for the root hint. Click OK in the New Name Server Record dialog box.
6. Click OK in the Properties dialog box for the server when you are finished.
7. Close DNS Manager.

A DNS server can function as a caching server. A **caching server** is used to provide fast queries, because the results of each query are stored in RAM. As more resolution queries are

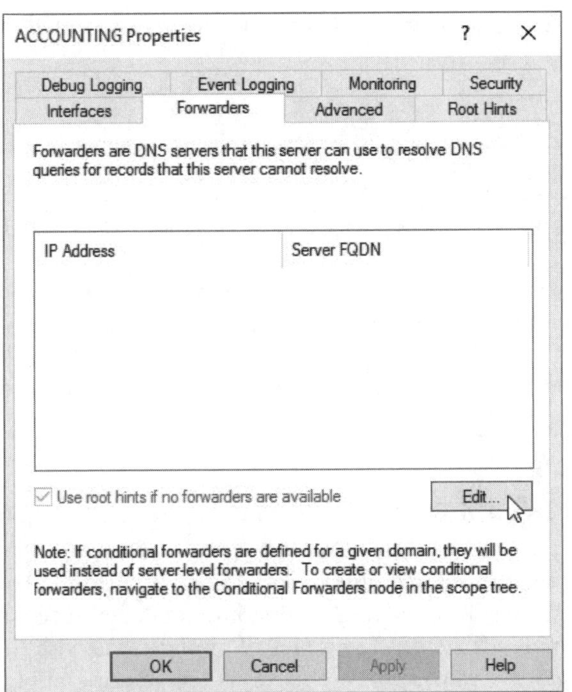

Figure 8-11 Configuring a forwarder

performed, a large set of information is stored in RAM for fast response to users. All DNS servers are also caching servers, but a DNS server without zones is a server that is caching-only. A **caching-only DNS server** queries a primary or secondary DNS server and caches the results to provide a fast response for the next identical query. Caching-only DNS servers are used as a way to reduce the number of secondary DNS servers and therefore reduce the extra network traffic that results because of replicating zones from the primary to the secondary servers. One limitation of using caching-only servers is that it takes time for each one to build up a comprehensive set of resolved names to IP addresses; every time a caching-only server goes down, it must rebuild its information from scratch.

Sometimes it is necessary to flush the DNS server cache, such as when your organization changes IP addressing or a DNS server has been configured incorrectly. The basic steps for clearing the cache are:

1. Open DNS Manager.
2. Right-click the server name in the left pane.
3. Click Clear Cache.

Alternatively, you can open a PowerShell window and use the *Dnscmd /ClearCache* command.

Windows workstation operating systems also cache DNS information, which might be corrupted or incorrect. If Windows 10, for example, is experiencing network or Internet connection problems, you might try clearing DNS cache by entering in the Command Prompt or PowerShell window, *ipconfig /flushdns*.

Table 8-2 summarizes elements of primary, secondary, AD integrated, and caching-only DNS servers.

Table 8-2 DNS server types

DNS server type	Description
Primary	An authoritative DNS server that is used to administer zones, including updating records in zones
Secondary	A DNS server that contains a backup of a primary DNS server and has read-only data
Active Directory Integrated	A primary DNS server that is also a domain controller and that has DNS zones designated to be replicated in Active Directory (and thus replicated to all domain controllers)
Caching-only	A DNS server without zones used to provide fast DNS queries, because query results are stored in RAM

Using DNS to Balance Application Access

Windows Server 2016 DNS offers an effective way to help spread the load for frequently used applications that have their own data sets: DNS round robin. DNS round robin is enabled by default on a Windows DNS server. By spreading the load, users experience faster response and network resources are used more efficiently. Examples of applications with their own data sets include Internet Information Services (IIS) for web servers, accounting applications in a large organization, customer service data sets, and proxy servers.

In **DNS round robin**, resource records are created for two or more servers that have different IP addresses but are associated with the same host name. Consider a situation in which an accounting system in a large organization can be run on an internal private network from any of four servers. The server IP addresses are 192.168.1.20, 192.168.1.21, 192.168.1.22, and 192.168.1.23. The host name assigned as an A or AAAA resource record is Accounting. This host name is associated with each of the four server addresses.

For example, when Client1 wants to access Accounting, that client is directed to the server at IP address 192.168.1.20. When Client2 accesses Accounting, Client2 is directed to the server at 192.168.1.21. The next two clients, Client3 and Client4 are directed to the servers at 192.168.1.22 and 192.168.1.23. Client5 is next connected to the server at 192.168.1.20 (starting from the beginning address in the round robin), Client6 is connected to the server 192.168.1.21, and so on. Through DNS round robin, access is evenly distributed among all four servers. No single server is loaded down with all users while the other servers sit idle. From each client's perspective, server and network response are efficient.

Next, consider a private network that is divided into two subnets, each with its own research server. The server IP addresses are 192.168.1.4 and 192.168.2.4 and both servers use the host name, *www.research.private*. Employing DNS round robin enables you to spread the load between subnets and servers. If you add the *netmask ordering* feature in DNS, this enables you to direct all clients on the 192.168.1 subnet to the server with the IP address 192.168.1.4. Also, clients on the subnet 192.168.2 are directed to the server at 192.168.2.4.

Another way to distribute the load among application servers is to use a Network Load Balancing (NLB) cluster. NLB is two or more computers that users see as a single computer. Each computer in the cluster runs the same application(s). NLB distributes client access requests between each computer in the cluster so that one or two computers do not handle all of the client load. An NLB cluster is a feature installed through Server Manager.

The general steps to configure DNS round robin and netmask ordering are as follows:

1. Open DNS Manager.
2. Right-click the server in the tree.

3. Click Properties.
4. Click the Advanced tab.
5. Ensure that the boxes are checked for *Enable round robin*, *Enable netmask ordering*, and *Secure cache against pollution* (see Figure 8-12).

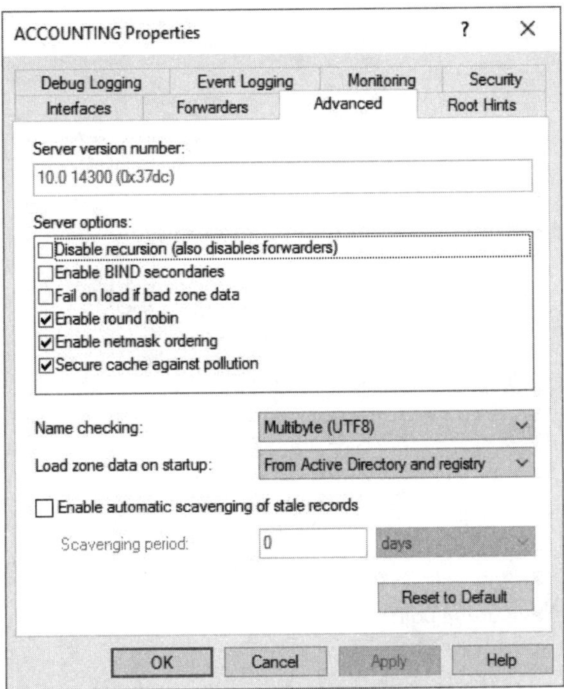

Figure 8-12 Configuring DNS round robin, netmask ordering, and secure cache against pollution

6. Click OK in the Properties dialog box for the server.
7. Close DNS Manager.

Whether or not you choose to use DNS round robin and netmask ordering, plan to make your implementation of DNS secure by using **DNS security extension (DNSSEC)**. DNSSEC ensures that records in all DNS zones use cryptographic digital signing, which is intended to reduce the opportunity for DNS information to be captured and modified by an attacker. Starting with Windows Server 2012, DNSSEC can be used with DNS dynamic updates. You can enable DNSSEC and configure DNSSEC settings as a group policy. Group policy is explained in Chapter 10, Securing Windows Server 2016. The general steps to enable DNSSEC through a group policy are (you may want to become familiar with group policy in Chapter 10 before trying these steps):

1. Right-click Start and click Run.
2. Enter MMC and click OK.
3. In the Console1—(Console Root) window, click File and click Add/Remove Snap-in.
4. Under Available snap-ins, double-click Group Policy Management Editor (the second Group Policy selection listed).
5. In the Select Group Policy Object dialog box, click Browse, select Default Domain Policy, and click OK. Click Finish.
6. Click OK in the Add or Remove Snap-ins dialog box.
7. Expanded the tree in the left pane to display Console Root\Default Domain Policy [*domainname*]\Computer Configuration\Policies\Windows Settings\Name Resolution Policy.

8

8. If necessary, click Name Resolution Policy in the left pane to see the Name Resolution Policy options in the middle pane.
9. Ensure the DNSSEC tab is displayed in the middle pane (see Figure 8-13).

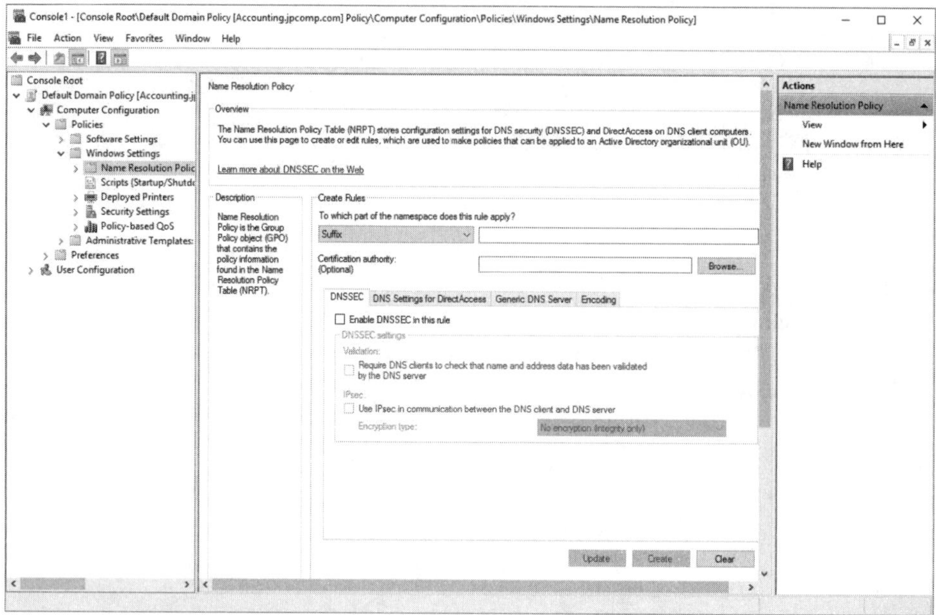

Figure 8-13 Configuring DNSSEC as a group policy

10. Specify the namespace and other information in the middle pane. Place a checkmark in the box for Enable DNSSEC in this rule and select the validation method.
11. Click the Update button in the middle pane (you may need to scroll down to see the Update button).
12. Close the Console1 window. Click No to save your settings.

Creating a DNS Implementation Plan

When you plan DNS implementation, consider the following best practices recommendations:

- Implement Windows Server 2016 DNS servers instead of other versions of DNS, if possible, and use Active Directory. The advantage is that the DNS servers, like the DCs, exist in a multimaster relationship. The multimaster relationship reduces the need to use caching servers because DNS zone transfers from DNS server to DNS server occur as a built-in process along with normal DC replication. Also, when you use Windows Server 2016 DNS server, you can take advantage of dynamic DNS updating, which will save you time as an administrator and make your DNS A, AAAA, and PTR resource records more accurate.
- The resource records and zones that can be set up for IPv4 can also be set up for IPv6. It also supports multimaster relationships when used with Active Directory. Dynamic DNS updating is additionally available for IPv6. (If you haven't started using IPv6, start working as soon as feasible on a plan to convert to IPv6 and include DNS and DHCP preparations in your plan.)
- Consider using namespaces to represent natural organizational boundaries, such as geographical, divisional, or departmental boundaries.

- Make sure the DNS servers on a private network are well secured in terms of Windows Server 2016 security options and physically in terms of where they are located and protected.
- Plan to locate a DNS server across most site links (see Chapter 4), just as you would locate DCs. The exceptions may be when there are not enough users across certain site links or when the site links are very reliable, high-speed links.
- Just as you should create two or more DCs per domain, also create two or more DNS servers to take advantage of the load balancing, the multimaster relationships, and the fault tolerance.
- When you have off-site links between different domains, designate one DNS server as a forwarder to reduce traffic over those links.
- The number of DNS servers that you set up can be related to your analysis of an organization. For example, an organization that is centralized will typically have fewer domains and, therefore, fewer DNS servers and DNS server administrators. An organization that is decentralized will likely have more domains, DNS servers, and DNS server administrators.
- If a branch location with a read-only domain controller (RODC) needs local DNS services because there are many users (say over 20 or 30 users), make the RODC a secondary DNS server and not a primary DNS server. This can speed up name resolution while also providing DNS backup services when a primary DNS server is overloaded or down. It also provides better security for DNS services.
- If you have multiple servers used for one application, such as for web access or accounting software, use DNS round robin to distribute the load.

DNS Enhancements in Windows Server 2016

The DNS role has several new enhancements in Windows Server 2016. Among the enhancements are DNS group policies, as you learned about in configuring DNSSEC. These group policies enable you to configure DNS settings in one domain, specific domains, or in all domains. Group policies are particularly important for establishing consistent security, as you learn in Chapter 10. There are now group policies for:

- Filtering malicious IP addresses and redirecting malicious clients to a dead end rather than to the computer they want to reach
- Redirecting clients to specific data sources or servers according to the time of day
- Managing client access to account for high traffic situations
- Directing clients to the best source for a specific application

Another enhancement is the ability for DNS to work with client computers that have more than one NIC. Further, for those who like using PowerShell to configure a server, Microsoft has added new cmdlets and new cmdlet parameters for configuring DNS.

Troubleshooting DNS

If DNS is installed, but is not resolving names or does not seem to be working, there are many steps you can take to troubleshoot the problem, such as restarting the DNS Server and DNS Client services. Another step is to check for the most recent log errors relating to DNS. Activity 8-5 shows you how to restart the DNS Server and Client services, and Activity 8-6 shows you how to check for DNS errors in the log information kept by Windows Server 2016. Also, Table 8-3 presents a full range of troubleshooting tips.

Table 8-3 **Troubleshooting DNS server problems**

DNS server problem	Solutions
DNS server is not responding with the correct information to DNS queries from clients.	Ensure that Dynamic DNS is enabled and configured correctly. Check manually added DNS host address records for accuracy. If the errors are related to one client, check the DNS client computer to ensure it is working correctly, including that the NIC and its driver are working correctly.
Users can contact the DNS server, but receive a permission denied message when trying to read DNS records.	Ensure that users have permission to read the DNS records, open DNS Manager, right-click the domain in the tree, click Properties, click the Security tab, and ensure that the Everyone group (and other general user groups) has *Allow* checked for the Read permission.
Users cannot access the DNS server.	Check the DNS server's connection to the network to ensure it is live on the network.
Users can access the DNS server, but DNS record information is not being processed.	Ensure that the DNS Server and DNS Client services are started and set to start automatically when the server is booted.
You have installed an update to the DNS server, but DNS response to clients is experiencing errors.	Reload the DNS server database, open the DNS tool, click the domain in the tree under Forward Lookup Zones, click the Action menu, and click Reload to reload the database.

Activity 8-5: Checking the DNS Server and DNS Client Services

Time Required: Approximately 5 minutes
Objective: Verify that the DNS Server and Client services are started.

Description: One troubleshooting tool for DNS is to ensure that the DNS Client and Server services are started. The DNS Client service enables DNS name queries to be cached. The DNS Server service enables name queries to be resolved and it enables dynamic DNS updating. You learn how to verify these services in this activity.

1. Open **Server Manager**, if it isn't open.
2. Click **Tools** and click **Services**.
3. Ensure the **Standard** tab is selected in the right pane of the Services window.
4. Scroll to find DNS Client and DNS Server.
5. Look under the Status column and determine if the DNS Client and DNS Server services are running (see Figure 8-14).
6. Double-click **DNS Client** in the right pane.
7. Ensure that *Startup type* is set to **Automatic**.
8. To stop and restart the service, click the **Stop** button, as shown in Figure 8-15 (unless the service is already stopped).
9. Click the **Start** button.
10. Click **OK**.
11. Double-click **DNS Server** in the middle pane.
12. Make sure that *Startup type* is set to **Automatic**.
13. To stop and restart the service, click the **Stop** button (unless the service is already stopped).
14. Click the **Start** button.
15. Click **OK**.
16. Close the Services window, but leave the Server Manager window open for the next activity.

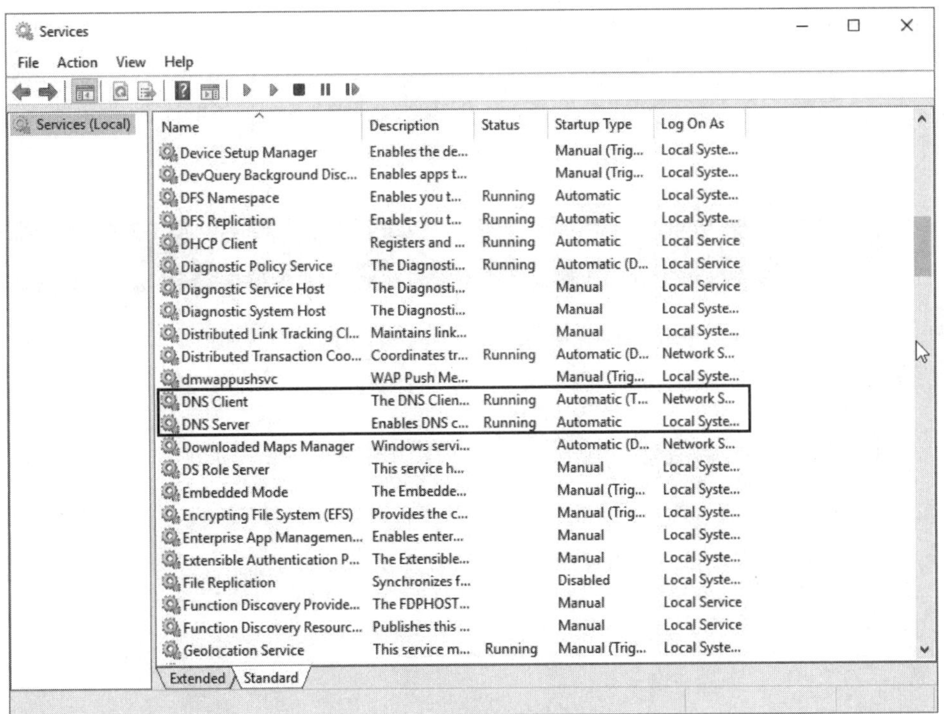

Figure 8-14 Viewing the status of the DNS Client and DNS Server services

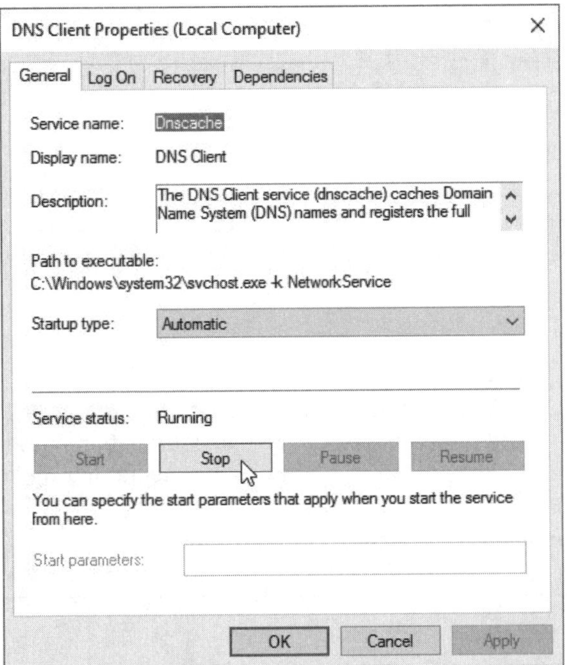

Figure 8-15 Stopping the DNS Client service

Activity 8-6: Checking Log Entries for DNS

Time Required: Approximately 10 minutes

Objective: Check the log information about possible DNS errors.

Description: You can use Server Manager to check the log information for any of the roles you have installed, including the DNS server role. In this activity, you check the most recent log entries for DNS services.

1. Open **Server Manager**, if it is not already open.
2. In the left pane, click **DNS**.
3. Scroll the right pane to view the EVENTS box (see Figure 8-16).

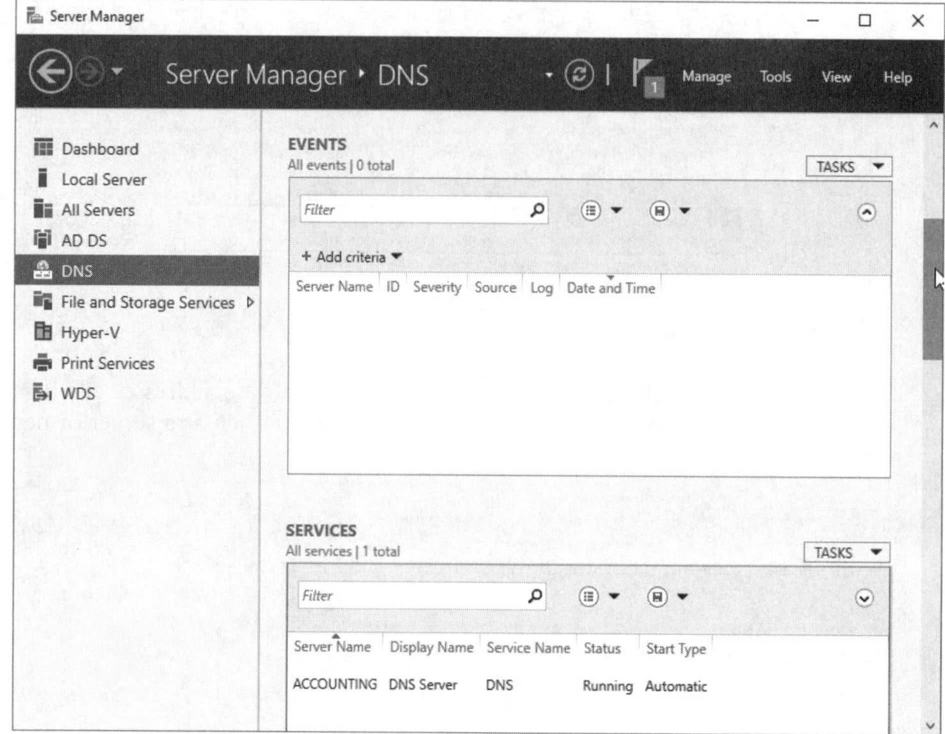

Figure 8-16 Checking for warning and error information for DNS in the EVENTS section

4. Notice if there are any errors reported in the EVENTS box. If you see an error, notice the severity, such as a warning. Double-click the error to view information about it.
5. Click the back arrow near the top of Server Manager to go back to the main display. Leave Server Manager open for the next activity.

In Chapter 12, Managing System Reliability and Availability, you learn about using the Event Viewer to see the information in the Windows Server 2016 logs for troubleshooting and monitoring the status of a server.

Implementing Microsoft DHCP

Dynamic Host Configuration Protocol (DHCP) enables a Windows Server 2016 server with DHCP services to detect the presence of a new workstation and assign an IP address to that workstation. This capability enables a network or server administrator to save hours of time by not having to keep track of IP addresses on a network and assign specific addresses to users and network devices. As you learned in Chapter 1, DHCP also saves users time because they don't have to configure their own IP addresses—DHCP can do this for them. When you set up a Windows 7, Windows 8/8.1, or Windows 10 client to automatically obtain an IP address, the client contacts a DHCP server to obtain that address. The DHCP server has a preassigned range of IP addresses that it can give to a new client. Each address is assigned for a specific period of time, such as eight hours, two weeks, a month, a year, or even permanently. A range of contiguous addresses is called the **scope**.

A Windows Server 2016 server can be configured in the role of a DHCP server using Microsoft DHCP services. When you set up a Microsoft DHCP server, you have the option to set it up to automatically register forward and reverse lookup zone records with a Microsoft DNS server. The DHCP server automatically updates the DNS server at the time it assigns an IP address. Using dynamic DNS updates can significantly save time in creating DNS lookup zone records. Further, a Microsoft DHCP server can be configured to dynamically register only address (A or AAAA) records—in cases where the DNS reverse lookup zone is not configured in DNS—or both address and PTR records.

Besides dynamic updating, a Microsoft DHCP server can:

- Reserve an IP address for a specific computer, such as for a server (servers should always use the same IP address to avoid network confusion).
- Update all computers on a network for a particular change in DHCP settings, which eliminates the need to manually update the computers.
- Provide DHCP services to multiple subnetworks (subnets), as long as routers can forward DHCP requests (routers should be compatible with RFCs 1541 and 1542, specifications that affect routing DHCP).
- Exclude certain IP addresses from a scope, so that these addresses can be used manually or statically set up on a particular computer or device, such as a server or network printer.

8

Importantly, you can configure DHCP failover for redundancy. DHCP failover consists of configuring two DHCP servers to lease IP addresses using the same subnet or scope. DHCP data is replicated between the two DHCP servers so that if one goes down, clients can still use the remaining live DHCP server. When you configure two DHCP servers for failover, you can also configure to use load-balancing so the two DHCP servers equalize the load, giving faster service to clients.

Multiple scopes are supported in a single Microsoft DHCP server because it is often necessary to assign different address ranges. You can accomplish this by creating two scopes, such as one range that is 192.168.10.1 to 192.168.10.122 and another that is 192.168.20.10 to 192.168.20.182. As this example illustrates, you can assign address ranges to reflect the network subnet structure or other network divisions. Alternatively, to consolidate management of scopes you can create one scope using the combined range of 192.168.10.1 to 192.168.20.182, and then exclude a range of addresses from within the scope.

If your network has Internet connectivity, make sure you obtain public IP address ranges from your Internet service provider, so that you use addresses that are specifically assigned to your organization and recognized as valid by the Internet community. Private networks use the address ranges of 10.0.0.0 to 10.255.255.255, 172.16.0.0 to 172.31.255.255, or 192.168.0.0 to 192.168.255.255 (see Chapter 1, Introduction to Windows Server 2016).

The installation steps for DHCP are similar to those for DNS, because both are installed as Windows Server 2016 roles.

Activity 8-7: Installing DHCP

Time Required: Approximately 15 minutes
Objective: Learn how to install the DHCP role.

Description: DHCP is installed as a server role in Windows Server 2016 using Server Manager. In this activity, you install DHCP.

1. Open **Server Manager**, if necessary.
2. Click **Manage** and click **Add Roles and Features**.
3. If you see the Before you begin window, click **Next**.
4. Make sure that **Role-based or feature-based installation** is selected in the Select installation type window. Click **Next**.

5. In the Select destination server window, ensure your server is selected and click **Next.**
6. Click the box for **DHCP Server** in the Select server roles window.
7. Click **Add Features** in the Add Roles and Features Wizard box (to install the DHCP management tool).
8. Click **Next** in the Select server roles window.
9. Click **Next** in the Select features window.
10. In the DHCP Server window (see Figure 8-17), read the information. Note the best practices advice to configure at least one static IP address for the DHCP server and to create and store a plan for subnets, scopes, and exclusions. Click **Next.**

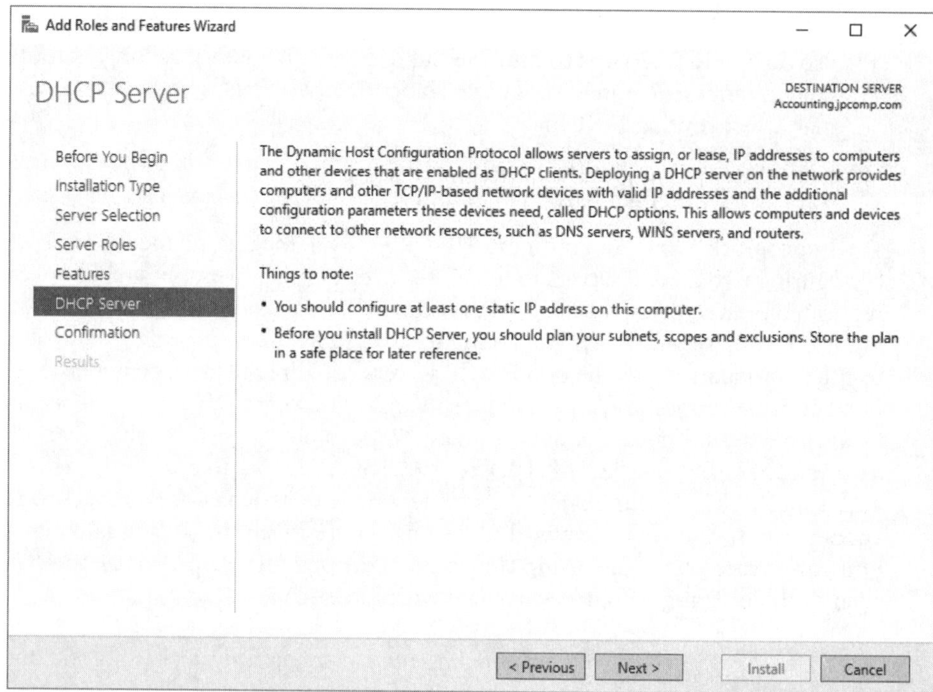

Figure 8-17 DHCP Server information window

11. Click **Install** in the Confirm installation selections window.
12. Click **Close.**
13. Leave Server Manager open.

Configuring a DHCP Server

After DHCP is installed, it is necessary to configure the DHCP server. First, set up one or more scopes of contiguous address ranges and activate each scope. Configuring a scope includes the following:

- Obtain the range of addresses to be used.
- Determine the subnet mask for the range of addresses.
- Decide on a name for the scope, such as naming it to reflect the name of a department or division in your organization.
- Decide how long to lease IP addresses.
- Determine whether to exclude specific addresses.

Second, authorize the DHCP server. The process of authorizing the server is a security precaution to make sure IP addresses are only assigned by DHCP servers that are managed by network and server administrators. The security is needed because it is critical for IP address leasing to be carefully managed through ensuring that only valid IP addresses are used and that there is no possibility that duplicate IP addresses can be leased. DHCP servers that are not authorized are prevented from running on a network.

Third, a step that is not required, but that saves time in managing DNS, is to configure the DHCP server and its clients to automatically update DNS records.

Only domain controllers and member servers can be authorized as DHCP servers when Active Directory is in use on the network. If Active Directory is not implemented, a standalone server can be authorized.

Activity 8-8: Configuring DHCP Scopes

Time Required: Approximately 15 minutes
Objective: Learn how to configure a DHCP scope.

Description: In this activity, you practice configuring a scope on a DHCP server. Before you start, obtain the address or computer name of a DNS server from your instructor (or use the address of this computer) and ask for a range of addresses for the scope, plus an address to exclude from the scope. You will also need to know the subnet mask. In the later steps of the activity you ensure that the DHCP server is authorized.

1. If necessary, open **Server Manager**.
2. Click **Tools** and click **DHCP**.
3. In the tree in the left pane of the DHCP window, double-click the name of the server under DHCP, such as *accounting* (or click the right-pointing arrow in front of the server name), to view IPv4 and IPv6 listed under the server name.
4. In the left pane, click **IPv4** to view the configuration information in the middle pane. Right-click **IPv4** and click **New Scope** (see Figure 8-18).

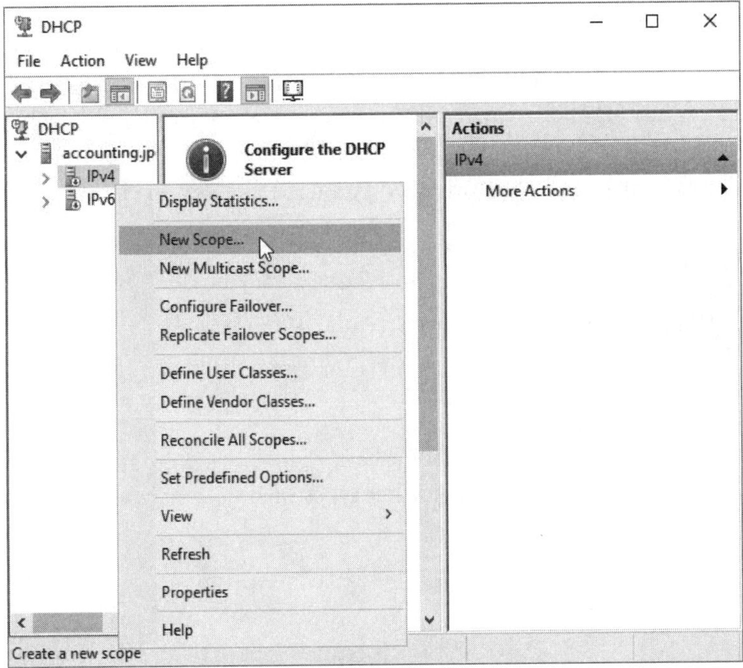

Figure 8-18 Configuring a new scope

5. Click **Next** after the New Scope Wizard starts.
6. Enter a name for the scope so it is easy for you to identify as you maintain it, such as Administration plus your initials (AdministrationJR), and enter a description for the scope, such as Admin area subnet. Click **Next**.
7. Enter the start and end IP addresses, such as 198.51.100.51 and 198.51.100.99. To go from field to field, press the period key (when you enter fewer than three numbers). If necessary, enter the subnet mask, such as 255.255.255.0 (see Figure 8-19). Click **Next**.

You can safely use the address range 198.51.100.51 through 198.51.100.99 for practice in this activity, because this is in the range reserved for documentation or practice uses.

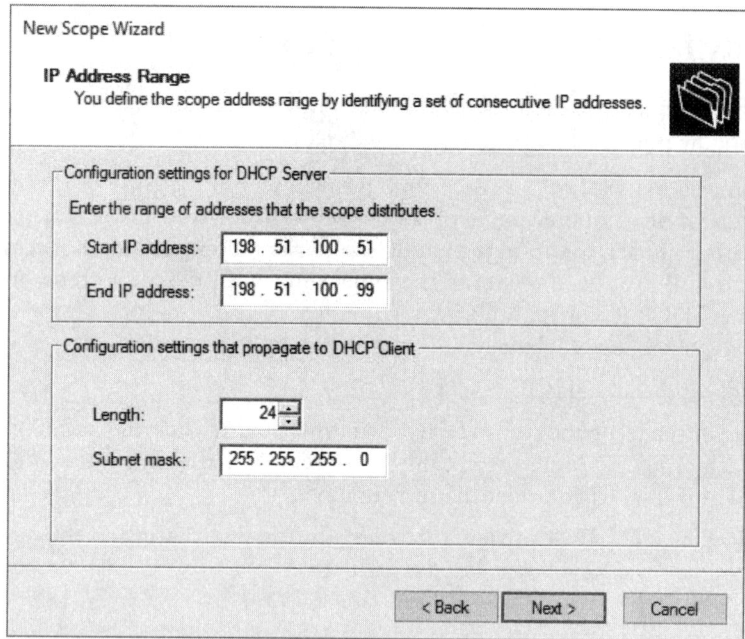

Figure 8-19 Establishing the IP address range

8. In the Add Exclusions and Delay window, enter an address to exclude, such as 198.51.100.70, in the Start IP address box and click **Add**.
   - What happens after you click Add? Do you need to enter an ending address?

When you statically assign IP addresses to servers on a network, use this feature to exclude those addresses from the DHCP address pool.

9. Click **Next**.
10. You can now configure the lease duration.
    - What is the default lease time? For what types of situations would this default be appropriate?

11. Change the default lease time to **16 days**. Click **Next**.
12. Ensure that **Yes, I want to configure these options now** is selected and click **Next**.
13. The next dialog box offers the ability to enter an IP address for a router (default gateway). You would configure this information if access to the addresses in this scope is through a router (default gateway). Click **Next**.
14. Enter the parent domain in which DNS name resolution will occur, such as *jpcomp.com* (your domain will be entered by default, but you can change it). Enter the name of the DNS server (check with your instructor or use the DNS server you have already set up) and click **Resolve**, or enter the DNS server's IP address. Click **Add** (unless the IP address is already displayed by default).
    - How would you enter more than one DNS server?
15. Click **Next**.
16. In the next dialog box, you can enter the names and IP addresses of WINS servers. This would be used on networks that have old Windows Server computers in which NetBIOS naming is used and so that these names can be mapped to IP addresses. (Entering the name of your WINS server is optional. If you do, click Resolve and then click Add.) Click **Next**. (If you see the WINS Servers dialog box, click **Next**.)
17. Ensure that **Yes, I want to activate this scope now** is selected and then click **Next** (or click **Cancel** if you do not have permission from your instructor to finish creating the scope).
18. Click **Finish**.
    - What now appears in the middle pane of the DHCP window? (You may need to select **Address Pool** in the left pane under Scope to view this.)
19. Your server may be authorized by default, but you will likely have to authorize it. You can verify this by right-clicking the server name in the tree. If you see the menu option *Unauthorize*, this means your server is already authorized and you should click an open space to close the menu. If instead you see *Authorize* in the menu, click this option to authorize the server.
20. Leave the DHCP window open for the next activity. Also, leave Server Manager open.

When it is installed, a DHCP server is automatically configured to register IP addresses at the DNS server, but you must also provide the DNS server's IP addresses when you configure each scope. Also, you can manually configure automatic DNS registration through a DHCP server, as you learn in the next activity.

Activity 8-9: Configuring Automatic DNS Registration

Time Required: Approximately 10 minutes
Objective: Verify that a DHCP server is configured to automatically register IP addresses with a DNS server.

Description: In this activity, you verify that the DHCP server you have configured is set up to automatically register with a DNS server the IP addresses that it leases and that it is configured for the types of clients on your network.

1. Open the **DHCP** tool, if it is not still open.
2. Ensure the server in the left pane is expanded to show the elements under it.
3. Double-click **IPv4** to select it.

4. Right-click **IPv4** and then click **Properties**.
5. Click the **DNS** tab (see Figure 8-20) and make sure that the box for **Enable DNS dynamic updates according to the settings below** is checked. Clients running the Windows 7, 8/8.1, 10, Server 2012/R2, and Server 2016 operating systems can request to update a DNS server. Ensure **Dynamically update DNS records only if requested by the DHCP clients** is selected. If older operating systems are connecting to the network, such as Windows 98 or Windows 95, which do not request to update a DNS server, click instead **Always dynamically update DNS records**—which means that the DHCP server takes the responsibility to update the DNS server's records every time a client obtains the IP address. Also, make sure that **Discard A and PTR records when lease is deleted** is checked, so that the DHCP server alerts the DNS server to delete a record each time a lease is up. If some older clients are running Windows 95, 98, and NT (unlikely but possible), also check **Dynamically update DNS records for DHCP clients that do not request updates (for example, clients running Windows NT 4.0)**.

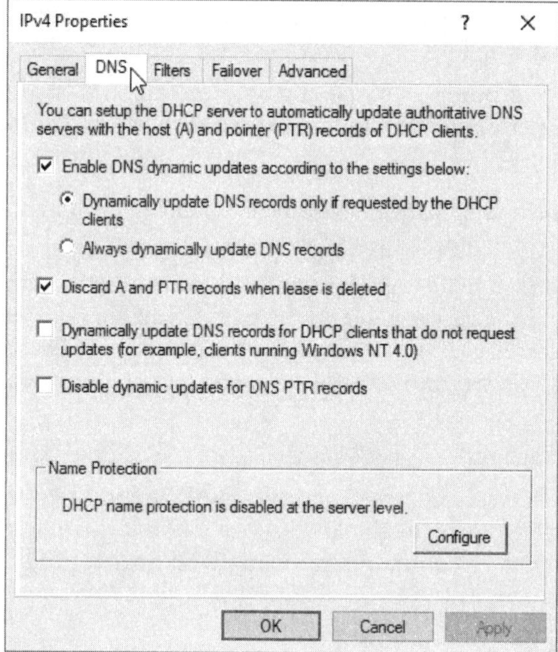

Figure 8-20 Configuring dynamic updates

6. Click **OK**.
7. Close the DHCP window.

Lease Times

Set the duration of a DHCP lease on the basis of the type of connection. In terms of best practices, Microsoft recommends the following:

- If you have a small network with no routers, a lease of 8 days or less is appropriate. On this type of network, you have less worry about extra traffic created by frequent contact with the DHCP server that also houses other resources.
- On a network with one or more routers, a larger number of clients, and client computers that generally stay put, set leases to expire after a longer period, such as from 16 to 24 days. This longer period helps to reduce extra traffic related to DHCP activity.

- On a network that has a large percentage of mobile devices, such as laptop and tablet computers, set leases to expire after the duration of the communication session, such as 8–24 hours for situations, such as when mobile workers are in the office for a day or two. Alternatively, consider 1–8 hours for high turnover of mobile users, such as in a library, doctor's office, or coffee shop.

Although not related to lease time, you should also consider that a DHCP server can have periods of high disk access activity when addressing requests for multiple resources, depending on the server. Employ storage solutions that provide faster disk access, such as traditional RAID level 5 or a disk storage pool using parity (see Chapter 7, Configuring and Managing Data Storage). Also, regularly optimize (defragment) magnetic disks.

DHCPv6 Support

Windows Server 2016 and Windows 10 both enable a network to use **Dynamic Host Configuration Protocol for IPv6 (DHCPv6)** for networks that are using IPv6. The Windows Server 2016 and Windows 10 implementation of DHCPv6 follows the official standard for DHCPv6 (as defined in Request for Comment 3315). The Microsoft implementation of DHCPv6 supports both stateful and stateless autoconfiguration.

Stateful autoconfiguration means that the computer or network device using IPv6 contacts a DHCP server for a leased address. In **stateless autoconfiguration**, the computer or network device assigns its own IPv6 address, which is constructed from the MAC address of its NIC (see Chapter 1) combined with the subnet designation obtained from communication with a router. Stateless autoconfiguration of an IPv6 address does not require a DHCP server but is included in the DHCPv6 standard for compliance with IPv6 capabilities.

To configure a DHCP scope for IPv6, right-click IPv6 in the tree in the DHCP tool, click New Scope, and follow the steps for configuring DHCP. To configure an IPv6 scope you will need:

- Name of the scope and description
- The prefix, such as 2001:db8::/32
- Start and end IPv6 addresses
- Address to be in the excluded range
- Lease time information
- Whether to activate the scope at the time it is configured

Activity 8-10: Configuring IPv6 to Use DHCP in a Client

Time Required: Approximately 10 minutes
Objective: Configure a client to obtain its IPv6 address from a DHCP server.

Description: A network connected computer can be configured to use an IPv6 address. In this activity, you use the autoconfiguration capability of IPv6 to configure an IPv6 address. In Step 5, if your network has a DHCPv6 server, then the client will obtain the IPv6 address from that server using stateful autoconfiguration. If there is no DHCPv6 server on the network, the client will configure its own IPv6 address using stateless autoconfiguration. The following steps can be used in Windows Server 2016, Windows 10, and Windows 8.1.

1. Right-click the **Start** button and click **Network Connections**.
2. In the Network Connections window, double-click the connection, such as **Wi-Fi** or **Ethernet**.
3. In the Status dialog box for the network connection, click **Properties**.

4. Under *This connection uses the following items:* in the Properties dialog box for the network connection, ensure that the box is checked for **Internet Protocol Version 6 (TCP/IPv6)**. Double-click **Internet Protocol Version 6 (TCP/IPv6)**.
5. In the Internet Protocol Version 6 (TCP/IPv6) Properties dialog box, select **Obtain an IPv6 address automatically** as in Figure 8-21. (This selection is the default.) Also, specify whether to **Obtain DNS server address automatically** or to **Use the following DNS server address** (the second selection requires you to enter the preferred and alternate DNS server addresses). Click **OK**.
   - How would you configure IPv4 to use DHCP?

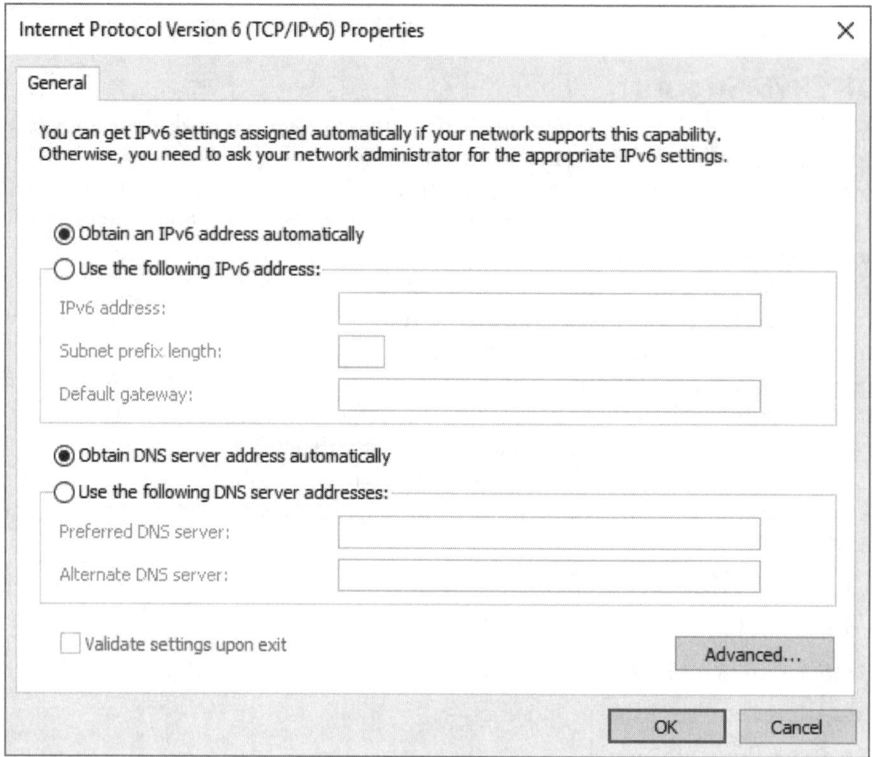

Figure 8-21 Selecting to obtain an IPv6 address automatically

6. Click **OK** in the Properties dialog box for the network connection.
7. Click **Close** in the Status dialog box for the network connection.
8. Close the Network Connections window.

Troubleshooting DHCP

When you set up a DHCP server, some problems may occur, such as the server stopping or not working, creating extra network traffic, or not automatically registering with DNS servers. Table 8-4 presents several typical problems and their resolutions.

Table 8-4 Troubleshooting a DHCP server

DHCP server problem	Solutions
The DHCP server will not start.	Use the Services tool to make sure that the DHCP Client and DHCP Server services are started and set to start automatically. If the DHCP Server service will not start, make sure that the COM+ Event System, Remote Procedure Call (RPC), Security Accounts Manager, TCP/IP Protocol Driver, and Windows Event Log services are already started, because the DHCP Server service depends on these services. Make sure that the DHCP server is authorized. Use Server Manager or Event Viewer to check the System log (see Chapter 12, Managing System Reliability and Availability).
The DHCP server creates extra or excessive network traffic (as determined by using the Performance Monitor as discussed in Chapter 11, Server and Network Monitoring).	Increase the lease period in each scope, so there is less traffic due to allocating new leases when the old ones expire.
The DNS lookup zone records are not automatically updated.	Make sure that DNS servers and IP addresses are set up in each DHCP scope. Make sure that the IPv4 and IPv6 properties are set up to automatically update the DNS server. Finally, enable DNS updating for clients that do not dynamically support it.
One of the leased IP addresses is conflicting with a permanent IP address leased to a computer, such as a server.	Exclude that IP address from the scope.
Your network has a large number of mobile laptop and tablet computers and is in short supply of IP addresses.	Reduce the lease duration so that leases expire sooner and can be reassigned.
The System log is reporting Jet database error messages.	The DHCP database is corrupted. Have users sign out from the network and disable the server's connection (right-click Start, click Network Connections, right-click the network connection, and click Disable). Use the DHCP management tool to reconcile the scopes (right-click IPv4 and IPv6 in the tree and click Reconcile All Scopes). Another option is to open the Windows PowerShell window, stop the DHCP service (use the command net stop dhcpserver) and use the Jetpack.exe program to repair the database.
The DHCP server is not responding.	Right-click Start, click Network Connections, double-click the network connection and notice the Activity section of the Status dialog box for the network connection to make sure the network connection is active. Use the Services tool to make sure that the DHCP Client and DHCP Server services are started and set to start automatically. Also, ensure that the DHCP server has a static IP address and not a dynamic IP address. Right-click Start, click Network Connections, double-click the network connection, click Properties, double-click Internet Protocol Version 4 (TCP/IPv4) or Internet Protocol Version 6 (TCP/IPv6) or both, and make certain a static address is specified.

8

IP Address Management

IP Address Management (IPAM) is a set of tools available in Windows Server 2016 to consolidate IP address management in one place. IPAM enables you to plan, configure, and manage IP addressing on your network. It can help you track all IP addresses that are deployed and to determine which addresses are currently not in use. IPAM monitors DHCP scopes so that you know when a scope needs to be increased. It also offers a central location for opening the DNS and DHCP tools. The IPAM tool is particularly useful for medium and large organizations that have lots of IP addresses and subnets to manage.

At this writing, there are some limitations to using IPAM, however, which is why there is not an activity in this book having you install and configure IPAM. First, IPAM does not work properly on a computer that is a domain controller. It can be installed, but it does not properly provision to implement all of its features. Second, discovery of DHCP servers on a network is turned off when IPAM is installed on a DHCP server. Third, IPAM must be installed on a non-DC server that is a member of an existing domain. Finally, IPAM does not link up with DHCP services built into network devices, such as routers and switches.

To install IPAM on a member server that is not a DC in a domain, follow these general steps:

1. Open Server Manager.
2. Click Manage and click Add Roles and Features.
3. If you see the Before you begin window, click Next.
4. Be certain that Role-based or feature-based is selected in the Select installation type window. Click Next.
5. Ensure your server is selected in the Select destination server window. Click Next.
6. Click Next in the Select server roles window.
7. Click the box for IP Address Management (IPAM) Server in the Select features window.
8. Click Add Features in the Add Roles and Features Wizard window.
9. Click Next.
10. Click Install.
11. Click Close.

After IPAM is installed, you can access it in Server Manager by clicking the IPAM selection in the left pane,

Redundancy Through NIC Teaming

When your server has two or more NICs, you can choose to configure NIC teaming for added redundancy. In **NIC teaming**, the congregated NICs operate as one logical connection. For the server administrator, NIC teaming has several benefits. It distributes the load (for NIC load balancing) among the teamed NICs to provide users faster access to the server. In NIC teaming, users still have access to the server even when one NIC fails. And, NIC teaming combines bandwidth for faster access. This means, if you have four 1 Gbps NICs in a team, the logical throughput is 4 Gbps.

Bluetooth is not supported in NIC teaming.

There are three NIC teaming configurations:

- *Static teaming*—All of the NICs are connected to the same intelligent (teaming capable) switch or router so that the switch can assist in the NIC teaming.
- *Switch-independent teaming*—Where the NICs can be connected to different switches (or routers) or the same switch, but regardless, the switch(s) do not assist in the NIC teaming.
- *Link Aggregation Control Protocol (LACP)*—In **Link Aggregation Control Protocol (LACP)**, the switch or switches are set to enable LACP so that the NICs are automatically teamed into a single logical connection, without the need for the network administrator to configure them.

When you configure NIC teaming, you also have three load-balancing methods from which to choose:

- *Hyper-V Port*—Intended for NIC teaming when the host is a virtual machine in Hyper-V
- *Address hash*—Inspects received packets to form a hashing algorithm to help establish which NIC in the team is used to communicate back with the client
- *Dynamic*—A new method that uses flowlets to reduce large-sized traffic into smaller elements for faster data transfer

The general steps for configuring a NIC team are:

1. Open Server Manager.
2. Click Local Server in the left pane.
3. In the right pane inside the PROPERTIES box, find NIC Teaming and click Disabled (see Figure 8-22).

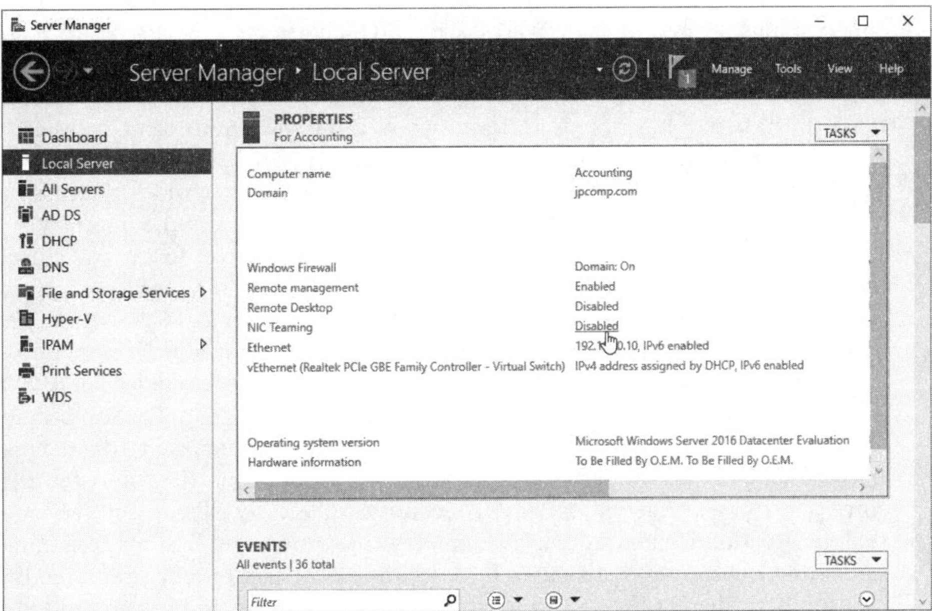

Figure 8-22 Configuring NIC teaming

4. In the NIC Teaming window and within the ADAPTERS AND INTERFACES box, hold down the Ctrl key and select the adapters to be in the team.
5. Right-click the highlighted adapters and click Add to New Team.
6. In the NIC Teaming dialog box, provide a name for the team and be certain the boxes in front of the NICs you want to include are checked.
7. Click the down arrow for Additional properties and select the teaming and load-balancing methods.
8. If you are using VLAN membership, click the down arrow in the text box for *Standby adapter:* and select the NIC for VLAN membership.
9. Click OK in the NIC Teaming box.
10. Close the NIC Teaming window.

8

Implementing Microsoft Internet Information Services

Microsoft **Internet Information Services (IIS)** is software included with Windows Server 2016 that enables you to offer a complete website. Your website might fulfill any number of functions. On a college campus, you might use it to enable applicants to apply for admission or to allow currently enrolled students to view their progress toward completing degree requirements. Many companies use their websites for multiple purposes, such as to announce new products, provide product support, take product orders, and advertise job openings. Another use is to provide training to company employees on using software, such as an inventory or order entry system.

IIS benchmarks prove these services are fast, and the software design enables the use of software applications to coordinate with an IIS server, such as a distributed client/server system that implements web-based features. One reason why IIS services are fast and can be integrated with other programs is the built-in **Internet Server Application Programming Interface (ISAPI)**. ISAPI is a group of DLL (dynamic link library) files that are applications and filters. The applications files enable developers to link customized programs into IIS and to speed program execution. IIS filters are used to automatically trigger programs, such as a Microsoft Access database lookup or a security program to authorize a user to access specific web functions. The Web Server (IIS) role contains the World Wide Web services, which are vital for a website. Another service that can be employed through IIS is the **File Transfer Protocol (FTP)** service. FTP is a TCP/IP-based application protocol that handles file transfers over a network. Additional services allow you to make an IIS server function as an email server using the **Simple Mail Transfer Protocol (SMTP)**. An SMTP server acts as an Internet gateway and in partnership with email services, such as Microsoft Exchange, to accept incoming email from the Internet and forward it to the recipient. It also forwards outgoing email from a network's email service to the Internet.

Windows Server 2016 is a good candidate for a web server for several reasons. One reason is that Windows Server 2016's privileged-mode architecture and fault-tolerance capabilities make it a reliable server platform. Another is that Windows Server 2016 is compatible with small databases, such as Microsoft Access, and large databases, such as SQL Server and Oracle. Also, users can sign in to a database through the IIS **Open Database Connectivity (ODBC)** drivers. ODBC is a set of database access rules used by Microsoft in its ODBC application programming interface (API) for accessing databases and providing a standard doorway to database data. This makes IIS very compatible with web-based client/server applications. IIS also is compatible with Microsoft Point-to-Point Encryption (MPPE) security, IP Security (IPsec), and the Secure Sockets Layer (SSL) encryption technique. SSL is a dual-key encryption standard for communication between a server and a client and is also used by Microsoft Edge and Internet Explorer. IIS enables security control on the basis of username and password, IP address, and folder and file access controls.

Even if you only want to support Internet printing, you'll need to install the Web Server (IIS) role along with the Internet Printing role service (refer Chapter 6, Configuring Windows Server 2016 Printing)—so it's useful for this reason alone to learn the basics about installing the Web Server (IIS) role.

IIS in Windows Server 2016 is broken into modules or features so that you can install only the features you need. This presents a smaller attack surface and makes IIS more efficient. Also, you can install IIS and most features in Windows Server Core and Nano Server, as well as in the full version of Windows Server 2016. Table 8-5 shows some of the role services that can be used with IIS.

Installing a Web Server

Installing and using IIS on the Internet requires the following:

- Windows Server 2016 installed on the computer to host IIS
- TCP/IP installed on the IIS host

Table 8-5 Internet Information Services role services (modules)

IIS features	Feature modules
Common HTTP features	Modules for publishing using common web document environments, such as HTML, designating a default web page, enabling directory browsing, enabling redirection to another URL, enabling HTTP error recording, and WebDAV publishing
Application development features	Modules for web application development tools including Common Gateway Interface (CGI) scripting, Active Server Pages (ASP), Internet Server Application Programming Interface (ISAPI) extensions and filters, Server Side Includes (SSI), ASP.NET, and .NET Extensibility
Health and diagnostics features	Modules for HTTP logging, tracing, tools for web server logs, ODBC logging for databases, and ability to create customized logging for specific needs
Security features	Modules to support multiple authentication techniques for public and private network use, including Centralized SSL Certification Support, IIS Client Certificate Mapping Authentication, Client Certificate Mapping Authentication, Digest Authentication, Windows Authentication, URL Authentication, and Basic Authentication; also includes request filtering and access limitations based on IP addresses and domain names
Performance features	Module for static content compression for content that does not change and that can be cached; also a module for dynamic content compression for content that changes—both forms of compression are intended to reduce the bandwidth load
IIS management features	Can install the IIS Management console, IIS management scripts and tools, and management service; you can also install management tools used in some earlier IIS versions
File Transfer Protocol (FTP) publishing features	Module to install FTP Server (for creation of an FTP site from which to upload and download files using FTP and includes an FTP management tool); and a module to install FTP Extensibility

8

- Access to an Internet service provider (ISP); ask the ISP for your IP address, subnet mask, and default gateway IP address
- Sufficient disk space for IIS and for website files (the required space depends on the number of web files that you publish)
- A method for resolving IP addresses to computer or domain names, such as DNS

Activity 8-11: Installing IIS

Time Required: Approximately 15 minutes
Objective: Learn how to install IIS.

Description: The Web Server (IIS) role is used to turn your Windows Server 2016 server into a website hosting server. In this activity, you use Server Manager to install the Web Server (IIS) role. (The Web Server (IIS) role should not already be installed on your server. If it is already installed, check with your instructor about removing it.)

1. Open **Server Manager**, if it is not open.
2. Click **Manage** and click **Add Roles and Features.**
3. If you see the Before you begin window, click **Next.**
4. Make certain **Role-based and feature-based installation** is selected in the Select installation type window and click **Next.**
5. Your server should be selected in the Select destination server window. Click **Next.**
6. Click the box for **Web Server (IIS)** in the Select server roles window.

7. So that you install the module for IIS Management Console, click **Add Features** in the Add Roles and Features Wizard.
8. Click **Next** in the Select server roles window.
9. Click **Next** in the Select features window.
10. Review the information window about Web Server Role (IIS) and then click **Next** (see Figure 8-23).

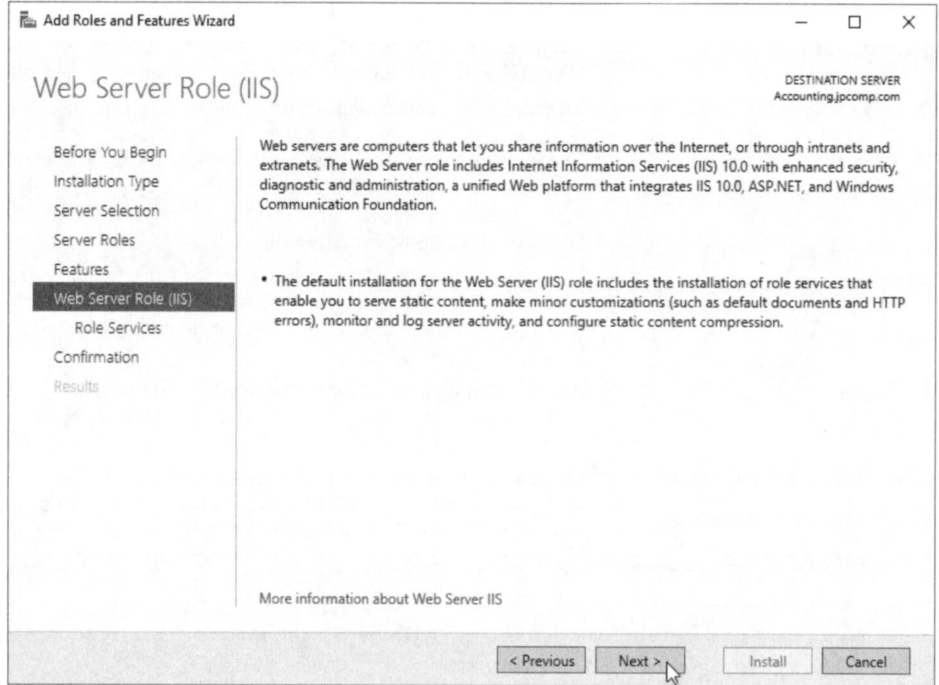

Figure 8-23 Information window for the Web Server Role (IIS)

11. Review the modules that are installed by default in the Select role services window.
    - Record the modules checked by default.
12. Under Security, click the box for **IIS Client Certificate Mapping Authentication** and read its description on the right side of the window. This selection enables you to use digital IDs for security.

Don't worry if you think you might need more modules. You can always install them later through Server Manager.

13. Click **Next** in the Select role services window.
14. Review your selections and click **Install.**
15. Click **Close.**
16. Leave Server Manager open for the next activity.

Web Server Best Practices

When you set up a web server, consider the following best practices ideas for your installation:

- Set the firewall on your network or server (or both) to block unneeded applications (and to close unused TCP and UDP communication ports), focusing on allowing primarily HTTP and HTTPS.
- Place the web server in a demilitarized zone (see Chapter 9, Configuring Remote Access Services, for more on the demilitarized zone and for an illustration).
- Use only those applications and services that are necessary on the web server, this includes omitting use of FTP services and applications, if FTP is not needed.
- Keep current with security patches to Windows Server 2016, IIS, and the applications on the web server.
- Keep logs of all user activity and regularly monitor those logs.
- Consider installing traps (sometimes called "honey pots") to help identify attacks when they occur. Some organizations install a web server that functions only as a honey pot, as a way to identify attackers and attacks to determine how to thwart them.
- Install and regularly use scanning, malware, and intrusion detection software.

Internet Information Services (IIS) Manager

The Internet Information Services (IIS) Manager is a complete tool for managing IIS (see Figure 8-24). Through this tool, you can do the following:

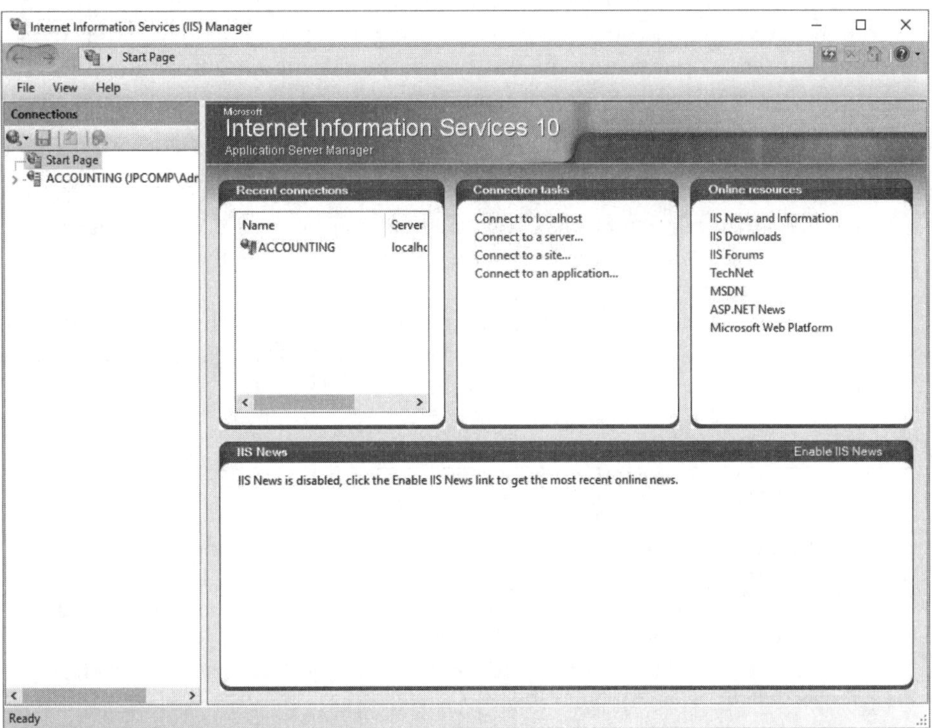

Figure 8-24 Internet Information Services (IIS) Manager

- Connect to a web server on your computer or remotely connect to a web server, an application, or site.
- Have connections to multiple web servers, applications, and sites.
- Manage a web server.

- Manage ASP.NET.
- Manage authorization for users and for specific web server roles.
- Manage web server logging.
- Compress web server files.
- Manage code modules and worker processes.
- Manage server certificates.
- Troubleshoot a web server.

This book is not intended to teach you how to fully implement and manage the Web Server (IIS) role. However, through the use of IIS Manager in the next sections, you get a small taste of this tool and how to manage a few web server tasks (to get you started).

For more information about IIS, visit *www.iis.net*.

Creating a Virtual Directory

A **virtual directory** is really a physical folder or a redirection to a **Uniform Resource Locator (URL)** that points to a folder, so that it can be accessed over the Internet, an intranet, or VPN. This means that the virtual folder can reside on the same computer that hosts IIS, or it can be on another computer. Of course, a URL is a special addressing format used to find, for example, particular web locations or FTP sites.

The reason for creating a virtual directory is to provide a shortcut path to specific IIS server content. For example, one reason for creating a virtual directory is to provide an easy way for multiple users to publish on the website, by modifying and uploading files to the virtual directory. In an organization with many departments or divisions that manage portions of a website, you might create a virtual directory for each one.

When you set up a virtual directory, you give it an alias, which is a name to identify it to a web browser. The URL format for accessing a file in a virtual directory entails providing the server name, the virtual directory alias, and the filename, such as \\Accounting\Webpub\Mypage.html. In this example, Accounting is the server name, Webpub is the alias of the virtual directory, and Mypage.html is the filename.

When you create a virtual directory, you can choose the permissions you want to apply, which are the same as permissions for a regular NTFS folder and files in the folder, including the ability to use advanced permissions as shown in Table 8-6.

Table 8-6 Virtual directory security options

Permission	Description	Applies to
Full control	Can read, add, delete, execute, and modify files plus change permissions and attributes, and take ownership	Folders and files
Modify	Can read, add, delete, execute, and modify files; cannot delete subfolders and their file contents, change permissions, or take ownership	Folders and files
Read & execute	Implies the capabilities of both List folder contents and Read (traverse folders, view file contents, view attributes and permissions, and execute files)	Folders and files
List folder contents	Can list (traverse) files in the folder or switch to a subfolder, view folder attributes and permissions, and execute files, but cannot view file contents	Folders only
Read	Can view file contents, view folder attributes and permissions, but cannot traverse folders or execute files	Folders and files
Write	Can create files, write data to files, append data to files, create folders, delete files (but not subfolders and their files), and modify folder and file attributes	Folders and files
Advanced permissions	Advanced permissions apply (see Table 5-2 in Chapter 5)	Folders and files

After a virtual directory is created, you can modify its properties in IIS Manager by clicking Default Web Site in the tree under the server, right-clicking the virtual directory's alias, such as WebPub, and then clicking Edit Permissions (see Figure 8-25; also, you perform these steps in Activity 8-12). Notice in Figure 8-25 that the folder's properties are similar to those for a regular folder.

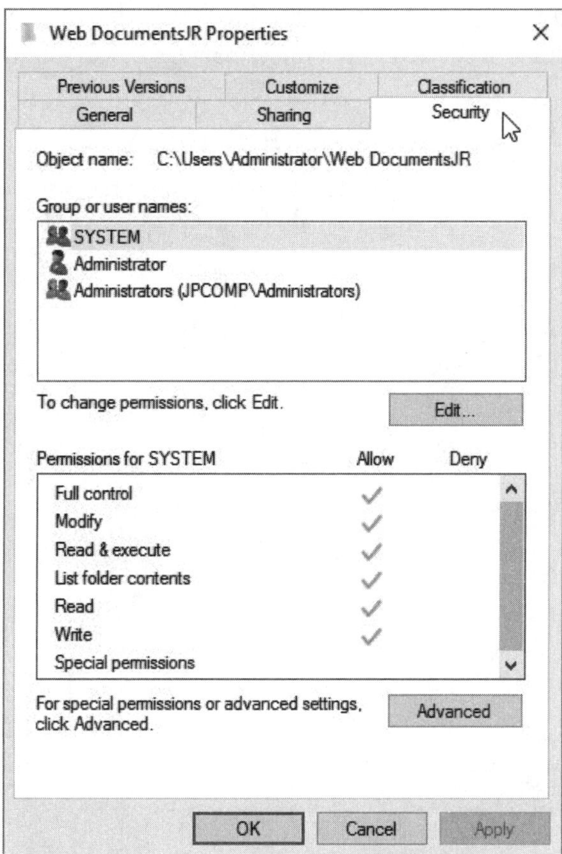

Figure 8-25 Properties of a virtual directory

You can set up the virtual directory to be shared so that users who need access to add contents to the directory can do this over the network. The share permissions are the same as those for a regular folder, as shown in Table 8-7.

Table 8-7 Virtual directory share permissions

Share permission	Description
Read	Permits groups or users to read and execute files, but they cannot add or delete files and folders and cannot modify files
Write	Enables groups or users to modify the contents of files
Change or Contribute	Enables groups and users to read, execute, and add files, but they can only modify and delete files provided by them
Custom	Means advanced permissions already apply on this folder or file
Full control	Permits groups or users to read, execute, add, delete, and modify files, and to create and delete subfolders and manage share permissions
Owner	Assigned to the owner of the folder, such as the folder's creator, and enables the owner to read, execute, add, delete, and modify files in the shared folder as well as create and delete subfolders and manage the share permissions

8

Activity 8-12: Creating a Virtual Directory

Time Required: Approximately 10 minutes
Objective: Set up a virtual directory.

Description: In this activity, you set up a virtual directory from which to publish documents for the IIS Web server that you installed in Activity 8-11. Before you start, create a folder under the \inetpub\wwwroot or \Users\Administrator folder under Local Disk (C:) and call the new folder Web Documents with your initials at the end of the folder name, such as Web DocumentsJR.

1. If necessary, open **Server Manager**.
2. Click **Tools** and click **Internet Information Services (IIS) Manager**.
3. Expand the tree in the left pane to view Default Web Site under the Sites folder. Right-click **Default Web Site** in the tree and click **Add Virtual Directory**, as shown in Figure 8-26.

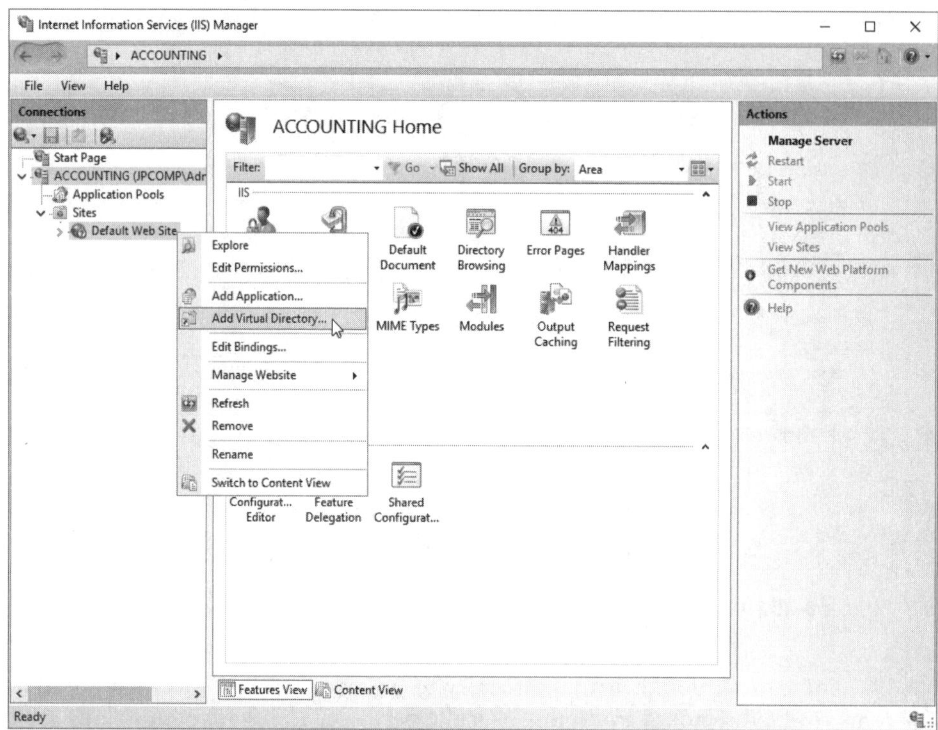

Figure 8-26 Adding a virtual directory

4. Enter an alias for the virtual directory, which users will employ to access it, such as *Webdoc* plus your initials at the end, such as *WebdocJR*. Also, enter the path to the physical folder you created before starting this assignment, such as *C:\Users\Administrator\Web DocumentsJR* (or use the Browse button to find it). Your entries should look similar to those in Figure 8-27. Click **OK**.
5. In the tree under Default Web Site (if necessary, click the right pointing arrow to expand it), right-click the virtual directory you created and click **Edit Permissions**.
6. Click the **Security** tab to view the current permissions (refer to Figure 8-25).
7. Click the **Sharing** tab.
   - How can you set up this folder for sharing?

8. Click **Cancel** in the Properties dialog box.
9. Leave the Internet Information Services (IIS) Manager window open for the next activity.

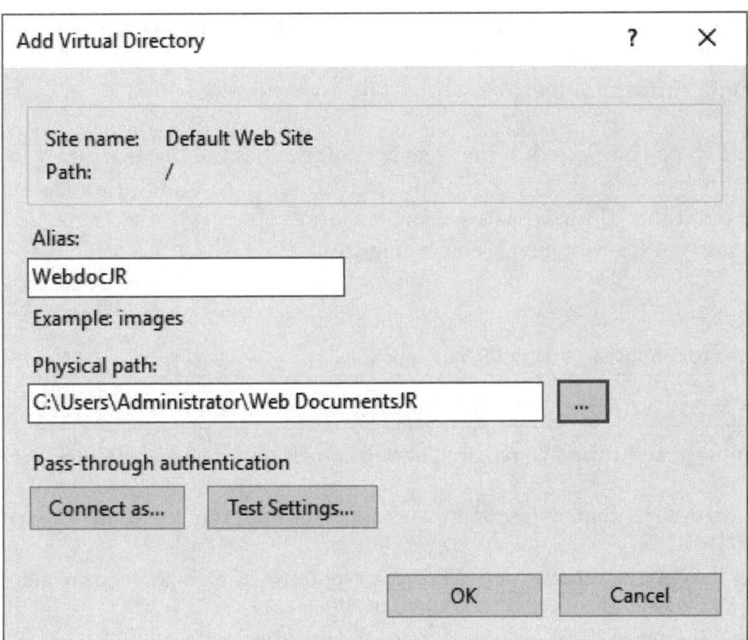

Figure 8-27 Add Virtual Directory dialog box

Managing and Configuring an IIS Web Server

After it is installed, you can manage a web server using IIS Manager, described in the previous section. The Internet Information Services Manager tool enables you to manage IIS components including the following:

- Application pools
- Sites
- SMTP email
- Certificates

Application pools enable you to group similar web applications into pools or groups for management, such as for common settings and for common worker processes. (A worker process is an ASP.NET process that runs on its own without using the same memory space as IIS.) Using application pools also ensures isolation between applications, so that a problem with one application does not affect another one. One application pool, called DefaultAppPool, is created automatically when you install the Web Server role. To configure this capability, click Application Pools in the tree under the server name (refer to Figure 8-26).

Sites is a folder used to manage multiple websites from one administrative web server, and the Default Web Site, which you worked with in Activity 8-12, is automatically set up within the Sites folder. You can choose to rename Default Web Site by right-clicking it in the tree and clicking Rename.

The SMTP E-mail Page feature is used to manage Internet email via email programs that take advantage of the application programming interface, system.net.mail. To use this capability, install SMTP Server as a feature via Server Manager. This feature can be used to configure the following:

- Reception of email
- The SMTP Server to receive email

- Authentication settings
- Storage of email messages
- Other email elements

Through the certificates feature, you can configure and monitor certificate security that is used with other websites. You can configure certificates and view certificate information including certificate names, to whom and by whom certificates are issued, and expiration date.

A website can be configured in many ways, but the best advice is to start by setting the basic properties and features, such as configuring performance to match the number of users, and a default web page. Table 8-8 lists many of the features you can configure through icons displayed in the middle pane of IIS Manager (refer to Figure 8-26).

Table 8-8 Sample website features to configure through IIS Manager

Feature	Purpose
Authentication	Configures the authentication required of web clients, with anonymous authentication configured as the default
Compression	Configures dynamic content (content that changes) or static content (content that does not change) compression
Default Document	Specifies the default webpage or pages that a client views, including, for example, default.htm, default.asp, indext.htm, index.html, and iistart.htm
Directory Browsing	Specifies information displayed when listing a folder's contents
Error Pages	Sets up error messages that are displayed in a client's browser when specific errors occur while accessing the web server
Handler Mappings	Configures the .dll files, code files, and other files used to fulfill client requests
HTTP Response Headers	Sets an expiration date on the directory contents, to set properties of headers that are returned to the client's browser, to set content ratings (such as for content limited to adults), and to specify Multipurpose Internet Mail Extensions (MIME)
Logging	Configures IIS logging of website access requests, including the location of the log file
MIME Types	Configures the accepted file extensions for files that don't change (static files)
Modules	Configures modules of code used when a client requests a specific website action
Output Caching	Configures how the output cache is used, such as storing a webpage in the web server memory so it is quickly available to the client when requested again
Request Filtering	Filters incoming HTTP requests to block harmful or unwanted requests from accessing the web server
SSL Settings	Configures Secure Sockets Layer (SSL) options, which enables data encryption between the server and the client over the Internet

Activity 8-13: Configuring a Website

Time Required: Approximately 15 minutes
Objective: Learn basic website configuration.

Description: In this activity, you practice configuring some basic parameters for the website you have installed.

1. Open **IIS Manager**, if you have closed it.
2. If necessary, expand the tree under the Sites folder to see Default Web Site.
3. Right-click **Default Web Site** to see the menu and review its contents (refer to Figure 8-26). Point to **Manage Website**.
   - How can you rename the website? Also, how can you restart the website if it is stopped?
4. Click the pointer in a blank area to close the open menu.

5. Double-click **Default Document** in the middle pane. Notice that Default.htm is set up to display first when the client connects to the website without specifying a file to access. Right-click **iisstart.htm** and notice there is an option to move it up the list.
6. Click the **back arrow** in the upper-left side of the Internet Information Services (IIS) Manager window.
7. Double-click **Directory Browsing** in the middle pane.
8. In the right pane, click **Enable** to enable directory browsing (see Figure 8-28).

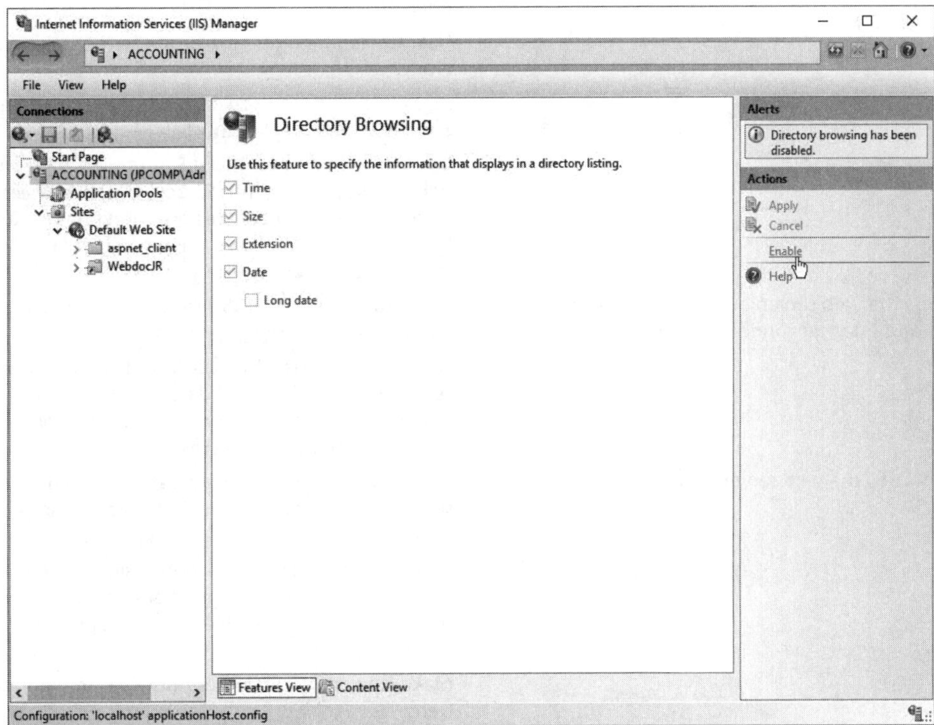

Figure 8-28 Enabling directory browsing

9. Click the **back arrow** in the upper-left side of the Internet Information Services (IIS) Manager window.
10. Right-click **Default Web Site** in the tree, click **Edit Permissions**, and click the **Security** tab (refer to Figure 8-25).
11. Click **Users (*domainname*\Users)** under *Group or user names:* to view the security given to general users in the domain.
12. Click **Cancel** in the Properties dialog box.
13. In the left pane, click **Default Web Site** in the tree, so that it is highlighted.
14. In the right pane, find the Configure section and click **Limits.**
15. Enter **240** in the *Connection time-out (in seconds):* box to increase the amount of time a user can be connected without taking action.
16. Click the box for **Limit number of connections.** Enter **500** as the number for simultaneous connections so you can control the load on the server. This is a number you should monitor in the future. If the server is frequently overloaded with users and performing slowly, you can reduce this number, for example, by 50 at a time, as needed. Click **OK.**
17. Close the Internet Information Services (IIS) Manager window.

Troubleshooting a Web Server

Occasionally a web server can experience problems, such as users not being able to connect to the server. Table 8-9 lists possible problems and their solutions.

Table 8-9 Troubleshooting IIS

Problem	Solution
The web server is not responding.	Right-click Start and click Network Connections to make sure that the server's connection to the network or Internet is enabled.
	Use Device Manager to ensure the NIC is connected and working.
	Right-click the web server in the tree of IIS Manager, click Manage Website, and click Start or Restart to start the IIS service.
	Use Server Manager (click IIS in the left pane and scroll the right pane to view the SERVICES box) or the Services tool to make sure the following services are running: World Wide Web Publishing Service, Application Host Helper Service, and Windows Process Activation Service.
No one can access the web server, but the server is booted and its network and Internet connections are enabled.	Make sure that the DNS server(s) is (are) connected and working on the network.
	Use a web browser from different computers and locations to test the connection, and determine if the problem is due to a network segment location, the Internet connection, or a specific client that cannot access the server.
Clients can connect to the web server, but cannot access its contents.	Make sure that the authentication and encryption set at the server matches the authentication and encryption properties that the client computers can support.
	Check the NTFS and share permissions on the web server and on virtual directories to make sure that they enable the appropriate client access, such as permissions to Allow for Read & Execute.
	Make sure that no NTFS permissions on web folders are set to Deny.
	Make sure that the \Inetpub\wwwroot folder is intact and contains all of the necessary HTML files (open IIS Manager, right-click Default Web Site, and click Explore to view the files).
	Make sure that the startup HTML file name is spelled correctly and is in the correct folder.

Chapter Summary

- DNS is used to resolve domain and computer names to IP addresses and vice versa.
- Before you install DNS, ensure that the server to house this role has a static or unchanging IP address. (All servers and other network devices that users regularly access should have a static or unchanging IP address.)
- After you install DNS as a server role, the next step is to configure forward and reverse lookup zones, as well as DNS resource records.
- When you configure Dynamic DNS, you enable automated IP address registration in a coordinated way with a DHCP server.
- Plan to set up two or more DNS servers on most networks to integrate DNS with Active Directory for DNS replication and load balancing.
- DHCP dynamically leases IP addresses to client computers, which saves the network administrator time and helps ensure reliable IP address assignment and configuration.

- Configuring DHCP involves configuring scopes that are IP address ranges from which addresses are leased to clients.
- Windows Server 2016 DHCP server supports both IPv4 and IPv6.
- IPAM is a set of tools you can use for IP address management, particularly for medium to large organizations that have lots of users and multiple DNS and DHCP servers.
- NIC teaming enables you to aggregate multiple NICs in a server to appear as one logical connection, with the advantage of faster network response and failover when a NIC malfunctions.
- To create a Windows Server 2016 web server, install the Web Server (IIS) role to implement Internet Information Services.
- Create IIS virtual directories to enable multiple users to publish information on a website.
- Use standard NTFS and share permissions to protect virtual directories so that only authorized users can publish in them.
- After you install a web server, configure it to customize features such as application pools, authentication, compression, default webpages, error pages, logging, and SSL security.

Key Terms

application pool Grouping of similar web applications in pools or groups for management, such as for common settings for common worker processes (ASP.NET processes).

caching server A DNS server function available in all DNS servers, that is used to provide fast queries because the results of each query are stored in RAM. As more resolution queries are performed, a large set of information is stored in RAM for fast response to users.

caching-only DNS server A DNS server without zones used to provide fast queries, because the results of each query are stored in RAM.

DNS dynamic update protocol A protocol that enables information in a DNS server to be automatically updated in coordination with DHCP.

DNS round robin Resource records are created for two or more servers that have different IP addresses but that are associated with the same host name, such as IP addresses 192.168.1.5 and 192.168.1.6 that are associated with the host name *researchserver*.

DNS security extension (DNSSEC) Ensures that records in all DNS zones use cryptographic digital signing, which is intended to reduce the opportunity for DNS information to be captured and modified by an attacker.

Dynamic DNS (DDNS) A form of DNS that enables client computers to update DNS registration information so that this does not have to be done manually. DDNS is often used with DHCP servers to automatically register IP addresses on a DNS server.

Dynamic Host Configuration Protocol for IPv6 (DHCPv6) A version of DHCP that can be used with IPv6 implementation on a network.

File Transfer Protocol (FTP) Available through the TCP/IP protocol suite, FTP enables files to be transferred across a network or the Internet between computers or servers.

forward lookup zone A DNS zone or table that maps computer names to IP addresses.

host address (A) resource record A record in a DNS forward lookup zone that consists of a computer or domain name correlated to an IP version 4 (or 32-bit) address.

Internet Information Services (IIS) A Microsoft Windows Server 2016 role that provides Internet, web, FTP, mail, and other services and that is particularly offered to set up a web server.

Internet Server Application Programming Interface (ISAPI) A group of dynamic link library (DLL) files that consists of applications and filters to enable user-customized programs to interface with IIS and to trigger particular programs, such as a specialized security check or a database lookup.

IP Address Management (IPAM) A set of tools available in Windows Server 2016 to consolidate IP address management in one place.

IPv6 host address (AAAA) resource record A record in a DNS forward lookup zone that consists of a computer or domain name mapped to an IP version 6 (or 128-bit) address.

Link Aggregation Control Protocol (LACP) Enables two or more NICs in a single computer to automatically be bundled into one logical connection.

NIC teaming The ability to join two or more network interface cards to work like one.

Open Database Connectivity (ODBC) A set of database access rules used by Microsoft in its ODBC application programming interface for accessing databases and providing a standard doorway to database data.

pointer (PTR) resource record A record in a DNS reverse lookup zone that consists of an IP (version 4 or 6) address correlated to a computer or domain name.

primary DNS server A DNS server that is used as the main server from which to administer a zone, such as updating records in a forward lookup zone for a domain. A primary DNS server is also called the authoritative server for that zone.

reverse lookup zone A DNS server zone or table that maps IP addresses to computer or domain names.

root hint A resource record to enable a DNS server to quickly find an authoritative DNS server in a zone that is not on the DNS server, and is used in particular to find an authoritative DNS server on the Internet.

scope A range of contiguous IP addresses that a DHCP server can lease to clients.

secondary DNS server A DNS server that is a backup to a primary DNS server and therefore is not authoritative.

Simple Mail Transfer Protocol (SMTP) An email protocol used by systems having TCP/IP network communications.

stateful autoconfiguration In IPv6, uses dynamic addressing for an IPv6 host by obtaining the IPv6 address through DHCPv6 and a DHCPv6 server.

statelesss autoconfiguration In IPv6, when a network host assigns its own IPv6 address without obtaining it from a DHCPv6 server.

stub zone A DNS zone that contains only the SOA record zone, name server (NS) records for authoritative servers, and A records for authoritative servers.

Uniform Resource Locator (URL) An addressing format used to find an Internet website or page.

virtual directory A URL-formatted address that provides an Internet location (virtual location) for an actual physical folder on a web server that is used to publish web documents.

zone A partition or subtree in a DNS server that contains specific kinds of records in a lookup table, such as a forward lookup zone that contains records in a table for looking up computer and domain names in order to find their associated IP addresses.

Review Questions

1. What step can you take when you install a DHCP server to ensure that IP addresses are only assigned by a DHCP server managed by a server administrator in your company?
   a. Certify the server as a managed container.
   b. Put a manager lock on the server.
   c. Authorize the server.
   d. Duplicate the server's key.
2. What is DHCPv6?

3. Because of budget constraints, your company has only one server. However, when it was purchased it was outfitted with a fast multicore processor and lots of memory. Often the network connection is the only bottleneck, with a capability of 1 Gbps. What relatively inexpensive addition can you make to the server to address this bottleneck?
   a. Implement the Network Express network role service.
   b. Add one or two additional NICs and configure NIC teaming.
   c. Configure DNS acceleration.
   d. Configure DNS to not replicate through Active Directory as a way to reduce network overhead.
4. Your colleague at another company has installed DNS, but it is not mapping computer names to IP addresses. Which of the following might be the problem? (Choose all that apply.)
   a. DNS lookup zone records are not set up to update automatically, and your colleague has not manually created any records.
   b. There is no WINS-R zone.
   c. The INIT record is missing.
   d. A single zone database can hold only 100 lookup records and there are over 100 records, so DNS has locked the zone.

5. Your company is located in Atlanta and has a branch location consisting of 35 employees in Greenville, South Carolina. The decision has been made to install a DNS server at the branch location. Which type of DNS server do you recommend installing at the branch location?
   a. A GlobalNames DNS server
   b. A netcast DNS server
   c. A primary DNS server
   d. A secondary DNS server
6. What is a root hint in DNS?
7. You work for an environmental consulting company in which most employees work in the field and then come back to the office for a day at a time. Consequently, the company only purchases laptop and tablet computers for its employees to accommodate their travel. When you set up the lease duration in DHCP, which of the following should you use?
   a. 24 hours
   b. 8 days
   c. 16 days
   d. 24 days
8. Explain stateful autoconfiguration and which Windows Server 2016 role enables use of this technology on a network.
9. The alumni development office at your university uses specialized software that can be accessed from two different servers. The software sometimes experiences slowdowns because it is used by the main alumni development office and by alumni development officers in every department throughout the university. What can you do to help reduce the periodic slowdowns by evenly distributing access of this software between the two servers?
   a. Use DHCPv6 instead of DHCP.
   b. Configure DNS round robin.
   c. Set up a DNS forwarder.
   d. Configure a DNS balancing zone.

10. Which of the following do you configure when setting up an IPv6 scope on a DHCP server? (Choose all that apply.)
    a. Start and end addresses
    b. Addresses in the excluded range
    c. Prefix
    d. Lease duration
11. The System log on your DHCP server is reporting DHCP database errors. Which of the following can you try first?
    a. Delete all scopes and recreate them.
    b. You must delete and reinstall the DHCP server role.
    c. You have a hung client IP connection. Disable connections to the server and then re-enable connectivity.
    d. Use the DHCP management tool to reconcile all scopes.
12. Which of the following are DNS resource records? (Choose all that apply.)
    a. Mail exchanger (MX)
    b. Name server (NS)
    c. Master browser (MB)
    d. Service locator (SRV)
13. Name three reasons to have a secondary DNS server.
14. Your large company has several thousand users and multiple DNS and DHCP servers. What tool should you install to better manage this conglomeration of network administration servers?
    a. Server Manager Plus
    b. ISCOPE
    c. IPAM
    d. Network Binder
15. Your website contains pages of special events. You don't always remember to deactivate these web pages and some remain available after the event has occurred. How can you prevent the display of webpages that are no longer current?
    a. Use the IIS scheduler to deactivate these pages.
    b. Configure the HTTP response headers function to expire specific documents.
    c. Configure the web alert feature in IIS to send you a reminder message to remove these pages.
    d. Use the IIS permission timeout setting to automatically deny the Read permission for a web document to be effective on a specified date.
16. Which of the following can you accomplish with IIS Manager? (Choose all that apply.)
    a. Manage streaming media speed
    b. Manage ASP.NET
    c. Manage logging of web server activities
    d. Manage server certificates
17. Which DNS zone holds host address records? Name two types of host address records.

18. Your school has a website with links for each department, such as for Math, Biology, English, Psychology, and so on. Each department wants to maintain its own portion of the site. Which of the following can you set up for each department to maintain its own web files?
    a. A virtual directory for each department
    b. A web partition for each department
    c. A web server for each department
    d. A web stub zone for each department
19. Which of the following applies to a DNS caching server? (Choose all that apply.)
    a. It eliminates the need to have DNS replication.
    b. It contains optimized DNS zone databases.
    c. It is used to enable fast DNS queries.
    d. It can help reduce the amount of network traffic generated by DNS servers.
20. Users complain that when an error occurs on your website, confusing messages are displayed. What IIS feature enables you to address this problem?

Case Projects

D'Amico Guitars manufactures acoustic and electric guitars along with guitar equipment such as cases, strings, and tuners. They are currently moving to new facilities that offer more space for production. The added space means they will be hiring new people, installing a new network, and purchasing new Windows Server 2016 servers. The company is anticipating growth to 428 employees and there will be over 300 client computers on the new network. They also will have 12 Windows Server 2016 servers by the time the move is completed.

The company has previously sold many guitars through third-party Internet distributors and has not had its own website. Online sales have been phenomenal, which has led them to decide to implement their own website to sell guitars and guitar equipment. As they transition to the new facilities, they regard their network and particularly the proposed website as essential to their business strategy.

D'Amico recently lost two server administrators who were hired by other companies. The loss of these administrators means they are shorthanded on people who know server and network administration, which is why they have contacted Aspen Consulting for your help. Your assignment is to assist with the setup of crucial network services.

Case Project 8-1: Planning Network Services

The Information Services Department director asks you to develop a report explaining how to plan the implementation of web, DNS, and DHCP services. In your report, address the following issues:

- In what order should the web, DHCP, and DNS services be implemented? Should all of these services be implemented on one server or on different servers?
- What setup elements should be planned in advance, such as DHCP scopes and other elements?
- What security issues should be addressed in the setup of these services?

If you have access to slide presentation software, consider preparing a slide presentation of your recommendations.

Case Project 8-2: Configuring a DNS Server

As you are demonstrating how to configure a DNS server to the new server administrators, one of them asks the following questions:

- What is the purpose of the reverse lookup zone?
- Can more than one DNS server be configured using Active Directory on the network and if so, what is the advantage?
- What is the most efficient way to update DNS records?

Case Project 8-3: DNS and DHCP Server Issues

After the DHCP server is configured and working, what other steps should be taken for reliable DNS server and DHCP server access?

Also, as you are considering the reliability issues, one of the Information Services Department employees calls to let you know that the DHCP server no longer seems to be issuing IP addresses, causing error messages. What do you do to solve this problem?

Case Project 8-4: Setting Up a Web Server

The D'Amico Guitar management team is considering options for the web server. They have asked you to write a report or create a slide show covering the following:

- What IIS features can benefit the company's plan to sell guitars and guitar equipment online?
- Is there an effective tool to manage the web server after it is installed? If so, what are its advantages?
- Does IIS provide security to protect the web-based assets, such as web documents, after they are set up?

chapter 9

Configuring Remote Access Services

After reading this chapter and completing the exercises, you will be able to:

- Understand Windows Server 2016 remote access services
- Implement and manage a virtual private network
- Configure a VPN server
- Implement a DirectAccess server
- Troubleshoot virtual private network and DirectAccess remote access installations
- Install and configure Remote Desktop Services

Networks have made today's on-the-go, always-connected computing lifestyle possible. Because of networks, we are able to telecommute, study, or conduct business at home, on the road, or even in the air. Through networks, many users are accessing servers at their place of business or school, either through the Internet or a remote wireless connection. Windows Server 2016 makes remote access possible by offering virtual private network and DirectAccess remote access capabilities.

In addition to remote access, Windows Server 2016 offers Remote Desktop Services, which enables organizations to save money on client computers and control how users run software applications. Remote Desktop Services can be accessed through a local network or remotely.

In this chapter, you learn to use Windows Server 2016 remote access services. You begin by learning the forms of remote access available in Windows Server 2016. You learn to install and configure a virtual private network for highly secure remote networking, and to install and configure the newer IPv6-based DirectAccess remote access capability. This chapter describes a range of hardware and software troubleshooting techniques for both virtual private networks and DirectAccess networking. Finally, you learn how to install, configure, and use Remote Desktop Services for running applications on a server.

Introduction to Remote Access

Today, people expect to use networks and servers anywhere there is access to the Internet. A college recruiter who travels throughout the country wants a way to remotely connect to servers on his main campus to obtain information for prospective students and update recruiting data. A traveling sales rep who sells tools to auto repair shops needs to access the home company's server to record sales information. A commuter student wants remote access to campus computers to obtain and turn in assignments, register for classes, and view her personal student information. These are examples of how remote access capabilities can put all kinds of people in touch with their home-based networks.

Windows Server 2016 meets this need with the **Remote Access** (**RAS**) role, which enables remote access through three means: virtual private networking, DirectAccess, and Web Application Proxy. A **virtual private network** (**VPN**) is like a tunnel through a larger network—such as the Internet, an enterprise network, or both—that is restricted to designated member clients only.

DirectAccess, which is built around IPv6, establishes two "tunnels" for connecting to a Direct Access server used in remote access and that is transparent to users and always on. **Web Application Proxy** entails publishing applications so that users external to an organization can access those applications on the organization's servers. This chapter focuses mainly on virtual private networking and DirectAccess as commonly used forms of remote access.

A VPN or DirectAccess user can remotely access the server through a network, the Internet, or a private intranet. The Web Application Proxy user typically accesses the applications through the Internet.

Implementing a Virtual Private Network

A VPN can use an Internet connection or an internal network connection as a transport medium to establish a connection with a VPN server. Figure 9-1 illustrates a VPN connection with four VPN tunnels, two through the outside Internet connections and two through the internal network. These tunnels connect to the Windows Server 2016 VPN server, which is in the **demilitarized zone** (**DMZ**). The DMZ is a portion of network that exists between two or more networks that have different security measures in place, such as the zone between the private network of a company and the public network of the Internet.

A VPN uses LAN protocols as well as tunneling protocols to encapsulate the data as it is sent across a public network such as the Internet. A benefit of using a VPN for remote access is that users can connect to a local ISP and connect through the ISP to the local network. The VPN is used to ensure that any data sent across a public network, such as the Internet, is secure. Security is achieved by having the VPN create an encrypted tunnel between the client and the RAS server.

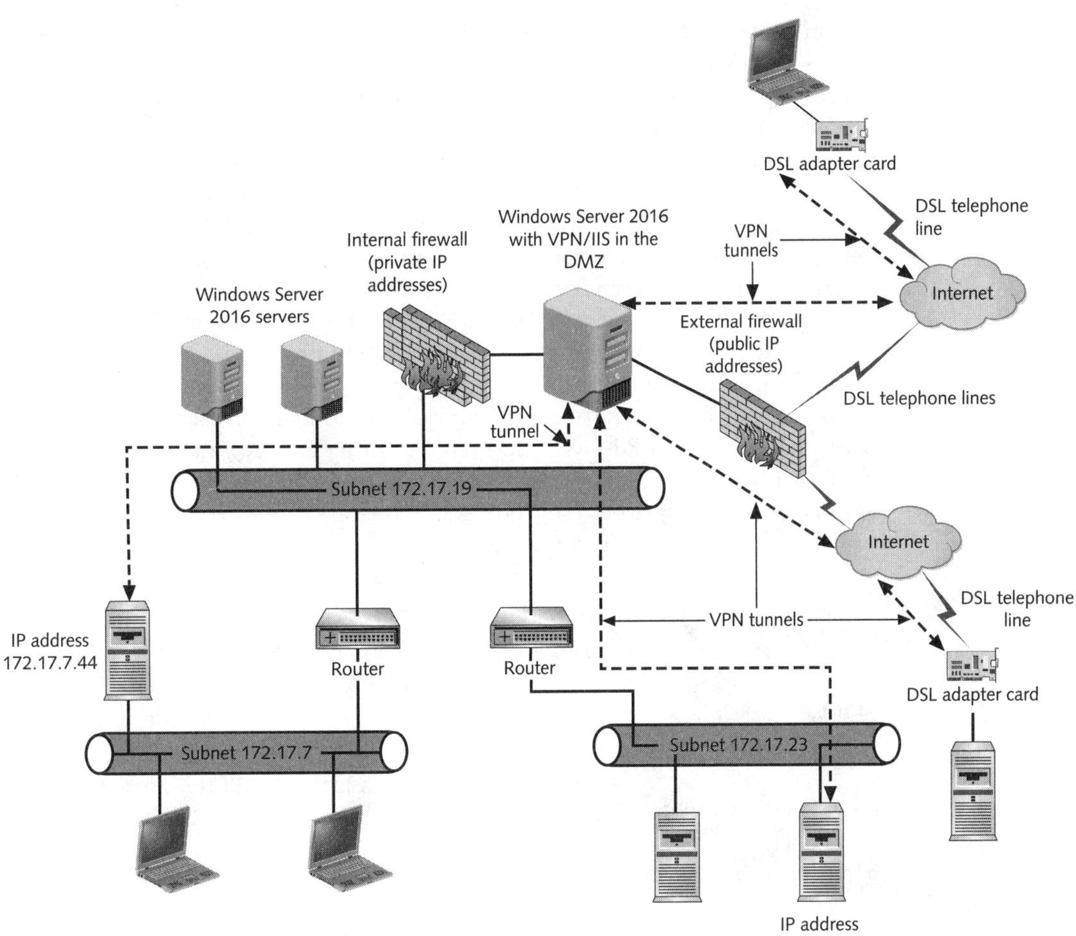

Figure 9-1 A VPN network

9

A VPN server uses two or more NICs for communications. One NIC is used to connect to the private network inside the organization that uses private IP addressing (see Table 1-3 in Chapter 1, Introduction to Windows Server 2016). The other NIC connects to the external public network, such as the Internet. To create this tunnel, the client first connects to the Internet by establishing a connection using a remote access protocol. Once connected to the Internet, the client establishes a second connection with the VPN server. The client and the VPN server agree on how the data will be encapsulated and encrypted across the virtual tunnel. Information can then be sent securely between the two computers because outsiders can't see into the tunnel.

Using Remote Access Protocols

The workhorse of a VPN connection is the remote access protocol because it carries the network packets over a wide area network (WAN) link. One function of the remote access protocol is to encapsulate a packet, such as an IP datagram, so that it can be transmitted from a point at one end of a WAN to another point—such as between two computers with DSL wide area network (WAN) adapters connected by a telecommunications line. IP is the most commonly used transport protocol, and so it is most typically encapsulated in a remote access protocol for transport over a WAN.

Several remote access protocols are used by Windows Server 2016 and its remote clients. An early basic remote access protocol in use is PPP. When a VPN is configured, tunneling protocols also come into play to enable the logical tunneling capability.

Point-to-Point Protocol (PPP) is used in legacy remote communications involving modems, such as in a convenience store that uses older technology and telecommunications lines to take your credit card. PPP enables the authentication of connections and encryption for the network communications, but is not considered to be as secure as more modern remote communications options. PPP is used, for example, for Internet connections and communications over telecommunications lines. PPP transports not only TCP/IP but also protocols that have been used on older Microsoft and NetWare servers, IPX and NetBEUI. PPP can automatically negotiate communications with several network communications layers at once, making it a versatile, although not particularly secure remote access protocol.

When you implement a Windows Server 2016 VPN server, one of three remote access tunneling protocols is used: Point-to-Point Tunneling Protocol, Layer Two Tunneling Protocol, and Secure Socket Tunneling Protocol.

Developed by a consortium of vendors including Microsoft, **Point-to-Point Tunneling Protocol (PPTP)** offers PPP-based authentication techniques and encrypts data carried by PPTP through using Microsoft Point-to-Point Encryption. **Microsoft Point-to-Point Encryption (MPPE)** is a starting-to-ending-point encryption technique that uses special encryption keys varying in length from 40 to 128 bits.

The specification for PPTP does not include mandatory encryption. Microsoft uses its own implementation of PPTP that follows the specification, but includes MPPE encryption as well.

Even with Microsoft's enhancements, PPTP is not considered a secure option because there are tools available to crack its encryption.

Modern Windows operating system implementations of PPTP, including in Windows 10 and Windows Server 2016, disable the use of MPPE 40- and 56-bit encryption keys through a Registry setting. This enforces the stronger 128-bit encryption. It is possible to reconfigure this Registry setting, but it is not recommended.

Layer Two Tunneling Protocol (L2TP) works similarly to PPTP. Both protocols use PPP authentication techniques and create special tunnels over a public network, such as the Internet, that reflect intranets and VPNs. Unlike PPTP, L2TP uses an additional network communications standard, called Layer Two Forwarding, that enables forwarding on the basis of MAC addressing (which is the physical address of the network interface) in addition to IP addressing. Also, L2TP uses IP Security for additional authentication and for data encryption. **IP Security (IPsec)** is a set of IP-based secure communications and encryption standards created through the Internet Engineering Task Force (IETF). Further, in Windows Server 2016, you can configure the security level of IPsec in a group policy (Chapter 10, Securing Windows Server 2016, provides more information about IPsec and contains an activity in which you configure an IPsec security policy).

Secure Socket Tunneling Protocol (SSTP) employs PPP authentication techniques. Also, it encapsulates the data packet in the Hypertext Transfer Protocol (HTTP) used through web communications. This gives VPN communications more versatility over all kinds of mobile connections and through firewalls. In some mobile situations the remote access network communications may be too locked down to permit PPTP or L2TP remote access, but they still allow web access through HTTP. SSTP additionally uses a Secure Sockets Layer channel for secure communications. **Secure Sockets Layer (SSL)** is a data encryption technique employed between a server and a client, such as between a client's browser and an Internet server. SSL has been a commonly used form of security for communications and transactions over the web and can be used by all web browsers. SSL has now evolved into **Transport Layer Security (TLS)**, so that TLS version 1.0 is considered to be the next step beyond SSL version 3.0

(where SSL has stopped). At this writing, TLS version 1.2 is available (TLS version 1.3 is in draft form).

SSTP is viewed as more secure than PPTP or L2TP because it encrypts using a 256-bit key. Also, SSTP authenticates users with 2048-bit key certificates. A disadvantage is that SSTP, at this writing, is not supported by Mac OS or Linux operating systems. PPP, PPTP, L2TP, and SSTP all support the additional remote access and VPN authentication measures described later in this chapter when you configure remote access communications. They also support synchronous and asynchronous communications, enabling connectivity through synchronous and asynchronous modems, cable modems, dial-up and high-speed leased telecommunication lines, T-carrier lines, DSL, ISDN, frame relay, and X.25 lines. See Table 9-1 for more information about these forms of connectivity.

Table 9-1 Communications technologies

Technology	Description
Asynchronous modem	A modem from which communications occur in discrete units, and in which the start of a unit is signalled by a start bit at the front, and a stop bit at the back signals the end of the unit
Cable modem	A digital modem device designed for use with the cable TV system, providing high-speed data transfer
Leased lines (dial-up and high speed)	Telecommunications lines or bandwidth on telecommunications lines that can be leased from a telecommunications company
Digital subscriber line (DSL)	A technology that uses advanced modulation techniques on regular telephone lines for high-speed networking at speeds of up to about 200 Mbps between subscribers and a telecommunications company
Frame relay	A WAN communications technology that relies on packet switching and virtual connection techniques to transmit at rates from 56 Kbps to 45 Mbps
Integrated Services Digital Network (ISDN)	A telecommunications standard for delivering data services over digital telephone lines with a current practical limit of 1.536 Mbps and a theoretical limit of 622 Mbps
Synchronous modem	A modem that communicates using continuous bursts of data controlled by a clock signal that starts each burst
T-carrier	A dedicated leased telephone line that can be used for data communications over multiple channels for speeds of up to 400.352 Mbps
X.25	An older packet-switching protocol for connecting remote networks at speeds up to 2.048 Mbps

On the client side, PPP, PPTP, and L2TP are available in Windows 2000 through Windows 10, and for server systems in Windows 2000 Server through Windows Server 2016. SSTP is available in Windows Vista through Windows 10 and in Windows Server 2008 through Windows Server 2016.

Configuring a VPN Server

Configuring a VPN server on a Windows Server 2016 network requires several general steps:

1. Installing the Network Policy and Access Services role
2. Configuring a Microsoft Windows Server 2016 server as a network's VPN server, including configuring the right protocols to provide VPN access to clients
3. Configuring a VPN server as a DHCP Relay Agent for TCP/IP communications
4. Configuring the VPN server properties
5. Configuring a remote access policy for security

When you configure a VPN server, Windows Server 2016 requires at least two network interfaces in the computer, one for the connection to the LAN and one for a connection to the physical VPN network.

Some steps in the activities in this book include bulleted questions for you to answer. Additionally, for all of the activities in this chapter, you'll need an account with Administrator privileges. These activities can be completed on a virtual machine or computer, such as in Hyper-V.

Activity 9-1: Installing Network Policy and Access Services and Remote Access

Time Required: Approximately 10 minutes

Objective: Learn how to install the Network Policy and Access Services and Remote Access roles.

Description: VPN servers enable remote users to access a Windows Server 2016 server through using secure tunneling protocols. In this activity, you install the Network Policy and Access Services role along with the Remote Access role as a first step in implementing a VPN server.

1. Open **Server Manager**, if it is not open.
2. Click **Manage** and click **Add Roles and Features.**
3. If you see the Before you begin window, click **Next.**
4. In the Select installation type window, ensure **Role-based or feature-based installation** is selected. Click **Next.**
5. Your server should be selected in the Select destination server window. Click **Next.**
6. Click the check box for **Network Policy and Access Services.**
7. Click **Add Features** to install the Network Policy and Access Services Tools in the Add Roles and Features Wizard dialog box.
8. Click the check box for **Remote Access** in the Select server roles window. The Network Policy and Access Services and Remote Access roles should now be selected as in Figure 9-2. Click **Next.**
9. Click **Next** in the Select features window.
10. Read the introductory information in the Network Policy and Access Services window. Click **Next.**
11. Read the introductory information in the Remote Access window. Click **Next.**
12. Click the box for **DirectAccess and VPN (RAS)** in the Select role services window.
13. Click **Add Features** in the Add Roles and Features Wizard dialog box.
14. Click **Next** in the Select role services window (see Figure 9-3).
15. Click **Install.**
16. Make sure the installation succeeded in the Installation progress window and then click **Close.** Leave Server Manager open for the next activity.

The next step in the process is to use the Remote Access tool to set up a VPN server.

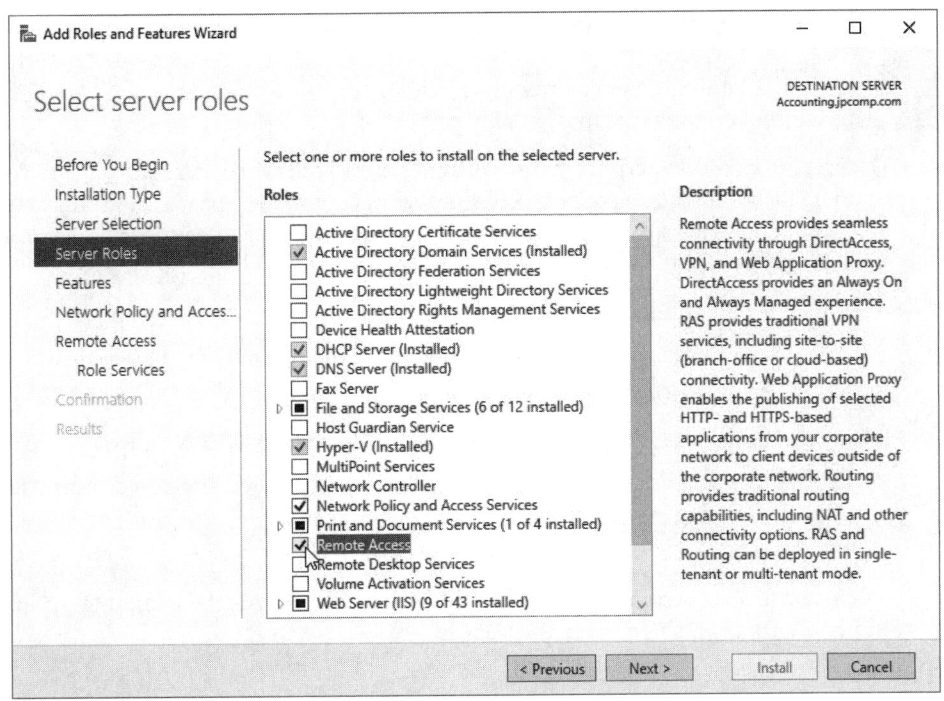

Figure 9-2 Network Policy and Access Services and Remote Access roles selected

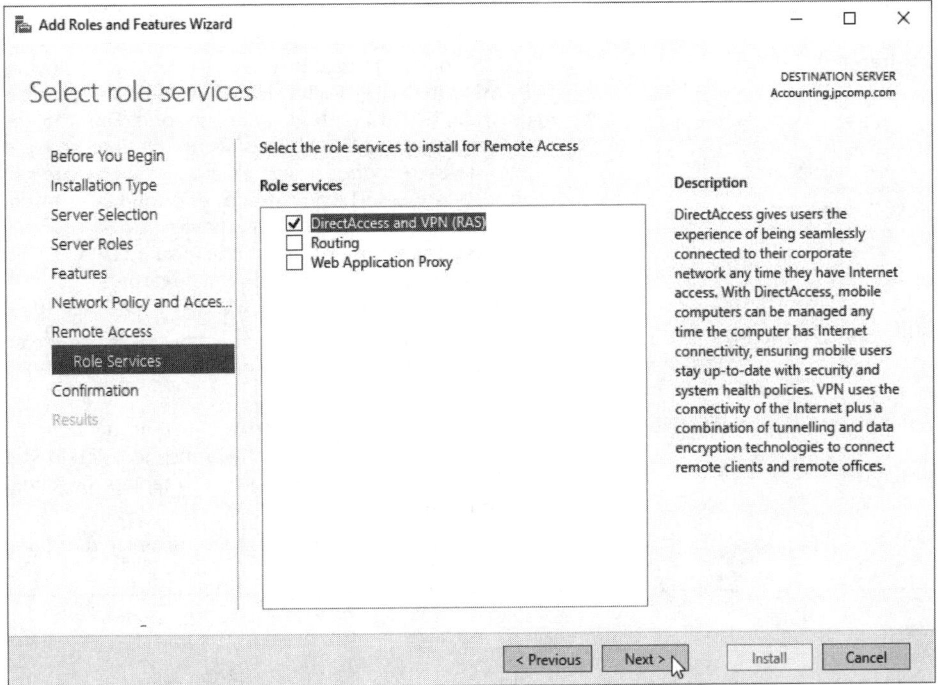

Figure 9-3 Select role services window

9

Activity 9-2: Setting Up a VPN Server

Time Required: Approximately 15 minutes
Objective: Initial setup of a VPN server.

Description: In this activity, you configure a VPN server for remote users to access. Because many readers may not have two NICs in the server used for practice, in this activity you perform a custom configuration, which enables you to still experience most configuration tasks while having only one NIC in your server.

1. Open **Server Manager**, if it is not open.
2. Click the **exclamation point** near Manage in the top part of the window.
3. Click **Open the Getting Started Wizard.**
4. In the Configure Remote Access window, select **Deploy VPN only.**
5. In the Routing and Remote Access window, right-click the server and click **Configure and Enable Routing and Remote Access.**
6. Click **Next.**
7. You can select from five options. Table 9-2 summarizes the available options. Click **Custom configuration.** Click **Next.**

Table 9-2 Routing and remote access options

Option	Description
Remote access (dial-up or VPN)	Use this option to set up remote access services to the network through a Windows Server 2016 server, using either a VPN or dial-up modems.
Network Address Translation (NAT)	Use this option to enable Internet access by employing **Network Address Translation (NAT)**. Used by Microsoft Remote Access Services and by firewalls, NAT translates IP addresses on an internal (private) network so that the actual IP addresses cannot be determined on the Internet, because each address is seen externally on the Internet as one or more decoy addresses. The advantages of using NAT include (1) addresses on the internal network do not have to be registered on the Internet, because they are only seen on the local internal network and (2) users on the internal network gain some measure of protection from Internet intruders. (You learn more about NAT in Chapter 10.)
Virtual private network (VPN) access and NAT	Use this option when you want to configure the server so that users can access it using a VPN and so that internal network VPN users take advantage of NAT.
Secure connection between two private networks	Use this option for secure communications between two servers over the Internet, such as one server at a branch location in St. Louis and another at the headquarters in Chicago (both servers must be configured with this option).
Custom configuration	Use this option when you want to customize the routing and remote access capabilities.

8. Click **VPN access** (see Figure 9-4).
9. Click **Next.**
10. Click **Finish.**
11. If you see the Routing and Remote Access box, click **OK.** (You'll address Windows Firewall issues in the next activity. You may see the box twice. Also, you may have to click Finish twice.)

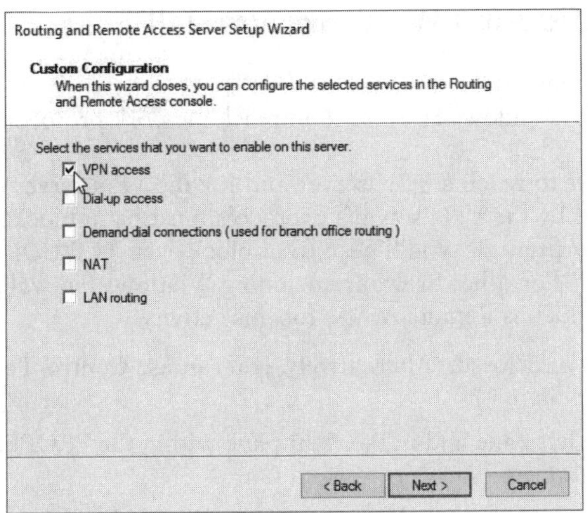

Figure 9-4 Selecting VPN access

12. Click **Start service** to start the Routing and Remote Access service.
13. Leave the Routing and Remote Access window open for Activity 9-4.

Configuring the Server's Firewall

The VPN server must be able to send communications through the network, which means an early configuration step is to make sure its communications can go through a firewall set up at the server. The communication services and protocols to allow through the firewall are shown in Table 9-3.

Table 9-3 **Ports to open in the Windows Firewall for a VPN**

Remote access protocol or service	Port(s)	Transport protocol
PPTP	1723	TCP
L2TP	500, 1701, and 4500 (4500 if you are using NAT)	UDP
SSTP (and SSL)	443	TCP
IKEv2 (Internet Key Exchange version 2; see the note after this table)	500, 1701, and 4500 (4500 if you are using NAT)	UDP
VPN	1194	TCP and UDP
DHCPv4 Relay Agent	67 and 68	UDP
DHCPv6 Relay Agent	547	UDP
Radius Server (for remote dial-up connections)	1812 and 1813	TCP and UDP

VPN communication protocols can use IPsec security that employs **Internet Key Exchange version 2 (IKEv2)**, which is the protocol that establishes security associations, including cryptographic keys, for IPsec secured communications. TCP and UDP ports are communications ports used for designated types of IP network communications.

If you are using the Windows Firewall on your server, the TCP and UDP ports used by VPN are unblocked by default when you configure a VPN server. However, it's important to make certain they are unblocked. You learn how to check in Activity 9-3.

Activity 9-3: Configuring Windows Firewall

Time Required: Approximately 10 minutes

Objective: Configure the Windows Firewall to unblock network protocol communications for a VPN server.

Description: To enable clients to reach a VPN server and for the VPN server to respond back, the TCP and UDP ports used by the VPN server's protocols must be unblocked by the server's firewall. For some third party firewalls, you'll need to unblock each TCP/UDP port for the designated VPN-based protocols. For other firewalls, including Windows Firewall, you can specify the application to unblock, which is Remote Access for this activity.

1. Open **Server Manager,** if it is closed. (Alternatively, you can use Control Panel to open Windows Firewall and skip to Step 3.)
2. Click **Local Server** in the left pane and in the right pane within the PROPERTIES box, click the Windows Firewall parameter, such as **Domain: On.**
3. In the Windows Firewall window, click **Allow an app or feature through Windows Firewall.**
4. In the Allowed apps window scroll to find **Remote Access** and ensure there is a check in its box and in the boxes for **Domain, Private,** and **Public.** Check the boxes for **Routing and Remote Access** and for **Secure Socket Tunneling Protocol,** if they are not checked. Make sure that **Domain, Private,** and **Public** are checked for these as well (see Figure 9-5). Click **OK.**

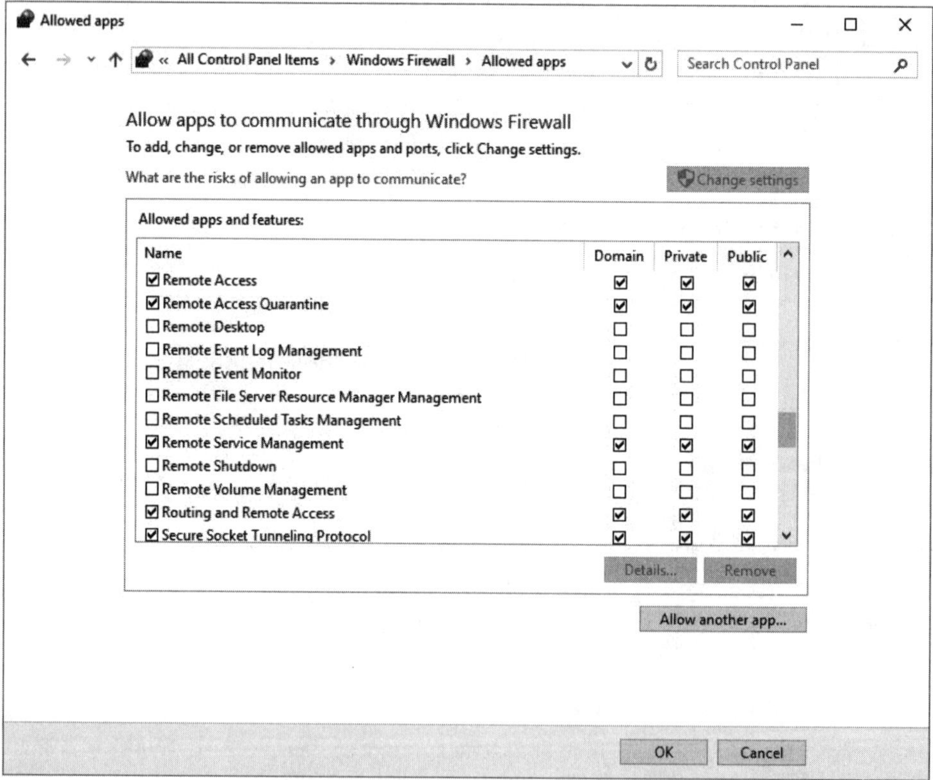

Figure 9-5 Configuring Windows Firewall

5. Close the **Windows Firewall** window but leave open Server Manager.

Configuring a DHCP Relay Agent

When a VPN server is initially configured, it is set up by default so that the IP addresses of clients are obtained automatically via a DHCP server. You can instead set the VPN server to have a pool of IP addresses to assign to clients, but in most cases it is less work to centralize IP leasing with your DHCP server. To coordinate the work of the DHCP server with the VPN server, you can set up the VPN server as a **DHCP relay agent.** A DHCP relay agent can be necessary, because some routers do not forward broadcast traffic, such as from a DHCP server, onto subnets. This is true for routers that are not RFC 1541 compliant, although today most routers are compliant. Check your router documentation to be sure.

If your routers are not RFC 1541 compliant, then you can configure a VPN server to act as a DHCP relay agent. A DHCP relay agent broadcasts IP configuration information between the DHCP server on a network and the client acquiring an address. In basic terms:

1. The client contacts the VPN server to make a connection.
2. The VPN server, as a DHCP relay agent, contacts the DHCP server for an IP address for the client.
3. The DHCP server notifies the VPN server of the IP address.
4. The VPN server relays this IP address assignment to the client.

You can use the Routing and Remote Access tool to configure a VPN server as a DHCP relay agent.

9

Activity 9-4: Configuring a DHCP Relay Agent

Time Required: Approximately 5 minutes
Objective: Set up a DHCP relay agent.

Description: In this activity, you configure the VPN server you set up to be a DHCP relay agent. Because you have already set up your server as a DHCP server in Activity 8-7 in Chapter 8, you can use the IP address of your server. Or ask your instructor what address to use for the DHCP server. (If you don't know the address of your server, click Start and click the Windows PowerShell tile, enter the command *ipconfig*, and record the IPv4 address.)

1. Access the **Routing and Remote Access** window, or if it is closed, access **Server Manager,** click **Tools,** and click **Routing and Remote Access.**
2. Double-click the name of the server in the tree in the left pane, if the items under the name are not displayed.
3. Double-click **IPv4** in the tree.
4. In the left pane, right-click **DHCP Relay Agent,** and click **Properties** (see Figure 9-6).
5. In the Server address box within the DHCP Relay Agent Properties window, enter the IP address of the DHCP server and click **Add,** as shown in Figure 9-7. (If the DHCP server's address has already been added automatically, you don't need to put it in.)
6. Click **OK.**
7. Leave the Routing and Remote Access window open for the next activity.

You can further configure the DHCP relay agent by specifying the maximum number of DHCP servers that can be reached through routers, which in this case Microsoft calls the hop count. You do this by configuring the network interface on the VPN server, such as the internal NIC.

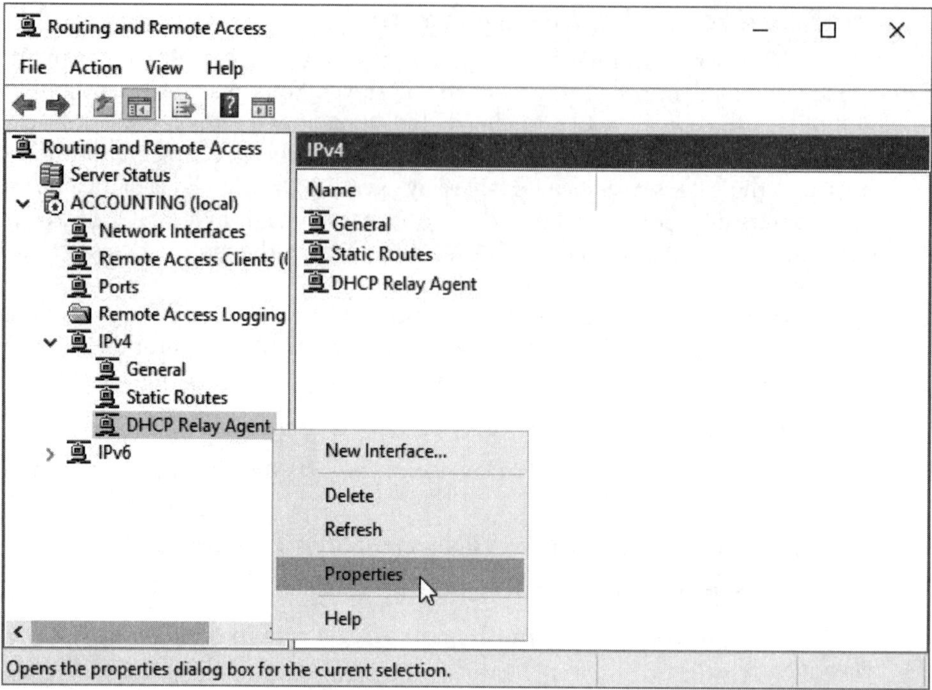

Figure 9-6 Configure a DHCP relay agent

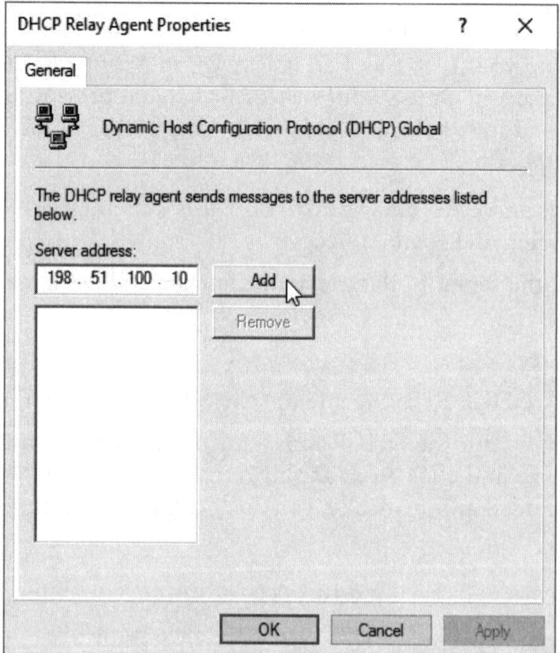

Figure 9-7 Entering the IP address of the DHCP server

Activity 9-5: Additional DHCP Relay Agent Configuration

Time Required: Approximately 5 minutes
Objective: Configure the DHCP relay agent hop count.

Description: In this activity, you configure hop count routing information for the DHCP relay agent.

1. Make sure the **Routing and Remote Access** window is open and that you see DHCP Relay Agent in the tree under IPv4.
2. Click **DHCP Relay Agent** in the tree.
3. In the right pane, right-click the interface, such as **Internal** and click **Properties.** (If no interface is shown, right-click **DHCP Relay Agent**, click **New Interface**, click an interface such as **Internal**, click **OK**, click **OK**, right-click the interface in the right pane, and click **Properties**.)
4. Be certain that the **Relay DHCP packets** box is checked.
5. In the Hop-count threshold text box, enter **2** for this activity. Note that the maximum number you can enter is 16.
6. If necessary, set the Boot threshold (seconds) value at **4** (the default). This parameter is used to give the DHCP server on the local network time to respond (in this case, four seconds) before a DHCP server on a remote network is contacted.
7. Click **OK**, as shown in Figure 9-8.

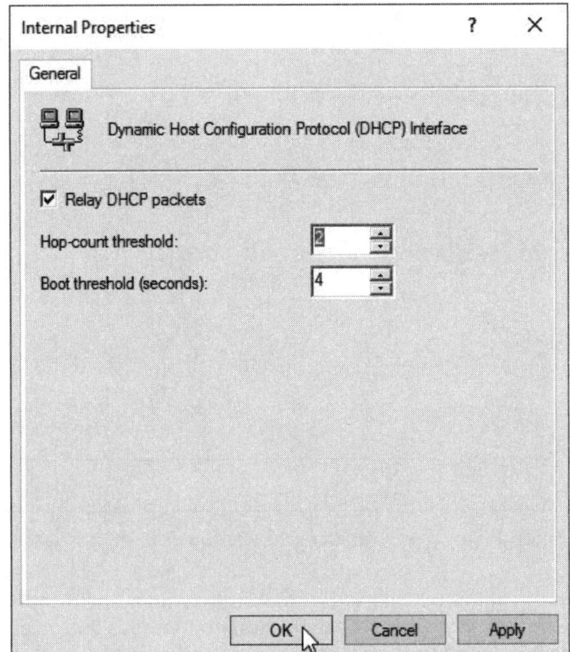

Figure 9-8 Configuring the interface properties

8. Leave the Routing and Remote Access window open for another activity.

Configuring VPN Properties

After the VPN server is set up, you can further configure it from the Routing and Remote Access window by right-clicking the VPN server in the tree and clicking Properties (see Figure 9-9). Table 9-4 summarizes the different property tabs available.

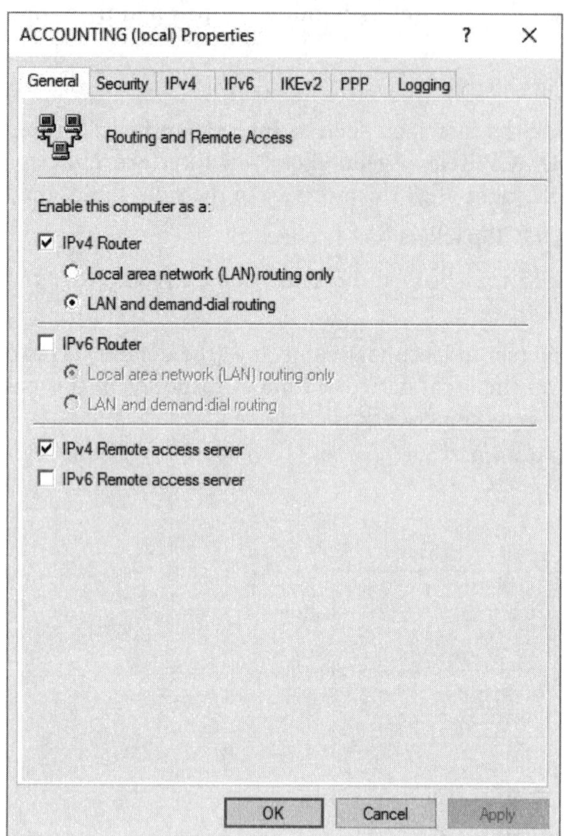

Figure 9-9 VPN server properties

Table 9-4 VPN server properties tabs

Property tab	Description
General	Allows you to enable the server as a router and/or a remote access server (by default, it is set up as an IPv4 router and remote access server)
Security	If Network Policy Server (NPS) is not installed, this tab allows you to configure an authentication provider and accounting provider (such as a RADIUS server); selecting the Authentication Methods button allows you to enable authentication protocols on the RAS server or enable unauthenticated access
IPv4	Allows you to enable IPv4 forwarding; from this tab, you can also change how IP addresses are assigned to clients using either a DHCP server or a static address pool
IPv6	Allows you to enable IPv6 forwarding and default route advertisement; also enables you to assign the IPv6 prefix
IKEv2	Enables you to set IKEv2 client controls, including idle timeout and network outage time; it also enables you to set the security association expiration time and data size limit
PPP	Allows you to enable PPP options such as Multilink or Multilink PPP (MPPP) connections; Multilink enables you to **aggregate lines or channels**, into one logical connection (if Multilink is used, the lines must be aggregated at the server and at the remote connection or device)
Logging	Allows you to enable PPP logging and specify what type of events to log

The General tab in Figure 9-9 enables you to configure the server as a router. Some network and server administrators prefer to avoid using a server as a router, because handling routing can create an extra burden on the server, slowing other services. Also, generally it is better to purchase a dedicated router that is connected between the VPN server and the network, Internet, WAN, or telecommunications connection. A dedicated router has an operating system designed for routing, including a full range of routing features and sophisticated firewall protection. However, if there is no router between your server and the Internet or WAN, for example, consider using the routing option in Figure 9-9. You would do this if your server directly connects to the Internet or WAN using a DSL adapter, for instance, and has a regular NIC to connect to the local network. A **DSL adapter** is a digital communications device that links a computer (or sometimes a router) to a DSL telecommunications line.

Configuring VPN Security

When a user accesses a VPN server through her account, that access is protected by the account access security that already applies, such as through a group policy or the default domain security policy. For instance, if account lockout is set up in a group policy, the same account lockout settings apply when a VPN user enters her account name and password (see Chapter 10 for more about security policies). In addition to the security policies already in place, you can set up VPN security through a remote access policy.

9

Elements of a Remote Access Policy Once Routing and Remote Access is enabled via setting up a VPN, a default remote access policy is created. You need to examine and change the policy to match your organization's needs. A remote access policy consists of several elements that must be evaluated before a user is granted remote access, as follows:

- Access permission
- Conditions
- Constraints
- Settings

The first step in evaluating access is to determine if access permission is enabled at the VPN server. The default permission for this policy is set to *Deny access*. You can change the default permission to *Grant access* (see Activity 9-6) in the default remote access policy; or for even more fine-grained security, leave it as *Deny access* in the default remote access policy and add new policies that apply to specific security groups.

The conditions of a remote access policy are a set of attributes that are compared with the attributes of the connection attempt. Conditions can include the vendor identification number of the network access server, for example. Each connection attempt is evaluated against the conditions of the remote access policy. The connection attempt must match all of the conditions of the policy or it will be rejected. If multiple policies are configured, the conditions of each policy are evaluated until a match is found. If no remote access policy is established, the connection attempt is rejected.

One way to manage users' access to a VPN server is to control access through the remote access policies. If you control access through the remote access policies, consider fine-tuning the management of user account access by creating groups. For example, create a universal or domain local group that has access to one or more VPN servers, and create a global group of the user accounts that you want to have the access. Make the global group a member of the universal or domain local group.

If the connection attempt matches the conditions of a remote access policy, the constraints are then evaluated. The constraints include the following:

- *Authentication methods*—The type of logon access, including access through a smart card
- *Idle Timeout*—How long a session can be idle before it is disconnected
- *Session Timeout*—Maximum time a user can be logged on during one session
- *Called Station ID*—Telephone number for the access server when a dial-up connection is used (rarely used today)
- *Day and time restrictions*—Days of the week and times of day when the remote access server is open to users
- *NAS Port Type*—Type of connection to the remote access server

Next, the settings in the remote access policy are examined. The settings include elements such as IP filters, encryption, IP settings, and others. The IP filters setting enables you to control which IP addresses can access the VPN, for example. Encryption is for setting a common encryption method for data sent between the server and the client. IP settings govern how an IP address is assigned to a connection.

Establishing a Remote Access Policy Once Routing and Remote Access is enabled, plan to create a remote access policy. You can use the Routing and Remote Access tool (accessed via Server Manager, the Start button Windows Administrative Tools folder, or as an MMC snap-in) to create and configure a remote access policy. To create a new remote access policy, click to activate and then right-click the Remote Access Logging & Policies folder in the tree under the VPN server and click Launch NPS to launch the Network Policy Server tool.

Activity 9-6: Configuring a Remote Access Policy

Time Required: Approximately 15 minutes
Objective: Configure a remote access policy.

Description: In this activity, you configure a remote access policy for the VPN server you have installed.

1. Open the **Routing and Remote Access** window, if it is not already open.
2. Make sure that the tree is expanded to show the elements under the server.
3. First click (to activate, if necessary) and then right-click the folder for **Remote Access Logging & Policies** and click **Launch NPS**. (NPS is the Network Policy Server, which is used in Windows Server 2016 to centralize management of security and other policies for network access servers.)
4. Be sure that the **Network Policies** folder in the left pane is highlighted, or click it if it is not.
5. In the right pane, right-click **Connections to Microsoft Routing and Remote Access server** and click **Properties**, as shown in Figure 9-10.
6. Click the **Overview** tab, if it is not displayed. In the Access Permission section, notice that access to the VPN server is denied by default. Click **Grant access. Grant access if the connection request matches this policy**.
7. Under the Network connection method section, make sure that **Type of network access server** is selected. Click the down arrow for the box associated with this option and click **Remote Access Server(VPN-Dial up)**, as shown in Figure 9-11.
8. Click the **Constraints** tab.

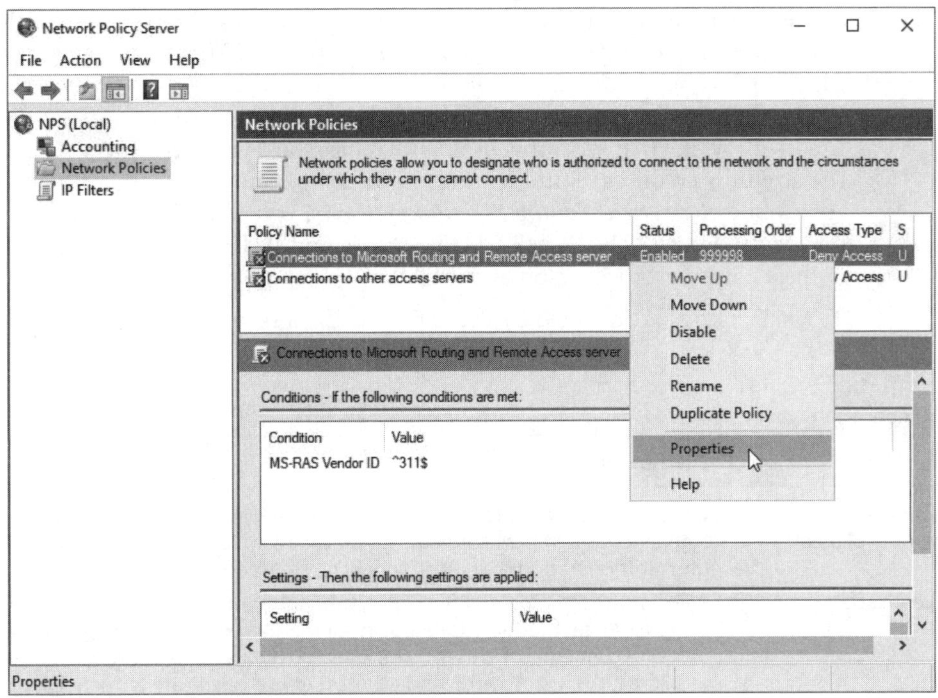

Figure 9-10 Configuring the remote access policy

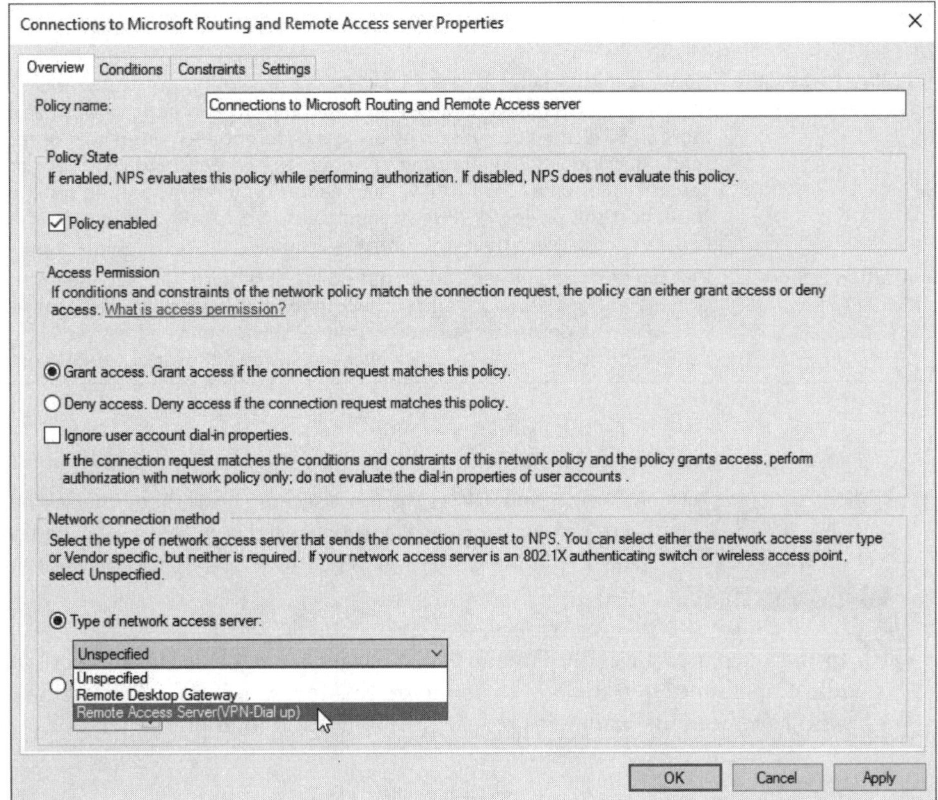

Figure 9-11 Selecting the type of network access server

9. In the left pane under Constraints, if necessary click **Authentication Methods**. Under *EAP Types*, notice that the two default selections are *Microsoft: Secured password (EAP-MSCHAP v2)* and *Microsoft: Smart Card or other certificate*. **Extensible Authentication Protocol (EAP)**, as explained in Table 9-5, is a strong form of authentication that can be used with MSCHAP v2 and is used with smart cards or certificates. A smart card is about the size of a credit card and is plugged into the computer to identify an authorized user. Also, under *Less secure authentication methods*, you can select from several authentication protocols: MS-CHAP-v2, MS-CHAP, CHAP, and PAP and SPAP. Table 9-5 describes these authentication protocols along with EAP.
   - What options are selected by default under *Less secure authentication methods*?

Table 9-5 Authentication types

Authentication protocol	Description
Challenge Handshake Authentication Protocol (CHAP)	CHAP requires encrypted authentication between the server and the client, but uses a generic form of password encryption that enables UNIX computers and other non-Microsoft operating systems to connect to a RAS server.
Extensible Authentication Protocol (EAP)	EAP consists of guidelines for negotiating authentication methods, and at this writing over 40 EAP methods are defined, including for wired and wireless authentication methods. One common use of EAP is for clients who access RAS through special devices such as smart cards, token cards, and others that use certificate authentication. If you click this option, then the Active Directory Certificate Services role should be installed so that you can configure it for a particular device or certificate type. The Active Directory Certificate Services role is installed through Server Manager.
MS-CHAP (also called **CHAP with Microsoft extensions version 1)**	MS-CHAP v1 and MS-CHAP v2 are set as the defaults when you install a VPN (RAS) server, which means that clients must use MS-CHAP with PPP. MS-CHAP is a version of CHAP that uses a challenge-and-response form of authentication along with encryption. Windows 95 through Windows 10 and Windows NT Server through Windows Server 2016 support MS-CHAP v1.
MS-CHAP v2 (also called **CHAP with Microsoft extensions version 2)**	Developed especially for VPNs, MS-CHAP v2 provides better authentication than MS-CHAP v1, because it requires the server and the client to authenticate mutually. It also provides more sophisticated encryption by using a different encryption key for receiving than for sending. Windows 2000 through Windows 10 and Windows 2000 Server through Windows Server 2016 support MS-CHAP v2; and earlier Windows operating systems can be updated to support this protocol. VPNs attempt to use MS-CHAP v2 with a client and then use MS-CHAP v1 if the client does not support version 2.
Password Authentication Protocol (PAP) and **Shiva PAP (SPAP)**	PAP can perform authentication, but does not require it, which means that operating systems without password encryption capabilities, such as MS-DOS, are able to connect to RAS. SPAP is a proprietary protocol used by Shiva remote access servers, such as Shiva LanRover (it is very unlikely you'll ever see Shiva LanRover or MS-DOS on a network today).

At this writing, EAP is the most secure choice. The other authentication types have weaknesses that experienced attackers can use to their advantage. CHAP, MS-CHAP, and MS-CHAPv2 are all susceptible to brute force attacks.

10. In the left pane, click **Idle Timeout**. In the right pane, click **Disconnect after the maximum idle time**. Enter 30 in the box to configure this for 30 minutes. This action disconnects users who have been idle and helps reduce the connection load on the server.

11. Click **Day and time restrictions** in the left pane. In the right pane, click **Allow access only on these days and at these times.**
12. Click the **Edit** button in the right pane. Notice that all of the times are blocked out as Permitted. Click the left most block under 12 for the Sunday row of times and drag your pointing device to block all of Sunday. Click **Denied**. Next, click the left most block for the Saturday row of times and drag the cursor to highlight the entire row. Click **Denied** (see Figure 9-12). This action secures the VPN server so that it cannot be accessed on the weekends. Click **OK**.

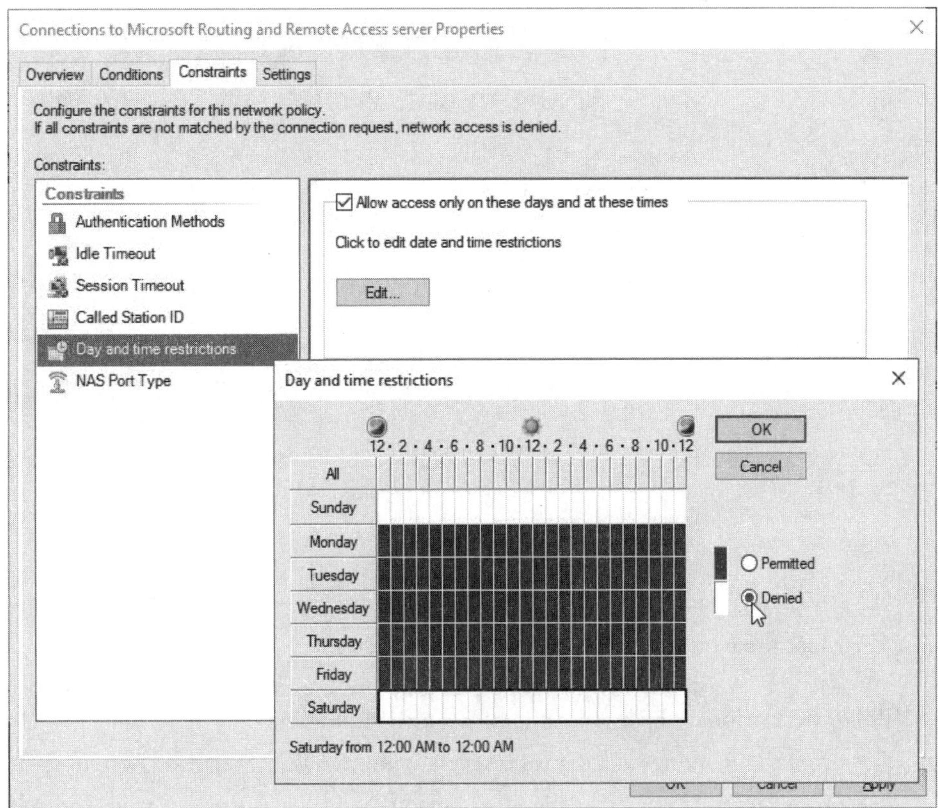

Figure 9-12 Securing the VPN server on weekends

13. Click **NAS Port Type** in the left pane. Under *Common dial-up and VPN tunnel types*, click **Virtual (VPN)**. Also, under *Common 802.1X connection tunnel types*, make the selection appropriate to your type of network. For example, a typical selection to make is *Ethernet*, for a wired network, or *Wireless—IEEE 802.11* for a wireless network (or select both, see Figure 9-13). Also, notice that under Others there are selections for DSL (ADSL), asynchronous modems, and cable WAN connections.
14. Click the **Conditions** and then the **Settings** tabs to see what they offer.
15. Click **OK** in the Connections to Microsoft Routing and Remote Access server Properties window to save your changes.

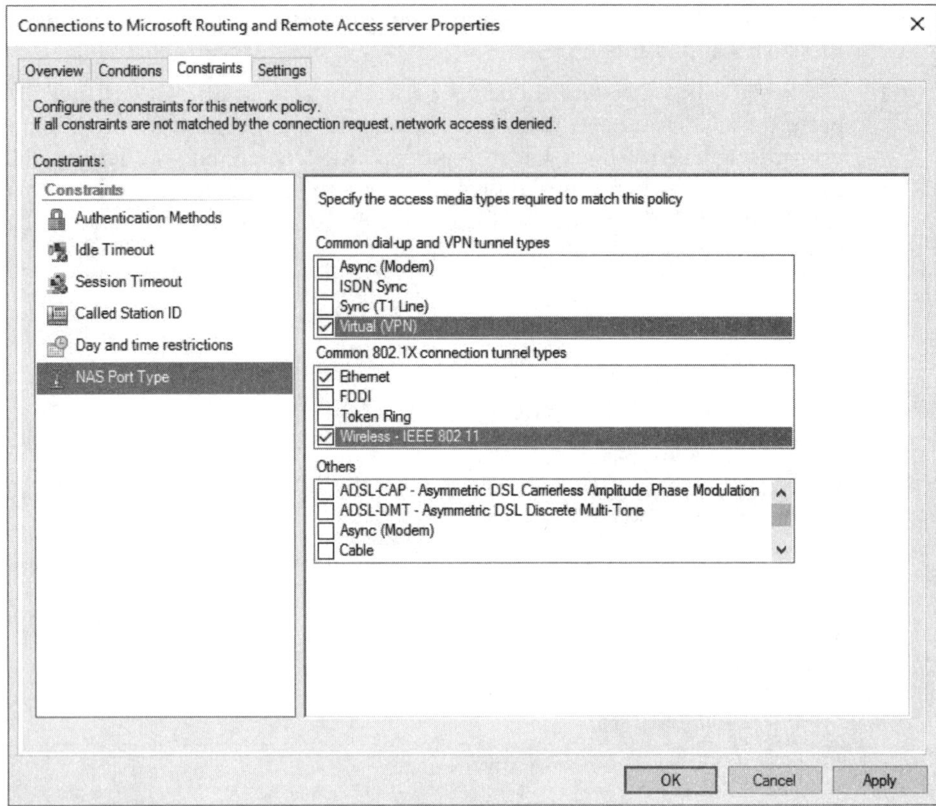

Figure 9-13 Configuring the access media types

16. Close the Network Policy Server window.
17. Close the Routing and Remote Access window.

After a remote access policy is created, you can always change it by using the Network Policy Server tool, which you can access in the following ways:

- From the Routing and Remote Access window (as in Step 3 of Activity 9-6)
- From Server Manager or the Start button/Windows Administrative Tools folder
- As an MMC snap-in

Monitoring VPN Users

After you have configured the VPN server and placed it in production, you should periodically monitor the users who are connected. You can use the Routing and Remote Access tool to monitor the connected users. With the tool open:

1. Expand the elements under the server name in the left pane.
2. Click Remote Access Clients in the left pane.
3. The right pane shows the users who are connected, including the user name, duration of the connection, number of ports used (for connections that use two or more ports through a multilink connection—but this is mainly for telecommunications clients, such as those using frame relay), and the active or idle status of the connection. If you want to disconnect a user, right-click that user and click Disconnect.

Multilink or Multilink PPP (MPPP) is a capability of a remote access server to aggregate multiple data streams into one logical network connection for the purpose of using more than one frame relay line, ISDN channel, modem, or other communications line in a single logical connection. Multilink works with **Bandwidth Allocation Protocol (BAP)**, which is a protocol that enables the bandwidth or speed of a remote connection to be allocated on the basis of the needs of an application, with the maximum allocation equal to the maximum speed of all channels aggregated via Multilink. **Bandwidth Allocation Control Protocol (BACP)** is similar to BAP but is able to select a preferred client when two or more clients vie for the same bandwidth.

Implementing DirectAccess

DirectAccess is built on using IPv6 and connecting to clients through the Internet. For the user and the server administrator, it has the advantage that the user connection is available as soon as the user turns on her or his computer. There is no need to sign in or enter a password, resulting in fewer calls to the server administrator from a user who can't sign in.

After the client computer operating system boots, the computer sets up an infrastructure tunnel to the organization's domain as well as to access DNS and DHCP servers. The client's computer can also be managed from the domain. Once the client is connected, an intranet tunnel is also set up, which gives the client access to the organization's web and email servers, databases, and other resources. The user can access a specific server by using its domain name, such as *research@jpcomp.com*, or its simple name, such as *research*.

To use DirectAccess, the server must have:

- IPv6 enabled at the server and clients.
- Applications that are IPv6 aware.
- Use of digital certificates that are either self-signed certificates or are managed through implementing a PKI to assign digital certificates.
- A security group containing the accounts of participating computers.
- Client computers running Windows 7 or above.
- Client computers that use Windows Firewall with the domain and public profiles configured to be on.

Computers running Windows 7 or above can use Microsoft DirectAccess Connectivity Assistant (DCA) version 2.0 to connect to Windows Server 2012 or above configured for DirectAccess. DCA can be downloaded from Microsoft's website for Windows 7 and is built into Windows 8 and above. Further, when you implement DirectAccess, the routers between client and server need to allow Internet Control Message Protocol for IPv6 (ICMPv6), IPsec Encapsulating Security Payload (ESP), and Internet Key Exchange—Authenticating Internet Protocol (AuthIP). AuthIP requires that UDP ports 500 and 4500 are open.

A **Public Key Infrastructure (PKI)** is achieved by having the Active Directory Certificate Services role installed to act as a certificate authority for managing and distributing digital certificates.

DirectAccess is installed using the Routing and Remote Access tool. If you have not previously installed a VPN server, open the Routing and Remote Access tool, right-click the server name in the tree, and click *Configure and Enable Routing and Remote Access*.

If you have previously installed a VPN, you can enable and install DirectAccess to work alongside VPN by using the Enable DirectAccess Wizard as in Activity 9-7.

Activity 9-7: Enabling DirectAccess

Time Required: Approximately 25 minutes
Objective: Enable DirectAccess after a VPN has been installed.

Description: For this activity, you enable DirectAccess. You can perform the activity using one NIC. However, before starting the activity, use the Active Directory Users and Computers tool to create a global security group, such as DirectAccess Users or DirectAccess Users plus your initials, such as *DirectAccess UsersJR*. Also, ensure that your server has a static IP address and that it is connected to the network.

1. Open the **Routing and Remote Access** tool.
2. Right-click the server in the left pane and click **Enable DirectAccess** (see Figure 9-14).

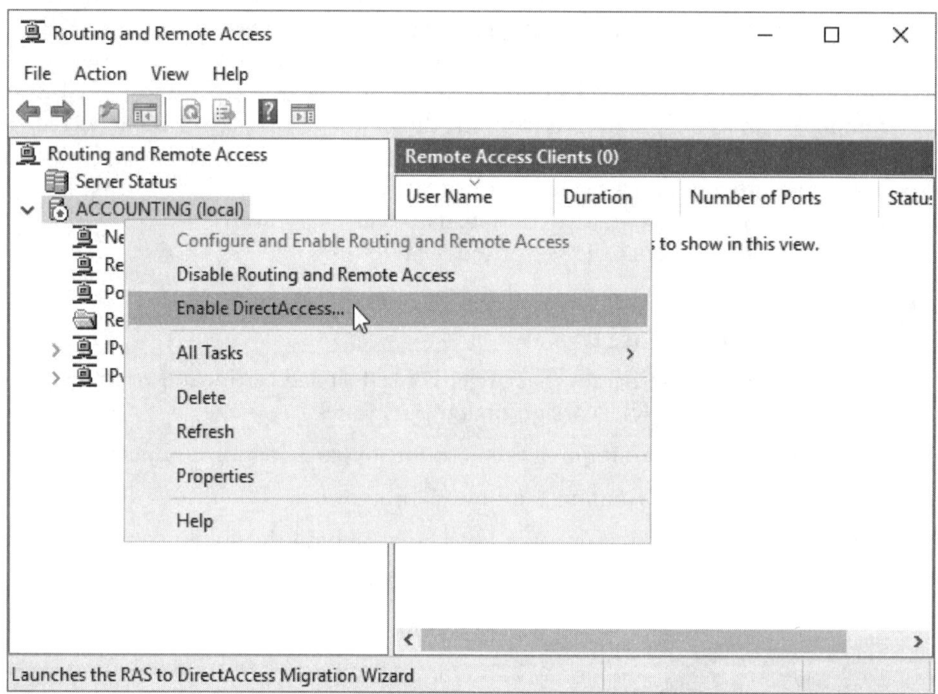

Figure 9-14 Selecting to enable DirectAccess

3. Click **Next** after the Enable DirectAccess Wizard starts.
4. If you see the DirectAccess Prerequisites window, check for warning or error messages. For example, the wizard will give a warning if a static IP address is not defined on the server or it will display an error message if there is no active network connection. You can still proceed if you see a warning, but the wizard won't let you proceed if there is an error, because you have to fix the error first. The error might be as simple as the need to connect the computer to the network.
5. In the DirectAccess Client Setup window, you need to designate a security group that you have already configured to contain computers that will be using DirectAccess. Click the **Add** button.

6. In the Select Groups dialog box, click **Advanced**, click **Find Now**, double-click the security group you have created, and click **OK**.
7. Click **Next** in the DirectAccess Client Setup window (see Figure 9-15).

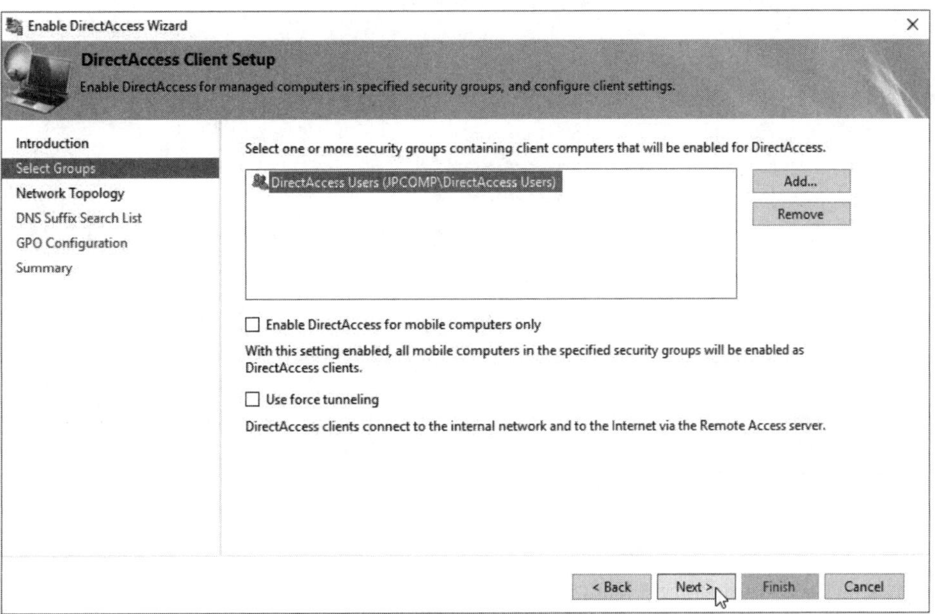

Figure 9-15 DirectAccess Client Setup window

8. Choose the network topology of the server. For this practice activity, select **Behind an edge device (with a single network adapter)**. An edge device may be a firewall or router configured to act like a firewall for example (refer to Figure 9-1, to view an example network topology). Note that the server can also be the edge device if it is directly connected to the Internet, for instance. (Further, you need to specify the public name or IPv4 address used by clients to connect to the RemoteAccess server, or try entering just the domain name, such as jpcomp.com.) Click **Next**.
9. In the Infrastructure Server Setup window, leave the default selection for now and click **Next**.
10. In the Configure Remote Access window, leave the default settings as in Figure 9-16, for group policy objects (GPOs, see Chapter 10 to learn more about group policies). Click **Next**.
11. In the Summary window, click **Finish**.
12. Click **Close** in the Enable DirectAccess Wizard Apply dialog box.
13. After you enable DirectAccess, the Remote Access Dashboard is displayed. You can use this tool to further configure DirectAccess and VPN. If you see the Manage Tracing dialog box click **Cancel**. In the left pane of Remote Access Dashboard, click **DirectAccess and VPN**.
14. In the Step 1 box, click **Edit** (see Figure 9-17).
15. Ensure that **Deploy full DirectAccess for client access and remote management** is selected. Click **Next**.
16. In the DirectAccess Client Setup window, ensure the security group you specified in Step 5 is displayed and click **Next**.
17. Leave the default selection in the next DirectAccess Client Setup window and click **Finish**.
18. Click the **Edit** button in the box for Step 2 to configure the remote access server.

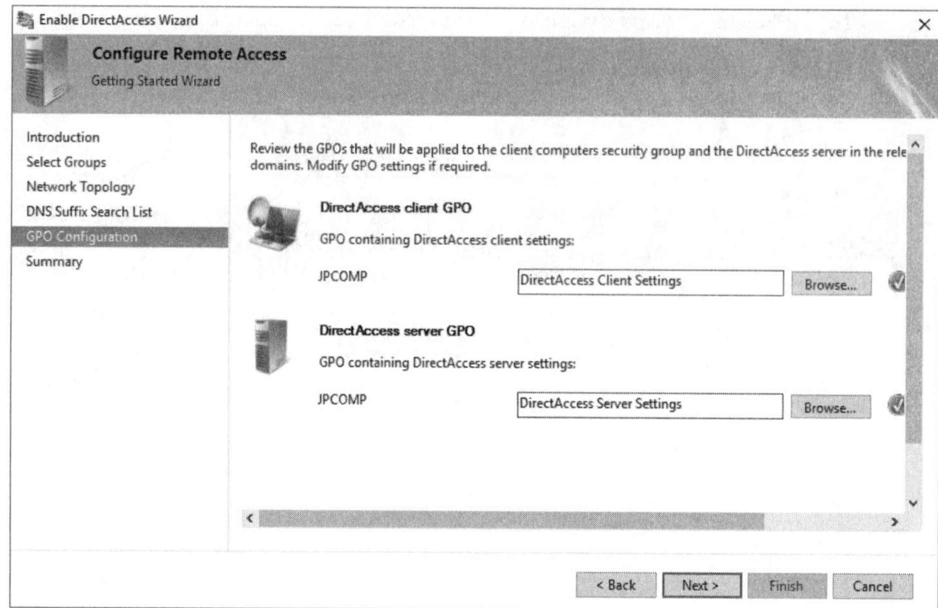

Figure 9-16 GPO configuration

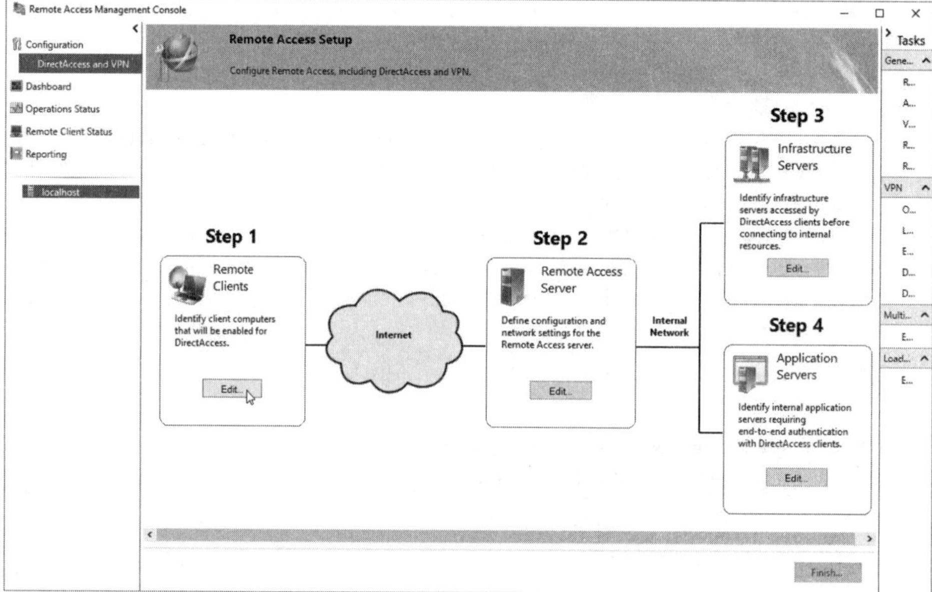

Figure 9-17 Remote Access Setup steps

19. In the Remote Access Server Setup window, leave the default for the public name or IPv4 address for the server and click **Next**.
20. Leave the defaults in the next Remote Access Server Setup window (see Figure 9-18). Notice that one default is to use self-signed certificates instead of PKI. Click **Next**.

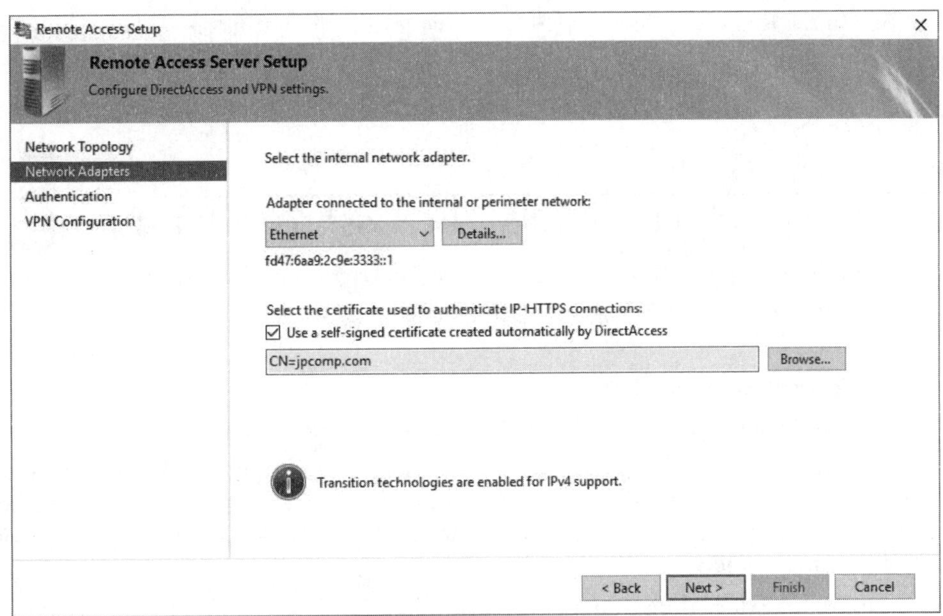

Figure 9-18 Network adapter configuration

21. Ensure that for User Authentication, **Active Directory credentials (username/password)** is selected and click **Next.**
22. In the next window, view the default selections for the IP Address Assignment method tab.
    - What is the default address assignment method?
23. Click **Finish.**
24. Click **Edit** in Step 3 to configure Infrastructure Servers.
25. In the first Infrastructure Server Setup window, notice that the default is to use a self-signed certificate. Click **Next.** (If you have problems proceeding because the Next button is inactive, click to remove the check from **Use a self-signed certificate.** Click to place the check again in the **Use a self-signed certificate** box. The CN parameter should change to CN=DirectAccess-NLS.localhost. Click **Next** again.)
26. Leave the default name suffix information for DNS in the next window and click **Next.**
27. In the next Infrastructure Server Setup window to add additional suffixes to the client suffix search list, click **Next.**
28. Click **Finish** in the next window.
29. Click **Edit** for Step 4 to configure application servers.
30. Notice that you can choose to extend authentication to the applications servers you add to the list in the DirectAccess Application Server Setup window. Click **Finish.**
31. Click **Finish** in the Remote Access Setup window. (If you close the window without clicking Finish first, you'll see a box indicating you have not saved your changes. In this box, click **No** and make sure you click the **Finish** button in the bottom right corner of the Remote Access Setup window.)

32. In the Remote Access Review window, review the settings and click **Apply**.
33. Click **Close**.
34. Close the **Remote Access Setup** window.

Troubleshooting VPN and DirectAccess Installations

Troubleshooting a VPN or DirectAccess server communications problem can be divided into hardware and software troubleshooting tips.

Hardware Solutions

If no one can connect to the VPN/DirectAccess server, try these hardware solutions:

- Use Device Manager to make sure network adapters and WAN adapters are working properly. Also, use Device Manager to make sure that an adapter has no resource conflicts (see Chapter 3, Configuring the Windows Server 2016 Environment). If a conflict exists, fix it immediately.
- For an external DSL adapter or a combined DSL adapter and router, make sure the device is properly configured and connected, and check its monitor lights for problems. Sometimes the easiest way to troubleshoot an external DSL adapter/router is to just unplug it, wait 30 seconds, and plug it back in.
- Call your ISP to determine if problems are present on the ISP's WAN.

Software Solutions

Try the following software solutions if no one can access the VPN/DirectAccess server:

- Use the Services tool or Server Manager to make sure the following services are running: IP Helper, Remote Access Connection Manager, IKE and AuthIP IPsec Keying Modules, Routing and Remote Access, Netlogon, Remote Access Management service, Base Filtering Engine, Windows Firewall, and Secure Socket Tunneling Protocol Service. Many of these services are dependent on other services, which you might need to start first.
- Ensure that the Windows Firewall is set up to allow remote access.
- Make sure that the VPN/DirectAccess server is enabled. To check, right-click the server in the Routing and Remote Access window, then click Properties and make sure that the *IPv4* (or *IPv6*) *Remote access server* box is checked on the General tab.
- Check the remote access policy to be sure that access permission is granted (see Activity 9-6, Step 6).
- Be certain that the VPN/DirectAccess server is started. To check, right-click the server in the Routing and Remote Access window, click All Tasks, and click Start or Restart.
- In the Routing and Remote Access tool, check the network interface. Under the server in the left pane, click Network Interfaces and make sure the network interface is enabled and connected. If not, right-click the interface and click Enable or Connect.
- Make sure that the IP parameters are correctly configured to provide an address pool for a VPN/Direct Access server. If IP configuration depends on DHCP, make sure that the DHCP server is working on the network and that you have configured a DHCP Relay Agent (with the correct hop-count threshold).
- Check to be sure the remote access policy is consistent with the users' access needs. For example, users may not be able to access a VPN/DirectAccess server because the server is

set to prevent access at certain times, or because certain users or computers are not in a security group that has access to the server.

- Open the Remote Access Management Console and click Dashboard in the left pane. Check the Operations Status and Configuration Status sections for problems, as indicated by an "x" within a red circle.

If only certain clients but not all are having connection problems, try these solutions:

- Make sure the clients are using the same communications protocol as the server, for example, PPP and PPTP, and that they are using an authentication and encryption method that is supported by the VPN/Direct Access server.
- If you manage access to a VPN/DirectAccess server by using security groups, make sure that each user account or computer account that needs access is in the appropriate group.

Connecting Through Remote Desktop Services

In addition to using Windows Server 2016 as a VPN/Direct Access server, you can also use it as a Remote Desktop Services (RDS) server. An RDS server enables clients to run session-based desktops, virtual desktops, and software applications on Windows Server 2016 instead of at the client. Using a session-based desktop, the client accesses an RDS server to run applications on that server during a connection session. Virtual desktops are used in association with accessing virtual machines on a virtual server through Hyper-V. Through a virtual desktop, the user can run applications on the remote server. Multiple virtual desktops can be in a pool of desktops for different purposes.

Nearly any type of operating system can access Windows Server 2016. The Windows Server 2016 Remote Desktop Services are used for three broad purposes: to run applications on a server instead of on the client, to support thin clients, and to centralize program access.

One of the reasons for using remote desktop services is to enable **thin clients**, such as downsized PCs that have minimal Windows-based operating systems, to access a Windows Server 2016 server so that most CPU-intensive operations, such as creating a spreadsheet, are performed on the server. Some examples of thin client computers are IO's Pro|Edge, Maxspeed's (Neoware) MaxTerm, IGEL's Thin Client series, and Wyse Technologies (purchased by Dell) Thin Clients. Thin client network implementations are generally used to save money and reduce training and support requirements. Also, they are used for portable field or handheld remote devices, such as remote hotel reservation terminals and inventory counting devices. Thin client computers typically cost hundreds of dollars less than a full-featured PC, and because the operating system is simpler, it is easier to train users. Thin client field devices can be made inexpensively and tailored for a particular use, such as taking inventory in warehouses. Or, if you've had a medical exam recently, you might have seen a thin client in the exam room used by a doctor or nurse.

Another reason for using an RDS server is to centralize control of how programs are used. Some organizations need to maintain tight control over certain program applications, such as sensitive financial applications, HIPAA and other healthcare forms, top-secret program development, word-processed documents, and spreadsheets. For example, a network equipment company that invents a switch that is 100 times faster than any other on the market can use an RDS server to closely guard access to design documents and programs. These are stored and modified only on the server, which can be configured to provide a high level of security.

Windows Server 2016 Remote Desktop Services not only support thin clients but also other types of client operating systems including Windows 10, Windows Server 2016, UNIX, UNIX-based X-terminals, Linux, Mac OS, and tablet operating systems including Android and iOS. Four main components enable remote desktop server connectivity, as shown in Table 9-6.

Table 9-6 Remote Desktop Services components

Component	Description
Windows Server 2016 multiuser Remote Desktop Services	These services enable multiple users to simultaneously access and run standard Windows-based applications on a Windows Server 2016 server.
Remote desktop services client	This client software runs on Windows 2000 through Windows 10 (but updates are only supported on recent operating systems, from Windows 7 on) and Windows Server 2003 through Windows Server 2016 to enable the client to run the Windows graphical user interface.
Remote Desktop Protocol (RDP)	This protocol is used for specialized network communications between the client and the server running Remote Desktop Services. RDP follows the International Telecommunications Union (ITU) T.120 standard to enable multiple communication channels over a single line.
Remote Desktop Services administration tools	These tools are used to manage Remote Desktop Services.

When you install RDS, you can install different role services for specific purposes. For example, the Remote Desktop Session Host role service is used for accessing an RDS server over a network. Another example is the Remote Desktop Web Access role service for accessing an RDS server through a web browser. Table 9-7 lists the role services that can be installed.

Table 9-7 Role services available through Remote Desktop Services

Role service	Description
Remote Desktop Session Host	Enables a remote desktop services server to offer session-based desktops and access to RemoteApp programs over a network so that clients can run applications on an RDS server
Remote Desktop Web Access	Enables clients to use a web browser or the Start menu to view a list of RemoteApp programs and to start RemoteApp programs on the RDS server; you need to install the Web Server (IIS) role with this and the Windows Process Activation Service (WPAS) feature
Remote Desktop Virtualization Host	Enables hosting virtual desktops and works with Hyper-V to enable you to set up different virtual desktops for users to access and from which to run applications
Remote Desktop Licensing	Handles Remote Desktop Services licenses needed by clients to enable access to the RDS server
Remote Desktop Gateway	Enables clients to establish an encrypted connection to virtual desktops and RemoteApp programs to an RDS server through the Internet using **Hypertext Transfer Protocol Secure (HTTPS)** for added security
Remote Desktop Connection Broker	Used when multiple RDS servers are on a network: (1) ensures that a client is connected or reconnected to the right RDS server and (2) that clients are load balanced across the RDS servers so that one or two servers do not bear most of the load

An RDS server employs RemoteApp, a feature that enables a client to run an application without loading a remote desktop on the client computer, which is particularly handy for web access. Previously with terminal services, users had two interfaces, one for the remote desktop and one that they had to access to still run programs at the local computer. The user then had to remember which desktop she was in, the one for the terminal server or the one for the local computer. In RDS, RemoteApp enables the user to run a program on the RDS server without having to load the remote desktop. The program appears to be just another program in a window running on the local computer, with no switching between the remote desktop and the local desktop.

A RemoteApp program is started by clients in the following ways:

- From an icon on the client's desktop
- From the client's Start menu
- As a link on a website via Remote Desktop Web Access
- As an .rdp (remote desktop protocol) file

Remote Desktop Gateway provides a secure way to use Remote Desktop Services over the Internet, which is vital for security conscious organizations. Remote Desktop Gateway is designed to work through firewall security and works on networks that use NAT (you learn about NAT in Chapter 10). Remote Desktop Gateway uses the time-tested HTTPS, which you have probably already used if you have purchased products over the Internet using your credit card. One of the reasons for offering Remote Desktop Gateway is to provide an alternative to using a VPN or DirectAccess server. Microsoft considers both Remote Desktop Web Access and Remote Desktop Gateway to be significant features of RDS because they make the services easier to use and more secure in a web-based and web browser environment already familiar to the user.

Installing Remote Desktop Services

When you install the Remote Desktop Services role, you also need to install the Remote Desktop Licensing role service to manage the number of user licenses you have obtained from Microsoft. If you have one or more RDS servers, there must be at least one Remote Desktop Licensing server. The Remote Desktop Licensing role server can be installed when you install the Remote Desktop Services role. Licenses can be purchased either per user account or by client device. The type of licensing you use depends on how users will access the Remote Desktop Services. If users access it through the Internet, then you'll want per-user licenses. If they access it through a local network, then licensing by device is often more suitable. You can initially install the Remote Desktop Licensing role service without having purchased the necessary licenses, but you'll need the licenses when Remote Desktop Services are made available to users in the production environment.

When you install the Remote Desktop Services role, you implement Network Level Authentication. **Network Level Authentication (NLA)** enables authentication to take place before the RDS connection is established, which thwarts would-be attackers. NLA is particularly designed to eliminate man-in-the-middle attacks in which an attacker redirects a client connection through his computer and then on to the terminal server, which enables the attacker to view all traffic between the client and the server. The authentication performed by NLA includes verifying the user account, the client computer, and the security credentials of the RDS server. These steps are all completed prior to starting the RDS network connection between the client and server. NLA can be used by Windows Server 2016 RDS servers and by server clients, including Windows 7, Windows 8/8.1, and Windows 10.

An element to consider before you install the Remote Desktop Services role is who will be allowed to access the RDS server. Create groups of user accounts in advance so that you can add these groups during the installation (you can add more groups later). If you are operating in an Active Directory environment, consider creating a domain local group, such as RDS Users. Next, create different global groups of users, such as a global group for each department that will access the RDS server(s). Next, add the appropriate user accounts for each department's global group. Finally, add the global groups to the single domain local group (you can probably use the global groups for other types of security access as well). See Chapter 4, Introduction to Active Directory and Account Management, to review global and domain local security groups.

Activity 9-8: Installing Remote Desktop Services

Time Required: Approximately 20 minutes
Objective: Learn how to install the Remote Desktop Services role.

Description: Using Remote Desktop Services can save a company money on client computer hardware, and it can be used for secure remote communications as an alternative to a VPN/DirectAccess server. Further, it offers a sound way to manage which applications users can access and how they use the applications. In this activity, you install the Remote Desktop Services role. You'll need to restart the server after you install the role.

1. Open **Server Manager**, if it is not open.
2. Click **Manage** and click **Add Roles and Features.**
3. If you see the Before you begin window, click **Next.**
4. Use **Role-based or feature-based installation** in the Select installation type window and click **Next.**
5. Make sure your server is highlighted in the Select destination server window and click **Next.**
6. In the Select server roles window, click the check box for **Remote Desktop Services** and click **Next.**
7. In the Select features window click **Next.**
8. Review the information about Remote Desktop Services and click **Next.**
9. In the Select role services window, click the check box for **Remote Desktop Connection Broker.**
10. Click the check box for **Remote Desktop Web Access.**
11. In the Add Roles and Features Wizard dialog box, click **Add Features.**
12. Click the check box for **Remote Desktop Session Host.**
13. In the Add Roles and Features Wizard dialog box, click **Add Features.**
14. Review your choices in the Select role services window (see Figure 9-19) and click **Next.**

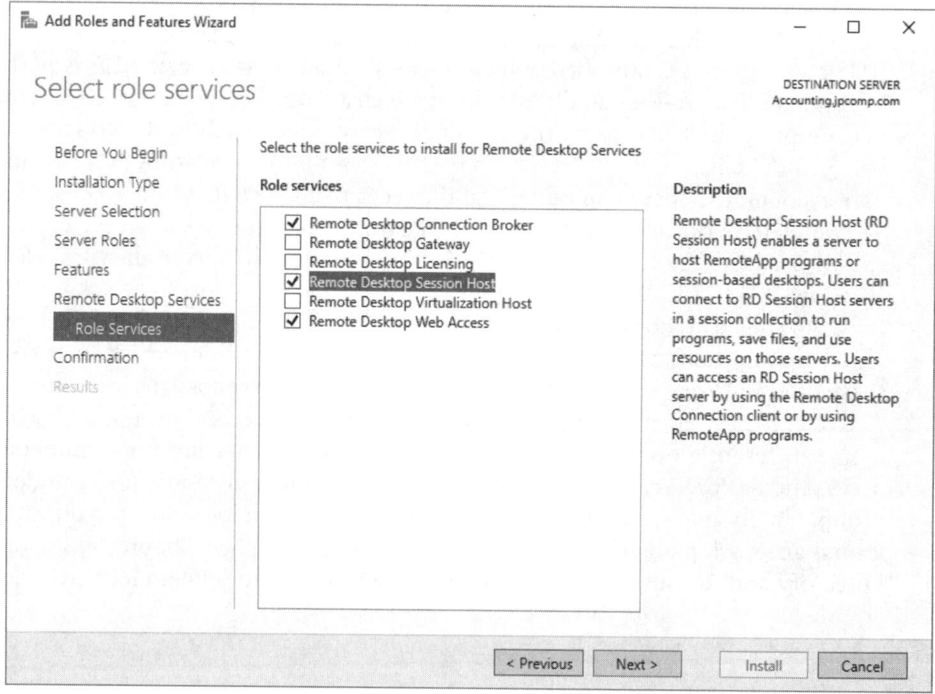

Figure 9-19 Select role services window

15. In the Confirm installation selections window, click **Install.**
16. Click **Close** when you see the message that you need to restart the server (under the blue bar).
17. Right-click the **Start** button, point to **Shut down or sign out,** and click **Restart.**
18. Specify the reason for the restart and click **Continue.** Wait for the server to restart and sign back in.
19. Open **Server Manager,** if necessary.
20. Click **Manage** and click **Add Roles and Features.**
21. If you see the Before you begin window, click **Next.**
22. Click **Remote Desktop Services installation** and click **Next.**
23. Ensure **Standard deployment** is selected in the Select deployment type window, as in Figure 9-20. Click **Next.**

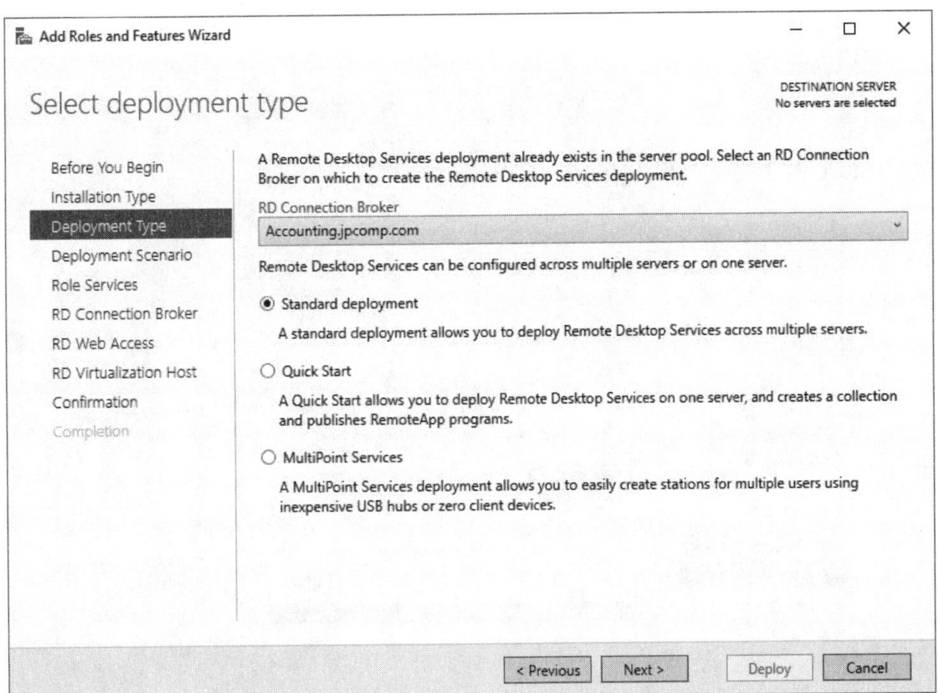

Figure 9-20 Selecting the deployment type

24. Click **Session-based desktop deployment** in the Select deployment scenario window (see Figure 9-21) and click **Next.**
25. In the Review role services window, notice that the role services listed are those you selected earlier: Remote Desktop Connection Broker, Remote Desktop Web Access, and Remote Desktop Session Host. Click **Next.**
26. Use your server as the selected broker server in the Server Pool box within the Specify RD Connection Broker server window; and, if necessary, click the **right-pointing arrow** between the boxes to add your server to the Selected box. Click **Next.**
27. Ensure your server is selected in the Specify RD Web Access server window in the Server Pool box. Click the **right-pointing arrow** between the boxes to add your server to the Selected box (see Figure 9-22). Click **Next.**

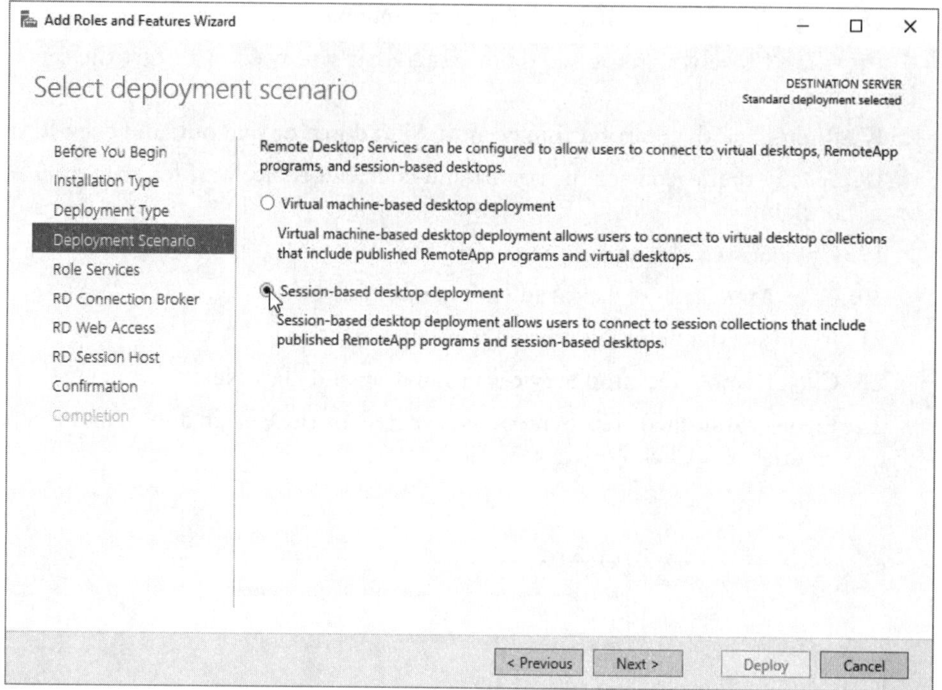

Figure 9-21 Select deployment scenario window

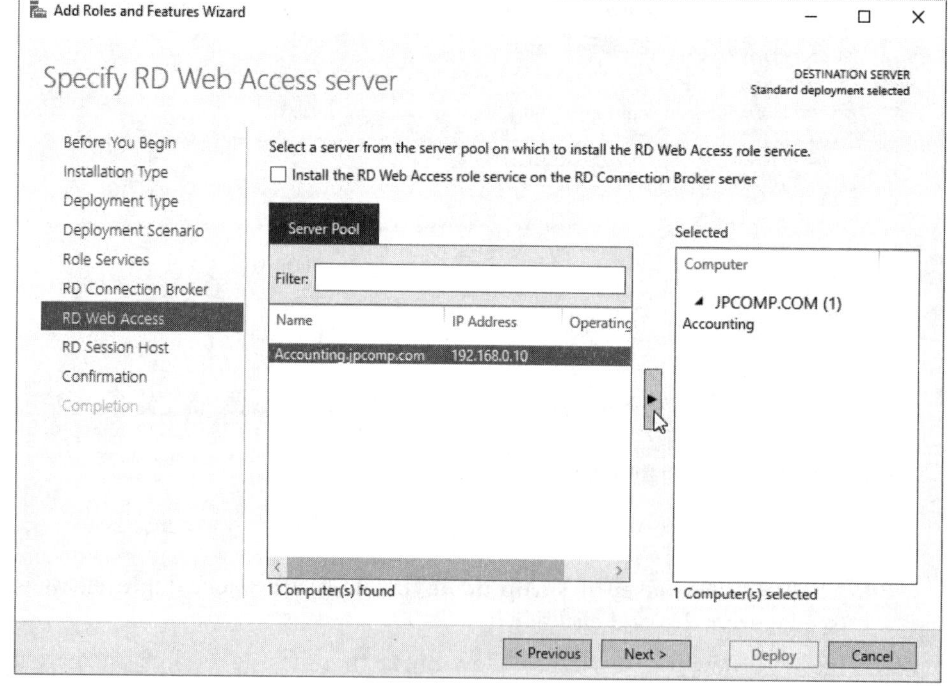

Figure 9-22 Selecting the server to add it to the selected box

28. Be sure your server is selected in the Specify RD Session Host servers window in the Server Pool box. Click the **right-pointing arrow** between the boxes to add your server to the Selected box. Click **Next.**
29. In the Confirm selections window, click the check box for **Restart the destination server automatically, if required.** Click **Deploy.**
30. In the View progress window, wait for the three role services to finish installing. Click **Close** (see Figure 9-23).

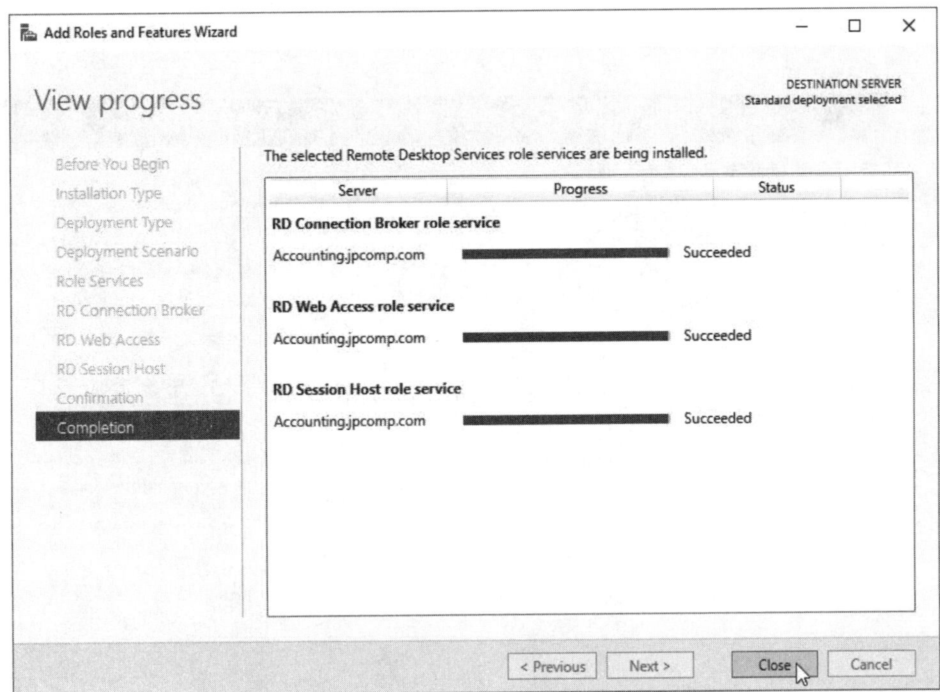

Figure 9-23 View progress window

31. Restart the server. Right-click the **Start** button, point to **Shut down or sign out,** and click **Restart.** Specify the reason for the restart and click **Continue.**

When you install an RDS server, the installation will automatically configure Windows Firewall to unblock communications for Remote Desktop Services. This includes Remote Desktop (for Windows Server to be a client), Remote Desktop Services, and Remote Desktop Web Services. If there is an occasion for which you need to configure Windows Firewall for Remote Desktop Services communications, refer to Activity 9-3.

Configuring Remote Desktop Services

After you have installed the RDS role and associated role services, use Server Manager to complete a basic configuration as in Activity 9-9.

Activity 9-9: Configuring Remote Desktop Services

Time Required: Approximately 15 minutes
Objective: Configure the RDS server.

Description: In this activity, you use Server Manager to perform a basic RDS server setup. The main parameter to set for this basic configuration is RDS licensing.

1. Open **Server Manager**, if it is not open.

   In the left pane, click **Remote Desktop Services** to see the Overview window as in Figure 9-24. (You may need to click **Remote Desktop Services** again after it connects.)

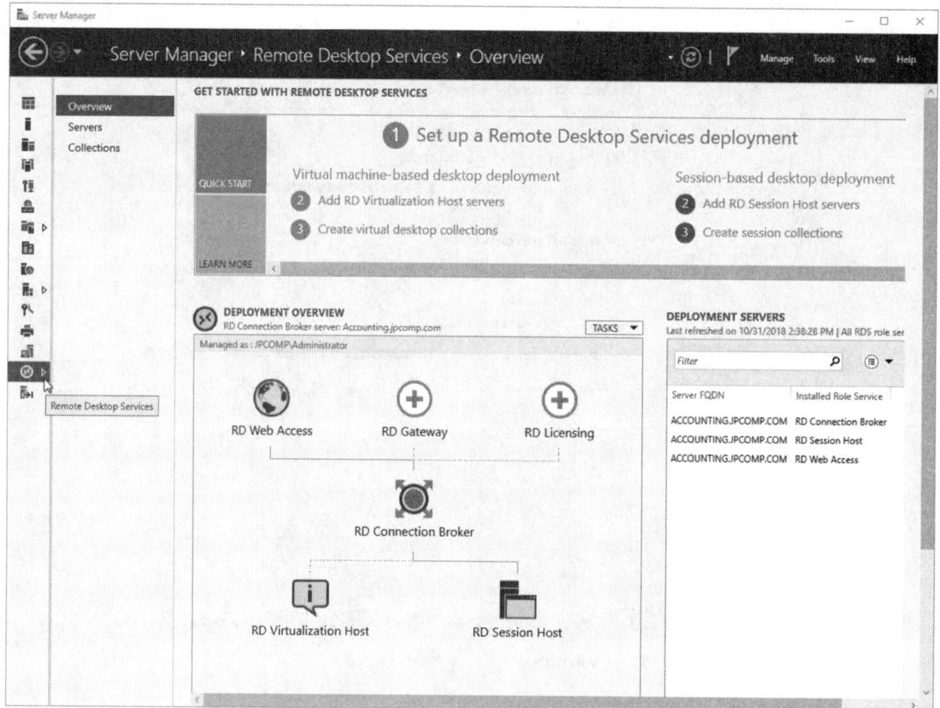

Figure 9-24 RDS Overview window

2. Notice that in the QUICK START section you have already completed the first step, which is to set up the RDS deployment. Also, you can decide to add RD session host servers or virtualization host servers (additional servers) in the second step, and you can create session collections or virtual desktop collections in the third step, which consists of pointing to disks that contain user profiles to be used. In this activity, we omit these last two steps because you can still have a basic setup without them.
3. Click the down-arrow for TASKS for the DEPLOYMENT OVERVIEW box, and click **Edit Deployment Properties.**
4. In the Configure the deployment box, leave **Do not use an RD Gateway server** selected as the default.
5. In the left pane, click **RD Licensing.** For this activity, select **Per User** (see Figure 9-25).
6. Click **RD Web Access** in the left pane.
   - What server is the default selection for web access?

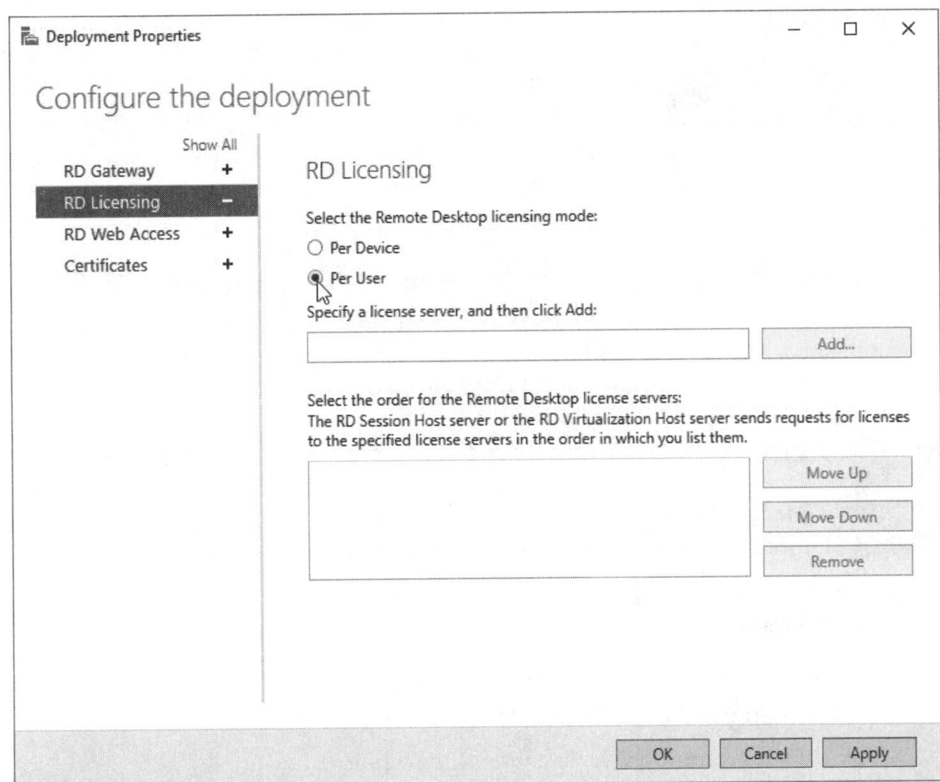

Figure 9-25 Configuring RD licensing

7. In the left pane, click **Certificates**. The Manage certificates window enables you to configure a certificate for security and to specify the certificate level.
8. Click **OK** in the Deployment Properties window.
9. In the DEPLOYMENT OVERVIEW box, notice that you can further configure RD Gateway (with a green plus sign) to add an RD gateway to the deployment. Also, you can further configure RD Licensing to add additional licensing servers.
10. Close **Server Manager.**

Accessing an RDS Server from a Client

Remote Desktop Services client computers can sign in using the **Remote Desktop Connection (RDC)** client. The RDC client is already installed in Windows Vista through Windows 10. It is also there in Windows Server 2016.

The general steps to start RDC client in Windows 10 or Windows Server 2016 are as follows:

1. Click Start and click the Windows Accessories folder.
2. Click Remote Desktop Connection.
3. Enter the name of the computer to access and click Connect.
4. Provide the username (if necessary) and password and click OK. (If you try now, you will likely see an access denied message because you have no licenses and no digital certificates configured.)

If you have trouble using Remote Desktop Connection from Windows 7, 8/8.1, or 10, configure Windows Firewall, similar to the Control Panel steps in Activity 9-3, to unblock Remote Desktop and any Remote Desktop Services application entries. Also, it may be necessary for router administrators to configure port forwarding, to ensure that there is a public IP address that allows the connection.

Publishing Applications for RemoteApp on an RDS Server

After you configure an RDS server, you can create a collection of RemoteApp programs that are published. The first step is to create a collection. Next, you select RemoteApps applications on the server to include in the collection, as in Activity 9-10.

Activity 9-10: Create a Collection and Publish RemoteApps

Time Required: Approximately 15 minutes
Objective: Create a collection and then select programs to publish.

Description: In this activity, you use Server Manager to create a collection and publish RemoteApp applications.

1. Open **Server Manager**, if necessary.
2. In the left pane, click **Remote Desktop Services.**
3. Click **Collections** on the left side of the window.
4. At the top of the window, click the down arrow for **TASKS** in the COLLECTIONS section and click **Create Session Collection.**
5. In the Before you begin window, click **Next.**
6. In the Name the collection window, enter a name for the collection, such as **RDS** plus your initials, such as *RDSJR*. Click **Next** (see Figure 9-26).

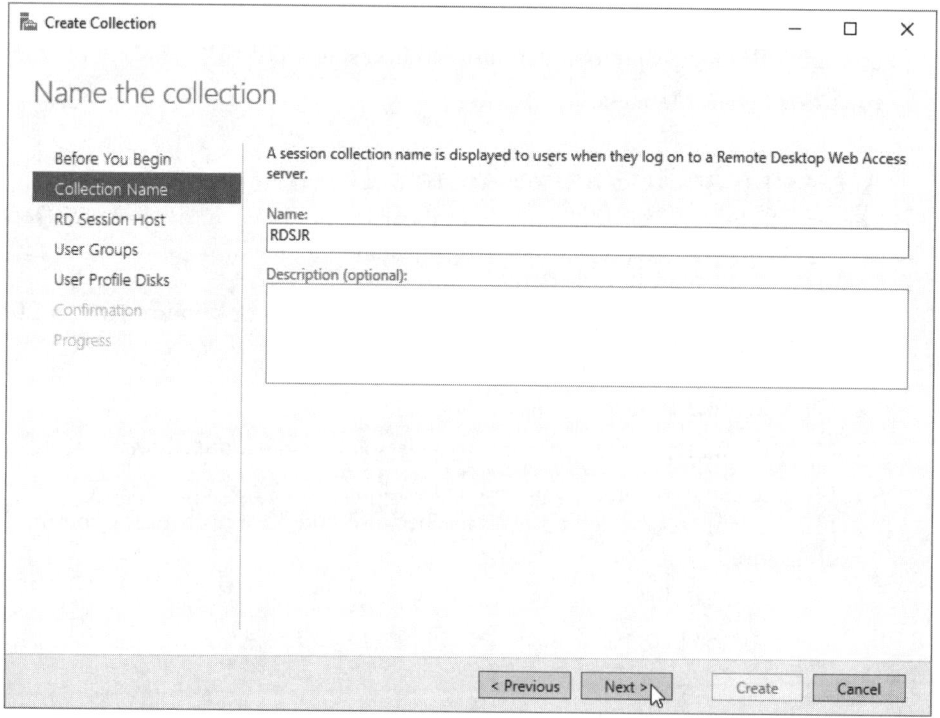

Figure 9-26 Name the collection window

7. In the Specify RD Session Host servers window, click the **right-pointing arrow** between the boxes to add your server to the Selected box. Click **Next.**
8. In the Specify user groups window, use the default Domain Users security group and click **Next.**
9. In the Specify user profile disks window, remove the check from the box for **Enable user profile disks.** Click **Next.**
10. In the Confirm selections window, click **Create.**
11. In the View Progress window, wait for the progress bars to complete and then click **Close.**
12. Now in Server Manager, the collection you created appears under Collections in the left side of the window. Click the collection, such as *RDSJR*.
13. At the top of the REMOTEAPP PROGRAMS box, click the **down-arrow** for **TASKS** and click **Publish RemoteApp Programs.**
14. Wait for a moment as the system finds programs that can be published and then scroll through the programs as in Figure 9-27.

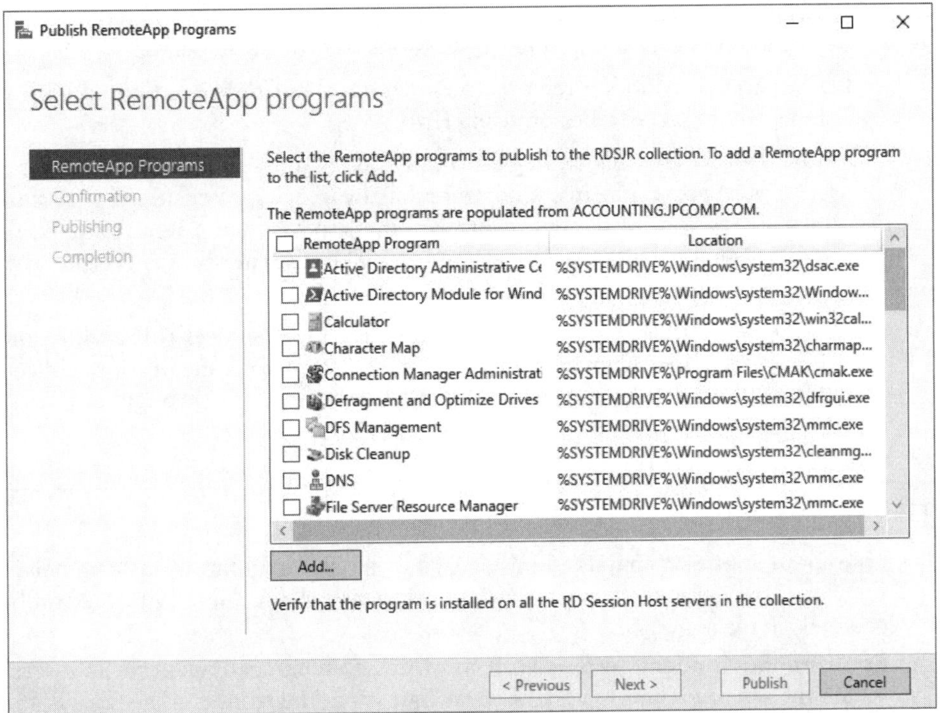

Figure 9-27 Select RemoteApp programs window

15. Click the check box for **Paint** in the Select RemoteApp programs window. Click **Next.**
16. In the Confirmation window, click **Publish.**
17. In the Completion window, click **Close.**
18. Notice that the Paint program appears in the REMOTEAPP PROGRAMS box in Server Manager.
19. Close **Server Manager.**

Chapter Summary

- Windows Server 2016 offers Remote Access Services to enable users to have remote access to a server.
- Remote Access Services includes virtual private network (VPN) and DirectAccess services that can be installed individually or together on a server.
- Remote access protocols include PPP, PPTP, L2TP, and SSTP. PPP provides the foundation for modern remote networking. PPTP, L2TP, and SSTP are tunneling protocols used by VPNs for security through public networks, including the Internet.
- Use Server Manager to install the Network Policy and Access Services and the Remote Access roles in Windows Server 2016.
- Use Server Manager to initially configure a VPN.
- After a VPN is installed, it should be configured to be a DHCP relay agent for IP address leasing to clients.
- A VPN has many properties that can be configured, including enabling the server, security, IPv4 and IPv6 properties, IKEv2, Multilink PPP, and logging.
- Plan to configure a remote access policy to govern how a VPN server is accessed, including using authentication and other restrictions to protect the server.
- DirectAccess is another remote access service that can be configured with VPN or standalone. DirectAccess relies on using IPv6.
- Many troubleshooting strategies can be used if your VPN or DirectAccess remote access server is having problems. A common hardware fix is to ensure that all communications links are working. A common software fix is to ensure the Windows Firewall is configured to allow remote communications and to make sure the services required by the VPN and DirectAccess remote access server are working.
- Use Server Manager to install the Remote Desktop Services role and to configure the role after it is installed. This configuration includes creating one or more collections containing published RemoteApp applications that users can access through an RDS server.

Key Terms

aggregate lines or channels Linking two or more communications channels, such as frame relay or ISDN channels, so that they appear as one channel, but with the combined speed of all channels in the aggregate.

asynchronous modem A modem from which communications occur in discrete units, and in which the start of a unit is signaled by a start bit at the front, and a stop bit at the back signals the end of the unit.

Bandwidth Allocation Control Protocol (BACP) Similar to BAP, but is able to select a preferred client when two or more clients vie for the same bandwidth. *See* Bandwidth Allocation Protocol (BAP).

Bandwidth Allocation Protocol (BAP) A protocol that works with Multilink in Windows Server 2016 to enable the bandwidth or speed of a remote connection to be allocated on the basis of the needs of an application, with the maximum allocation equal to the maximum speed of all channels aggregated via Multilink.

cable modem A digital modem device designed for use with the cable TV system, providing high-speed data transfer.

Challenge Handshake Authentication Protocol (CHAP) An encrypted handshake protocol designed for standard IP- or PPP-based exchange of passwords. It provides a reasonably secure, standard, cross-platform method for sender and receiver to negotiate a connection. *See also* MS CHAP and MS-CHAPv2.

demilitarized zone (DMZ) A portion of network that exists between two or more networks that have different security measures in place, such as the zone between the private network of a company and the public network of the Internet.

DHCP relay agent On a VPN server, relays IP lease assignments between a DHCP server and the network client computer.

digital subscriber line (DSL) A technology that uses advanced modulation techniques on regular telephone lines for high-speed networking at speeds of up to about 52 Mbps between subscribers and a telecommunications company.

DirectAccess Built around IPv6, establishes two "tunnels" for connecting to a DirectAccess server used in remote access and that is transparent to users and always on.

DSL adapter A digital communications device that links a computer (or sometimes a router) to a DSL telecommunications line.

Extensible Authentication Protocol (EAP) Consists of guidelines for negotiating authentication methods, and at this writing over 40 EAP methods are defined, including for wired and wireless authentication methods. EAP can also be used with security devices such as smart cards, token cards, and others that use certificate authentication.

frame relay A WAN communications technology that relies on packet switching and virtual connection techniques to transmit at rates from 56 Kbps to 45 Mbps.

Hypertext Transfer Protocol Secure (HTTPS) A secure form of HTTP that uses Secure Sockets Layer to implement security.

Integrated Services Digital Network (ISDN) A telecommunications standard for delivering data services over digital telephone lines with a current practical limit of 1.536 Mbps and a theoretical limit of 622 Mbps.

Internet Key Exchange version 2 (IKEv2) A protocol that establishes security associations, including cryptographic keys, for IPsec secured communications.

IP Security (IPsec) A set of IP-based secure communications and encryption standards created through the Internet Engineering Task Force (IETF).

Layer Two Tunneling Protocol (L2TP) A protocol that transports PPP over a VPN, an intranet, or the Internet. L2TP works similarly to PPTP, but uses an additional network communications standard, called Layer Two Forwarding, that enables forwarding on the basis of MAC addressing. *See* Point-to-Point Tunneling Protocol (PPTP).

leased lines Telecommunications lines or bandwidth on telecommunications lines that can be leased from a telecommunications company.

Microsoft Point-to-Point Encryption (MPPE) A starting-to-ending-point encryption technique that uses special encryption keys varying in length from 40 to 128 bits.

MS-CHAP (CHAP with Microsoft extensions version 1) A Microsoft-enhanced version of CHAP that can negotiate encryption levels and that uses the highly secure RSA RC4 encryption algorithm to encrypt communications between client and host. MS-CHAP is no longer considered secure and is susceptible to brute force attacks.

MS-CHAP v2 (CHAP with Microsoft extensions version 2) An enhancement of MS-CHAP that provides better authentication and data encryption and that is especially adapted for VPNs. MS-CHAPv2 is no longer considered secure and is susceptible to brute force attacks.

Multilink or Multilink PPP (MPPP) A capability of a remote access server to aggregate multiple data streams into one logical network connection for the purpose of using more than one modem, ISDN channel, or other communications line in a single logical connection.

Network Address Translation (NAT) Used by Microsoft Routing and Remote Access Services and by firewalls, NAT translates IP addresses on an internal or local network so that the actual IP addresses cannot be determined on the Internet, because the address seen on the Internet is a decoy address.

Network Level Authentication (NLA) A security method that enables authentication to take place before a Remote Desktop Services connection is established and that involves verifying the user account, client computer, and network server.

Password Authentication Protocol (PAP) A nonencrypted plaintext password authentication protocol. This represents the lowest level of security for exchanging passwords via PPP or TCP/IP.

Point-to-Point Protocol (PPP) A legacy remote communications protocol that transports IP as well as legacy protocols such as IPX and NetBEUI. PPP can automatically negotiate communications with several network communications layers at once, and it supports connection authentication. PPP has historically been used for dial-up connections between a client and server.

Point-to-Point Tunneling Protocol (PPTP) A remote communications protocol that enables connectivity to a network through the Internet and connectivity through intranets and VPNs. PPTP is no longer considered secure.

Public Key Infrastructure (PKI) Implementation of hardware and software to distribute, manage, and expire digital certificates, such as through implementing the Active Directory Certificate Services role.

Remote Access (RAS) A role that enables Windows Server 2016 to provide remote access so that off-site clients have access to a Windows Server 2016 network through the Internet, such as through a virtual private network. *See* virtual private network.

Remote Desktop Connection (RDC) Software on a client computer that enables it to connect to a terminal server. This was originally called Remote Desktop Services Client.

Secure Sockets Layer (SSL) A data encryption technique employed between a server and a client, such as between a client's browser and an Internet server. SSL is a commonly used form of security for communications and transactions over the web and can be used by all web browsers.

Secure Socket Tunneling Protocol (SSTP) A remote access communications protocol used in VPN communications and that employs PPP authentication techniques along with web-based communications transport and encryption through Hypertext Transfer Protocol and Secure Sockets Layer. *See* Secure Sockets Layer (SSL).

Shiva PAP (SPAP) A proprietary version of Password Authentication Protocol used on Shiva systems. *See* Password Authentication Protocol (PAP).

synchronous modem A modem that communicates using continuous bursts of data controlled by a clock signal that starts each burst.

T-carrier A dedicated leased telephone line that can be used for data communications over multiple channels for speeds of up to 400.352 Mbps.

thin client A specialized personal computer or terminal device that has a minimal Windows-based operating system. A thin client is designed to connect to a host computer that does most or all of the processing. The thin client is mainly responsible for providing a graphical user interface and network connectivity.

Transport Layer Security (TLS) A data encryption technique that has evolved from and replaced SSL. *See* SSL.

virtual private network (VPN) A private network that is like a tunnel through a larger network—such as the Internet, an enterprise network, or both—that is restricted to designated member clients only.

Web Application Proxy Entails publishing applications so that users external to an organization can access those applications on the organization's servers.

X.25 An older packet-switching protocol for connecting remote networks at speeds up to 2.048 Mbps.

Review Questions

1. Your company's management wants to install a VPN server and use web access to the VPN. They also want to use the same protocol as is used for secure transactions on the web. Which of the following protocols can you install to provide this security?
   a. SSN
   b. SSTP
   c. PPP/HTTP
   d. 3DES
2. You have set up a VPN, but no one can access it on the network. Your analysis at the VPN server shows that it is installed correctly and is enabled. Which of the following are services needed by a VPN server that should be checked to be sure they are working? (Choose all that apply.)
   a. Routing and Remote Access
   b. Remote Access Connection Manager
   c. Netlogon
   d. WAN sockets
3. You are planning for a DirectAccess server. Which of the following must you take into account in your planning? (Choose all that apply.)
   a. Client computers need to use Windows Firewall.
   b. Windows 8/8.1 clients are not compatible with DirectAccess, which means clients must have Windows 10.
   c. DirectAccess needs to be configured for IPv4 address piping.
   d. Either self-signed or managed digital certificates must be used.
4. A VPN server needs at least __________ NICs.
5. When you configure a VPN server to use the L2TP protocol, what UDP port(s) must be opened at the server's firewall to enable VPN communications to go through to the network? (Choose all that apply.)
   a. 500
   b. 802
   c. 1701
   d. 4500 (if NAT is also used)
6. What is the purpose of a DHCP relay agent?
7. Your company works with classified government information and wants to use smart cards for accessing its secure VPN server. What authentication should be configured at the VPN server to enable smart card use?
   a. EAP
   b. S-CHAP
   c. VPNSecure
   d. SPAP
8. To monitor users on a VPN server, use the __________.

9. You are configuring a DirectAccess server. Which of the following must your network use?
   a. Static IP addresses at the clients
   b. DNS reversing
   c. IPv4
   d. IPv6
10. ________ is already installed in Windows 7 through Windows 10 to enable users to access an RDS server.
11. The RDS role service that enables you to set up different virtual desktops is the ________ role service and works with ________.
12. A DirectAccess server is enabled through which of the following tools?
   a. Routing and Remote Access tool
   b. DirectAccess tool
   c. Remote Access Management and Configuration tool
   d. Remote Services tool
13. The ________ protocol is used for specialized network communications between a client and an RDS server.
14. Which of the following is true of Remote Desktop Gateway? (Choose all that apply.)
   a. It eliminates the need for ActiveX controls.
   b. It works for both VPN and Remote Desktop Services servers when they are configured to use the PPP protocol.
   c. It uses HTTPS.
   d. It enables clients to have encrypted connections with RemoteApp programs.
15. Your colleague has just installed a VPN server and now wants to establish a remote access policy. Where is the remote access policy configured?
   a. Active Directory organizational unit
   b. Remote Policy Log
   c. Network Policy Server
   d. Domain Registry
16. Layer Two Tunneling Protocol (L2TP) uses which of the following? (Choose all that apply.)
   a. MAC addressing
   b. IPsec
   c. TCP encryption
   d. IP addressing
17. What are the four basic elements of a remote access policy?
18. Users often load up the connections on your company's VPN server because many just leave their connections on all of the time, including overnight, on weekends, and while they are not doing work on the VPN. Your IT manager views this as a security risk, and it places an unnecessary load on the server and network. Which of the following remote access policy elements can you configure to address the problem? (Choose all that apply.)
   a. Change the NAS port duration time.
   b. Configure the idle timeout.
   c. Configure session timeout.
   d. Configure day and time restrictions.

19. Secure Socket Tunneling Protocol uses __________ for data encryption between a VPN server and a client's web browser.
20. When you want to install a remote access server, such as a VPN server, what role should be installed as well as the Remote Access role?
    a. Active Directory Remote Tools
    b. Network Policy and Access Services
    c. Active Directory Lightweight Directory Services
    d. Network Security Protocol Services

Case Projects

Cryp Code is a new firm that has recently been contracted by the FBI and CIA to write security programs for their computer systems. All of the programmers who work for Cryp Code must qualify for a security clearance before they can go to work. This means that Cryp Code is currently shorthanded as the company tries to find qualified programmers. The company staff works in a secure office area where they develop and test computer code and programs.

When programmers are working in the FBI and CIA headquarters, they need secure remote access to their company's servers on which they develop computer code. This enables them to view program design documents, research notes, program flow charts, and program source files.

Cryp Code uses Windows Server 2016 servers, and the programmers use Windows 10 client computers. Because they are short-staffed, Cryp Code has retained Aspen Consulting to implement remote access communications. As the only consultant who already has a security clearance, you have been chosen to work with Cryp Code.

Case Project 9-1: VPN Issues

The partners who own Cryp Code are interested in having you install a VPN, but first they want to know more about VPN structural elements. The partners are programmers and not operating system experts, and this is why they want to know more. Create a white paper, slide show, or both to discuss the following elements of a Windows Server 2016 VPN server that particularly apply to their company's needs:

- Remote access protocols
- IP addressing considerations
- Remote access policies
- Authentication
- Encryption

Case Project 9-2: VPN Tools and Installation

The partners are also interested in having you include in your presentation the following information about a Windows Server 2016 VPN:

- What tools are available for configuring and managing a VPN?
- What are the general steps required to install a VPN?

Case Project 9-3: Troubleshooting a VPN Problem

You have installed and configured the VPN without difficulty. However, when you test it remotely you cannot connect because no VPN server seems to be available. What steps do you take to troubleshoot the problem?

Case Project 9-4: Addressing a Security Need

The CIA has a very secret security program that nine Cryp Code programmers are working on. It is important that computer code and programs only be located on a secure server that is in a controlled and locked computer room with camera monitors. The programmers are not allowed to have any of the code on their own computers or to test the programs on their computers. At this point, the programmers are taking turns working around the clock on the server console in the computer room. The Cryp Code partners ask if you have a recommendation to enable the programmers to work on this project from their own computers without having the code on their computers. What do you suggest and what are the advantages of your suggestion? Provide as much detail as you can.

chapter 10

Securing Windows Server 2016

After reading this chapter and completing the exercises, you will be able to:

- Understand how Windows Server 2016 uses Group Policies
- Understand and configure security policies
- Implement Active Directory Rights Management Services
- Manage security using the Security Templates and Security Configuration and Analysis snap-ins
- Configure security policies for client computers
- Use the *cipher* command for encryption
- Use BitLocker Drive Encryption
- Configure Network Address Translation
- Configure Windows Firewall
- Use Windows Defender

No one wants confidential files and information to be stolen. No one wants his or her computer to be compromised by an attacker. No network administrator wants a network intrusion. For these reasons, Windows Server 2016 is equipped with an arsenal of security tools. The tools range from security policies to Windows Firewall and Windows Defender. It doesn't matter if you work with a small office network or a multicampus corporate network; it pays to learn about and use the Windows Server 2016 security features.

In this chapter, you start by discovering the security features in Windows Server 2016. You might think of these features as ways in which Microsoft has learned from experience to bolster server defenses. You learn how to put security policies to work and how to implement Rights Management Services. You learn to use the Security Templates and Security Configuration and Analysis tools to create defenses and to analyze the defenses you have already set up.

Windows Server 2016 Group Policies can be configured to enforce security on client computers, and you learn how to use this feature for a more secure network. You learn to use the *cipher* command for encrypting files and folders and how to use BitLocker Drive Encryption to protect entire drives. You set up Network Address Translation to hide IP addresses from intruders, and you find out how to configure basic and advanced Windows Firewall capabilities, as well as how to use Windows Defender.

An Overview of Security Features in Windows Server 2016

Windows Server 2016 was created to emphasize security. In surveys of computer professionals about Windows Server systems, security typically has ranked as a number one concern. Some of the popular security features of Windows Server 2016 that help address those concerns include:

- Reduced attack surface of the kernel through Server Core and Nano Server
- Expanded and evolving Group Policies
- Windows Firewall
- Windows Defender
- Security Templates and Security Configuration and Analysis tools
- User Account Control
- BitLocker Drive Encryption

Microsoft offers Server Core for organizations that want a Windows Server 2016 server, but with a much smaller attack surface. As you learned in Chapter 1, Introduction to Windows Server 2016, Server Core eliminates most of the GUI portion of the operating system and Nano Server eliminates even more. This makes the Windows kernel much smaller, presenting a minimal attack surface. Server Core or Nano Server can be a good solution, particularly for a server that handles critical network operations such as DNS and DHCP. They also can be a good solution for a web or other server in the demilitarized zone (DMZ) of a network, which is a portion of a network that is between two networks, such as between a private network and the Internet. Computers in the DMZ generally have fewer security defenses via routers and firewalls, for example. When an organization plans security, Server Core or Nano Server should be considered as a serious option. The smaller kernels in Server Core and Nano Server also can offer better performance and lead to fewer problems.

The security value of a smaller attack surface is also the reason why Windows Server 2016 is designed to be role based. As a role-based operating system, you select only the server role modules, and portions of modules, that you need. Additionally, you choose the individual features to install.

Group Policy is a way to bring consistent security and other management to Windows Server 2016 and to clients connecting to a server. Microsoft introduced Group Policy with Windows Server 2000 and has been building more functionality with each new version of the Windows

Server operating system, including in Window Server 10. In Windows Server 2016, Microsoft adds more policies for Group Policy management and several new policy settings.

In Windows Firewall and IPsec, settings are merged for consistency. Also, Windows Firewall protects incoming and outgoing communications. As you have learned in previous chapters, you can customize Windows Firewall to allow specific applications and to block others, which in part means that certain TCP or UDP ports are opened only for the specific applications that you allow.

Windows Defender is software that scans for viruses, spyware, and malware. Windows Server 2016 is the first Windows Server operating system to include Windows Defender, so that you don't have to download it separately or buy antivirus software. Windows Defender can remove or quarantine viruses and other malware to keep them from doing harm.

The Security Templates and the Security Configuration and Analysis tools enable you to configure server-wide security. Plan to use these tools from the beginning to configure security, to update security periodically, and to ensure your security settings are keeping pace with changes you make to a server.

User Account Control (UAC) is designed to keep the user running in the standard user mode as a way to more fully insulate the kernel, which runs in privileged mode (see Chapter 1), and to keep operating system and desktop files stabilized. Prior to Windows Server 2008 and Windows Vista, when devices and software were installed or changed, users could potentially negatively alter a system or introduce malware. This is because users performed these actions with extensive access to the system, going beyond standard user mode. UAC was first introduced in Windows Vista and later in Windows Server 2008 so that software and device drivers could be installed from an account running in standard user mode. Although the operating system allows this (with the right permissions), the installation still requires authorization from the server administrator. UAC means there is little chance that the installation can destabilize the operating system, because the installation takes place only with the proper authorization and in standard user mode.

Another element of UAC is the Administrator Approval Mode. For example, even though you are on the Administrator account when you run a typical program, Windows Server 2016 runs that program with standard user permissions in the standard user mode—insulating the operating system from extensive access. If the program needs to run in a mode as Administrator with more permissions and extensive access, the operating system displays a message box or prompt via UAC and you must respond. This security measure helps prevent malware or an intruder from acquiring control through a back door without the administrator knowing.

BitLocker Drive Encryption prevents an intruder from bypassing access control list (ACL) file and folder protections. If a drive is protected using BitLocker Drive Encryption, no one can access information without proper authentication even if the drive has been stolen. The data on the drive is encrypted and protected against tampering. You learn more about BitLocker Drive Encryption later in this chapter.

Introduction to Group Policy

The use of **Group Policy** in Windows Server 2016 enables you to standardize the working environment of clients and servers by setting policies in Active Directory. Hundreds of policies can be configured through Group Policy to help you manage desktop configurations, logon security, resource auditing, software availability, and many other functions.

Group Policy is set for many environments, ranging from client desktops to account policies to remote installation of Windows 10 on clients. Group Policies are secured so that they cannot be changed by individual users. The defining characteristics of Group Policy are as follows:

- *Group Policy can be set for a site, domain, OU, or local computer*—Group Policy can be linked to any site, domain, OU, or local computer. An OU is the smallest Active Directory container with which a Group Policy is linked. Group Policy is not linked to security groups directly, but it can be filtered through these groups. Also, when the first domain is created, the Default Domain Policy is automatically associated with that domain.

The Default Domain Policy is, by default, inherited by child domains but can be changed so that a child domain has a different Group Policy than its parent domain.

- *Group Policy cannot be set for non-OU folder containers*—Default containers that are folders instead of OUs, such as the Builtin, Computers, ForeignSecurityPrincipals, Managed Service Accounts, and Users folders, in the Active Directory Users and Computers tool are not truly OUs; therefore, you cannot link Group Policy with these containers.
- *Group Policy settings are stored in Group Policy Object*—A **Group Policy Object (GPO)** is an Active Directory object that contains Group Policy settings (a set of Group Policies) for a site, domain, OU, or local computer. Each GPO has a unique name and globally unique identifier (GUID). When Active Directory is installed, one local GPO is created for every Windows Server 2016 server. A server can also be governed by Active Directory GPOs for sites, domains, and OUs.
- *GPOs can be local and nonlocal*—The local GPO applies to the local computer. Nonlocal GPOs apply to sites, domains, and OUs. When multiple GPOs are present, their effect is incremental (local GPO first, default domain GPO next, domain controller GPO next, site GPO next, and the GPOs for OUs next).
- *Group Policy can be set up to affect user accounts and computers*—Group Policy is set up to affect user configuration, computer configuration, or both, as illustrated in the Default Domain Policy shown in Figure 10-1. If a policy is set up for users but is not the same as a policy set up for computers, then the policy set up for computers prevails over the policy for user accounts.

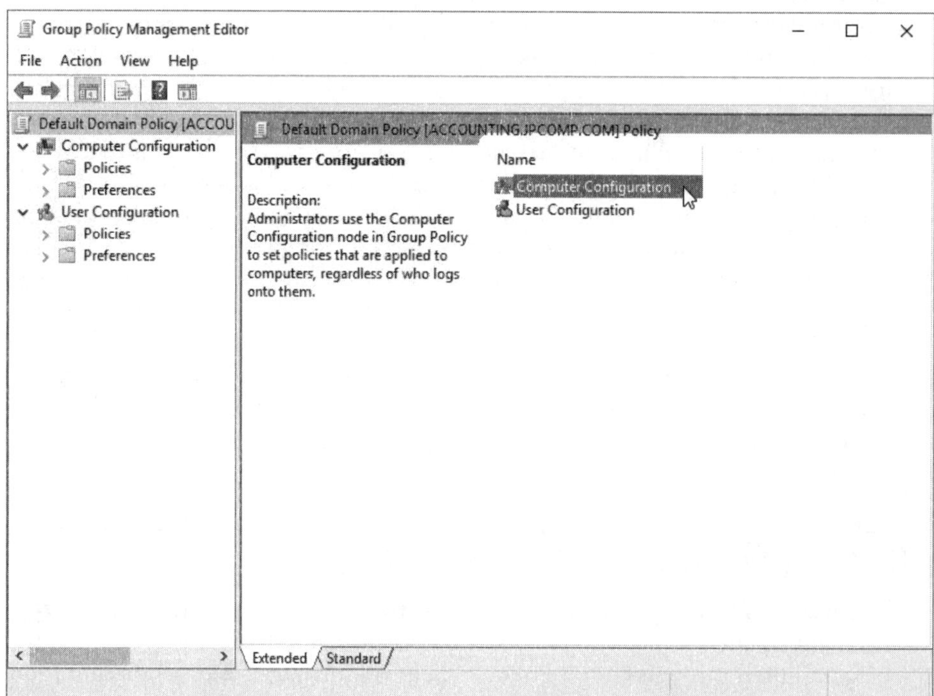

Figure 10-1 Default Domain Policy

- *When Group Policy is updated, old policies are removed or updated for all clients*—Each time you update Group Policy, the new information is updated for clients and the old information that no longer applies is removed. Figure 10-1 shows the Group Policy Management Editor set up to edit the Default Domain Policy.

Securing Windows Server 2016 Using Security Policies

Security policies are a subset of individual policies within a larger Group Policy for a site, domain, OU, or local computer. Windows Server 2016 has many individual security policies that you can configure; this chapter offers you a taste of some of the most important ones. In the next sections, you learn how to establish the following security policies:

- Account policies
- Audit policy
- User rights
- Security options
- IP security policies

Always make sure you configure the security policies on the local computer (the server as a computer on the network) within the Default Domain Policy prior to releasing a server for use. By configuring security policies in the Default Domain Policy, you ensure that they apply to all in the domain and apply through new DCs as they are added.

Before learning about security policies, it is important to become familiar with the Group Policy Management tool and the Group Policy Management Editor.

Some steps in the activities in this book include bulleted questions for you to answer. Additionally, for all of the activities in this chapter, you'll need an account with Administrator privileges. These activities can be completed on a virtual machine or computer, such as in Hyper-V.

Activity 10-1: Using the Group Policy Management Tool

Time Required: Approximately 10 minutes
Objective: Learn how to use the Group Policy Management tool.

Description: Group Policy can be configured using the Group Policy Management tool and the Group Policy Management Editor. In this activity, you practice accessing features in the Group Policy Management tool and the Group Policy Management Editor. Make sure DirectAccess is already installed (see Activity 9-7 in Chapter 9), so that you use it in this activity to configure Group Policy. Also, for this activity, Internet Explorer Enhanced Security Configuration should be turned off (which is the default) to avoid viewing Internet Explorer security warnings. If you need to turn it back on after you finish the activities in this chapter, repeat Steps 1–3, but set it to *On* rather than *Off*.

1. Open **Server Manager**, if it is not open.
2. Click **Local Server** in the left pane.
3. In the right pane, find IE Enhanced Security Configuration. If it is set to On, click **On** and in the Internet Explorer Enhanced Security Configuration dialog box, click **Off** for both Administrators and for Users. Click **OK**.
4. In Server Manager, click **Tools** and click **Group Policy Management**.

5. Click the **right-pointing arrows** to expand to see the items under Domains and then under the domain name, such as *jpcomp.com* as in Figure 10-2.

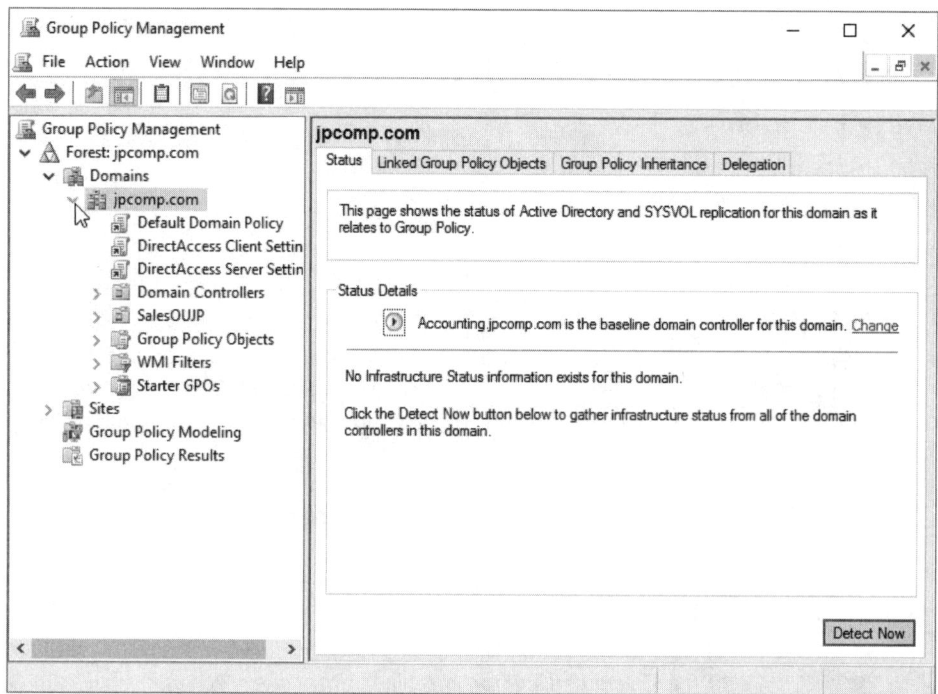

Figure 10-2 Using the Group Policy Management tool

6. Click **Default Domain Policy** and then click **OK** in the Group Policy Management Console box.
7. In the right pane, click the **Settings** tab.
8. In the right pane, click **show** for Windows Settings, if necessary (do not click if it says hide, you can go between hide and show).
9. Click **show** for Security Settings under Windows Settings, if the settings are not displayed.
10. Click **show** for Account Policies/Password Policy.
    - What is the minimum required length for a password? What is the maximum time a password can be used before the account holder needs to change the password?
11. In the tree in the left pane, click **DirectAccess Server Settings** and click **OK** in the Group Policy Management Console box.
12. In the right pane, ensure that the **Settings** tab is selected and if necessary, click **show** for Windows Settings.
13. Click **show** for Security Settings in the right pane under Windows Settings.
14. Click **show** for Windows Firewall with Advanced Security.

15. Click **show** for Inbound Rules in the right pane under Windows Firewall with Advanced Security.
16. Scroll to view the settings for Inbound Rules.
    - What protocols are allowed?
17. In the left pane, click **Default Domain Policy** and click **OK**.
18. Right-click **Default Domain Policy** in the left pane and click **Edit** to open the Group Policy Management Editor (refer to Figure 10-1).

You also can open the Group Policy Management Editor as an MMC. See Chapter 5, Configuring, Managing, and Troubleshooting Resource Access, and review Activity 5-6.

19. In the right pane, expand the tree under Computer Configuration to see **Policies, Windows Settings, Security Settings** as in Figure 10-3.

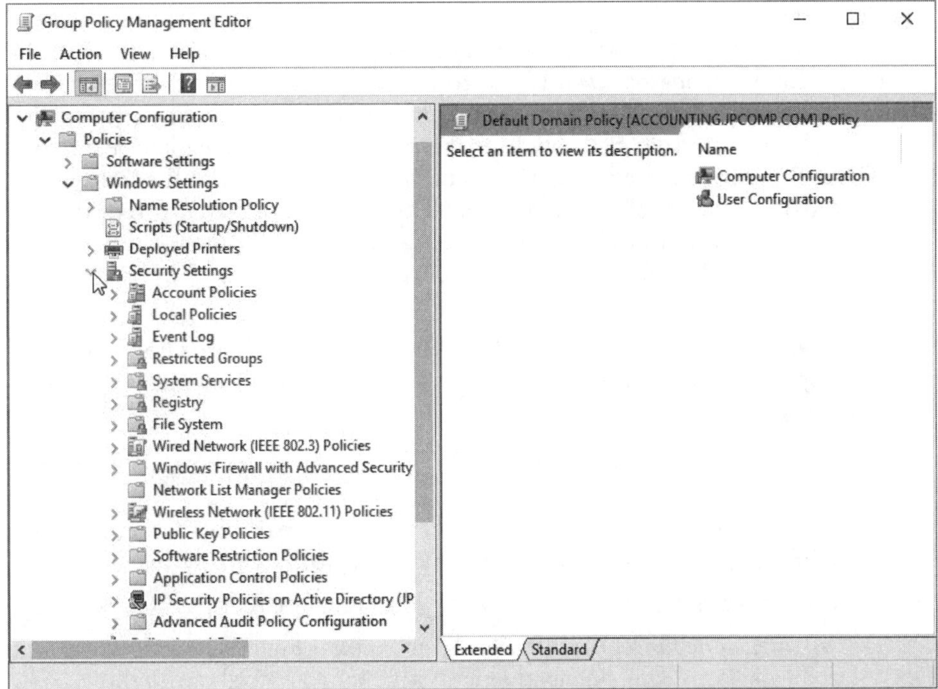

Figure 10-3 Accessing Security Settings in the Default Domain Policy

20. Leave the Group Policy Management Editor window, as well as the Group Policy Management window, open for the next activity.

Establishing Account Policies

Account policies are security measures set up in a Group Policy that applies to all accounts or to all accounts in a container, such as a domain, when Active Directory is installed. The account policies are located in the following path in the tree of the Default Domain Policy: Computer

Configuration, Policies, Windows Settings, Security Settings (refer to Figure 10-3). This is what you will have observed in Steps 18 and 19 of Activity 10-1, using the Group Policy Management Editor. The account policy options that you can configure affect three main areas:

- Password security
- Account lockout
- Kerberos security

Each of these is described in the next sections.

Password Security A first line of defense in Windows Server 2016 is password security. One option is to set a password expiration period, requiring users to change passwords at regular intervals. Many organizations use this feature, for example, requiring that users change their passwords every 45 to 90 days.

Server administrators should consider changing passwords every month or sooner for the Administrator account and other accounts that can access sensitive information.

Some organizations require that all passwords have a minimum length, such as seven characters (for a "strong password" Microsoft recommends a minimum of seven characters, but others consider nine characters better). This requirement makes passwords more difficult to guess. Another option is to have the operating system "remember" passwords that have been used previously. For example, the system might be set to recall the last ten passwords, preventing a user from repeating one of these. Password recollection forces the user to change to a different password instead of reusing the same one when a new one is set. An account lockout option can also be configured. The specific password security options that you can configure are as follows:

- *Enforce password history*—Enables you to require users to choose new passwords when they make a password change, because the system can remember the previously used passwords
- *Maximum password age*—Permits you to set the maximum time allowed until a password expires
- *Minimum password age*—Permits you to specify that a password must be used for a minimum amount of time before it can be changed
- *Minimum password length*—Enables you to require that passwords are a minimum length
- *Passwords must meet complexity requirements*—Enables you to create a filter of customized password requirements that each account password must follow
- *Store password using reversible encryption*—Enables passwords to be stored in reversible encrypted format (similar to clear-text passwords) and used when applications or application processes must employ user passwords

Microsoft does not recommend enabling *Store password using reversible encryption* unless absolutely necessary for an application you must use. This setting weakens password security.

Activity 10-2: Configuring Password Security

Time Required: Approximately 10 minutes

Objective: Configure password security in the default domain security policy.

Description: In this activity, you configure the password security for a domain.

1. Open the **Group Policy Management Editor**, if it is not open and expand the tree to view the elements under Account Policies (which is under Computer Configuration, Policies, Windows Settings, Security Settings, Account Policies; see Activity 10-1, Step 1-19).
2. Click the **down arrow** for Account Polices in the left pane, to display the items under Account Policies. Click **Password Policy.**
3. Double-click **Enforce password history** in the middle pane.
4. Ensure that **Define this policy setting** is checked. The default setting is **24** passwords remembered, which is the maximum. Assume you work for a company that has a policy to set this number at 15. Enter **15** in the box, as shown in Figure 10-4. Click **OK.**

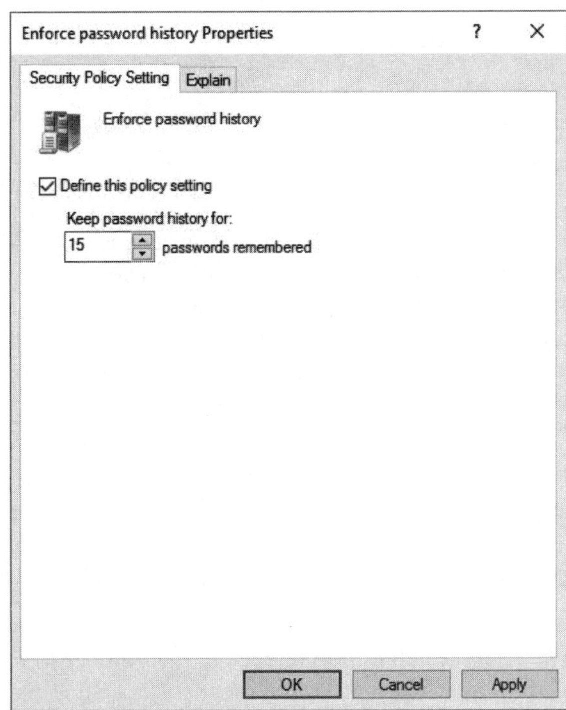

Figure 10-4 Configuring password history

5. Double-click **Maximum password age** and ensure that **Define this policy setting** is checked. Change the **days** text box to **60** and click **OK.**
6. Double-click **Minimum password length.** Be sure that **Define this policy setting** is checked and set the *characters* text box to 8. Click **OK.** The Default Domain Security Settings window should now look similar to the one in Figure 10-5.
7. Leave the Group Policy Management Editor window open for the next activity.

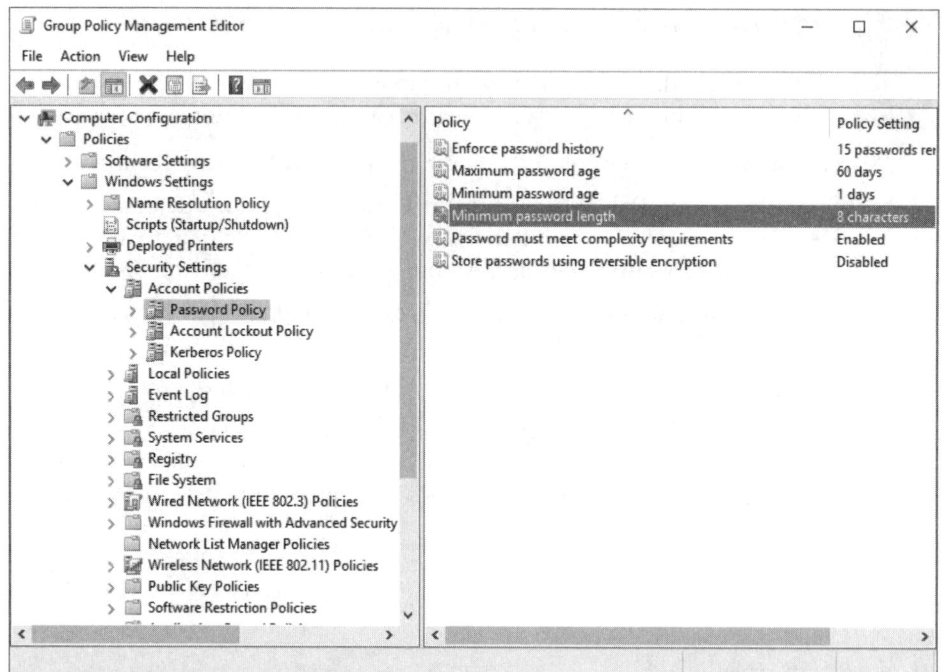

Figure 10-5 Password policy configuration

Account Lockout The operating system can employ **account lockout** to bar access to an account (including the true account owner) after a number of unsuccessful tries. The lockout can be set to release after a specified period of time or by intervention from the server administrator.

A common policy is to have lockout go into effect after five to 10 unsuccessful logon attempts. Also, an administrator can set lockout to release after a designated time, such as 30 minutes. The 30 minutes creates enough delay to discourage intruders, while giving some leeway to a user who might have forgotten a recently changed password. The following are the account lockout parameters that you can configure in the account lockout policy:

- *Account lockout duration*—Permits you to specify in minutes how long the system will keep an account locked out after reaching the specified number of unsuccessful logon attempts.
- *Account lockout threshold*—Enables you to set a limit to the number of unsuccessful attempts to sign in to an account.
- *Reset account lockout count after*—Enables you to specify the number of minutes to wait after a single unsuccessful logon attempt before the unsuccessful logon counter is reinitialized to 0.

Account lockout is especially targeted to thwart a brute force attack, which usually involves software that continues to try different password combinations until finding the right one to break into an account. Some server administrators feel that setting account lockout very high, such as to 50 or more, is still enough to discourage brute force attacks, while at the same time reducing calls to user support personnel because users are locked out of their accounts due to difficulty remembering their passwords.

Activity 10-3: Configuring Account Lockout Policy

Time Required: Approximately 10 minutes

Objective: Configure account lockout policy in the default domain security policy.

Description: In this activity, you configure the account lockout policy settings.

1. Open the **Group Policy Management** tool and then the **Group Policy Management Editor** from which to configure the Default Domain Policy, if the Group Policy Management Editor is not still open after Activity 10-2.
2. Click **Account Lockout Policy** in the tree under Computer Configuration, Policies, Windows Settings, Security Settings, and Account Policies.
3. Double-click **Account lockout duration** in the right pane.
4. Check the box for **Define this policy setting**, if it is not already checked. Enter **40** in the minutes text box (see Figure 10-6), and click **OK**.

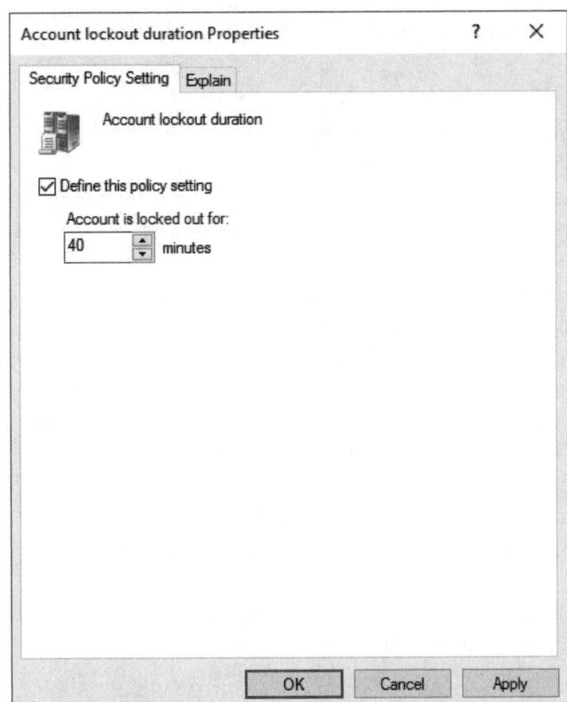

Figure 10-6 Configuring account lockout duration

5. You should see the Suggested Value Changes box.
   - What changes are suggested?
6. Click **OK** in the Suggested Value Changes box. In the middle pane, notice that your change plus the suggested changes have been implemented.
7. Leave the Group Policy Management Editor window open for the next activity.

Kerberos Security **Kerberos** security involves the use of tickets that are exchanged between the client who requests logon and network services access and the server or Active Directory that grants access. On a network that does not use Active Directory, each standalone Windows Server 2016 server can be designated as a Kerberos key distribution center, which means that the server stores user accounts and passwords. When Active Directory is used, then each domain controller is a key distribution center. When a user signs in, the client computer sends an account name and password to the key distribution center. The key distribution center responds by issuing a temporary ticket that grants the user access to the Kerberos ticket-granting service on a domain controller (or standalone server), which then grants a permanent ticket to that computer. The permanent ticket, called a **service ticket**, is good for the duration of a logon session (or for another period of time specified by the server administrator in the account policies) and enables the computer to access network services beginning with the Logon service. The permanent ticket contains encrypted information such as a session key, an ID for the user account, IDs for services the user account can access, and the IP address of the user's computer. When the user seeks to access a service, the permanent ticket information is decrypted to validate the user and the services the user is permitted to use. You might think of a Kerberos ticket as similar to one you would purchase to enter a concert; the ticket is good for the duration of that event and for entry to refreshment and merchandise booths, but you must purchase a new ticket to attend a concert on another date.

Windows Server 2016 uses Kerberos version 5 (V5). This version of Kerberos authenticates both the user requesting server access and the server. Also, on every domain controller (DC), the Kerberos Key Distribution Center service must be running. If this service is not started, users cannot sign in to the network. You can verify the service using the Services tool.

Kerberos on Windows Server 2016 and Windows 10 is enhanced to provide even stronger security. One significant enhancement is the use of **Advanced Encryption Standard (AES)** encryption, which is the standard deployed by the U.S. federal government and is intended to be more secure than DES. In addition to offering strong security, AES is fast and uses a minimal amount of memory. Kerberos also offers improved security in branch offices that use read-only domain controllers (RODCs), (see Chapter 4, Introduction to Active Directory and Account Management).

When Active Directory is installed, the account policies enable Kerberos, which is the default authentication. If Active Directory is not installed, Kerberos is not included by default in the account policies because the default authentication is through **Windows NT LAN Manager version 2** (**NTLMv2**). NTLM is not as robust as Kerberos, but it is compatible with all versions of Windows, including legacy Windows systems such as Windows NT.

The following options are available for configuring Kerberos:

- *Enforce user logon restrictions*—Turns on Kerberos security, which is the default.
- *Maximum lifetime for service ticket*—Determines the maximum amount of time in minutes that a service ticket can be used to continually access a particular service in one service session.
- *Maximum lifetime for user ticket*—Determines the maximum amount of time in hours that a ticket can be used in one continuous session for access to a computer or domain.
- *Maximum lifetime for user ticket renewal*—Determines the maximum number of days that the same Kerberos ticket can be renewed each time a user signs in.
- *Maximum tolerance for computer clock synchronization*—Determines how long in minutes a client will wait until synchronizing its clock with that of the server or Active Directory it is accessing.

If getting users to sign out when they go home at night is a problem, limit the maximum lifetime for service ticket or maximum lifetime for user ticket values to a certain number of hours, such as 10 or 12.

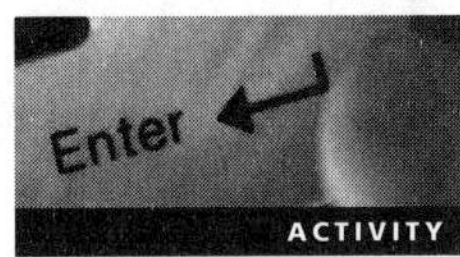

Activity 10-4: Configuring Kerberos Security

Time Required: Approximately 10 minutes
Objective: Configure Kerberos in the default domain security policy.

Description: In this activity, you configure the Kerberos policy settings for a company in which people work 10- and 12-hour shifts (setting Kerberos for up to 12 hours).

1. Open the **Group Policy Management Editor** to the same place where you left off in Activity 10-3 for the Default Domain Policy.
2. Click **Kerberos Policy** in the tree under Computer Configuration, Policies, Windows Settings, Security Settings, and Account Policies.
3. Double-click **Maximum lifetime for service ticket** in the right pane. Ensure the box for **Define this policy setting** is checked. Enter **720** in the minutes text box. Click **OK**.
4. Click **OK** in the Suggested Value Changes dialog box to also set *Maximum lifetime for user ticket* to 12 hours. When you are finished, the right pane should look similar to Figure 10-7.

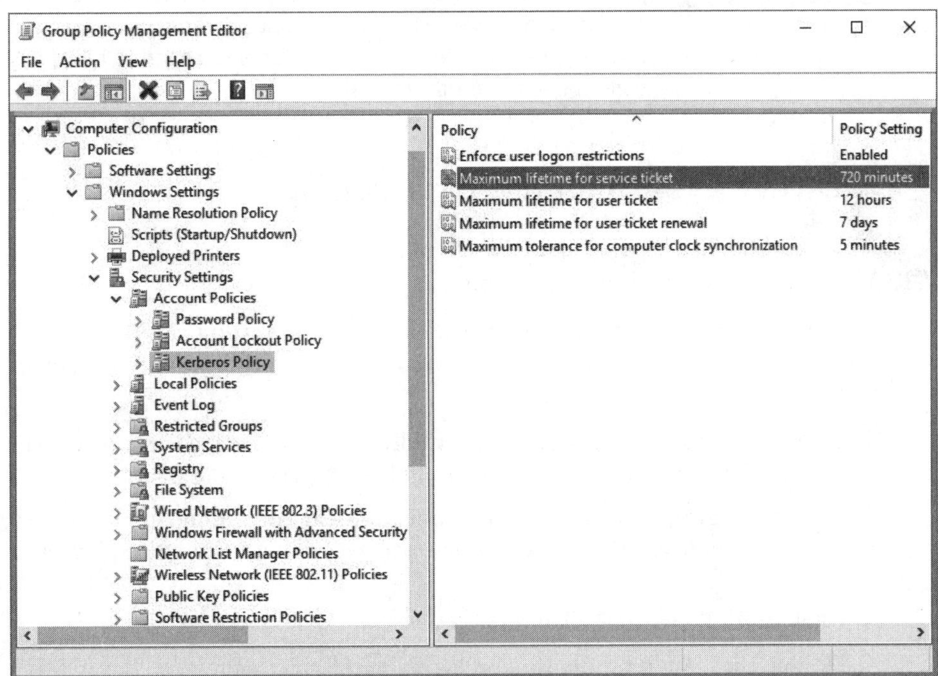

Figure 10-7 Configuring Kerberos Policy

5. Leave the Group Policy Management Editor window open for the next activity.

Establishing Audit Policies

After accounts are set up, you can specify account auditing to track activity associated with those accounts. For example, some organizations need to track security changes to accounts, while others want to track failed logon attempts. Some server administrators track failed logon attempts for the Administrator account, to be sure an intruder is not attempting to access the server. Accounts that access an organization's financial information often are routinely audited to protect their users as well as the information they access. Examples of events that an organization can audit are as follows:

- Account logon (and logoff) events
- Account management

- Directory service access
- Logon (and logoff) events at the local computer
- Object access
- Policy change
- Privilege use
- Process tracking
- System events

Each listed activity is audited in terms of the success or failure of the event. For example, if account logon attempts are audited, a record is made each time someone signs into an account successfully or tries to sign in but fails.

Use auditing sparingly. Each audited event causes a record to be made in the Security event log. For example, if you audit all logon attempts of 1000 domain accounts, the server log will quickly become loaded down just from auditing events. Reviewing all of the audit data can be time consuming, and the data can consume valuable disk space. Excessive auditing can backfire and consume so many server resources that the server can barely be used for other activities.

Activity 10-5: Configuring Auditing

Time Required: Approximately 10 minutes
Objective: Configure an audit policy.

Description: Assume that the IT manager in your organization wants to track the logon activity of all accounts in the domain over a 24-hour period. In this activity, you enable account logon auditing to facilitate that request.

1. Open the **Group Policy Management Editor** window to the same place where you left off in Activity 10-4 for the Default Domain Policy, if it is not already open.
2. Click the **right-pointing arrow** in front of **Local Policies** in the tree under Computer Configuration, Policies, Windows Settings, and Security Settings to display the items under Local Polices.
3. Click **Audit Policy** in the left pane.
4. Double-click **Audit account logon events** in the right pane.
5. Click the box for **Define these policy settings.**
6. Ensure that both the **Success** and **Failure** boxes are checked, as shown in Figure 10-8.
7. Click **Apply** to have these take effect immediately and then click **OK.**
   - If you were concerned about tracking changes to Group Policy, what would you audit?
8. Leave the Group Policy Management Editor window open for the next activity.

If you want to audit activity on a particular object, such as a folder, file, or printer, enable Audit object access. Next, in the object's properties, such as the properties for a folder, specify the accounts or groups you want to audit. For a folder, you would do this by right-clicking the folder in File Explorer and clicking Properties. Click the Security tab, the Advanced button, and the Auditing tab. (See Chapter 5, Configuring, Managing, and Troubleshooting Resource Access, and review Activity 5-6.)

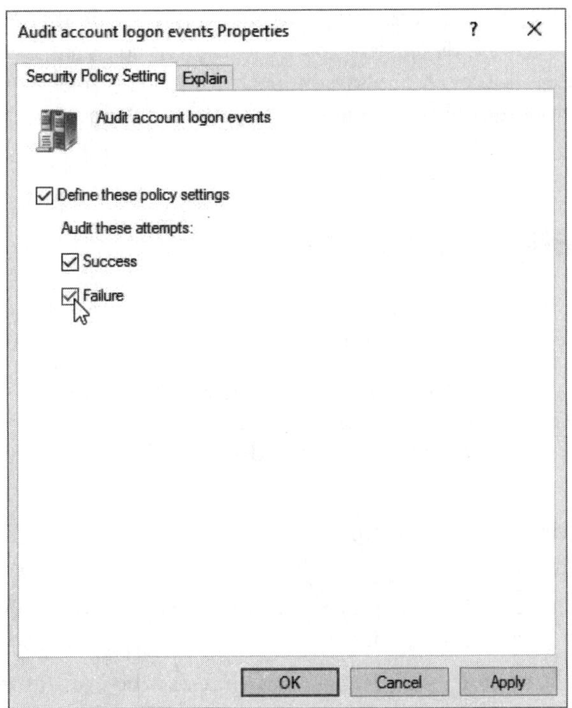

Figure 10-8 Configuring account logon auditing

Configuring User Rights

User rights enable an account or group to perform predefined tasks. The most basic right is the ability to access a server. More advanced rights give privileges to create accounts and manage server functions. Although not specifically differentiated when you set them up, two general categories of rights are established: privileges and logon rights. Privileges generally relate to the ability to manage server or Active Directory functions, and logon rights are related to how accounts, computers, and services are accessed. Both types of rights are established through setting up the user rights assignment in a Group Policy.

Some examples of privileges include the following:

- Add workstations to domain
- Back up files and directories
- Change the system time
- Create permanent shared objects
- Generate security audits
- Load and unload device drivers
- Perform volume maintenance tasks
- Shut down the system

Examples of logon rights are as follows:

- Access this computer from the network
- Allow logon locally
- Allow logon through Remote Desktop Services
- Deny access to this computer from the network
- Deny logon as a service
- Deny logon locally
- Deny logon through Remote Desktop Services

The most efficient way to assign user rights is to assign them to groups instead of to individual user accounts. When user rights are assigned to a group, then all user accounts (or groups) that are a member of that group inherit the user rights assigned to the group, making these **inherited rights**.

Activity 10-6: Configuring User Rights

Time Required: Approximately 15 minutes
Objective: Learn how to configure user rights.

Description: This activity enables you to view the existing user rights and restrict local logon access to this server to the Administrator account, the Administrators group, and the Server Operators group. Also, you restrict the ability to shut down the server to the Administrators group.

1. Open the **Group Policy Management Editor** window to edit the Default Domain Policy, if the window is not already open.
2. Click **User Rights Assignment** in the tree under Computer Configuration, Policies, Windows Settings, Security Settings, and Local Policies.
3. Scroll through the middle pane to view the rights that can be configured, as shown in Figure 10-9.

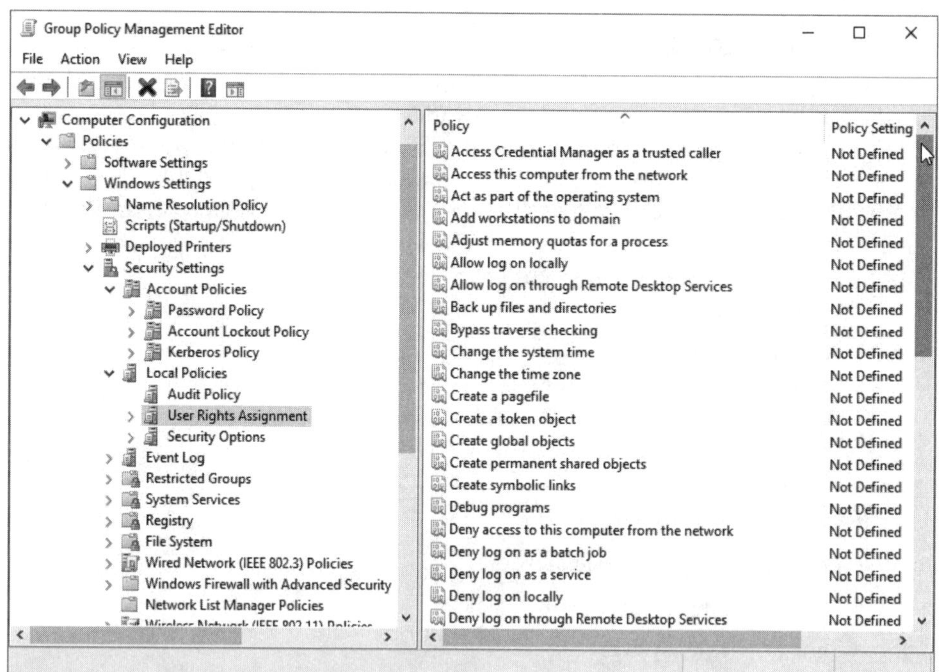

Figure 10-9 User Rights Assignment policy options

4. Double-click **Allow log on locally.**
5. Check the box for **Define these policy settings.**
6. Click **Add User or Group,** as shown in Figure 10-10.
7. Click the **Browse** button in the Add User or Group box.

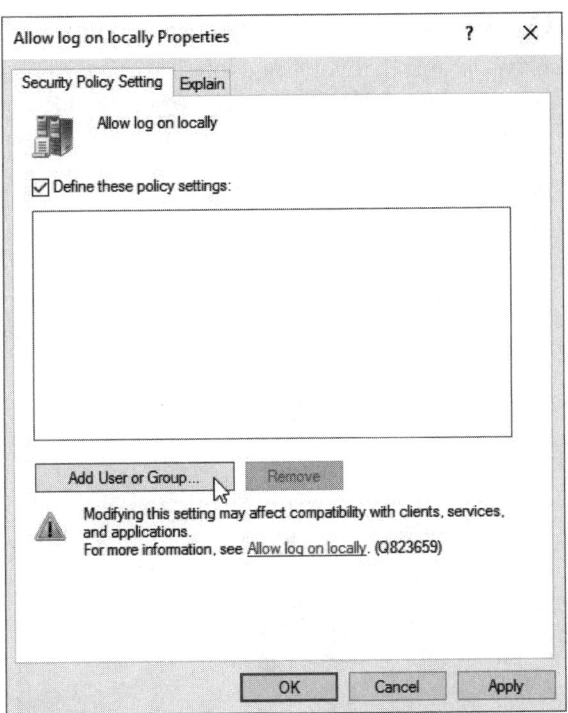

Figure 10-10 Adding a user or group to make a rights assignment

8. Click the **Advanced** button in the Select Users, Computers, Service Accounts, or Groups dialog box.
9. Click the **Find Now** button in the Select Users, Computers, Service Accounts, or Groups dialog box.
10. Hold down the **Ctrl** key and click **Administrator, Administrators**, and **Server Operators** (you can release the **Ctrl** key temporarily to scroll to Server Operators). Ensure that Account Operators is not selected at the top of the listing. If it is selected, continue holding down the **Ctrl** key and click **Access Control Assistance Operators** to deselect it. Click **OK**.
11. Click **OK** in the Select Users, Computers, Service Accounts, or Groups dialog box.
12. Click **OK** in the Add User or Group box.
    - What now appears in the text box on the Allow log on locally Properties dialog box?
13. Click **OK** in the Allow log on locally Properties dialog box.
14. Double-click **Shut down the system**. Place a check in the box for **Define these policy settings**.
15. Click **Add User or Group**.
16. Click the **Browse** button in the Add User or Group box.
17. Click the **Advanced** button in the Select Users, Computers, Service Accounts, or Groups dialog box.
18. Click **Find Now** in the Select Users, Computers, Service Accounts, or Groups dialog box.
19. Double-click **Administrators**.
20. Click **OK** in the Select Users, Computers, Service Accounts, or Groups dialog box.
21. Click **OK** in the Add User or Group box.
22. Click **OK** in the Shut down the system Properties dialog box.
23. Leave the Group Policy Management Editor window open for the next activity.

Configuring Security Options

There are many specialized security options that you can configure in a Group Policy, such as the Default Domain Policy, in Windows Server 2016. These options are divided into the following categories:

- Accounts
- Audit
- DCOM
- Devices
- Domain controller
- Interactive logon
- Microsoft network client
- Network access
- Network security
- Recovery console
- Shutdown
- System cryptography
- System objects
- System settings
- User Account Control

Each category has specialized options. For example, if you are concerned about intruders attempting to access the Administrator account, you can use the *Accounts: Rename administrator account* policy to disguise the Administrator account with another name. In another example, if you want only the Server Operators group to format and eject CDs and DVDs, configure *Devices: Allowed to format and eject removable media*. Or, if you have configured specific logon hour controls so that users cannot log on during certain times, then you can force off users who have not logged off after hours by configuring *Network security: Force logoff when logon hours expire*.

Activity 10-7: Configuring Security Options

Time Required: Approximately 10 minutes

Objective: Examine Security Options and configure an option.

Description: In this activity, you view all of the Security Options that can be set up as policies. Next, you rename the Guest account to designate it for use by vendors who visit your organization, and then you create a message for users who sign in to the server or network.

1. If necessary, open the **Group Policy Management Editor** window to edit the Default Domain Policy.
2. Click **Security Options** in the tree under Computer Configuration, Policies, Windows Settings, Security Settings, and Local Policies. You should see a window similar to Figure 10-11.
3. Scroll through the options.
   - What option would you use to restrict access to the CD/DVD drive in the computer so that it can only be accessed by someone logged on locally? How can you set up the system so that it can be shut down without first having someone logged on locally?
4. Double-click **Accounts: Rename guest account**.

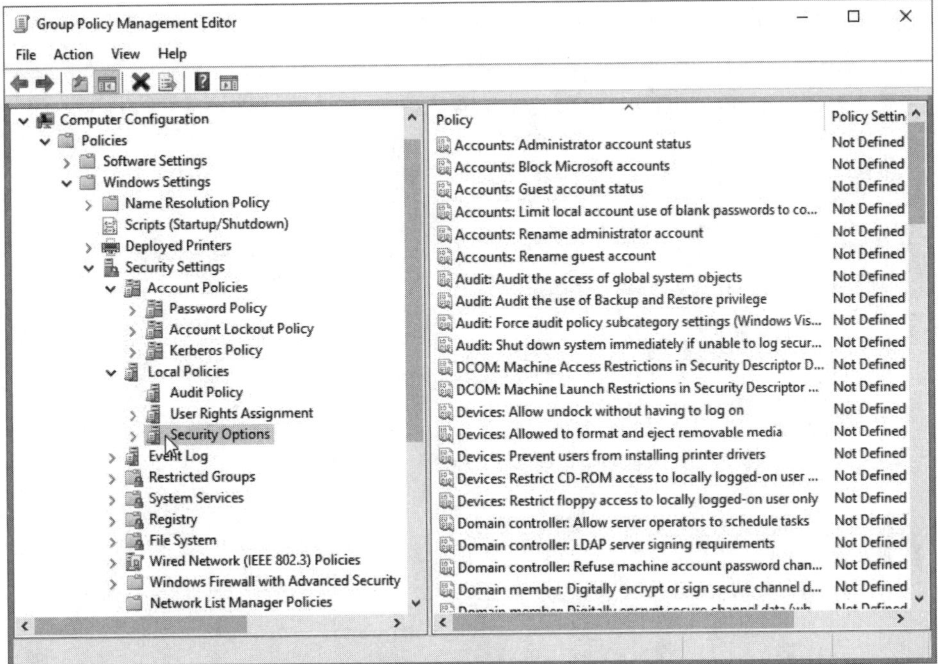

Figure 10-11 Accessing Security Options

5. Check the box for **Define this policy setting.**
6. Enter the name **Vendors** in the text box. Click **OK.**
7. Double-click **Interactive logon: Message text for users attempting to log on.**
8. Check the box for **Define this policy setting in the template.**
9. Click at the beginning of the text box and enter a message, such as **Welcome to our company network!** (press **Enter** for a new line) **Authorized Users Only** (see Figure 10-12).
10. Click **OK.** Notice how the Policy Setting column is changed for the policies you configured.
11. Leave the Group Policy Management Editor window open for the next project.

Using IP Security Policies

Windows Server 2016 supports the implementation of **IP security (IPsec)**, which is a set of IP-based secure communications and encryption standards created through the Internet Engineering Task Force (IETF). When an IPsec communication begins between two computers, the computers first exchange certificates or passwords/pre-shared keys to authenticate the receiver and sender. Next, data is encrypted at the NIC of the sending computer as it is formatted into an IP packet, which consists of a header containing transmission control information, the actual data, and a footer with error-correction information. IPsec can provide security for all TCP/IP-based application and communications protocols, including FTP and HTTP, which are used in Internet transmissions. IPsec policies for a domain can be managed through the Default Domain Policy. A computer that is configured to use IPsec communication can function in any of three roles:

- *Client (Respond Only)*—When Windows Server 2016 is contacted by a client using IPsec, it will respond by using IPsec communication.
- *Secure Server (Require Security)*—Windows Server 2016 will only respond using IPsec communication, which means that communication via any account and with any client is secured through strict IPsec enforcement.

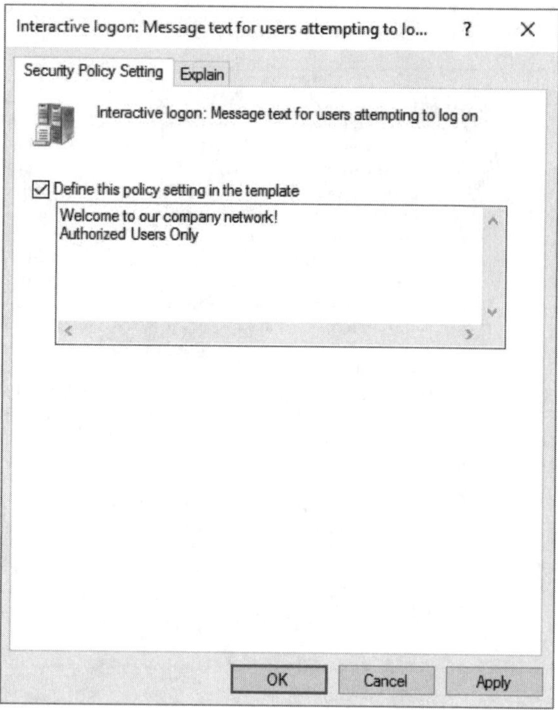

Figure 10-12 Configuring a logon message

- *Server (Request Security)*—When Windows Server 2016 is first contacted or when it initiates a communication, it will use IPsec by default. If the responding client does not support IPsec, Windows Server 2016 will switch to the clear mode, which does not employ IPsec.

IPsec security policies can be established through the Default Domain Policy. IPsec security policies can also be configured through the IP Security Policy Management MMC snap-in so that specific security standards apply to all computers that sign in to a domain in Active Directory.

Activity 10-8: Configuring IPsec in the Default Domain Policy

Time Required: Approximately 10 minutes
Objective: Configure IPsec Group Policy elements.

Description: In this activity, you learn how to configure a server to use IPsec.

1. If necessary, open the **Group Policy Management Editor** window to edit the Default Domain Policy.
2. Click **IP Security Policies on Active Directory** (*domainname*) in the tree under Computer Configuration, Policies, Windows Settings, and Security Settings (see Figure 10-13).
3. Double-click **Secure Server (Require Security)**. The Rules tab lists the IP Security rules already configured (see Figure 10-14). To create a new rule, you would click the **Add** button to start the Create IP Security Rule Wizard.
4. Double-click **All IP Traffic** to view the properties of a rule that is already created.
5. Click each tab to view the properties.

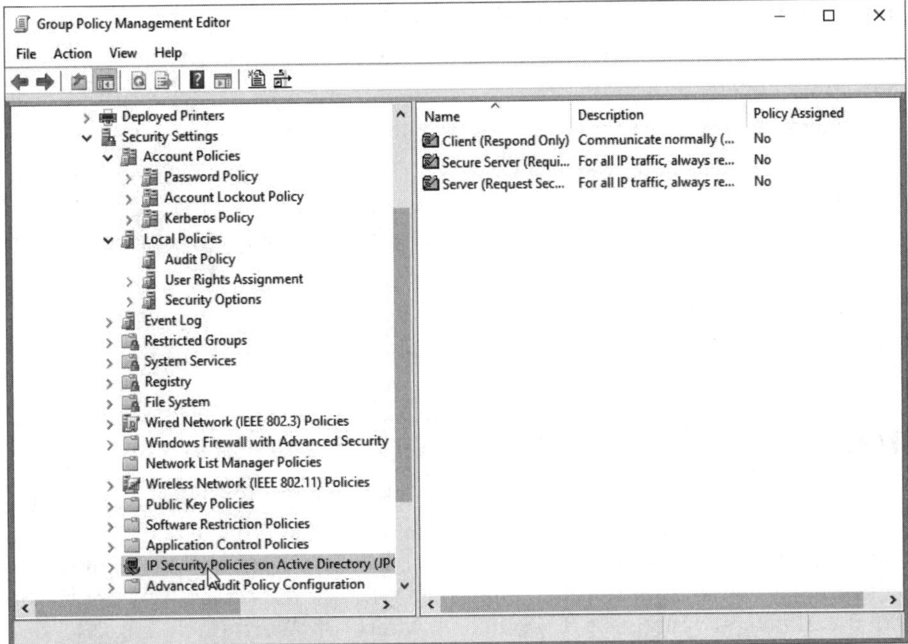

Figure 10-13 Configuring IPsec policies

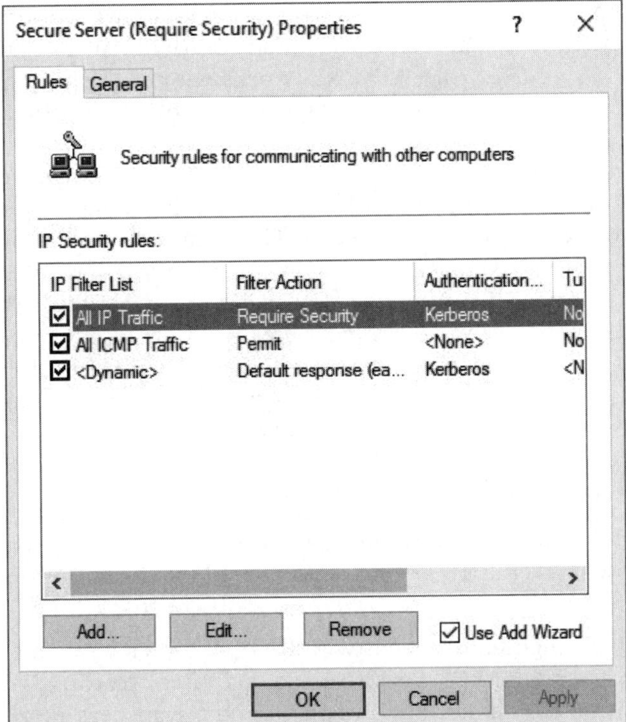

Figure 10-14 IP Security rules

- When you view the Filter Action tab, what Filter Action is selected? On the Connection Type tab, what connection types can be selected? What tab would you use to configure IPsec for tunneling, such as over a VPN? What Authentication Methods are used?

6. Click **Cancel** in the Edit Rule Properties dialog box.
7. Click the **General** tab on the Secure Server (Require Security) Properties dialog box. Review the contents of this tab.
8. Click **Cancel** in the Secure Server (Require Security) Properties dialog box.
9. In the Group Policy Management Editor window, right-click Secure **Server (Require Security)**, and click **Assign**. This policy is now assigned so that it will take effect for the server. (Check with your instructor about whether to leave it assigned. You can follow similar steps to Unassign the policy.)
10. Close the Group Policy Management Editor window.
11. Close the Group Policy Management window, if it is still open.

Active Directory Rights Management Services

Active Directory Rights Management Services (AD RMS) is a server role to complement the client applications that can take advantage of Rights Management Services safeguards. **Rights Management Services (RMS)** are security rights developed by Microsoft to provide security for documents, spreadsheets, email, and other types of files created by applications. Applications that can take advantage of RMS include Microsoft Word (including XPS documents), PowerPoint, Excel, SharePoint, Outlook, Edge, and Internet Explorer. Also, software developers can use Microsoft application development tools to implement RMS capabilities in the software they write.

RMS information protection goes beyond ACLs and the Windows Firewall. It uses security capabilities such as encryption, user authentication, and security certificates to help safeguard information. When used as a server role, AD RMS works with enabled programs to build in an extra layer of protection and offer multiple ways to control how information is used and distributed.

RMS works by implementing rights that manage who can read, modify, copy, save, print, forward, and manipulate a document, spreadsheet, email, web document, and other types of files. Rights are given to user accounts and groups. This means that an engineer working on a confidential company project can email sensitive information to a boss or coworker and set security so that the email cannot be printed or forwarded to anyone other than the intended recipient or recipients. The U.S. federal government uses RMS because it employs AES encryption and digital certificates. Even if Windows Firewall does not keep a sensitive email from being forwarded without authorization, RMS can block the forwarding attempt. Even though an organization may not check printouts employees take home or pass on to someone else, RMS can block the information from even being printed.

Here are the general steps used in RMS security:

1. A user creates a Word document, for example, and uses RMS via Word to give a single user account on a Windows Server 2016 server access to read the document (but no other RMS access rights).
2. In the process of protecting the document with RMS, Word encrypts the document using an AES key and an additional RSA key. **RSA** (named after creators Rivest, Shamir, and Adleman) is an encryption technique that uses public and private keys along with a computer algorithm that relies on factoring large prime numbers. Also, Word provides a certificate-based identity license for the document to a Windows Server 2016 server that has the AD RMS role installed.
3. The AD RMS server issues an identity license to the client who can access the document.
4. When the authorized client attempts to read the document using Word, that client shows the AD RMS server its license to access the document.
5. The AD RMS server authenticates the client and determines the level of access. Next, the server issues a use license to the authorized client. Because the client has read access, the

client can decrypt the document to read it using Word, but cannot copy, print, modify, or do other actions on the document.

If you work in an organization that needs RMS-based security and has applications to employ it, use Server Manager to install the AD RMS role in Windows Server 2016 to take advantage of RMS.

For organizations that participate in cloud-based services, Microsoft offers the Azure RMS service. For organizations that use Office 365 Enterprise, Azure RMS is integrated with services such as Microsoft Office client applications, including Microsoft Word and Exchange Online Mail. Another way to have Azure RMS is by subscribing to the Enterprise Mobility Suite of cloud-based applications from Microsoft. Third, Azure RMS is available as a "standalone subscription" for organizations that use Microsoft products on their own site.

Managing Security Using the Security Templates and Security and Configuration Analysis Snap-Ins

Windows Server 2016 offers the Security Templates MMC snap-in that enables you to create one or more security templates to house in Active Directory. This snap-in enables you to set up security to govern the following:

- Account policies
- Local policies
- Event log tracking policies
- Group restrictions
- Service access security
- Registry security
- File system security

The Security Templates snap-in is particularly useful when you have multiple Group Policies to maintain or when you have multiple OUs, but many of those OUs share the same Group Policy. For example, if you have 20 OUs set up in a domain and use one security policy for eight OUs, a different one for eight OUs, and still another one for four OUs, then you would create three security templates.

Activity 10-9: Using the Security Templates Snap-In

Time Required: Approximately 15 minutes

Objective: Learn to use the Security Templates snap-in.

Description: In this activity, you learn how to use the Security Templates snap-in.

1. Right-click **Start**, click **Run**, type **mmc** in the *Open* text box and click **OK.**
2. Click **File** and click **Add/Remove Snap-in.**
3. In the Add or Remove Snap-ins dialog box, click **Security Templates** and click the **Add** button. Now click **Security Configuration and Analysis** and click the **Add** button.
4. Click **OK.**
5. Click **Security Templates** in the tree.

6. In the middle pane, right-click the path to the Templates folder, such as **C:\Users\Administrator\Documents\Security\Templates** and click **New Template** (see Figure 10-15).

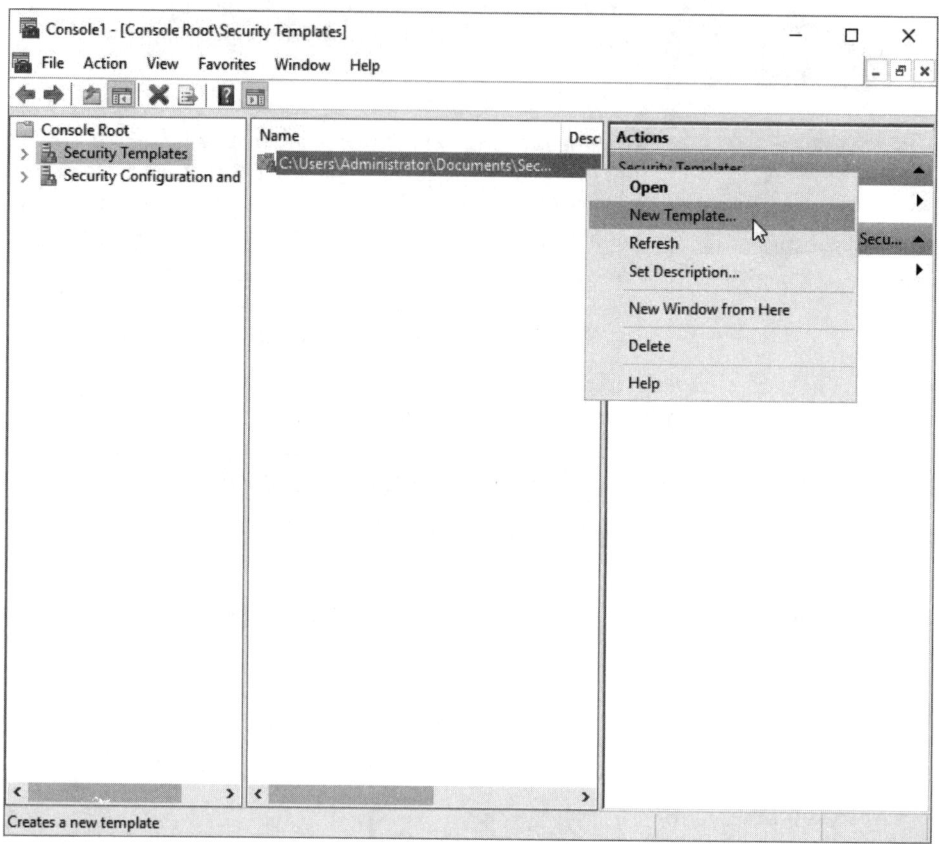

Figure 10-15 Creating a new security template

7. In the *Template name* box, enter the word **Template** plus your initials, such as *TemplateJR*. In the *Description* box, enter **Practice template.** Click **OK.**
8. In the left pane under Console Root, Security Templates, click the path to the template in the tree, such as **C:\Users\Administrator\Documents\ Security\Templates,** to ensure the new template is displayed in the middle pane.
9. Double-click the template name in the middle pane, such as *TemplateJR*.
   - What Group Policy elements are displayed in the middle pane that you can now configure?
10. Double-click **Account Policies** in the middle pane.
11. Double-click **Password Policy** in the middle pane.
12. Configure *Enforce password history* to **20** passwords remembered and click **OK** in the Enforce password history Properties dialog box. Next, configure *Maximum password age*

to **45** days. If you see the Suggested Value Changes box to set the *Minimum password age* to 30 days, click **OK** (or manually configure *Minimum password age* to 30 days). Further, configure *Minimum password length* to **eight** characters (see Activity 10-2 if you want to review how to configure these). If necessary you can position the cursor over the line in the box separating the middle pane from the right pane and drag the line to the right to view the settings for the parameters in the middle pane—or maximize the window.

13. Click **Account Lockout Policy** in the tree.
14. Configure *Account lockout duration* to **40** minutes and after you click **OK** in the Account lockout duration Properties dialog box, click **OK** in the Suggested Value Changes dialog box to use the suggested values for *Account lockout threshold* (five invalid logon attempts) and *Reset account lockout counter after* (30 minutes)—refer to Activity 10-3.
15. Click the template in the tree, such as *TemplateJR*. Configure any other policies as desired in the middle pane.
16. Leave the console window open for the next activity; or if you have to close it now, close the console window and click **Yes** in the Microsoft Management Console window, click **Desktop** in the left pane of the Save As window, use the file name **Security Tools** plus your initials, such as *Security Tools JR* and click **Save**.
17. If you see the Save Security Templates box, click **Yes**.

After you create a security template, you can install it using the Security Configuration and Analysis MMC snap-in. You can also use this snap-in to analyze your current security parameters.

10

Activity 10-10: Using the Security Configuration and Analysis Snap-In

Time Required: Approximately 20 minutes
Objective: Explore the features of the Security Configuration and Analysis snap-in.

Description: The Security Configuration and Analysis snap-in enables you to import a security template, apply the template, and analyze security. In this activity, you learn how to use this tool.

1. From the desktop, open the **Security Tools** console you created in Activity 10-9, if it is closed.
2. Click **Security Configuration and Analysis** in the tree in the left pane.
3. Right-click **Security Configuration and Analysis** in the left pane and click **Open Database**.
4. In the *File name* text box, enter a database name consisting of **Domain** plus your initials, such as *DomainJR* (see Figure 10-16), and then click **Open**.
5. In the Import Template dialog box, notice that the template you created in Activity 10-9 is listed. Click the template, such as *TemplateJR*, and click **Open**.
6. Right-click **Security Configuration and Analysis** in the left pane of the console window and click **Analyze Computer Now**.
7. In the Perform Analysis box, notice that the error log is created in the path \Users\Administrator\Documents\Security\Logs and the log file name uses the name of your database, such as *DomainJR.log*. Click **OK**.
8. Right-click **Security Configuration and Analysis** in the left pane of the console window and click **View Log File**. You see the log file contents to review security analysis information. Use the scroll bar to view the contents, as shown in Figure 10-17. (Because you generated a sample database for demonstration purposes, your results don't necessarily reflect actual errors on your system.)

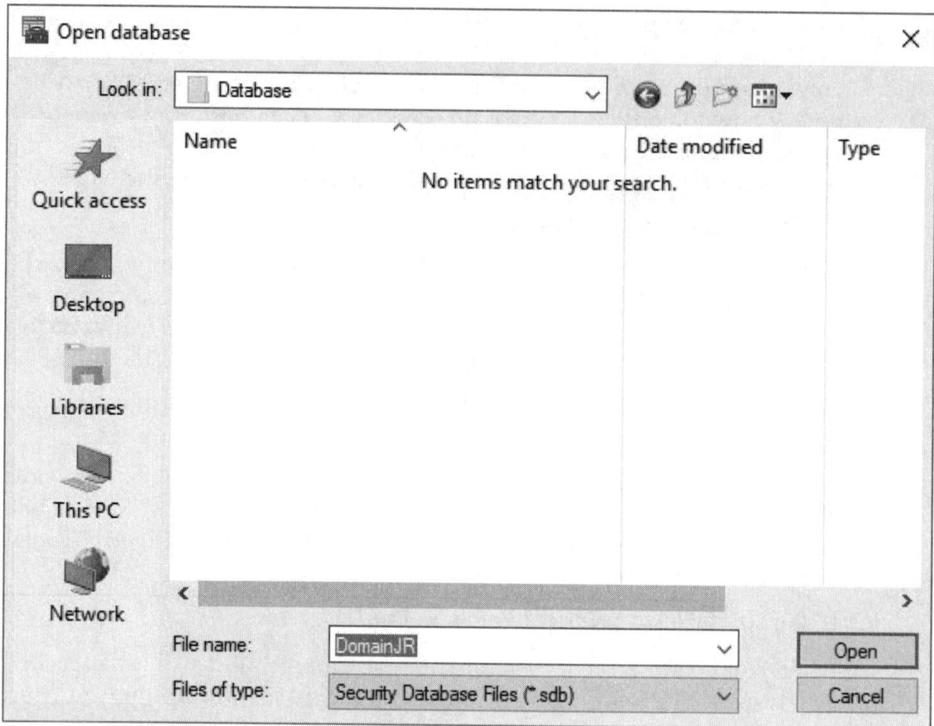

Figure 10-16 Creating a security database

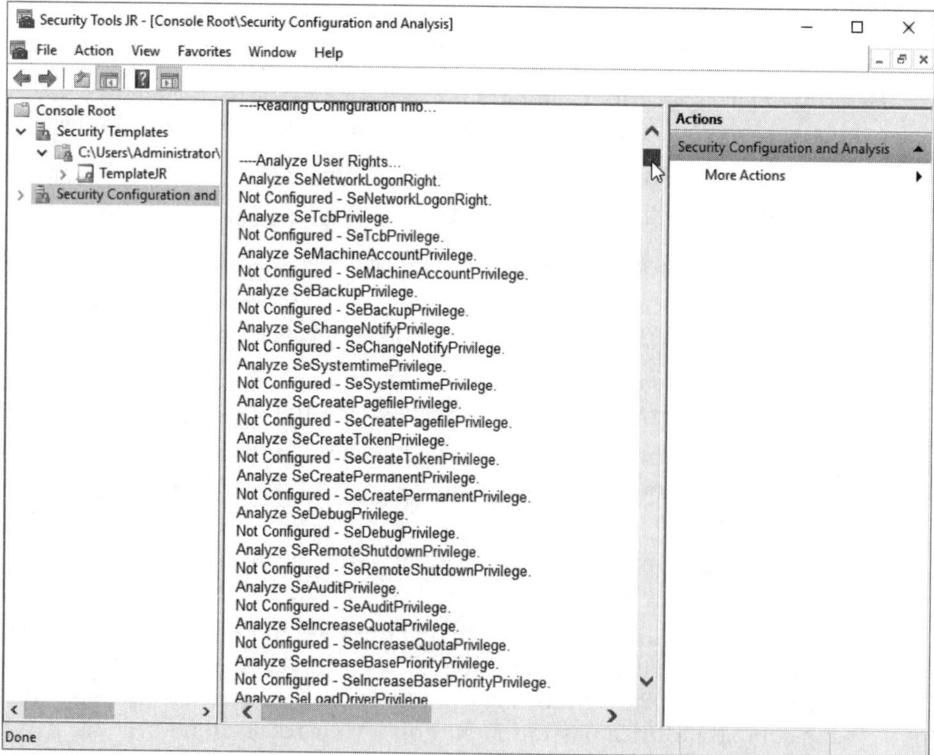

Figure 10-17 Log file contents

9. To configure your system using the imported template, right-click **Security Configuration and Analysis** and click **Configure Computer Now**, then click **OK** in the Configure System dialog box.
10. Notice that the log contents in the middle pane are now changed to show the successful configuration of security policies.
11. Close the console window and click **Yes**. If you did not close and save the console in Activity 10-9, in the *File name* box, enter **Security Tools** plus your initials, such as *Security Tools JR* and then click **Desktop** in the left pane. Click **Save**.
12. If you see the Save Security Templates box, click **Yes**.

When you apply a security template, it incrementally updates the Group Policy Object to which it is applied.

Configuring Client Security Using Policies in Windows Server 2016

You can customize desktop and other settings for client computers that access Windows Server 2016 networks. Customizing settings used by clients offers several advantages, including enhanced security and providing a consistent working environment in an organization. The settings are customized by configuring policies on the Windows Server 2016 servers that the clients access. When the client signs in to the server or the network, the policies are applied to the client.

For example, you can configure a policy that disables Control Panel or specific Control Panel options on particular clients or all clients. Another policy might be configured to ensure that all clients have an icon on their desktop that starts the same application in the same way. If a client inadvertently deletes the icon, it is reapplied the next time the client signs in. In some organizations, it is important to store sensitive information on a server to enhance security and conformity of use. If this is the case, you can use folder redirection, so that a folder appears on the clients' desktops that really points to a secure folder on the server. Windows Server 2016 offers literally hundreds of ways to configure clients through modifying Group Policies.

Manually Configuring Policies for Clients

You always have the option to manually configure policies that apply to clients, in order to accomplish specific purposes. For example, sometimes the management of an organization will make a decision to standardize a specific item, such as the use of certain printers or the implementation of specific software. In other cases, it might be necessary to prevent users from having access to specific functions because those functions are a security risk or a distraction.

You can manually configure one or more policies that apply to clients by using the Group Policy Management tool or the Group Policy Object Editor snap-in. In either tool, you customize the desktop settings for client computers by using the Administrative Templates Policy object under User Configuration and Policies in a Group Policy Object, such as the Default Domain Policy (see Figure 10-18).

Table 10-1 presents very general descriptions of the Administrative Templates options under User Configuration.

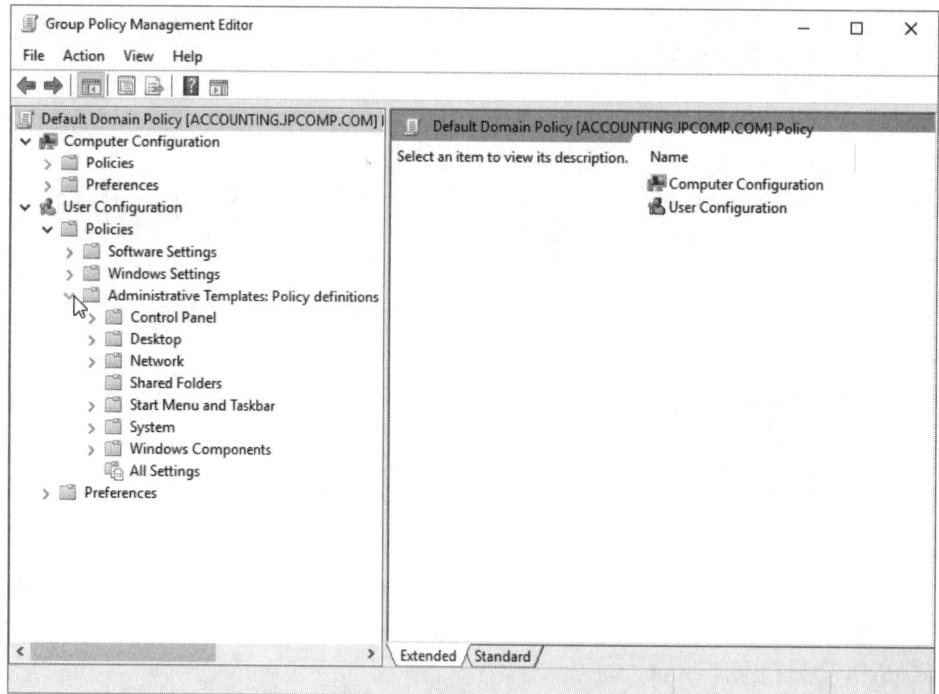

Figure 10-18 Group Policies for clients

Table 10-1 Options for configuring administrative templates settings under User Configuration

Component	Description
Control Panel	Controls access to Control Panel functions such as Default Programs, Devices and Printers, Display, Programs and Features, Internet Options, Language, and so on; plus the ability to prohibit access to Control Panel or to hide or display only specific Control Panel icons
Desktop	Controls access to desktop functions, including specified desktop icons (such as Microsoft Edge or Internet Explorer), the ability to adjust desktop toolbars, access to specific icons on the desktop, use of the Desktop Recycle Bin, the ability to delete desktop items, and many others
Network	Controls access to many network access and configuration functions, such as the ability to configure TCP/IP, access to setting up a new network connection, access to offline files, and many others
Shared Folders	Controls the ability to publish DFS roots and shared folders
Start Menu and Taskbar	Controls the ability to configure the Start menu and taskbar, the ability to access program groups from the Start menu, and the ability to use Start menu options including Run, Programs and Features, System, File Explorer, and others; also controls the ability to configure the taskbar
System	Controls access to logon/logoff capabilities, scripts, driver installation, removable storage access, Group Policy refresh rate, slow link detection, and other system functions
Windows Components	Controls access to installed software such as AutoPlay policies, Internet Explorer, File Explorer, MMC, Task Scheduler, Windows Installer, Windows Media Player, Windows PowerShell, and many others
All Settings	Controls a wide variety of settings, including access to data sources, access to processes, scripting options, cut/copy/paste operations, file downloads, installation of desktop items, use of the screen saver, configuring toolbar buttons, logon options, use of ActiveX controls, Internet Explorer use and maintenance, and many others

Activity 10-11: Configuring Policies to Apply to Clients

Time Required: Approximately 10 minutes
Objective: Learn how to configure a Group Policy to apply to Windows Server 2016 clients.

Description: This activity gives you experience configuring policies to apply to clients. For this activity, you set up File Explorer so that a confirmation dialog box is displayed when a user deletes a file. Also, as a result of users configuring their own computers, the user support group has had to work overtime on unnecessary problems, and some security breaches have occurred. In response, the organization's management has decided to prohibit access to Control Panel on every client computer.

1. Open **Server Manager,** if it is not open.
2. Click **Tools** and click **Group Policy Management.**
3. Expand the tree in the left pane to view Default Domain Policy under Domains and the domain name.
4. Right-click **Default Domain Policy** and click **Edit** to open the Group Policy Management Editor window (refer to Figure 10-1).
5. If necessary, click the **right-pointing arrow** in front of **User Configuration** in the tree to display the elements under it.
6. Click the **right-pointing arrow** in front of **Policies** under User Configuration.
7. Double-click **Administrative Templates: Policy definitions (ADMX files) retrieved from the local computer** in the tree to display its contents.
8. Double-click **Windows Components** in the tree. Notice the range of folders that appear in the left and right panes.
9. Double-click **File Explorer** in the left pane to view the settings you can configure (see Figure 10-19).

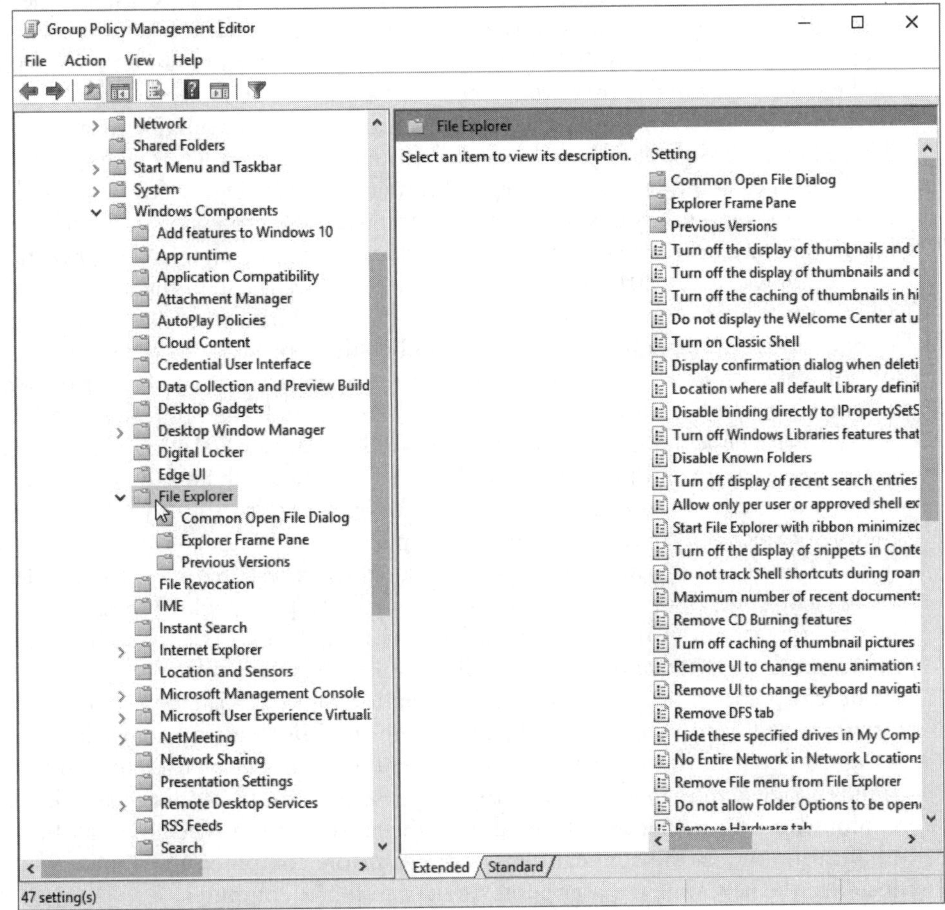

Figure 10-19 File Explorer policies

10. In the right-pane, click **Display confirmation dialog when deleting files**. View the information in the right pane that describes what this setting does. Double-click **Display confirmation dialog when deleting files**. Click the option for **Enabled** in the Display confirmation dialog when deleting files window. Click **OK**.
11. In the left pane under *User Configuration\Policies\Administrative Templates: Policy definitions (ADMX files) retrieved from the local computer\Windows Components*, click **Network Sharing**.
    - How would you keep users from sharing files within their profile?
12. In the left pane under *User Configuration\Policies\Administrative Templates: Policy definitions (ADMX files) retrieved from the local computer*, click **Control Panel**. Click **Prohibit access to Control Panel and PC settings**. View the explanation to see what this option does.
    - How would you enable this policy?
13. In the left pane, click each of the main folders under *User Configuration\Policies\Administrative Templates: Policy definitions (ADMX files) retrieved from the local computer* that you have not yet opened to view their contents (**Desktop**, **Network**, **Shared Folders**, **Start Menu and Taskbar**, **System**, and **All Settings**).
14. Leave the Group Policy Management Editor window open for the next activity.

Publishing and Assigning Software

For some organizations, one of the most important concerns is that their users employ the same software with the same software settings, for the sake of productivity and security. This can be particularly important for applications that have frequent version changes, such as Microsoft Word or Excel. Another important element is to make it possible for users to deploy this software without sending a user support professional to configure each workstation. This approach offers several advantages. One is that users can be more productive, because they use the same software in the same way, whether they are on their own computer or someone else's. Also, because all users have the same software setup, a large body of individuals is available to support their colleagues. These factors are great for ensuring user productivity. Another advantage is that data security weaknesses caused by users installing and configuring their own software are reduced. Further, the load on user support professionals is eased, because these professionals do not have to individually install software or troubleshoot problems created by users who install their own software.

Windows Server 2016 addresses all of these issues through the ability to configure policies for client software use. Two very effective ways to control client software use are by publishing applications and assigning applications. **Publishing applications** (or software) involves setting up software through a Group Policy so that the application is available for users to install from a central application distribution server, such as through the Programs and Features capability via the user's desktop (in Windows 10 and Windows Server 2016, right-click **Start** and click **Programs and Features**). An additional option is to automatically install an application on the client when a user opens a document formatted for that application, such as Microsoft Word for a .docx document. Technically, a published application is assigned to the user's account. **Assigning applications** means an application is automatically represented on the user's desktop, for example, as a Start menu option or as an icon on the desktop, and which initially is really a link to the central application distribution server. The first time the user tries to open the application on her computer is the point at which it is fully installed from the distribution server and can be used from that point on (as long as the application is assigned to the user account). Alternatively, the program and document files can be used from the Microsoft cloud, such as for Office 365. An assigned application can be assigned to either the computer or user account. When the application is assigned to the user account, the advertisement for the application follows the user to any computer and is installed on demand from the Start menu or when the user first tries to open the application. When the application is assigned to the computer, the application is automatically installed the next time the user boots or signs in to the computer.

The user or the user's organization is responsible for ensuring proper licensing for every application installation.

Activity 10-12: Configuring Software Installation

Time Required: Approximately 5 minutes
Objective: Learn where to set up software installation in a Group Policy.

Description: In this activity, you view where to configure software to be published or assigned.

1. Open the **Group Policy Management Editor** for the Default Domain Policy, if it is not open.
2. Under *User Configuration\Policies* in the tree, click **Software Settings**.
3. In the right pane, right-click **Software installation**, and then click **Properties**.
4. Make sure that the **General** tab is displayed in the Software installation Properties dialog box (see Figure 10-20). Notice that you can use the *Default package location* box to specify the location of the software that users will install, which can be on this server or on a different server in the network. Also, among the *New packages* parameters, there are options to *Publish* or *Assign* software.

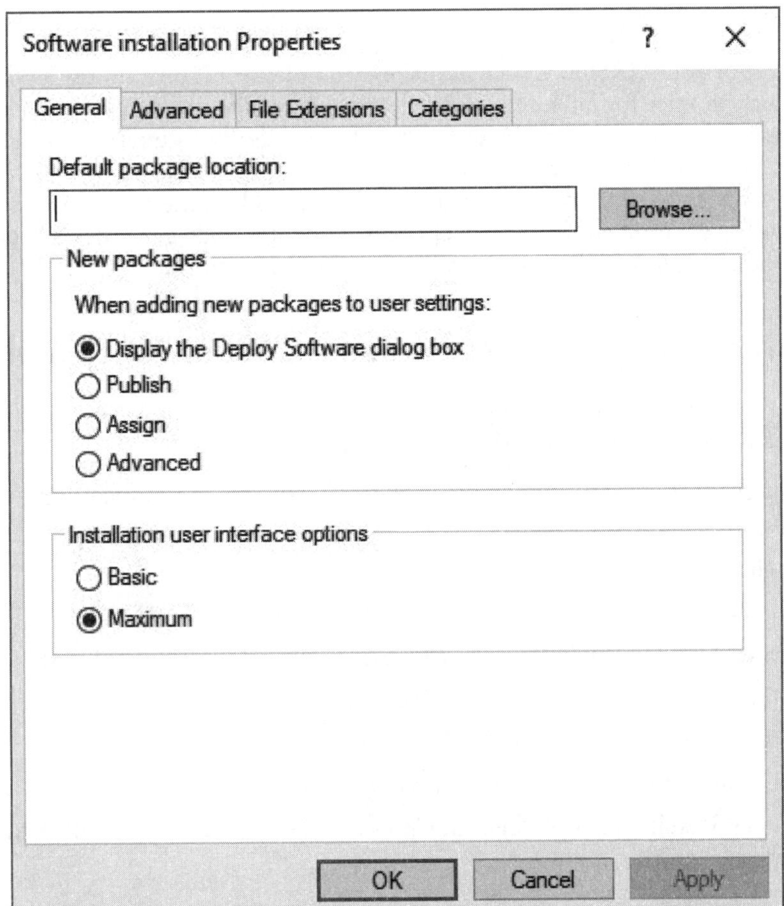

Figure 10-20 Software installation Properties dialog box

5. Click each of the **Advanced, File Extensions,** and **Categories** tabs to view the properties that can be configured on these tabs.
6. Click **Cancel.**
7. To view from where to set up published or assigned software, in the right pane right-click **Software installation,** point to **New,** and notice the Package option. If you were publishing or assigning software, from this point you would click **Package,** use the **Open** window to locate the installer package for the software, click **Open,** select **Publish** or **Assigned,** click **OK,** and complete the setup steps.
8. Click in an open location on your desktop to close the menus.
9. Close the Group Policy Management Editor window.

In small to large server environments, you can add additional security for applications by using Microsoft's Enhanced Mitigation Experience Toolkit (EMET). EMET is a free download from Microsoft's Download Center and can be installed on your server. EMET works independently of your programs to build in extra security without significant overhead. In a program that is not tightly written or that is not updated, vulnerabilities can exist in how the program handles and returns memory. EMET blocks these vulnerabilities so that attackers and malware can't take advantage of them.

Resultant Set of Policy

Resultant Set of Policy (RSoP) is used to make the implementation and troubleshooting of Group Policies much simpler for an administrator. When multiple Group Policies are applied, configuration settings and conflicts can be difficult to track. RSoP can query the existing policies that are in place and then provide reports and the results of policy changes.

RSoP supports two modes: planning and logging. Planning mode generates a report and provides the result of proposed policy changes. Logging mode generates a report based on the current policies in place and provides the resulting policy settings.

Activity 10-13: Using the Resultant Set of Policy Tool

Time Required: Approximately 10 minutes
Objective: Learn how to use the Resultant Set of Policy tool.

Description: In this activity, you create an RSoP report using the logging mode to review the policies you have set in this chapter.

1. Right-click **Start** and click **Run.**
2. Enter **mmc** in the *Open* text box and click **OK.**
3. Maximize the console window, if necessary.
4. Click the **File** and click **Add/Remove Snap-in.**
5. Click **Resultant Set of Policy** and click the **Add** button.
6. Click **OK** in the Add or Remove Snap-ins window.
7. Right-click **Resultant Set of Policy** in the tree and click **Generate RSoP Data.**
8. Click **Next** after the Resultant Set of Policy Wizard starts.
   - What two modes can you select to use on the Mode Selection dialog box?
9. Select **Logging mode,** if it is not selected already. Click **Next.**

10. In the Computer Selection dialog box, ensure that **This computer** is selected, and click **Next.**
11. For this activity, use the default settings for User Selection, which are **Display policy settings for** and **Current user.** Click **Next.**
12. Review the summary of the selections you have made in the Summary of Selections window (see Figure 10-21) and click **Next.** It will take a few moments for the tool to create the report.

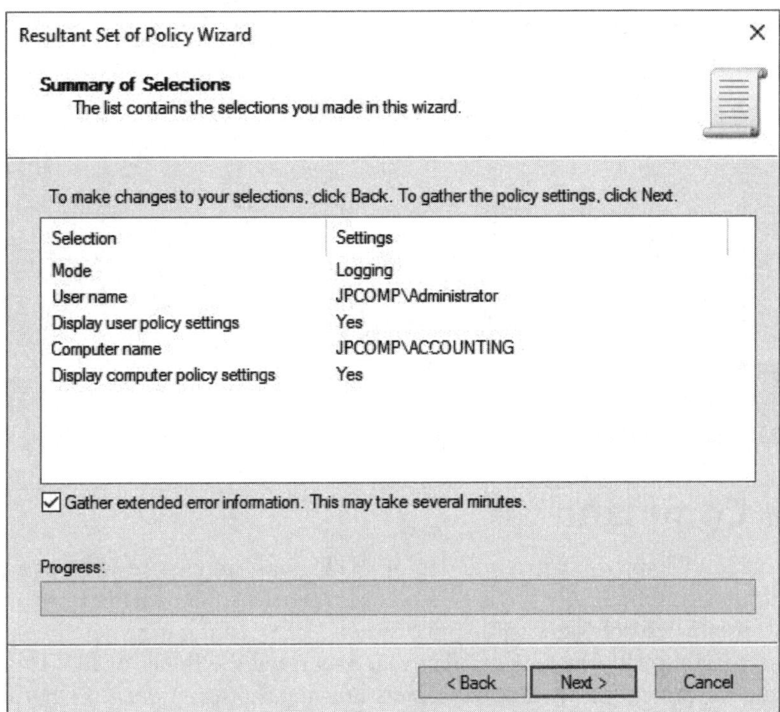

Figure 10-21 Summary of Selections window

13. Click **Finish.**
    - What are the options now displayed in the middle pane?
14. In the middle pane, double-click **Computer Configuration.**
15. Double-click **Windows Settings.**
16. Double-click **Security Settings.** You'll see the security settings options displayed in the middle pane, as shown in Figure 10-22.
17. Double-click **Account Policies** in the middle pane and then double-click **Password Policy.** You should see a report of the same policies you configured earlier in this chapter for the domain, with no conflicts.
18. Close the console window and click **No** (to not save the settings).

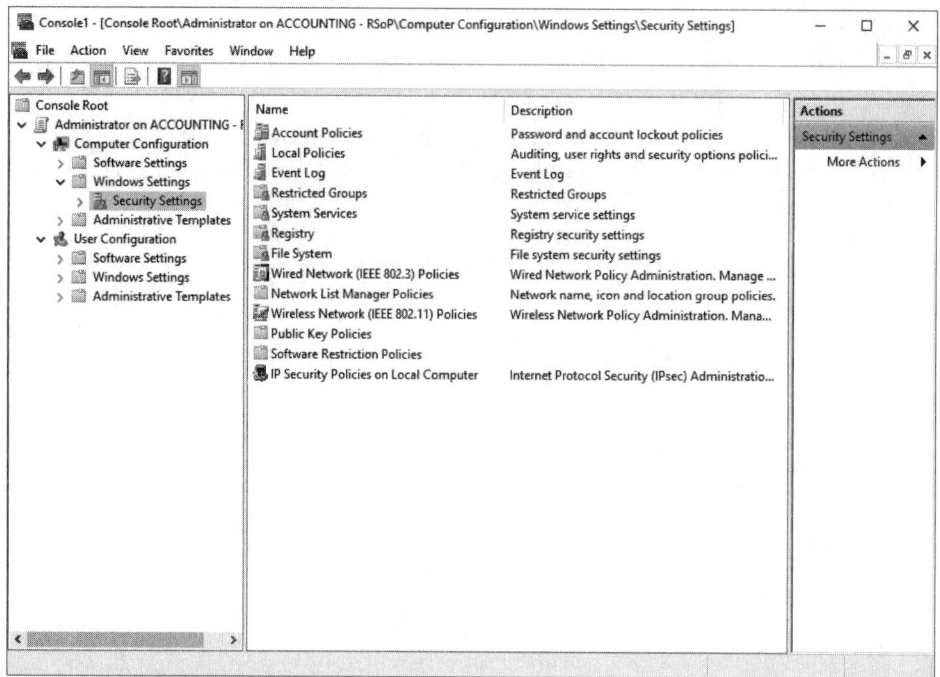

Figure 10-22 RSoP report for security settings

Using the *cipher* Command

As you learned in Chapter 5, when you deploy NTFS you can use the Encrypt attribute to protect folders and files, enabling only the user who encrypts the folder or file to read it. An encrypted folder or file uses Microsoft's Encrypting File System (EFS), configuring a unique private encryption key that is associated with the user account that encrypted the folder or file. This capability might be used at a government facility that has servers housing top secret data. If a hard drive is stolen or discarded because it is malfunctioning, data on the hard drive is protected from unauthorized users.

In Chapter 5, you learned that you can set the Encrypt attribute on a folder or file through working with that folder's or file's properties. Another option that you learn in this section is to use the *cipher* command from the Windows PowerShell or Command Prompt window. You can use the *cipher* command with the parameters listed in Table 10-2. If you do not specify any parameters with the command, it displays the encryption status of the current folder.

Table 10-2 Common *cipher* command-line parameters

Parameter	Description
/?	Lists the *cipher* command options
/e	Encrypts the specified folder so any files added to the folder are encrypted
/d	Decrypts the contents of the specified folder and sets the folder so that any files added to the folder are not encrypted
/s	Applies other *cipher* options used with the /s option to the contents of the current folder and the contents of subfolders under it
/h	Enables you to view which folders and files use the hidden or system attributes
/k	Provides the account employing *cipher* with a new encryption key, meaning that previous keys associated with other accounts are no longer valid—use with extreme caution
/n	With the /u option, ensures that encryption keys are not modified, but that you can view the currently encrypted folders and files
/u	Updates the *cipher* user's encryption key
/r	Invokes a recovery agent key so that the server administrator can set up a recovery policy
/w	Purges data from disk space that is flagged as unused (but which still contains data that could be recovered)
/x	Copies encryption key and certificate data to a file that is encrypted for use by the *cipher* user

Activity 10-14: Using the *cipher* Command

Time Required: Approximately 10 minutes
Objective: Use the *cipher* command in the Windows PowerShell window.

Description: This activity enables you to use the *cipher* command to view which folders and files are encrypted on your system.

1. Click the **File Explorer** icon on the taskbar.
2. In File Explorer, double-click an NTFS formatted volume on which you can create a folder, such as **Local Disk** (C:).
3. Browse to the **/Users/Administrator/Documents** folder (or to your account's Documents folder, if you are not using the Administrator account). Create a new subfolder called **Encrypt** plus your initials, such as *EncryptJR* (right-click in a blank area, point to **New**, click **Folder**, and enter the name of the folder). Press **Enter**.
4. Right-click the folder you created and click **Properties**.
5. On the **General** tab, click **Advanced**.
6. Click **Encrypt contents to secure data**. Click **OK**.
7. Click **OK** in the folder's Properties dialog box and close **File Explorer**.
8. Click **Start** and click the **Windows PowerShell** tile; or click **Start**, click the **Windows PowerShell** folder, and click **Windows PowerShell**.
9. At the prompt, type **cd documents** and press **Enter** to change to the documents subdirectory.
10. Type **cipher** and press **Enter**.
    - Do you see any files or folders that are encrypted, as signified by an E? How do you know if a file or folder is not encrypted?
11. Close the Windows PowerShell window.

Using BitLocker Drive Encryption

BitLocker Drive Encryption is another effective tool for protecting data on hard drives, including removable hard drives connected through a USB port. Windows Server 2016 BitLocker Drive Encryption also supports EFI-based computers as well as computers using BIOS.

BitLocker Drive Encryption uses Trusted Platform Module for one approach to security. **Trusted Platform Module (TPM)** is a security specification for a hardware device that can be used to secure information on a different hardware device, such as a hard drive. The hardware device with the security specification can be a chip or microcontroller on a motherboard that contains the security capabilities. When used to protect a hard drive, TPM verifies that the computer to which the hard drive is connected has authority to access that hard drive. This means if a hard drive is stolen, it cannot be accessed by another computer. Security at the hardware level, such as TPM, is thought to be more foolproof than software security.

TPM security chips can be obtained from companies such as Broadcom, Infineon, and STMicroelectronics. Server manufacturers including Dell and Hewlett-Packard offer server models that have a TPM chip.

If a computer is not equipped with a TPM chip, BitLocker Drive Encryption can be used with a USB flash drive that contains a personal identification number (PIN). When the computer is booted, the user must insert the flash drive, or else hard drives cannot be accessed and the operating system does not start. Additionally, if the computer has gone into hibernation, it is necessary to insert the flash drive to resume computer operation.

BitLocker Drive Encryption encrypts the entire drive, including the operating system, programs, and data files. When the system is booted and while the system is running, BitLocker Drive Encryption checks to ensure that files have not been tampered with or accessed by any sources that do not have the proper physical-device key. If it detects unauthorized access, it locks the files on the drive.

You will need to disable BitLocker Drive Encryption when you update the operating system and then enable it after the update.

Activity 10-15: Installing BitLocker Drive Encryption

Time Required: Approximately 10 minutes
Objective: Set up BitLocker Drive Encryption.

Description: This activity enables you to install BitLocker Drive Encryption. You will need to reboot the computer after it is installed, so make sure you have no other open programs or windows before you start. You do not need a TPM chip or flash drive with a PIN for this activity, because you do not enable BitLocker Drive Encryption after it is installed.

1. Open **Server Manager**, if it is not open.
2. Click **Manage** and click **Add Roles and Features.**
3. If you see the Before you begin window, click **Next.**
4. In the Select installation type window, ensure that **Role-based or feature-based installation** is selected. Click **Next.**
5. Make sure your server is selected in the Select destination server window and click **Next.**
6. In the Select server roles window, click **Next.**
7. Click the box for **Bitlocker Drive Encryption** (note that you can also install BitLocker Network Unlock, which can be needed after performing server maintenance and restarting a server).
8. Click **Add Features** in the Add Roles and Features Wizard.
9. Click **Next.**
10. Click the box for **Restart the destination server automatically if required.** Click **Yes** and then click **Install.**
11. Your computer should now reboot automatically.
12. Sign back in. (You might see the Add Roles and Features Wizard again when you reboot. Make sure the installation succeeded and click **Close.**)
13. Control Panel now has a new configuration utility for configuring BitLocker Drive Encryption. Because your computer might not be equipped with a TPM chip or you might not have a flash drive with a PIN, you will only view where to configure these. Right-click **Start** and click **Control Panel.**
14. Set Control Panel to the **Large icons** or **Small icons** view. Look for the *BitLocker Drive Encryption* applet (see Figure 10-23). (If you don't see the applet, reboot the computer and look again in Control Panel.)
15. Close **Control Panel.**

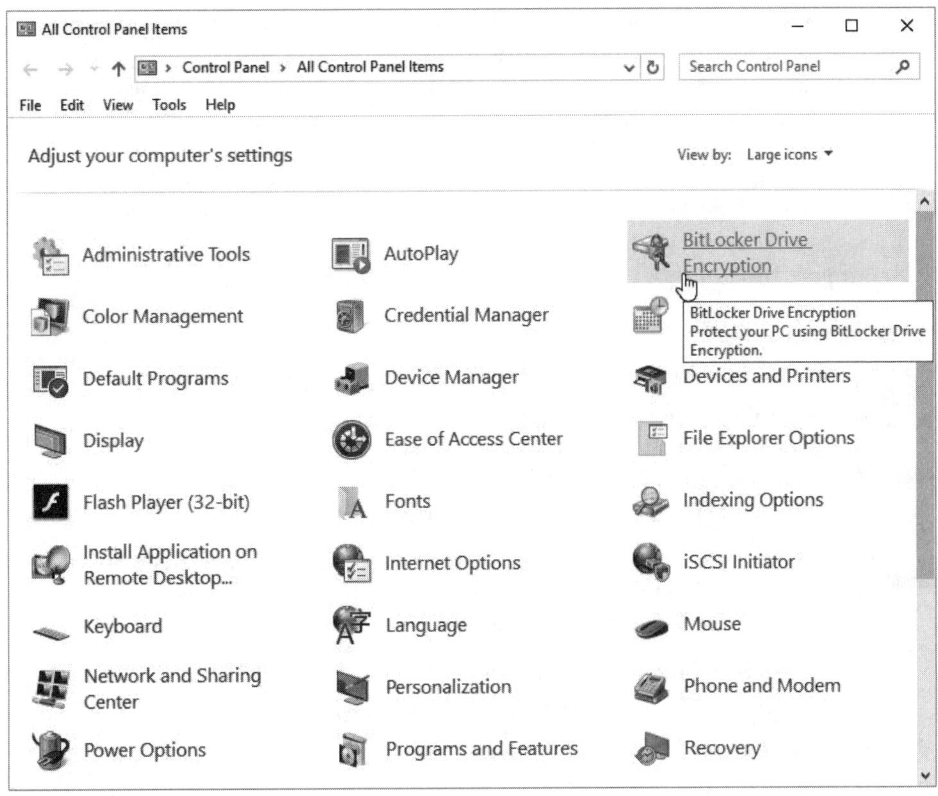

Figure 10-23 BitLocker Drive Encryption applet in Control Panel

In Step 14, if your system has a TPM chip or a flash drive with a PIN, you can click BitLocker Drive Encryption, select the drive on which to use BitLocker Drive Encryption, click Turn on BitLocker, and follow the steps to configure BitLocker Drive Encryption.

Configuring NAT

Network Address Translation (NAT) serves two important functions:

- It enables an organization to automatically assign its own private IP addresses on an internal network without having to set up many globally unique addresses for use over external networks.
- It protects computers on an internal network so that computers on external networks, including the Internet, cannot identify their true IP addresses on the internal network.

NAT uses a pool of private addresses for its internal network, which is a network separated from the outside world by a router or firewall, for example. Because the internal addresses are not viewed by the outside world, there is no need to have a large pool of IP addresses that can also be used over an external network. Only one or a very small pool of globally unique IP addresses are needed for outside communications. As a by-product, this means that fewer IPv4 global addresses are needed, which has helped to keep the networking world from running out of the limited number of globally available IPv4 addresses.

One reason for developing IPv6 was to enable the use of more globally available IP addresses. The widespread use of NAT has contributed to organizations delaying going to IPv6.

NAT is also a good security technique because internal IP addresses are concealed from the outside world. In a typical installation, NAT acts like a firewall so that the outside world (external networks) sees only one address, such as 198.51.100.1. However, the internal network contains many computers with addresses such as 192.168.22.1, 192.168.22.2, 192.168.22.3, 192.168.22.4, and so on. When the computer with IP address 192.168.22.4 sends a communication to the outside world, it's translated into the address 198.51.100.1, for example. (NAT can also use a set of addresses for translation to the outside world.)

When you install the Remote Access role and then use the Getting Started Wizard, you can configure to setup NAT (see Activities 9-1 and 9-2 in Chapter 9). If you don't set up NAT at that time, you can add NAT as a role service.

Activity 10-16: Adding NAT as a Role Service and Configuring NAT

Time Required: Approximately 15 minutes
Objective: Add NAT as a role service in the Remote Access Services role.

Description: This activity enables you to install and configure NAT on an existing VPN. Before you start, the Remote Services role should already be installed as well as having a VPN server set up as in Activities 9-1 and 9-2 in Chapter 9.

1. Open **Server Manager**, if it is not open.
2. Click **Manage** and click **Add Roles and Features.**
3. Click **Next,** if you see the Before you begin window.
4. Make sure **Role-based or feature-based installation** is selected in the Select installation type window and click **Next.**
5. Be sure your server is selected in the Select destination server window and click **Next.**
6. In the Select server roles window, click the **right-pointing arrow** in front of Remote Access to display the role services under it. Select the box for **Routing** and click **Next.**
7. Click **Next** in the Select features window.
8. Click **Install** in the Confirm installation selections window.
9. Click **Close** in the Installation progress window.
10. In Server Manager, click **Tools** and click **Routing and Remote Access.**
11. If necessary, click the **right-pointing arrow** in front of the server to expand the items under it so you can view IPv4.
12. Click the **right-pointing arrow** in front of IPv4, if necessary to view the items under it.
13. Right-click **General** under IPv4 and click **New Routing Protocol** in the menu.
14. Double-click **NAT,** as shown in Figure 10-24.
15. In the tree under IPv4, right-click **NAT** and click **New Interface.**
16. Select the interface, such as **Ethernet** and click **OK.**
17. In the Network Address Translation Properties dialog box, click **Private interface connected to private network,** if it is not already selected. Note that the other selection is *Public interface connected to the Internet,* which enables you to shield internal network addresses from Internet-based attackers. Click **OK.**
18. Close the Routing and Remote Access window.

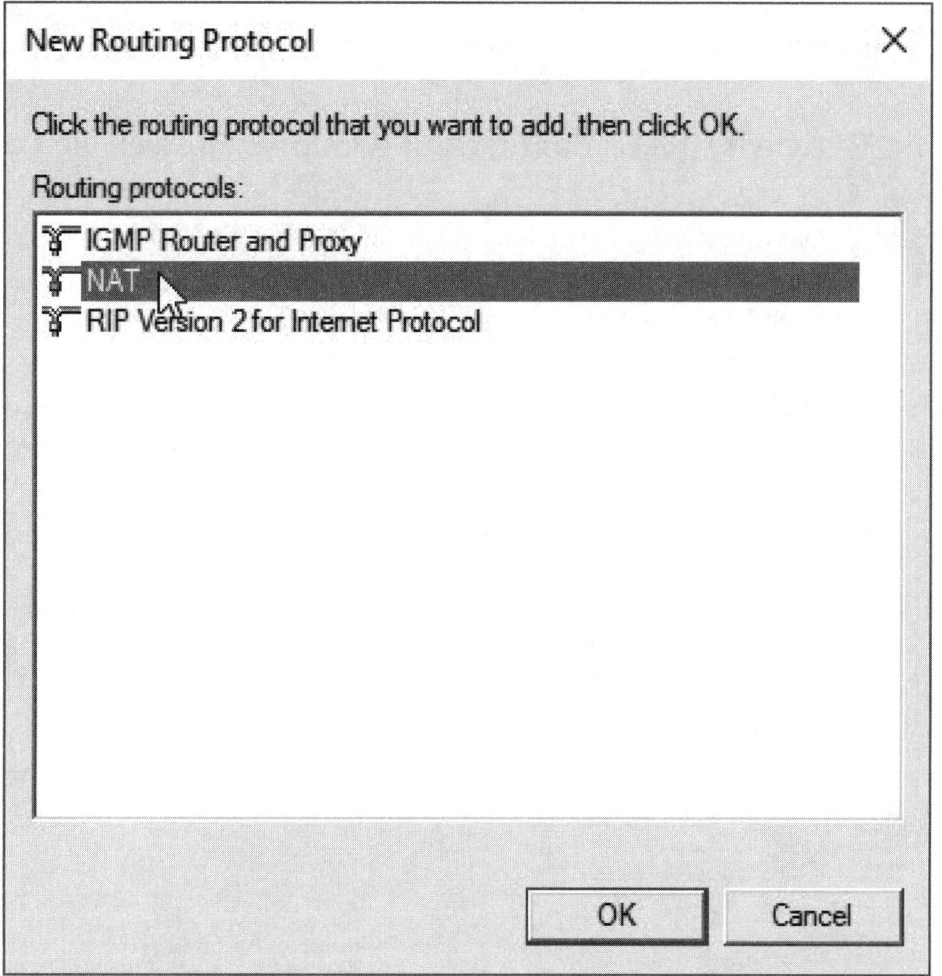

Figure 10-24 Selecting NAT

Windows Firewall

Windows Firewall offers the following advantages:

- Protects incoming and outgoing communications
- Merges firewall filters with IPsec settings to avoid settings conflicts
- Includes the *Windows Firewall with Advanced Security* MMC snap-in
- Has firewall exceptions or rules for several kinds of managed objects and applications

In Chapter 2, Installing Windows Server 2016, you enabled Windows Firewall as one of the first configuration settings for a server. Another step is to configure exceptions and advanced features. You have previously configured exceptions in earlier chapters of this book. Exceptions are programs that you choose to allow through the firewall in both directions (incoming and outgoing communications). When considered as a group, the exceptions are a set of rules. They can be configured for the following:

- TCP and UDP ports
- All or only specified ports
- IPv4 and IPv6
- All or only specified network interfaces
- Services by providing the path to the service

You can configure basic exceptions and advanced features from Control Panel or Server Manager. Specific inbound and outbound communications can also be configured from the Windows Firewall with Advanced Settings MMC snap-in.

Activity 10-17: Configuring Windows Firewall via Control Panel

Time Required: Approximately 10 minutes
Objective: Configure Windows Firewall from Control Panel.

Description: In this activity, you configure Windows Firewall exceptions and network connections through Control Panel.

1. Right-click **Start** and click **Control Panel.**
2. In the Control Panel Large icons or Small icons view, click **Windows Firewall.**
3. Click **Allow an app or feature through Windows Firewall.**
4. Scroll through the apps and features that can be marked as exceptions.
   - How is VPN access allowed through the firewall? What options are available for DHCP related activities?
5. Click **Allow another app** to view how you can browse for other programs that can be added to the exceptions. Click **Cancel.**
6. Click **Cancel** in the Allowed apps window.
7. In the Windows Firewall window, click **Advanced settings.**
8. Click **Inbound Rules** in the left pane (see Figure 10-25). Scroll to view the inbound rules in the middle pane.

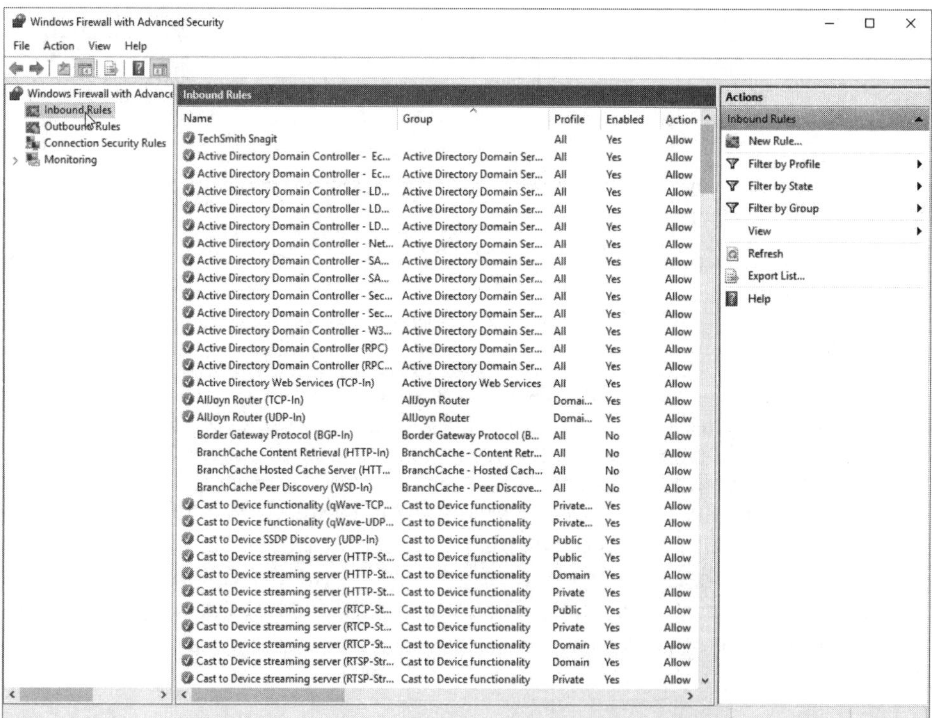

Figure 10-25 Viewing inbound rules in the advanced settings of Windows Firewall

9. Click **Outbound Rules** in the left pane and scroll to view these rules.
10. In the right pane, click **New Rule.**
11. In the New Outbound Rule Wizard (see Figure 10-26), notice that you can set rules for programs, TCP and UDP ports, as well as to use predefined rules and to set up custom rules. Click **Port.** Click **Next.**

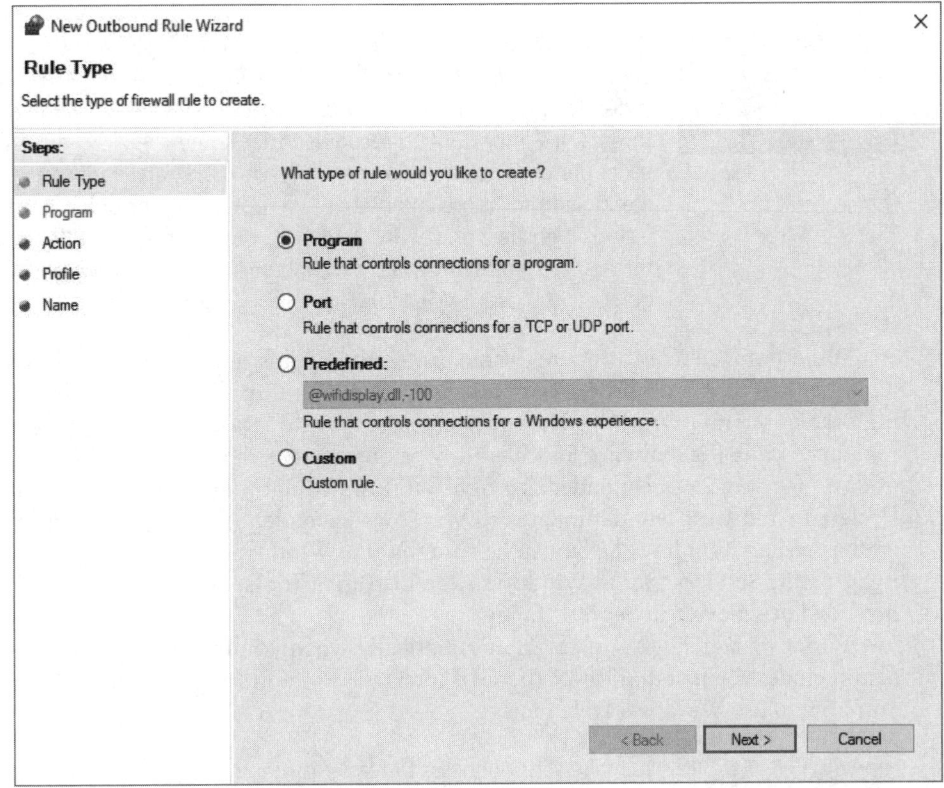

Figure 10-26 Rule Type window

12. In the Protocol and Ports window, click **UDP** and enter the port number **205**, which is an unused port for the AppleTalk protocol that we are using for practice (you can find a listing of TCP and UDP ports at *www.iana.org/assignments/service-names-port-numbers/service-names-port-numbers.xhtml?&page=1*). Click **Next.**
13. Click **Allow the connection** in the Action window. Click **Next.**
14. Notice the options you can set in the Profile window.
    - In what circumstances can you set the rule to take effect?
15. Leave the default selections in the Profile window and click **Next.**
16. In the Name text box, enter **AppleTalk Unused.** Click **Finish.**
17. Close the Windows Firewall and Windows Firewall with Advanced Security windows.

Windows Defender

Windows Defender is a security program that comes with Windows Server 2016. It protects against malware, viruses, spyware, and other threats. Historically, Windows Defender has come with Windows 7, Windows 8, and Windows 8.1. In many circumstances, it has come disabled when sold through OEMs to enable the OEM to install trial versions of other virus checking software. Windows Defender also can be downloaded to operate in Windows Server 2008/R2 and Windows Server 2012/R2. Windows Server 2016 is the first Windows Server system that includes Windows Defender.

Windows Defender in Windows 7 only protects against spyware. In Windows 8 through Windows 10 and in Windows Server 2016, Windows Defender includes protection from viruses, malware, spyware, and other threats. It's important to recognize that some client system and server users prefer installing third-party antivirus and malware software. They are looking for more comprehensive protection, including blocking suspicious websites, preventing malicious downloads, and other sources of threats. Third-party software may also include a firewall with features that go beyond those in Windows Firewall.

Windows Defender offers real-time protection against malware, so that malware is blocked when it tries to install into an operating system. If an application tries to change an operating system setting, Windows Defender gives you notification in real-time. Windows Defender regularly scans for malware and has the option to run a manual scan. Microsoft sends regular updates for Windows Defender through Windows Update. Ensure that you configure Windows Update to allow automatic updates to Windows Defender. Also, if you are using Windows Firewall as well as Windows Defender, be sure that the Windows Firewall Service is running, such as by using the Services tool in Windows Administrative Tools, or by using the Services information box for Local Server in Server Manager.

Windows Defender is installed automatically when you install Windows Server 2016, which also includes the installation of the GUI interface for Windows Defender. Activity 10-18 shows you how to use Windows Defender.

To make sure Windows Defender is running, right click **Start**, click **Command Prompt (Admin)**, type ***sc*** *query windefend* in the Command Prompt Window, and press **Enter**. The STATE parameter should be set to RUNNING. If the STATE is STOPPED, use the Services tool in Windows Administrative Tools or the Services information box for Local Server in Server Manager to start the Windows Defender Service, and ensure this service is set to start automatically. Also, even though Windows Defender is running, the Windows Defender Network Inspection Service may be configured to start manually, and thus be stopped. If you want to use the Windows Defender Network Inspection Service to guard against attacks through a network protocol opening, use the Services tool in Windows Administrative Tools to start the service and then configure the Windows Defender Inspection Service to start automatically.

Activity 10-18: Using the Windows Defender GUI

Time Required: Approximately 15 minutes
Objective: Use the Windows Defender GUI.

Description: In this activity, you learn how to use **Windows Defender**.

1. Right-click **Start** and click **Control Panel**.
2. Set View by to **Large icons** or **Small icons** and click **Windows Defender**.

3. If this is the first time you've started Windows Defender, read the What's new in Windows Defender box. If you are interested in using the Cloud Protection and Automatic Sample Submission options, click the **Turn on** button and click **Close**.
4. In the Windows Defender window with the **Home** tab selected (see Figure 10-27), notice the Scan options on the right side of the window: Quick, Full, and Custom. Also, notice there is information to show if real-time protection is turned on and if virus and spyware definitions are current. Note that on the Home tab, if your virus and spyware definitions are out of date, you'll see the Update definitions button that you can click to download the new definitions.

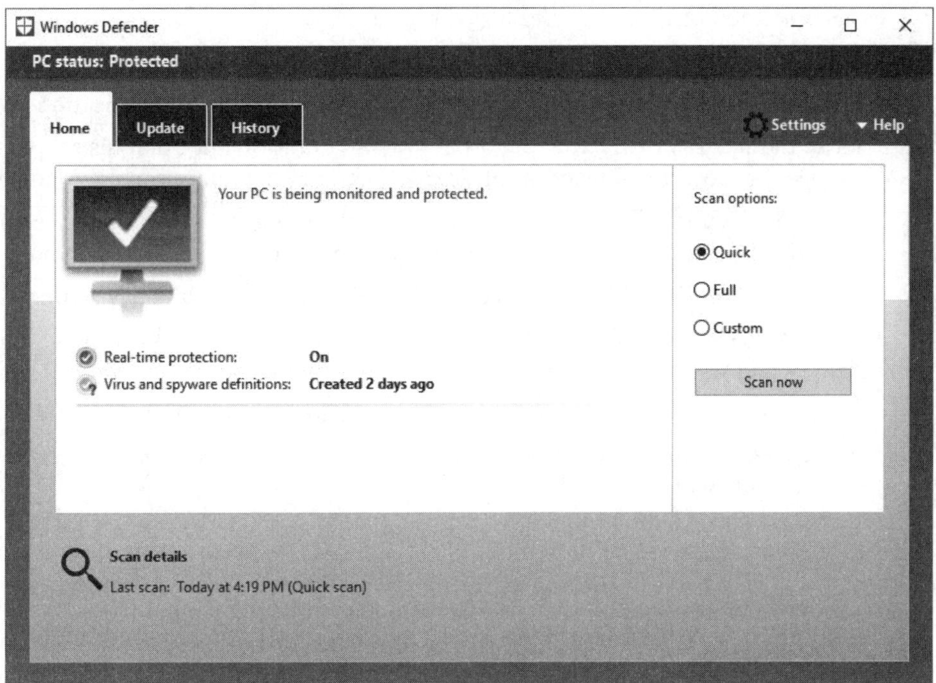

Figure 10-27 Windows Defender GUI

5. Click the **Update** tab. You can use the Update definitions button on this tab to get the latest updates for Windows Defender, including new virus definitions.
6. Click the **History** tab, which has options for viewing malware items that have been detected and to see the actions taken.
7. Click **Settings** in the top right portion of the window. Ensure the sliding button for **Turn on real-time protection** is set to **On**. Notice the other options that can be configured for Windows Defender. Close the Settings window.
8. Click the **Home** tab. Ensure that **Quick** is selected and click **Scan now**.
9. After the scan is complete, close Windows Defender.
10. Close the All Control Panel Items window.

Chapter Summary

- Windows Server 2016 has many important security features. These include Server Core, Group Policy options, Windows Firewall, Windows Defender, the Security Configuration and Analysis snap-in, User Account Control, and BitLocker Drive Encryption. Some of these features are discussed earlier in the book and others are introduced in this chapter.
- Group Policy offers a way to standardize security across a domain, OU, site, or local server.

- Configure account policies to include security features such as password security, account lockout, and Kerberos authentication.
- Use audit policies to track how resources are accessed, such as folders, files, or user accounts.
- User rights policies enable you to create specific security controls over privileges and logon access.
- Security options are specialized policies for accounts, auditing, devices, domain controllers, logon, clients, network security, system shutdown, system settings, and others. Windows Server 2016 offers many specialized policies.
- Configure IPsec security policy for strong client authentication.
- Implement Active Directory Rights Management Services for application-level security.
- Use the Security Templates and Security Configuration and Analysis snap-ins to configure consistent security policies for an Active Directory container such as a domain.
- For better control over the activities of clients, configure security policies on the local server or in the domain that applies to clients, such as through the Default Domain Policy.
- Use Resultant Set of Policy to plan and troubleshoot Group Policy settings.
- The *cipher* command is a valuable tool for implementing the Encrypting File System from the Windows PowerShell or Command Prompt windows.
- BitLocker Drive Encryption is a security measure for protecting entire hard drives.
- Network Address Translation is used to disguise IP addresses on an internal network from the outside world.
- Windows Firewall can be configured to allow traffic exceptions and to manage incoming and outgoing traffic, so you can use the applications you need but still close doors that don't need to be open to attackers.
- Windows Defender is included with Windows Server 2016 to protect against malware, viruses, spyware, and other threats.

Key Terms

account lockout A security measure that prevents access to a user account, such as after a specified number of unsuccessful logon attempts. Account lockout is often used to prevent brute force attacks that repeatedly try password combinations to attempt to break into an account.

Active Directory Rights Management Services (AD RMS) A server role that works with client applications that can take advantage of RMS safeguards. *See* Rights Management Services (RMS).

Advanced Encryption Standard (AES) A relatively new encryption standard adopted by the U.S. government to replace DES and 3DES and that employs a private-key block-cipher form of encryption.

assigning applications (or software) Means an application is automatically represented on the user's desktop, for example, as a Start menu option or as an icon on the desktop, and which initially is really a link to a central application distribution server. When the application is assigned to the computer, it is automatically installed when the user boots or signs in to the computer. When assigned to the user account, the first time the user tries to open the application, such as from the Start menu, is the point at which it is fully installed from the distribution server.

BitLocker Drive Encryption A security measure for protecting hard drives in Windows 7, 8/8.1, and 10 as well as in Windows Server 2016. It can use a TPM chip on a computer or a flash drive with a PIN to enforce security. *See* Trusted Platform Module (TPM).

Group Policy A set of policies that govern security, configuration, and a wide range of other settings for objects within containers in Active Directory.

Group Policy Object (GPO) An object in Active Directory that contains Group Policy settings for a site, domain, OU, or local computer.

inherited rights User rights that are assigned to a group and that automatically apply to all members of that group.

IP security (IPsec) A set of IP-based secure communications and encryption standards created through the Internet Engineering Task Force (IETF).

Kerberos A security system developed by the Massachusetts Institute of Technology to enable two parties on an open network to communicate without interception from an intruder, by creating a unique encryption key for each communication session.

publishing applications (or software) Involves setting up software through a Group Policy so that the application is available for users to install from a central distribution server, such as through the Programs and Features capability via the user's desktop.

Resultant Set of Policy (RSoP) A Windows Server 2016 tool that enables you to produce reports about proposed or current Group Policy settings for the purpose of planning and troubleshooting when multiple Group Policies are in use (such as for OUs and domains).

Rights Management Services (RMS) Security rights developed by Microsoft to provide security for documents, spreadsheets, email, and other types of files created by applications.

RSA Developed by Rivest, Shamir, and Adleman, an encryption technique that uses public and private keys along with a computer algorithm that relies on factoring large prime numbers.

service ticket In Kerberos security, a permanent ticket good for the duration of a logon session (or for another period of time specified by the server administrator in the account policies) that enables the computer to access network services beginning with the Logon service.

Trusted Platform Module (TPM) A security specification for a hardware device used to secure information on another device, such as on a hard drive. The TPM hardware device is typically a chip.

User Account Control (UAC) Enables software and device installations in standard user mode while still ensuring authorization from the administrator. UAC is intended to further remove these activities from access to the kernel to protect the operating system and make it difficult to destabilize through malware and intrusions.

Windows Defender Software that scans for and removes viruses, spyware, and malware. Windows Defender is included with Windows Server 2016.

Windows Firewall Windows software that manages incoming and outgoing communications through opening or blocking TCP and UDP communication ports and specific applications—to limit the attack surface and thwart attackers and malware.

Windows NT LAN Manager version 2 (NTLMv2) An authentication protocol used in legacy Windows NT Server systems and retained in all Windows systems for backward compatibility for clients that cannot support Kerberos.

Review Questions

1. Kerberos on Windows Server 2016 authenticates which of the following? (Choose all that apply.)
   a. The TCP communications port
   b. The client requesting server access
   c. The Group Policy that applies to the client requesting server access
   d. The server the client is trying to access

2. In your organization, the server administrators perform server maintenance once a week or more in the early morning hours before users come in for work. They often encounter users who are still signed in to the servers. Which of the following is one way in Kerberos to make sure that users are not still signed in during the earlier morning hours?
   a. Limit the maximum lifetime for service tickets.
   b. Set the Kerberos duration threshold to *minimum*.
   c. Have the Kerberos Monitor automatically sign out users at 10 PM.
   d. Use Kerberos Manager to freeze sign-in access.
3. You have received a Word memo from your supervisor outlining the five-year strategic plan for your company, which operates in a very competitive field. When you try to copy the memo or print it out, you discover you don't have the rights to complete these actions. What Windows Server 2016 and Word capability did your supervisor use to safeguard the memo?
   a. NAT application protection
   b. GUID access
   c. Rights Management Services
   d. XPS View Control
4. What is a TPM chip and how is it used with Windows Server 2016?
5. Your company is considering the use of Network Address Translation for remote access communications. Which of the following are advantages of Network Address Translation? (Choose all that apply.)
   a. It doubles the speed of network protocol transfer.
   b. It enables an organization to automatically assign its own IP addresses on an internal network without having to obtain a globally unique address.
   c. It broadcasts the IP addresses of internal network computers so they can be registered on DNS servers throughout the Internet for faster lookup.
   d. It changes MAC addresses to the loopback address for disguising clients.
6. Security definition updates for Windows Defender are performed through the __________ function in Windows Server 2016.
7. You need to lock down a server and ensure that only necessary TCP and UDP port communications are used for inbound and outbound network communications. What tool enables you to lock down communications through these ports?
   a. Port Switch Service
   b. NAT
   c. Windows Firewall
   d. Group Policy Editor
8. The GUI used to manually perform scans via Windows Defender is installed as a __________ through Server Manager.
9. When users change passwords on your organization's server, they frequently go back to passwords they have used before in the last few months. What Group Policy element for the Default Domain Policy can you configure to prevent users from repeating the same passwords so frequently?
   a. Set *maximum password age* to a lower value.
   b. Turn off *password repeat*.
   c. Turn on *store password*.
   d. Increase the setting for *enforce password* history.

10. Which of the following can you configure when creating a security template? (Choose all that apply.)
    a. File system security
    b. Group restrictions
    c. Account policies
    d. Event log tracking policies
11. You are in the Windows PowerShell window and decide to encrypt a folder. Which of the following commands do you use?
    a. *cipher /e*
    b. *attrib /s*
    c. *cipher /k*
    d. *attrib /c*
    e. There is no Windows PowerShell command to encrypt a folder.
12. AD RMS is installed as a _________ through _________.
13. You have configured security policies for the domain and for nested OUs. After completing the configuration, users in two OUs do not have the access to resources that they need. What tool can you use to quickly troubleshoot the problem?
    a. Security Templates snap-in
    b. Resultant Set of Policy tool
    c. Network Access Protection Analysis tool
    d. Group Policy Object Editor

10

14. Your organization has a DHCP server, but users cannot access it after another server administrator worked on the DHCP server last night. Which of the following might you check on the DHCP server as a step in troubleshooting the problem?
    a. New Windows Defender virus definitions
    b. Application exceptions that are configured in Windows Firewall
    c. DHCP access time windows
    d. Group policy auditing settings for DHCP
15. Name two advantages of Advanced Encryption Standard (AES).
16. Your company employs a part-time person whose sole job is to install software for users. That person is now leaving and the company wants to automate the process so that users can reliably install their own software. Which of the following Windows Server 2016 capabilities can you use?
    a. Pushing applications
    b. Automated Application Installation Wizard
    c. Publishing applications
    d. GPO application installation
17. Your assistant wants to audit all kinds of activities on a server, from every time someone accesses the server to every time a file or printer is used. What is your response?
    a. Auditing all of these activities is vital for good server security.
    b. It is not possible to audit logon events.
    c. Auditing access to all processes should be added to the list.
    d. Use auditing sparingly; it creates high maintenance for the security logs.

18. Group policies can be set for which of the following? (Choose all that apply.)
    a. Local computer
    b. OU
    c. Site
    d. Domain
19. Name two Internet communications protocols that IPsec can help secure.
20. In Windows Defender, where can you view malware items that have been detected or quarantined to find out how Windows Defender has addressed them?

Case Projects

People's Bank and Trust is a full-service, privately owned community bank. The bank is divided into the following departments: Customer Service, Loans, Business Services, and Investment Services. The bank is presently upgrading its servers from Windows Server 2008 to Windows Server 2016. Also, it is gradually upgrading client computers from a mix of Windows 7 and 8 to Windows 10. The cash drawers at the tellers' booths are connected to Windows 7 computers, which are networked into the servers. The bank uses Active Directory with one small domain and with OUs for each department. All of the servers at the bank are configured as DCs.

In addition to walk-in and drive-up services, People's Bank and Trust offers ATM services and Internet banking. The Internet banking is performed through a Windows Server 2008 web server located at the bank. The bank also offers automated telephone banking services that are tied into its Windows servers.

The bank auditors have recently raised concerns in several areas of computer and network security that the bank wants to address at the same time as it upgrades the client and server computers. The IT director at the bank has retained you via Aspen Consulting to assist with the transition to Windows Server 2016 and to help resolve the security issues raised by the audit.

Case Project 10-1: Password Security

Inadequate password security is one of the areas that the auditors believe needs improvement. A former server administrator acquiesced to bank employees' complaints about frequent password changes and set very lax account policies for passwords. The audits raised the following concerns:

- Some bank employees have used the same user account password for several years.
- Many of the existing passwords are only four or five characters in length.
- Several bank employees regularly change their passwords but rotate between the same three or four passwords with each change.
- An employee who has forgotten a password can keep trying different combinations for as long as they like, until they hit upon the password or give up trying.

What capabilities in Windows Server 2016 enable the bank to address the auditors' concerns? Create a detailed report of your recommendations for the bank's Audit Response Committee. Also, for the IT manager who is a committee member, note what tool can be used to implement your recommendations.

Case Project 10-2: Using Windows Server 2016 Auditing

The Audit Response Committee would like to know in what ways Windows Server 2016 can provide audit information, because no auditing is currently in use. The committee would like you to create a report that provides examples of what can be audited. Also, the IT director wants you to create a set of general instructions for how to set up auditing changes to files.

Case Project 10-3: Managing Client Computers

The auditors would like to see more standardization of each user's desktop and curtail the ability to change some important settings. Specifically they would like to:

- Prevent Windows 7, 8, and 10 clients from using Control Panel after computers have been set up.
- Ensure that all Windows clients start the most recent version of Microsoft Excel when they click on a file with an .xlsx extension.
- Prevent users from changing information about their network connections.
- Remove the Music icon from the Start menu.

For any of these that are possible, include general instructions for the IT Department about how to implement them.

Case Project 10-4: Responding to a Security Alert

The bank auditors have become aware that the banking software vendor for the bank has issued a security alert that their last software update inadvertently unblocks the TCP and UDP ports for FTP and telnet (ports 20, 21, 23, and 24). The bank has ignored this alert. What immediate steps can be taken to block these ports (assume that the bank uses the port blocking capabilities that come with Windows 10)?

Server and Network Monitoring

After reading this chapter and completing the exercises, you will be able to:

- Understand the importance of server monitoring
- Use Resource Monitor
- Monitor server services and solve problems with services
- Use Task Manager for server monitoring
- Configure and use Performance Monitor
- Set up and use Data Collector Sets for performance and diagnostic information
- Implement the SNMP service for network management

When you hike a favorite trail repeatedly, you grow in your knowledge and appreciation for that trail. You come to understand and see things on your hikes that newcomers or those who aren't paying attention miss completely. The same thing is true about monitoring a server and its network over time. The more you use monitoring tools, the more you come to understand how a server and its network perform in all kinds of situations. This chapter introduces you to tools that enable you to truly know your server and network as an expert. After your server is up and running, this knowledge will make you a proficient server administrator who can quickly spot and solve problems, often before anyone experiences them.

In this chapter, you begin by learning about the importance of monitoring. You learn to monitor server services and how to fix problems with the services. You go on to use Task Manager as a basic tool for monitoring and managing applications, processes, services, system performance, network performance, and users. Next, you learn to use Performance Monitor, which is a versatile tool you'll come to rely on for monitoring your server and network inside and out. Along with Performance Monitor, you can use Data Collector Sets to check on server and network performance and to quickly diagnose problems. Finally, you implement the SNMP service for network management.

Introduction to Server Monitoring

Server monitoring is performed for several reasons. One reason is to establish a baseline of performance, so problems can be more easily identified when they occur. It may be difficult to diagnose a problem or determine if there is a resource shortage unless you first know what performance is typical for your server. Other reasons to monitor servers are to prevent problems before they occur and to diagnose existing problems. Monitoring enables you to pinpoint problems and identify solutions, for example, by tracking disk errors and replacing a hard disk before it fails.

The most important way to get to know your server is to use monitoring tools to establish normal server performance characteristics. This is a process that involves establishing benchmarks. **Benchmarks (or baselines)** provide a basis for comparing data collected during problem situations with data showing normal performance conditions. This creates a way to diagnose problems and identify components that need to be upgraded or replaced.

The best way to get a feel for a server's performance is to establish a baseline and then frequently monitor server performance, comparing the data collected with that in the baseline. Performance indicators can be confusing at first, so the more time you spend observing them, the better you'll understand them.

Sample benchmarks that you might establish include the following:

- Test benchmarks of disk, CPU, memory, and network response before releasing a new operating system, server hardware, or a complex application to users
- Slow, typical, and heavy usage of disk, CPU, memory, and other server resources for each server
- Slow, typical, and heavy usage of the combined network and server resources
- Growth of use of network and server resources at specific intervals, such as every 6 months to a year

In the sections that follow, you'll explore all types of techniques to monitor resources for benchmarks, to help avoid problems, and to fix problems as they occur.

Using Resource Monitor

Resource Monitor can be a good starting place for monitoring a server. Resource Monitor provides a real-time snapshot for monitoring the following resources (see Figure 11-1):

- CPU
- Memory
- Disk
- Network

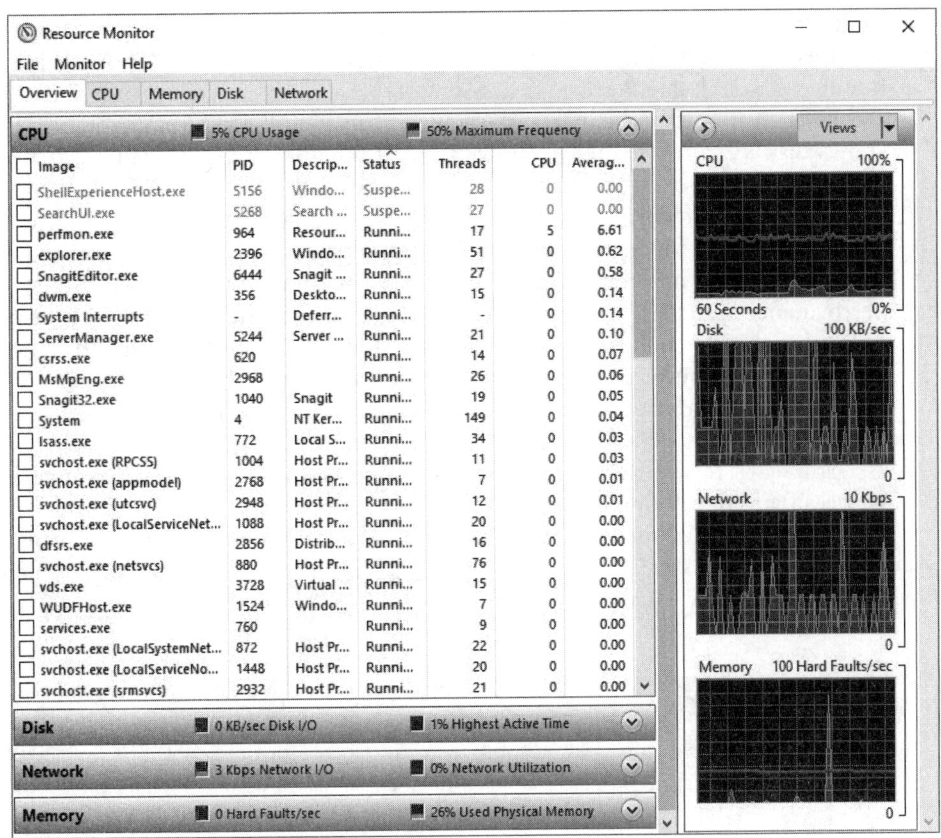

Figure 11-1 Resource Monitor

This tool can be very useful for a first quick analysis of a problem, such as when users report that their connection response to the server is slow. Slow response could be related to CPU use, memory, disk use, network activity, or a combination of these. If you receive a call from a user about slow response, you can quickly look at these statistics to get a general idea of the problem or an initial clue, which might consist of one or a combination of factors. For example, a Remote Desktop Services user might experience slow response because the application she is using maximizes CPU use, creates excessive network activity at the server, or both. Or, the application might be very memory-intensive. If the NIC on the server is malfunctioning by sending out constant network communications, you can get a first clue about this problem by checking the Network tab in Resource Monitor. In this case, the only high-use area might be the network utilization as measured at the server.

In another scenario, you might find that data needs to be redistributed among disks or that you need to restructure DFS (Distributed File System), as indicated by looking at disk I/O (input/output) in Resource Monitor.

When you monitor a server for problems, the main problem sources are those monitored by Resource Monitor: CPU, memory, disk, and network. Added to these are the actual processes or services running on the server, which are displayed according to these four main categories.

The processor(s) in a server can be a bottleneck for a couple of reasons. One reason is simply that the processor does not have enough processing speed or that combined processors still do not have the total processing speed/power needed. A second reason is that one or more applications are inefficient or poorly programmed. As suggested by Microsoft, if the total average CPU usage is frequently over 85 percent, it is likely that it is time to upgrade to one or more faster CPUs.

Memory bottlenecks can be caused by insufficient memory or inefficient programs. Further, if there is not enough memory, disk I/O activity can increase, thus affecting disk performance. If the percentage of total used physical memory is frequently over 80 percent, and memory hard faults/sec is often high, additional memory is likely needed. This situation means you should consider using Performance Monitor to do a more detailed examination of memory performance (see the section, Using Performance Monitor).

Hard disk bottlenecks particularly affect the overall server performance. Resource Monitor shows disk I/O and the highest active time. If the disk I/O, as measured in KB/sec is frequently high, such as 80 percent, consider purchasing faster disks.

Network performance is still another possible bottleneck that can affect all server users. Problems to look for include a problem with a server NIC or a network that is saturated with traffic, similar to being stuck in rush-hour traffic in a city. Resource Monitor shows network performance statistics in terms of I/O in Kbps/sec and percent network utilization. Network utilization that is regularly over 60–70 percent is a cause for concern and signals the need to use Performance Monitor to track down problems in detail. Network utilization over 90 percent is very serious and signals an urgent need to locate problem sources or to determine network design bottlenecks.

You learn to use Resource Monitor in Activity 11-1. Be sure to notice the processes and services that are running in each tab display in Resource Monitor and notice the amount of the particular resource, such as CPU, they use. If you are monitoring for a problem, such as slow server response, consider going to Resource Monitor first and then use it as a springboard to the Services tool, Task Manager, or Performance Monitor to gather more information.

Some steps in the activities in this book include bulleted questions for you to answer. Additionally, for all of the activities in this chapter, you'll need an account with Administrator privileges. These activities can be completed on a virtual machine or computer, such as in Hyper-V.

Activity 11-1: Using Resource Monitor

Time Required: Approximately 10 minutes
Objective: Use Resource Monitor for an initial server assessment.

Description: In this activity, you open Resource Monitor to assess current CPU, memory, disk, and network activity in Windows Server 2016.

1. Open **Server Manager**, if it is not open.
2. Click **Tools** and click **Resource Monitor.**
3. Be sure the **Overview** tab is selected.
4. Click the **down arrow** for **CPU**, if necessary, to view processes associated with CPU activity (refer to Figure 11-1).
   - What is the % CPU Usage? What is the % Used Physical Memory (shown in the Memory section of Resource Monitor)?
5. Click the **CPU** tab.
   - What four sections of information do you see to view information about CPU activity?
6. Under the Processes section in the CPU tab, right-click a process, such as *Server Manager.exe*.
   - What actions can you take from this menu?
7. Click the **Memory** tab. Notice the MB in Use and the MB Available data associated with the Physical Memory section. Also, notice the active memory-related graphs in the right pane.
8. Click the **Disk** tab. Click the **down arrows** to expand the **Disk Activity** and **Storage** sections. Review the information in each of these sections. View the graphs in the right pane showing real-time disk activity information.

9. Click the **Network** tab.
   - What is the current % Network Utilization? Which section of information in the left pane enables you to determine TCP and UDP ports that are active and allowed or not allowed through Windows Firewall?
10. Close Resource Monitor, but leave Server Manager open for the next activity.

Monitoring Server Services

Servers are always running a number of services. The exact number of services depends on the number and types of components you have installed. Table 11-1 presents a small sampling of some of the services typically in use in Windows Server 2016.

Table 11-1 Sample Windows Server 2016 services

Service	Description
Active Directory Domain Services	Enables Active Directory services for a network and must be running to enable users to sign in to the network (when Active Directory is installed)
Computer Browser	Keeps a listing of computers and domain resources to be accessed
DHCP Server	Enables clients to obtain leased IP addresses (when the DHCP Server role is installed)
DNS Server	Enables resolution of DNS names and IP addresses (when the DNS Server role is installed)
File Replication	Replicates the Active Directory elements on multiple DCs (when Active Directory is installed)
Intersite Messaging	Transfers messages between different Windows Server 2016 sites
IPsec Policy Agent	Enables IPsec security and enforces IPsec policies
Kerberos Key Distribution Center	Enables Kerberos authentication and the server as a center from which to issue Kerberos security keys and tickets
Microsoft iSCSI Initiator Service	Manages access to iSCSI devices, such as hard drives in a Storage Area Network (SAN)
Netlogon	Maintains logon services such as verifying users who are signing in to the server or a domain
Network List Service	Keeps information about the networks the server connects to and communicates network information to applications on the server
Optimize drives	Optimizes files in storage to help server performance
Plug and Play	Enables automatic detection and installation of new hardware devices or devices that have changed
Print Spooler	Enables print spooling
Remote Procedure Call (RPC)	Provides remote procedure call services
Remote Registry	Enables the Registry to be managed remotely
Resultant Set of Policy Provider	Enables use of Resultant Set of Policy to determine Group Policy settings
Security Accounts Manager	Keeps information about user accounts and their related security setup
Server	A critical service that supports shared objects, logon services, print services, and remote procedure calls
System Event Notification Service	Enables the detection and reporting of important system events, such as a hardware or network problem
Task Scheduler	Used to start a program at a specified time and works with the software Task Scheduler
TCP/IP NetBIOS Helper	Activated when TCP/IP is installed, and used to enable NetBIOS name resolution and NetBIOS network transport
User Profile Service	Loads and unloads user profiles and is necessary for users to sign in or out
Windows Event Log	Enables server events to be logged for later review or diagnosis in case problems occur
Windows Firewall	Enables Windows Firewall to control incoming and outgoing communications
Windows Time	Enables updating the clock
Windows Update	Enables the operating system to obtain updates
Workstation	Enables network communications and access by clients over the network via the Server Message Block (SMB) protocol (SMB is used to access shared resources such as folders and printers)

Accessing Server Services

As you have learned previously, you can access server services through Server Manager or the Computer Management tool (see Figure 11-2).

When you click the Standard tab, the services are displayed in the right pane of the Services window in five columns of information, as shown in Figure 11-2. The Name column shows services listed alphabetically. A short description of each service is provided in the Description column. The Status column indicates the current status of the service as follows:

- *Running* shows that the service is started and active.
- *Paused* means that the service is started, but is not available to users.
- A blank means that the service is halted or has not been started.

The Startup Type column shows how a service is started when the computer boots. Many services are started automatically when the server is booted. Some services are started manually because they might not be needed until a given time. Services that are not set to start automatically or manually are disabled. The Log On As column specifies the account under which the service is running. Most services log on to a Local System account. Some network-related services, such as IPsec Policy Agent, log on to a Network Service account.

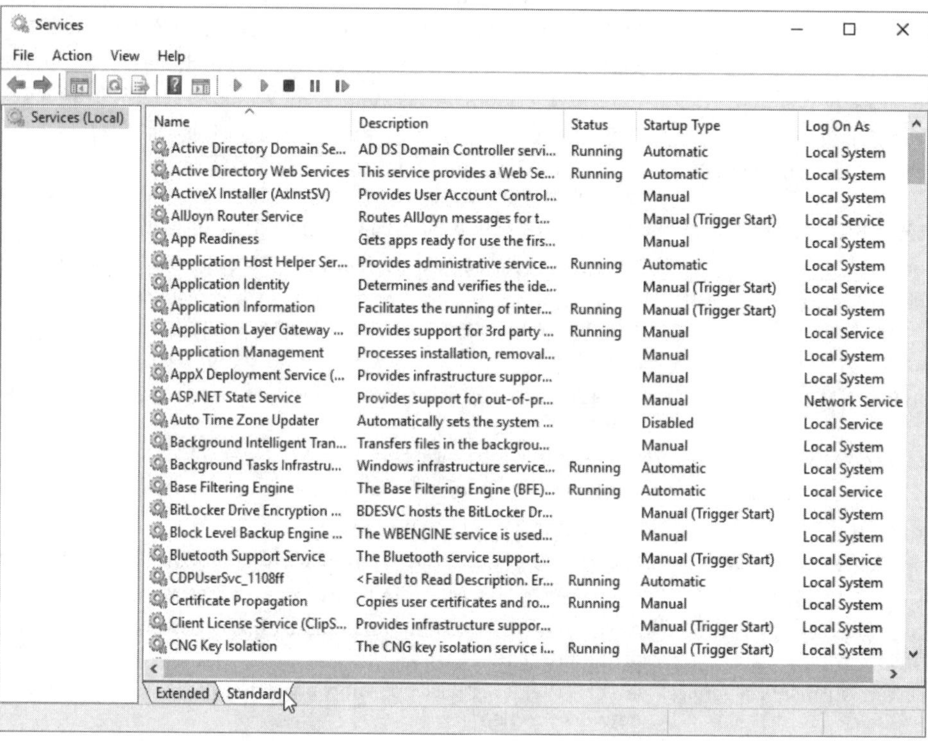

Figure 11-2 Services window

Solving a Problem with a Service

When you experience a problem on a server that is associated with a service, check the status of the service to make sure that it is running or set to start automatically. You can start, stop, pause, resume, or restart a service by right-clicking it and clicking any of these options—however, you can use only those options that are activated. For example, occasionally a service does not start properly when the server is booted or hangs while the server is running, such as the Print Spooler service. The Services and Computer Management tools provide a way to monitor this situation. Even if the Print Spooler shows that it is running, if you determine that you want to restart it, right-click the service and click Restart (keep in mind, though, that you will lose print jobs in the print queue and so you should only try this solution as a last resort).

Use the Stop option carefully, because some services are linked to others. Stopping one service will stop the others that depend on it. For instance, stopping the Workstation service affects these other services: Computer Browser, DFS Namespace (if DFS is installed), Netlogon, and Remote Desktop Configuration. The system gives you a warning when other services are affected by stopping a particular service.

You can check dependencies by double-clicking a service and clicking the Dependencies tab (see Figure 11-3).

Several services are linked to the Server and Workstation services, including signed-in users. If it is necessary to stop one of these services—for example, to diagnose a problem—give the users advance warning or stop the service after work hours.

Pausing a service takes it offline to be used only by Administrators or Server Operators. A paused service is restarted by right-clicking it and clicking Restart.

Another way to manage a service is to double-click it to view that service's properties (see Figure 11-3). For example, you can set a service to start automatically by double-clicking the service, accessing the General tab, and setting the Startup type box to Automatic.

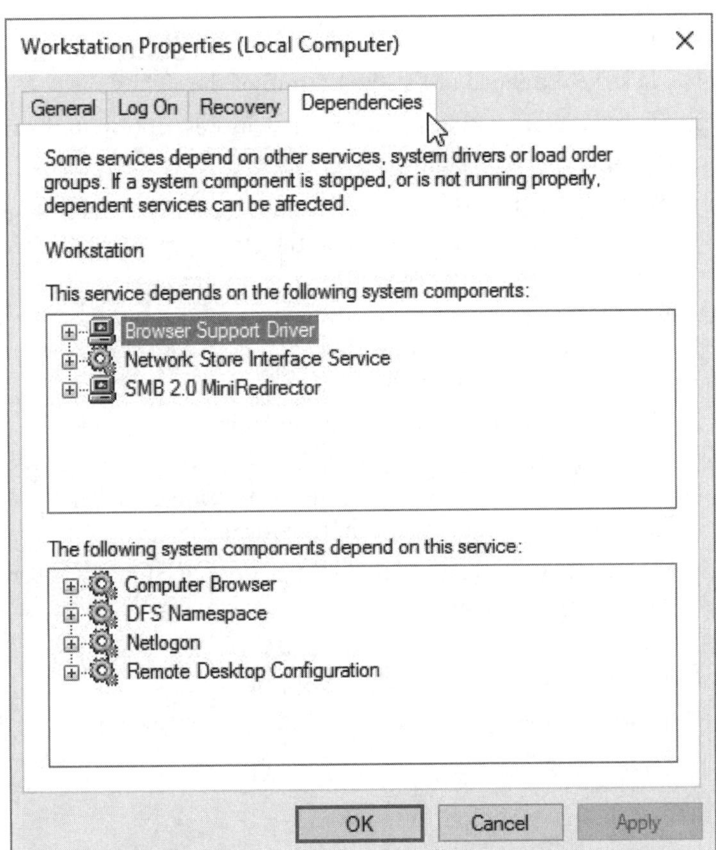

Figure 11-3 Workstation service dependencies

Activity 11-2: Monitoring and Managing a Service

Time Required: Approximately 10 minutes
Objective: Use the Services tool to monitor and manage a Windows Server 2016 service.

Description: In this activity, you practice monitoring, starting, and stopping a service. You also view a service's dependencies.

1. Open **Server Manager**, if it is not open.
2. Click **Tools** and click **Services**. (Alternatively you can right-click **Start**, click **Computer Management**, double-click **Services and Applications** in the tree in the left pane, and click **Services** in the tree to see a three-pane window, in which you execute the steps below in the middle pane instead of in the right pane.)
3. Ensure that the **Extended** tab is selected at the bottom of the right pane in the Services window.
4. Scroll to and click the **Server** service. Read the description of this service in the right pane in the Services window.
5. Click the **Standard** tab at the bottom of the right pane.
6. If necessary, stretch the border of the right pane over to the right so that you can see the five columns in the pane.
7. Scroll through the services and notice the information available in the columns.
8. Double-click the **Server** service.
9. Click the **Dependencies** tab and wait for a few seconds.
   - What services depend on the Server service? On what services does the Server service depend?
10. Click **Cancel**.
11. Click the **Extended** tab at the bottom of the right pane.
12. Click the **Workstation** service to view its description in the right pane.
    - Why is this service important?
13. Double-click the **Microsoft iSCSI Initiator Service**. Set this service to start when the server is booted by selecting **Automatic** in the Startup type list box (it is set to Manual by default), as shown in Figure 11-4. Click **Apply**.
14. Click the **Dependencies** tab to determine if any other service(s) must be started prior to starting this service. Notice that this service does not depend on any other services and no other services depend on it.
15. Click the **General** tab and then click **Start**.
16. Click **OK** in the Microsoft iSCSI Initiator Service Properties (Local Computer) dialog box. Click the **Standard** tab in the right pane. Notice that the Microsoft iSCSI Initiator Service is now running and set to start automatically.
17. Click the **Extended** tab. With the Microsoft iSCSI Initiator Service selected (or click the service, if necessary), click **Stop** to the left of the Name column in the right pane to stop the service.
    - Even though the service is stopped now, what will happen when you reboot the computer?
18. Close the Services (or Computer Management) window.

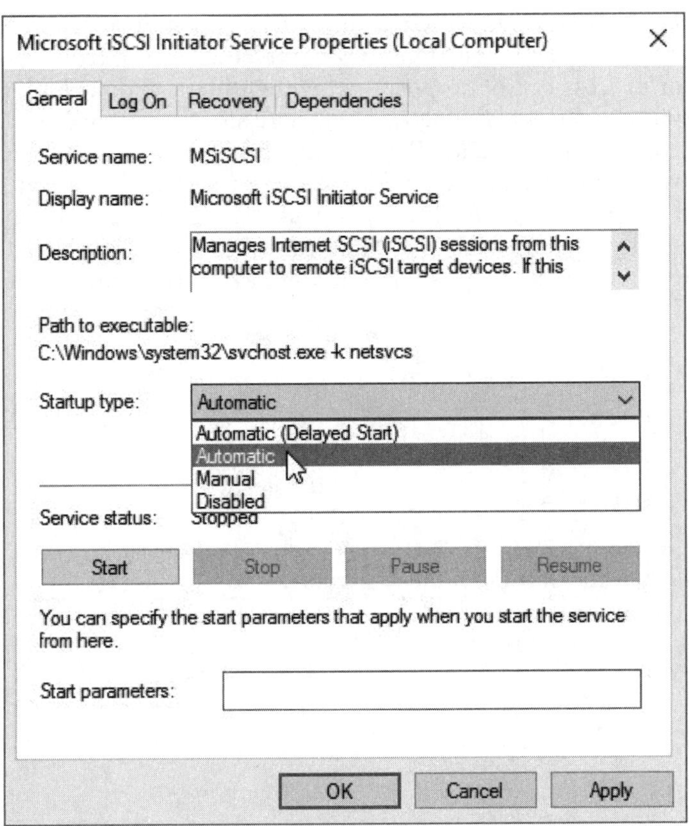

Figure 11-4 Configuring the Microsoft iSCSI Initiator Service to start automatically

Frequently monitor services to learn which ones you need and which you don't need. Disable services you don't need. This not only helps your server boot faster and run more efficiently, it also provides better security because it closes possible entryways that an attacker or malware can use to access your system.

Using Task Manager

Sometimes a server component, such as an application or process, hangs or consumes server resources, slowing overall server performance. Windows Server 2016 includes the Task Manager tool that can be used to monitor applications and processes running on a server.

Monitoring Applications

You can use Task Manager to view applications running on the server by pressing Ctrl+Alt+Delete while signed in as Administrator or as a member of the Administrators group. Click Task Manager. If necessary, click the down arrow for *More details* to see the full Task Manager window with five tabs: Processes, Performance, Users, Details, and Services.

An alternate way to start Task Manager is to right-click an open space on the taskbar and click Task Manager.

When you view the Processes tab, shown in Figure 11-5, you'll see all of the software applications, background processes, and Windows processes running from the server console. Any application or process can be stopped by highlighting it and clicking the End task button. If an application or process is hung (no longer responding to user input), you can select that application or process and click End task to stop it and release server resources. The Processes tab shows the name of the application or process, the percent of CPU it is using in real time, and the percentage of memory it is using. When you right-click an application or process and click *Go to details*, Task Manager takes you to the Details tab so you can view the actual process name highlighted, if you don't know the name of the application or process.

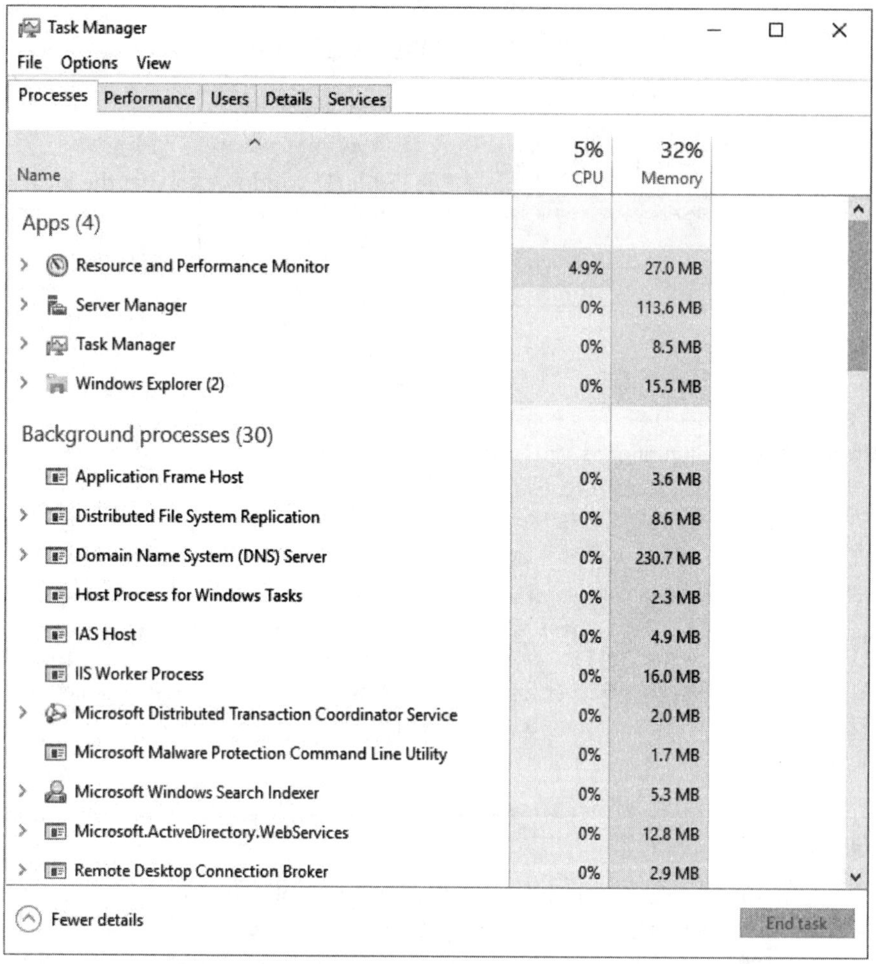

Figure 11-5 Task Manager Processes tab

If you right-click an application, several active options appear in a menu, as follows:

- *Expand*—Available for applications or processes so you can view elements associated with them (the same as clicking the right-pointing arrow in front of the application or process). For example, if you are running the background process Domain Name System (DNS) Server, the element under it is DNS Server.

- *Restart*—Only available when the application or process allows its use for a restart.
- *End task*—Stops the application or process.
- *Resource values*—Focuses on the resources actively used, such as memory, in percentage or value.
- *Create dump file*—Creates a dump file to reflect activity by the application or process, which is stored by default in \Users\ADMINISTRATOR\AppData\Local\Temp\ *dumpfolder#*\ as the file named *programprocessname*.DMP. For example, if you make this selection for the Command Prompt program, the dump file is called cmd.DMP and is placed in dump folder 1 for the first saved instance, dump folder 2 for the second saved instance, and so on. Creating a dump file is useful when you are having a problem with an application or process, for example, if the application crashes or freezes and you want to look for error information in the dump file as a clue to the problem.
- *Go to details*—Takes you to the Details tab and highlights the specific process associated with the program or process's general name. For example, if you select this option for the background process, Domain Name System (DNS) Server, you go to the Details tab, which highlights dns.exe.
- *Open file location*—Opens a File Explorer window showing the location of the file used for the application or process, For instance, if you make this selection for the background process Domain Name System (DNS) Server, File Explorer goes to C:\Windows\System32\dns.exe.
- *Search online*—Opens your browser to show the search results for the application or process.
- *Properties*—Opens a properties dialog box for the application or process.

When you create a dump file (.dmp), you'll need a debugging tool to open and read the file. Use a 32-bit debugging tool for 32-bit programs and a 64-bit debugging tool for 64-bit programs and processes. You can obtain debugging tools, such as WinDBG from Microsoft's download website, such as *www.microsoft.com/en-us/download.*

11

Activity 11-3: Working with Applications in Task Manager

Time Required: Approximately 10 minutes
Objective: Use Task Manager to monitor and manage applications.

Description: In this activity, you start an application and then use it to learn about Task Manager functions for controlling applications and processes, including ending an application or process.

1. Click **Start**, click the **Windows Accessories** folder, and click **Wordpad**.
2. Press the **Ctrl+Alt+Delete** keys at the same time.
   - What options are displayed on the screen?
3. Click **Task Manager**.
4. Click the **down arrow** for **More details**, if necessary.
5. Click the **Processes** tab, if it is not displayed already.
6. Right-click **Windows Wordpad Application** and notice the active options on the menu (see Figure 11-6).

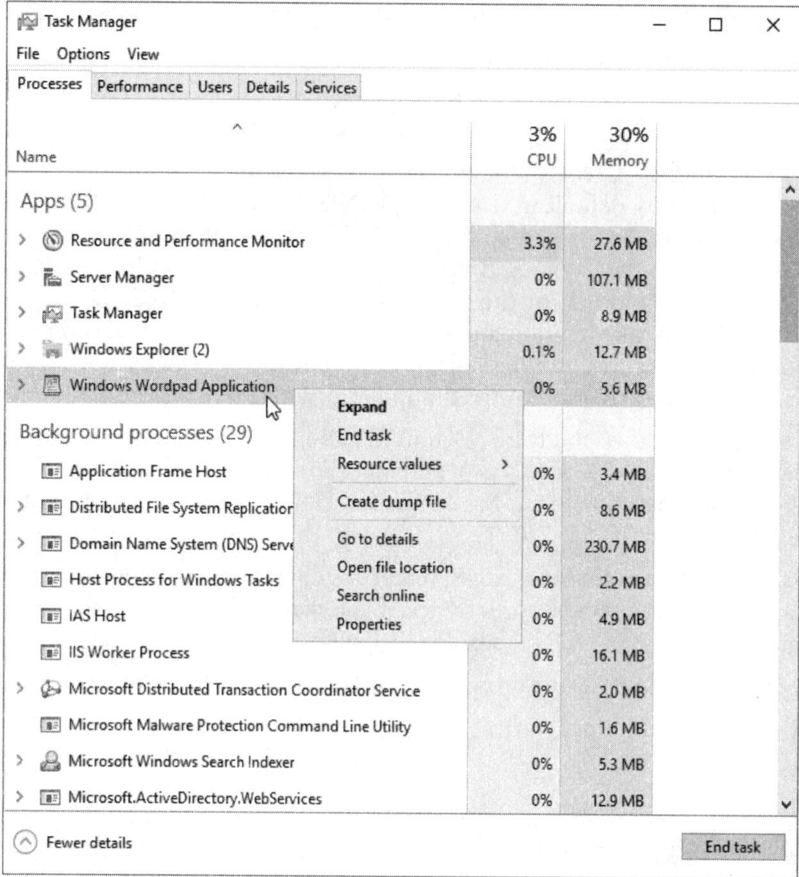

Figure 11-6 Opening the menu of options

7. Click **Go to details.**
   - What happens?
8. Click the **Processes** tab in Task Manager.
9. Spend a few moments to view the CPU and Memory columns for the Apps and processes.
10. Click **Windows Wordpad Application,** if it is not still selected. Click **End task** to close Windows Wordpad Application. (It's better to close an application or process by using its normal method to close or sign out, but keep in mind you can use this action when an application or process is not responding.)
11. Leave Task Manager open for the next activity.

Monitoring Processes

The Details tab lists the processes in use by all running applications (see Figure 11-7). If you need to stop a process, simply highlight it and click End task. The Details tab also shows information about each started process, as summarized in Table 11-2.

Many different processes may be running on a system, with some variation related to the Windows operating system, Microsoft, and third-party applications that are running. Table 11-3 presents some common processes that you may see on your system.

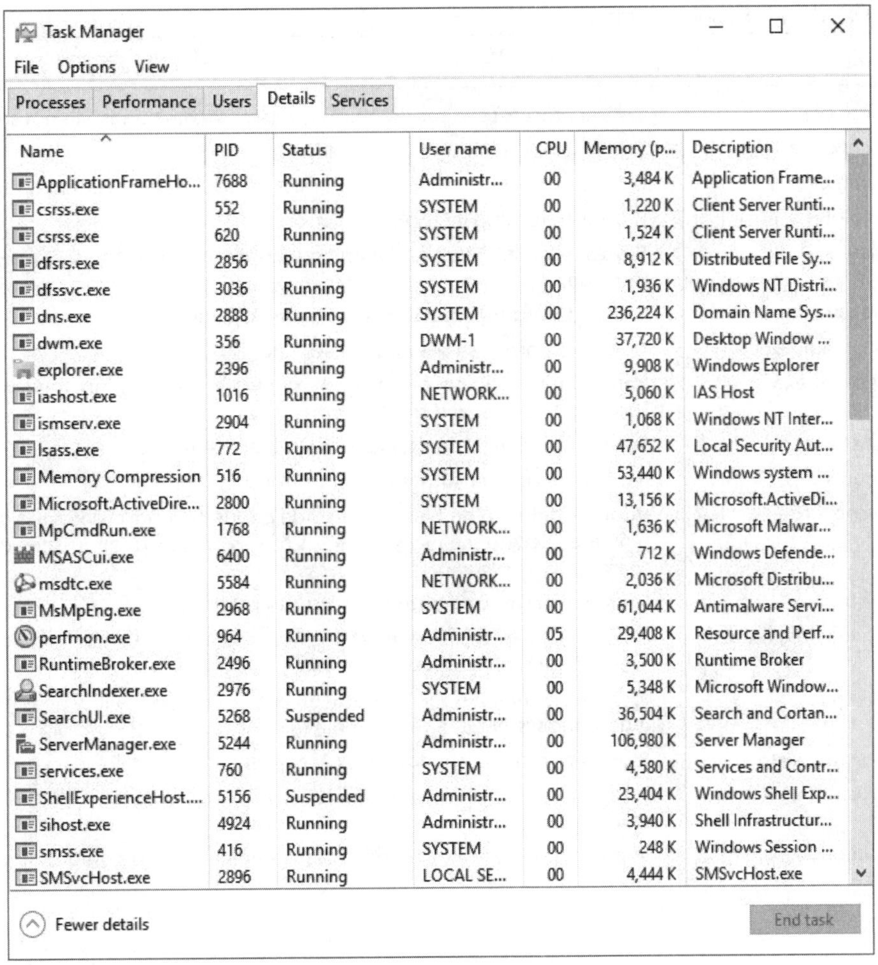

Task Manager

File Options View

Processes | Performance | Users | Details | Services

Name	PID	Status	User name	CPU	Memory (p...	Description
ApplicationFrameHo...	7688	Running	Administr...	00	3,484 K	Application Frame...
csrss.exe	552	Running	SYSTEM	00	1,220 K	Client Server Runti...
csrss.exe	620	Running	SYSTEM	00	1,524 K	Client Server Runti...
dfsrs.exe	2856	Running	SYSTEM	00	8,912 K	Distributed File Sy...
dfssvc.exe	3036	Running	SYSTEM	00	1,936 K	Windows NT Distri...
dns.exe	2888	Running	SYSTEM	00	236,224 K	Domain Name Sys...
dwm.exe	356	Running	DWM-1	00	37,720 K	Desktop Window ...
explorer.exe	2396	Running	Administr...	00	9,908 K	Windows Explorer
iashost.exe	1016	Running	NETWORK...	00	5,060 K	IAS Host
ismserv.exe	2904	Running	SYSTEM	00	1,068 K	Windows NT Inter...
lsass.exe	772	Running	SYSTEM	00	47,652 K	Local Security Aut...
Memory Compression	516	Running	SYSTEM	00	53,440 K	Windows system ...
Microsoft.ActiveDire...	2800	Running	SYSTEM	00	13,156 K	Microsoft.ActiveDi...
MpCmdRun.exe	1768	Running	NETWORK...	00	1,636 K	Microsoft Malwar...
MSASCui.exe	6400	Running	Administr...	00	712 K	Windows Defende...
msdtc.exe	5584	Running	NETWORK...	00	2,036 K	Microsoft Distribu...
MsMpEng.exe	2968	Running	SYSTEM	00	61,044 K	Antimalware Servi...
perfmon.exe	964	Running	Administr...	05	29,408 K	Resource and Perf...
RuntimeBroker.exe	2496	Running	Administr...	00	3,500 K	Runtime Broker
SearchIndexer.exe	2976	Running	SYSTEM	00	5,348 K	Microsoft Window...
SearchUI.exe	5268	Suspended	Administr...	00	36,504 K	Search and Cortan...
ServerManager.exe	5244	Running	Administr...	00	106,980 K	Server Manager
services.exe	760	Running	SYSTEM	00	4,580 K	Services and Contr...
ShellExperienceHost....	5156	Suspended	Administr...	00	23,404 K	Windows Shell Exp...
sihost.exe	4924	Running	Administr...	00	3,940 K	Shell Infrastructur...
smss.exe	416	Running	SYSTEM	00	248 K	Windows Session ...
SMSvcHost.exe	2896	Running	LOCAL SE...	00	4,444 K	SMSvcHost.exe

Fewer details End task

Figure 11-7 Details tab

Table 11-2 Task Manager Details tab information

Process information	Description
Name	The process name, such as winword.exe for Windows Microsoft Office Word
PID (process ID)	The identification number the operating system has assigned to the process
Status	Operation status, such as Running
User Name	The user account under which the process is Running (started) or paused
CPU	The percentage of the CPU resources used by the process
Memory (private working set)	The amount of memory the process is using
Description	Full or formal name of the process, such as Client Server Runtime Process

Table 11-3 Sample processes

Process	Description
csrss.exe	Critical process used for graphics and graphic commands (do not stop)
dfssvc.exe	Enables the Distributed File System
dwm.exe	Desktop Window Manager for the GUI effects of open windows (do not stop)
explorer.exe	Process that runs File Explorer
lsass.exe	Process for implementing logon and security policies that is vital to the server (do not stop)
mcc.exe	Process to run the Microsoft Management Console
SearchIndexer.exe	Noncritical process for Windows searches
services.exe	Important service for starting and stopping processes while the operating system is running, booting, and shutting down (do not stop)
smss.exe	Session Manager Subsystem and a vital service for a server (do not stop)
spoolsv.exe	Part of the spooler subsystem for printing
svchost.exe	Vital for running .dll files that provide a foundation for Windows operating systems (you are likely to see many instances of this process running and you should not stop them)
System	Windows kernel and system process (do not stop)
System Idle Process	Shows a tally of the amount of the CPU resources available for use (not truly a process and cannot be stopped)
takeng.exe	Process that enables the Task Scheduler to run tasks when scheduled, such as backing up the system at a certain time (do not stop)
Taskmgr.exe	Process to run the Windows Task Manager
TrustedInstaller.exe	Used for Windows operating system and software updates, when they occur (do not stop)
winlogon.exe	Important process that enables users to sign in to and sign out of the system (do not stop)

Regularly monitoring processes enables you to learn which ones are normal for your system. If you see a process you cannot identify, check it out because it could be malware. You can find out more about processes by visiting *www.processlibrary.com*.

Setting Priorities

Using the Details tab within Task Manager, you can also increase the priority of a process (or processes) in the list so that it has more CPU priority than what is set as its default. Suppose, for example, that you want to increase the priority for File Explorer, which is process explorer.exe. To start, right-click explorer.exe, displaying a menu in which you can choose from the following:

- End task
- End process tree (end that process and all subprocesses associated with it)
- Set priority
- Set affinity (displayed if your server has two or more processors and allows you to select the CPU on which to run the process)
- Analyze wait chain (shows the threads or processes that are blocking your process)
- UAC virtualization (activated only if applicable)

- Create dump file
- Open file location
- Search online
- Properties
- Go to service(s) takes you to the Services tab

When you point to Set priority, you can use the priority options to allocate more or less CPU priority to that process (see Figure 11-8).

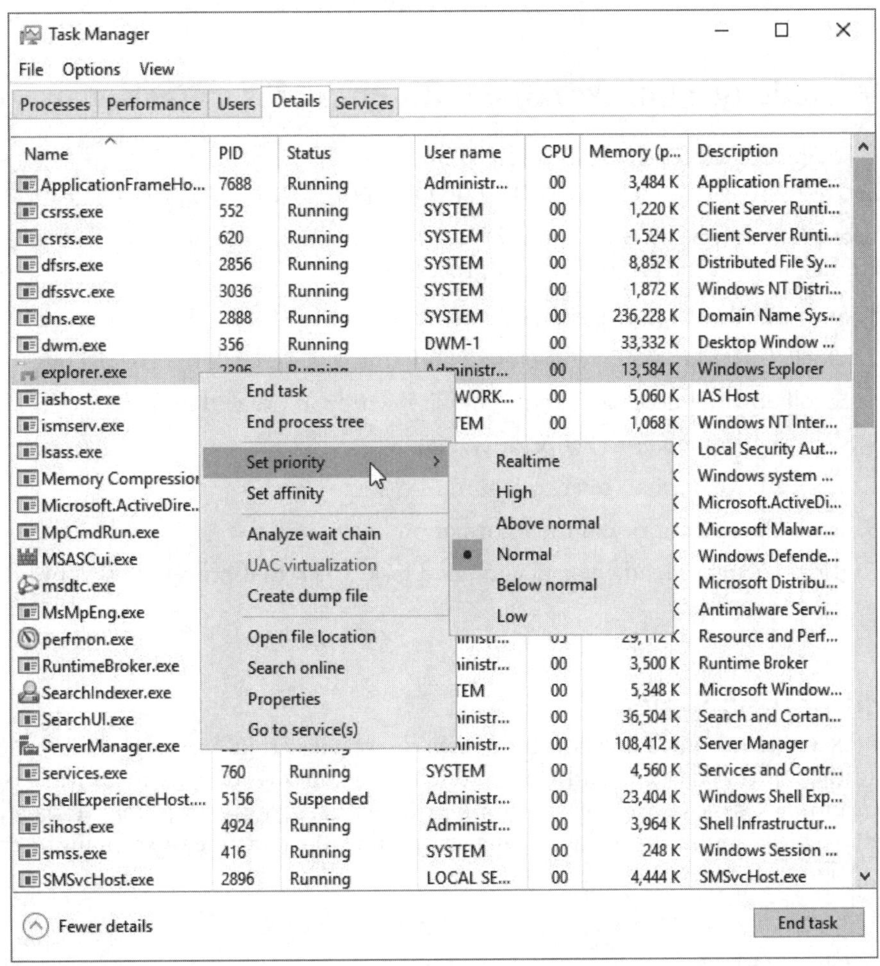

Figure 11-8 Setting the priority of a process

Normally, the priority at which a process runs is set in the program code of the application, which is called the **base priority class**. If the base priority class is not set by the program, a normal (average) priority is set by the system. The server administrator always has the option to set a different base priority. As shown in Figure 11-8, the administrator can change the priority to any of six options: Low, Below normal, Normal, Above normal, High, or Realtime. You might think of these processes as being on a continuum, with Normal as the midpoint, which is 0. Low is 2, Below normal is 1, Above normal is +1, and High is +2. Realtime is given an extra advantage at +15. For example, a Low priority means that if a process is waiting in a queue—for example, for processor time, disk access, or memory access—all processes with a higher priority will go first. The same is true for Below normal, except that processes with this priority will run before those set at Low, and so on.

Use the Realtime priority with great caution, because it is like running on steroids. If assigned to a process, that process may completely take over the server, preventing work by any other processes. For instance, you might want to assign a Realtime priority when you detect a disk drive that is about to fail and you want to give all resources over to the backup process so you can back up files before the disk fails.

Activity 11-4: Working with Processes in Task Manager

Time Required: Approximately 10 minutes

Objective: Use Task Manager to monitor processes and to reset the priority of a process.

Description: In this activity, you use Task Manager to learn about how a process is functioning and then to reset the priority of that process.

1. Start the **Wordpad** program, as you did in Activity 11-3.
2. Open **Task Manager,** if it is closed, and, if necessary, click the **Details** tab.
3. Scroll down, if necessary, and right-click **wordpad.exe** and notice the options.
4. On the menu, point to **Set priority.**
5. Click **Above normal** (refer to Figure 11-8).
6. Click **Change priority** in the information box.
7. Right-click **wordpad.exe** and click **End task.** Click **End process** in the information box.
8. Close Task Manager.

Monitoring Services

The Services tab in Task Manager shows the services that are started, stopped, or paused. In addition to the Services and Computer Management tool, this is another place where you can monitor services. However, unlike the Services and Computer Management tools, the management options from Task Manager are limited to starting or stopping a service. To start or stop a service, you do the following:

1. Right-click the service.
2. Click Start, Stop, or Restart (see Figure 11-9).

If you want to manage services using more management options, right-click the service in the Services tab and click *Open Services* (see Figure 11-9) to open the Services tool.

The services on the Services tab might not be displayed in alphabetical order. You can put them in alphabetical order by clicking the Name column heading.

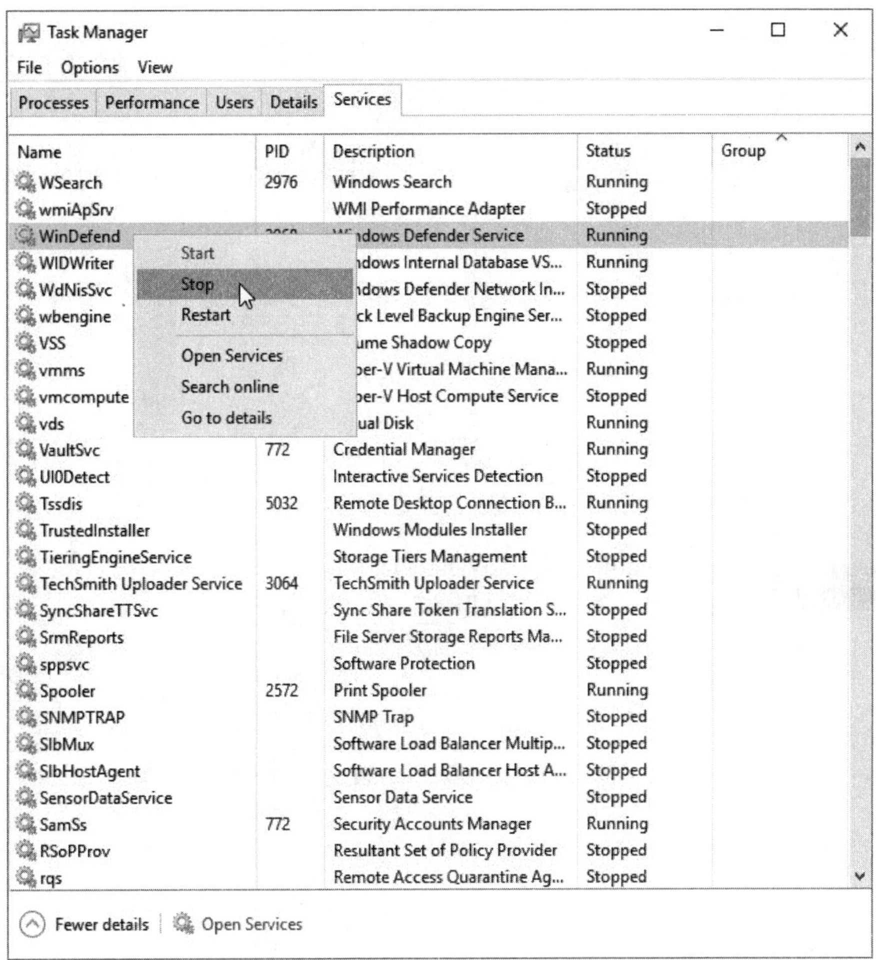

Figure 11-9 Stopping a service on the Services tab

Monitoring Real-Time Performance

The Task Manager Performance tab shows vital CPU, memory, and network (such as Ethernet) performance information through graphs and performance statistics (see Figure 11-10).

You can select to view information by clicking CPU, Memory, or Ethernet (for a cabled network connection), as shown in Figure 11-10. The top portion of the window shows a line graph of real-time activity. Below the line graph are performance statistics. For example, the CPU statistics include information about the actual CPU utilization as a percentage, the CPU speed, the number of processes running, and the number of threads and handles. A **handle** is a resource, such as a file, used by a program and having its own identification so the program is able to access it. **Threads** are blocks of code within a program.

The Memory display shows memory usage in real time. The Memory composition graph shows how memory is allocated and is shaded for differentiating each allocation. You can view a specific memory allocation by moving the pointer to that area, such as to the beginning gray shaded portion as shown in Figure 11-11. The memory statistics at the bottom of the window show information about the amount of memory in use, memory available, total of memory cached, committed memory, the size of the paged pool and non-paged pool. **Committed memory** is the number bytes a process has designated for use and that are promised by the operating system to a designated portion of the page file. The **paged pool** represents data that can be stored in the paging file and so can be paged in and out of the virtual memory (a page file on disk). The **non-paged pool** holds the operating system kernel and device drivers that cannot be paged out,

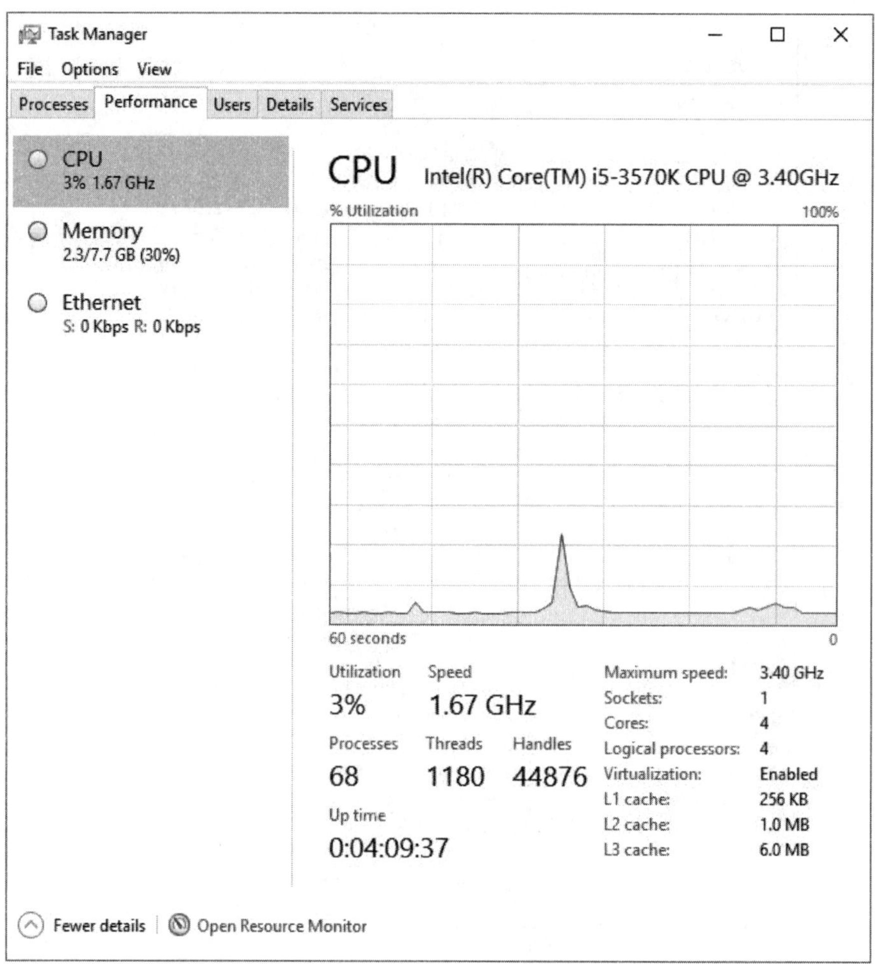

Figure 11-10 Monitoring CPU activity using the Performance tab

and so these processes and threads are always kept in physical memory or RAM to assure faster, uninterrupted performance. Page faults are not allowed in the non-paged pool. A **page fault** occurs whenever memory pages are called by a program or process from the paging file on disk. Consider reviewing the discussion of virtual memory in Chapter 3, Configuring the Windows Server 2016 Environment.

The network performance information shows real-time send and receive throughput on the network. This information is shown in the graph at the top of the window and in the statistics below the graph, as in Figure 11-12. Also, Figure 11-12 illustrates that if the computer has more than one NIC or is configured to have a virtual NIC for Hyper-V, which is the case in Figure 11-12, there are options in the left portion of the window to view network performance data for each NIC.

The network performance data can be a quick diagnostic tool not only to determine if the network is busy but also to ensure that the NIC is connected and working. A NIC that is disconnected, for example, because the network cable is loose, will show up on this display. Also, note that a connected NIC may show 0 percent throughput even though computers are connected to the server. The NIC is simply handling the traffic efficiently, because the clients are not using significant bandwidth.

This information can be valuable if you suspect there is a problem with a NIC in the server and you want an immediate determination if it is working. The information on the tab also can be an initial warning that something is causing prolonged high network utilization—80–100 percent, for instance.

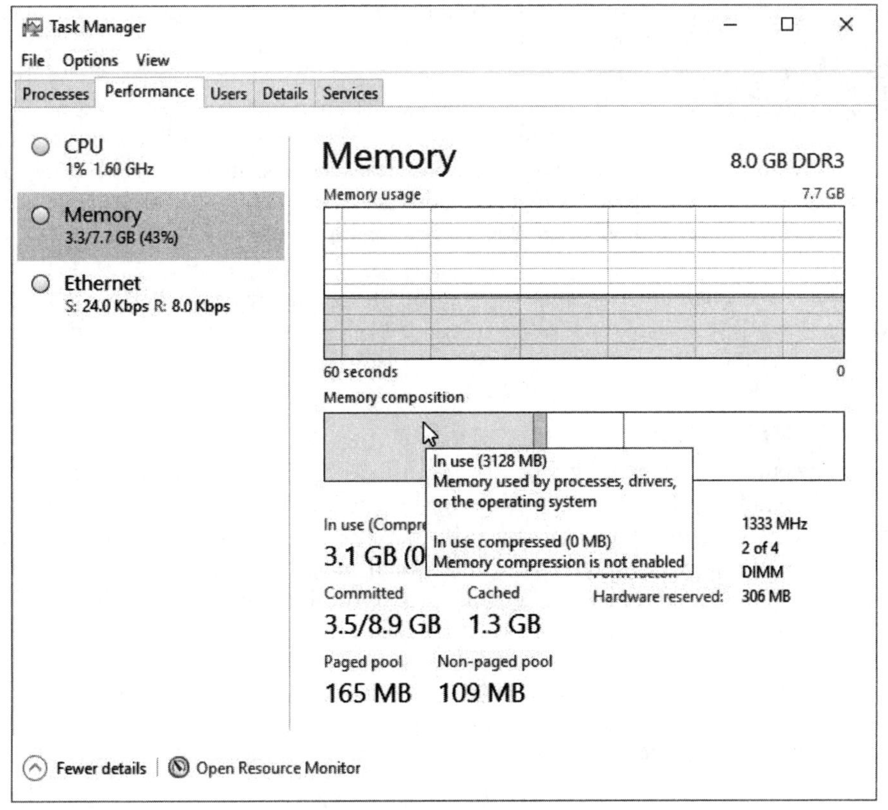

Figure 11-11 Viewing memory composition in the front-most grey shaded area

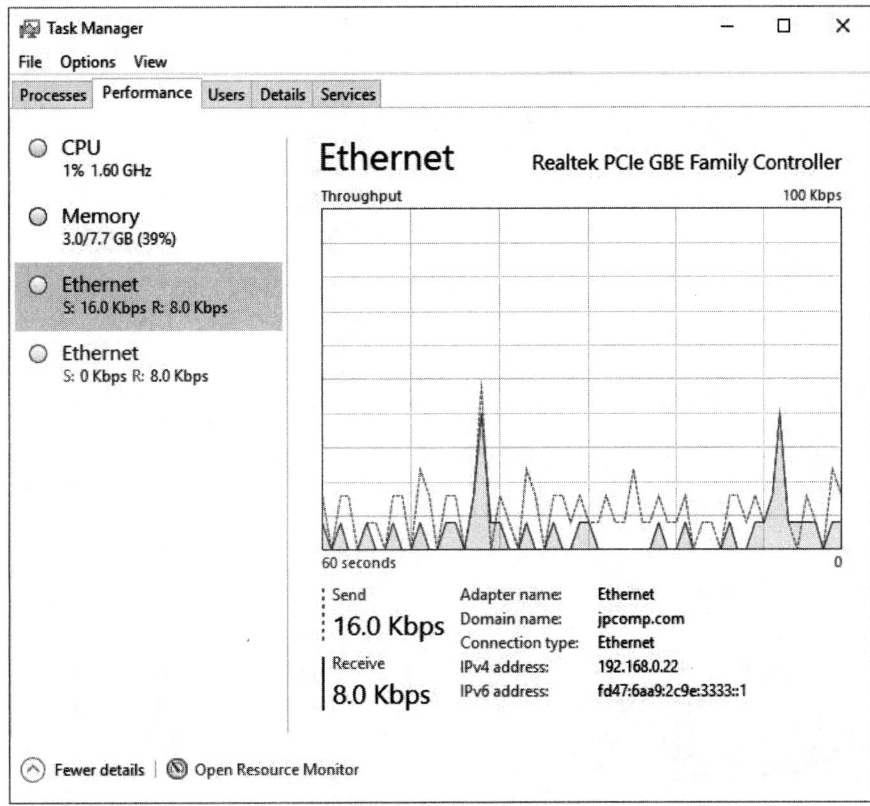

Figure 11-12 Network throughput information on the Performance tab

If the percent of network utilization is frequently over 40 percent, that means the network is experiencing high traffic and there may be bottlenecks due to the network design, possibly indicating the need to create subnets. Network utilization that is regularly over 60–70 percent indicates a serious need to modify the network to address bottlenecks or increase network speed. Network utilization that is over 90 percent for a sustained period requires immediate attention in terms of locating the network problem or redesigning the network.

When you click Open Resource Monitor, at the bottom of the Performance tab, the Resource Monitor window is displayed (refer to Figure 11-1, but the Network tab will be displayed instead of the Overview tab).

Monitoring Users

The Users tab in Task Manager provides a list of the users currently signed in. You can sign out a user by clicking that user and clicking the Disconnect button, which ensures that any open files are closed before the user is signed out. Also, to view the programs in use and the amount of CPU or memory occupied by an individual program, right-click a user and click Expand. Figure 11-13 shows the activities when just the Administrator account is signed in.

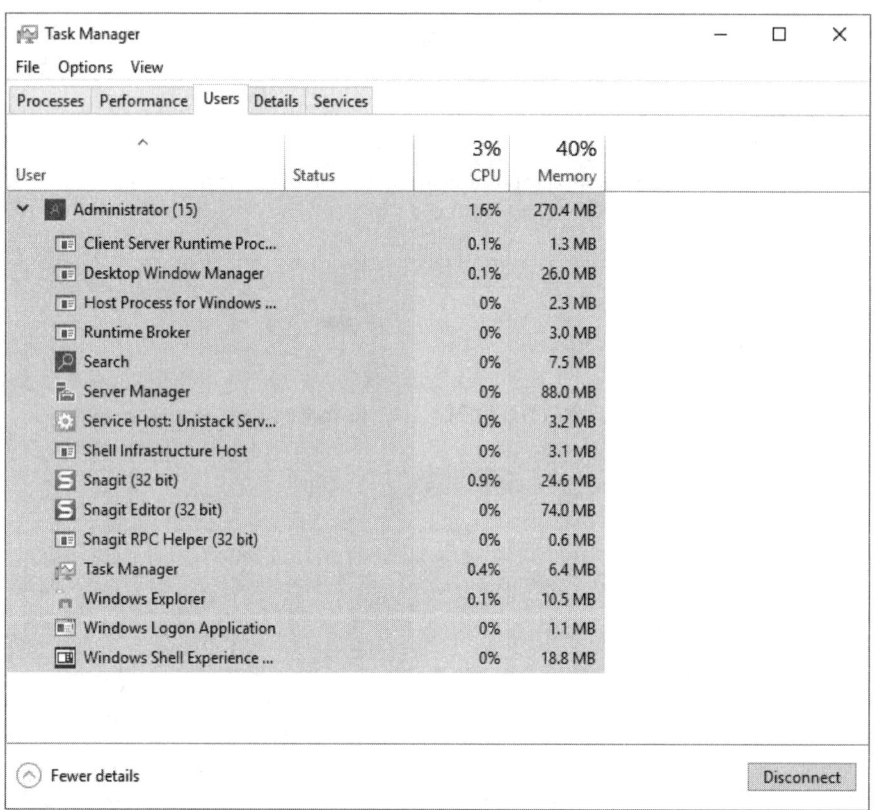

Figure 11-13 Activities of the Administrator account

Plan to regularly monitor the users on a server. Over time, this gives you a good idea about user load at particular times of day. If you see the user load increasing, you can take this into consideration as you plan hardware and software upgrades for your server. Also, regularly monitoring users makes it easier to identify suspicious use of an account, such as when an attacker has taken over an account.

Using Performance Monitor

One of the most versatile tools used to help detect and troubleshoot performance issues on a Windows Server 2016 server is **Performance Monitor**. Performance Monitor can be used to monitor components such as hard disks, memory, the processor, a network interface, a started process, and the paging file. For example, you might monitor memory and the paging file to determine if you have fully tuned the paging file for satisfactory performance and to determine if you have adequate RAM for the server load.

Capturing Data Using Performance Monitor

Performance Monitor is a powerful monitoring tool that you can open from Server Manager, the Windows Administrative Tools folder through the Start button, or as an MMC snap-in. After you open the Performance Monitor, expand the tree in the left pane, if necessary, and click Performance Monitor under Monitoring Tools, as in Figure 11-14.

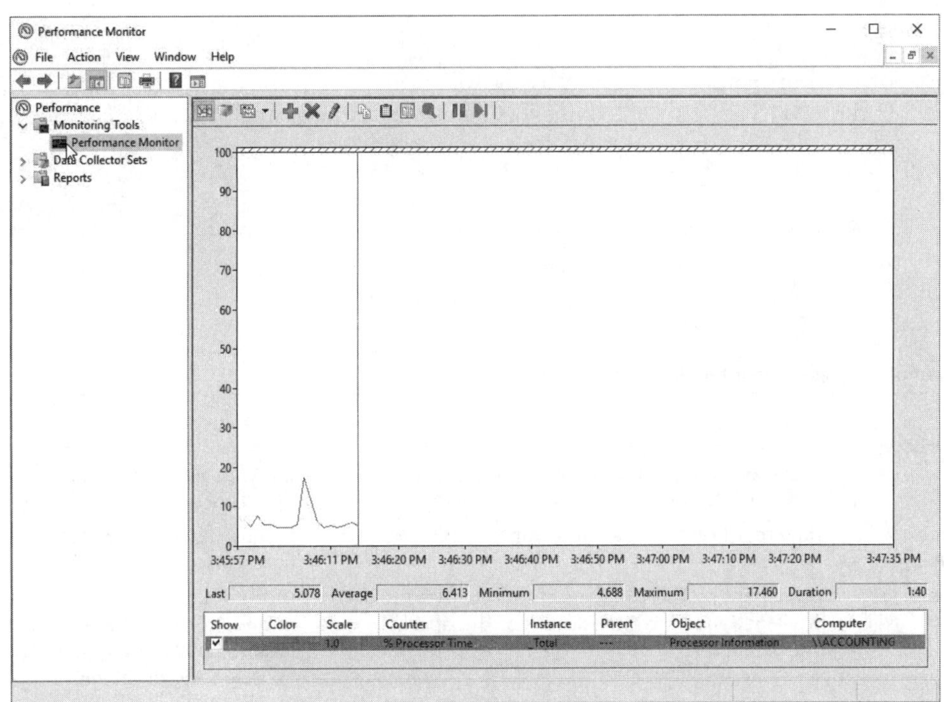

Figure 11-14 Starting Performance Monitor

The default view is in the line mode, showing a grid that you use for graphing activities on the server. In Figure 11-14, Performance Monitor is just beginning to graph the % Processor Time that is in use. When you gather data for your analysis, select one or more objects to monitor. A Performance Monitor object may be memory, the processor, or another part of the computer. Other objects are added as you install services and applications.

For each object, one or more counters can be monitored. A **counter** is an indicator of a quantity of the object that can be measured in some unit, such as percentage, rate per second, or peak value, depending on what is appropriate to the object. For example, the % Processor Time counter for the Processor object measures the percentage of processor time that is in use by nonidle processes. (It is not uncommon for % Processor Time to occasionally be very high, but this often just means that an application is using the processor very efficiently.) Figure 11-15 shows % Processor Time selected under Processor while configuring Performance Monitor. Pages/sec is an example of a counter for the Memory object that measures the number of pages written to or read from virtual memory per second. The processor is one of the common objects to monitor when a server is slow. Table 11-4 gives examples of some of the most frequently used counters for the Processor object.

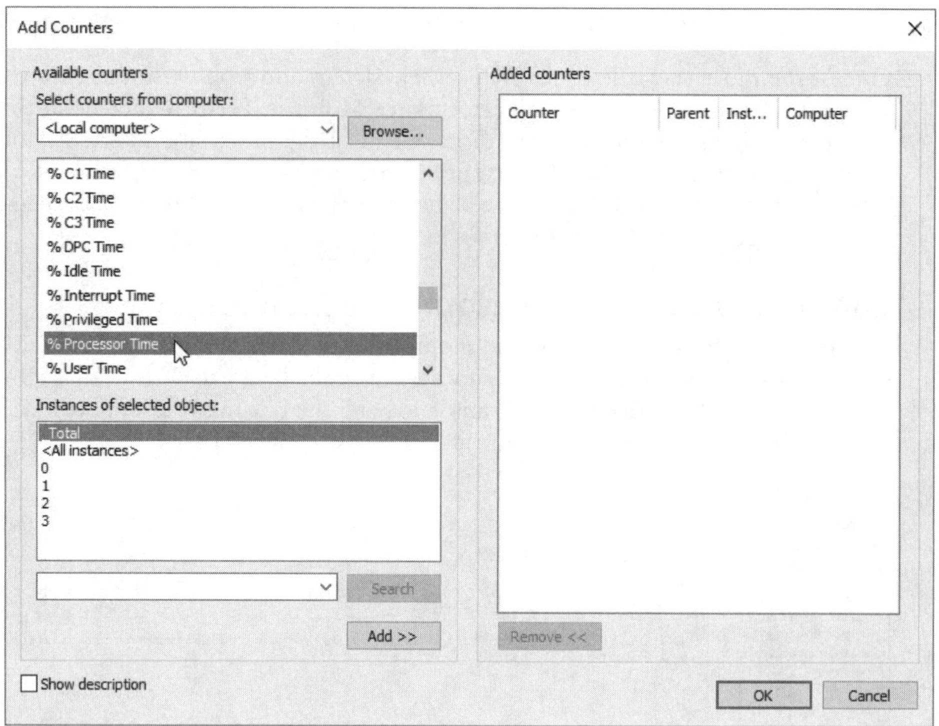

Figure 11-15 Selecting % Processor Time

Table 11-4 Sample processor counters in Performance Monitor

Counter	Description	Recommendations
% DPC Time	Processor time used for deferred procedure calls, for example, for hardware devices	Look for a CPU bottleneck, hardware, or running process problems if regularly over 15%
% Interrupt Time	Time spent on hardware interrupts by the CPU	Frequently over 15% indicates there may be a hardware problem
% Privileged Time	Time spent by the CPU for system activities in privileged mode, which is used for the operating system	If this is relatively high, such as 40% or more, and % Processor Time is high (over 60–70%), look for a Windows service or a device driver experiencing problems
% Processor Time	Time the CPU is busy on all nonidle activities	Problems may be indicated when 70% or higher
% User Time	Time spent by the CPU in user mode running software applications and system programs	Can be relatively high on Remote Desktop Services servers because more time is spent on user mode than kernel mode services
Interrupts/sec	Number of device interrupts per second	Values over 1000 may indicate a hardware problem

When you regularly see % Processor Time at 70% or more, investigate the other counters shown in Table 11-4 as well as the System object using the Processor Queue Length counter. For example, when the % Processor Time is regularly at 80% or higher and the System object Processor Queue Length counter is often over 4, it is likely time to upgrade to more or faster processors (or both) on a server to handle the load. Also, the % Cx Time counters shown in Figure 11-15 track when a specific processor is in a low-power idle state. These counters work only for processors designed to have this state.

If % DPC Time is frequently over 50% for a specific processor and much less for all other processors on a server with only one NIC, consider adding one or two additional NICs (if the network bandwidth can handle more NICs), which should help spread the NIC overhead to the other processors—as a processor load balancing strategy.

Sometimes instances are associated with a counter. An **instance** exists when there are different elements to monitor, such as individual processes when you use the Process object or when a process contains multiple threads or runs subprocesses under it for the Thread object. Other examples are when it is possible to monitor two or more disks or multiple processors. In many cases, each instance is identified by a unique number for ease of monitoring.

Performance Monitor offers several buttons to choose actions and to set display options. After the tool is opened, click the Add button (represented by a green plus sign) on the button bar just above the tracking window (refer to Figure 11-14). This opens the Add Counters window (refer to Figure 11-15) from which to select objects to monitor, counters, and instances.

You can monitor one or more objects at a time as a way to get a better understanding of how particular objects interact, for example, by monitoring both memory and the processor. Also, you can monitor the same object using different combinations of counters. You stop monitoring by clicking the Delete button (represented by an X) on the button bar.

You can use three view modes when monitoring objects: line, histogram bar, and report.

- The line mode is a running line chart of the object that shows distinct peaks and valleys. For example, when you use the line mode and monitor for different objects, a line with a unique color, such as red or green, represents each object (Figure 11-14 shows the line mode).
- The histogram bar mode is a running bar chart that shows each object as a bar in a different color.
- The report mode simply provides numbers on a screen, which you can capture to put in a report.

11

Each of these options is set from the Change graph type button on the button bar just above the tracking window. You can change the view mode at any time by clicking the appropriate selection. Figure 11-16 illustrates the use of the histogram bar mode to monitor several counters.

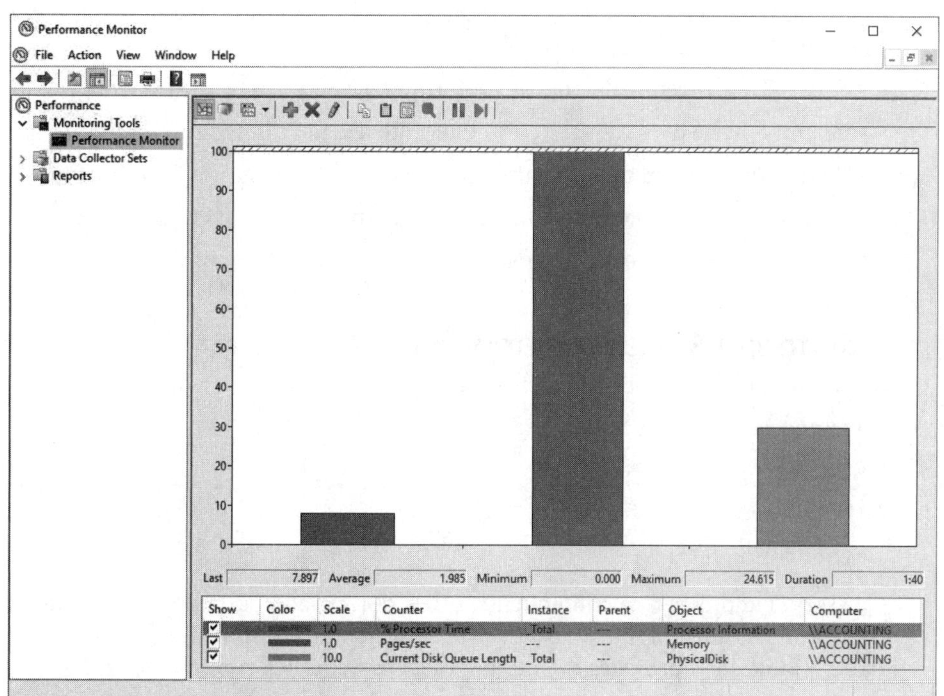

Figure 11-16 Histogram bar mode

Each object combination is displayed using a different color, so they are easily identified. For example, if Figure 11-17 (shown in larger view to see the full line graph) were in color, you would see that each object is a different color.

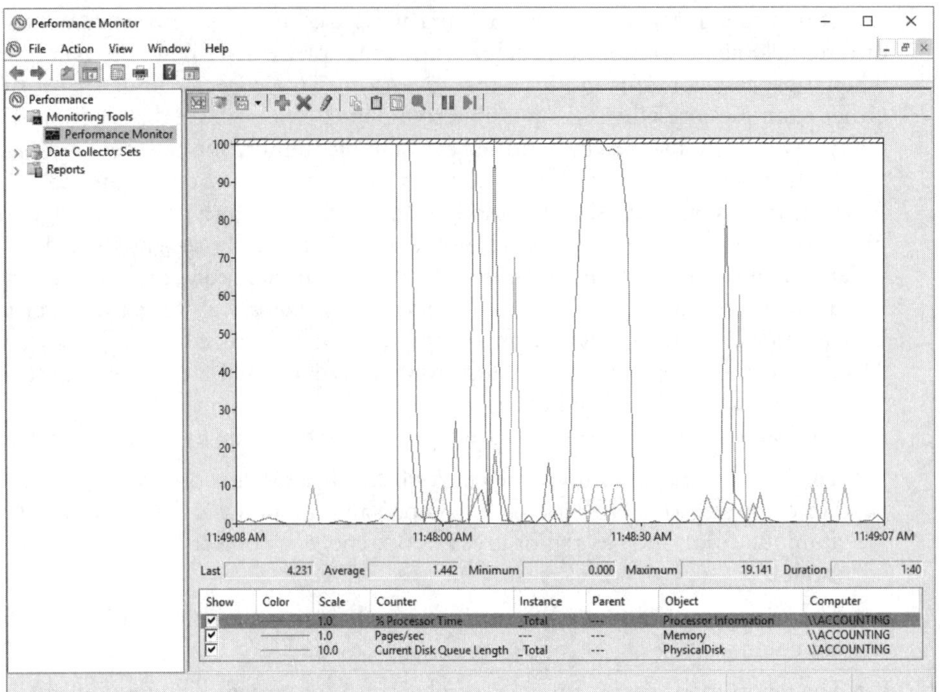

Figure 11-17 Monitoring multiple objects in line mode

The counters are shown at the bottom of the screen with a key to indicate the graphing color for each one. When you click a counter, the status information just above the counters shows the following for that counter:

- *Last*—The current value of the monitored activity
- *Average*—The average value of the monitored activity for the elapsed time
- *Minimum*—The minimum value of the activity over the elapsed time
- *Maximum*—The maximum value of the activity over the elapsed time
- *Duration*—The amount of time to complete a full graph of the activity

Monitoring System Components

When monitoring the performance of a server, four objects are often used:

- Processor
- Memory
- Physical disk
- Network interface

As you add different components, other objects and counters will be added that can also be important to monitor, but these four are particularly important for monitoring server performance. Table 11-5 provides a sampling of object/counter combinations that you can use initially for monitoring computer system performance.

Table 11-5 **Sample objects and counters for performance monitoring**

Object	Counters / Descriptions
Processor	% Processor Time—Percentage of time for threads to process
	% Privileged Time—Time spent by the CPU for system activities in privileged mode
	% User Time—Percentage of time spent processing user threads
Memory	Available Bytes—Physical memory currently available for use
	Committed Bytes—Amount of virtual memory currently being used
	Pages/sec—Number of hard page faults per second
Physical Disk	% Disk Time—Amount of time the disk spends working
	Avg. Disk Bytes/Transfer—Average number of bytes transferred between memory and disk during read and write operations
	Disk Bytes/sec—Speed at which bytes are transferred
	Current Disk Queue Length—Number of requests waiting to be processed
Network Interface	Bytes Total/sec—As measured across the NIC, number of bytes sent and received per second

Activities 11-5 and 11-6 enable you to explore how to use Performance Monitor and then how to troubleshoot processor difficulties. In Activity 11-7, you'll learn how to enable Performance Monitor to track disk activity through activating the Disk Performance Statistic Driver.

Activity 11-5: Exploring Performance Monitor

11

Time Required: Approximately 10 minutes
Objective: Examine available options in Performance Monitor.

Description: This activity gives you an opportunity to practice viewing objects, counters, and instances in Performance Monitor.

1. Open **Server Manager**, if it is not open.
2. Click **Tools** and then click **Performance Monitor**.
3. When the tool starts, ensure that **Performance** is selected in the left pane and read the Overview of Performance Monitor.
4. Next, scroll through the System Summary to review basic information about your server.
   - What are the main categories of information provided in the System Summary?
5. If necessary, expand the tree in the left pane and click **Performance Monitor** under Monitoring Tools.
6. In the right pane, move your pointer over each of the buttons on the button bar to view its description.
7. Click the **Add** button (a plus sign) in the button bar in the right pane.
   - What computer is selected by default for monitoring? How would you monitor activity on a different computer?
8. Scroll through the objects in the box under the computer that is selected.

9. Click the **down arrow** to the right of **Processor.** Scroll to view the counters associated with the Processor object. After you answer the following question and are done viewing, collapse the list by clicking the **up arrow** to the right of Processor.
   - What are the first five counters listed? Click a counter. What instances are listed in the Instances of selected object box? (There should be enough to represent each processor in the server.)
10. Next, select to view the Server counters under **Server** (click the **down arrow**). Scroll through the counters for Server to view them all. Collapse the list for Server after you are finished viewing.
11. Select to view **Process** as the object and view the counters associated with Process. Collapse the list under Process.
12. Choose to view the **TCPv4** object and the counters for this object. Click the **Segments/sec** counter and click the **Show description** check box. Notice the description of this counter displayed at the bottom of the window.
13. Observe two more objects and their associated counters and instances.
14. Click **Cancel** in the Add Counters window, but leave the Performance Monitor window open for the next activity.

Activity 11-6: Monitoring for Processor Problems

Time Required: Approximately 15 minutes
Objective: Learn how to monitor for processor bottlenecks.

Description: In this activity, you use Performance Monitor to check for processor bottlenecks, such as the processor's ability to handle the server load and possible problems caused by hardware.

1. Make sure that the **Performance Monitor** window is already open, and if not, open it to display Performance Monitor.
2. If any object/counter combinations are currently running—by default % Processor Time should still be running—right-click anywhere in the right pane, click **Remove All Counters** (see Figure 11-18), and click **OK.**

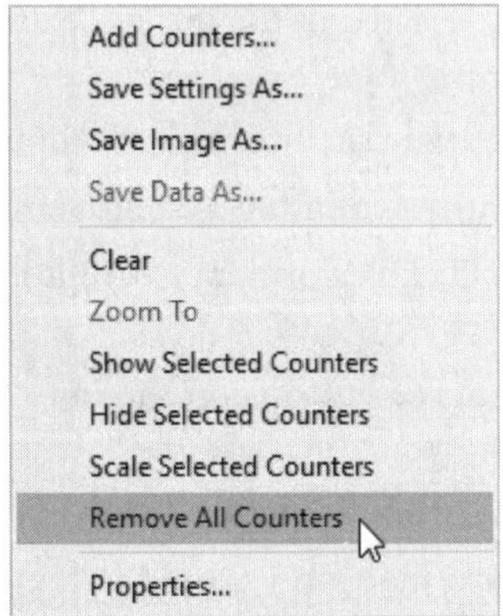

Figure 11-18 Removing counters

3. Click the **Add** button in the button bar to add counters.
4. Scroll to find **Processor** and click its **down arrow**.
5. Click **% Processor Time** (refer to Figure 11-15). Leave **_Total** as the default for instances.
   - What information does this counter provide for the Processor object? How would you find out, if you didn't know?

When you monitor % Processor Time, sustained values of 80–85% or higher indicate a heavily loaded machine; consistent readings of 95% or higher may indicate a machine that needs to have its load reduced or its capabilities increased (with a new machine, a motherboard upgrade, or a faster CPU).

6. Click the **Add** button in the Add Counters dialog box.
7. Click **% Interrupt Time** as the counter for Processor and leave **_Total** as the instance. Click **Add.**

% Interrupt Time is useful to monitor because it measures the amount of the processor's time that is used to service hardware requests from devices such as the NIC, disks, optical drives, and USB connected peripherals. A high rate of interrupts when compared with your baseline statistics indicates a possible hardware problem, such as a malfunctioning NIC.

8. Scroll the counters list for the Processor object and click **Interrupts/sec.** Leave **_Total** as the instance and click **Add.**

The Interrupts/sec counter measures the average number of times per second that the CPU is interrupted by devices requesting immediate processing. Network traffic and system clock activity establish a kind of background count against which this number should be compared. Problem levels occur when a malfunctioning device begins to generate spurious interrupts or when excessive network traffic overwhelms a network adapter. In both cases, this usually creates a count that's five times or greater than a lightly loaded baseline situation.

9. Scroll to find the **System** object and click its **down arrow.**
10. Click **Processor Queue Length.** Click **Add.**

The Processor Queue Length counter for the System object measures the number of execution threads waiting for access to a CPU. If this value is frequently over 4 on a single CPU, it indicates a need to distribute this machine's load across other machines or the need to increase its capabilities, usually by adding an additional CPU or by upgrading the machine or the motherboard. When the value is over 2 per CPU on multiple-processor systems, you should consider adding processors or increasing the processor speed.

11. The Add Counters dialog box should now look similar to the one in Figure 11-19.
12. Click **OK.**
13. Monitor the system for several minutes to determine if there are any processor problems. Record any problems that you diagnose from using Performance Monitor.
14. Click the **Change graph type** button **down arrow** just to the right of the graph's box and click **Histogram bar** to see this mode. Monitor in this mode for a few minutes.
15. Click the **Change graph type** button **down arrow** and click **Report** to see this mode. Monitor in this mode for a few minutes.
16. Click the **Change graph type** button **down arrow** and click **Line.**
17. Right-click anywhere in the right pane, click **Remove All Counters,** and click **OK.**

18. Leave the Performance Monitor window open.

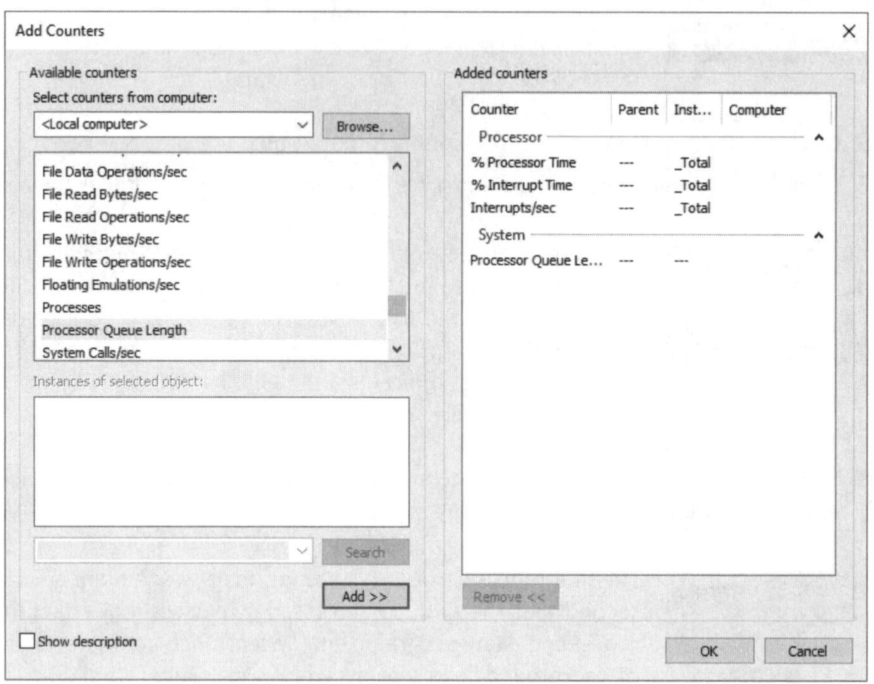

Figure 11-19 Selections in the Add Counters window

Activity 11-7: Verifying the Disk Counters

Time Required: Approximately 5 minutes
Objective: Learn to check the status of *diskperf*.

Description: Monitoring disks through Performance Monitor is accomplished by using the Disk Performance Statistic Driver, which is enabled through the command-line program *diskperf*. Normally, hard disk Performance Monitor counters are enabled by default. If they are not enabled, you can start them by typing *diskperf -y* and pressing Enter in the Windows PowerShell or Command Prompt window. To disable the disk counters, you would type *diskperf -n*. In this activity, you use *diskperf* to verify the status of the hard disk performance counters to see if they are enabled.

1. Click **Start** and click the **Windows PowerShell** tile; or click **Start**, click the **Windows PowerShell** folder, and click **Windows PowerShell**.
2. In the Windows PowerShell window, type **diskperf** and press **Enter**. If the disk counters are enabled, you'll see the counters are automatically enabled on demand.
3. Close the Windows PowerShell window.

Keep in mind that performance monitoring can impact the overall performance of the server. If you write lots of information to disk while monitoring, this can also affect disk performance. And if you monitor remotely, you can impact network performance. Plan to use performance monitoring judiciously.

Using Data Collector Sets

The Data Collector Sets tool is another vehicle that is used to monitor performance and to consolidate performance information. A **data collector set** is a collection of diagnostic and performance information in the form of a report or log. There are three basic types of data collection tools and formats:

- Performance counters and performance counter reports
- Traces and trace reports
- System configuration data

One data collector set can produce only one type of log or it can produce data for all three reporting formats. A **performance counter report** tracks information using objects, counters, and instances. A **trace** monitors particular events, and a **trace report** contains only those instances when the events occur. For example, you could create a trace to record each time disk input/output activity occurs or when an Active Directory Kerberos security event is triggered.

The system configuration data that can be obtained using data collector sets includes information on the following:

- Operating system
- Processor
- System services
- BIOS
- Controllers
- Port classes
- Storage classes
- Printing classes
- Video classes
- User accounts
- Startup programs
- Disk settings
- Processes

Data collector sets can be created in several ways. One way is to use a predefined data collector set, such as the following:

- Active Directory Diagnostics (if Active Directory is installed)
- Basic (creates a basic data collector set)
- System Diagnostics (focuses on hardware and system resources as well as processes)
- System Performance (focuses on identifying performance issues related to hardware, system response, and running processes)
- WDAC Diagnostics (used to analyze Windows Data Access components, which are technologies, such as ActiveX data objects and Open Database Connectivity (ODBC) used in data-intense client/server applications)

Using a predefined data collector set helps to take the guesswork out of what to monitor. However, when you select any of the predefined data collector sets, you still can configure specific counters from Performance Monitor to include in your collector set. The Data Collector Sets tool also enables you to start a wizard and select a template to use for creating a data collector set. Templates are XML files that are stored on the local computer. In addition to using templates that come with your operating system, you can import a template created on another computer. Yet another way to create a data collector set is to do so manually.

In addition to using counters, traces, and system information, each data collector set consists of properties that you can configure as follows:

- *General*—Enables you to create a description for the data collector set and add keyword descriptors or use a default description. You can also specify from which user account to run the data collection process, but the account must have Administrator privileges (the default account is System).
- *Directory*—Enables you to specify the directory path and naming convention for the reports after they are generated.
- *Security*—Enables you to set up permissions to control who can run the data collector set for creating a report.
- *Schedule*—Enables you to create a regular schedule on which to run the data collector set, such as at 10:00 AM every weekday.
- *Stop Condition*—Enables you to specify conditions under which to stop or limit the duration of the data gathering, such as when the report contents reach a specific size.
- *Task*—Enables you to specify a task that runs as soon as the data collection stops.

After a data collector set has been configured, you can start it and collect data for a specific period of time, such as 5 minutes, as configured in the properties of the set. The data collector set process also can be manually stopped before the preset stop time. You can run a data collector set session multiple times or on a regular schedule to take snapshots of a server system. Also, you can view the report results from Performance Monitor after a data collection session is stopped.

Using a Wizard and a Template to Create a Data Collector Set

One of the easiest ways to get started using the Data Collector Sets tool is to rely on a predefined template. Templates that are similar to the predefined data collector sets mentioned earlier can be deployed from the Create new Data Collector Set Wizard:

- *Active Directory Diagnostics*—Collects data about Active Directory activities and can combine performance counters and trace events
- *Basic*—Collects data using performance counters
- *System Diagnostics*—Collects information about the status of processes, hardware, system response times, and other measures, and provides ideas for improving system performance
- *System Performance*—Collects information similar to the System Diagnostics template and reports problem areas
- *WDAC Diagnostics*—Analyzes Windows Data Access components, including ActiveX data objects and Open Database Connectivity (ODBC) for applications that use one or more databases

The Create new Data Collector Set Wizard steps you through deploying one of these templates, or you can skip the templates and use the wizard to manually configure your own options.

To start the wizard, right-click the User Defined folder under Data Collector Sets in the Performance Monitor tool, point to New, and click Data Collector Set.

Activity 11-8: Using a Template for a Data Collector Set

Time Required: Approximately 25 minutes
Objective: Create a data collector set from a template.

Description: In this activity, you use the System Performance template to create a data collector set.

1. Ensure that the **Performance Monitor** window is already open, and if not, open it.
2. Click the **right-pointing arrow** in front of **Data Collector Sets** in the tree in the left pane, if necessary, to see the items under it.
3. Right-click **User Defined**, point to **New**, and click **Data Collector Set.**
4. In the *Name* box, enter **System Performance** plus your initials, such as *System Performance JR*.
5. Ensure that **Create from a template (Recommended)** is selected, as shown in Figure 11-20.

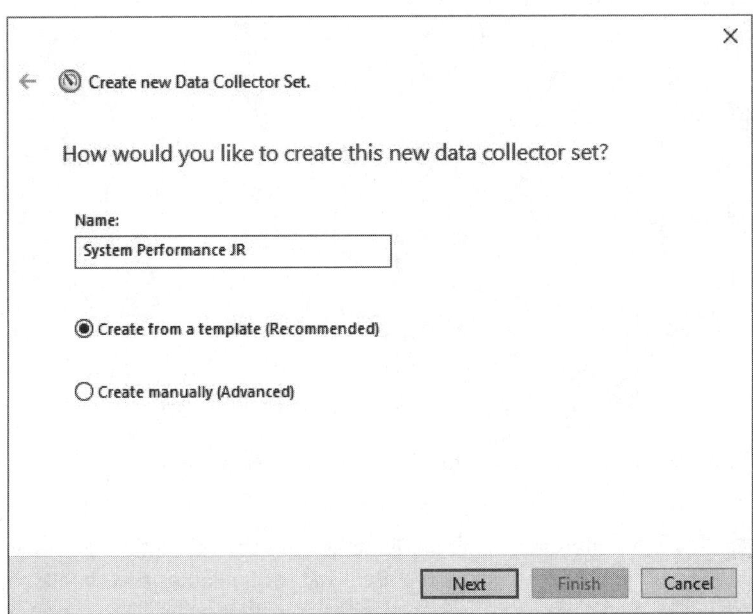

Figure 11-20 Selecting to use a template for the data collector set

6. Click **Next.**
7. Click **System Performance** under Template Data Collector Set and click **Next.**
8. Use the default location in which to save the data and click **Next.**
9. Click **Save and close,** if it is not selected already.
10. Click **Finish.**
11. Click the **right-pointing arrow** in front of **User Defined** in the tree, if it is not expanded, and notice the data collector set that you created is listed under User Defined.
12. Click the data collector set you created in the tree. In the right pane, notice that it includes *NT Kernel*, which incorporates a trace session of real-time CPU activity, memory, disk, and network activity. The second tracking element is *Performance Counter*, which is a combination of counters for processes, physical disk, CPU, memory, system, server, and many network counters.
13. Right-click the data collector set you created, such as *System Performance JR*.
    - What options do you see enabled on the menu?
14. Click **Properties.** On the General tab, read the description of the template.
15. Click the **Stop Condition** tab.

11

16. Under *Overall duration*, set the value to **5** and leave the *Units* value as **Minutes**. This means 5 minutes of data is collected each time you start the data collector set (see Figure 11-21).

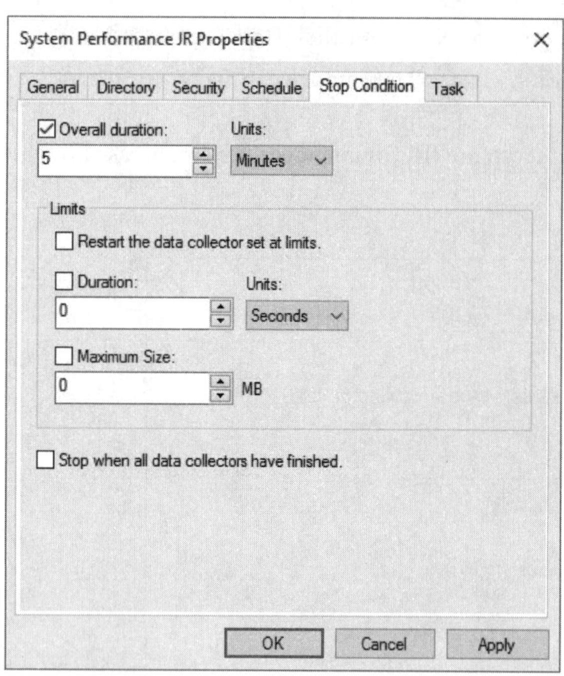

Figure 11-21 Establishing the duration of the data collection session

An alternative is to set limits for the data collection. For example, you might set the duration under Limits as 5 minutes and choose to have the data collector set restart right after it stops. Or, if disk space is a concern, you might have the data collector set stop after the log size reaches 5 MB.

17. Click the **Schedule** tab. This tab enables you to schedule a regular start time for collecting data.
18. Click the **Add** button on the Schedule tab.
19. In the Folder Action dialog box, the default time is 12:00 AM. However, because you are monitoring system performance, it makes more sense to gather data when the system is in full work mode, such as at 10:00 AM or 2:00 PM or whatever time is more appropriate for your organization. For this activity, change the Start time to **10:00:00 AM**. Also, remove the check marks from Saturday and Sunday.
20. Click **OK** in the Folder Action dialog box.
21. Click **OK** in the System Performance (your initials) Properties dialog box.
22. In the tree, right-click the data collector set you created, such as *System Performance JR*, and click **Start** to commence gathering data.
23. Wait a few minutes (you don't have to wait for five minutes because you can manually stop the data collection sooner). Right-click the data collector set in the tree and click **Stop.**
24. Right-click the data collector set in the tree again and click **Latest Report.**
25. In the right pane, you'll see the report of information you have collected so far (see Figure 11-22).

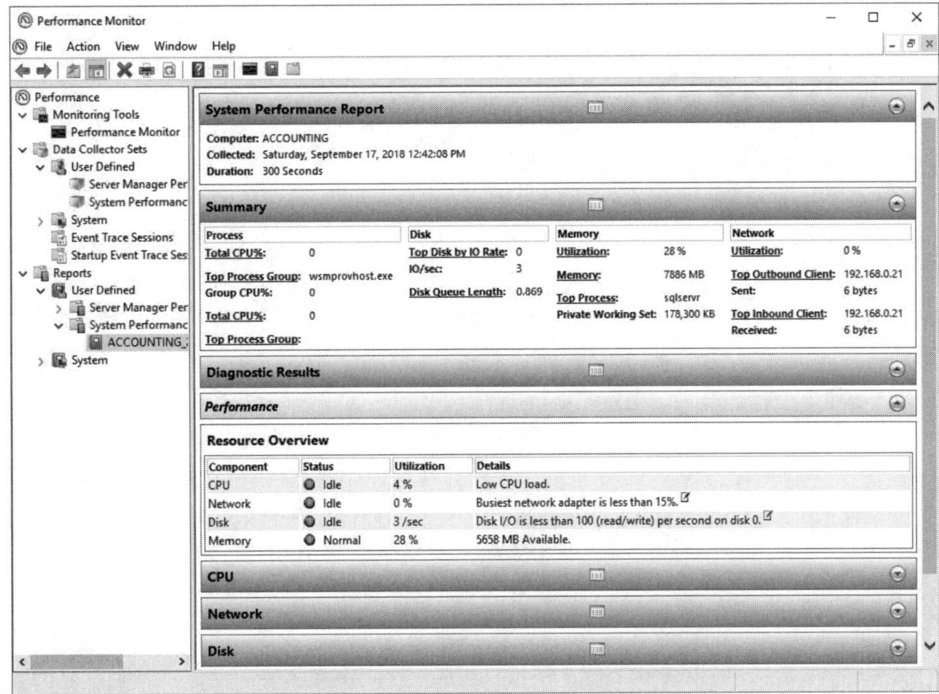

Figure 11-22 Viewing the data collection report

26. Use the scroll bar in the right pane to view the report information. Click the **CPU** heading if it is not expanded. Notice that CPU information is divided into Process, Service, Services, and System. Click the down arrow for **Services** under CPU to expand its view and notice the services listed and CPU% value for each service. Click the **up arrow** to close the view of **Services**.
27. Click the **down arrow** for **Memory**. Click the **down arrow** for **Counters**.
    - How many performance counters are used for the memory object? How many handle count instances are monitored?
28. Click the **down arrow** for **Report Statistics** and review the information about the report, including the Computer Information and Collection Information. Notice you can determine how long the data collector set gathered information by looking under Collection Information.
29. In the tree, click the data collector set you created, such as *System Performance JR*.
30. In the right pane, right-click **Performance Counter** and click **Properties**.
31. In the Performance Counter Properties dialog box, notice that the counters preselected by the template you used are listed under *Performance counters*. If you wanted to remove a particular counter from the data collector set, you could click it and click **Remove**.
32. Click the **Add** button.
33. In the next window, you can select one or more performance counters to add to the data collector set, as shown in Figure 11-23. Click **Cancel**.
34. Click **Cancel** in the Performance Counter Properties dialog box.
35. Leave the Performance Monitor window open for the next activity.

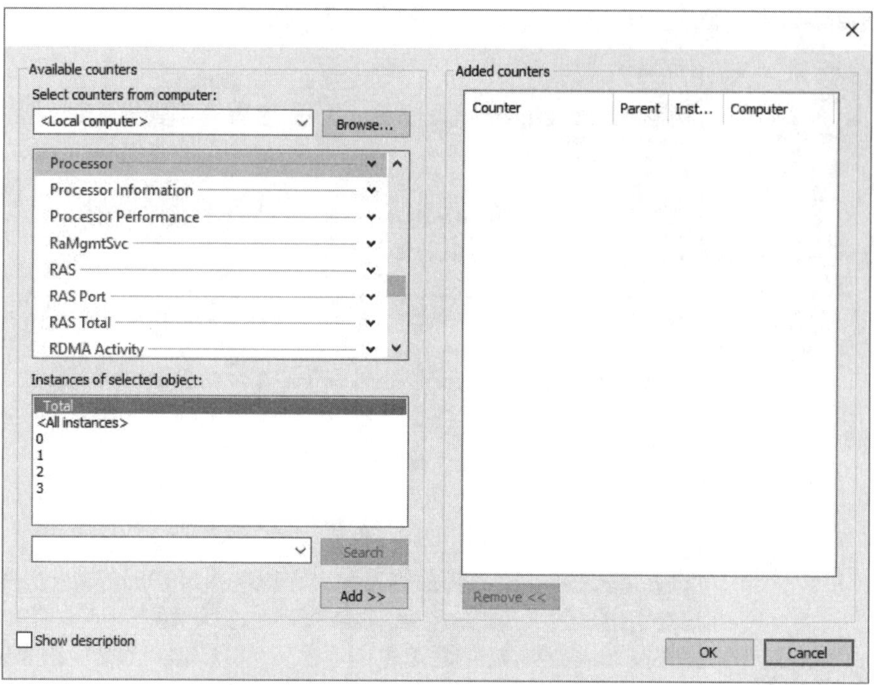

Figure 11-23 Window for adding performance counters

Returning to a Report and the Importance of Network Data

After you create a report, you can go back to it by finding that report under Reports in the tree within the Performance Monitor tool. For example, the report you created in Activity 11-8 contains valuable information about network performance. Monitoring the network is one of the monitoring tasks you should set out to do early on. This is important because it provides a way to determine baselines and later to compare baseline data with current system performance statistics to locate a problem source. For example, consider a workday afternoon on which several users call to report that the system is slow. Your next step is to determine if the source of the problem is the network or the server. If you regularly monitor the network and the server, you can view your data collector set reporting data to help locate the problem source faster.

For network performance, it helps to establish baselines from which to diagnose problems. Plan to gather data such as the following:

- *Network Interface performance counter*—Shows network traffic at the network interface (NIC), including bytes and packets sent and received, bandwidth data, and network error data
- *IPv4 and IPv6 performance counters*—Show inbound and outbound IPv4 and IPv6 traffic and packet errors
- *TCPv4 and TCPv6 performance counters*—Show connection and transmission data, including active connection data, and connection failures

Begin gathering benchmarks so that you have an understanding of what network activity is typical. Also, gather benchmarks on typical network error levels, so that you know at what point an increase in network errors signals a problem.

The report you created in Activity 11-8 contains NIC, IP, and TCP information about network performance that you can use to help create network performance baseline data.

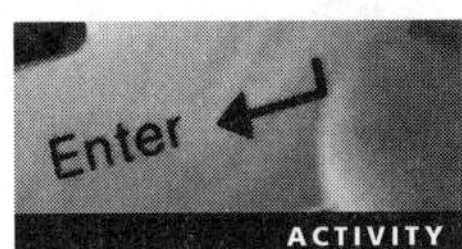

Activity 11-9: Viewing a Report

Time Required: Approximately 5 minutes
Objective: Learn how to go back to view a report you have already created.

Description: In this activity, you reopen the report you created in Activity 11-8 so that you can review the network performance data.

1. Open **Performance Monitor** if it is not still open.
2. In the tree in the left pane, click the **right-pointing arrow** for **Reports**, if necessary.
3. Also in the tree, click the **right-pointing arrows** for **User Defined** then for **System Performance**, if necessary. Click **System Performance** (with your initials) in the tree.
4. In the right pane, you will see one report listed with a green icon and a number that represents the date of the report, such as 20180917 for September 17, 2018, and a version number, such as 000001. Double-click the report. (If the Performance Monitor tool has gotten out of sync due to multiple activities and does not display the report, close the Performance Monitor window, open it, and try opening the report again.)
5. Scroll down to the **Network** category and click its **down arrow**. You'll see categories of information for Interface (the NIC), IP, TCP, and UDP.
6. Click the **down arrow** for **IP**. Notice the counters showing performance data for IPv4 and for IPv6 (if it is enabled).
7. Click the **down arrow** for **TCP**. Review the performance data for TCPv4 and TCPv6.
   - What data might you use to determine if there are connection problems?
8. Leave Performance Monitor open for the next activity.

Using a Predefined Data Collector Set

As you learned earlier, Performance Monitor has several predefined data collector sets that you can run at any time without first creating them through the Create new Data Collector Set Wizard. Several of the templates, such as the System Performance template you used in Activity 11-8, are based on these predefined data collector sets.

For diagnosing system and network problems, the predefined System Diagnostics data collector set is particularly valuable. Activity 11-10 enables you to use the System Diagnostics data collector set (but similar steps can be used to run any of the predefined data collector sets).

Activity 11-10: Using the System Diagnostics Data Collector Set

Time Required: Approximately 15 minutes
Objective: Use the predefined System Diagnostics data collector set.

Description: The System Diagnostics data collector set offers a good starting point for monitoring your system and network and gathering benchmarks about system and network use. This data collector set combines the use of performance counter, trace and configuration information into one report. This activity assumes you are using a wired network connection. If you are using a wireless connection, look for appropriate options to view information about that type of connection.

1. Open the Performance Monitor if it is not already open.
2. Click the **right-pointing arrow** in front of **System** (use System under Data Collector Sets, not System under Reports) in the tree.
3. Notice the predefined data collector sets you can run from under the System folder in the tree.
4. Click **System Diagnostics** in the tree.

5. In the right pane, notice the combination of Trace, Configuration, and Performance Counter elements included in the System Diagnostics data collector set under the Type column.
6. Right-click **Performance Counter** in the right pane and click **Properties.**
7. On the Performance Counters tab, scroll through the preselected performance counters for system and network monitoring, as shown in Figure 11-24. The asterisk at the end of each object means to use all of the counters for that object. Click **Cancel** in the Performance Counter Properties dialog box.

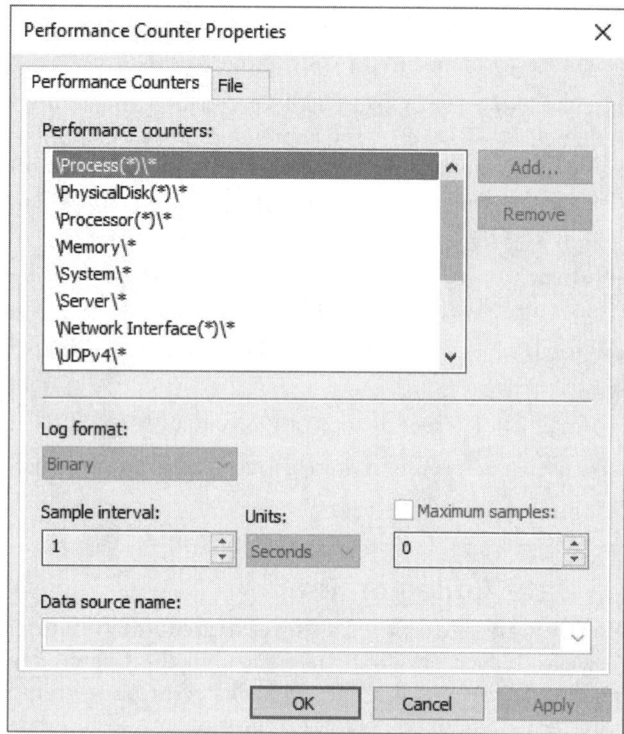

Figure 11-24 Preselected performance counters

8. Right-click **System Diagnostics** in the tree in the left pane and click **Start.**
9. Wait for a few minutes.
10. Right-click **System Diagnostics** in the tree and click **Stop.**
11. Right-click **System Diagnostics** in the tree and click **Latest Report.**
    - Were any problems found under the Diagnostic Results category? Did the system pass all tests as reported under Basic System Checks?
12. Review the report information for **Hardware Configuration** and for **Network.** Review any other results that interest you.
13. Close Performance Monitor.

If you discover performance problems while using Performance Monitor and Data Collector Sets, consider using Event Viewer to check for important event messages that may show an error condition, for example. Also, for specific server roles, remember you can use Server Manager to view reported events related to a role. Finally, Resource Monitor can also give you more clues in helping to make sense of problems indicated through Performance Monitor.

Implementing the SNMP Service

A part of the TCP/IP suite of protocols, the **Simple Network Management Protocol** (**SNMP**) is used for network management on TCP/IP-based networks. It provides administrators with a way of centrally managing workstations, servers, switches, and routers from a central computer running management software. SNMP can be used for the following:

- Configuring network devices
- Monitoring the performance of a network
- Locating network problems
- Monitoring network usage

SNMP provides network management services through agents and management systems. The SNMP management system (a computer running management software) sends and requests information from an SNMP agent. The SNMP agent (any computer or network device running SNMP agent software) responds to the management system's request for information. The management systems and agents can be grouped into communities for administrative and security purposes. Only those management systems and agents in the same community can communicate with each other.

Some examples of network management systems and software applications that use SNMP include WebNMS (commercial software), Multi Router Traffic Grapher (open source software), Spiceworks Network Monitoring (free software), Nagios (open source), OpenNMS (open source), and Message Analyzer (network monitoring software available from Microsoft that replaces Network Monitor and can be downloaded from Microsoft's Download Center).

When a network management station is set up on a network, the following Microsoft operating systems and components are compatible with SNMP:

- All versions of Windows Server operating systems from Windows 2000 Server to Windows Server 2016
- All versions of Windows workstation operating systems from Windows 2000 to Windows 10
- WINS servers
- DHCP servers
- Web (IIS) servers
- Microsoft Remote Access servers

At this writing, Windows Server 2016 does not come with a full-fledged SNMP network management system application. However, the Windows Management Instrumentation (WMI) Software Development Kit (SDK) enables SNMP applications to access SNMP data.

Activity 11-11: Installing SNMP Services

Time Required: Approximately 5 minutes
Objective: Install SNMP.

Description: In this activity, you use Server Manager to install the SNMP Service feature in Windows Server 2016.

1. Open **Server Manager,** if it is not open.
2. Click **Manage** and then click **Add Roles and Features.**
3. If you see the Before you begin window, click **Next.**

4. Use **Role-based or feature-based installation** in the Select installation type window. Click **Next**.
5. Be sure your server is highlighted in the Select destination server window and click **Next.**
6. Click **Next** in the Select server roles window.
7. In the Select features window, click the box for **SNMP Service.**
8. Click **Add Features** in the Add Roles and Features Wizard.
9. Click **Next** in the Select features window.
10. Click **Install.**
11. Click **Close.**
12. Leave Server Manager open for the next activity.

After you install the SNMP service, make sure that it is started, is set to start automatically, and is set up to have a **community** of hosts that share use of the service and a **community name,** which is similar to having a rudimentary password used among the hosts.

Activity 11-12: Configuring SNMP Services

Time Required: Approximately 10 minutes
Objective: Learn how to configure SNMP services.

Description: In this activity, you learn how to configure SNMP service and the SNMP Trap service.

1. Open **Server Manager,** if it is not already open.
2. Click **Tools** and then click **Services.**
3. In the right pane of the Services window, double-click **SNMP Service.**
4. On the General tab, make sure *Startup type* is set to **Automatic** and that the service is started.
5. Click the **Security** tab (see Figure 11-25). From here you can configure the accepted communities for the agent. For example, Public is a community name that is often accepted by SNMP implementations. You would click the Add button in the upper half of the dialog box to configure community names. Also, by default the SNMP agent is configured to accept SNMP packets from localhost. You can configure the SNMP agent to accept SNMP packets from additional hosts by clicking the Add button in the lower half of the dialog box. Additional hosts are specified by host name or IP address of the host from which the agent can accept SNMP packets.
6. Click the **Traps** tab. When a certain type of event occurs on an SNMP agent (such as the system being restarted), the agent can send a message known as a **trap** to a management system. The management system that receives the trap is known as the trap destination. To configure a trap, you would type in the name of the community that the SNMP agent will send trap messages to and click *Add to list*. Next, you would click *Add* in the Trap destinations and type in the host name or IP address of the management system that will receive the trap messages.
7. Click **Cancel** in the SNMP Service Properties (Local Computer) dialog box.
8. Double-click the **SNMP Trap** service in the Services window. If you plan to create traps, you need to configure this service, which is set to Manual by default. Set the *Startup type* to **Automatic,** so that you do not have to remember to start the service after every reboot of the system. Click **Apply.**
9. Click **Start.**
10. Click **OK** in the SNMP Trap Properties (Local Computer) dialog box.

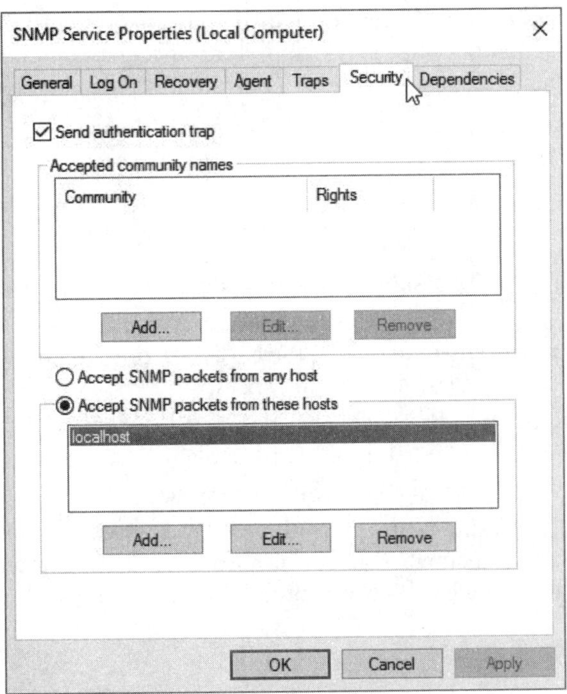

Figure 11-25 SNMP security parameters

11. Close the Services window. Also, close Server Manager.

11

Chapter Summary

- Server monitoring enables you to establish benchmarks or baselines to help identify areas that need improvement and to identify problem areas.
- Resource Monitor is a tool you can use to gain an initial picture of how CPU, memory, disk, and network resources are employed and to use as a springboard to troubleshooting server problems.
- A server has many services running at the same time. Services can be monitored to ensure the necessary ones are started and working correctly and unnecessary services are turned off. Monitoring services also enables you to determine what services depend on others.
- Task Manager enables you to monitor applications, processes, services, CPU and memory performance, network performance, and signed-in users. If a problem is occurring with a particular application or process, you can use Task Manager to stop the application or process. Task Manager can help identify system performance problems, show if more memory is needed for the computer, or even be used to sign out a hung user connection.
- Performance Monitor uses objects such as the processor or memory for monitoring. For each object, you can monitor from an array of counters that are specialized measurement options. Performance Monitor offers the ability to monitor your system and network in depth, to set baselines, and to troubleshoot problems.
- A data collector set is a tool associated with Performance Monitor that enables you to collect data about a server or network and compile the data into a report. The type of data compiled and how it is rendered into a report is established through creating the data collector set. Several predefined and template-based data collector sets are available to help you get a running start with this powerful tool.

- Windows Server 2016 offers the SNMP service, which you can choose to install. The SNMP service enables network agents to gather network performance data on TCP/IP networks for use by network management software. It also provides a way to manage and configure specific network devices.

Key Terms

base priority class The initial priority assigned to a program process or thread in the program code.

benchmark (or baseline) A measurement standard for hardware or software used to establish performance measures under varying loads or circumstances.

committed memory The number bytes a process has designated for use and that are promised by the operating system to a designated portion of the page file.

community A group of hosts that share the same SNMP services.

community name In SNMP communications, a rudimentary password (name) used by network agents and the network management station (or software) in the same community so that their communications cannot be easily intercepted by an unauthorized workstation or device.

counter Used by Performance Monitor, a measurement technique for an object, for example, for measuring the processor performance by percentage in use.

data collector set A combination of techniques for gathering performance and diagnostic data that is rendered in a report or log format. The basic data gathering techniques can be one or a combination of performance counters, event traces, and system configuration data.

handle A resource, such as a file, used by a program that has its own identification so the program is able to access it.

instance An individual occurrence of an element that is being monitored in Performance Monitor; exists when two or more types of elements can be monitored, such as two or more CPUs, threads, or disk drives.

non-paged pool Holds the operating system kernel, device drivers, and other key elements that cannot be paged out, and so these processes and threads are always kept in physical memory or RAM.

page fault Event that occurs whenever memory pages must be called from disk (from the paging file).

paged pool Contains data that can be stored in the paging file, and so can be paged in and out of the virtual memory (a page file on disk).

performance counter report Output of information gathered via Performance Monitor objects, counters, and instances configured within a data collector set.

Performance Monitor The Windows Server 2016 utility used to track system or application objects. For each object type, one or more counters can be logged via a data collection set for later analysis or tracked in real time for immediate Performance Monitoring.

Simple Network Management Protocol (SNMP) Used for network management and performance monitoring on TCP/IP-based networks.

thread A block of program code executing within a running process. One process may launch one or more threads.

trace Capture of a specific event when it occurs, such as a page fault or input to a disk.

trace report Contains results of monitored trace events generated by a data collector set and contains only those instances when the events occur, such as creating a trace to record each time disk input/output activity occurs or when an Active Directory Kerberos security event is triggered. *See* trace.

trap A specific situation or event detected by SNMP that a network administrator may want to be warned about or to track via network management software, for example, when a network device is unexpectedly down or offline. *See* Simple Network Management Protocol (SNMP).

Review Questions

1. You need the ability to monitor a network and network devices, such as routers, through using a network management system. Which of the following elements supported by Windows Server 2016 can you install to work with the network management system?
   a. NTLM hosts file
   b. SNMP service
   c. Kerberos network protocol
   d. IPsec monitor service
2. Your company uses an inventory program that seems to be stuck in a programming loop and will not let you shut it down. What tool can you use to immediately shut down this program which is consuming CPU resources?
   a. Server Monitor
   b. Performance Monitor
   c. Task Manager
   d. Control Panel System and Maintenance option
3. Your advertising firm is expecting a new client to visit in about 15 minutes. In preparation, you have been printing out reports and graphics for the meeting, but the print process has been slow because the server is so busy. What can you do to best help ensure the printouts are finished on time?
   a. Decrease the priority of all processes, except the print spooler process, to Low.
   b. Sign out all other users, even if there is not time to give them sufficient notification
   c. Quickly increase the page file size by 1–2 MB to handle the printouts.
   d. Increase the priority of the print spooler process to Above normal or High.
4. Briefly explain the concept of a thread and mention where you can monitor thread activity in Windows Server 2016.
5. One of the marketing people in your company occasionally runs multiple huge database queries in the middle of the workday, sometimes causing a server to slow affecting the work of other users. What tool can you use to determine if that user is running database queries and the amount of CPU and memory resources occupied by that user?
   a. Task Manager
   b. SNMP counter in Performance Monitor
   c. Services tool
   d. Active Directory Users and Computers tool
6. What general monitoring information can you obtain by using the TCPv4 and TCPv6 performance objects in Performance Monitor?
7. Which of the following can be an SNMP agent? (Choose all that apply.)
   a. Windows Server 2016
   b. Windows 10
   c. DHCP servers
   d. Web (IIS) servers

11

8. Name three predefined data collector sets.
9. While practicing, your assistant changed the priority of File Explorer and now the server response for all users is extraordinarily slow. What priority did he or she most likely set?
   a. High
   b. Normal
   c. Realtime
   d. Low
10. Briefly explain how to view users who are signed in and how to disconnect a user.
11. Your IT department head wants you to gather daily performance data on system performance for a new Windows Server 2016 server. You create a data collector set for this purpose. How can you set the data collector set to run at 2:00 PM every workday?
   a. Use the Performance Monitor Schedule option to schedule the start and stop times of the data collector set.
   b. Use the Monitor Scheduler MMC snap-in.
   c. Set the new Task Clock in Windows Server 2016.
   d. Set a schedule and stop condition in the properties of the data collector set.
12. Your server is running slowly and you suspect that a disk drive is the bottleneck. You've decided to use Performance Monitor to monitor the disk drive. Which of the following do you set up in Performance Monitor?
   a. The Harddisk instance
   b. The Physical Disk counter
   c. The MemDisk counter
   d. The % Disk Write counter
13. Which of the following tools do you use to configure a data collector set?
   a. Even Viewer
   b. Task Manager
   c. Resource Monitor
   d. Performance Monitor
14. Which of the following are counters associated with the processor object used for monitoring? (Choose all that apply.)
   a. Processor Overload Count
   b. % Privileged Time
   c. Interrupts/sec
   d. % Application Use
15. Name three things that can be done with SNMP.
16. While you are checking to ensure you can see all network servers from your Windows 10 workstation, you notice that one of the servers seems to disappear, then reappear, then disappear. You decide to go to the console of that server to run some diagnostics. Which of the following tools can you use to help diagnose a network connectivity or resources access problem at the server? (Choose all that apply.)
   a. Services listing accessed through the Services tool
   b. Event Diagnostics template used as a data collector set

c. Performance tab in Task Manager
d. Network Interface counter in Performance Monitor

17. An application developer in the IT department at your company has written a purchase order program that often stops responding when the Vendor Listing screen is displayed. Which of the following can you offer to do to help her diagnose the problem with this program? (Choose all that apply.)
    a. Use Task Manager to lower the priority of the *appmanager* service, which is used to run all applications in Windows Server 2016.
    b. Use Performance Monitor to allocate more memory to the program so that it has more reserved memory.
    c. Use Task Manager to print a dump file for the program.
    d. Use Performance Monitor to create a *diskperf* report showing the interaction between disk speed and application access timing.
18. Your organization is implementing a new customer service application and you want to monitor how your current configuration for virtual memory is performing while the new application is in use. Which of the following Performance Monitor elements do you use? (Choose all that apply.)
    a. Processor object and % User Time counter
    b. Memory object and Committed Bytes counter
    c. Processor object and % Privileged Time counter
    d. Memory object and Pages/sec counter
19. Name the three modes you can use to view Performance Monitor activity.
20. Which is the only tab in Task Manager that does not show information about CPU and memory use?
    a. Performance
    b. Processes
    c. Details
    d. Services

Case Projects

Alterrain manufactures high-end mountain bikes with models for general recreational use and specialty models for racing. Alterrain products are sold throughout North America and Europe. The company operates from an office building adjacent to its manufacturing building. A centralized server and network operations room in the office building is fully networked, as is the manufacturing building.

The office building houses management along with the Marketing, Accounting, and Research and Design departments. The Manufacturing, Inventory, and Shipping departments are housed in the manufacturing building. Network communications in the office building are largely wireless, but the servers use cable connections to the network and are protected behind a router. The manufacturing building has a cable network because the machinery used in the building and the building structure are not well suited for dependable wireless communications.

Alterrain has 12 Windows Server 2016 servers. The company employees use a combination of Windows 8.1, Windows 10, and Linux desktop and laptop computers.

Because the company has recently experienced network and server problems, management has decided to launch a proactive network and server resource efficiency initiative. The goal of this program is to minimize computer interruptions and maximize user productivity. As part of the initiative, they have hired you through Aspen Consulting to help put into place efficiency measures.

Case Project 11-1: Obtaining Baselines

The Alterrain IT Department does little server monitoring because most of its time has been spent upgrading servers and network equipment as well as responding to user needs. You recommend starting the proactive network and server resource efficiency initiative by developing a plan for gathering baseline performance data on each server. Prepare a report or slide presentation for the IT director that describes the baseline data you would gather.

Case Project 11-2: Using Monitoring Tools

Alterrain is hiring a new computer administrator who will have computer efficiency and resource reliability as one of her job duties. In preparation for her arrival, the IT director asks you to prepare an overview for her of Windows Server 2016 monitoring tools, which includes:

- Task Manager
- Performance Monitor
- Data Collector Sets

Case Project 11-3: Monitoring a Problem in the Inventory Department

A group of users in the Inventory Department has expressed a concern that one or more of the Inventory Department users are playing games on their workstations and that besides interfering with work, the game playing is making the inventory data query and database system slow. What tool do you use to monitor the activity of users in this department to identify the game players? Explain why this tool can be effective in this situation.

Case Project 11-4: Creating a Performance Monitor Strategy

The IT director asks you to prepare a document to help the company standardize Performance Monitor data gathered from each server. Create a recommendation for consistent use of five or six Performance Monitor objects that can be used to help establish baseline data and enable fast troubleshooting of problems that may develop in the future. For each object you propose using, also discuss two or three counters to use with those objects.

chapter 12

Managing System Reliability and Availability

After reading this chapter and completing the exercises, you will be able to:

- Understand general problem-solving strategies
- Resolve boot problems
- Use and configure Event Viewer
- Troubleshoot network connectivity
- Remotely administer one or more servers

The most successful server and network administrators are often barely known to the users who rely on them. This means the users' systems work reliably or are fixed nearly as soon as they break down. You can be this kind of administrator once you perfect your problem-solving skills and learn to use the tools in Windows Server 2016 to diagnose and fix problems. In Chapter 11, Server and Network Monitoring, you learned how to use several tools to address server problems. This chapter teaches problem-solving skills and gives you more tools for your arsenal.

In this chapter, you learn to develop basic problem-solving strategies, including techniques for solving problems step-by-step. Boot problems can represent a serious risk, so you learn how to troubleshoot a server that won't boot. You learn to use Event Viewer, which is the repository of logs used for troubleshooting problems. You also learn many tools for diagnosing network connectivity problems. Finally, you learn to use tools for remotely managing a server to give you greater flexibility compared with working only from the server console.

General Problem-Solving Strategies

The best approach to solving server and network problems is to develop effective problem-solving strategies. Four general strategies are:

- Understanding how a server and the network interact
- Training your users to help you solve problems
- Solving problems step-by-step
- Tracking problems and solutions

Understanding How Servers and the Network Interact

You can take various steps to better understand the environment in which a server operates. Many server and network administrators create a diagram of the entire network or diagrams of different portions of a network and then update the diagrams each time an aspect of the network changes. Figure 12-1 is a sample diagram of a portion of a network that shows cabled and wireless links.

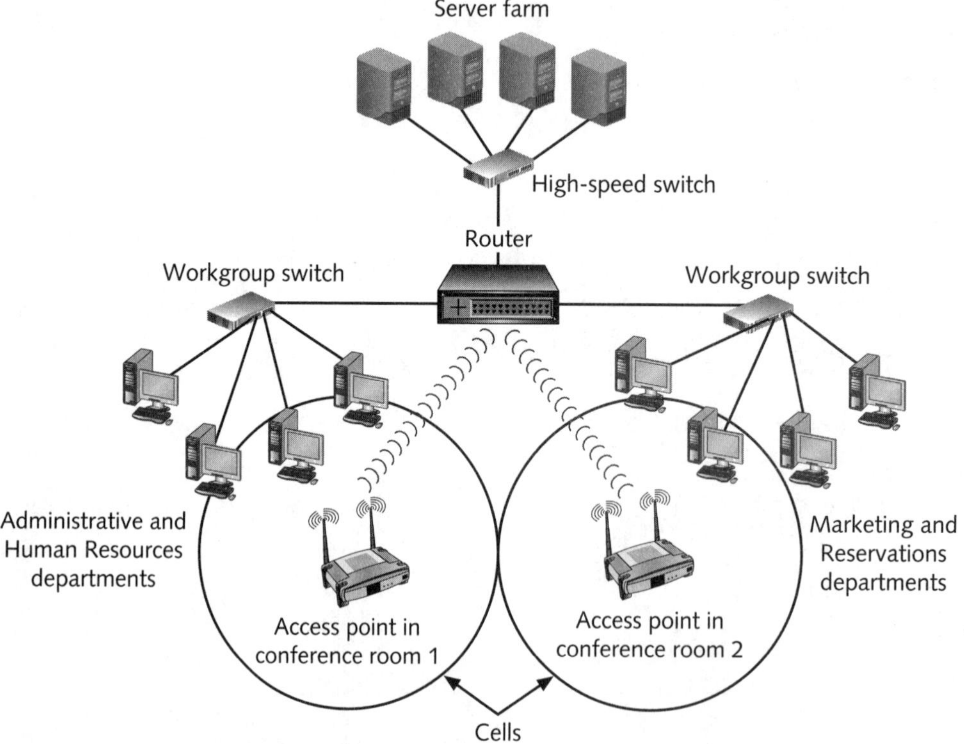

Figure 12-1 Sample network diagram

A network diagram should include the following elements:

- Servers (and any mainframes/supercomputers)
- Workstations and network printers (unless the network is too large to include these)
- Wireless network devices
- Cabled network devices
- Telecommunications links
- Wireless and cabled links
- Remote links
- Building locations

A server does not exist in a vacuum, but is a member of a larger community of networked workstations and users. Gathering benchmarks, as discussed in Chapter 11, helps you understand your server and how it is affected by the network context. For example, slow server performance can look like a network problem, and slow network performance can look like a server problem. The more you know about the server's network context, the faster you'll be able to resolve a problem, such as slow server performance.

Understanding the community that uses a server is vital. For example, because users are dependent on a server, it is important to wait until off-peak hours to perform server maintenance, including software upgrades or the installation of new devices. Some organizations reserve specific off-peak hours for server maintenance, such as very early in the morning, and users know in advance that they cannot access servers during those hours.

Training Users to Help

Another valuable strategy is to train network users to be your partners in reporting problems. If you encourage users to be troubleshooting allies, they are more likely to feel they can take action to deal with a problem, rather than wait impatiently for you to detect and solve it. When you train users to gather information and report it to you, they become troubleshooting partners who can advance you several steps toward the solution. You can train users to take a variety of actions to help you and themselves. For example, they should:

- Save their work at the first sign of a problem
- Record information about a problem as the problem is occurring
- Report any protocol information, such as error messages about a protocol or an address
- Quickly report a problem by text message, by telephone, or by voice mail if you cannot be reached immediately
- Avoid sending email about urgent problems

Solving Problems Step-by-Step

Equipped with knowledge of your network context and help from trained users, you can use the following step-by-step techniques to solve server and network problems:

1. Get as much information as possible about the problem. If a network user reports the problem, listen carefully to his or her description. Even if he or she does not use the correct terminology, the information is still valuable. Part of your challenge is to ask the right questions to get as much information as possible.
2. Record the error message at the time it appears or when a user reports it to you. This is an obvious but sometimes overlooked step. If you try to recall the message from memory, you

might lose some important information. For example, the error "Network not responding" can lead you to a different set of troubleshooting steps than the message "Network timeout error." The first message might signal a damaged NIC, whereas the second message could mean that a database server is overloaded and the application is waiting to obtain data.

3. Determine if anyone else is experiencing the problem. For example, several people might report they cannot load a statistical analysis package. This might be due to a problem at the server or in a cloud connection they use to load the software. If only one person is experiencing this problem, it might point to trouble on her or his workstation.
4. Check the Windows Server 2016 event logs for signs of a problem (it's always a good idea to regularly check the logs anyway; you'll learn how to do this later in the chapter).
5. Use Performance Monitor, Data Collector Sets, Task Manager, Server Manager, and the Computer Management tool to help you troubleshoot problems.
6. Check for power interruptions. Power problems are a common source of server and network difficulties. Even though the server is on an uninterruptible power source (UPS), its network connection can still be a source of problems, because a network cable can carry current to the server's NIC during a lightning storm or because of a major power-related problem.
7. Take the information you have gathered and define the problem, such as that the server is not connecting to the network.
8. Determine possible solutions for the problem.
9. Consider the best or most likely solutions, which may well be the simplest ones. For example, the solution to a problem might be as simple as connecting a cable or power cord.

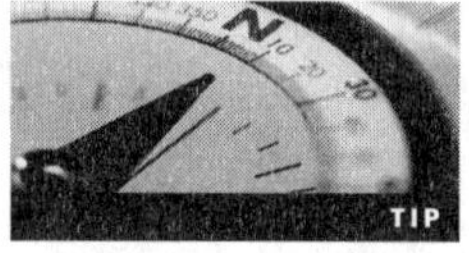

In some cases, you might be completely stumped by a problem, for example, because it is a rare problem or a bug that only the vendor knows how to fix. In these cases, contact the vendor for solutions. It can be less expensive for you to contact the vendor sooner and pay a modest support fee than to spend hours working on a problem that you might not be able to solve alone.

10. Determine how the solution will affect users. For example, if the solution is to install an operating system update, plan to implement it when the server is not busy or during regularly scheduled server maintenance time when no one expects to use the server. Test important updates before bringing them into production.
11. After your solution is implemented, continue monitoring the server to ensure there are no further problems.

One experienced Windows Server instructor teaches students to do the following when deciding on the best solution: Know what to do, know how to do it, and consider the consequences for users before implementing a solution.

Tracking Problems and Solutions

An effective troubleshooting tool is to keep a log of all network problems and their solutions. Some server administrators log problems in a database created for that purpose. Others build problem logging into help desk systems maintained by their organization. A **help desk system** is application software designed to maintain information on computer systems, user questions, problem solutions, and other information that members of the organization can reference.

The advantage of tracking problems is that you soon accumulate a wealth of information on solutions. For example, to jog your memory about a solution, you can look up how you handled a similar problem 6 months ago. The log of problems also can be used as a teaching tool and reference for other computer support staff. Problems that show up repeatedly in the log might indicate that special attention is needed, such as replacing a server that experiences frequent hardware problems.

It is also good practice to keep a change log, a record of changes made to a server's hardware and software. Sometimes problems arise when configuration changes are made to a server, such as the installation of new hardware and/or software or a change in settings. Documenting changes provides a reference for troubleshooting if problems should arise later. This is especially important if you are not the only server administrator and someone else is also troubleshooting the problem.

Resolving Boot Problems

Sometimes a server encounters a hardware problem and cannot be booted, displays an error screen during the boot process, or hangs. Several things can lead to boot problems, such as the installation of new software, drivers, or hardware problems. Some of the common causes of boot failures include the following:

- Disk failure on the drive or drives containing the system and boot files
- A corrupted partition table
- A corrupted boot file
- A corrupted Master Boot Record
- A disk read error

In most cases, the first step is to power off the computer and try rebooting it. Often this will work in instances where there is a temporary disk read error or memory error during the first boot attempt, which is corrected on the second try. Also, one or more data storage registers might be out of synchronization in the CPU, causing a transient problem. Rebooting resets the CPU registers. If the computer has multiple drives, a disk controller might need to be reset, which is accomplished by rebooting.

The best way to reboot for clearing a temporary error is to turn the power off, wait several seconds for the hard disk drives to fully come to a stop, and then turn on the power. This causes all components to completely reset. If, instead, you reboot using a reset button, some components might not fully reset.

Troubleshooting by Using Safe Mode

If a simple reboot does not fix the problem, or if you have installed new software or drivers or changed the server configuration and the server does not properly boot, try using the advanced options for booting—accessed by pressing F8 as soon as the computer boots—which include starting the computer in Safe Mode. **Safe Mode** boots the server using the most generic default settings (for example, for the display, disk drives, and pointing device) and only those services needed to boot a basic configuration. After you boot into Safe Mode, you have the opportunity to further troubleshoot the problem.

For example, if you install software or a driver that causes a problem with the boot process, then you can boot into Safe Mode and remove or disable that software or driver. Or, perhaps you have replaced the mouse with a trackball and installed the new driver for the trackball, but after you reboot, there is no pointer on the screen when you move the new trackball. You can boot into Safe Mode, reinstall the old driver and mouse, and contact the trackball vendor for a solution or new driver. Or, if you changed the server's configuration, for example, by setting up an additional page file or installing a Windows component, and the server does not properly boot, you can restore the original page file settings or remove the Windows component while in Safe Mode.

If you contact a Microsoft technician for help with a server problem, often she or he will ask you to boot in Safe Mode in order to execute troubleshooting steps.

Table 12-1 lists the advanced booting options available when you press F8 at the beginning of the boot process.

Table 12-1 Advanced Boot Options menu options

Booting option	Description
Repair Your Computer	Enables you to access system recovery and restore tools as well as diagnostics
Safe Mode	Boots the system using the minimum configuration of devices and drivers, and does not have network connectivity
Safe Mode with Networking	Boots the system using the minimum configuration of devices and drivers, and does have network connectivity
Safe Mode with Command Prompt	Boots the system into the command mode using the minimum prompt configuration of devices and drivers, and does not have network connectivity
Enable Boot Logging	Creates a record of devices and drivers that started, so you can check a log for points of failure—look for the log in the \Windows folder with the name ntbtlog.txt
Enable low-resolution video	Boots the system using the fewest resources for video
Last Known Good Configuration (advanced)	Boots the system using the last configuration before any changes to the configuration were made and implemented in the Registry
Directory Services Repair Mode	Reboots the server into a local mode so that the server is not available to users as a domain controller; enables the administrator to log on to validate, work on, or restore the Active Directory database (only available when AD DS is installed)
Debugging Mode	Boots the system while transmitting debug data to be viewed at another computer over a serial or USB connection, which can be used by Microsoft technicians to troubleshoot problems
Disable automatic restart on system failure	Does not automatically restart the system if it fails
Disable Driver Signature Enforcement	Enables drivers without the proper digital signature to be installed (which might be needed on older hardware or when you have a driver you know is safe, but does not have a digital signature)
Disable Early Launch Anti-Malware Driver	Anti-malware driver is disabled so that other drivers needed to boot the operating system can initialize without being scanned for malware
Start Windows Normally	Starts the system without any special options

To access the Advanced Boot Options menu:

1. Reboot the computer. (Be sure all users are signed out before doing this.)
2. Press F8 as soon as the computer boots.
3. Select the option you want to use, such as Safe Mode, and press Enter.

Use the advanced option that is the most appropriate for the kind of problem you are troubleshooting. For example, if the problem is only that you have installed a new monitor driver and cannot use or see the display when you boot, select *Enable low-resolution video*. If the problem is related to the most recent software or configuration change you have made, such as installing an additional SCSI adapter or an additional network interface, boot using the *Last Known Good Configuration (advanced)*. The *Last Known Good Configuration (advanced)* is the Windows Server 2016 configuration that is stored in the Registry

(HKEY_LOCAL_MACHINE\System\CurrentControlSet). This configuration is the one in effect prior to making a system, driver, or configuration change after the last time the computer was booted. For those times when you are not sure why the system is having problems, or you have installed multiple new drivers or several new software programs, use the *Safe Mode* or the *Safe Mode with Networking* option so that you can access the Windows Server 2016 desktop to work on the problem.

If you use Safe Mode but are unable to troubleshoot the problem, or a failed driver message is displayed during the boot process, use the *Enable Boot Logging* option so that you can create a log that you can later check for problems. For example, you might boot so that the log is created and then boot again into Safe Mode so that you can view the contents of the log.

The *Safe Mode with Command Prompt* option is particularly useful when you can solve a problem by executing a command, such as by running *chkdsk* to repair damaged files or by running *sfc* to locate critical system files that have been overwritten and then restore them.

If you have Active Directory installed and suspect that it is damaged, or that the **SYSVOL** shared volumes (see the following Note) are corrupted, use the *Directory Services Repair Mode* to restore damaged files and folders.

When you set up Active Directory, a domain controller is automatically set up with the SYSVOL shared folder, which contains scripts, Group Policy Objects (GPOs), and software distribution files. The GPOs can be important for access to the domain. SYSVOL is technically recognized as part of the operating system. The contents of SYSVOL are replicated between DCs using the Windows Server 2016 Distributed File System (DFS) Replication capability (when the domain functional level is set to Windows Server 2008 or above) for reliable and efficient replication.

Some steps in the activities in this book include bulleted questions for you to answer. Additionally, for all of the activities in this chapter, you'll need an account with Administrator privileges. These activities can be completed on a virtual machine or computer, such as in Hyper-V.

12

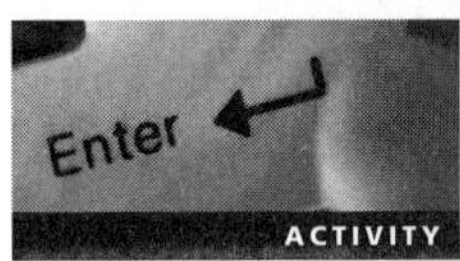

Activity 12-1: Booting into Safe Mode

Time Required: Approximately 15 minutes
Objective: Learn how to boot into Safe Mode.

Description: In this activity, you practice accessing the advanced boot options on a server and then you boot into the Safe Mode.

1. Make sure all users are signed out from Windows Server 2016.
   - What tool would you use to check that all users are signed out?
2. Shut down and then reboot the computer (right-click **Start**, point to **Shut down or sign out**, and click **Restart.** Select the appropriate reason for the shutdown and click **Continue**).
3. Press **F8** as soon as the computer boots.
   - What option would you use to boot to fix a monitor driver problem? Which one would you use to run *chkdsk*?
4. Select **Safe Mode** and press **Enter.**
5. Press **Ctrl+Alt+Delete** and sign in with your username and password.
   - How is the Windows Server 2016 desktop display different in Safe Mode from when you boot normally? What else is different in Safe Mode?
6. Shut down the computer and then reboot normally.

Troubleshooting by Using the Repair Your Computer Option or Installation DVD

In Windows Server 2016, you can access repair options when you select Repair Your Computer from the Advanced Boot Options menu or when you boot from an installation DVD (or thumb drive) and select the option to Repair your computer. —The options that are available, for example, when you select *Repair Your Computer* after you press F8 when booting are:

- *Continue*—which exits the repair options menu and continues to boot into Windows Server 2016
- *Use another operating system*—so that you can select to boot from another operating system on the same computer, when that computer is installed with multiple operating systems
- *Troubleshoot*—which goes to another menu with the selections: System Image Recovery (used to restore from an image backup), Command Prompt (from which to execute commands), and Startup Settings (to change startup actions)
- *Turn off your PC*—to shut down the computer

When you boot from the installation DVD and select *Repair your computer* instead of the Install Now button, you see the options: *Continue*, *Troubleshoot*, and *Turn off your PC*. When you select *Troubleshoot* you can select from the options: *System Image Recovery* or *Command Prompt* (see Figure 12-2).

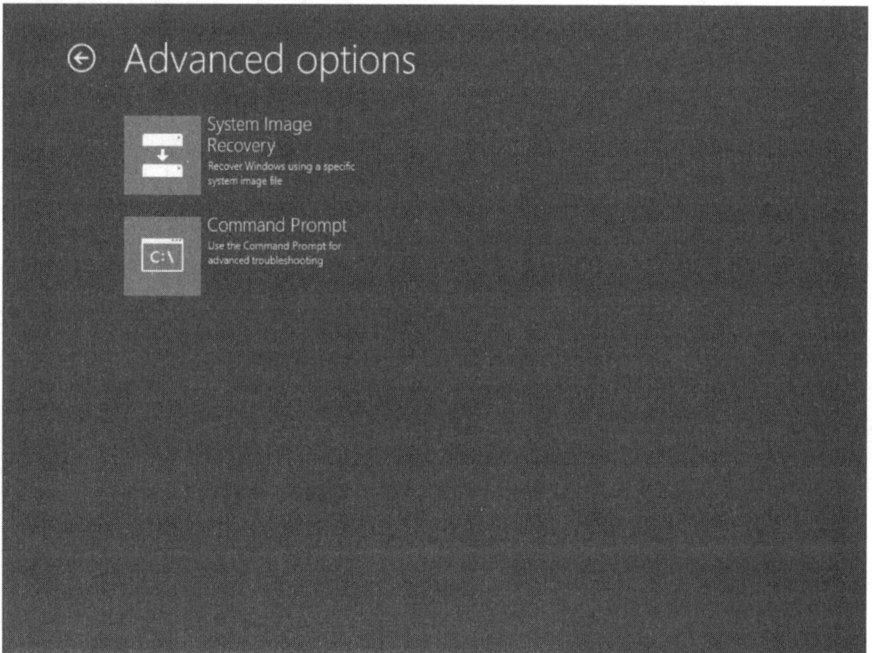

Figure 12-2 Repair your computer Advanced options

System Image Recovery The System Image Recovery option requires that you have previously taken an image (binary backup for what is sometimes called a bare metal recovery). This type of backup is used for a full restore of all the files on a server using a complete image, like a picture, of all folders and files as of the time of the backup. This is an all or none type of restore, so you cannot simply restore selected folders or files, because the information is not stored in the backup as files, but as bits. Review the Backup Options section in Chapter 7, Configuring and Managing Data Storage. Creating a binary backup is discussed in Chapter 7 as a custom backup method (also see Activity 7-9) in the Windows Server Backup tool.

When you select System Image Recovery, you can choose from different operating system versions, if you have multiple Windows operating systems on a dual boot computer. After selecting the operating system, such as Windows Server 2016, you see the *Select a system image backup* dialog box that enables you to specify the location of the backup data or to select from multiple binary backups. Click Next in the dialog box and follow the steps to perform the restore.

Note that besides application and data files, a binary backup also contains the system state data stored on the server. The **system state data** includes the operating system plus extra components and information that reflect the currently configured state of the server, depending on what features are installed. This includes elements such as the following:

- System and boot files
- Protected system files
- Active Directory
- SYSVOL folder (when Active Directory is installed)
- Registry
- COM+ Class Registration information
- DNS zones (when DNS is installed)
- Certificate information (when certificate services are installed)
- Server cluster data (when server clustering is used)
- IIS metadirectory (if the Web Server role is installed)

All of the system state data is backed up as a group because many of these entities are interrelated.

When you back up the system state data, you also are backing up the system protected files, which are the files used to start up the operating system when you boot. 12

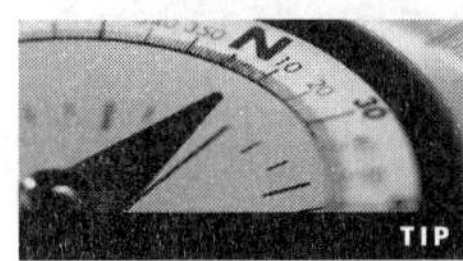

Chapter 7 also discusses how to back up only the system state data with system protected files. Be sure you periodically create a backup of the system state data, so that you have a faster alternative for a restore instead of performing the more drastic full image restore.

Activity 12-2: Using the Installation DVD for an Image Restore

Time Required: Approximately 10 minutes
Objective: Learn from where to perform an image restore.

Description: In this activity, you learn how to access the Repair option from a Windows Server 2016 installation DVD and how to use it to start an image restore. You will need the Windows Server 2016 installation DVD (or thumb drive). You do not need an image backup, because you simply learn from where to start it. Note that your computer's BIOS should also be set to try to boot first from the medium you use, such as an optical drive (see Chapter 2, Installing Windows Server 2016, and refer to Activity 2-1). Alternatively, on a virtual machine, your system should be able to recognize the installation medium, such as a DVD in an optical drive.

1. Insert the Windows Server 2016 installation DVD or a bootable Windows Server 2016 installation thumb drive.
2. Right-click the **Start** button, point to **Shut down or sign out**, and click **Restart**.

3. When the computer reboots, press **Enter** or another key at the message or prompt to press a key to boot from a CD or DVD or thumb drive (or on a virtual machine, you may just see a blinking prompt, which implies that if you press a key it will start from the removable storage medium, such as a DVD).
4. Press **Next** in the Windows Setup window to configure the language, time and currency, and keyboard or input method options.
5. In the Windows Setup window with the Install now button, click **Repair your computer.**
6. On the Choose an option screen, click **Troubleshoot** (see Figure 12-3).

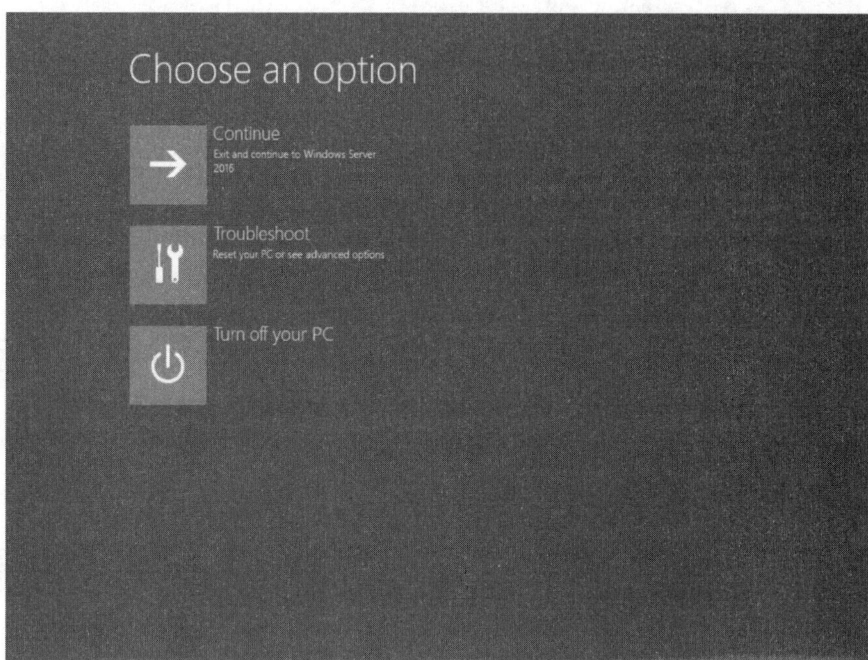

Figure 12-3 Choose an option screen

7. On the Advanced options screen (refer to Figure 12-2), click **System Image Recovery.**
8. On the System Image Recovery screen, click the appropriate operating system (a computer can have more than one operating system installed).
9. If you see an error message box that Windows cannot find a system image, click **Cancel.**
10. In the Select a system image backup dialog box (see Figure 12-4), you can specify the image or image location. To actually start the backup you would click Next and complete the guided steps to start the backup. However, do not perform an image backup at this time.
11. Click **Cancel.**
12. Leave the Choose an option screen open for the next activity. (Or if you have to stop now select the Turn off your PC option.)

Using the Command Prompt When you select to use the Command Prompt option from Advanced Options, you can use this option to access the command prompt so that you can repair a disk problem or copy a critical file back to the server. Another reason for using the

Figure 12-4 Select a system image backup dialog box

command prompt is to copy off the server important files you have not yet backed up because the system failed before starting the backup. The command prompt capability can be vital when you cannot boot into your server.

When you open the Command Prompt window, you start in the \Sources folder on the Windows Server 2016 installation DVD. You can execute many commands from the command prompt, such as the *copy* command to copy a file or the *chkdsk* command to check for disk errors and repair them. For any command, you can enter *help /?* to view its online documentation. Table 12-2 provides a sampling of the commands.

Table 12-2 Sample command prompt commands

Command	Description
attrib	Manages folder and file attributes
cd	Changes to a different directory (folder), to the parent directory, or shows the directory you are in
chkdsk	Verifies and fixes files (requires access to the Autochk.exe file)
cls	Reinitializes the display
copy	Copies files
del	Deletes files
dir	Lists the contents of a directory (folder)
diskpart	Partitions a disk and manages multiple partitions on a system
exit	Closes the Command Prompt window and returns to the Advanced Options box
expand	Uncompresses a file
format	Formats a drive
md (mkdir)	Creates a new directory
more	Shows a file's contents one screen at a time
rd (rmdir)	Deletes a directory
ren (rename)	Modifies a file's name
type	Shows a file's contents

Activity 12-3: Using the Command Prompt

Time Required: Approximately 15 minutes

Objective: Learn how to access the command prompt from the Windows Server 2016 installation DVD.

Description: If you have an area of disk damage or a corrupted system file and cannot boot a server, using the installation DVD to access the command prompt can be critical. In this mode you can attempt to replace a system file, fix the boot problem, or copy important files off of the server. In this activity, you use the Windows Server 2016 installation DVD to access the command line.

1. Ensure that the **Choose an option** screen is displayed. If it is not and you have to go back into the repair mode, follow Steps 1-5 in Activity 12-2.
2. Click **Troubleshoot** in the Choose an option screen (refer to Figure 12-3).
3. Click **Command Prompt** in the Advanced options screen (refer to Figure 12-2).
4. You'll see a command prompt window similar to Figure 12-5 (you'll see a screen that has a black background and white text; the properties of the screen in Figure 12-5 are changed for easier print reproduction).

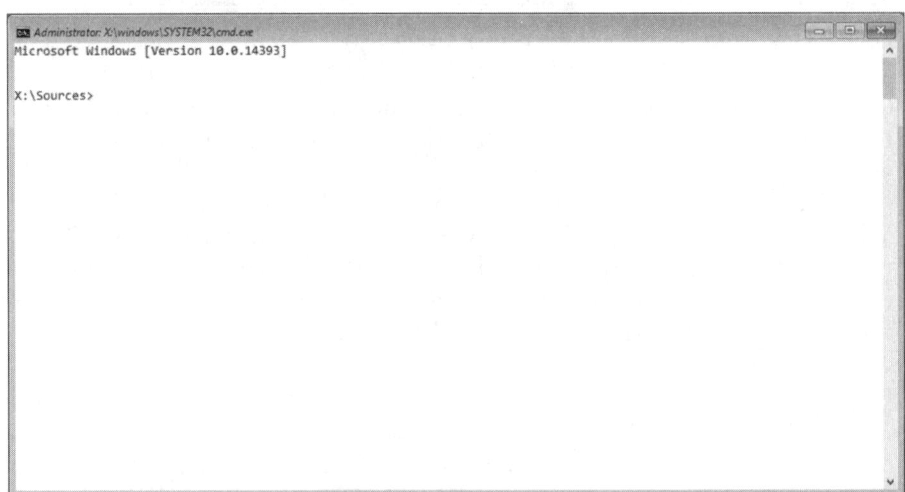

Figure 12-5 Command prompt window in the repair mode

5. Type **dir \Windows** and press **Enter** to view the files and subdirectories in the \Windows directory (containing system files).
6. Type **copy /?** and press **Enter** to view the documentation for the copy command. Press the **spacebar**, if necessary, to display the remaining documentation.
7. Type **chkdsk** to check the file system and press **Enter**.

When *chkdsk* is finished, you are likely to see the message "Failed to transfer logged messages to the event log with status 50." because *chkdsk* cannot write to the event log in this mode. Also, if errors are found, you'll see a message that you can use *chkdsk /f* to fix file system errors. See Chapter 7 to review using *chkdsk*.

8. Type **exit** and press **Enter** to close the Command Prompt window.
9. On the Choose an option screen (refer to Figure 12-3), click **Turn off your PC.**
10. Boot up your system and sign back in.

General Tips for Fixing Boot Problems

Using the Safe Mode, the Windows Server 2016 installation DVD, and other techniques, Tables 12-3 and 12-4 provide tips for fixing boot problems and responding to Stop messages. A Stop message is an error message displayed when the server experiences a serious problem and then stops functioning.

Table 12-3 Troubleshooting boot problems

Boot problem	Solutions
A message appears when booting, such as one of the following: Inaccessible Boot Device; Invalid Partition Table; Hard Disk Error; Hard Disk Absent or Failed.	The boot sector on the NTFS partition is corrupted or the hard drive is damaged. This can be caused by a virus, a corrupted partition table, a BIOS setting change, or a corrupted disk. Check the BIOS setup to make certain it is correct. Correct any improper settings (also make sure the CMOS battery is working—it is not working if the BIOS settings are zero, null, or incorrect).
	If no BIOS problems are present, use the Windows Server 2016 installation DVD to boot the system into the command prompt, then run a virus scanner on the server or insert a virus scanner in an optical drive and attempt to scan the hard disk for viruses. If a virus is found, remove it.
	If the disk cannot be accessed, determine if the problem is the hard disk, disk controller, or a SCSI adapter and replace the defective part (if necessary, make sure to check that a SCSI adapter is properly terminated). If the hard disk must be replaced, reinstall the operating system.
The system hangs when booting.	Power off and on the computer to reboot. Try rebooting a couple of times.
	If rebooting does not work, check the BIOS settings to be sure they have not changed and that the CMOS battery is working. If many of the BIOS settings are incorrect, replace the battery and restore the proper settings.
	For an SMP computer, the hal.dll file might be corrupted. Boot from the Windows Server 2016 installation DVD into the command prompt from the repair mode. Reinstall the hal.dll file from the manufacturer's CD/DVD or thumb drive.
Changes were made to the system configuration when last logged on and now the computer will not boot.	Stop the boot process immediately and reboot using the Last Known Good Configuration (advanced) option (press F8 when you boot) on the Advanced Boot Options screen. Once logged on, check the configuration and fix any problems, such as a bad or removed device driver.
The screen display goes blank or is jumbled as the computer begins booting into Windows Server 2016.	Immediately stop the boot process. Restart the computer, accessing the BIOS setup before starting Windows Server 2016. Check the video BIOS setup to make sure it is correct and restore any settings that are changed. Reboot the computer.
	If no BIOS problems are present, reboot using the Enable low-resolution video option on the Advanced Boot Options screen (press F8 when you boot). Once logged on, check and reinstall the display driver. Alternatively, boot into the command prompt repair mode from the Windows Server 2016 installation DVD and reinstall the display driver.
A driver is missing, but you are not sure which one, or the operating system is having trouble recognizing all hardware components on the computer when it boots.	Access the Advanced Boot Options screen and use the Enable Boot Logging option to boot and examine the \Windows\ntbtlog.txt file. (The ntbtlog.txt file is a log of drivers that are successfully loaded or not loaded when Windows Server 2016 boots.)

Table 12-4 Troubleshooting boot problems associated with Stop messages

Stop message*	Solutions
0x00000023 NTFS File System	Boot into Safe Mode or the command prompt via the Windows Server 2016 installation DVD and run *chkdsk /f* to repair any damaged files. If you have recently installed a virus scanner or a disk defragmenter that is not from Microsoft or compatible with Windows Server 2016, boot into Safe Mode or using Last Known Good Configuration (advanced) and remove that software.
0x0000001E and the message Kmode_Exception_Not_Handled	If you have recently installed a new video system and associated drivers, remove the new hardware, and reboot into the Safe Mode to remove the new drivers (or boot using the Enable low-resolution video option on the Advanced Boot Options screen). Do the same if you have installed any new drivers. Verify the video setup in the computer's BIOS or install any updated BIOS software offered by the computer vendor. Reboot using Safe Mode or the command prompt from the Windows Server 2016 installation DVD and make sure that you are not out of disk space. (From the command prompt, type *dir* and press Enter to view if free disk space is available.)
0x000000B4 and the message Video Driver Init Failure	If you have recently installed a new video system and associated drivers, remove the new hardware, and reboot into the Safe Mode to remove the new drivers (or boot using the Enable low-resolution video option on the Advanced Boot Options screen).
0x0000007B and the message Inaccessible_Boot_Device	Boot into Safe Mode or boot into the command prompt via the Windows Server 2016 installation DVD and check for a virus. Boot into Safe Mode or boot into the command prompt via the Windows Server 2016 installation DVD and run *chkdsk /f* to repair any damaged files.
0x0000002E and the message Data Bus Error Or 0x0000007F and the message Unexpected Kernel Mode Trap	Use a memory diagnostic tool and replace any defective memory.
0x0000000A and the message IRQL Not Less or Equal	Suspect a hardware resource conflict caused by a new device or card you have added. If you can boot using the Safe Mode, check the system log. If you cannot boot into Safe Mode, remove the new device or devices and boot using Last Known Good Configuration (advanced).
0x00000058 and the message Ftdisk Internal Error	Suspect that the main volume in a mirrored set has failed. Boot using the secondary volume and use the Disk Management tool to attempt to repair the main volume and resynchronize it with the secondary volume. If you cannot repair the volume, use the Disk Management tool to break the mirrored set, replace the damaged disk, and then recreate the mirrored set.
0x000000BE and the message Attempted Write to Readonly Memory	Boot using the Enable Boot Logging option and then boot again into Safe Mode (or the command prompt) so you can examine the \Windows\ntbtlog.txt log for a driver that did not start or that is causing problems, then reinstall or replace the driver using the Safe Mode or by copying it into the system using the command prompt via the Windows Server 2016 installation DVD.

*Information in this table is based on Microsoft's help documentation.

Using and Configuring Event Viewer

A valuable tool for diagnosing all kinds of server problems is Event Viewer (see Figure 12-6). Event Viewer houses the **event logs** that record information about all types of server events, in the form of errors, warnings, and informational events. Windows Server 2016 event logs are divided into three general categories: Windows logs, applications and services logs, and Microsoft logs.

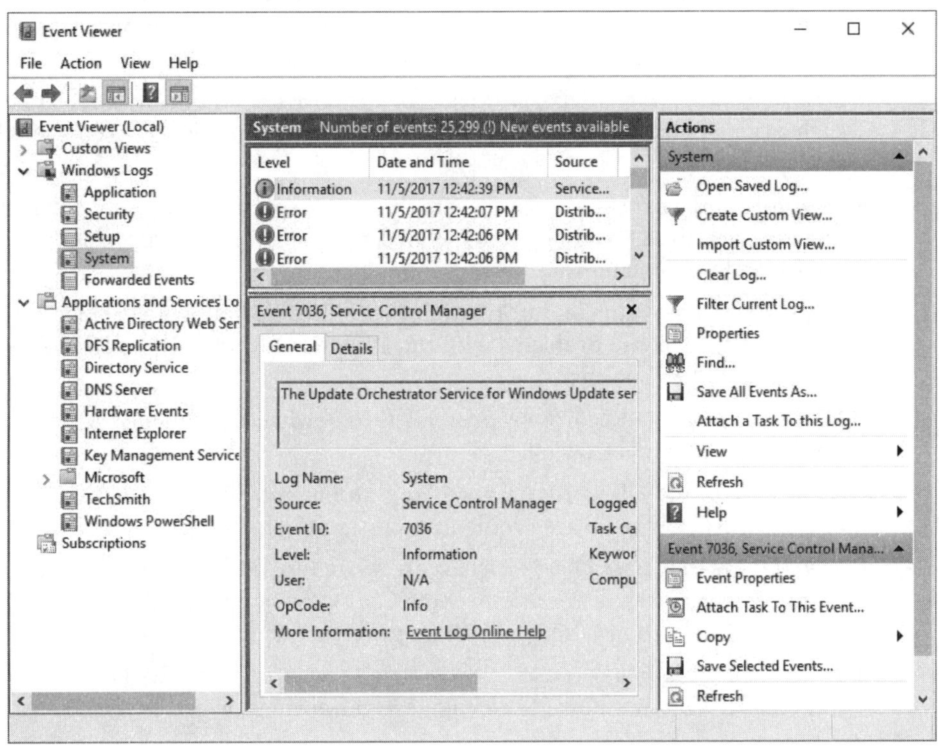

Figure 12-6 Event Viewer

Windows generates four logs for reporting general operating system and software application events:

- **Application log**—Records information about how software applications are performing, if the programmer has designed the software to write information into the log.
- **Security log**—Records access and security information about logon accesses and file, folder, and system policy changes. If you have auditing set up, for instance, file auditing, use the security log to track each audited event, such as a successful or failed attempt to access a file. If you choose to audit an account or folder, the audit data is recorded in the security log.
- **Setup log**—Contains a record of installation events, such as installing a role or feature through Server Manager. For example, if a software error occurs, it may be recorded in the log.
- **System log**—Records information about system-related events such as hardware errors, driver problems, and hard drive errors.
- **Forwarded events log**—Contains events recorded by remote computers and forwarded to this computer, which is called the collector computer.

The applications and services logs are largely a combination of what Microsoft calls admin and operational logs. **Admin logs** are designed to help give the system administrator information about a specific problem and its causes and may suggest how to solve the problem. For example, it might report that the DFS Replication service (for DFS and DC replication) has failed and that this might be caused by the Windows Firewall configuration. An **operational log** tracks occurrences of specific operations, such as when a disk drive is added.

The specific applications and services logs available in Event Viewer depend in part on which roles and features are installed. Here is a sampling of these logs:

- *Active Directory Web Services log*—Records events associated with the Web Server role, such as when the server is started, when there are certificate problems, when there are problems loading a configuration file, and so on.
- *DFS Replication log*—Records events for the Distributed File System Replication services, such as when DFS Replication service is started and records any events in which the service fails.
- *Directory Service log*—Records events that are associated with Active Directory, such as updates to Active Directory, events related to the Active Directory database, replication events, and startup and shutdown events.
- *DNS Server log*—Provides information about instances in which (1) DNS information is updated, (2) there are problems with the DNS service, and (3) the DNS Server has started successfully after booting.
- *Hardware Events*—Records events related to hardware including the CPU, disk drives, memory, and other hardware.
- *Internet Explorer*—Records events related to Internet Explorer, including if it terminates unexpectedly or if there are problems accessing the Internet.
- *Key Management Service*—Tracks events related to Kerberos key distribution, when a server functions as a key distribution center. Check this log if users are having trouble logging on, for example, to be sure there are no problems with the key distribution services.
- *Windows PowerShell*—Tracks events related to use of Windows PowerShell, including the state of the Windows PowerShell engine and information about certificates needed.

In addition to the logs already described, you also can choose whether to display the analytic and debug logs. These logs are mentioned last because they contain more complex information. The **analytic logs** relate to how programs are operating and are typically used by application or system programmers. The **debug logs** are used by application developers to help trace problems in programs so they can fix program code or program structures.

Several elements are related to working with event logs and are discussed in the next sections:

- Viewing log events
- Creating filters
- Maintaining event logs

Viewing Log Events

Log events are displayed in Event Viewer with an icon that indicates the seriousness of the event. An informational message, such as notification that a service has been started, is prefaced by a blue "i" displayed in a white comment circle; a warning, such as that a device driver failed to load, is depicted by a black "!" (exclamation point) that appears on a yellow caution symbol; and an error, such as a defective disk adapter, is indicated with a white exclamation point that appears inside a red circle (Figure 12-6 shows examples of the icons).

Each log displays descriptive information about individual events, such as the following information provided in the system log:

- Description of the event
- Name of the log in which the event is recorded
- Source of the event, which is the software application or hardware reporting it
- Event ID, so the event can be tracked if entered into a database (associated events might have the same number)
- Level of the event—information, warning, error
- User associated with the event, if any
- OpCode of the event
- Link for more information
- Date and time the event was logged
- Task category of the event, if one applies, such as a system event or logon event
- Keywords associated with the event
- Name of the computer on which the event occurred

Event Viewer can be opened from Server Manager, the Windows Administrative Tools folder from the Start button, as an MMC snap-in, from the Computer Management tool, and by right-clicking Start and clicking Event Viewer. Event Viewer contains options to view all events or to set a filter so only certain events are viewed, such as error events.

To view the contents of a log, click that log in the tree under Event Viewer. To view the detailed information about an event, double-click the event (see Figure 12-7). Read the description of the event for more information.

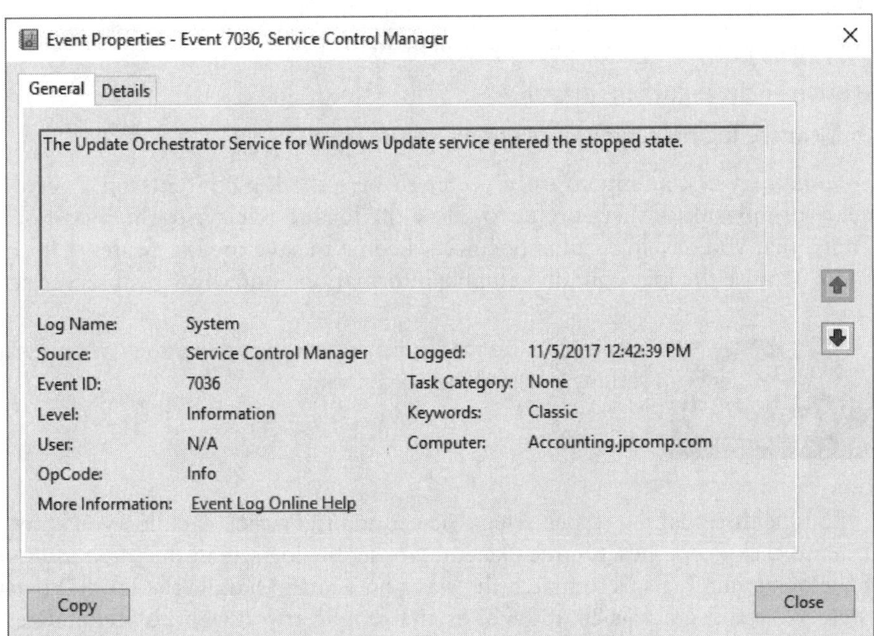

Figure 12-7 Viewing an event

The event logs are a good source of information to help you troubleshoot a software or hardware problem. For example, if Windows Server 2016 crashes unexpectedly, reboot and look at the logs as a first step. A memory allocation or disk problem can be found quickly through the help of the system log. If a software application hangs, check the application log for information.

Using the Event Viewer Filter Option

All of the event logs in Event Viewer have a filter option to help you quickly locate a problem. For example, you can set up a filter to show only events associated with a particular user or only events that occurred on the previous afternoon. The events can be filtered on the basis of the following criteria:

- When the event was logged, such as in the last 7 days
- Event level, such as information, warning, error, critical, and verbose
- By log, such as the system or security log
- By source of the event, such as a particular service or software component
- Task category of the event, such as a security change
- Keywords, such as Audit Failure and Audit Success
- User associated with the event
- Computer associated with the event
- Date and time ranges

Maintaining Event Logs

The event logs quickly fill with information, and you should establish from the beginning how you want the logs maintained. Logs can be maintained using several methods, as follows:

- Size each log to prevent it from filling too quickly.
- Overwrite the oldest events when the log is full.
- Archive the log when it is full.
- Clear the log manually (does not overwrite events).

Some network administrators prefer to save the log contents on a regular basis, such as weekly or monthly. Others prefer to allow the logs to overwrite the oldest events. It is recommended that you develop a maintenance schedule to save the log contents for a designated time period, because the logs contain valuable information about historical server activity.

Some organizations print certain logs daily, such as the system and security logs, and then clear them.

To tune the event logs, open Event Viewer and right-click each log you want to tune, one at a time, and click Properties. On the General tab, set the log size in the *Maximum log size (KB)* box. Set the maximum log size to match the way you want to handle the logs. The default size for the System log, for instance, is 20,480 KB. As an example, if you want to accumulate 2 weeks of information, set the size to enable that much information to be recorded, such as 24,000 KB. You will need to test this setting for a few weeks to make sure that the size you set is adequate. A common way to make sure that an event log is never completely filled is to use one of these options: *Overwrite events as needed (oldest events first)* or *Archive the log when full, do not overwrite events*.

If the server is a busy domain controller on which auditing is enabled, even a large-sized security log might contain only enough space to record a few hours of audited events. In this situation, besides setting a large log size, consider auditing only what is necessary or regularly viewing the log for the information you are seeking.

Options to save and clear the individual logs are also available. To save a log, right-click the log in the tree, click *Save All Events As*, enter a name for the log file, and click Save. You can save the log as one of the following kinds of files:

- *.evtx*—which is saved in event log format
- *.xml*—which is saved in XML format
- *.txt*—which is saved as a tab-delimited text file that can be imported into a spreadsheet
- *.csv*—which is saved as a comma-delimited text file that can be imported into a spreadsheet

When you are signed in as Administrator, the event log files are saved by default in the folder \Users\Administrator\AppData\Roaming\Microsoft\Windows\Libraries\Documents. To clear a log, right-click the log in the tree and click *Clear Log*. You'll see options to save the log before you clear it, to clear the log without first saving it, and to cancel.

Activity 12-4: Using Event Viewer

Time Required: Approximately 15 minutes
Objective: Use Event Viewer to view system log events.

Description: In this activity, you use Event Viewer to examine system log events, and you practice using a filter.

1. Open **Server Manager**, if it is not open.
2. Click **Tools** and click **Event Viewer**.
3. In Event Viewer, click the **right-pointing arrow** in front of **Windows Logs** (under Event Viewer (Local), refer to Figure 12-6).
   - What logs do you see?
4. Click each log to view the information displayed for it in the middle pane.
5. Click the **right-pointing arrow** in front of **Custom View** in the left pane.
6. Click **Administrative Events** under Custom View in the left pane. The middle pane shows a compilation of errors and warnings from all administrative logs. Administrative Events is a default filter created for viewing important events and can be a good place to start looking for a problem.
7. Click **System** in the left pane to view the system log contents (refer to Figure 12-6). In the middle pane, briefly scroll through the listed events.
   - Are any errors or warnings reported? If so, find out more about one or two of the errors or warnings by clicking them and viewing the details.
8. Click the **right-pointing arrow** in front of **Applications and Services Logs** in the left pane. Click each log to view its contents in the middle pane and click on one or two events for each log.

12

9. Click the **View** menu at the top of the window and click **Show Analytic and Debug Logs,** if there is no check mark already in front of this selection.
10. Right-click **System** under Windows Logs in the tree and click **Properties** (see Figure 12-8).

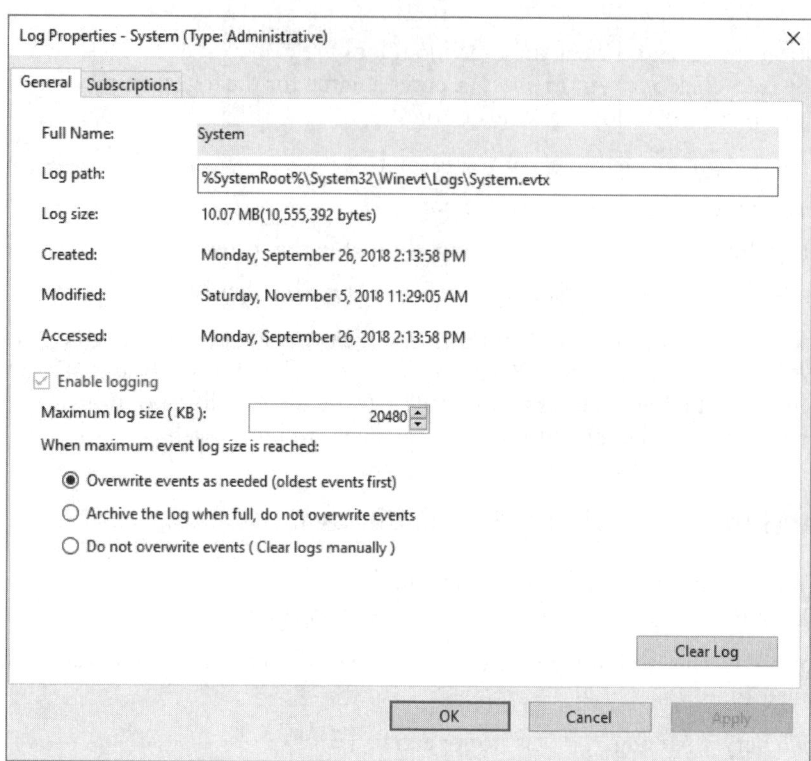

Figure 12-8 System log properties

11. In the Log Properties—System (Type: Administrative) dialog box, the default selection for managing the system log is to *Overwrite events as needed (oldest events first)*. Click **Archive the log when full, do not overwrite events.** This option enables you to keep historic log information, but you will need to periodically delete archived logs you do not need. Notice the location of the system log as shown in the *Log path* box. This is useful information so that you know where to maintain the logs.
12. Change the **Maximum log size (KB)** to **22016.**
13. Click **OK** in the Log Properties—System (Type: Administrative) dialog box.
14. Click **System** under Windows Logs in the tree, if it is not already selected.
15. In the right pane, click **Filter Current Log.**
16. Click the **down arrow** for **Event sources** to view the options you can use for filtering. If you were to select one or more of these options, only events for these sources would be displayed in the system log (but the events for other sources would still be tracked and saved so you could change the filter to view them later). Click the pointer in a blank area of the dialog box to close the listing.
17. Click the **down arrow** for **Keywords** and notice the keywords you can use to build a filter (events containing the keywords you select would be displayed). Click the pointer in a blank area of the dialog box to close the listing of keywords.
18. Assume that you only want to view the error messages in the system log. Click the box for **Error,** as shown in Figure 12-9.

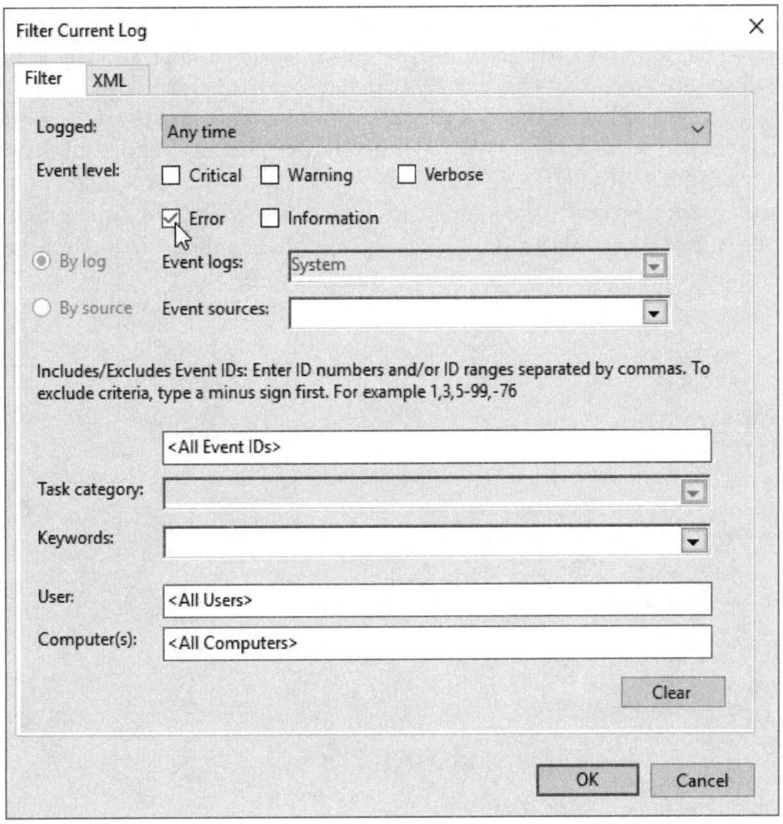

Figure 12-9 Creating a filter

19. Click **OK** in the Filter Current Log dialog box.
    - How does using the filter change what you view in the system log? Does this mean that the events you viewed before creating the filter are deleted, or simply not displayed?
20. Close Event Viewer.

Troubleshooting Connectivity

One area that server and network administrators often troubleshoot is TCP/IP connectivity. For instance, one problem is the use of duplicate IP addresses. This can happen in situations where static IP addressing is used, with the network administrator or user typing in the IP address and subnet mask when the computer is set up. Alternatively, a user might decide to experiment with the NIC configuration and change the TCP/IP settings to those that conflict on the network or no longer work. If two computers are using the same IP address, one or both will not be able to connect to the network at the same time; or both are likely to experience unreliable communications such as sudden disconnections.

Both command-line tools and graphical tools are available for troubleshooting Windows Server 2016 connectivity. You learn about these tools in the next sections.

Command-Line Tools Windows server and workstation operating systems come with tools you can use to help test network connectivity. For example, you can test the IP address of a Windows computer (when you are at that computer), such as Windows Server 2016 or Windows 10, by opening the Windows PowerShell or the Command Prompt window and typing *ipconfig* to view a dialog box showing the adapter address (MAC or Ethernet), IP address, subnet mask, and other information for that computer (see Figure 12-10). If the server is using an IP address that is identical to the address used by another networked computer that is turned on, the subnet mask value is 0.0.0.0 when you run one of these utilities. Also, *ipconfig* shows when there are multiple network adapters in a computer and it can show when the media is disconnected.

Figure 12-10 Using *ipconfig* in Windows PowerShell

Another tool for testing TCP/IP connections is the *ping* utility. You can poll the presence of another TCP/IP computer from the Windows Server 2016 or Windows 10 Windows PowerShell or Command Prompt window by typing *ping* and the IP address or computer name of the other computer. Many server administrators use *ping* to quickly test the presence of a server or computer from their office when there are reports of connection problems to that computer. Pinging a server on a network in another state or remote location also enables you to quickly test if your Internet connectivity is accessible from your office workstation. Figure 12-11 illustrates the *ping* utility as used from Windows Server 2016.

The *ping* utility may be blocked by Windows Firewall. If this is the case on your server or workstation, configure the inbound and/or outbound rules in Windows Firewall to allow ICMPv4 and ICMPv6 (refer to Activity 10-17 in Chapter 10, Securing Windows Server 2016).

netstat is a utility available in Windows Server 2016, Windows 10, and other Windows operating systems and is a quick way to verify that a workstation or server has established a successful TCP/IP connection. This utility provides information about TCP and UDP connectivity. Sometimes a TCP/IP session to a server or other computer hangs. You can determine

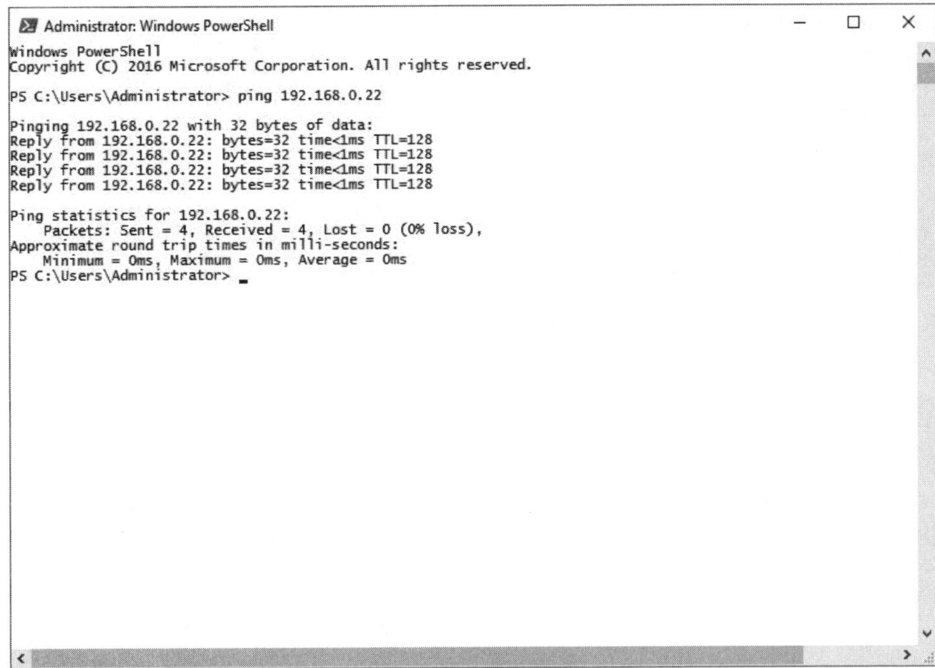

Figure 12-11 Using *ping* in Windows PowerShell

this by entering *netstat -e* from the Windows PowerShell or Command Prompt window at that computer (see Figure 12-12). Two columns of received and sent data are displayed. If these columns contain 0 bytes, it is likely the connection is hung. If the connection is hung, use the Network Connection window (in Windows Server 2016 and Windows 10), as described in the Graphical Tools section, to disable the computer connection and then to reconnect.

The *netstat -e* command also provides a quick indication of the number of transmission errors and discarded packets detected at that computer's NIC. For a more comprehensive listing of communication statistics, type *netstat -s*. Table 12-5 lists some useful diagnostics available from the Windows PowerShell and Command Prompt windows in Windows Server 2016, Windows 10, and other Windows versions.

Activity 12-5: Using TCP/IP Connectivity Troubleshooting Tools

Time Required: Approximately 10 minutes
Objective: Learn how to use *nbtstat* and *netstat*.

Description: In this activity, you have an opportunity to use *nbtstat* to view computers (NetBIOS names) on the network and then *netstat* to view all connections.

1. Click **Start** and click the **Windows PowerShell** tile; or click **Start**, click the **Windows PowerShell** folder, and click **Windows PowerShell**.
2. At the command prompt, enter **nbtstat -n** and press **Enter**.
   - What information is displayed?
3. Next, type **nbtstat -s** and press **Enter**.
   - What information is displayed by this command?

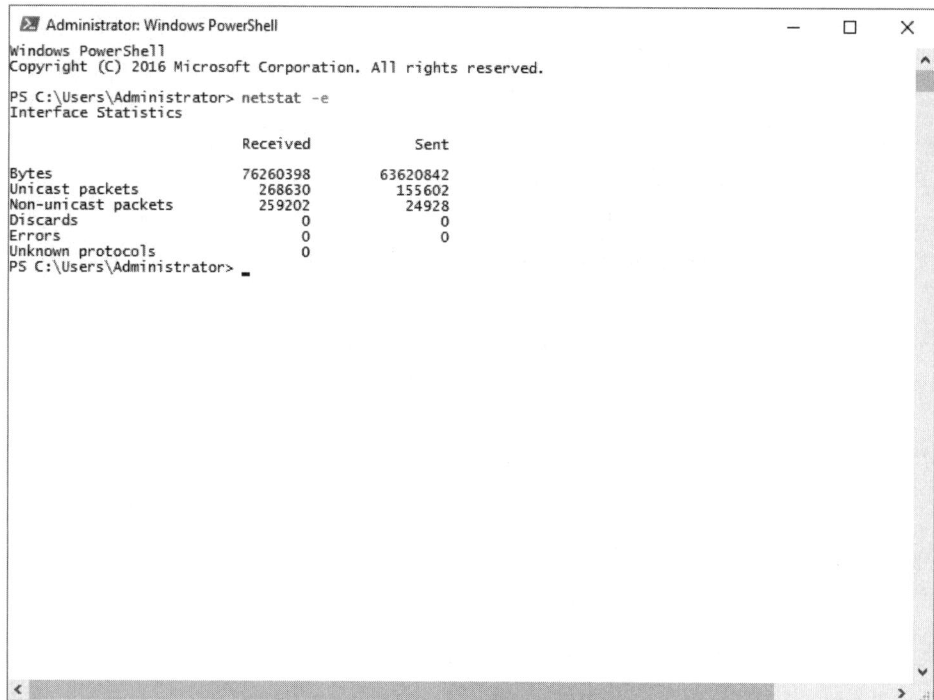
Administrator: Windows PowerShell

```
Windows PowerShell
Copyright (C) 2016 Microsoft Corporation. All rights reserved.

PS C:\Users\Administrator> netstat -e
Interface Statistics

                           Received            Sent

Bytes                      76260398        63620842
Unicast packets              268630          155602
Non-unicast packets          259202           24928
Discards                          0               0
Errors                            0               0
Unknown protocols                 0
PS C:\Users\Administrator> _
```

Figure 12-12 Using *netstat–e* in Windows PowerShell

Table 12-5 **Windows Server 2016 and Windows 10 diagnostic commands for TCP/IP connectivity**

Diagnostic command	Function
arp	Displays Address Resolution Protocol (ARP) information, such as using the *arp -a* command to view the arp cache information at a computer (see Chapter 1)
ipconfig	Displays information about the TCP/IP setup at that computer (enter *ipconfig /?* to view all of the options for this command)
nslookup	Shows information about DNS servers
pathping	Polls another TCP/IP node showing the path through routers along the way (including packet loss through routers; see Chapter 1)
ping	Polls another TCP/IP node to verify you can communicate with it (enter only *ping* to view all of the options for this command)
netstat (-a, -e, -n, -s)	Displays information about the TCP/IP session from that computer (enter *netstat /?* to view all of the options for this command); *netstat -a -n* can be helpful in looking for malware vulnerability by enabling you to view which ports are listening
nbtstat (-n)	Shows the server and domain NetBIOS names registered to the network (enter only *nbtstat* to view all of the options for this command)
tracert (server or host name)	Shows the number of hops and other routing information on the path to the specified server or host (enter only *tracert* to view all of the options for this command)

4. Now type **netstat -a | more** at the command prompt and press **Enter**. Tap the space bar to advance through additional screens of information. You can press **Ctrl + C** to quit without going through all lines of information.
   - What information is produced by this command?
5. Type **ipconfig** and press **Enter** to view the results of this command.
6. Find your IP address from the *ipconfig* results. Type **ping** plus your IP address and press **Enter**.
   - How can you use the *ipconfig* command to verify your own TCP/IP connection? What is the purpose of the *ping* command?
7. Close Windows PowerShell.

Graphical Tools

In addition to using commands from the Windows PowerShell or Command Prompt window, you can use a GUI (graphical user interface) tool for diagnosing and repairing network problems. For example, if you use the *netstat -e* command as described earlier and determine that a network connection is hung, use the Network Connections window to disable and then enable the connection. Disabling and enabling the connection resets the NIC and the TCP/IP connectivity to make sure you have a clean connection. (Rebooting produces the same result, but is more drastic and time consuming.) You can also use the Network Connection window to diagnose a network problem.

Activity 12-6: Disable and Enable a Network Connection and Then Diagnose a Connectivity Problem

Time Required: Approximately 10 minutes
Objective: Learn how to disable and enable a network connection to reset it and how to diagnose a connectivity problem.

12

Description: In this activity, you disable your own network connection and then enable the connection as practice in resetting a hung connection. You also practice using the diagnostic tool to troubleshoot a connection problem. Before starting, use Task Manager to make sure no one is signed in to the server you use for practice.

1. Right-click **Start** and click **Network Connections**.
2. Right-click the connection, such as **Ethernet**, and click **Disable** (see Figure 12-13).
3. Right-click the connection again and click **Enable**.
4. To practice using the connection diagnostic, right-click the network connection and click **Disable**.
5. Right-click the connection and click **Diagnose this connection**.
   - Briefly describe what happens.
6. Click **Close** in the Windows Network Diagnostics box.
7. Close the **Network Connections** window.

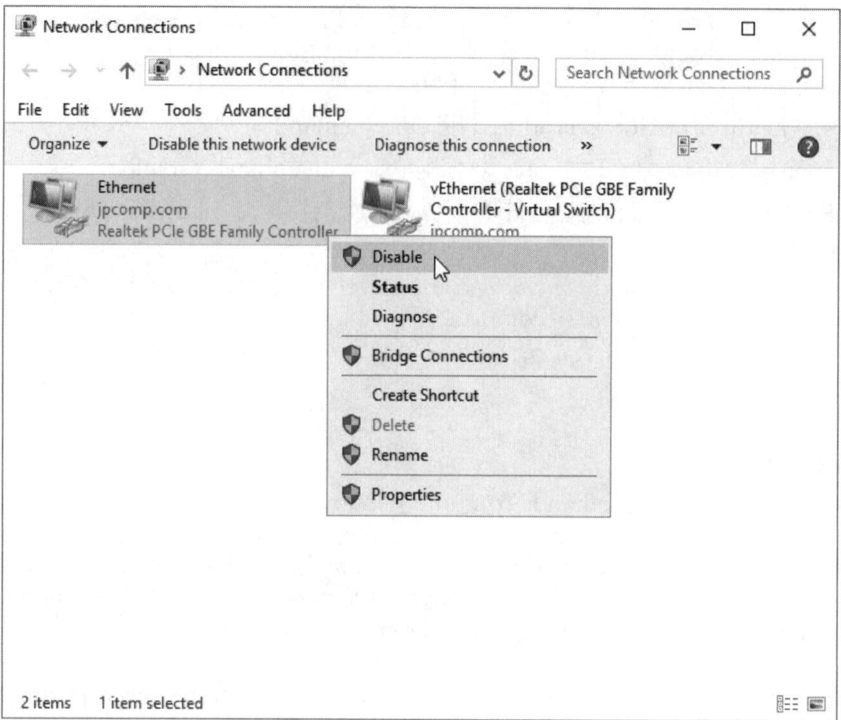

Figure 12-13 Disabling the network connection

Using the System Configuration Tool

Some server administrators like using the system configuration tool, *msconfig*, to help troubleshoot a problem. You can start *msconfig*, by typing this command in the Windows PowerShell or Command Prompt windows. Alternatively, right-click Start, click Run, enter *msconfig* in the Open box, and click OK.

The System Configuration window has five tabs that can be helpful for troubleshooting situations (see Figure 12-14):

- *General*—Enables you to perform one of three types of startups: normal, diagnostic, or selective. The diagnostic startup loads basic devices and services, so you can troubleshoot from a basic system. The selective startup enables you to select which elements to load at startup, including system services and startup programs, and whether to use the original boot configuration.
- *Boot*—Enables you to specify which items to use to boot: no GUI, create a boot log, base video (minimal VGA mode), and display OS boot information (displays driver names as they are loaded). You can also select to boot using a Safe boot with options such as a minimal boot (Safe Mode with no networking), alternate shell (command prompt in Safe Mode), boot into Active Directory repair, and boot while also enabling network connectivity (Safe Mode with networking). Also, there are advanced options you can configure for booting, including the number of processors used (on a multiprocessor system), the maximum amount of RAM to use for the OS, and other options.

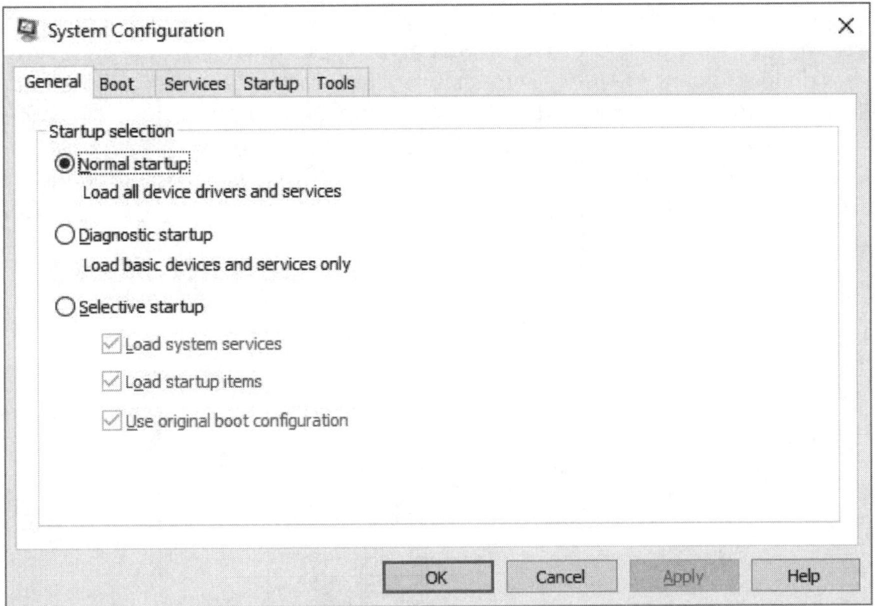

Figure 12-14 System Configuration window

- *Services*—Shows the installed services that start when the server starts and which ones are running, paused, or stopped. You can enable or disable any of the services. Use caution when disabling a service, because an application you need might not work when you reboot.
- *Startup*—This function is now deferred to Task Manager.
- *Tools*—Enables you to open a range of diagnostic tools, such as the Windows Troubleshooting Diagnostic, the Computer Management tool, Event Viewer, Performance Monitor, Resource Monitor, Command Prompt, Registry Editor, and others. To open a tool, select it from the list and click Launch.

When you configure the General, Boot, or Services tabs, it's important to remember that the actions you configure take effect when you restart the server. To discontinue such actions for the next restart, you will need to reconfigure them using the *msconfig* tool and then restart the computer.

Remotely Administering a Server

It is useful for server administrators to be able to remotely access a server in order to manage it or solve a problem. The remote access may be from another building, from home, or while traveling. The primary way to facilitate remote access is through using the Remote Desktop client capability.

You can use the Remote Desktop client to remotely access and manage the server, such as through a VPN server or Internet connection. Use the Remote Desktop client at your workstation to sign in to your regular account that you use for administration (see Chapter 9, Configuring Remote Access Services).

You can configure Remote Desktop using Server Manager or the System applet in Control Panel to access the System Properties dialog box, as shown in Figure 12-15. In the System Properties dialog box, click *Allow remote connections to this computer* and *Allow connections only from computers running Remote Desktop with Network Level Authentication (recommended)*. As you learned in Chapter 9, Network Level Authentication (NLA) is designed to discourage man-in-the-middle attacks and is supported by Windows Server 2016, as well as Windows 7 through Windows 10.

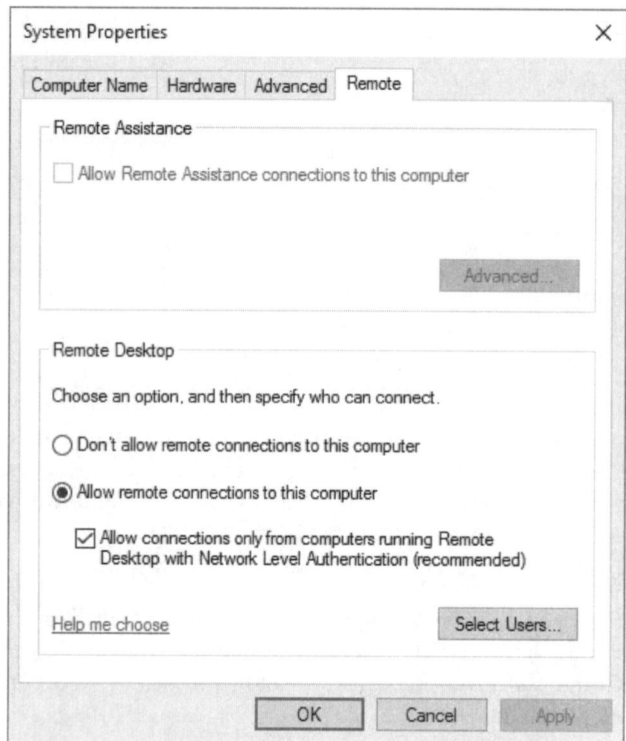

Figure 12-15 System Properties dialog box

Also, make sure that you have configured a strong password for the account from which you perform administration. As a review, Microsoft defines the following characteristics of a strong password:

- Contains seven or more characters (eight or more is better)
- Does not reflect qualities about you that others might guess, such as your name, information about your family, or the name of your organization
- Is not a word that could be found in a dictionary
- Is changed at regular intervals without repeating a previously used password
- Contains a combination of upper- and lowercase characters, numbers, and symbols

Activity 12-7: Configuring to Enable Remote Access Through Remote Desktop

Time Required: Approximately 10 minutes

Objective: Enable access to Windows Server 2016 through Remote Desktop.

Description: In this activity, you configure Windows Server 2016 to be accessed from Windows workstations, such as Windows 10, through Remote Desktop and using NLA.

1. Open **Server Manager,** if it is not open.
2. In the left pane, click **Local Server.**
3. In the right pane, click the setting for Remote Desktop, such as **Disabled** (if it is enabled already, click **Enabled**).
4. In the System Properties dialog box with the Remote tab displayed, ensure that **Allow remote connections for this computer** is selected as well as **Allow connections only from computers running Remote Desktop with Network Level Authentication (recommended)**, if it is not already selected (refer to Figure 12-15).
5. Click **Select Users.**
6. Click **Add** in the Remote Desktop Users dialog box.
7. In the Select Users or Groups dialog box, click **Advanced.**
8. Click **Find Now.**
9. Click the **Administrator** account or the account you are using (or press and hold **Ctrl** and click all of the accounts to have access).
10. Click **OK.** (If you see an error box, click **Close.** This may be a programming error to be fixed in an update, but it is likely to still add the account or group you selected.)
11. Click **OK** again in the Select Users or Groups dialog box.
12. Click **OK** in the Remote Desktop Users dialog box
13. Click **OK** in the System Properties dialog box.
14. In the right pane of Server Manager, click the setting for Windows Firewall, which should be **Domain: On.**
15. Click **Allow an app or feature through Windows Firewall.**
16. Ensure the boxes are checked for **Remote Desktop** and for **Windows Remote Management** (including checks in their Domain, Private, and Public boxes), if they are not checked (see Figure 12-16).
17. Click **OK** in Allowed apps window. Close Windows Firewall.

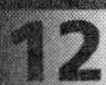

Remote Server Administration Tools

Remote Server Administration Tools (RSAT) enable you to manage multiple servers from one Windows Server 2016 server. These tools raise important possibilities. For example, you might have one server in a computer operations room that is used round-the-clock by server operators to manage other servers, so that the operators do not have to go to the console of a specific server. Another possibility is to have a Windows Server 2016 server in your office that you use as a personal workstation and from which to manage servers in a remote computer room; or you might use it to manage servers in different locations throughout a company. Remote Server Administration Tools can make you more productive by allowing you to remain in one location to administer remote servers.

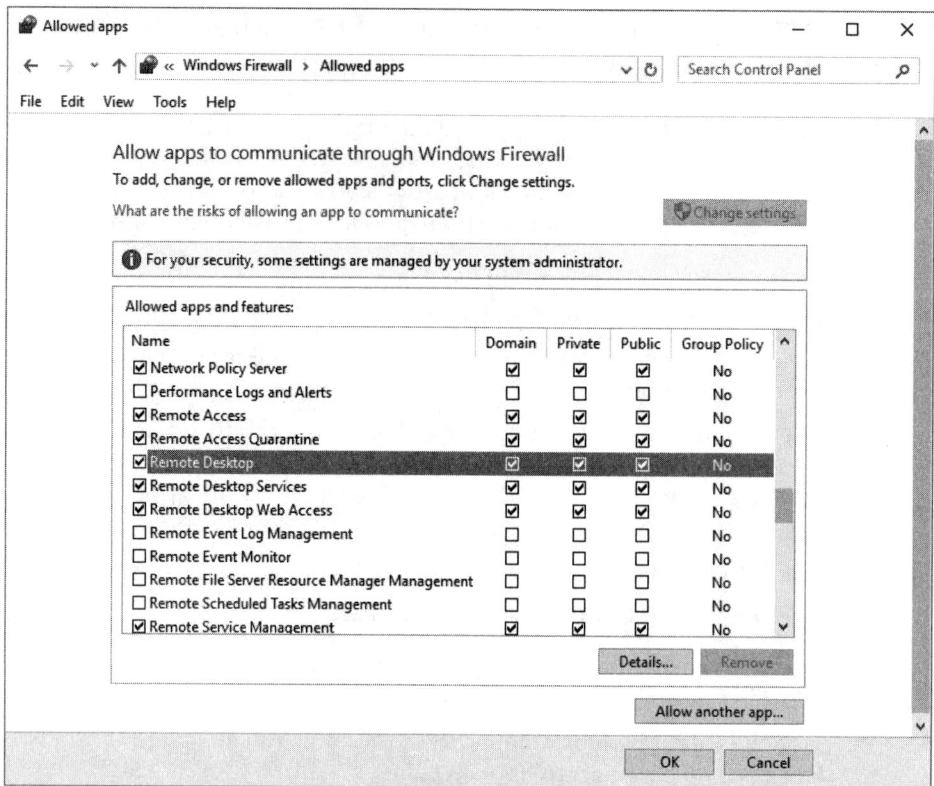

Figure 12-16 Configuring Windows Firewall

Managing a server from Remote Desktop takes the administration to the server and has the advantage of generally better performance for data-intensive administration activities, such as for using Event Viewer. Further, Remote Desktop can be better to use through a remote connection, such as from the administrator's home. RSAT can be more efficient when used in a LAN environment, such as from the server administrator's office connected to the LAN. Also, it can be more efficient for administrative tasks that are less data intensive, such as configuring a service in the Services window.

The Remote Server Administration Tools are offered through Server Manager. A subset of the Remote Server Administration Tools, called the Role Administration Tools, is typically automatically installed, but only for managing Active Directory DS, Active Directory LDS, and DNS Server (and other selected remote management tools that may be installed at the time you install the specific role). You can install more role management tools through Server Manager. You can additionally use Server Manager to install the Feature Administration Tools, which are an additional subset of the Remote Server Administration Tools. You'll also need to have the Web Services (IIS) role installed first.

Using the Remote Server Administration Tools, you can remotely manage any of Windows Server 2016, Windows Server 2012/R2, and Windows Server 2008/R2 servers. Because Windows Server 2016 is role-based, the Remote Server Administration Tools enable you to manage roles and features that are installed on a server. This includes the following role-based management tools:

- Active Directory Certificate Services Tools
- Active Directory Domain Services Tools

- Active Directory Lightweight Directory Services Tools
- Active Directory Rights Management Services Tools
- DHCP Server Tools
- DNS Server Tools
- FAX Server Tools
- File Services Tools
- Hyper-V Management Tools
- Network Controller Management Tools
- Network Policy and Access Services Tools
- Print and Document Services Tools
- Remote Access Management Tools
- Remote Desktop Services Tools
- Volume Activation Tools
- Windows Deployment Services Tools
- Windows Server Host Guardian Service Tools

Most Windows Server 2016 servers also have a combination of features installed as well as roles. To accommodate remote administration of features, the Remote Server Administration Tools also include the following tool sets, when the Feature Administration Tools subset is installed:

- BitLocker Drive Encryption Tools
- BITS Server Extensions Tools
- Failover Clustering Tools
- IP Address Management (IPAM) Client
- Network Load Balancing Tools
- Shielded VM Tools
- SMTP Server Tools
- Storage Replica Management Tools
- WINS Server Tools

To use these feature-based tools, you first need to use Server Manager to install the Feature Administration subset of RSAT and select the specific tools to install. You can install additional tools at any time through Server Manager.

In addition to all of these tools, you can use other management tools remotely. For example, you can use Event Viewer to view logs on a remote server. Or, you can use Performance Monitor to monitor a remote server.

If a tool that you want is not at your disposal, because it is not installed, you can use the following general steps to load it (the Web Services (IIS) role should be installed first):

1. Open Server Manager, if it is not open.
2. Click Manage.
3. Click Add Roles and Features.
4. Click Next, if you see the Before you begin window.

5. Ensure that Role-based or feature-based installation is selected in the Select installation type window and click Next.
6. Be sure your server is selected and click Next in the Select destination server window.
7. Click Next in the Select server roles window.
8. Click the right-pointing arrow in front of Remote Server Administration Tools (*x* of 42 installed)
9. If you want to use Feature Administration tools click its box (and click Add Features, if you see there are additional Web Services (IIS) tools to add) and click its right-pointing arrow to select the specific tools to install.
10. Click the right-pointing arrow in front of Role Administration Tools (*x* of 27 installed) as in Figure 12-17. Select the boxes for any of these tools you wish to install (if they are not already installed). You may need to click Add Features, if you see there are additional Web Services (IIS) tools to add.

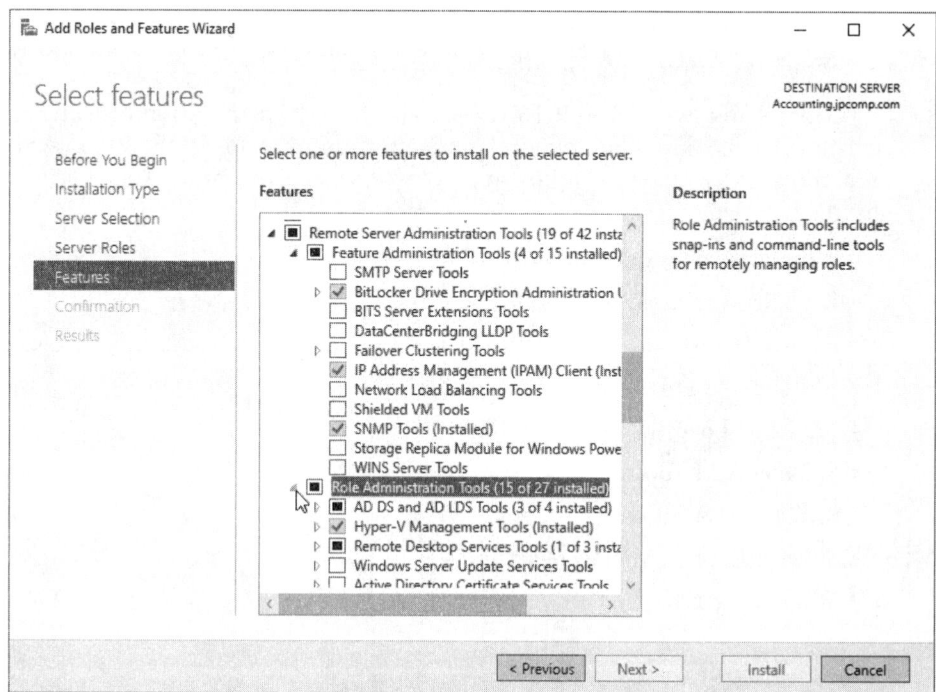

Figure 12-17 Installing Feature Administration Tools and Role Administration Tools

11. Click Next in the Select features window.
12. Click Install and then click Close

In general, when you install a role, such as DHCP Server, or certain features, such as SNMP, and you select to Add Features in the Add Roles and Features Wizard, the appropriate Remote Server Administration Tools are installed along with that role or feature.

With the Remote Server Administration Tools installed, managing remote services is relatively transparent. All you have to do is to open the management tool you need to use and indicate that you want to connect to a specific remote Windows Server 2016 (or other Windows server).

Activity 12-8: Using the Remote Server Administration Tools

Time Required: Approximately 10 minutes
Objective: Learn how to use the Remote Server Administration Tools capability.

Description: Many of the MMC snap-ins can be implemented using the Remote Server Administration Tools capability. In this activity, you learn how to use the remote administration capability via two sample snap-ins, the DNS and the Performance Monitor MMC snap-ins. It is not necessary to have another server to remotely access, because you'll simply learn how to use the remote access capability.

1. Right-click **Start** and click **Run.**
2. Type **mmc** in the Open text box and click **OK.**
3. Click the **File** menu and click **Add/Remove Snap-in.**
4. In the Add or Remove Snap-ins dialog box, click **DNS** and click the **Add** button.
5. Click **Performance Monitor** and click **Add.**
6. Click **OK** in the Add or Remove Snap-ins dialog box.
7. In the Console1—[Console Root] window, click **DNS** in the tree.
8. Click the **Action** menu and click **Connect to DNS Server.**
9. You see the Connect to DNS Server dialog box (see Figure 12-18). To connect to another server that offers DNS services, you would click the option button for *The following computer* and then enter the name of the server on which to use the DNS management tool. In this case, the Connect to DNS Server dialog box represents the implementation of the Remote Server Administration Tool, DNS Server Tools (which is transparent other than using this dialog box to remotely connect). Click **Cancel.**

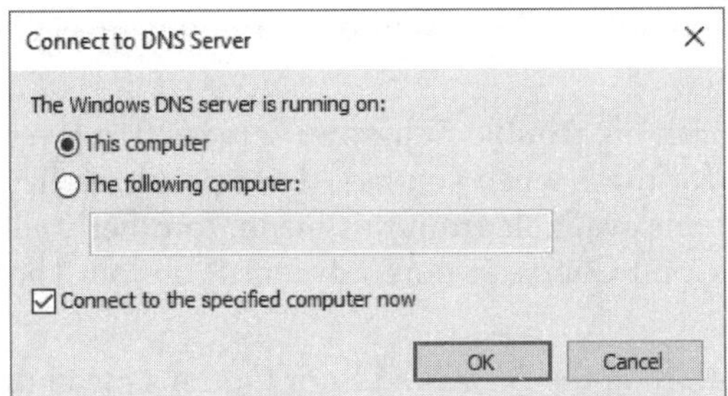

Figure 12-18 Connect to DNS server dialog box

10. Another way to remotely connect to a server to use the DNS Server Tools is to use the right pane. In the right pane, click **More Actions** under DNS and click **Connect to DNS Server.**
11. When you see the Connect to DNS Server dialog box, click **Cancel.**
12. Click **Performance (Local)** in the tree.
13. Click the **Action** menu and click **Connect to another computer.**

14. You see the Select Computer dialog box (see Figure 12-19). In this dialog box you can select to connect to the local computer or to a remote computer. To connect to a remote computer, you can type its name in the box or use the Browse button to find and select the local computer on the network.

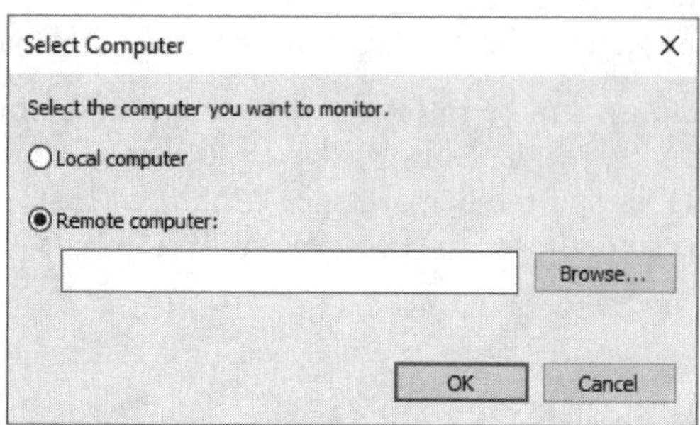

Figure 12-19 Select Computer dialog box

15. Click **Cancel** in the Select Computer dialog box.
16. Click **More Actions** in the right pane and click **Connect to another computer** to view another way to open the Select Computer dialog box.
17. Click **Cancel** in the Select Computer dialog box.
18. Close the Console1 – [Console Root] window.
19. Click **No** so that the console settings are not saved.

Chapter Summary

- Before problems occur, develop a problem-solving strategy that includes understanding your server and network, training users to help, step-by-step problem solving, and tracking problems.
- A server that won't boot can mean big trouble. Windows Server 2016 gives you the Advanced Boot Options menu for times when you have boot problems. The Safe Mode is one of the most recognized options available from this menu. Another well-known option is to boot using the Last Known Good Configuration (advanced) option. These are just a few of the options available.
- The Repair Your Computer option on the Advanced Boot Options menu or using the same option from the Windows Server 2016 installation DVD offers tools to recover a system, or work with a system that won't boot.
- Regularly perform an image backup, which includes system state data, so that you can fully recover a system that has failed.
- Event Viewer is a storehouse of logs from which you can monitor a system and diagnose problems. The three main categories of logs are Windows logs, applications and services logs, and Microsoft logs.

- Regularly use Event Viewer to monitor the contents of logs. Also, learn to maintain the logs and to set filters to make the information in logs more useful for specific situations.
- Windows Server 2016 contains command-line and graphical tools for troubleshooting network connectivity problems. Some command-line tools, such as *ping*, enable you to test the connectivity of remote computers as well as the local computer. The GUI tools can analyze a connection and give you a short diagnostic report with suggestions for fixing a problem.
- Windows Server offers Remote Server Administration Tools that enable you to manage a server remotely. You can install these through Server Manager.
- You can use the Remote Desktop client capability, such as from Windows 10, to remotely manage a Windows Server 2016 server. MMCs can also be used to remotely manage a server.

Key Terms

admin log A type of event log that gives the system administrator information about a specific problem and its causes, and might also suggest how to solve the problem.

analytic log An event log often used by application and system programmers to help analyze how specific programs are running and to identify problems with those programs.

application log An event log that records information about how software applications are performing.

debug log An event log used by application developers to help trace problems in programs so they can fix program code or program structures.

event logs Logs that you can view through Event Viewer that record information about server events, such as errors, warnings, or informational events.

forwarded events log Contains events recorded by remote computers and forwarded to one computer, which is called the collector computer.

help desk system Application software designed to maintain information on computer systems, user questions, problem solutions, and other information that members of an organization can reference.

operational log A type of event log that tracks occurrences of specific operations, such as when a disk drive is added.

Safe Mode A boot mode that enables Windows Server 2016 to be booted using the most generic default settings, such as for the display, disk drives, and pointing device—and only those services needed to boot a basic configuration.

security log An event log that records access and security information about logon accesses, file, folder, and system policy changes.

setup log An event log that contains a record of installation events, such as installing a role or feature through Server Manager.

system log An event log that records information about system-related events such as hardware errors, driver problems, and hard drive errors.

system state data Operating system and boot files, plus extra components and information that reflect the currently configured state of the server, depending on what features are installed. The system state data can be backed up using the Windows Server Backup tool.

SYSVOL A shared folder set up when Active Directory is installed that contains scripts, Group Policy Objects (GPOs), and software distribution files, several of which are needed for domain access. SYSVOL folders are replicated among DCs.

Review Questions

1. Your server has some damaged disk areas and won't boot or run *chkdsk* automatically when you try to boot. Which of the following options should you try to fix the disk?
   a. Boot from the BIOS boot mode and run the analyze disk option in the BIOS.
   b. Boot from a Windows 10 DVD boot disc and run *diskpart*.
   c. Each Windows Server 2016 drive has a boot sector. Change the BIOS to boot from the boot sector of a different drive.
   d. Boot from a Windows Server 2016 installation DVD and access the command prompt to run *chkdsk*.
2. Which of the following options can be found on the Advanced Boot Options menu? (Choose all that apply.)
   a. Partition Table Repair
   b. Safe Mode with Networking
   c. Disable Driver Signature Enforcement
   d. Repair Your Computer
3. What keyboard key or key combination enables you to boot into the Advanced Boot Options menu when initially booting Windows Server 2016?
   a. F2
   b. F8
   c. Ctrl+Alt
   d. Shift+Esc
4. Name three problem-solving strategies for addressing a problem with Windows Server 2016.
5. The system log contains hundreds of entries. However, you only want to track events that have happened in the last 24 hours. Which of the following can you use?
   a. Set up a filter.
   b. Set up a trap.
   c. Turn off recording of all other events related to other user accounts.
   d. View the log using Reliability Monitor.
6. Name five elements that compose system state data.
7. After you boot a server, you see a message that SYSVOL may be damaged. What tool can you use to try to repair the damage?
   a. *nbtstat -S*
   b. *chkdsk /sectors*
   c. Directory Services Restore Mode on the Advanced Boot Options menu
   d. SYSVOL option in Replication Services management tool
8. Name two options that are available when you boot into the repair mode from the Windows Server 2016 installation DVD.
9. Which of the following might be part of your problem-solving strategy? (Choose all that apply.)
   a. Regularly check the logs.
   b. Reboot the server once or twice a day to prevent problems and reset all registers.
   c. Use the Computer Management tool to periodically stop and restart the Workstation, Server, and Logon services throughout the day.
   d. Look for the simple solutions first.

10. What information are you likely to find in the security log?
11. Your Windows Server 2016 server is having trouble booting, and you suspect that it is related to a driver or service that is not properly starting. How can you track each of the startup actions of the server so that you can later go back and review each one for problems?
    a. Select the Debugging Mode from the Advanced Boot Options menu options when you boot.
    b. Enable Boot Logging as a Group Policy and examine the file boot.log after the system is rebooted.
    c. Select Enable Boot Logging from the Advanced Boot Options menu options when you boot.
    d. Configure driver signing to be in the verbose mode.
12. Your company's server won't boot. The Management Council just completed the 5-year strategic plan and placed the only copy on the server before it crashed. Which of the following can you do to try and retrieve the file containing the plan?
    a. Boot into Safe Mode to obtain a copy of the plan from the application log.
    b. Boot into Disk Mode and perform a disk dump onto a DVD.
    c. Use the Recovery repair option to recover the file onto a flash drive.
    d. Boot into the command line and use the *copy* command to copy the file off of the disk.
13. How can you manually empty the contents of an event log?
    a. Use the Event Log applet in Control Panel.
    b. In the Event Log window, right-click the log and click Clear Log.
    c. In the Event Log window, click File, select the log, and click Delete.
    d. As a security measure, event logs cannot be emptied other than by first setting an event log maintenance Group Policy.

14. Which of the following are components of a strong password? (Choose all that apply.)
    a. Does not contain a word that can be found in a dictionary.
    b. Contains no personal information about you, your family, or business that others might guess.
    c. Must be 25 characters or more.
    d. Contains numbers, symbols, and upper- and lowercase characters.
15. When you use Remote Desktop client from Windows 10 to remotely access Windows Server 2016, plan to use it with ________ Authentication for stronger security.
16. Which of the following are Feature Administration Tools that can be installed as a part of Remote Server Administration Tools? (Choose all that apply.)
    a. BitLocker Drive and Encryption Tools
    b. Network Load Balancing Tools
    c. Failover Clustering Tools
    d. Storage Replica Management Tools
17. Your server is not successfully using Windows Update to update the operating system when you try to do a manual update. It appears that it is connecting to the local network, but not to the Internet. Which of the following tools can you use to help diagnose the problem? (Choose all that apply.)
    a. Network Connection window
    b. *ping* command
    c. *net test* command
    d. *nbtest* command

18. You want to set up a command center for the server operators in your company so they can use one Windows Server 2016 server to monitor the other 28 servers in the operations room and spread throughout the company. Which of the following features should you make sure is installed at the command center server?
    a. Universal Server Manager tool
    b. Active Directory Computers tool
    c. Remote Server Administration Tools
    d. Remote Console Tool
19. What information is provided by the *netstat* command, including information about two protocols that work alongside IP?
20. Users report that they cannot sign in to a server because they are getting messages about a Kerberos error. Which of the following can best help you track down the problem?
    a. *tracert* command-line command
    b. DFS Replication log
    c. *ping* command-line command
    d. Key Management Service log

Case Projects

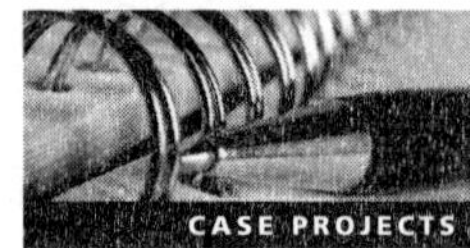

Chelos is a chain of popular Mexican food restaurants throughout the southwestern United States. The restaurant headquarters is in Dallas. The Chelos national headquarters is in one multistory building that houses the management offices and the Chelos Kitchens. The management offices consist of the Marketing and Franchising, Accounting, Operations, and IT departments. The Chelos Kitchens unit produces a variety of prepackaged foods used by all Chelos restaurants.

Each department and the Chelos Kitchens unit have Windows Server 2016 servers at their locations. An additional small computer operations center contains the web, email, DNS, DHCP, and master Active Directory servers. All servers in the company have recently been put under the control of a small team of server operators who work in two shifts. The company has a total of 22 Windows Server 2012 and 2016 servers.

The two system programmers who set up the servers and were responsible for training the server operators have just left to start their own business. Chelos has hired two new system programmers, but they are new to Windows Server 2016, although they have some experience with Windows Server 2012.

The IT director has retained you through Aspen Consulting to assist with the training of the system programmers and to help develop troubleshooting expertise among the system programmers and server operators. Network problems and problems with hardware failures that have delayed operations have been reported, and Chelos wants to improve the server support so that problems are solved more quickly.

Case Project 12-1: Developing a Troubleshooting Strategy

When you arrive at Chelos, your first analysis of their situation is that very few of the IT staff have much troubleshooting expertise. Most of the troubleshooting done in the past was by the two system programmers who have moved on. You decide to develop a written troubleshooting strategy customized for Chelos that can be used by the new system programmers and the server operators. Create a strategy that can be presented either in a document, a slide presentation, or both.

Case Project 12-2: Troubleshooting a Hardware Crash

While you are at the Chelos headquarters, one of the servers suddenly crashes with what appears to be a disk failure. Because you are working on the problem, you also see this as an opportunity to help train the system programmers and server operators currently on duty. Address the following questions as you are working with these staff members:

- Where would you look first for a clue about what happened?
- How would you explain the steps and tools you would use in handling the crash?
- If it is truly a system disk crash, how can you restore the system?

Case Project 12-3: Using Event Viewer

The system programmers and server operators are not very familiar with using Event Viewer to be proactive to prevent problems or even for using it to diagnose a problem. They ask you to develop a report or slide show that addresses the following:

- Different ways to open Event Viewer
- Key Windows logs to check in Event Viewer
- The kinds of information available in Event Viewer
- How to quickly view only specific events
- Developing a regular schedule of checking logs

Case Project 12-4: Working with a Connectivity Problem

As you are discussing event logs with one of the server operators, several calls come in that a server in the Marketing Department cannot be contacted over the network. When the server operator calls someone in the Marketing Department, it is reported that the server seems to be up and running normally but not accessible through the network. What tools can you use to immediately test connectivity from the server operator's location several floors below the Marketing Department? If the server operator decides she has to go to the server to fix it, what command-line and GUI tools can she run to diagnose possible connection problems?

Case Project 12-5: Server Management

It is inconvenient and time consuming for the server operators to go all over the building to manage the servers in each department. What is your recommendation to them for reducing the trips they have to make to the servers spread throughout the building?

appendix A

Windows Server 2016 Virtualization and Hyper-V

It's hard to pick up a computer publication or go to a computing news website without seeing many stories about virtualization. So what is virtualization? This appendix gives you a short background of virtualization and introduces Microsoft Hyper-V virtualization software that is included with the principal Windows Server 2016 editions.

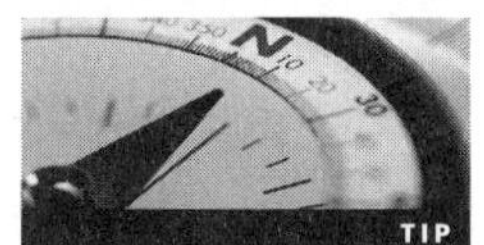

Client Hyper-V is also included with Windows 10 Professional and Enterprise and can be used with Windows 8.1 Professional and above. You learn how to enable it in the section, Installing Client Hyper-V in Windows 8.1 or Windows 10. If you have these operating systems on your computer, you can use Client Hyper-V to create a virtual machine on which to run Windows Server 2016 for the activities in this book.

What Is Virtualization?

Virtualization involves turning a single computing platform, such as an operating system or computer, into two or more virtual computing platforms. The popular application of this is to use virtualization to run multiple operating systems from a single physical computer running one native operating system. Instead of one operating system running on a single computer, two, three, or more operating systems can be running on one physical computer. For example, if three operating systems are running on one physical computer, this means there are three virtual machines running inside one virtual server. The virtual server software is an application or server role running on one native (non-virtual) machine.

Several recognized forms of virtualization include:

- *Server virtualization*—Running multiple server operating systems on a single server computer. For instance, this form of virtualization might include having two Windows Server 2016 operating systems and one Linux operating system on one server. Microsoft Hyper-V is an example of server virtualization.

As you learned in Chapter 1, Introduction to Windows Server 2016, a virtual server is a computer running virtual server software that enables configuring multiple virtual machines, each running its own operating system. A virtual machine is an instance of a discrete operating system running within virtual server software on one computer. Multiple virtual machines can run within the virtual server software on one computer.

- *Workstation or PC virtualization*—Running multiple workstation operating systems, such as Windows 8.1, Windows 10, and Linux, on one computer. Microsoft Client Hyper-V running on Windows 10 Professional is one example of this approach. However, Client Hyper-V also enables you to create virtual machines for Windows Server systems as well as Windows workstation operating systems.
- *Application virtualization*—Running single applications in their own virtual machine environments. On an operating system, this means running applications to have their own file system and Registry. For example, if you are converting to a new accounting system, you might have the old accounting software in one virtualized application environment and the new accounting software in another virtualized application environment on the same physical computer. The old accounting software is used until the new software system is fully tested and operational. Application virtualization is now available in Windows Server 2016 through containers, such as through Hyper-V containers.
- *Storage virtualization*—Setting up multiple networked disk storage units to appear as one unit, such as in Storage Area Networks (SAN).
- *Hardware or CPU virtualization*—Using the CPU to perform virtualization tasks by having virtualization processes work inside a specially designed CPU. AMD implements this through AMD-V technology in some of its CPUs, and Intel does the same through Intel Virtualization Technology (VT) in some CPUs.
- *Network virtualization*—Dividing a single network into multiple channels or bandwidths so that the network appears as multiple networks.

Of these options, server virtualization has aroused significant interest among those who work with server operating systems and is the focus of Microsoft Hyper-V. In the next section, you learn why server virtualization has sparked so much interest.

Advantages of Virtual Servers

Server virtualization offers several advantages, including the following:

- Enables server consolidation
- Uses hardware effectively
- Provides hardware independence
- Enables using different operating systems on one computer
- Provides effective development environments
- Offers a foundation for cloud computing
- Offers business advantages

Each of these advantages is discussed in the following sections.

Ability to Consolidate Servers

One of the reasons why virtual servers are appealing is that they offer the ability to reduce the number of servers needed to run a business. Over time, businesses and organizations continue to add servers for new functions. For example, this can include adding a web server (or servers), additional DNS servers, and servers for new databases and software. The sprawl of servers has become known as a server farm, because servers seem to sprout up everywhere.

Server proliferation requires more work in maintaining servers, resulting in the need to hire additional people to manage them. Locating space to store the servers is also a problem. As the number of servers grows, it doesn't take long until space runs out in an operations center or server room; it becomes necessary to invest in more space. Additional expenses are incurred for physical security, air conditioning, and heating to keep the servers in a secure, controlled environment. Further, the cost of electricity is rising, and more server hardware translates into higher electric bills.

The use of virtual servers enables an organization to consolidate servers into fewer physical computers, generally cutting the number of computers by two-thirds or three-fourths. Server consolidation means that significant money can be saved on personnel, space, security, and electricity.

Uses Hardware Effectively

An organization might have a number of computers that are underutilized. For example, many individual file servers, DNS servers, DHCP servers, and other servers barely take advantage of the full power of their hardware. Making these systems virtual servers can save money on hardware and hardware maintenance, because hardware can be used to capacity.

Enables Hardware Independence

The specific hardware used to house virtual machines in one virtual server is less important, because the operating system runs inside the virtual machine. The hardware is primarily important to the virtual server host operating system. For example, if the host is Windows Server 2016 in the Hyper-V role, then the computer must be compatible with Windows Server 2016 and Hyper-V. The server operating systems running inside Hyper-V are not as affected by hardware compatibility, other than to make sure that sufficient RAM, disk space, and network connectivity are available. This also means that you can move a virtual server from one host computer to another without worrying about hardware compatibility.

Freedom from hardware compatibility issues has several advantages. One advantage is that it makes disaster recovery easier. If a computer operating as a virtual server host goes down at one site, such as due to a tornado or flood, the virtual machines that it hosts can be exported to other off-site host computers (such as through backups) with fewer hardware concerns. Your organization might even use off-site virtual machines as standby backup computers, so the organization has very little downtime when a disaster strikes.

Another advantage is that hardware upgrades are smoother. When you upgrade the hardware, such as for more processing power or disk space, it is easier to transfer a virtual server from one computer to another. The operating system in the virtual machine needs little or no reconfiguration.

Although virtual computing provides hardware independence, you still need to pay close attention to the hardware needed on a computer that hosts multiple virtual machines. The virtual machines on the host will share the same processor(s) used by the host. Make sure you outfit the host computer with one or more fast processors. Another important factor to consider is the RAM installed in the host. Calculate the RAM that you need for each virtual machine and for the host virtual server, and come up with the total amount of RAM—adding a little extra RAM to accommodate growth.

Ability to Use Multiple Operating Systems

Many organizations use a combination of operating systems, such as Windows Server 2012 R2, Windows Server 2016, and Linux. These organizations can reduce the number of servers they maintain by using virtual server systems that support the implementation of different operating systems on the same computer.

This is a major improvement from the days when you had to have certain hardware for each operating system, such as a specialized computer for a Linux-based web server and a different type of computer for Windows Server systems. Dedicated hardware often meant an organization had to have specialized staff to manage each type of system and its hardware. Also, each type of hardware required separate support agreements. All of this translated into higher expenses.

Provides Effective Development Environments

Many organizations develop their own software. Other organizations purchase software packages, but need to test those packages before bringing them into live production. In the past, organizations have purchased separate computers for software development and testing. Some organizations with limited budgets have even performed development on production computers, which is a risky approach.

Organizations that use a separate development server can spend considerable time adapting the development software to a new computer system. Using a virtual server as a development environment can ease the hassles of bringing new software live. Developing software on a virtual server presents few or no hardware considerations because you simply transfer the newly developed software to another virtual server. Further, before the software is brought into production, users can test it in a server environment that already looks similar or identical to the one they are accustomed to using. When the new software is brought into live production, users will need to make fewer adjustments.

Organizations that purchase software packages can use a virtual server to test the packages before bringing them into production. Users who help with the testing can do so in a safe environment and take their time to get used to the new software. Bringing the new software into production is simpler and cleaner, just as it is for organizations that develop their own software on a virtual server.

Offers a Foundation for Cloud Computing

Most implementations of cloud computing, including from Microsoft, are built on virtual servers and machines that offer the application and storage services that are the trademark of cloud computing. Virtual server technology enables the costs of cloud computing to be kept lower, because the outlay for machine resources is lower. If you store your personal or business files in the cloud or if you use a cloud-based application, then you are interacting with a virtual machine (as well as virtual storage) in the cloud to facilitate your computing.

Offers Business Advantages

To stay competitive and attractive to stockholders, businesses must always pay attention to the bottom line. Any business that requires multiple servers can typically save money by deploying virtual servers. You've already learned some of the ways virtual servers can save money, but it's important to reiterate that savings can come from:

- Lower hardware costs
- Paying lower utility bills, including costs for running computers, air conditioning, and heating
- Reduced staff costs

- Reduced costs for space
- Reduced software development costs
- Reduced software implementation costs
- Reduced costs for implementing systems on new hardware
- More disaster recovery options

Disadvantages of Virtualization

When an organization considers the advantages of virtualization, it is also important to be aware of the disadvantages. One disadvantage is that the server hardware can be a single point of failure. Plan to build in hardware fault tolerance and disaster recovery to reduce the impact of hardware failure. For example, consider purchasing server hardware that contains redundant power supplies, CPUs, memory, network interfaces, and RAID level 1 or level 5 disk storage fault tolerance or virtual storage. Another option is to have a backup server computer on hand in case the main one fails. As a disaster recovery step, the backup computer might already be set up with virtual machines to match those on the primary server; you can regularly back up data from the virtual machines on the primary server to those on the backup server. If the primary server goes down, the backup server can take over. For better disaster recovery, place the backup server computer in a different location from the primary server.

Another disadvantage of virtualization is that backing up all of the virtual machines on a single computer can be a much slower process than backing up a single server with a single operating system and no virtual machines.

Several Microsoft software partners offer backup software for virtual systems, including Acronis, Altaro, UltraBac, Veeam, and others.

Features of Hyper-V

Windows Server 2016 Hyper-V offers features to make this a strong virtual machine platform now and into the future. These features include the following:

- Ability to load 32-bit and 64-bit guest operating systems
- Option to load Windows Server, Windows workstation/client, and Linux operating systems on the same computer (See Tables A-1 and A-2)
- Enhanced access of the CPU, video, disk, removable storage, and networking capabilities of the host computer
- Ability to perform network load balancing through the use of its virtual switch capabilities, so the load can be spread equally among virtual servers
- Option to scale up to larger and faster hardware platforms and capabilities for implementing more virtual machines
- Option to migrate virtual machines to other Hyper-V virtual servers, including live migration
- Ability to resize a virtual disk
- Support for failover clustering
- Hyper-V Manager tool for installation and management of virtual machines

- Ability to take virtual machine snapshots of a particular virtual server state, so that you can quickly return to a prior working state if configuration changes create a problem or don't work (also important for creating backups that can return to a prior state)
- Designed so that third-party vendors can develop tools and specialized utilities for Hyper-V

Table A-1 Windows guest operating systems compatible with Hyper-V*

Guest operating system	Virtual processors upper limit	Server or workstation operating system
Windows Server 2016	64	Server
Windows Server 2012 or 2012 R2	64	Server
Windows Server 2008 R2 with Service Pack 1	64	Server
Windows Server 2008 with Service Pack 2	4	Server
Windows Home Server or Small Business Server 2011	2 to 4 depending on the edition	Server
Windows Server 2003 or 2003 R2 with Service Pack 2	2	Server
Windows 10	32	Workstation (all editions)
Windows 8 or 8.1	32	Workstation (all editions)
Windows 7	4	Workstation (Ultimate, Enterprise, or Professional Editions; 32- or 64-bit)
Windows Vista with Service Pack 2	2	Workstation (Business, Enterprise, and Ultimate Editions)
Windows XP with Service Pack 3 (32-bit) and Windows XP with Service Pack 2 (64-bit)	2	Workstation (Professional Edition)

*Applies to Windows Server 2016 Hyper-V and to Windows 8.1/10 Client Hyper-V

Table A-2 Linux guest operating system distributions compatible with Hyper-V**

Guest operating system	Version
Red Hat Enterprise Linux	5.5 and above
CentOS Linux (free distribution compatible with Red Hat Enterprise Linux)	5.5 and above
SUSE	11 and above
Ubuntu	12.04 and above
Debian	7.0 and above
FreeBSD	8.4 and above
Oracle	6.4 and above

**Applies to Windows Server 2016 Hyper-V and to Windows 8.1/10 Client Hyper-V

Other Windows and Linux operating systems may work as guest operating systems to some extent, but you may have to experiment with installation and functionality.

Windows Server 2016 adds several new features to Hyper-V that are attractive to server administrators. One feature is host resource protection. This feature ensures that a virtual machine does not use more host computer resources, such as memory, than are allocated to that virtual machine. If a virtual machine shows extra levels of activity, then the host computer can scale back the resources given to that virtual machine so that other functions on the host, such as running other virtual machines, are not degraded. Also in Windows Server 2016, Hyper-V now supports hot add and remove, which means that a virtual machine does not have to be shut down to add or remove a network adapter or memory. Additionally, more or less memory can be allocated from the host to a virtual machine without having to shut down that virtual machine.

Two other features new to Hyper-V in Windows Server 2016 are shielded virtual machines and containers. The ability to shield a virtual machine means that the data and the running state on the virtual machine can be encrypted. Shielding is used as a security measure so that it is more difficult for malware or even an inexperienced administrator to interfere with the smooth running of the shielded virtual machine.

Still another new addition is direct access to some hardware devices for faster performance. To take advantage of this capability, the virtual server's processor must have either Intel-based Extended Page Table (EPT) or AMD-based Nested Page Table (NPT), which are virtualization technologies for memory management of paging and page tables.

The introduction of containers to Hyper-V is the most heralded new feature. Containers enable an isolated application to run on a single computer system or virtual machine. Hyper-V containers are explained next.

Hyper-V Containers

A Hyper-V container offers an application its own environment in which to run. Each container runs in a dedicated virtual machine and the container provides a home to an application that is isolated from outside interference. Each container has its own kernel, which means the application housed in the container does not face competition for access to the kernel or kernel resources. The bottom line is that an application can run faster and more efficiently.

There are several different components of a Hyper-V container. First, there is the *host virtual machine* running in Hyper-V. Inside the virtual machine, there are layers needed to form the container. For instance, there is a *container operating system image* that provides the operating system to run in the virtual machine. Another component layer is a *container image* that houses the operating system and application(s). You might think of the container operating system image and the container image as outside and inside layers of a container. All container images are stored in a container registry and each container image is downloaded as needed. Finally, a docker file is accessed and installed at the beginning of the steps to create a container and is used to facilitate the creation of a container image.

Creating a container is a more complex undertaking than space allows for in this appendix. However, if you want to practice creating a container, visit the Microsoft Developers Network website at *msdn.microsoft.com/en-us/default.aspx* and search for Windows containers documentation or examples. The website will have the most current example steps and download files, such as docker file downloads and image downloads. You'll find these are compatible with your installation of Windows Server 2016 Standard or Datacenter Edition.

Requirements of Hyper-V

Hyper-V can be installed on a computer that matches the basic requirements for Windows Server 2016 systems (see Tables 1-1 and 1-2 in Chapter 1, Introduction to Windows Server 2016). Beyond this, the requirements are as follows (also applicable to Client Hyper-V in Windows 10 Professional and Enterprise):

- An ×64 computer (second-level address translation (SLAT) is required in the processor if you want to use Hyper-V virtualization elements, such as hypervisor which gives guest OSs a virtual operating environment)

- Data Execution Prevention (DEP) enabled (see Activity 3-6 in Chapter 3, Configuring the Windows Server 2016 Environment)
- A processor with AMD-V or Intel VT (hardware virtualization)
- At least 4 GB of RAM
- For Windows Server 2016, a clean installation for the edition that you use—not really required, but highly recommended by Microsoft

Installing Hyper-V in Windows Server 2016

In Windows Server 2016, Hyper-V is a role that you install through Server Manager. The general steps for installing Hyper-V are as follows:

1. Open Server Manager.
2. Click Manage and click Add Roles and Features.
3. If you see the Before you begin window, click Next.
4. Make sure Role-based or feature-based installation is selected in the Select installation type window and click Next.
5. Ensure your server is selected in the Select destination server window and click Next.
6. Click the box for Hyper-V in the Select server roles window.
7. Click Add Features in the Add Roles and Features Wizard.
8. Click Next in the Select server roles window.
9. Click Next in the Select features window.
10. Read the information window for Hyper-V (see Figure A-1) and click Next.

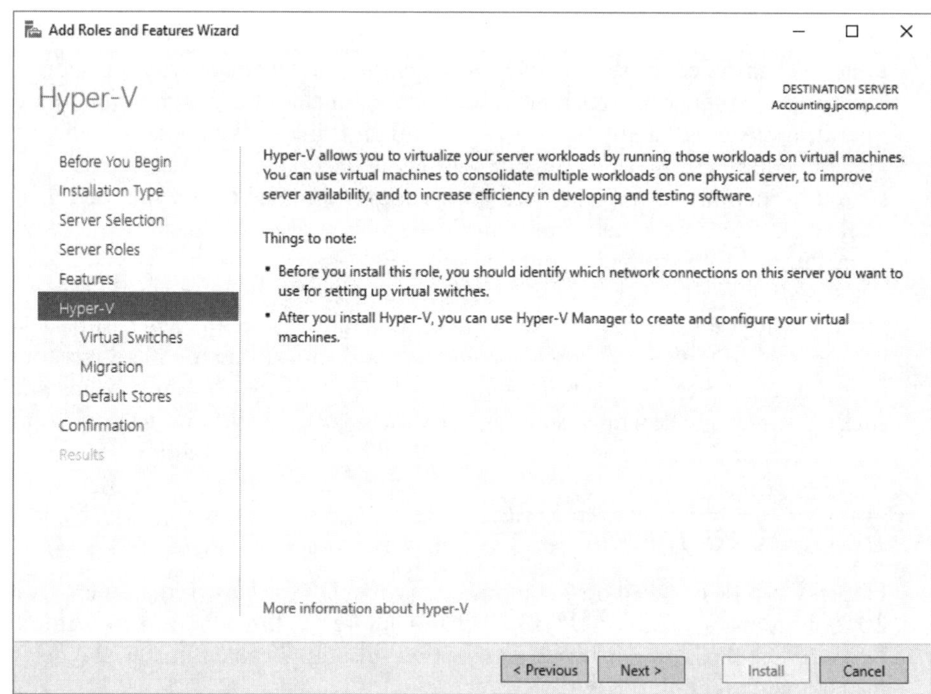

Figure A-1 Hyper-V information window

11. If you have already determined which NIC to use as a virtual switch, select it in the Network adapters box in the Create Virtual Switches window. Click Next.
12. In the Virtual Machine Migration window, you can select whether to allow the server to send and receive live migrations. Click Next after you have made your selection.
13. Use the Default Stores window to select the locations for storing virtual hard disk files and virtual machine configurations, or use the default locations as shown in Figure A-2. Click Next.

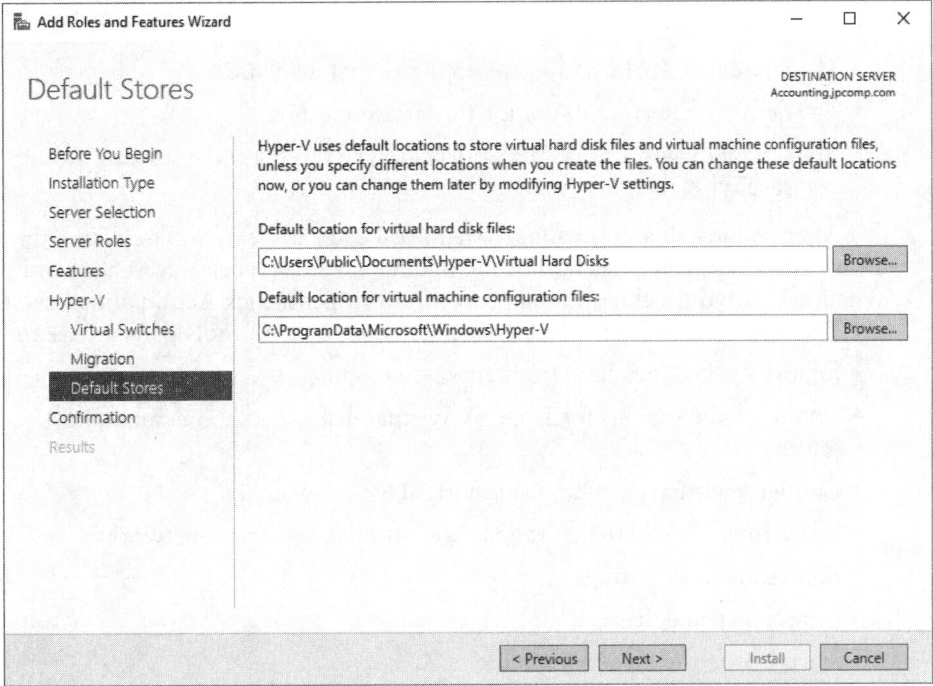

Figure A-2 Default Stores window

14. In the Confirm installation selections window, click Install.
15. Click Close.
16. Use Task Manager to make sure all users are signed out and then restart the server.

In Windows PowerShell, you can install the Hyper-V role and then restart the computer by using the command: Add-WindowsFeature Hyper-V – restart

Using Hyper-V Manager

After Hyper-V is installed, you can access the Hyper-V Manager tool from Server Manager, from the Windows Administrative Tools folder from the Start button, from the Start button menu, or as an MMC snap-in. With Hyper-V Manager you can:

- Install virtual machines
- Configure virtual machines

- Install guest operating systems
- Manage virtual machines, including starting and stopping them
- Manage network communications through virtual machines
- Troubleshoot virtual machines
- Remotely manage Hyper-V on earlier versions of Windows, such as Hyper-V in Windows Server 2012 or Windows Server 2012 R2. You can also manage Hyper-V running on Windows 8, 8.1, or 10. This capability is new to Windows Server 2016.

In Chapter 2, Installing Windows Server 2016, you learned how to install Windows Server 2016 as a virtual machine in Hyper-V by using Hyper-V Manager. When you create a virtual machine, you specify:

- The amount of RAM to allocate to the virtual machine
- The network interface to use for the virtual machine
- The virtual disk to use, such as a disk attached to the server or disk storage in a location you specify

After you install an operating system, you can start it by right-clicking the operating system in the Virtual Machines section of the middle pane of Hyper-V Manager and clicking Connect. When the Virtual Machine Connection window opens, click Action and click Start.

The right pane in Hyper-V Manager provides links to tools you can use to:

- Import a virtual machine from another computer
- Configure the settings for Hyper-V (virtual disks, virtual machines, keyboard, and other settings)
- Configure virtual switches using Virtual Switch Manger
- Use Virtual SAN Manager to manage virtual storage area networks
- Edit virtual disk settings
- Inspect a virtual disk
- Start or stop the Hyper-V service
- Remove a server
- Refresh the view
- Configure the view
- Access help information

When you manage a specific virtual machine from the right pane, the options depend on if the virtual machine is started. For example, if it is not started, you can:

- Connect to the virtual machine
- Change the settings
- Start the virtual machine
- Move, export, rename, or delete the virtual machine
- Go to help documentation

If the virtual machine is started, you can do the following from the links in the right pane of Hyper-V Manager: (see Figure A-3):

- Connect to the virtual machine (which opens the window from which to access it)
- Configure settings
- Turn off the virtual machine
- Shut down the virtual machine

- Save the virtual machine
- Pause the virtual machine
- Reset the virtual machine
- Create a checkpoint (snapshot of the current state of the virtual machine)
- Move or export the virtual machine
- Rename the virtual machine
- Enable replication

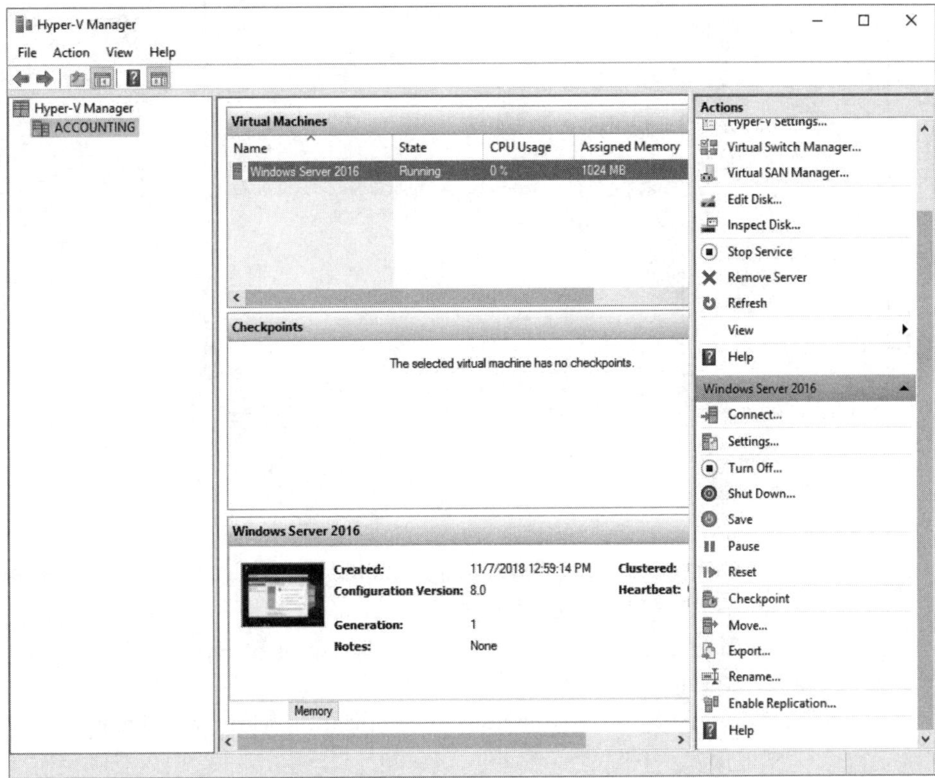

Figure A-3 Hyper-V Manager

When you open a window to connect locally to the virtual machine, you can maximize the window so that you have a full view of the operating system you are using through the virtual machine. A control bar remains at the top of the screen to minimize the window or close it.

Creating a Virtual Machine

The general steps to create a virtual machine using Hyper-V Manager are:

1. Open Server Manager, if it is not open.
2. Click Tools and click Hyper-V Manager.
3. In the left pane, right-click the server name under Hyper-V Manager, point to New, and click Virtual Machine (see Figure A-4).
4. If you see the Before You Begin screen in the New Virtual Machine Wizard, click Next.
5. In the Specify Name and Location window, enter the name for the virtual machine, such as Windows Server 2016, and click Next.

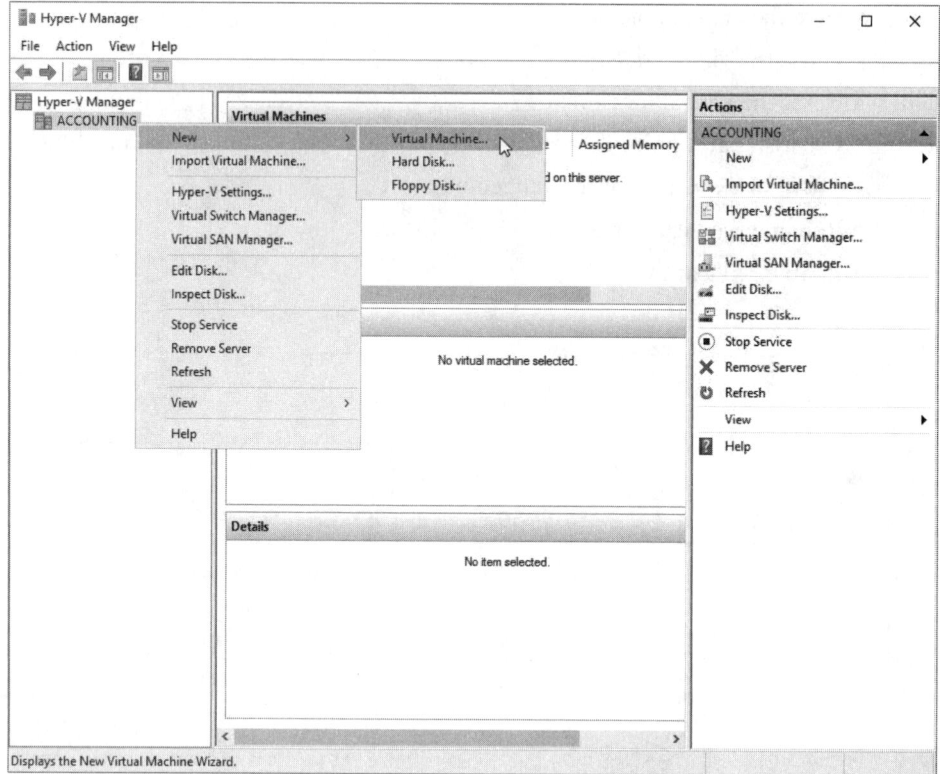

Figure A-4 Creating a new virtual machine

6. In the Specify Generation window, select the Hyper-V generation you want to use from the following choices and then click Next.
   - Generation 1: compatible with previous versions of Hyper-V and supports 32-and 64-bit guest operating systems
   - Generation 2: supports the newer virtualization features and supports only 64-bit guest operating systems
7. In the Assign Memory window (see Figure A-5), specify the amount of RAM to allocate for the guest operating system (check the minimum and desired RAM needs for the operating system with the specific functions or roles you plan to use—512 MB is the minimum requirement for Windows Server 2016, but you should plan on using more RAM). Click Next.
8. In the Configure Networking window, select the NIC connection, or create a virtual switch after you finish configuring the virtual machine. Click Next.
9. In the Connect Virtual Hard Disk window, configure the virtual hard disk (such as using the *Create a virtual hard disk* option, specifying the name, location, and size parameters for the virtual hard disk). Click Next.
10. In the Installation Options window, select the desired installation mode. For example, if you have an installation DVD, use the *Install an operating system from a bootable CD/DVD-ROM* option and select the physical CD/DVD drive or to use an .iso image file. (If you are using a CD/DVD, load it now.) Click Next.
11. Click Finish.
12. If you loaded a CD/DVD, and the virtual machine window is not displayed, click the new virtual machine under Virtual Machines in Hyper-V Manager, click the Action menu in Hyper-V, and click Connect.

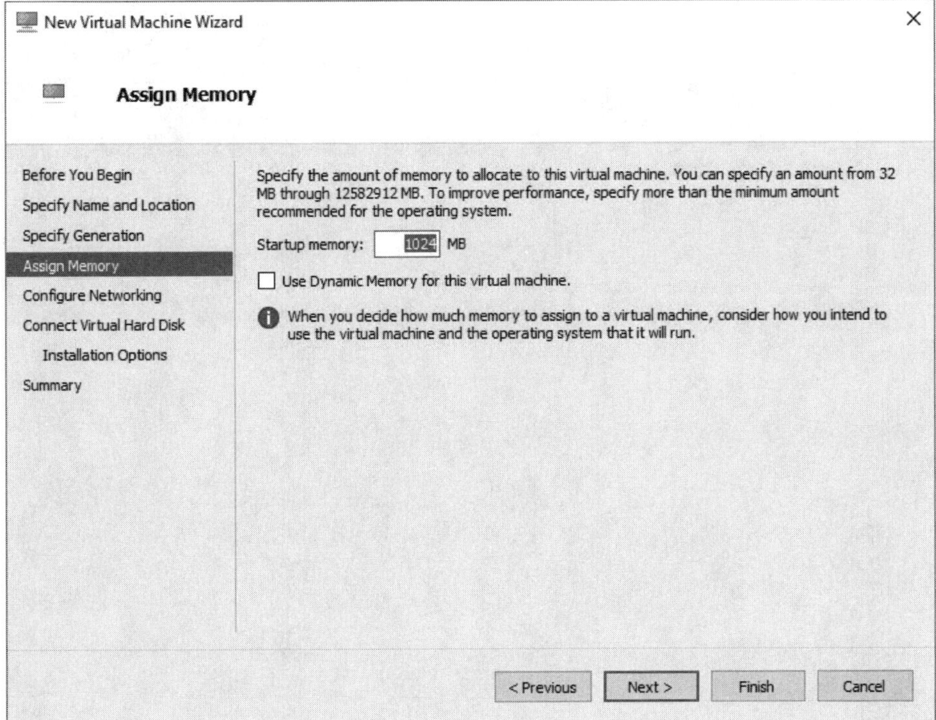

Figure A-5 Assigning memory for the virtual machine

13. In the Virtual Machine Connection window, click the Action menu and click Start (you may need to press Enter to have the virtual machine boot from the installation CD/DVD).
14. Follow the steps to load the operating system.

After the virtual machine is installed, you may choose to create a virtual switch, which determines how the virtual machine(s) communicate. There are three virtual switch settings:

- *External*—Enables the virtual switch to bind to the host computer's NIC so that the virtual machine can communicate through the physical network connected to the NIC.
- *Internal*—Does not provide network connectivity, but does give the virtual machine a connection to a virtual adapter that is used by other virtual machines on the computer, so the virtual machines can communicate with each other and with the parent physical computer.
- *Private*—Enables virtual machines in the same virtual server to communicate with each other, but not with the parent physical computer or with the network connected to the parent physical computer.

The general steps for setting up a virtual switch are:

1. Open Hyper-V Manager.
2. In the right pane click Virtual Switch Manager.
3. In the Virtual Switch Manager window for the host computer, select the virtual switch setting (see Figure A-6) and click Create Virtual Switch.
4. Click OK.
5. Click Yes in the Apply Network Changes dialog box and notice the warning that Pending changes may disrupt network connectivity.
6. Click OK in the Virtual Switch Manager window, if necessary.

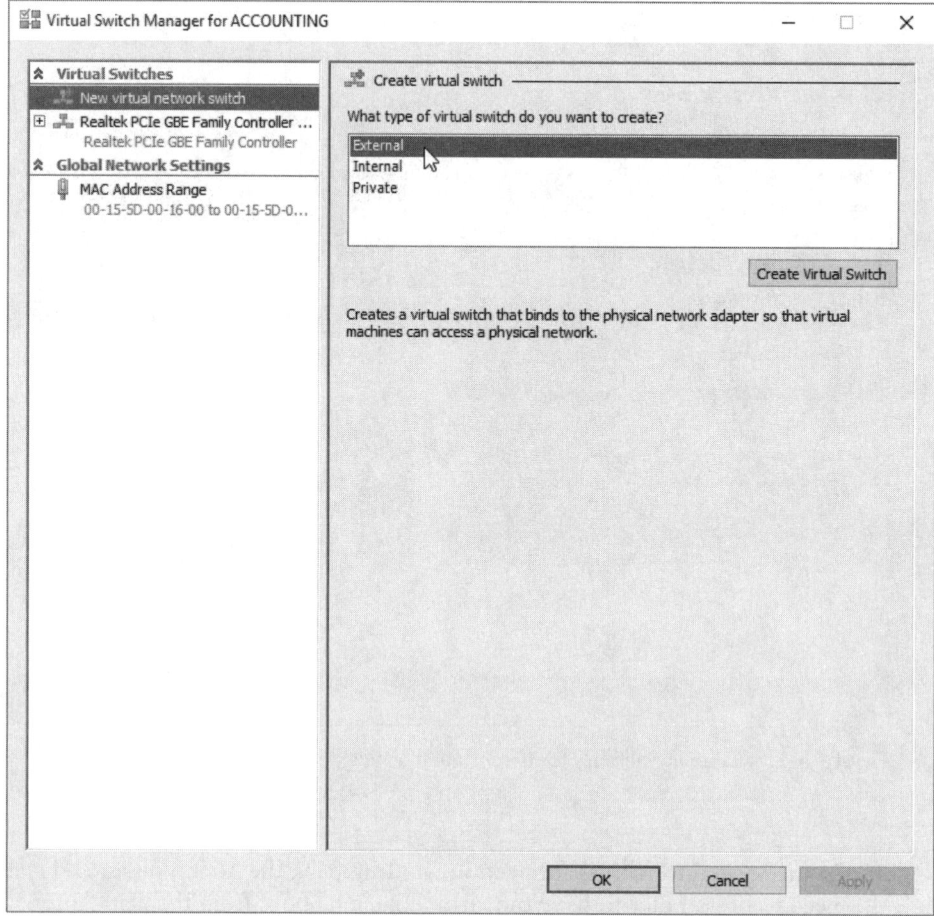

Figure A-6 Configuring a virtual switch

Configuring a Virtual Machine

After the virtual machine is created and the operating system is installed, you can configure or reconfigure the virtual machine settings. Before you configure the settings, shut down the virtual machine window by clicking Action and clicking Shut Down or shutdown the operating system in the virtual machine window. (To restart it, click the virtual machine in Hyper-V Manager and click Connect. In the virtual machine window, click Action and click Start).

The general steps for configuring a virtual machine are:

1. Click the virtual machine under Virtual Machines in Hyper-V Manager.
2. In the right pane of Hyper-V Manager, click Settings.
3. In the Settings window for the virtual machine (see Figure A-7), select the element you want to configure in the left pane, such as Add Hardware or Memory. Change or add to the present configuration.
4. After the configuration is complete, click OK in the Settings window for the virtual machine.

If you prefer using Windows PowerShell commands to configure Hyper-V and a virtual machine, visit: *technet.microsoft.com/en-us/library/hh848559.aspx* for instructions.

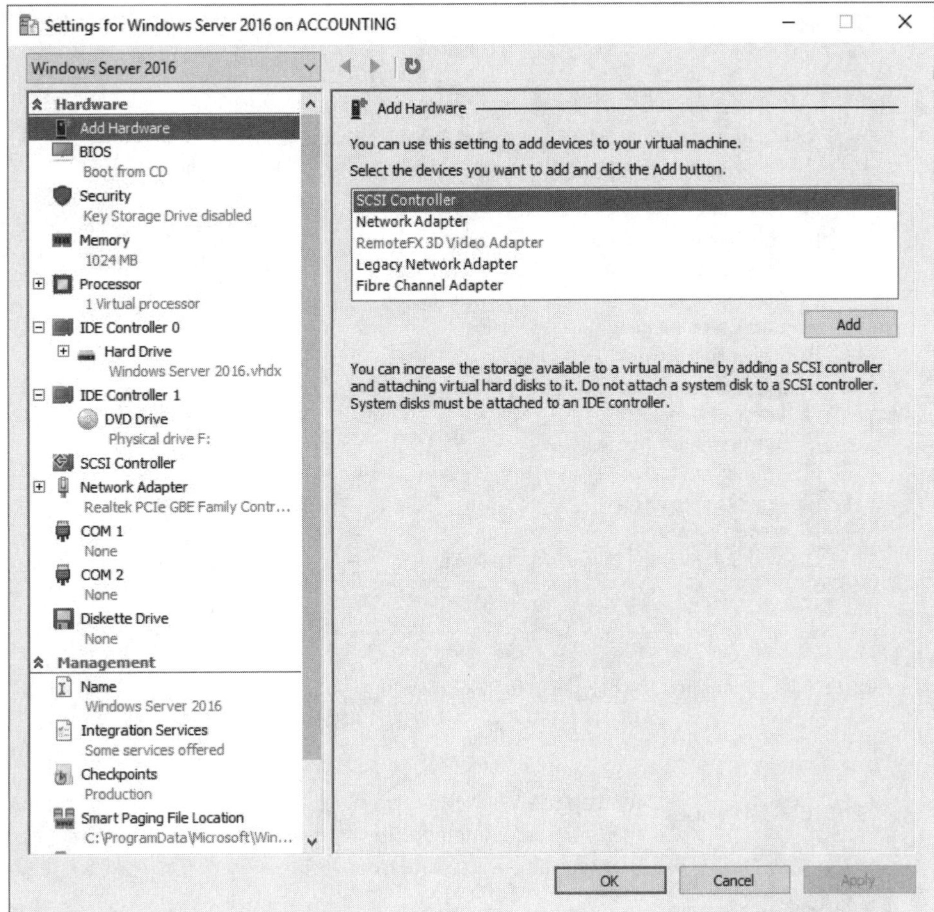

Figure A-7 Configuring settings for a virtual machine

Installing Client Hyper-V in Windows 8.1 or Windows 10

Client Hyper-V is available for Windows 8.1 or Windows 10, if you have the Professional Edition or above. Client Hyper-V comes with Windows 10 and you can select to enable it. In Windows 8.1, you may need to download and install Client Hyper-V from the Microsoft Download Center at *www.microsoft.com/en-us/download/*.

To enable Client Hyper-V in Windows 8.1 or 10, use these general steps:

1. Right-click Start and click Programs and Features.
2. Click Turn Windows features on or off.
3. In the Windows Features dialog box, click the box for Hyper-V (see Figure A-8). Click OK.
4. Close the Programs and Features window.
5. If necessary, wait for Client Hyper-V to install the necessary components.
6. Restart the computer.
7. Click Start and click Hyper-V Manager to get started in Windows 8.1 or Windows 10. Or in Windows 8.1 or Windows 10 press the WIN key and Q at the same time, type Hyper-V in the Search or Ask me anything box, and click Hyper-V Manager from the displayed options.
8. Use Hyper-V as you would in Windows Server 2016.

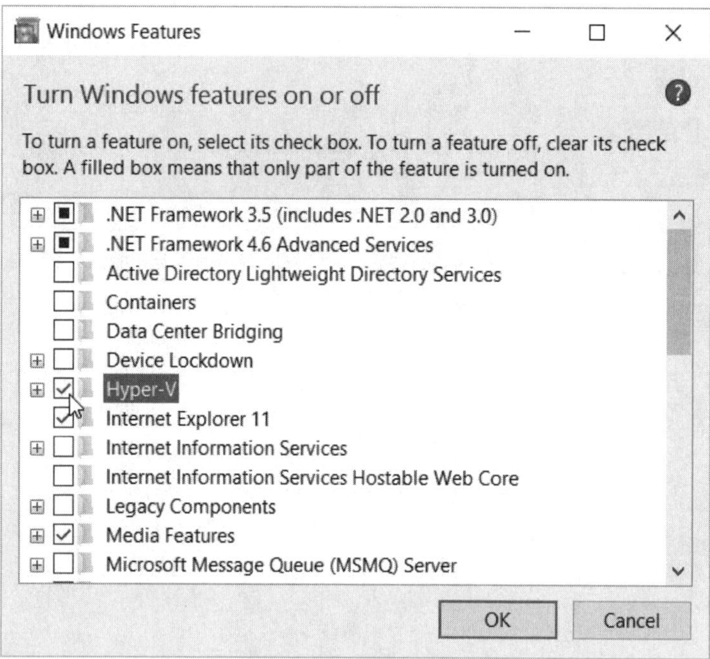

Figure A-8 Enabling Client Hyper-V in Windows 10

You can use Windows PowerShell in Windows 8.1 and Windows 10 as an alternative setup method. The command is: Enable-WindowsOptionalFeature –FeatureName Microsoft-Hyper-V -All

For the activities in this book, you can obtain the free Windows Server 2016 evaluation installation DVD from Microsoft or make an installation DVD from an .iso file downloaded from Microsoft's download website. Then use Client Hyper-V in Windows 8.1 Professional or above or in Windows 10 Professional or above to create a Windows Server 2016 virtual machine.

Summary

The Hyper-V role is popular because it enables server administrators to run several operating systems on one computer. Many organizations use Hyper-V to run multiple Windows Server 2016 virtual machines on one physical computer to save money on the purchase of computers and to make running multiple servers more convenient. Hyper-V also provides a foundation for cloud computing.

Windows 8.1 and 10 users who have the Professional Edition or higher can install Client Hyper-V on their workstations. In this context, it is useful for remotely managing multiple servers from a virtual machine housing Windows Server 2016 on a server administrator's workstation. Client Hyper-V is also useful for running or learning about different computer operating systems.

appendix B

Sample Windows PowerShell Cmdlets

This appendix is a quick reference providing sample Windows Server 2016 PowerShell cmdlets, to help you become familiar with using cmdlets.

Table B-1 lists cmdlets alphabetically by category. The categories are file-processing cmdlets, system-related cmdlets, network utilities, and security utilities. Rather than to simply list cmdlets, this table shows a specific action you can take with a cmdlet, such as how to stop a specific service or how to copy a particular file from one folder to another. You can take a cmdlet example and extrapolate it to a similar task that you want to perform.

Following Microsoft's convention, the cmdlets are presented using initial capital letters, but keep in mind that cmdlets are not actually case sensitive. If you wish to view the online documentation for a cmdlet, enter Get-Help [cmdlet], such as Get-Help Get-Acl to see the online documentation for the Get-Acl command.

When you want to repeat a command you've just typed, or perhaps you made a misspelling in a command you just executed and want to correct it to run again, press the up arrow on your keyboard. The last command you ran is displayed on the command line. Press the up arrow two times and the second to last command is displayed, and so on.

Table B-1 **Windows PowerShell cmdlet examples by category**

Cmdlet	Brief description of function
File-processing cmdlets	
Clear-Content c:\work\myfile.txt	Erases the contents of myfile.txt, without deleting the file
Copy-Item c:\work\myfile.txt c:\docs	Copies myfile.txt from the \work folder to the \docs folder
Copy-Item c:\work*.docx c:\docs	Copies all files in the \work folder with the .docx suffix to the \docs folder
Get-Content c:\work\myfile.txt	Displays the contents of the myfile.txt file
Invoke-Item c:\programs\test\test.exe	Runs the test.exe program
Move-Item c:\work\mydata.txt c:\data	Moves the file mydata.txt from the \work folder to the \data folder
Move-Item c:\work\newdata.txt c:\docs\mydata.txt	Moves the newdata.txt file from the \work folder to the \docs folder and renames the file to mydata.txt in the \docs folder
New-Item c:\work\spreadsheets -type directory	Creates the new folder (directory), spreadsheets within the \work folder
New-Item c:\work\newfile.txt -type file	Creates a new file called newfile.txt in the \work folder
Remove-Item c:\work\junk	Deletes the junk folder within the \work folder (if there are files in the junk folder, you will see a prompt to confirm if the files should be deleted—to avoid the prompt, end the cmdlet with the -recurse parameter)
Rename-Item c:\work\yourfile.txt myfile.txt	Renames the file, yourfile.txt to myfile.txt, keeping the renamed file in the /work folder
Test-Path c:\work\myfile.txt	Returns True if the file exists or False if it does not exist
System-related cmdlets	
Add-Computer -ComputerName PC120 -DomainName Ourdomain	Adds the computer "PC120" to the "Ourdomain" domain
Install-WindowsFeature DNS	Installs the DNS server role
Clear-Eventlog -LogName system	Clears the system log
Get-ChildItem	Lists the objects in the current folder, such as files and subfolders (similar to using the *dir* command at the command line to list directory contents)
Get-Command	Lists the Windows Powershell cmdlets (add the | *more* parameter to display one screen at a time)
Get-Culture	Shows the language and country settings
Get-Eventlog -list	Lists the event logs, including the number of entries and the configuration for when a log fills up
Get-Eventlog system | more	Shows the contents of the system log, one screen-full at a time (press the spacebar to advance; press Ctrl + C to exit)
Get-Eventlog system -newest 10	Displays the last 10 events recorded in the system log
Get-History	View a list of Windows PowerShell commands you have recently used
Get-Process	Shows the processes running, including the handles, process ID, and CPU use for each process
Get-Service	Shows information about all installed services, including the status and description
Get-Service | Where-Object {$_.status -eq "running"}	Shows only services with the status running
Get-Service | Where-Object {$_.status -eq "stopped"}	Shows only services with the status stopped
Get-WindowsFeature	Displays the server roles and features that are available to install
Get-WindowsFeature DNS	Shows the installation status of the DNS role
Invoke-Expression c:\scripts\myscript.ps1	Run the script, myscript.ps1
Restart-Computer	Restarts the computer
Resume-Service AxInstSV	Resumes the AxInstSV service
Set-Date -date "8/15/2018 11:45 AM"	Sets the date and time
Set-Service AxInstSV -startuptype "automatic"	Configure the AxInstSV service to start automatically when the system is booted
Set-Service AxInstSV -startuptype "manual"	Configure the AxInstSV service to start manually

Cmdlet	Brief description of function
System-related cmdlets (continued)	
Start-Service AxInstSV	Starts the AxInstSV service
Stop-Service AxInstSV	Stops the AxInstSV service
Stop-Process -processname explorer.exe	Stops the file explorer process by using the process name, explorer.exe
Stop-Process 4022	Stops process number 4022
Suspend-Service AxInstSV	Pause the AxInstSV service (see the Resume-Service cmdlet to resume the service)
Uninstall-WindowsFeature DNS	Uninstalls the DNS role
Get-WindowsSearchSetting	Shows the settings for Windows Search, such as if Search is enabled
Network utilities	
Backup-DhcpServer -Path c:Windows\DHCP	Backs up the DHCP server to c:\Windows\DHCP
Disable-NetAdapter -Name 'Wi-Fi'	Disables the wireless network adapter
Enable-NetAdapter -Name 'Wi-Fi'	Enables the wireless network adapter
Get-NetIPAddress	Shows the IPv4 and IPv6 address configuration of the computer
Get-NetIPConfiguration	Shows IP configuration information along with virtual switch, Bluetooth, wireless and wired information, domain or workgroup name, and the connection status of each network connection option (similar concept to the *ipconfig* command-line command)
Get-NetIPInterface	Shows information about the network interface (NIC) IPv4 and IPv6 properties, including if DHCP is enabled and the connection state of the NIC
Get-NetRoute	Shows IP routing table data, including next hop IP addresses and destination prefixes (similar to the *route* command-line command)
Get-NetRoute -Protocol local -DestinationPrefix 192.168*	Shows the IP routes within the local network system
Get-NetTCPConnection | Group State, RemotePort | Sort Count | FT Count, Name -Autosize	Shows the present TCP/IP network connections, including established, timewait, and listening connections (similar to the *netstat* command-line command)
Get-NetTCPSetting	Displays the current TCP settings, and can show a specific setting by using the *SettingName* option—important for optimizing network throughput and identifying possible sources of congestion
New-NetIPAddress -InterfaceAlias "Ethernet" -IPv4Address "192.168.0.52" -PrefixLength 24 -DefaultGateway 192.168.0.254	Creates or changes the IPv4 address of the computer to 192.168.0.52; note the PrefixLength 24 parameter is in CIDR notation and sets the subnet mask to 255.255.255.0
Restart-NetAdapter	Restarts the network adapter
Resolve-DnsName www.mycompany.com	Resolves the DNS name for www.mycompany.com, (similar to using the *nslookup* command-line command)
Test-Connection -ComputerName PC120	Tests the network connection to the computer named "PC120" (similar to the *ping* command-line command)
Test-NetConnection www.mycompany.com -TraceRoute	Shows the network route (hops) to the destination www.mycompany.com (similar concept to the *traceroute* command-line command)
Security utilities	
Get-Acl c:\windows	Provides a simple listing of access/permissions security for the \Windows folder
Get-Acl c:\windows | Format-List	Provides more detailed information about access/permission security for the \Windows folder
Get-Acl c:\work\spreadsheets*.*	Provides information about access/permissions security for the contents of the \work\spreadsheets folder
Get-NetFirewallRule | more	Displays the Windows Firewall rules one screen at a time (press the spacebar to advance)
Set-NetFirewallProfile -Profile Domain,Public,Private -Enabled True	Enables Windows Firewall (to turn off Windows Firewall replace -Enabled with -False)

Glossary

access-based enumeration When enabled, permits the user to view only shared folders and files for which they have permissions.

access control list (ACL) A list of all security descriptors that have been set up for a particular object, such as for a shared folder or a shared printer.

account lockout A security measure that prevents access to a user account, such as after a specified number of unsuccessful logon attempts. Account lockout is often used to prevent brute force attacks that repeatedly try password combinations to attempt to break into an account.

Active Directory A central database of computers, users, shared printers, shared folders, other network resources, and resource groupings that is used to manage a network and enable users to quickly find a particular resource.

Active Directory Rights Management Services (AD RMS) A server role that works with client applications that can take advantage of RMS safeguards. *See* Rights Management Services (RMS).

active partition The partition from which a computer boots.

Address Resolution Protocol (ARP) A protocol in the TCP/IP suite that enables a sending station to determine the MAC or physical address of another station on a network.

admin log A type of event log that gives the system administrator information about a specific problem and its causes, and might also suggest how to solve the problem.

Advanced Encryption Standard (AES) A relatively new encryption standard adopted by the U.S. government to replace DES and 3DES and that employs a private-key block-cipher form of encryption.

aggregate lines or channels Linking two or more communications channels, such as frame relay or ISDN channels, so that they appear as one channel, but with the combined speed of all channels in the aggregate.

American National Standards Institute (ANSI) An organization that works to set standards for all types of products, including network equipment.

analytic log An event log often used by application and system programmers to help analyze how specific programs are running and to identify problems with those programs.

anycast A packet that goes only to the closest interface and does not attempt to reach other interfaces with the same address.

application log An event log that records information about how software applications are performing.

application pool Grouping of similar web applications in pools or groups for management, such as for common settings for common worker processes (ASP.NET processes).

Assessment and Deployment Kit (ADK) Tools and documentation targeted to help you use and customize a specific Windows operating system.

assigning applications (or software) Means an application is automatically represented on the user's desktop, for example, as a Start menu option or as an icon on the desktop, and which initially is really a link to a central application distribution server. When the application is assigned to the computer, it is automatically installed when the user boots or signs in to the computer. When assigned to the user account, the first time the user tries to open the application, such as from the Start menu, is the point at which it is fully installed from the distribution server.

asynchronous modem A modem from which communications occur in discrete units, and in which the start of a unit is signaled by a start bit at the front, and a stop bit at the back signals the end of the unit.

attribute A characteristic associated with a folder or file used to help manage access.

auditing In Windows Server 2016, a security capability that tracks activity on an object, such as reading, writing, creating, or deleting a file in a folder.

Automatic Private IP Addressing (APIPA) Windows Server 2016 supports Automatic Private IP Addressing (APIPA) to automatically configure the TCP/IP settings for a computer. The computer assigns itself an IP address in the range of 169.254.0.1–169.254.255.254, if a DHCP server is not available.

Bandwidth Allocation Control Protocol (BACP) Similar to BAP, but is able to select a preferred client when two or more clients vie for the same bandwidth. *See* Bandwidth Allocation Protocol (BAP).

Bandwidth Allocation Protocol (BAP) A protocol that works with Multilink in Windows Server 2016 to enable the bandwidth or speed of a remote connection to be allocated on the basis of the needs of an application, with the maximum allocation equal to the maximum speed of all channels aggregated via Multilink.

base priority class The initial priority assigned to a program process or thread in the program code.

basic disk In Windows Server 2016, a partitioned disk that can have up to four partitions and that uses logical drive designations. This type of disk is backward compatible with previous versions of Windows client and server operating systems and MS-DOS and supports multi-boot with other operating systems.

basic input/output system (BIOS) A program on a read-only or flash memory chip that establishes basic communication with a computer's components such as the monitor and disk drives. The advantage of a flash chip is that you can update the BIOS.

benchmark (or baseline) A measurement standard for hardware or software used to establish performance measures under varying loads or circumstances.

Best Practices Analyzer (BPA) Analyzes the installed server roles to report if they are set up to conform to Microsoft's best practices for roles.

bidirectional printing Ability of a printer to conduct two-way communication between the printer and the computer, such as to provide out-of-paper information; also, bidirectional printing supports Plug and Play and enables an operating system to query a printer about its capabilities.

BitLocker Drive Encryption A security measure for protecting hard drives in Windows 7, 8/8.1, and 10 as well as in Windows Server 2016. It can use a TPM chip on a computer or a flash drive with a PIN to enforce security. *See* Trusted Platform Module (TPM).

boot partition Partition on basic disks that holds the Windows Server 2016 \Windows folder containing the system files.

boot volume Volume on dynamic disks that holds the \Windows folder of system files.

bridgehead server A domain controller at each Active Directory site with access to a site network link, which is designated as the DC to exchange replication information. There is only one bridgehead server per site. *See* site.

broadcast A message sent to all computers on a network (but usually blocked to other networks by a router).

cable modem A digital modem device designed for use with the cable TV system, providing high-speed data transfer.

caching-only DNS server A DNS server without zones used to provide fast queries, because the results of each query are stored in RAM.

caching server A DNS server function available in all DNS servers, that is used to provide fast queries because the results of each query are stored in RAM. As more resolution queries are performed, a large set of information is stored in RAM for fast response to users.

Challenge Handshake Authentication Protocol (CHAP) An encrypted handshake protocol designed for standard IP- or PPP-based exchange of passwords. It provides a reasonably secure, standard, cross-platform method for sender and receiver to negotiate a connection. *See also* MS CHAP and MS-CHAPv2.

client A computer that accesses resources on another computer via a network or direct cable connection.

client access license (CAL) A license to enable a workstation to access a Windows server.

cloud computing Providing a host of scalable web-based applications and services (including cloud storage) over the Internet or a private network that are used by clients through web browsers and downloadable apps.

clustering Linking two or more discrete computer systems so they appear to function as though they are one, thus increasing the ability to access server resources and provide fail-safe services.

cmdlet A command-line tool available in Windows PowerShell. *See* Windows PowerShell.

committed memory The number bytes a process has designated for use and that are promised by the operating system to a designated portion of the page file.

community A group of hosts that share the same SNMP services.

community name In SNMP communications, a rudimentary password (name) used by network agents and the network management station (or software) in the same community so that their communications cannot be easily intercepted by an unauthorized workstation or device.

connectionless communication Also called a connectionless service, a communication service that provides no checks (or minimal checks) to make sure that data accurately reaches the destination node.

connection-oriented communication Also called a connection-oriented service, this service provides several ways to ensure that data is successfully received at the destination, such as requiring an acknowledgement of receipt and using a checksum to make sure the packet or frame contents are accurate.

container (1) An Active Directory object that houses other objects, such as a tree that houses domains or a domain that houses organizational units. (2) An operating environment that enables applications to run in an isolated fashion and provides the ability to execute multiple applications on one computer system.

contiguous namespace A namespace in which every child object has a portion of its name from its parent object.

counter Used by Performance Monitor, a measurement technique for an object, for example, for measuring the processor performance by percentage in use.

cryptoprocessor A processor that enables hardware to be protected through using cryptographic keys employing the Trusted Platform Module security specification. *See* Trusted Platform Module (TPM).

custom backup Enables you to configure backups differently for each volume, using either a full backup or an incremental backup.

data collector set A combination of techniques for gathering performance and diagnostic data that is rendered in a report or log format. The basic data gathering techniques can be one or a combination of performance counters, event traces, and system configuration data.

Data Encryption Standard (DES) A network symmetric-key encryption standard developed by the National Institute of Standards and Technology (NIST) and the American National Standards Institute (ANSI).

Data Execution Prevention (DEP) A security feature that monitors how programs use memory and stops programs that attempt to use memory allocated for system programs and processes. This is intended to foil viruses, Trojan horses, and worms that attempt to invade system memory.

data type Way in which information is formatted in a print file.

debug log An event log used by application developers to help trace problems in programs so they can fix program code or program structures.

default gateway The IP address of the router that has a connection to other networks. The default gateway address is used when the host computer you are trying to contact exists on another network.

defragmenting A software process that rearranges data to fill in the empty spaces that develop on disks and makes data easier to obtain.

demilitarized zone (DMZ) A portion of network that exists between two or more networks that have different security measures in place, such as the zone between the private network of a company and the public network of the Internet.

Desired State Configuration A feature of Windows Server 2016 that enables monitoring of specific server states and roles to ensure that desired server states are not inadvertently altered.

Device Specific Module (DSM) A software interface between the Multipath I/O capability in Windows Server 2016 and the hard disk hardware.

DFS Replication A role service you can install within the File and Storage Services role, so that shared folders offered through DFS are backed up to protect against data loss, such as through hardware failure, and to provide redundancy. *See* Distributed File System (DFS).

DFS topology Applies to a domain-based DFS model and encompasses the DFS namespace root, shared folders, and replication folders.

DHCP relay agent On a VPN server, relays IP lease assignments between a DHCP server and the network client computer.

digital certificate A set of unique identification information that is typically put at the end of a file or that is associated with a computer communication. Its purpose is to show that the source of the file or communication is legitimate.

digital subscriber line (DSL) A technology that uses advanced modulation techniques on regular telephone lines for high-speed networking at speeds of up to about 52 Mbps between subscribers and a telecommunications company.

DirectAccess Built around IPv6, establishes two "tunnels" for connecting to a DirectAccess server used in remote access and that is transparent to users and always on.

directory service A large container (database) of information about network data and resources, such as computers, printers, user accounts, and user groups, that enables management and fast access to those resources.

discretionary ACL (DACL) An access control list that manages access to an object, such as a folder, and that is configured by a server administrator or owner of the object.

disjointed namespace A namespace in which the child object name does not resemble the parent object name.

disk duplexing A fault-tolerance method similar to disk mirroring in that it prevents data loss by duplicating data from a main disk to a backup disk, but disk duplexing places the backup disk on a different controller or adapter than is used by the main disk.

disk mirroring A fault-tolerance method that prevents data loss by duplicating data from a main disk to a backup disk. Some operating systems also refer to this as disk shadowing.

disk quota Allocating a specific amount of disk space to a user or application with the ability to ensure that the user or application cannot use more disk space than is specified in the allocation.

Distributed File System (DFS) A system that enables folders shared from multiple computers to appear as though they exist in one centralized hierarchy of folders instead of on many different computers.

distribution group A list of users that enables one email message to be sent to all users on the list. A distribution group is not used for security and thus cannot appear in an access control list (ACL).

DNS dynamic update protocol A protocol that enables information in a DNS server to be automatically updated in coordination with DHCP.

DNS round robin Resource records are created for two or more servers that have different IP addresses but that are associated with the same host name, such as IP addresses 192.168.1.5 and 192.168.1.6 that are associated with the host name *researchserver*.

DNS security extension (DNSSEC) Ensures that records in all DNS zones use cryptographic digital signing, which is intended to reduce the opportunity for DNS information to be captured and modified by an attacker.

domain A grouping of resource objects—for example, servers, computers, and user accounts—to enable easier centralized management of these objects. On Windows Server 2016 networks, a domain is contained within Active Directory as a higher-level representation of how a business, school, or government agency is organized.

domain-based DFS model A DFS model that uses Active Directory and is available only to servers and workstations that are members of a particular domain. The domain-based model enables a deep, root-based, hierarchical arrangement of shared folders that is published in Active Directory. DFS shared folders in the domain-based model can be replicated for fault tolerance and load balancing.

domain controller (DC) A Windows 2000 Server or above server that contains a full copy of the Active Directory information, is used to add a new object to Active Directory, and replicates all changes made to it so the changes are updated on every DC in the same domain.

domain functional level Refers to the Windows Server operating systems on domain controllers and the domain-specific functions they support. Depending on the functional level, one, two, or all of the following operating systems are supported: Windows 2000 Server, Windows Server 2003, Windows Server 2008/R2, Windows Server 2012/R2, and Windows Server 2016.

domain local security group A group that is used to manage resources—shared folders and printers, for example—in its home domain and that is primarily used to give global groups access to those resources.

Domain Name System (DNS) Also called Domain Name Service, a TCP/IP application protocol that enables a DNS server to resolve (translate) domain and computer names to IP addresses or IP addresses to domain and computer names.

dotted decimal notation An addressing technique that uses four octets, such as 10000110.11011110.01100101.00 000101, converted to decimal (e.g., 134.222.101.5) to differentiate individual servers, workstations, and other network devices.

driver signing A digital signature incorporated into driver and system files as a way to verify the files and to ensure that they are not inappropriately overwritten.

DSL adapter A digital communications device that links a computer (or sometimes a router) to a DSL telecommunications line.

dynamic addressing An IP address that is automatically assigned to a client from a general pool of available addresses and that might be assigned each time the client is started, or it might be assigned for a period of days, weeks, months, or longer.

dynamic disk In Windows Server 2016, a disk that does not use traditional partitioning, which means that there is no restriction to the number of volumes that can be set up on one disk or to the ability to extend volumes onto additional physical disks. Dynamic disks are compatible with Windows Server 2016 back through Windows 2000 Server.

Dynamic DNS (DDNS) A form of DNS that enables client computers to update DNS registration information so that this does not have to be done manually. DDNS is often used with DHCP servers to automatically register IP addresses on a DNS server.

Dynamic Host Configuration Protocol (DHCP) A network protocol that provides a way for a server to automatically assign an IP address to a workstation on its network.

Dynamic Host Configuration Protocol for IPv6 (DHCPv6) A version of DHCP that can be used with IPv6 implementation on a network.

Encrypting File System (EFS) Set by an attribute of NTFS, this Microsoft file system enables a user to encrypt the contents of a folder or a file so that it can only be accessed via private key code by the user who encrypted it. EFS adheres to the Data Encryption Standard's expanded version for data protection.

enhanced metafile (EMF) A data type for printing used by modern Windows operating systems, such as Windows 10 and Windows Server 2016. EMF print files offer a distinct advantage in Windows operating system environments because they are very portable from computer to computer.

event logs Logs that you can view through Event Viewer that record information about server events, such as errors, warnings, or informational events.

extended partition A partition that is created from unpartitioned free disk space and is linked to a primary partition in order to increase the available disk space.

Extensible Authentication Protocol (EAP) Consists of guidelines for negotiating authentication methods, and at this writing over 40 EAP methods are defined, including for wired and wireless authentication methods. EAP can also be used with security devices such as smart cards, token cards, and others that use certificate authentication.

fault tolerance Techniques that employ hardware and software to provide assurance against equipment failures, computer service interruptions, and data loss.

file system cache An area designated in physical computer memory that is used in Windows operating systems to help speed up reading and writing to hard disk.

File Transfer Protocol (FTP) A TCP/IP application protocol that transfers files in bulk data streams and that is commonly used on the Internet.

fine-grained password policies Used so that different security groups can have different password policies.

Flexible Authentication Secure Tunneling (FAST) Used in Kerberos security to establish a secure channel or communications tunnel between a client seeking authentication for access to a computer service and the server providing access keys for secure communications. Also called Kerberos armoring.

folder target A path in the Universal Naming Convention (UNC) format, such as to a DFS shared folder or to a different DFS path.

forest A grouping of Active Directory trees that each have contiguous namespaces within their own domain structure but that have disjointed namespaces between trees. The trees and their domains use the same schema and global catalog.

forest functional level A forest-wide setting that refers to the types of domain controllers in a forest, which can be any combination of Windows 2000 Server, Windows Server 2003, Windows Server 2008/R2, Windows Server 2012/R2, or Windows Server 2016. The level also reflects the types of Active Directory services and functions supported.

formatting A process that prepares a hard disk partition for a specific file system.

forward lookup zone A DNS zone or table that maps computer names to IP addresses.

forwarded events log Contains events recorded by remote computers and forwarded to one computer, which is called the collector computer.

fragmented Having files spread throughout a disk with empty pockets of space between files; a normal and gradual process in the functioning of an operating system, addressed by using a defragmentation utility.

frame A unit of data that is transmitted on a network that contains control and address information, but not routing information.

frame relay A WAN communications technology that relies on packet switching and virtual connection techniques to transmit at rates from 56 Kbps to 45 Mbps.

full backup A backup of an entire system, including all system files, programs, and data files.

Generic Routing Encapsulation (GRE) tunneling A protocol that encapsulates a packet payload for transport through a private tunnel over a network that goes from one point to another. One advantage of GRE tunneling is the ability to enable virtual private networks to use a private tunnel over an external network, such as through a wide area network.

global catalog A repository for all objects and the most frequently used attributes for each object in all domains. Each forest has a single global catalog that can be replicated onto multiple servers.

globally unique identifier (GUID) A unique number, up to 16 characters long, that is associated with an Active Directory object.

Globally Unique Identifier (GUID) Partition Table (GPT) A method for partitioning disks that allows for theoretically unlimited partitions and use of larger disks. In Windows Server 2016, the maximum number of partitions on a GPT disk is 128, and the maximum partition size is up to 18 exabytes.

global security group A group that typically contains user accounts from its home domain and that is a member of domain local groups in the same or other domains, so as to give that global group's member accounts access to the resources defined to the domain local groups.

graphics device interface (GDI) An interface on a Windows network print client that works with a local software application, such as Microsoft Word, and a local printer driver to format a file to be sent to a local printer or a network print server.

Group Policy A set of policies that govern security, configuration, and a wide range of other settings for objects within containers in Active Directory.

Group Policy Object (GPO) An object in Active Directory that contains Group Policy settings for a site, domain, OU, or local computer.

handle A resource, such as a file, used by a program that has its own identification so the program is able to access it.

hard link Enables you to create one file and then establish links to that file in other folders, as though the file is in all of the folders.

help desk system Application software designed to maintain information on computer systems, user questions, problem solutions, and other information that members of an organization can reference.

hive A set of related Registry keys and subkeys stored as a file.

home directory or home folder A server folder that is associated with a user's account and that is a designated workspace for the user to store files.

host address (A) resource record A record in a DNS forward lookup zone that consists of a computer or domain name correlated to an IP version 4 (or 32-bit) address.

Hypertext Transfer Protocol (HTTP) A protocol in the TCP/IP suite of protocols that is used to transport Hypertext Markup Language (HTML) documents and other data transmissions over networks and the Internet for access by web-compliant browsers.

Hypertext Transfer Protocol Secure (HTTPS) A secure form of HTTP that uses Secure Sockets Layer to implement security.

Hyper-V Virtualization software developed by Microsoft that is included with Windows Server 2016 Standard and Datacenter Editions. *See* virtualization.

Hyper-V Extensible Virtual Switch Protocol Used with the Hyper-V role at the server's network interface card(s) (NICs) to bind or associate the virtual network services to the NIC and enable the use of a virtual switch between the parent partition containing the main operating system, Windows Server 2016, and child partitions containing other operating systems.

incremental backup Backs up only files that are new or that have been updated.

inherited permissions Permissions of a parent object that also apply to child objects of the parent, such as to subfolders within a folder.

inherited rights User rights that are assigned to a group and that automatically apply to all members of that group.

instance An individual occurrence of an element that is being monitored in Performance Monitor; exists when two or more types of elements can be monitored, such as two or more CPUs, threads, or disk drives.

Integrated Services Digital Network (ISDN) A telecommunications standard for delivering data services over digital telephone lines with a current practical limit of 1.536 Mbps and a theoretical limit of 622 Mbps.

Internet Information Services (IIS) A Microsoft Windows Server 2016 role that provides Internet, web, FTP, mail, and other services and that is particularly offered to set up a web server.

Internet Key Exchange version 2 (IKEv2) A protocol that establishes security associations, including cryptographic keys, for IPsec secured communications.

Internet Printing Client A software plug-in to enable handling Internet printing through IPP and HTTP Internet communications. *See* Internet Printing Protocol (IPP).

Internet Printing Protocol (IPP) A protocol that is encapsulated in HTTP and that is used to print files over the Internet.

Internet Protocol (IP) The Internet layer protocol responsible for addressing packets so that they are delivered on the local network or across routers to other networks or subnets.

Internet Protocol Version 4 (IPv4) The most commonly used version of IP, which has been in use for many years. IPv4 has a limitation in that it was not designed to anticipate the vast numbers of networks and network users currently in existence.

Internet Protocol Version 6 (IPv6) The newest version of IP that is designed for enhanced security and that can handle the addressing needs of growing networks.

Internet Server Application Programming Interface (ISAPI) A group of dynamic link library (DLL) files that consists of applications and filters to enable user-customized programs to interface with IIS and to trigger particular programs, such as a specialized security check or a database lookup.

Internet Small Computer System Interface (iSCSI) A high-speed technology used in SANs that employs TCP/IP communications and SCSI disk drives. *See* Storage Area Network (SAN).

interrupt request (IRQ) line A hardware line that a computer component, such as a disk drive or serial port, uses to communicate to the processor that it is ready to send or receive information. Intel-based computers have 16 IRQ lines, with 15 available for computer components to use.

I/O address The address in memory through which data is transferred between a computer component and the processor.

IP address A logical address assigned to each host on an IP network. It is used to identify a specific host on a specific network.

IP Address Management (IPAM) A set of tools available in Windows Server 2016 to consolidate IP address management in one place.

IP security (IPsec) A set of IP-based secure communications and encryption standards created through the Internet Engineering Task Force (IETF).

IPv6 host address (AAAA) resource record A record in a DNS forward lookup zone that consists of a computer or domain name mapped to an IP version 6 (or 128-bit) address.

journaling The process of keeping chronological records of data or transactions so that if a system crashes without warning, the data or transactions can be reconstructed or backed out to avoid data loss or information that is not properly synchronized.

Kerberos A security system developed by the Massachusetts Institute of Technology to enable two parties on an open network to communicate without interception from an intruder, by creating a unique encryption key for each communication session.

Kerberos armoring *See* Flexible Authentication Secure Tunneling (FAST).

Kerberos transitive trust relationship A set of two-way trusts between two or more domains (or forests in a forest trust) in which Kerberos security is used.

kernel An essential set of programs and computer code that allows a computer operating system to control processor, disk, memory, and other functions central to its basic operation.

latency The time it takes for information to travel from the transmitting device to the receiving device.

Layer Two Tunneling Protocol (L2TP) A protocol that transports PPP over a VPN, an intranet, or the Internet. L2TP works similarly to PPTP, but uses an additional network communications standard, called Layer Two Forwarding, that enables forwarding on the basis of MAC addressing. *See* Point-to-Point Tunneling Protocol (PPTP).

leased lines Telecommunications lines or bandwidth on telecommunications lines that can be leased from a telecommunications company.

Link Aggregation Control Protocol (LACP) Enables two or more NICs in a single computer to automatically be bundled into one logical connection.

Linux Integration Services (LIS) Services for Hyper-V that support Linux virtual machines and Linux clients.

load balancing On a single server, distributing resources across multiple server disk drives and paths for better server response; and on multiple network servers, distributing resources across two or more servers for better server and network performance.

local area network (LAN) A network of computers in relatively close proximity, such as on the same floor or in the same building.

local print device A printer, such as a laser printer, physically attached to a port on the local computer.

local security group A group of user accounts that is used to manage resources on a stand-alone computer.

local user profile A desktop setup that is associated with one or more accounts to determine what startup programs are used, additional desktop icons, and other customizations. A user profile is local to the computer in which it is stored.

logical processor A core within a multi-core processor that can run its own executable threads.

mandatory user profile A user profile set up by the server administrator that is loaded from the server to the client each time the user logs on; changes that the user makes to the profile are not saved.

Master Boot Record (MBR) Data created in the first sector of a disk, containing startup information and information about disk partitions.

media access control (MAC) address Also called a physical or device address, the hexadecimal number permanently assigned to a network interface and used by the MAC sublayer (a communications sublayer for controlling how computers share communications on the same network).

member server A server on an Active Directory managed network that is not installed to have Active Directory.

Microsoft Azure Active Directory An Active Directory service that an organization can use for online cloud applications, such as Office 365. Microsoft Azure Active Directory is a directory service that provides user authorization and identity management for organizations that subscribe to Microsoft cloud services.

Microsoft Passport A new authentication technique that replaces the use of passwords with a two-step authentication process that combines verifying a device is enrolled in the domain and that the device has a personal identification number.

Microsoft Point-to-Point Encryption (MPPE) A starting-to-ending-point encryption technique that uses special encryption keys varying in length from 40 to 128 bits.

mirrored volume Two dynamic disks that are set up for RAID level 1 so that data on one disk is stored on a redundant disk.

mounted drive A physical disk, CD/DVD, removable drive, or other drive that appears as a folder and that is accessed through a path like any other folder.

MS-CHAP (CHAP with Microsoft extensions version 1) A Microsoft-enhanced version of CHAP that can negotiate encryption levels and that uses the highly secure RSA RC4 encryption algorithm to encrypt communications between client and host. MS-CHAP is no longer considered secure and is susceptible to brute force attacks.

MS-CHAP v2 (CHAP with Microsoft extensions version 2) An enhancement of MS-CHAP that provides better authentication and data encryption and that is especially adapted for VPNs. MS-CHAPv2 is no longer considered secure and is susceptible to brute force attacks.

multicast A single message is sent from one location and received at several different locations that are subscribed to receive that message.

Multilink or Multilink PPP (MPPP) A capability of a remote access server to aggregate multiple data streams into one logical network connection for the purpose of using more than one modem, ISDN channel, or other communications line in a single logical connection.

multimaster replication Windows Server 2016 networks can have multiple servers called DCs that store Active Directory information and replicate it to each other. Because each DC acts as a master, replication does not stop when one DC is down and updates to Active Directory continue, for example, when creating a new account.

Multipath I/O A set of drivers in Windows Server 2016 that can be used with device and network architecture to set up multiple paths between a server and its disk storage to achieve fault tolerance.

multitasking The capability of a computer to run two or more programs at the same time.

multithreading Running several program processes or parts (threads) at the same time.

name resolution A process used to translate a computer's logical or host name into a network address, such as to a dotted decimal address associated with a computer—and vice versa.

namespace A logical area on a network that contains directory services and named objects and that has the ability to perform name resolution.

namespace root The main Active Directory container that holds DFS links to shared folders in a domain.

National Institute of Standards and Technology (NIST) Established by the United States Congress, this agency is a physical science laboratory that works to research and standardize measurements and applied technologies. NIST is part of the U.S. Department of Commerce and was first created to help make U.S. businesses more competitive.

NetBIOS name A name or identifier used in older Windows systems to uniquely identify a computer.

.NET Framework An environment that is built into Windows Server 2016 that is used to develop and execute applications.

network A communications system that enables computer users to share computer equipment, software, data, voice, and video transmissions.

Network Address Translation (NAT) Sometimes used by firewalls, proxy servers, and routers, NAT translates IP addresses on an internal or local network so that the actual IP addresses cannot be determined on the Internet, because the address seen on the Internet is a decoy address used from a pool of decoy addresses.

network discovery The ability to view other network computers and devices.

Network File System (NFS) protocol A file transfer protocol common to UNIX and Linux systems that transfers information in record streams instead of in bulk file streams.

network interface card (NIC) An adaptor board or device to connect a workstation, server, or other network device to a network medium. The connection can be wired or wireless.

Network Level Authentication (NLA) A security method that enables authentication to take place before a Remote Desktop Services connection is established and that involves verifying the user account, client computer, and network server.

network print device A printing device, such as a laser printer, connected to a print server through a network.

New Technology File System (NTFS) File system that is native to Windows Server systems and that supports features such as security, compression, disk quotas, encryption, self-healing from disk damage, and others.

NIC teaming The ability to join two or more network interface cards to work like one.

non-paged pool Holds the operating system kernel, device drivers, and other key elements that cannot be paged out, and so these processes and threads are always kept in physical memory or RAM.

Non-volatile Memory Express (NVMe) A communications protocol and interface created for SSD to enable much faster data access and to reduce data latency.

object A network resource, such as a server or a user account, that has distinct attributes or properties, is defined in a domain, and exists in Active Directory.

Open Database Connectivity (ODBC) A set of database access rules used by Microsoft in its ODBC application programming interface for accessing databases and providing a standard doorway to database data.

operational log A type of event log that tracks occurrences of specific operations, such as when a disk drive is added.

organizational unit (OU) A grouping of objects within a domain that provides a means to establish specific policies for governing those objects and that enables object management to be delegated.

ownership Having the privilege to change permissions and to fully manipulate an object. The account that creates an object, such as a folder or printer, initially has ownership.

packet A unit of data transmitted on a network that contains control and address information as well as routing information.

paged pool Contains data that can be stored in the paging file, and so can be paged in and out of the virtual memory (a page file on disk).

page fault Event that occurs whenever memory pages must be called from disk (from the paging file).

paging Moving blocks of information, called pages, from RAM to virtual memory (the paging file) on disk.

paging file Disk space, in the form of a file, for use when memory requirements exceed the available RAM.

parallel rebuild A Windows Server 2016 feature that enables a failed disk in RAID (a set of disks for redundant storage) to be rebuilt significantly faster.

parallelized repair A process in Storage Spaces that causes the data on a failed disk to be automatically spread over all of the remaining functioning disks.

partition table Table containing information about each partition on a disk, such as the type of partition, size, and location. Also, the partition table provides information to the computer about how to access the disk.

partitioning Allocating a group of tracks and sectors on a disk to be used by a particular file system, such as NTFS.

Password Authentication Protocol (PAP) A nonencrypted plaintext password authentication protocol. This represents the lowest level of security for exchanging passwords via PPP or TCP/IP.

peer-to-peer networking A network on which any computer can communicate with other networked computers on an equal or peer basis without going through an intermediary, such as a server or host.

performance counter report Output of information gathered via Performance Monitor objects, counters, and instances configured within a data collector set.

Performance Monitor The Windows Server 2016 utility used to track system or application objects. For each object type, one or more counters can be logged via a data collection set for later analysis or tracked in real time for immediate Performance Monitoring.

permissions In Windows Server 2016, privileges to access and manipulate resource objects, such as folders and printers; for example, the privilege to read a file or to create a new file.

physical processor A processor chip plugged into a processor socket on a motherboard in a computer.

Plug and Play (PnP) Ability of added computer hardware, such as an adapter or modem, to identify itself to the computer operating system for installation. PnP also refers to the Intel and Microsoft specifications for automatic device detection and installation. Many operating systems, such as Windows-based, Mac OS X, and UNIX/Linux, support PnP.

Point and Print Implements the v4 driver model, so that a print server does not have to provide clients with printer drivers for specific models of printers.

pointer (PTR) resource record A record in a DNS reverse lookup zone that consists of an IP (version 4 or 6) address correlated to a computer or domain name.

Point-to-Point Protocol (PPP) A legacy remote communications protocol that transports IP as well as legacy protocols such as IPX and NetBEUI. PPP can automatically negotiate communications with several network communications layers at once, and it supports connection authentication. PPP has historically been used for dial-up connections between a client and server.

Point-to-Point Tunneling Protocol (PPTP) A remote communications protocol that enables connectivity to a network through the Internet and connectivity through intranets and VPNs. PPTP is no longer considered secure.

portable operating system interface (POSIX) Standards set by the Institute of Electrical and Electronics Engineers (IEEE) for portability of applications.

PostScript (PS) printer A printer that has special firmware or cartridges to print using a page-description language (PDL).

Preboot Execution Environment (PXE) An environment in which a client computer has software or hardware to enable its network interface card to connect to the network and communicate with a server (or boot from the server) without having to first boot from an operating system on the client's hard disk.

preemptive multitasking Running two or more programs simultaneously so that each program runs in an area of memory separate from areas used by other programs.

primary DNS server A DNS server that is used as the main server from which to administer a zone, such as updating records in a forward lookup zone for a domain. A primary DNS server is also called the authoritative server for that zone.

primary partition Partition or portion of a hard disk that is bootable.

print client Client computer or application that generates a print job.

print job A document or items to be printed.

print queue A stack or lineup of print jobs, with the first job submitted at the top of the stack and the last job submitted at the bottom, and all of the jobs waiting to be sent from the spooler to the printer. On a Windows Server 2016 print server, the priority of a print job can be changed so that a job that is not at the top of the queue can be printed right away.

print server Network computer or server device that connects printers to the network for sharing and that receives and processes print requests from print clients.

Printer Control Language (PCL) A printer language used by non-PostScript Hewlett-Packard and compatible laser printers.

printer driver Contains device-specific information that Windows Server 2016 requires to control a particular print device, implementing customized printer control codes, font, and style information so that documents are converted into a printer-specific language.

printer pooling Linking two or more identical printers with one printer setup or printer share.

privileged mode A protected memory space allocated for the Windows Server 2016 kernel that cannot be directly accessed by software applications.

process A computer program or portion of a program that is currently running. One large program might start several smaller programs or processes.

processor socket A receptacle on a computer motherboard into which a processor chip is plugged.

protected users global group A global group that is created by default and enforces strict locked-in security that cannot be reconfigured.

protocol A strictly defined set of rules for communication across a network that specifies how networked data is formatted for transmission, how it is transmitted, and how it is interpreted at the receiving end.

Public Key Infrastructure (PKI) Implementation of hardware and software to distribute, manage, and expire digital certificates, such as through implementing the Active Directory Certificate Services role.

publish Making an object, such as a printer or shared folder, available for users to access when they view Active Directory contents and so that the data associated with the object can be replicated.

publishing applications (or software) Involves setting up software through a Group Policy so that the application is available for users to install from a central distribution server, such as through the Programs and Features capability via the user's desktop.

RAID (redundant array of inexpensive [or independent] disks) A set of standards designed to extend the life of hard disk drives and to prevent data loss from a hard disk failure.

RAID-5 volume Three or more dynamic disks that use RAID level 5 fault tolerance through disk striping and creating parity blocks for data recovery.

RAW A data type often used for printing UNIX and Linux print files and legacy Windows operating system print files.

Read-Only Domain Controller (RODC) A domain controller that houses Active Directory information but cannot be updated, such as to create a new account. This specialized domain controller receives updates from regular DCs but does not replicate to any DCs because it is read-only by design. *See* domain controller (DC).

Registry A database used to store information about the configuration, program setup, devices, drivers, and other data important to the setup of Windows operating systems, such as Windows Server 2016.

Registry entry A data parameter in the Registry stored as a value in hexadecimal, binary, or text format.

Registry key A category of information contained in the Windows Registry, such as hardware or software.

Registry subkey A key within a Registry key, similar to a subfolder under a folder.

Reliable Multicast Protocol Used on Windows-based networks to facilitate multicast transmissions for multimedia communications.

Remote Access (RAS) A role that enables Windows Server 2016 to provide remote access so that off-site clients have access to a Windows Server 2016 network through the Internet, such as through a virtual private network. *See* virtual private network.

Remote Desktop Connection (RDC) Software on a client computer that enables it to connect to a terminal server. This was originally called Remote Desktop Services Client.

replication group A grouping of shared folders in a DFS namespace root that are replicated or copied to all servers that participate in DFS replication. When changes are made to DFS shared folders, all of the participating servers are automatically or manually synchronized so that they have the same copy.

Resilient File System (ReFS) A Microsoft file system introduced with Windows 8 and Windows Server 2012 with the goal of better performance and faster repair of disk errors than NTFS. *See* New Technology File System.

resource On a network, this refers to an object, such as a shared printer or shared directory, which can be accessed by users. On workstations as well as servers, a resource is an IRQ line, I/O address, or memory that is allocated to a computer component, such as a disk drive or communications port.

Resultant Set of Policy (RSoP) A Windows Server 2016 tool that enables you to produce reports about proposed or current Group Policy settings for the purpose of planning and troubleshooting when multiple Group Policies are in use (such as for OUs and domains).

reverse lookup zone A DNS server zone or table that maps IP addresses to computer or domain names.

Rights Management Services (RMS) Security rights developed by Microsoft to provide security for documents, spreadsheets, email, and other types of files created by applications.

roaming profile Desktop settings that are associated with an account so that the same settings are employed no matter which computer is used to access the account (the profile is downloaded to the client from a server).

root hint A resource record to enable a DNS server to quickly find an authoritative DNS server in a zone that is not on the DNS server, and is used in particular to find an authoritative DNS server on the Internet.

root key Also called a subtree, the highest category of data contained in the Registry. There are five root keys.

router A device that connects networks, is able to read IP addresses, and can route or forward packets of data to designated networks.

RSA Developed by Rivest, Shamir, and Adleman, an encryption technique that uses public and private keys along with a computer algorithm that relies on factoring large prime numbers.

Safe Mode A boot mode that enables Windows Server 2016 to be booted using the most generic default settings, such as for the display, disk drives, and pointing device—and only those services needed to boot a basic configuration.

schema Elements used in the definition of each object contained in Active Directory, including the object class and its attributes.

scope A range of contiguous IP addresses that a DHCP server can lease to clients.

scope of influence (scope) The reach of a type of group, such as access to resources in a single domain or access to all resources in all domains in a forest (see domain local, global, and universal security groups). (Another meaning for the term *scope* is the beginning through ending IP addresses defined in a DHCP server for use by DHCP clients; see Chapter 8).

script A file of shell commands that are run as a unit within the shell. The shell interprets the commands to the operating system one line at a time. To run the contents of a script, the name of that script usually must be entered at the command line. Scripts save time because commands don't have to be typed individually by the user. Another advantage is that the users do not have to memorize the exact sequence of a set of commands each time they want to accomplish a certain task.

secondary DNS server A DNS server that is a backup to a primary DNS server and therefore is not authoritative.

Secure Sockets Layer (SSL) A data encryption technique employed between a server and a client, such as between a client's browser and an Internet server. SSL is a commonly used form of security for communications and transactions over the web and can be used by all web browsers.

Secure Socket Tunneling Protocol (SSTP) A remote access communications protocol used in VPN communications and that employs PPP authentication techniques along with web-based communications transport and encryption through Hypertext Transfer Protocol and Secure Sockets Layer. *See* Secure Sockets Layer (SSL).

security group Used to assign a group of users permission to access network resources.

security log An event log that records access and security information about logon accesses, file, folder, and system policy changes.

Serial Advanced Technology Attachment (SATA) A high-speed serial interface technology for hard disks.

Serial Attached SCSI (SAS) An update to parallel SCSI that uses serial communications and does not require terminators as with the older parallel SCSI technology.

server A single computer that provides extensive multiuser access to network resources.

server-based networking A model in which access to the network and resources, and the management of resources, is accomplished through one or more servers.

Server Manager A comprehensive server management tool offered through Windows Server 2016.

Server Message Block (SMB) protocol Used by default on Microsoft systems, enables an operating system to offer shared files, folders, printers, serial ports, and other shared elements on a network.

Server Message Block version 3 (SMBv3) Version 3 of the SMB protocol native to Windows operating systems that is used for sharing folders and files on a network as well as for communications between nodes in Storage Spaces Direct.

service pack (SP) A major update for an operating system that includes fixes for known problems and provides product enhancements.

Service Principal Name (SPN) An identification number for a network service that employs Kerberos security.

service ticket In Kerberos security, a permanent ticket good for the duration of a logon session (or for another period of time specified by the server administrator in the account policies) that enables the computer to access network services beginning with the Logon service.

setup log An event log that contains a record of installation events, such as installing a role or feature through Server Manager.

shared directory A directory on a networked computer that other computers on the network can access.

share permissions Permissions that apply to a particular object that is shared over a network, such as a shared folder or printer.

shell A command-line environment, also called a command interpreter, that enables communication with an operating system. Commands that are run within a shell are typically specific to that shell (although different shells sometimes use the same or similar commands, particularly in UNIX and Linux).

Shiva PAP (SPAP) A proprietary version of Password Authentication Protocol used on Shiva systems. *See* Password Authentication Protocol (PAP).

Sigverif A tool used to verify system and other critical files to determine if they have a signature.

Simple Mail Transfer Protocol (SMTP) An email protocol used by systems having TCP/IP network communications.

Simple Network Management Protocol (SNMP) Used for network management and performance monitoring on TCP/IP-based networks.

simple volume A portion of a disk or an entire disk that is set up as a dynamic disk.

site An option in Active Directory to interconnect IP subnets so that the server can determine the fastest route to connect clients for authentication and to connect DCs for replication of Active Directory. Site information also enables Active Directory to create redundant routes for DC replication.

Small Computer System Interface (SCSI) A 32- or 64-bit computer adapter that transports data between one or more attached devices, such as hard disks, and the computer using parallel communications technology.

software-defined storage (SDS) Managing data storage with software that is independent of the actual storage hardware.

solid state drive (SSD) A fast storage technology based on using semiconductors for storage, similar to flash drives.

spanned volume Two or more Windows Server dynamic disks that are combined to appear as one disk.

spool file A print file written to disk until it can be transmitted to a printer.

spooler In the Windows environment, a group of DLLs, information files, and programs that process print jobs for printing.

spooling A process working in the background to enable several print files to go to a single printer. Each file is placed in temporary storage until its turn comes to be printed.

SQL Server A relational database system from Microsoft that is used to build enterprise databases.

stand-alone DFS model A DFS model in which no Active Directory implementation is available to help manage the shared folders. This model provides only a single or flat-level share.

stateful autoconfiguration In IPv6, uses dynamic addressing for an IPv6 host by obtaining the IPv6 address through DHCPv6 and a DHCPv6 server.

stateless autoconfiguration In IPv6, when a network host assigns its own IPv6 address without obtaining it from a DHCPv6 server.

static addressing An IP address that is assigned to a client and remains in use until it is manually changed.

Storage Area Network (SAN) A grouping of storage devices that forms a subnet. The storage devices are available to any server on the main network and appear to the user as though they are attached to the server they are accessing.

storage pinning Used with storage tiering to enable you to move specific files to a given storage location and ensure that those files are always kept in that location.

storage pool (1) Storage capacity that can be set up from different physical and virtual disks to store specific information, such as inventory programs under development for a business. (2) **Used in Storage Spaces, a grouping of physical disks and disk space to be managed by a Windows Server 2016 server as a virtual disk.**

Storage Spaces **A Windows Server 2016 technology that enables multiple physical disks to be formed into individual storage pools.** *See* storage pool.

Storage Spaces Direct Software-defined storage that is intended to make storage more versatile through making it easier to add storage as needed, to access storage, and to use new storage capabilities. *See* Storage Spaces.

storage tiering A Windows Server 2016 feature that allows selected blocks of data to be moved to specific locations, such as to solid state storage instead of disk storage.

stripe set Two or more basic disks set up so that files are spread in blocks across the disks.

striped volume Two or more dynamic disks that use striping so that files are spread in blocks across the disks.

striping A data storage method that breaks up data files across all volumes of a disk set to minimize wear on a single volume.

stub zone A DNS zone that contains only the SOA record zone, name server (NS) records for authoritative servers, and A records for authoritative servers.

subnet mask Used to distinguish between the network part and the host part of the IP address and to enable networks to be divided into subnets.

subtree Same as root key.

symmetric multiprocessor (SMP) computer A computer that uses more than one processor.

sync share A server folder that holds work files for mobile and stationary devices. *See* work folders.

synchronous modem A modem that communicates using continuous bursts of data controlled by a clock signal that starts each burst.

system control ACL (SACL) An access control list that contains settings to audit the access to an object, such as a folder.

system environment variables Variables defined by the operating system and that apply to any user signed in to the computer.

system log An event log that records information about system-related events such as hardware errors, driver problems, and hard drive errors.

system partition Partition on basic disks that contains boot files.

system state data Operating system and boot files, plus extra components and information that reflect the currently configured state of the server, depending on what features are installed. The system state data can be backed up using the Windows Server Backup tool.

system volume Volume on dynamic disks that is used to boot the computer.

SYSVOL A shared folder set up when Active Directory is installed that contains scripts, Group Policy Objects (GPOs), and software distribution files, several of which are needed for domain access. SYSVOL folders are replicated among DCs.

T-carrier A dedicated leased telephone line that can be used for data communications over multiple channels for speeds of up to 400.352 Mbps.

terminal A device that consists of a monitor and keyboard to communicate with host computers that run the programs. The terminal does not have a processor to use for running programs locally.

TEXT A data type used for printing text files formatted using the ANSI standard that employs values between 0 and 255 to represent characters, numbers, and symbols.

thin client A specialized personal computer or terminal device that has a minimal Windows-based operating system. A thin client is designed to connect to a host computer that does most or all of the processing. The thin client is mainly responsible for providing a graphical user interface and network connectivity.

thread A block of program code executing within a running process. One process may launch one or more threads.

tiered storage places In Storage Spaces, the ability to have slow tiers (slow disk technology, such as SATA) for less frequently accessed data and fast tiers (faster disk technology, such as SSD) for more frequently accessed data.

total cost of ownership (TCO) The cost of installing and maintaining computers and equipment on a network, which includes hardware, software, maintenance, and support costs.

trace Capture of a specific event when it occurs, such as a page fault or input to a disk.

trace report Contains results of monitored trace events generated by a data collector set and contains only those instances when the events occur, such as creating a trace to record each time disk input/output activity occurs or when an Active Directory Kerberos security event is triggered. *See* trace.

transitive trust A trust relationship between two or more domains in a tree, in which each domain has access to objects in the others.

Transmission Control Protocol/Internet Protocol (TCP/IP) The default protocol suite installed with Windows Server 2016 that enables network communication.

Transmission Control Protocol (TCP) This transport protocol, which is part of the TCP/IP suite, establishes communication sessions between networked software application processes and provides for reliable end-to-end delivery of data by controlling data flow.

Transport Layer Security (TLS) A data encryption technique that has evolved from and replaced SSL. *See* SSL.

trap A specific situation or event detected by SNMP that a network administrator may want to be warned about or to track via network management software, for example, when a network device is unexpectedly down or offline. *See* Simple Network Management Protocol (SNMP).

tree Related domains that use a contiguous namespace, share the same schema, and have two-way transitive trust relationships.

Trusted Platform Module (TPM) A security specification for a hardware device used to secure information on another device, such as on a hard drive. The TPM hardware device is typically a chip.

two-way trust A domain relationship in which both domains are trusted and trusting, enabling one to have access to objects in the other.

unicast A message that goes from one single computer to another single computer.

Unified Extensible Firmware Interface (UEFI) A firmware alternative to BIOS that includes the use of GPT disks. *See* Globally Unique Identifier (GUID) Partition Table (GPT).

Uniform Resource Locator (URL) An addressing format used to find an Internet website or page.

Universal Naming Convention (UNC) A naming convention that designates network servers, computers, and shared resources. The format for a UNC name is, for example, \\servername\namespace\folder\file.

Universal PnP (UPnP) A supplementation to PnP that enables automated configuration for devices connected through a network.

universal security group A group that is used to provide access to resources in any domain within a forest. A common implementation is to make global groups that contain accounts members of a universal group that has access to resources.

upstream server A server that has the Windows Server Update Services role installed and that is designated to obtain patches and service packs from Microsoft. Once it obtains the patches or service packs, it automatically makes them available to specific servers on the network.

User Account Control (UAC) Enables software and device installations in standard user mode while still ensuring authorization from the administrator. UAC is intended to further remove these activities from access to the kernel to protect the operating system and make it difficult to destabilize through malware and intrusions.

User Datagram Protocol (UDP) A connectionless protocol that can be used with IP, instead of TCP.

user environment variables Environment variables that are defined on a per-user basis.

virtual desktop Enables you to run different desktops side-by-side, such as having one desktop working with programming tools and another desktop using server administration tools.

virtual directory A URL-formatted address that provides an Internet location (virtual location) for an actual physical folder on a web server that is used to publish web documents.

virtual disk As used in Storage Spaces, a grouping of different kinds of physical disks, also known as a storage pool, that are combined on a server to appear to the user or to an application as one disk. *See* storage pool and Storage Spaces.

virtual machine An instance of a discrete operating system running within virtual server software on one computer. Multiple virtual machines can run within the virtual server software on one computer.

virtual memory Disk storage allocated to link with physical RAM to temporarily hold data when there is not enough free RAM.

virtual private network (VPN) A private network that is like a tunnel through a larger network—such as the Internet, an enterprise network, or both—that is restricted to designated member clients only.

virtual processor A logical processor in a computer that is used by a virtual machine.

virtual server A computer running virtual server software that enables configuring multiple virtual machines. *See* virtual machine.

virtualization Software that enables one computer to run two or more operating systems that are live at the same time and in which one application running in one operating system does not interfere with an application running in a different operating system.

volume A logical designation of one or more physical disks partitioned and formatted with one file system. One volume can be composed of one or more partitions. In Windows Server 2016, a volume can be a basic disk partition that has been formatted for a particular file system, a primary partition, a volume set, an extended volume, a stripe set, a stripe set with parity, or a mirror set. A volume can also be a dynamic disk that is set up as a simple volume, spanned volume, striped volume, RAID-5 volume, or mirrored volume.

volume set Two or more formatted basic disk partitions (volumes) that are combined to look like one volume with a single drive letter.

Volume Shadow Copy Service (VSS) Backup service used in Windows Server 2016 to create stable images of files and folders on servers based on the point in time when the image is made.

Web Application Proxy Entails publishing applications so that users external to an organization can access those applications on the organization's servers.

Web Services for Devices (WSD) A technology in which devices, such as printers, can use web-based services to inform clients of their capabilities.

Windows Defender Software that scans for and removes viruses, spyware, and malware. Windows Defender is included with Windows Server 2016.

Windows Deployment Services (WDS) Services in Windows Server 2016 that enable Windows Server 2016 and Windows 10 (and certain other Windows operating systems) to be installed on multiple computers using automated techniques.

Windows Firewall Windows software that manages incoming and outgoing communications through opening or blocking TCP and UDP communication ports and specific applications—to limit the attack surface and thwart attackers and malware.

Windows Internet Name Service (WINS) A Windows Server service that enables the server to convert NetBIOS computer names to IP addresses for network and Internet communications. (NetBIOS is an applications programming interface to provide programs with a consistent command set for using network services.)

Windows Nano Server An installation option in Windows Server 2016 that provides an even smaller footprint than Windows Server Core and is intended for a remotely administered server in a cloud or datacenter.

Windows NT LAN Manager version 2 (NTLMv2) An authentication protocol used in legacy Windows NT Server systems and retained in all Windows systems for backward compatibility for clients that cannot support Kerberos.

Windows PowerShell A Windows command-line interface that offers scripting capabilities as well.

Windows Server Catalog A list of computer hardware and software tested by Microsoft and determined to be compatible with a specific Windows Server operating system, such as Windows Server 2016.

Windows Server Core A minimum Windows Server 2016 configuration, designed to function in a fashion similar to traditional UNIX and Linux servers by offering a command-line interface and only the minimum services needed to get the job done.

Windows System Image Manager (Windows SIM) A tool in the Windows Server 2016 Assessment and Deployment Kit used to create and manage answer files for an unattended Windows operating system installation through Windows Deployment Services. *See* Assessment and Deployment Kit (ADK) and Windows Deployment Services (WDS).

work folders A feature of the File and Storage Services role that enables users to access and synchronize work folders through using all types of devices, mobile and stationary, such as tablet PCs, laptops, and stationary PCs. Work folders are designed to accommodate the bring-your-own-device (BYOD) environment common to many places of work.

workgroup As used in Microsoft networks, a number of users who share drive and printer resources in an independent peer-to-peer relationship.

workstation A computer that has its own central processing unit (CPU) and can be used as a stand-alone or network computer for word processing, spreadsheet creation, or other software applications.

X.25 An older packet-switching protocol for connecting remote networks at speeds up to 2.048 Mbps.

XML Paper Specification (XPS) An advanced way of printing documents for multiple purposes, including viewing electronic pages and printing pages in a polished format.

XPS Viewer Enables you to view a file saved in the XPS format.

zone A partition or subtree in a DNS server that contains specific kinds of records in a lookup table, such as a forward lookup zone that contains records in a table for looking up computer and domain names in order to find their associated IP addresses.

Index

D

E

F

J

K

L

O

P

R

S

T

X

Z